Outlook® 2007 All-in-One Desk Reference For

Managing Your Mail

After you start getting a bunch of e-mail messages, it's easy to feel buried under a mountain of mail. Luckily, Outlook makes it easy to review incoming messages and deal with any attachments they may have.

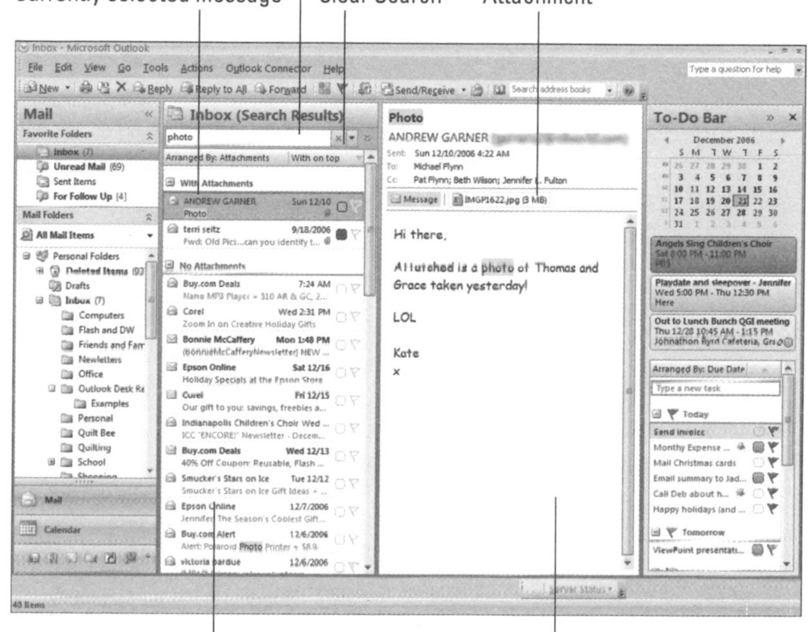

To Do This . . .	*Do This . . .*
View the Reading pane.	Choose View⇨Reading Pane⇨Right *or* Bottom (to indicate the position on-screen).
View a message in the Reading pane.	Click the message header in the list.
Display the contents of the next message in the list.	Press the down arrow key.
Open a message in its own window.	Double-click the message header.
Preview an attachment.	Click the attachment name in the Reading pane.
Open an attachment.	Double-click the attachment.
Save an attachment.	Right-click the attachment and choose Save As.
Search for e-mail.	Type some text in the Search box and press Enter.
Clear a search.	Click the Clear Search button.

Outlook® 2007 All-in-One Desk Reference For Dummies®

Cheat Sheet

Getting to Know the Outlook 2007 Interface

In order to create a new Outlook item, you enter details into a form, such as the Message form shown here. The forms may change a bit depending on the type of item you're working on, but some things, like the elements listed here, always stay the same.

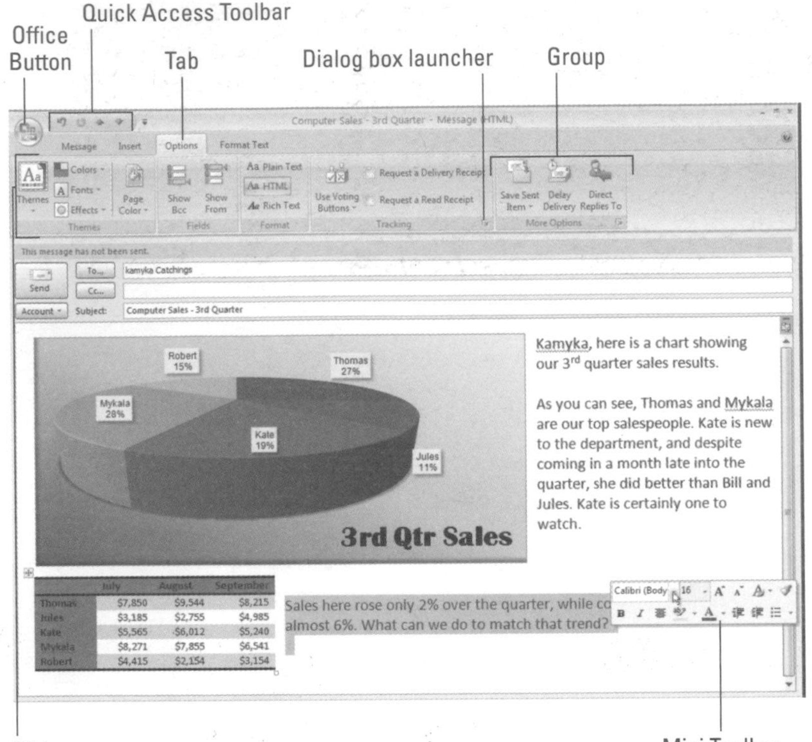

Element	What It Does
Office Button	Click this button to display a menu containing all the file-related commands, such as New, Save, Save As, Print, and Close.
Quick Access Toolbar	This toolbar contains buttons for common commands like Save, Undo, and Redo.
Ribbon	This special toolbar is arranged as a series of tabs and contains buttons for commands ranging from creating or changing an item to formatting text.
Group	Ribbon buttons are arranged in groups, such as Themes, Fields, Format, and so on.
Dialog box launcher	Clicking this button displays a dialog box with additional options for the current group.
Mini Toolbar	This toolbar appears when you type some text, select it, and move the mouse pointer up just a little. It contains command buttons for applying formatting to the selected text.

For Dummies: Bestselling Book Series for Beginners

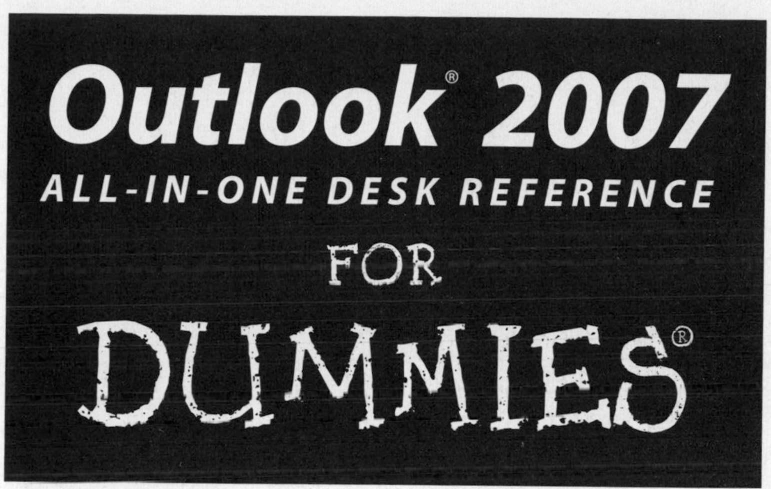

by Jennifer Fulton and Karen S. Fredricks

Wiley Publishing, Inc.

Outlook® 2007 All-in-One Desk Reference For Dummies®

Published by
Wiley Publishing, Inc.
111 River Street
Hoboken, NJ 07030-5774

www.wiley.com

Published by Wiley Publishing, Inc., Indianapolis, Indiana

Published simultaneously in Canada

For general information on our other products and services, please contact our Customer Care Department within the U.S. at 800-762-2974, outside the U.S. at 317-572-3993, or fax 317-572-4002.

For technical support, please visit www.wiley.com/techsupport.

Wiley also publishes its books in a variety of electronic formats. Some content that appears in print may not be available in electronic books.

Library of Congress Control Number: 2006939601

ISBN: 978-0-470-04672-2

Manufactured in the United States of America

10 9 8 7 6 5 4 3 2 1

About the Authors

Jennifer Fulton, iVillage's former "Computer Coach," is an experienced computer consultant and trainer with over 20 years in the business. Jennifer is a best-selling author of over 100 computer books for the beginner, intermediate, and advanced user, ranging from the self-motivated adult business user to the college, technical, high-school, or middle school student. Jennifer is also a computer trainer for corporate personnel, teaching a variety of classes including Windows, Microsoft Office, Paint Shop Pro, Photoshop Elements, and others.

Jennifer is a self-taught veteran of computing, which means, of course, that if something *can* happen to a computer user, it has probably happened to her at one time or another. Thus Jennifer brings what's left of her sense of humor to her many books, including: *Adobe Photoshop Elements 4 in a Snap, How to Use Macromedia Dreamweaver 8 and Fireworks 8, Adobe Photoshop Elements 3 in a Snap, Digital Photography with Photoshop Album in a Snap, Paint Shop Pro 8 in a Snap, Learning Office 2003, Learning Excel 2003*, and *Multimedia Basics*.

Karen S. Fredricks began her life rather non-technically growing up in Kenya. She attended high school in Beirut, Lebanon, where she developed her sense of humor while dodging bombs. After traveling all over the world, Karen ended up at the University of Florida and has been an ardent Gator fan ever since. In addition to undergraduate studies in English, Theater, and Accounting, Karen has a master's degree in Psycholinguistics. Beginning her career teaching high school English and theater, Karen switched to working with the PC during its inception in the early '80s and has worked as a full-time computer consultant and trainer ever since.

Karen is an ACT! Certified Consultant, an ACT! Premier Trainer, a Microsoft Office User Specialist, and a QuickBooks Pro Certified Advisor. She is the author of four *For Dummies* books on ACT! In addition, she has written *Outlook 2007 Business Contact Manager For Dummies* and is completing work on *Microsoft Office Live For Dummies*. A true fan of the *For Dummies* series, she helped organize *The Authors Unconference,* the first ever gathering of *For Dummies* authors.

Karen resides in Boca Raton, Florida. Her company, Tech Benders, specializes in contact management software and provides computer consulting, support, and training services. She is also a regular guest on several syndicated computer radio talk shows. In her spare time, Karen loves to spend time with family and friends, play tennis, work out, road bike, and write schlocky poetry.

Karen loves to hear from her readers. Feel free to send her your comments about the book to `dummies@techbenders.com` or visit her Web site `www.techbenders.com` to learn more about the products listed in this book.

Dedication

Jennifer Fulton: To my husband Scott, who patiently and lovingly supported me while I worked feverishly on this book.

Karen S. Fredricks: To Gary Kahn, who loves and encourages me every step of the way!

Authors' Acknowledgments

Jennifer Fulton: I would like to thank all the wonderful people at Wiley Publishing who worked hard under a very tight deadline to guide this book through to its completion. I would especially like to thank Greg Croy, for giving me this opportunity, and Kim Darosett, for her keen eye as an editor and her patience as this project went through numerous revisions.

Karen S. Fredricks: This is my sixth book for Wiley Publishing and as usual they've made writing this book a pleasure! Thanks to Greg Croy, my acquisitions editor, for believing in me; I look forward to working with you on many more titles! Special thanks to my project editor, Kim Darosett. Heidi Unger, Mary Lagu, Barry Childs-Helton, Colleen Totz, and Kelly Ewing, the copy editors, had the unenviable task of making me look good; their edits were always right on! Technical editor Lee Musick's sharp eye helped to spot all the changes between the beta and final versions of Outlook 2007. It was an honor to work with Jennifer Fulton, my co-author; I hope we work on more titles together again in the future!

Rich Tennant is the coolest cartoonist ever. I am astounded by the thought, research, and time that he devotes to each one of his cartoons. I'm not sure which is funnier — his cartoons — or his stories about creating his cartoons!

The most important acknowledgment of all goes out to all of the readers of the *For Dummies* series, and more specifically, the readers of this book. I hope you'll enjoy *reading* this book as much as I enjoyed *writing* it!

Publisher's Acknowledgments

We're proud of this book; please send us your comments through our online registration form located at www.dummies.com/register/.

Some of the people who helped bring this book to market include the following:

Acquisitions, Editorial, and Media Development

Project Editor: Kim Darosett

Executive Editor: Greg Croy

Copy Editors: Barry Childs-Helton, Kelly Ewing, Mary Lagu, Colleen Totz, Heidi Unger

Technical Editor: Lee Musick

Editorial Manager: Leah Cameron

Media Development Manager: Laura VanWinkle

Editorial Assistant: Amanda Foxworth

Sr. Editorial Assistant: Cherie Case

Cartoons: Rich Tennant (www.the5thwave.com)

Composition Services

Project Coordinator: Kristie Rees

Layout and Graphics: Claudia Bell, Carl Byers, Shawn Frazier, Denny Hager, Stephanie D. Jumper, Barbara Moore, Melanee Prendergast, Heather Ryan, Erin Zeltner

Proofreaders: Aptara, Christy Pingleton

Indexer: Sherry Massey

Anniversary Logo Design: Richard Pacifico

Special Help: Rebecca Senninger

Publishing and Editorial for Technology Dummies

Richard Swadley, Vice President and Executive Group Publisher

Andy Cummings, Vice President and Publisher

Mary Bednarek, Executive Acquisitions Director

Mary C. Corder, Editorial Director

Publishing for Consumer Dummies

Diane Graves Steele, Vice President and Publisher

Joyce Pepple, Acquisitions Director

Composition Services

Gerry Fahey, Vice President of Production Services

Debbie Stailey, Director of Composition Services

Contents at a Glance

Introduction 1

Book I: Getting Started 9

Chapter 1: An Insider's Look at the Outlook Interface 11

Chapter 2: Outlook, Quick and Dirty 33

Chapter 3: Setting Up Your E-Mail Accounts 53

Chapter 4: Importing Data into Outlook 69

Book II: E-Mail Basics 83

Chapter 1: Creating New Messages: Beyond the Basics 85

Chapter 2: Reading and Replying to E-Mail 113

Chapter 3: Making Your E-Mail Look Professional and Cool 127

Chapter 4: Repeating Yourself Easily with Signatures and Templates 161

Book III: Über E-Mail 171

Chapter 1: Controlling the Sending and Receiving of Messages 173

Chapter 2: When You Have to Know Now: Instant Messaging 189

Chapter 3: Getting the Latest News Delivered Right to Your Inbox 195

Chapter 4: Sending Mass Mailings 205

Chapter 5: Managing Multiple E-Mail Accounts 213

Book IV: Working with the Calendar 231

Chapter 1: Getting Familiar with the Calendar 233

Chapter 2: Going Further with the Calendar 251

Chapter 3: Calendar Collaboration 263

Chapter 4: All About Meetings 301

Chapter 5: Making the Calendar Your Own 327

Book V: Managing Contacts 349

Chapter 1: Getting in Contact 351

Chapter 2: Working with Your Contacts 363

Chapter 3: Dealing with Business Cards 375

Chapter 4: Contacts Collaboration 385

Book VI: Tracking Tasks, Taking Notes, and Recording Items in the Journal 395

Chapter 1: Creating Tasks with the To-Do Bar 397
Chapter 2: Dealing with More Complex Tasks 413
Chapter 3: Spreading the Joy: Task Assignments 425
Chapter 4: Taking Notes 447
Chapter 5: Taking Notes in Overdrive: OneNote 455
Chapter 6: Maximizing the Power of OneNote 489
Chapter 7: Making History in the Journal 521

Book VII: Working with Business Contact Manager 535

Chapter 1: Minding Your Business Contact Manager 537
Chapter 2: Introducing the Basic Business Contact Manager Elements 551
Chapter 3: Working with Opportunities 567
Chapter 4: Reports and Dashboards 577

Book VIII: Customizing Outlook 589

Chapter 1: Organizing Items with Categories 591
Chapter 2: Changing Your View on Outlook 603
Chapter 3: Customizing Outlook Forms 621

Book IX: Managing Your Outlook Stuff 635

Chapter 1: Finding a Place for Your Stuff 637
Chapter 2: Playing by the Rules 661
Chapter 3: Making Mincemeat Out of Spam 677
Chapter 4: Seek and Ye Shall Find 689
Chapter 5: Securing Outlook E-Mail 707

Book X: Out and About: Taking Outlook on the Road 725

Chapter 1: Staying in Touch No Matter Where You Are 727
Chapter 2: Turning Your E-Mail Accounts into Roadies 751
Chapter 3: Printing Your Stuff and Taking It with You 767

Index 783

Table of Contents

Introduction *1*

About This Book..2
Conventions Used in This Book 3
Foolish Assumptions 4
How This Book Is Organized...4
Book I: Getting Started...5
Book II: E-Mail Basics 5
Book III: Über E-Mail...5
Book IV: Working with the Calendar 6
Book V: Managing Contacts 6
Book VI: Tracking Tasks, Taking Notes, and Recording Items in the Journal.....6
Book VII: Working with Business Contact Manager 6
Book VIII: Customizing Outlook..6
Book IX: Managing Your Outlook Stuff..7
Book X: Out and About: Taking Outlook on the Road 7
Icons Used in This Book..7
Where to Go from Here..8

Book I: Getting Started *9*

Chapter 1: An Insider's Look at the Outlook Interface **11**

What Can Outlook Do for Me? 11
Heeeerrre's Outlook!..13
Getting Around with the Navigation Pane 14
Viewing Mail with the Reading Pane..17
Previewing with AutoPreview 19
Sneaking a peek at attachments 20
Having Fun with the Folder List 22
Your Week in a Nutshell: The New To-Do Bar..24
Getting a Snapshot of Your Day with Outlook Today 26
Sizing Things Up in the Outlook Window...27
Minimizing Outlook to a Taskbar Icon..28
Taking a Shortcut to Your Favorite Folders 30

Chapter 2: Outlook, Quick and Dirty **33**

Creating Outlook Items: The Common Factors 33
Wow! There's a New button!...33
Using forms to create items 34
Editing an item...36
Deleting an item..37

Adding a Quick Contact 38
Sending a Fast E-Mail 39
Reading and Replying to Incoming Messages 41
Creating a Simple Appointment 42
Adding a Quick Task 44
Taking a Note 45
Drag and Drop and How It Saved My Life 46
    Understanding how it works 47
    Creating Outlook items with drag and drop 47
    Reorganizing Outlook items with drag and drop 51

Chapter 3: Setting Up Your E-Mail Accounts .53

Understanding the E-Mail Process 53
    Obtaining an e-mail account 54
    Knowing the e-mail flavors 54
Configuring Your E-Mail Accounts 56
    Having Outlook do the heavy lifting 57
    Configuring your e-mail account manually 60
Maintaining Your E-Mail Accounts 62
    Changing your e-mail password 62
    Changing your e-mail account name or reply info 64
Changing Your ISP Information 65
    Changing your account information 66
    Changing your connection type 66

Chapter 4: Importing Data into Outlook 69

Importing E-Mail from Outlook Express/Windows Mail or Eudora..........69
    Importing e-mail from Outlook Express or Windows Mail 70
    Grabbing Outlook Express/Windows Mail account information 71
    Grabbing Eudora Pro or Eudora Light e-mail and account info 75
    Grabbing Eudora 5.0–6.0 e-mail and account info..........................75
Importing Contacts 78
Importing Other Data 79

Book II: E-Mail Basics 83

Chapter 1: Creating New Messages: Beyond the Basics 85

Creating a Message, Step by Step 85
    Step 1: Display the message form 85
    Step 2: Address the e-mail 86
    Step 3: Send extra copies of the message 87
    Step 4: Enter a subject and a message..88
    Step 5: Send it off 89
Retrieving Your Mail 90
    Going through the mail..91
    Fast ways to review mail 92

Working with Address Books....94
Attaching a new address book to Outlook....95
Choosing which address book is the boss....98
Resolving to Find the Right E-Mail Address....99
Understanding how Outlook verifies addresses....99
Searching for an address in your address book....101
Sending Carbon Copies (Ccs) and Blind Carbon Copies (Bccs)....103
Formatting Text to Make Your Messages Stand Out....104
Understanding message formats: HTML, RTF, and plain text....104
Applying formatting to a message....106
Attaching a File to a Message....108
Best practices for working with attachments....108
Attaching files....109
Saving a Message So You Can Send It Later....111
Saving a draft....111
Changing the Drafts folder....112

Chapter 2: Reading and Replying to E-Mail....113

Finding the Messages You Want to Read: Changing the View....113
Dealing with E-Mails That Use Pictures....114
Opening E-Mail Attachments....116
Saving E-Mail Attachments....117
Replying versus Replying to All....118
Controlling how text is quoted in a reply....120
Adding your name to a reply....122
Viewing a conversation....123
Forwarding an E-Mail....125
Resending an E-Mail Message....125

Chapter 3: Making Your E-Mail Look Professional and Cool....127

Checking Your Ignorance at the Door with Spelling and Grammar Checking....128
Checking spelling....129
Checking grammar....132
Using Stationery to Add Flair....134
Taking a stationery out for a test run....135
Selecting your everyday stationery....136
Applying a Word Theme....137
Applying a Color, Font, or Effects Set....138
Creating a custom set of colors or fonts....139
Customizing your look....141
Simply Colorizing the Background....142
Color is a solid choice....142
Why not try a gradient, texture, pattern, or image?....143
Inserting an Image....145

Illustrating Your Point 147
 Tabling the notion 147
 Charting the way 148
 Getting your message to take shape 149
 Getting smart with SmartArt 150
Manipulating Objects 152
Linking to the Outside World 154
Inserting an Outlook Item 156
Playing with Text 157
 Adding headings and other QuickStyles 157
 Dealing with bulleted and numbered lists 159
 Placing text exactly where you want it with a text box 159

Chapter 4: Repeating Yourself Easily with Signatures and Templates 161

Adding Your Signature 161
 Creating a signature 162
 Adding the signature to e-mail messages 165
Repeating the Same Stuff Over and Over 166
 Saving reusable text and images as a Quick Part 166
 Inserting a Quick Part into an Outlook item 168
Using a Template to Create a Reusable Message 168

Book III: Über E-Mail 171

Chapter 1: Controlling the Sending and Receiving of Messages . . .173

How Can I Tell If You Read This? 173
 Making what you send look really important 174
 Flagging messages for yourself 176
 Tracking when messages are delivered and read 177
Getting Out the Vote 179
Controlling Message Delivery 181
 Delaying when messages are sent 182
 Setting messages to expire after a certain date 182
 Recalling and replacing messages 183
 Changing how Outlook tells you e-mail has arrived 185
Stopping a Long E-Mail Download 188

Chapter 2: When You Have to Know Now: Instant Messaging 189

Understanding the Magic 189
Compatible IM Services 190
Sending an Instant Message 191
Controlling Your Online Status 194

Chapter 3: Getting the Latest News Delivered Right to Your Inbox 195

Adding News Feeds..196
Manually adding a news feed..196
Adding a recommended feed...197
Adding a news feed through Internet Explorer 199
Changing or removing a feed...201
Reading News Feeds 202
Sharing News Feeds 203
Sharing a feed by e-mail..203
Importing/exporting a news feed list 204

Chapter 4: Sending Mass Mailings 205

Creating a Distribution List...205
Using a distribution list to send e-mails 208
Making changes to a distribution list 208
Creating a Mass Mailing in Word Using Your Contacts 209

Chapter 5: Managing Multiple E-Mail Accounts 213

Controlling Sending and Receiving 213
Creating Send/Receive groups..214
Now, let's go get that mail! 218
Selecting Your Default E-Mail Account 220
Changing the Order in Which Accounts Are Checked 221
Sending from a Specific E-Mail Account...222
Directing Incoming Mail to a Specific Folder 223
Directing Sent Messages to a Different Folder...226
Having Replies Sent to Another Address 228
Dealing with Multiple People, Multiple Accounts, and One Little Ol' Computer 229

Book IV: Working with the Calendar............................231

Chapter 1: Getting Familiar with the Calendar 233

Appointments, Meetings, and Events — What's the Difference?...........233
Understanding Day/Week/Month View 234
Day view 235
Week view..238
Month view...239
Navigating around the Calendar 241
Creating a Complete Appointment 243
Dealing with a Reminder When It Rears Its Ugly Head...................................247
Planning an All-Day Event 247

Chapter 2: Going Further with the Calendar .251

Scheduling a Recurring Appointment, Meeting, or Event......................251
Making Changes to a Recurring Item......................253
Changing Appointments or Events......................254
Removing an Appointment or Event......................255
Reorganizing Your Time......................256
Adding Holidays to the Calendar......................258
Creating Your Own Holiday List......................260

Chapter 3: Calendar Collaboration 263

Sharing Your Calendar via Exchange......................264
    Sharing a calendar with everyone......................264
    Sharing a calendar with specific people......................266
    Changing permissions or stopping sharing......................269
Viewing Someone Else's Calendar......................270
    Accessing someone's main Calendar folder......................270
    Accessing someone's custom calendar......................273
Managing Your Time......................274
Creating a Group Schedule......................277
Forwarding Appointments to Others......................280
Sharing a Calendar in iCalendar Format......................281
Inserting Calendar Information into an E-Mail......................283
Publishing a Calendar to Microsoft Office Online......................286
Publishing a Calendar to Any Web Server......................290
Sharing a Calendar through Google......................292
    Exporting one of your calendars to Google Calendar......................292
    Importing a Google calendar......................296
    Subscribing to a Google calendar......................298

Chapter 4: All About Meetings 301

Scheduling a Meeting......................301
    Scheduling a meeting on an Exchange network......................302
    Scheduling a meeting when you don't use Exchange......................306
    Changing a meeting......................308
    Canceling a meeting......................311
Sending a Message to All Attendees......................313
Dealing with Meeting Requests......................314
    Accepting, tentatively accepting, or declining a meeting......................314
    Proposing a new meeting time......................316
    Automatically handling meeting requests......................318
Checking on Meeting Responses......................319
    Accepting or declining a time proposed by others......................320
    Automatically handling meeting responses......................322
    Preventing replies for a meeting request......................323
    Preventing time change proposals for a meeting request......................325

Chapter 5: Making the Calendar Your Own .327

Creating Multiple Calendars 328
Adding Internet Calendars 329
Displaying Multiple Calendars 332
Grouping Calendars by Type or Purpose 334
Customizing the Calendar 338
Establishing the work week and work days 338
Changing the time grid 339
Setting the default reminder time 343
Changing the calendar color 344
Customizing the Date Navigator 345
Displaying the View List on the Navigation Pane 348

Book V: Managing Contacts 349

Chapter 1: Getting in Contact 351

Adding a Complete Contact 351
Changing Contact Information 355
Basing a Contact on an Incoming E-Mail 357
Creating Another Contact from the Same Company 358
Getting Rid of Duplicate Contacts 359

Chapter 2: Working with Your Contacts 363

Picking a View That Suits Your Needs 363
Locating a Contact 365
Viewing a Map to a Contact's Address 368
Browsing to a Contact's Web Page 369
Calling a Contact 371
Viewing Activity Associated with a Contact 374

Chapter 3: Dealing with Business Cards 375

Editing a Contact's Business Card 375
Creating a Reusable Business Card 378
Creating a new business card template 378
Using a template to create a new contact 380
Applying a new template to an old contact 380
Sharing Business Cards 381
Creating a Contact from a Business Card Sent to You 382
Displaying More Business Cards 383

Chapter 4: Contacts Collaboration 385

Sharing Your Contacts 385
Sharing contacts with everyone 386
Sharing contacts with specific people 388
Changing permissions or stopping sharing 390

Viewing Contacts Shared by Others 392
Accessing someone's main Contacts folder....................392
Accessing someone's custom Contacts folder 393

Book VI: Tracking Tasks, Taking Notes, and Recording Items in the Journal....................395

Chapter 1: Creating Tasks with the To-Do Bar 397

Using the To-Do Bar to Track Tasks....................397
Turning an incoming e-mail into a To-Do bar item....................399
Turning a contact into a To-Do bar item 401
Setting the Quick Click Flag 402
Changing the Flag You've Assigned 403
Changing the Task Name on the To-Do Bar 404
Dealing With To-Do Items You've Finished or No Longer Want to Flag....................404
Marking a To-Do item as finito....................404
Removing a flag instead of marking it complete 405
Deleting a To-Do item....................406
Finding Flagged Messages....................406
Customize the To-Do Bar 408
Creating a Task Using the Daily Task List in the Calendar....................410

Chapter 2: Dealing with More Complex Tasks 413

Creating a Detailed Task....................413
Turning an e-mail into a task....................416
Linking an appointment or meeting to a task....................416
Scheduling a Recurring Task 417
Working with Tasks....................419
Changing the color of overdue tasks 420
Sorting and rearranging tasks....................421
Updating what you've done 422
Marking a task as complete....................422
Using To-Do List view....................423

Chapter 3: Spreading the Joy: Task Assignments 425

Assigning a Task to Someone Else 425
Reclaiming a Task You Tried to Reassign....................428
Checking the Progress of an Assigned Task 429
Dealing with Task Assignments Sent to You 431
Accepting or declining a task....................432
Sending a status report on an assigned task 433
Reassigning a reassigned task 435

Forwarding a Task Instead of Reassigning It 436
Sharing Your Tasks List 438
- Sharing tasks with everyone 439
- Sharing tasks with specific people 441
- Changing permissions or stopping sharing 443

Viewing Tasks Shared by Others 444
- Accessing someone's main Tasks folder 444
- Accessing someone's custom task folder 445

Chapter 4: Taking Notes 447

Creating a Complete Note 447
Organizing Notes with Categories 449
Selecting a Notes View 450
Making Notes Look the Way You Like 451
Sticking Notes to Your Desktop 453
Passing Notes 453

Chapter 5: Taking Notes in Overdrive: OneNote 455

Organizing in OneNote 456
Navigating in OneNote 457
Creating a Notebook 459
Adding a New Page 463
- Saving yourself from boredom with templates 463
- Discovering the subtle truth about subpages 465

Adding a Section 466
Adding a Section Group 467
Taking a Note 468
- Formatting text 469
- Creating a table 470
- Other stuff you can do with a new page 471

Creating a Quick Side Note From Any Program 473
Writing and Drawing Notes by Hand 474
- Adding rules to a page 476
- Converting handwriting to editable text 476
- Drawing by hand 477

Inserting Images 478
Inserting a Screen Shot 480
Adding Audio or Video 482
Inserting a Document or File 484
Inserting a Picture of a Document 485
Adding Links to Other Pages, Files, or the Internet 487
- Linking to other notebook pages 487
- Linking to files, documents, or Web pages 488

Chapter 6: Maximizing the Power of OneNote 489

Inserting Details of an Appointment or Meeting into a Note................490
Creating an Outlook Task on a Page 491
Creating an Outlook Contact from OneNote..492
Creating an Appointment or Meeting from OneNote.............................493
Creating Notes about Outlook E-Mail, Contact, Appointment, or Meeting 494
Sending a Page to Someone 495
Sharing Notes...497
Sharing a few pages...497
Blogging your notes 498
Sharing notebooks 500
Hosting a Live Sharing Session...502
Creating a live session 502
Joining a live session 504
Securing Your Notes 505
Reorganizing Your Notes...509
Selecting pages 509
Moving pages and notes...509
Moving sections...511
Tagging Important Information 511
Searching for Data..513
Finding notes you wrote recently...518
Finding tagged items...519

Chapter 7: Making History in the Journal 521

Tracking Activities in Your Journal...521
Automatically tracking activities...522
Adding previous activities to the Journal 524
Tracking Journal entries manually..525
Logging phone conversations...526
Changing the Journal View 528
Customizing the timeline...529
Using a list view 530
Turning Off Journal Tracking..531
Removing Journal Entries 533

Book VII: Working with Business Contact Manager......535

Chapter 1: Minding Your Business Contact Manager 537

Comparing BCM and Outlook? 537
Knowing Who Should Use BCM...538

Getting Started in BCM 539
Creating a database 540
Opening a database 542
Finding your current database 542
Deleting a database 543
Importing Contacts into BCM 544
Determining your data type 545
Importing data 547
Moving contacts from Outlook 550

Chapter 2: Introducing the Basic Business Contact Manager Elements 551

Working with Business Contacts 551
Adding a new Business Contact 552
Making changes to a Business Contact 554
Adding a Business Contact from an Account record 554
Getting the 411 on Accounts 555
Entering Accounts 556
Creating an Account from an existing Business Contact 558
Editing an existing Account 559
Linking Outlook to BCM Records 559
Linking existing Outlook items to a BCM record 560
Linking a BCM Record to a new Outlook item 561
Turning Your Business into a Major Project 562
Projecting your Business Projects 562
Chipping away at a Business Project 564
Tracking your project progress 565
Bidding your project adieu 565

Chapter 3: Working with Opportunities 567

Creating a New Opportunity 567
Finding More Opportunity in Your Opportunities 570
Wrapping a ribbon around an opportunity 570
Editing an opportunity 571
Closing the deal 572
Deleting an opportunity 572
Adding Products and Services to an Opportunity 573
Editing or Deleting a Product or Service 575

Chapter 4: Reports and Dashboards 577

Knowing the Basic BCM Reports 577
Running a BCM Report 580
Giving Your Reports a Facelift 581
Modifying an existing report 581
Filtering out the bad stuff 583

Drilling for Dollars in Your Reports 585
Giving your reports a helping hand 585
Having a refreshing look at your report 586
Working with Dashboards 587

Book VIII: Customizing Outlook 589

Chapter 1: Organizing Items with Categories 591

Adding a Category to an Open Outlook Item..591
Adding a Category to an Item without Opening It 593
Assigning a Quick Click Category to an Item..594
Removing a Category from an Item 596
Managing Your Categories 597
Renaming a category 598
Assigning shortcut keys to categories..598
Assigning new colors to categories 599
Creating new categories 600
Removing a category 601

Chapter 2: Changing Your View on Outlook 603

Changing Your Outlook Today..603
Reading Can Be a Pane 605
Joining the Group..607
To group or not to group 607
Getting in with the In Group..607
Viewing Outlook in a Whole New Light 609
Tabling the Table View 611
Adding a column to a table 611
Removing columns..612
Moving a column 612
Resizing a column..612
Sort of sorting your column..612
Sorting Your Data 613
The View from the Top 614
Tweaking an existing view..614
Resetting a standard view 616
Changing the name of a custom view 616
Creating a view from scratch 617
Deleting a custom view..618
Displaying All the Messages in a Folder..618
Reading in the Reading pane 619
Manually marking messages 620

Chapter 3: Customizing Outlook Forms 621
Making Quick Changes to the Quick Access Toolbar 621
Adding a Quick Access toolbar command from the Ribbon.........622
Quickly adding Quick Access toolbar commands 623
Playing with Forms 625
Creating a new form using existing fields...................................625
Form Beautification 101 628
Adding custom-defined fields 631
Using Custom Forms..632
Making your form the default 632
Deleting a form..634

Book IX: Managing Your Outlook Stuff........................635

Chapter 1: Finding a Place for Your Stuff 637
Developing an Outlook Filing System..637
Creating a new folder 638
Moving an item to another folder 639
Rearranging your folders...640
Giving folders the heave-ho 640
Moving an item to a different type of folder 641
Getting Organized with the Organize Feature 642
Playing Favorites with Your Favorite Folders...............................643
Adding folders to your Favorite Folders 644
Finding your favorites..644
Changing the order of your Favorite Folders 644
Linking a Web page to a Favorite Folder 645
Cleaning Up Your Mess..647
Giving your folders a bit of spring cleaning.................................647
Sending your data to the trash compactor...................................650
Emptying the trash...652
This is one for the archives..652

Chapter 2: Playing by the Rules 661
Making Up the Rules as You Go..661
Creating the basic game plan...661
Adding bells and whistles to your rules..665
Taking Rules the Whole Nine Yards 668
Bending the Rules 672
Running with the rules..672
Cheating with the rules...673
Throwing your rules out the window 676

Chapter 3: Making Mincemeat Out of Spam 677

Maintaining Your Junk 677
Changing the level of protection in the junk e-mail filter 677
Giving senders your seal of approval 679
Ensuring that your recipients make the list 680
Blocking a name from your Inbox 681
Putting Junk in Its Place 682
Delegating a message to the junk pile 683
Sorting through your junk mail 684
Taking out the trash — permanently 684
Protecting Yourself from Phishing Attacks 685
Changing the phishing options 686
Enable or disable links in phishing e-mail messages 686
Giving Your Mail a Postmark 688

Chapter 4: Seek and Ye Shall Find 689

Getting Instant Gratification with Instant Searching 689
Enabling Instant Search 690
Fiddling with the Instant Search options 690
Searching instantly 692
Refining your Instant Search 692
Searching through the Search Folders 694
Adding a predefined Search Folder 695
Creating a customized Search Folder 697
Deleting a Search Folder 699
Searching 101 — Finding Names in the Address Book 699
Taking the Pain out of the Navigation Pane 701
Getting turned on by the Navigation pane 701
Playing hide and seek with the Navigation pane 701
Finding your way around the Navigation pane buttons 702
Fiddling with the Folder List 704
Working with Shortcuts and Shortcut Groups 704
Creating a Shortcut 705
Tweaking a Shortcut 705
Creating a group of Shortcuts 706
Tweaking a Shortcut group 706

Chapter 5: Securing Outlook E-Mail 707

Working with Passwords 707
Guarding Your Privacy 709
Grappling with Macros 711
Handling a macro security warning 711
Changing the macro settings in the Trust Center 711

Help! Someone's Sending E-Mail on My Behalf....712
Answering the security warning....713
Preventing future security warnings....713
Kicking the HTML out of Your E-Mail....715
Sending via Certified E-Mail....716
Getting a digital ID from a certifying authority....716
Putting your digital ID to work....717
Exchanging e-mail certificates....718
Sending Encrypted or Digitally Signed E-Mail....719
Encrypting or using a digital signature....719
Sending a message with an S/MIME receipt request....720
Setting a message expiration date....721
Understanding the Information Rights Management Program....721
How IRM watches your back....722
When you need to watch your own back....722
Configuring your computer for IRM....723
Sending a message with restricted permissions....723
Using a different account for IRM e-mail....724
Viewing messages with restricted permissions....724

Book X: Out and About: Taking Outlook on the Road.....725

Chapter 1: Staying in Touch No Matter Where You Are 727

Letting the Out of Office Assistant Handle Mail While You're Gone....727
Turning the Assistant on or off....728
Letting rules control the Assistant....730
Changing the rules....732
What to do if you have a POP3 or IMAP e-mail account....734
Assigning a Delegate to Handle E-Mail and Appointments While You're Gone....737
Assigning a delegate....737
Changing a delegate's permission levels....741
Managing Someone Else's E-Mail and Calendar....742
Displaying somebody else's folders....742
Dealing with meetings and tasks as a delegate....746
Dealing with e-mail as a delegate....748
Dealing with appointments as a delegate....750

Chapter 2: Turning Your E-Mail Accounts into Roadies 751

Taking E-Mail on the Road....751
Getting e-mail messages on a second computer without deleting them....752
Downloading message headers only....754

Taking Microsoft Exchange on the Road....757
Downloading the Offline Address Book....757
Changing the Cached Exchange Mode settings to download headers only....760
Using Web Mail as a Solution....762
Creating a Web-Outlook connection....763
Checking on your Web connection....765
Importing Outlook contacts to Windows Live Mail....765

Chapter 3: Printing Your Stuff and Taking It with You....767

Printing a Message and Any Attached Documents....768
Printing the Contents of Any Other Single Item....772
Printing a List of Items....773
Printing Contact Names and Mailing Addresses....776
Printing Contact Names and E-Mail Addresses....779
Printing a Blank Calendar....781

Index....783

Introduction

Life in the digital age seems so complicated to me. When I was younger, life was simple: Go to school, do your homework fast, then play, play, play until Mom calls you in for dinner. Then go back out and play until just past dark. We didn't need a lot of fancy electronics — just something resembling a ball (even if it was a bit deflated), a set of ever-changing rules, and a big backyard.

As an adult, things have gotten much too hurry-up-and-wait, if you know what I mean. Sure, it's nice to have all the latest gadgets — I don't know what I'd do without my cell, PDA, or laptop with its wireless Internet connection. But I find it ironic that the tools that were supposed to make life easier have made it more complex. Sure, having a cell phone means I can get through to my daughter when needed and get help in case of an emergency. It also means that my boss can find me even when I go out on the weekends, or that a client can track me down at all hours and give me new things to get done by the end of the day.

If your life runs nonstop like mine, you're probably overwhelmed with lists, lists, lists. You keep notes to remind you to pick up milk on the way home and to keep track of your client's cell number, your best friend's new address, and directions to that restaurant where you're meeting your boss for an employee review. Rather than filling your purse, wallet, or pockets with a bunch of notes, I recommend turning the whole mess over to Microsoft Outlook. I'm pretty confident you'll find that Outlook is a much better organizer.

Outlook includes several parts, or *modules*; each module keeps track of an important aspect of your busy, busy life:

- **Mail** stores incoming and outgoing e-mail messages in folders you create. It also lets you quickly find e-mail based on content and re-sort messages however you want, and provides a quick and easy way of previewing e-mail attachments without having to open them completely (and possibly infect your system with a virus).
- **Calendar** stores all your appointments, meetings, and day-long events and displays them in daily, weekly, or monthly format. It also displays the Daily Tasks list, in case you don't have enough going on in your day.

- **Contacts** helps you remember the important facts about the people you know, such as their name, phone number, address, e-mail address, cell number, and Web page address. This module also helps you track important trivia, such as the name of their spouse, children, and family pet.
- **Tasks** tracks all the things you need to get done, now or someday. Tasks are divided into two groups: to-do items, which are basically quick notes about things to do, and tasks, which contain more detailed info such as task start date, due date, number of hours spent on the task, status, percent complete, priority, and reminder.
- **Notes** tracks small bits of stray info, like your locker combination and super-secret decoder password. You can even post these notes on your Windows desktop if you need them to be more "in your face."
- **Journal** is a "module wanna be." Journal isn't used much, although there's no particular reason why it can't be useful, since it tracks activities related to selected contacts and provides an easy way to review them. Snoopy Journal tracks all sorts of activities, such as e-mails sent to and from a specific contact, appointments made with a contact, phone calls made to a contact, and Office documents associated with that contact, such as Excel workbooks and Word documents.

Now, most of you will be completely satisfied with this group of six hardworking modules. But for those of you for whom nothing is ever enough — well, depending on your version of Office, Outlook comes with several companion programs that expand its functionality:

- **OneNote** is Notes on steroids. With this creature, you can create notebooks on any subject and fill their pages with text, graphics, sound recordings, screen captures, Web links, and links to Outlook items such as appointments and tasks.
- **Business Contact Manager** (BCM to its friends) can help you manage numerous hot and cold leads, important contacts and their accounts, and several money-generating projects.

Along the way, there's lots of hand-holding. Steps are written clearly, with explanations and lots of pictures to help you see if you're getting it right.

About This Book

Even though Outlook is made up of lots of parts, such as Mail, Contacts, and Calendar, most people use it at first only to manage e-mail. That's okay; Outlook's a big boy and can take the fact that you think it's only an e-mail program. Once you get used to using Outlook, though, you'll find that it's pretty handy for all sorts of things — except maybe taking out the garbage and clearing a drain.

Don't let all those Outlook modules overwhelm you at first; you can get to each of them in your own sweet time. And the way this book is organized will help you. Each chapter is written with a kind of "I don't know much" attitude, so if you want to jump over to one of the Calendar chapters and start there, you can. If something you need to know is located in a different chapter, I'll tell you about it. Don't worry.

Along the way, there's lots of hand-holding. Steps are written clearly, with explanations and lots of pictures to help you see if you're getting it right.

Conventions Used in This Book

The new Office Ribbon may throw you at first, but Book I, Chapter 2, helps you get over any trepidations you may have. Frankly, I found the Ribbon a bit overwhelming at first, because its purpose is to show you every command you might ever want to use. However, after a second or so, I found it the smartest design change Microsoft could have ever made. The Ribbon makes it quite easy to locate the command you need, such as Send (for sending a message) or Attach File (for adding an e-mail attachment such as a picture or a workbook).

You don't see the Ribbon when you first start Outlook. Nope — the Ribbon doesn't make an appearance until you try to create something using a special window that Outlook calls a *form*. So, if you create a message or an appointment, you'll see the Ribbon. If you're wondering what the Ribbon looks like, there's a picture of it in Book I, Chapter 2, so the two of you can get properly introduced. Go ahead and take a look; the Introduction will still be here when you get back. While you're looking, I want you to notice a few things, such as the tabs along the top that allow you to display different sets of buttons, and the group name that appears under each group of similar buttons. The group name is important when you want to follow the steps in this book, as you'll see in a moment.

Every book has its own way of showing you how to do stuff. In this book, if I want you to select a command on the Ribbon, I give you the sequence of things to click, like this:

Message⇨Include⇨Attach File

This sequence tells you what to click and in what order. First, click the Message tab, and then in the Include group, click the Attach File button. So the sequence again is: Click the Message tab, look for the Include group (don't click it), and click the Attach File button. Got it? Great.

The Ribbon does not appear in the main Outlook window where you switch from module to module; you'll see instead the basic menu system you're used to. If I need you to select a command from a menu, you'll see something like this:

View⇨Current View⇨Messages with AutoPreview

Here, the sequence is less mysterious: Open the View menu, click Current View, and then click Messages with AutoPreview on the submenu that appears. By clicking, I mean pointing at something on the screen and pressing down that left mouse button. (Right-clicking involves pointing and pressing the right mouse button instead.)

Underneath the menu in the main Outlook window, you'll find the Standard toolbar, and using it should be pretty familiar since just about every program designed today has a toolbar. (Soon they'll all be sporting Ribbons, though.) Anyway, if you need to activate a command from the toolbar, I'll tell you to click a certain button. All you gotta do at that point is click the right picture-button.

Foolish Assumptions

Well, maybe it is foolish for me to assume something about you since we've never actually met, but I'm betting that you're a Windows user and therefore at least a little familiar with basic Windows stuff like windows, minimizing and maximizing, and using menus. I'm also assuming that you know how to use a mouse and to click and double-click.

I guess I wouldn't be far off in assuming that you have an e-mail account somewhere and that you want to send and receive e-mail messages. That's what Outlook is more or less known for. I won't assume, however, that you've set up Outlook to get messages; instead, I show you how to do that in Book I, Chapter 3.

Finally, when I show you something, I won't assume you know anything about Outlook other than its name, or how to use Outlook to do anything.

How This Book Is Organized

Although Outlook is actually a pretty complex, fully-fledged program, don't let its power overwhelm you. It's remarkable how little you actually need to know to get started, and I've stuck it all in Book I, "Getting Started." In fact, you don't even have to read all four chapters in Book I. I recommend at least glancing through Chapters 1 and 2, though, because they teach you the basics of how to navigate and use Outlook.

So, with two little chapters, you're off to the races. From there, you can skip around to whichever chapter deals with a topic of interest. Not sure where to find stuff? Don't worry; I've got it pretty well organized so you can find what you need quickly. First off, this book is divided into minibooks. There are nine of them, each focusing on a particular aspect of Outlook. In each book are chapters, numbered from 1 to whatever. So when I say, go look in Book II, Chapter 4, I mean the fourth chapter in the second minibook. You can always tell what book and chapter you're in by looking for that gray box on the right-hand page. Here's what each book is about:

Book I: Getting Started

This minibook covers the basics of the Outlook window, such as how to use the Navigation pane, the Reading pane, and the Ribbon. Chapter 2 shows you how to quickly create just about any item in Outlook, such as a quick message or appointment. Obviously, there's more to creating items than what's covered in Chapter 2, so from there you can jump to the book that covers that item in more depth, such as Calendar. This minibook also includes stuff you might not need to do because someone's already done it for you, such as adding your e-mail account information and importing data from your old e-mail program.

Book II: E-Mail Basics

This minibook shows you how to use the Mail module. You see how to create more than just simple e-mail messages, read and reply to e-mail you get, make your messages look snappy, and repeat the same information (such as your name and phone number) in all outgoing e-mails without retyping it all the time.

Book III: Über E-Mail

This minibook covers more than the need-to-know stuff, moving into the cool-to-know area of e-mail. In this minibook, you see how to manage multiple e-mail accounts, control when e-mail is sent or received, use Outlook to send instant messages (yes, you can!), and blanket the Internet with a single message. Okay, I don't show you how to generate spam (mass junk e-mail); I show you how to send a single message to multiple people in your Contacts list.

Book IV: Working with the Calendar

As you might expect, this minibook focuses on the part of Outlook that keeps track of appointments, meetings, and such: Calendar. You see how to display Calendar in a bunch of different ways; create appointments, meetings, and day-long events; make those items repeat in your calendar without retyping them; make changes to appointments, meetings, and events; share your calendar with other people in your company; add cool stuff like Internet calendars; and customize the way Calendar looks and operates.

Book V: Managing Contacts

This minibook focuses on the Contacts module, showing you the basics in adding contacts and displaying them in a variety of ways. You also see how to work your contacts, pulling up an associated Web site or a map of their location. You'll also learn cool stuff like creating mock business cards and sharing contacts with colleagues and friends.

Book VI: Tracking Tasks, Taking Notes, and Recording Items in the Journal

This minibook covers a lot of ground — the Tasks module, where you create tasks and to-do items (think mini-tasks), the Notes module, where you can create quick Post-it-like short notes, and the Journal, where you can track activity related to particular contacts. You also see how to use OneNote, a cool add-on program that allows you to gather Outlook items like tasks and meeting details into one place, alongside your notes from the meeting, handouts, graphics, audio notes, and other minutiae.

Book VII: Working with Business Contact Manager

This minibook focuses on another Outlook add-on program called Business Contact Manager. You see how to use it to manage business contacts, business accounts, and the revenue they generate. You also see how to keep track of the details surrounding large projects that involve multiple contacts, a myriad of tasks, and who knows how much record keeping.

Book VIII: Customizing Outlook

Jump to this minibook to see how to create categories for grouping Outlook items together; change your view of messages, tasks, contacts, appointments, and such; and customize the basic working window, the *form* (the window in which you create an item such as an outgoing e-mail message or a new contact).

Book IX: Managing Your Outlook Stuff

After creating tons of Outlook items, including contacts, e-mail messages, and tasks, you will realize that you need to organize them. You can approach this problem in several ways, all of which are covered in this minibook. You see how to create new folders to put stuff in, move or copy items from folder to folder, and clean up your mailbox. You also see how to complete handy tasks, such as using rules to automatically sort incoming mail; deal with *spam* (junk e-mail); locate the stuff you've created; and make Outlook more secure.

Book X: Out and About: Taking Outlook on the Road

This book covers ways to manage the problem of getting e-mail when you're out of the office, how to deal with incoming messages automatically when you're on vacation (or how to get someone to do it for you), and how to print stuff like e-mail messages or contact info.

Icons Used in This Book

As you browse through this tome, your thoughts will be occasionally interrupted by little pictures (icons) in the margin. These icons point out important things you should know.

These paragraphs contain shortcuts and other tips that help you get something done quickly and get back to enjoying life.

These icons point you toward other important information in the book, or they may just contain important things to make a note of.

Watch out for this information, as it may very well prevent you from making a common mistake.

Technical Stuff paragraphs contain interesting but not vital information, such as the reasons behind a particular task, or the ways to deal with a particular situation that applies to only a select few. Don't feel compelled to read these tidbits unless you're truly interested in the topic at hand.

Where to Go from Here

The best place to start if you are new to Microsoft Outlook is Book I, Chapter 1. Then move on to Book I, Chapter 2. Those two chapters give you the basic stuff you need to know to start using Outlook right away. From there, just jump around to the chapters that interest you, or that point you to the ways to solve the problem you're dealing with at the moment, such as how to get an appointment to appear somewhere else on your calendar, or change somebody's e-mail address in the Contacts list.

Book I

Getting Started

The 5th Wave
By Rich Tennant
RICHTENNANT
It's an e-mail from my mother. She wants me to know how happy she is for us.

Contents at a Glance

Chapter 1: An Insider's Look at the Outlook Interface.....11

Chapter 2: Outlook, Quick and Dirty.....33

Chapter 3: Setting Up Your E-Mail Accounts.....53

Chapter 4: Importing Data into Outlook.....69

Chapter 1: An Insider's Look at the Outlook Interface

In This Chapter

- Getting comfortable with the Outlook interface
- Moving from place to place within Outlook
- Getting a handle on today's events
- Making everything the right size for you
- Moving Outlook out of the way as you do other work

I'm always hearing that this is the Information Age — what an understatement! Right now, I'm sitting here wondering exactly how much information a single adult needs just to get through any given day. Given all the phone numbers, cell numbers, e-mail addresses, meetings, appointments, and lists of things to get done before the boss catches on, I bet it's a lot. Actually, let me look up that exact figure — it's probably right here at my fingertips along with the thousands of other highly useful bits of my life's daily trivia.

If ever a program was designed for the Information Age, it's Outlook. I'll bet the people at Microsoft created Outlook just so they could see their desks every once in a while. As you'll discover in this chapter, Outlook is pretty handy for managing the tons of data that clutter your desk on a daily basis — the hundreds of messages, appointments you better not miss, names you better not forget, and things you better do.

What Can Outlook Do for Me?

That's a good question. No sense in letting Outlook sit around on your Windows desktop if it won't at least help you clean up your *real* desktop once in a while.

As you probably already know, Outlook handles e-mail messages, both coming and going. What you might not know, however, is that it integrates nicely with other forms of electronic communication, including instant messaging, text messaging, and electronic news feeds (RSS). All this communicating takes place within the confines of Outlook's Mail module — which happens to be the module that's displayed when you start Outlook, as shown in Figure 1-1.

The Mail module is so handy that it takes two minibooks to tell you all about it: Books II and III.

In addition to the Mail module, Outlook has five other modules, each one designed to help you manage a different part of your busy life:

✦ **Calendar:** The life's work of the Calendar module is to keep track of all your appointments, meetings, and day-long events such as birthdays and seminars. And the magic doesn't stop there. The Calendar can help you easily manage multiple calendars — from the busy schedules of your children to the central calendar for your department. You find the nitty-gritty details for using the Calendar in Book IV.

✦ **Contacts:** The Contacts module organizes the details you need to remember about all the people in your life, from your favorite plumber's emergency phone number to the name of your boss's spouse. You can use it to keep track of important business contacts, even grouping people from the same company together. And when you're running late for a meeting, Contacts can quickly provide a map to the meeting's location. The Contacts module is the star of Book V.

✦ **Tasks:** In the Tasks module, you find all those things you need to do whenever you find the time. You can quickly arrange tasks by due date, priority, or any other category you can think of (such as Pass On to Some Unsuspecting Fool). You master multitasking in Book VI.

✦ **Notes:** In the Notes module, you keep track of, well, your notes. I know you prefer little bits of scrap paper, the back of cash-register receipts, empty envelopes, and Kleenexes, but why not give the Notes module a shot? See Book VI for help.

✦ **Journal:** Playing a background role is the Journal, which you can program to track your activities. I know you're thinking, "My busybody neighbor in the next apartment is already doing a pretty good job of that." Using the Journal, however, you can quickly locate the e-mail, appointments, to-do items, and even documents associated with a particular client. (The Journal module is discussed in-depth in Book VI.)

Outlook is a part of Microsoft Office, so it's designed to play nicely with its brothers and sisters. Throughout this book, you find many ways to use the various Office components — Word, Excel, PowerPoint, and so on — with Outlook. For example, you might want to use the addresses in Contacts to create form letters in Word, or you might want to insert Excel data into an e-mail message in Outlook. Whether your goal is to get data into or out of Outlook, you can find a simple way to accomplish your task within these pages.

You can jump between modules — Mail, Calendar, Contacts, Tasks, Notes, and Journal — by choosing the module you want from the Go menu. Most people, however, take the freeway when traveling between Outlook modules:

the Navigation pane, which is described in more detail later (in the section "Getting Around with the Navigation Pane").

When you change to a different module in Outlook, the buttons on the Standard toolbar and the commands on the Actions menu (shown in Figure 1-1) change. For example, if you jump to the Calendar, you find buttons for displaying today's schedule and accessing the Address Book. On the Actions menu, you find commands related to Calendar tasks, such as creating an appointment or setting up a meeting.

Heeeerrre's Outlook!

Like most Web pages, Outlook's window (see Figure 1-1) contains a navigation system on the left and a viewing area on the right. The viewing area changes a bit as you move from module to module, but basically you'll see the items in that module (such as all your tasks if you're in the Tasks module) in a big long list.

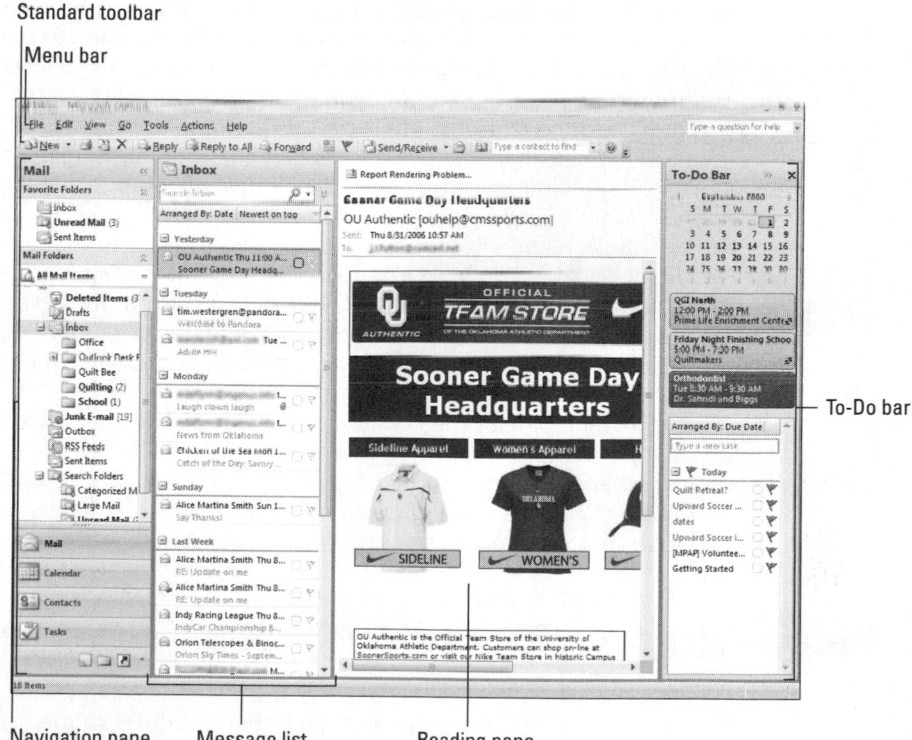

Figure 1-1: Outlook handles e-mail and more.

You can choose a view to display the items in the current module however you want. To select an arrangement, choose it from the View menu (choose View⇨Current View). For example, when you open the Mail module, it displays e-mail using the Messages view, which sounds like all your messages are just dumped in a pile and then thrown on the screen. Instead, Messages view simply arranges your mail in the order in which you received it, grouped by day. With a click or two, you can easily group the messages in a different way — for example, by putting all the messages from the same person together; you find out how to do this in Book II, Chapter 2. Picky viewers can customize a view to suit their exacting needs. For example, in the Mail module, you might customize the Messages view to show only e-mails with files attached to them. (See Book VIII, Chapter 2 for details.)

So to recap, the viewing area is located on the right, and it changes depending on which module you're in. The left side of the Outlook window is where the navigation system (the Navigation pane) resides. As you discover in the next section, the Navigation pane helps you get around the various modules in Outlook.

At the top of the Outlook window, you might recognize the menu bar (which includes the File, Edit, and View menus), and below it, the Standard toolbar. The Standard toolbar keeps buttons like the Print, Move to Folder, and Delete buttons close at hand so you can call on them whenever you want. The number and type of buttons appearing on the Standard toolbar change as you move around Outlook. The New button, on the far left, is always there no matter where you go. Click it to create a new something in the current module. For example, if you click New while in Contacts, you create a new contact. Want to send a message while in Contacts? Then click the arrow on the New button and choose New Message from the list.

As you might expect, if you don't know what a button does, just hover the mouse over it for a second, and a ScreenTip appears, displaying the name of the button. (It's nice how all the Office programs dress and work alike, isn't it?)

On the far right side of the Outlook window, you find the To-Do bar. This guy doesn't automatically show up in every module, although you can make him appear whenever you want. As you might gather by looking at Figure 1-1, he's there to remind you of upcoming appointments and things you better get done. You read more about the To-Do bar later in this chapter.

Getting Around with the Navigation Pane

I don't know where they got the name, because the Navigation pane (see Figure 1-2) definitely isn't a pain. In fact, it couldn't be simpler to use. To jump to a different module in Outlook, just click that module's button. For example, click the Calendar button to see all the appointments, meetings, and other things you've got to do today. If you get depressed when you look at all the stuff you have to get done by Friday, you can jump over to Tasks (by clicking the Tasks button) and make a note to book a vacation — soon. You'll find the navigation buttons at the bottom of the Navigation pane.

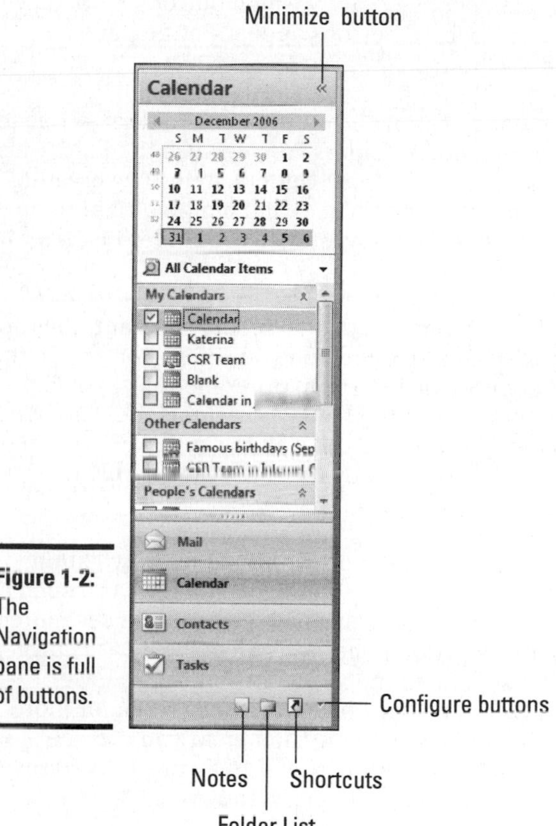

Figure 1-2: The Navigation pane is full of buttons.

Below the Tasks button (refer to Figure 1-2), you find a group of these small icons:

- **Notes:** Takes you to the Notes module. You find out how to take notes in Book VI, Chapter 4.
- **Folder List:** Displays the Folder List.

✦ **Shortcuts:** Lets you easily access your favorite folders. You find out how to take such shortcuts later in this chapter.

✦ **Configure buttons:** Click this down-arrow button to see a menu with commands that control the number and type of module buttons on the Navigation pane and to perform other tweaks. Choose Show More Button on this menu to display more buttons on the pane; choose Show Less Buttons to reduce the number of buttons shown. If you choose Add or Remove Buttons, you can choose exactly which buttons to display or remove. Choose the order in which buttons appear on the pane by choosing Navigation Pane Options.

What's the Folder List? It's a handy list of all your Outlook folders — one for each Outlook module plus other special folders. You can use the Folder List to perform neat tricks such as organizing your Outlook items (by creating new folders or moving items from place to place) and jumping right to an e-mail folder from any other module. You investigate the Folder List later in this chapter.

Although the bottom half of the Navigation pane remains constant, the top portion of the Navigation pane changes depending on where you are. In the Mail module, it displays a list of e-mail folders. In other modules, you'll probably see a list of views that you can use to change how items are displayed. For example, in Tasks, you can choose to display all the tasks due within the next seven days or just those that are already overdue. Now if only there was an Easy button somewhere on the Navigation pane.

By the way, if you see some blue text in the upper half of the Navigation pane, feel free to click it; the blue text is just a link to a related task, such as Browse Calendars Online. If you find yourself wishing you could see more of what's going on in the upper Navigation pane, you can make its area bigger by dragging the blue bar that separates the upper area from the lower module buttons downward. (Drag the bar upward to make room for more module buttons.) To make the Navigation pane thinner so you can see more of the viewing area, click its Minimize button. (Refer to Figure 1-2.) To restore the pane to its normal self, click the Expand button shown in Figure 1-3.

If space is really a problem, you can remove the Navigation pane altogether and use the Go menu to get around. To banish the Navigation pane from the screen, choose View➪Navigation Pane➪Off, or just press Alt+F1. To compromise between pane space and viewing space, resize the Navigation pane, as described later in this chapter.

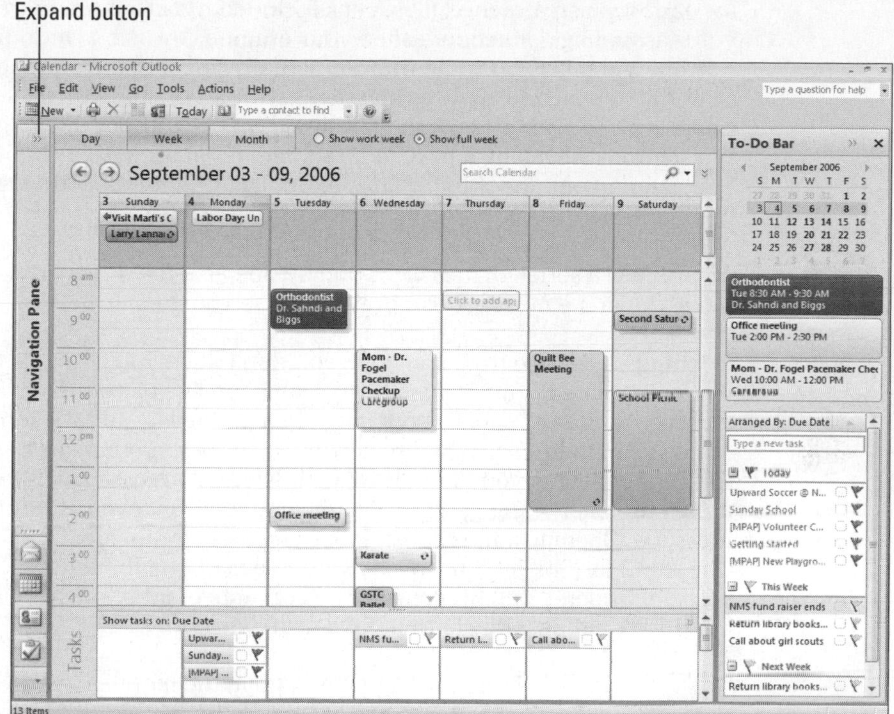

Figure 1-3: Minimize the Navigation pane to make more viewing room.

Viewing Mail with the Reading Pane

If you get a lot of e-mail messages (and who doesn't these days?), you have to deal with them as they come in, or they quickly pile up. Using the Reading pane, you can preview the contents of a message without wasting time opening it. Here's how it works: When you jump to Mail, you see several columns to the right of the Navigation pane, as shown in Figure 1-4. The first column lists the messages in the current e-mail folder. (You find out how to create e-mail folders in Book IX, Chapter 1.) The second column is the Reading pane, where you can preview messages.

In Mail, just click a message header to preview its contents in the Reading pane, as shown in Figure 1-4. If needed, use the Reading pane's scroll bars to scroll through the e-mail. While previewing the message, you can reply to it, forward it, open attached files, click included hyperlinks, and even cast a vote (assuming the sender asked your opinion) by using Outlook's voting buttons. All this is possible without actually opening the message. To find out how to read and reply to messages without opening them, see Book I, Chapter 2. To find out how to view attachments without opening them, see the section, "Sneaking a peek at attachments," later in this chapter for help. You can find out about hyperlinks in Book II, Chapter 3, and voting in Book III, Chapter 1.

To preview a series of messages one by one, use the down-arrow key to move down the message list, previewing as you go.

Opening a message from someone you don't know might unleash an unruly virus on your computer, possibly causing damage to your files. Previewing a message is not the same as opening it, so previewing allows you to keep the bad guys in their cages. By previewing a message, you might be able to tell if the sender means you harm. If so, just delete the message without opening it. Be careful of opening any attachments, however, even after previewing a message. Opening a file can set loose any monster inside it. See Book II, Chapter 2 for tips on how to safely open e-mail attachments; see the next section for details on previewing the contents of attachments without opening them (and possibly letting out a nasty virus).

The gold bar that sometimes appears above the message contents is called the InfoBar. (See Figure 1-5.) True to its name, it provides information about the message, such as whether it contains evil attachments, images, or audio files that were blocked because they might cause problems on your system if they scurry about willy-nilly.

You can use the InfoBar to download the images and audio files in messages that were blocked by Outlook; see Book II, Chapter 2 for how-tos.

You can hide the Reading pane if you don't want to use it by choosing View➪Reading Pane➪Off. Bring the pane back out of hiding by choosing View➪Reading Pane➪Right (to position the Reading pane to the right of the message list) or View➪Reading Pane➪Bottom (to position the Reading pane at the bottom of the Outlook window, below the message list).

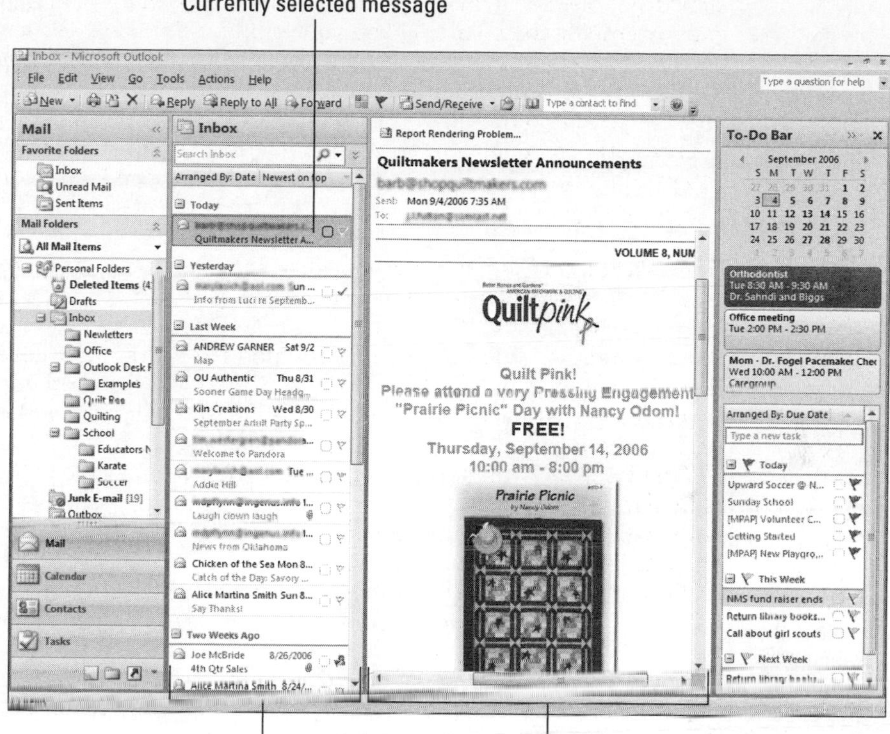

Figure 1-4: Deal with incoming messages fast by previewing them.

Previewing with AutoPreview

Even if the Reading pane is hidden, you can still preview the contents of messages, although in a slightly different way, using a little gadget called AutoPreview. To turn on AutoPreview, choose View⇨AutoPreview. When AutoPreview is on, the first three lines of each message appear just below the message's header, as shown in Figure 1-5. This allows you to quickly scan the message list and decide which ones you want to open.

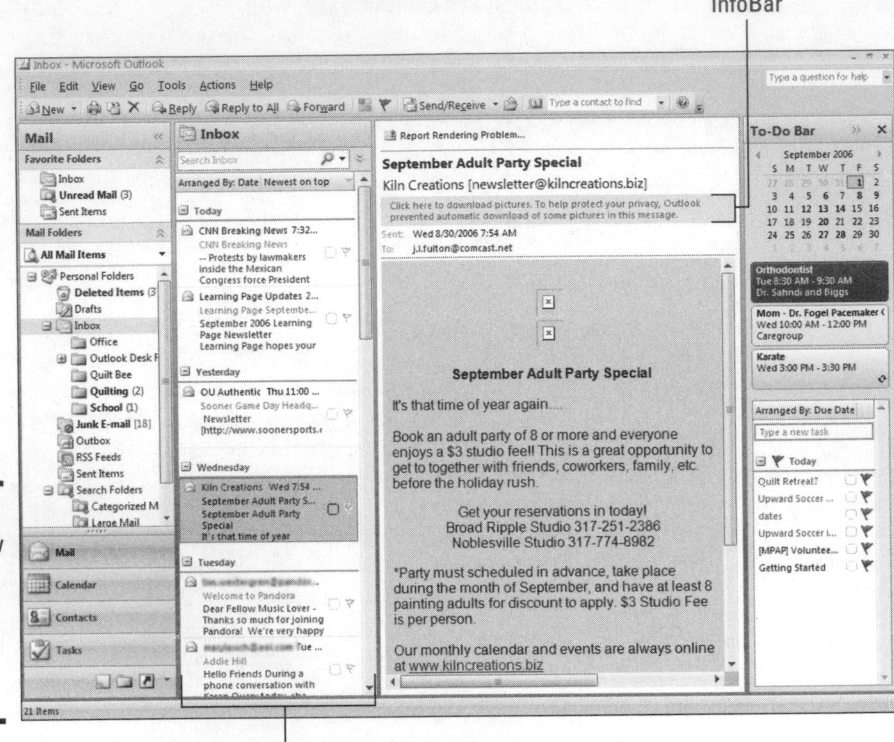

Figure 1-5: AutoPreview provides an alternative to using the Reading pane.

Sneaking a peek at attachments

Opening *attachments* (images, documents, and other files sent with an e-mail) can sometimes cause problems on your system, given that the attached files might contain macros, scripts, and ActiveX controls with evil on their minds. These potential monsters are basically an automated series of actions that might damage your files if you set them loose. One way to protect your computer is to preview an attachment rather than open it. When an attachment is previewed in Outlook, any macros, scripts, or ActiveX controls it might contain are automatically restrained in little puppy cages so they can do no damage.

Messages that have attachments are shown in the message list with a small paper clip icon, as shown in Figure 1-6. To preview an attachment, just click the file's name, which is displayed just above the message contents in the Reading pane. If you see a warning, click the Preview File button that appears in the Reading pane to view the file's contents. If someone's sent you a message with lots of attachments, you might have to scroll the list to find the attachment you want to preview. To view the message contents again, click the message button on the InfoBar.

When you preview an attachment, you might not see the complete, final contents of the file. To be absolutely sure you're seeing everything, you should open the attachment. See Book II, Chapter 2 for details.

Of course, some attachments can't be previewed because Outlook doesn't know how to properly decipher their contents. Outlook can easily preview Office documents (duh) and image files, so you won't have any problems there. To view the contents of other attachments, you must open them manually — after running your virus detector over them, of course. See Book II, Chapter 2 for help.

If a message was sent using Rich Text Format (RTF) instead of HTML or plain text format, then you won't be able to preview any attachments (although you can open them easily). The type of format used to send a message appears in the message title bar when the message is opened in its own window. So if you have trouble previewing an attachment that you think Outlook should be able to display, you can always open the message and check its format. Of course, you can't change the format of a message that was sent to you, but after opening the message, at least you'll know why you can't preview the attachments that the message contains.

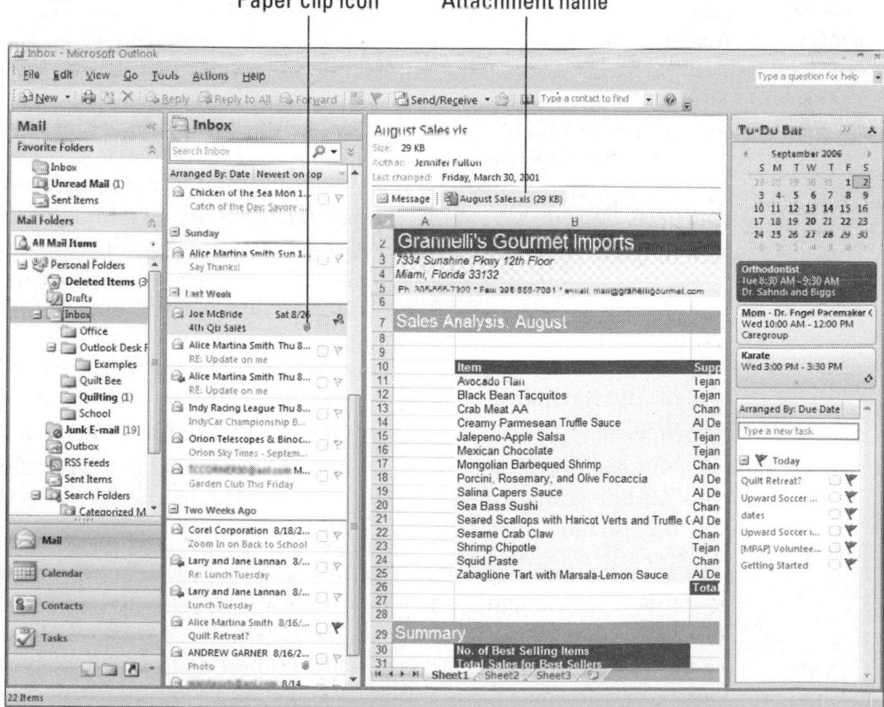

Figure 1-6: Preview attachments rather than opening them.

By the way, you can also preview an attachment in a message that's already open (assuming Outlook knows how to display the attachment, of course). Again, in the open message, just click the name of the attachment (you can find it below the Subject box). To redisplay the message contents, click the Message icon. In order to entice you to read more of this book, I've cleverly hidden the directions for opening messages in the next chapter.

If necessary, you can easily display all your messages that have attachments. See Book VIII, Chapter 2 for help.

Having Fun with the Folder List

The Folder List displays all of your Outlook folders — not only your e-mail folders, but also a folder for each Outlook module, such as Contacts. You also find some special folders hanging around the Folder List, such as search folders. Search folders are linked to specific search criteria; when you open a search folder, it displays any e-mail that currently matches the criteria — such as all your unread mail. You find out how to create your own search folders in Book IX, Chapter 4.

To make the Folder List appear within any module, just click the Folder List button at the bottom of the Navigation pane, as shown in Figure 1-7. Your folder listing then appears at the top of the Navigation pane.

You probably won't use the Folder List much because you can jump to most folders pretty easily without it. I tend to use the Folder List when jumping back and forth between other modules and my e-mail. I use a lot of e-mail folders to help me organize my mail better. When I'm in Calendar or Contacts, I like to be able to jump right to the exact e-mail folder I need, instead of to whatever e-mail folder I was using last.

If you decide to use the Folder List, here are some things to remember:

✦ If you display the Folder List and then click a different module button on the Navigation pane (such as the Contacts button), the Folder List disappears.

✦ You can keep the Folder List on-screen by clicking the folder for the module you want to use from those in the list. So, to keep the Folder List up and move to Contacts, click the Contacts folder.

✦ As with any Windows folder listing, if you want to see subfolders, click a folder's plus sign. To collapse a folder and hide its subfolders, click the folder's minus sign.

- You won't see shared folders in the Folder List. So, to browse through your boss's Calendar, you'll have to click the Calendar button to access the link to the shared calendar.
- Remember that if you drag down the bar just above the module buttons on the Navigation pane, you can make more room to display the Folder List. You also make less room to display the module buttons, so if you drag the border all the way down to the bottom of the Navigation pane, all the module buttons change to tiny icons. You can still use them, however (assuming you can see them).
- To remove the Folder List and return to normal, just click any of the module buttons. For example, click the Contacts button to remove the Folder List and replace it with view options and handy links for using Contacts.

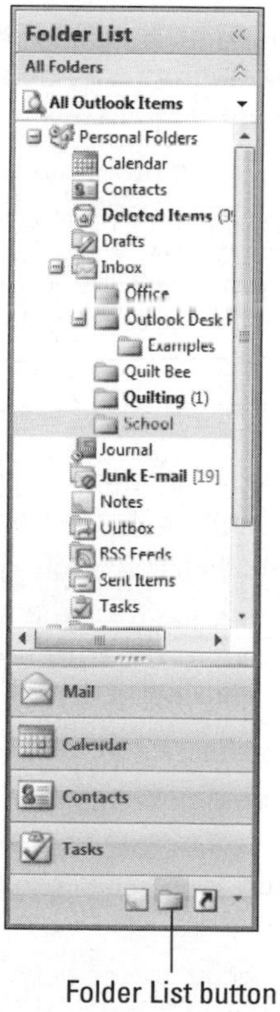

Folder List button

Figure 1-7: The Folder List displays all your Outlook folders.

Your Week in a Nutshell: The New To-Do Bar

Nowadays it's common for a person to wear lots of hats: project leader, department head, soccer mom, PTA queen, party girl, and occasional community volunteer. Although Outlook doesn't provide a closet for all your hats, you might find that it does a good job of helping you keep track of them — plus all the meetings, appointments, events, and tasks that come with wearing so many. Outlook gathers your stuff together in one place on the To-Do bar. There, you can find today's due-soon-or-even-sooner list of appointments, meetings, and tasks.

You'll also find tasks listed along the bottom of the Calendar and in the Tasks module.

Note that Outlook categorizes your things to do in two groups:

- **Tasks:** A task is something you create, typically, while in the Tasks module. It usually has both a starting and ending (due) date associated with it, and its information is fairly complete.
- **To-Do items:** A To-Do item is created from some other Outlook item, when you flag it. For example, if an e-mail message comes in reminding you to bring that sales report to the planning meeting, you can flag the message and create an instant reminder in the To-Do list. By default, items flagged this way are considered due today, although you can tweak the timing as needed.

You find out the nitty-gritty of flagging stuff to create To-Do items in Book VI, Chapter 1. All you need to know right now is that both your To-Do items and your Tasks show up on the To-Do bar.

The To-Do bar, shown in Figure 1-8, appears nightly in the Mail room, along its right side. You can make the To-Do bar appear in any other module by choosing View➪To-Do Bar➪Normal from the menu bar. Turn it off again by choosing View➪To-Do Bar➪Off. This turns the bar off in the current module only. To minimize the bar to a skinny column along the right side that you can instantly expand with a single click, choose View➪To-Do Bar➪Minimize. You can also minimize the bar by clicking its Minimize button.

Here's a closer look at the different parts of the To-Do bar, as shown in Figure 1-8:

- **Date Navigator:** You can use this navigator to jump over to the Calendar so you can look at tasks and appointments for a different day, week, or month. You'll find out how to navigate the Navigator in Book IV, Chapter 1.

- **Appointments:** This section is where your next three appointments or meetings are listed in order by date. It's probably important to note that day-long events don't show up in the To-Do bar, although that shouldn't matter much because such events are typically things like birthdays and anniversaries. (Note to Microsoft: As a wife, I believe you might want to rethink your idea of not showing events on the To-Do bar — because forgetting certain events might cause the belongings of your clients to be thrown out on the lawn. Just a thought.)
- **Tasks and To-Do Items:** Below the Appointments section, you find your complete list of tasks and to-do items. Notice how the thoughtful folks at Microsoft added a scroll bar, just in case you have a long, long list of things to do.

You can customize the To-Do bar to change the number of months and appointments shown. You can also control whether the task list appears on the To-Do bar. See Book VI, Chapter 1 for details.

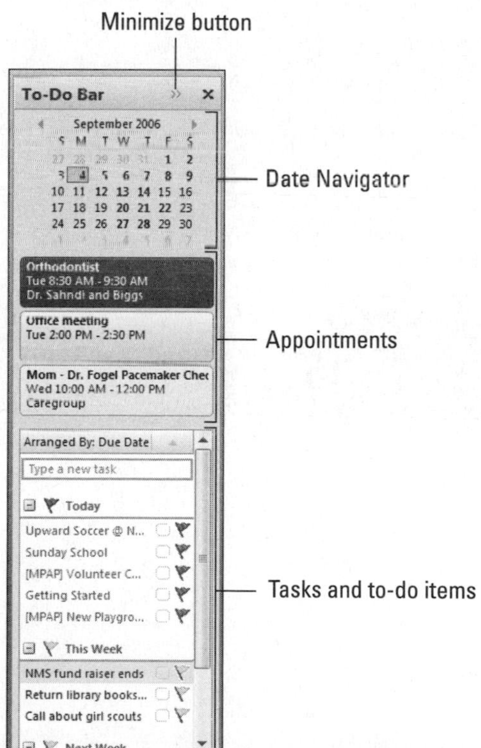

Figure 1-8: Step right up to the To-Do bar.

Getting a Snapshot of Your Day with Outlook Today

As with just about everything Microsoft creates, Outlook often offers you a thousand different ways to perform the same task. In other programs, this might provide you with many opportunities to mess something up. Luckily, Outlook is both flexible and childproof.

Outlook Today is just another example of such flexibility. You can display Outlook Today by following these steps:

1. **Click the Mail button on the Navigation pane to change to Mail if needed.**
2. **Click the root folder for your mail.**

   In most cases, the root folder shows up as Personal Folders in the mail folder list. (See Figure 1-9.) If you're on an Exchange network, the root folder shows up as `Mailbox - Jennifer Fulton` or something similar.

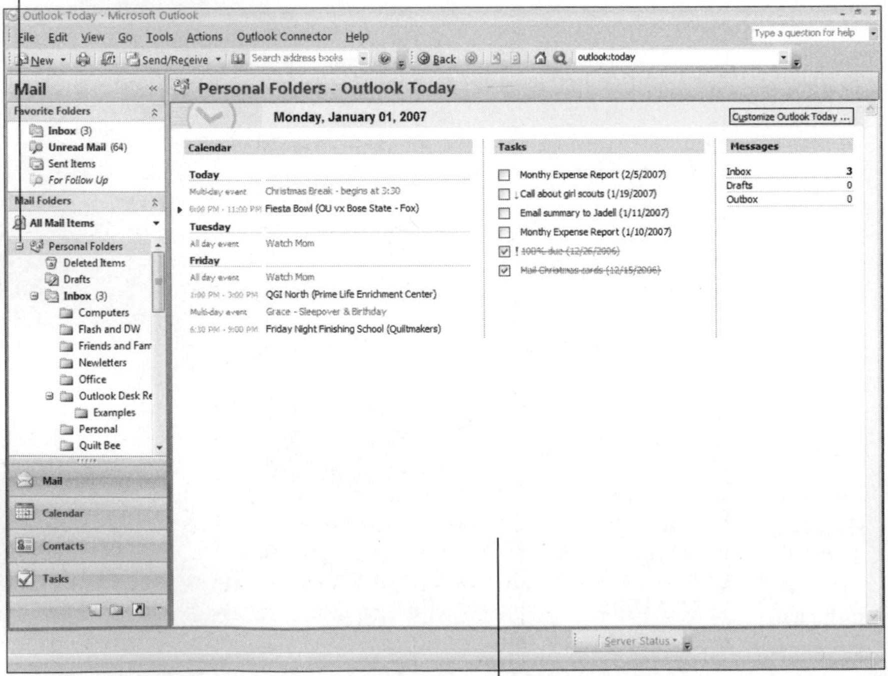

Root folder

Outlook Today

Figure 1-9: The Outlook for today is pretty good.

Although the To-Do bar is pretty good at giving you an idea of what you have coming up, it mostly focuses on what's going on today. Despite its name, Outlook Today actually presents you with more of a weekly overview of your upcoming appointments, meetings, all-day events, and tasks. It also kindly reminds you exactly how many e-mails in your Inbox you haven't read yet, how many saved but unsent e-mails in the Drafts folder you still need to finish, and how many e-mails in the Outbox await actual transmission to the mail server. The one thing it doesn't show is your To-Do items (Outlook messages, contacts, and the like that you've flagged for follow-up).

You can use Outlook Today to open anything you see mentioned there. Just click any event, appointment, meeting, or task you see listed, and the associated item opens for you. To check your unread messages, click the Inbox link; to finish an e-mail, click the Drafts link; to check on unsent messages, click the Outbox link.

You can customize the Outlook Today page somewhat; you can even make it the first thing you see when you start Outlook. Just click the Customize Outlook Today link at the top of the Outlook Today page, and choose the options you want from the page that appears. Click the Save Changes link at the top of the options page to save your choices and return to the Outlook Today page.

Sizing Things Up in the Outlook Window

After you're familiar with the way Outlook looks on a normal day, you can begin to make a few changes so that it works better for you. For example, at times you might find yourself wishing that the Navigation pane took up a little less room so you can see more of whatever's in the viewing area. As it turns out, this is an easy fix: Simply move the mouse over the divider between the Navigation pane and the viewing area, and after the cursor changes to a double-headed pointer, drag the divider to the left to make the pane smaller and the viewing area larger. See Figure 1-10.

If you're in Mail or Tasks, you might want to resize the Reading pane (assuming you have it on) by dragging the divider between the message header list and the Reading pane. To make the pane larger and the list narrower, drag the divider to the left. To make the message headings easier to read, drag the divider to the right to make the listing wider. You can also make the Reading pane wider by minimizing the To-Do bar as described earlier in this chapter. If you want to keep the To-Do bar on-screen and yet increase the size of the viewing area, you can make the pane narrower by dragging the divider between the viewing area and the bar to the right.

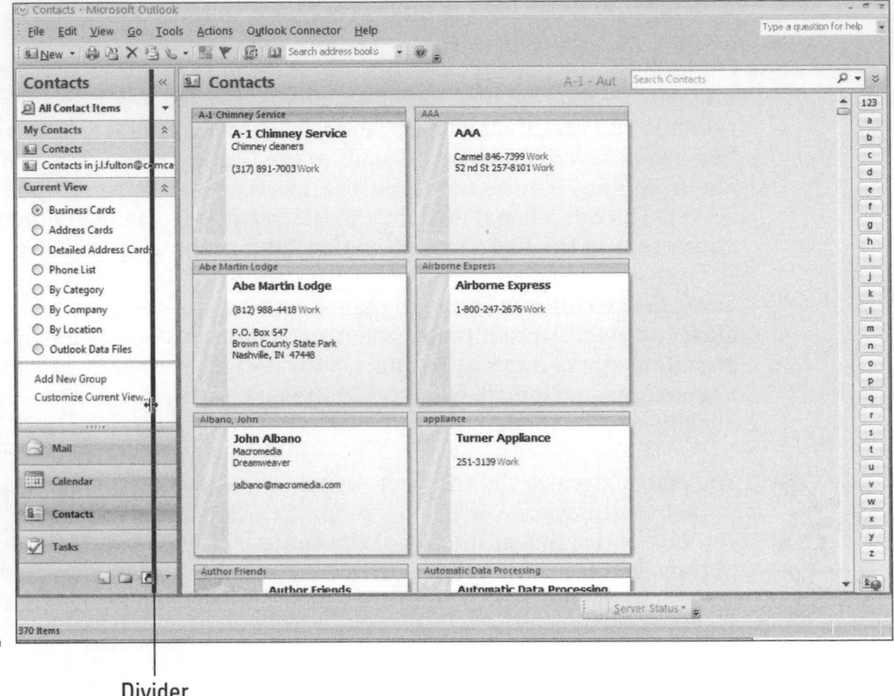

Figure 1-10: Resize any area in Outlook to make it the size you want.

In Calendar, make the calendar viewing area larger and the Daily Task List (which appears below the calendar) smaller by dragging the divider that separates them downward. In any module that uses a list view with columns to display items (such as the Phone List view in Contacts), you can resize the width of any column.

You can also resize the Outlook window by dragging one of the window's corners. To resize Outlook so you have as much room as possible to work, click the window's Maximize button (located in the upper-right corner).

Minimizing Outlook to a Taskbar Icon

In order to have Outlook automatically check for e-mail at periodic intervals, Outlook must be open. That doesn't mean, however, that you have to let Outlook have the run of the place. If you need to get on with other tasks, you can minimize Outlook to remove it from the screen: Simply click the Outlook window's Minimize button, which is located in the upper-right corner. Doing so reduces the Outlook window to a button on the Windows taskbar. If you often run a lot of programs, however, putting one more button on an already-crowded taskbar is not always the best answer.

Outlook works a bit differently from other Windows programs, so it allows you to really get it out of the way (and off the taskbar) when you want. Whenever Outlook is running, it puts an icon for itself in the Windows system tray, as shown in Figure 1-11. When new mail arrives, a chime sounds, and an envelope icon (the New Mail icon) joins the Outlook icon on the system tray so you know right away that you've got new messages. Just in case you don't get the subtle hint of an envelope icon, a notification for each incoming message briefly appears. You can click a notice to switch to Outlook and view that message. At any other time, even if the taskbar button for Outlook is removed, you can still access the program by clicking the Outlook system-tray icon or the envelope icon (if visible).

You can change how Outlook lets you know that you have mail; see Book III, Chapter 1.

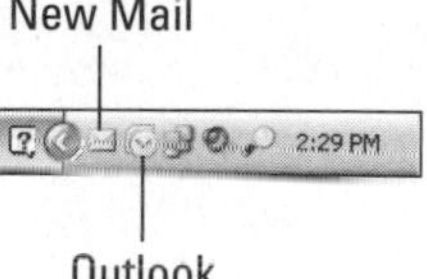

Figure 1-11: You've got mail.

To prevent the Outlook button from appearing on the taskbar whenever the program is minimized:

1. **Right-click the Outlook system tray icon.**
2. **Choose Hide When Minimized.**

If your Windows system tray is crowded, you can hide the Outlook icon when it's resting and make it appear only when new mail comes in. Here's how:

1. **Right-click the system tray and choose Properties.**
2. **Choose Taskbar⇨Hide inactive icons.**
3. **Click Customize.**
4. **Select Microsoft Office Outlook from the Current Items list.**
5. **Select Hide When Inactive from the Behavior list.**
6. **Click OK and then click Apply.**

Taking a Shortcut to Your Favorite Folders

When the Navigation pane is maximized, you'll see several small icons along its bottom. On the far right is the Shortcuts button (it features a right pointing arrow), which provides quick access to your favorite Outlook folders. To create a shortcut to a favorite folder:

1. **Click the Shortcuts button.**

   Again, you'll find the button hiding on the far right, at the bottom of the Navigation pane.

2. **Click Add New Shortcut.**

   The Navigation pane displays two links: Add New Shortcut and Add New Group. Click the Add New Shortcut link. The Add to Navigation Pane dialog box appears, as shown in Figure 1-12.

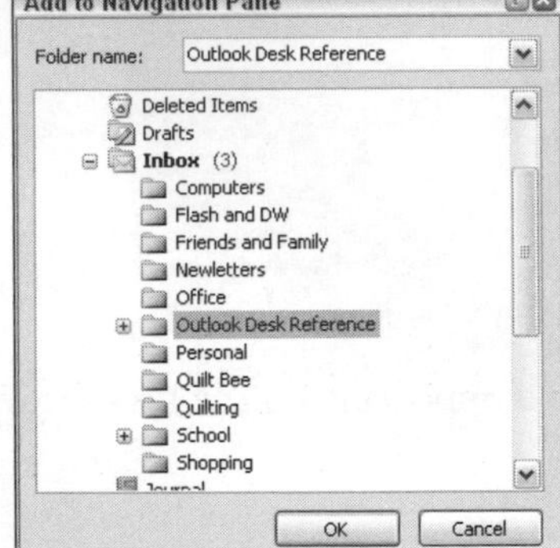

Figure 1-12: Add a favorite folder to the Navigation pane.

3. **Select a folder and click OK.**

   Select a folder from the list and click OK. The folder appears at the top of the Shortcuts list on the Navigation pane.

You can create new folders for special stuff like personal e-mail or your boss's calendar, and then add shortcuts to them. See Book IX, Chapter 1 for help.

To use the shortcuts you've set up, click the Shortcuts button, and a list of the shortcuts you've created appears on the Navigation pane, as shown in Figure 1-13. As you might gather from the description of the News and Work headings, you can group shortcuts to organize them. To create a shortcut group:

1. **Click the Add New Group link.**

   If needed, click the Shortcuts button at the bottom of the Navigation pane, and there you'll find the Add New Group link.

2. **Type a name for the group and press Enter.**

   The group name appears in a blue band, just below the Shortcuts list. (See Figure 1-13.)

3. **Drag shortcuts into the group.**

   To add a shortcut into the new group, drag and drop it on the group name.

When you've got a few shortcuts and you've grouped similar ones together, here's how to work with them:

- To open a group (such as the News group) and display its shortcuts, click the down arrow at the end of the group name.
- To hide a group's shortcuts (such as the Work group) and make the shortcuts list smaller, click the group's up arrow.
- To use a shortcut, click it. The corresponding folder is then displayed. For example, if the shortcut points to an e-mail folder where you keep personal correspondence, Outlook jumps over to Mail and displays your personal e-mail.

Figure 1-13: Why not take a shortcut?

Chapter 2: Outlook, Quick and Dirty

In This Chapter

- What all Outlook items have in common
- The fastest way to add a new contact or send an e-mail
- The simplest way to schedule an appointment
- The easiest way to record something to do or to make a note
- Using drag and drop to get almost anything done quickly

It doesn't take long after you realize how Outlook can help you manage information — thousands of appointments, phone numbers, e-mail addresses, and tasks — that you start wishing I'd just shut up and show you how to get that pile off your desk and into Outlook. Well, in this chapter I grant your wish, at least kinda: I can't promise I'll shut up, but I can promise that you'll find out how to create every kind of Outlook item quickly.

Creating Outlook Items: The Common Factors

Even though Outlook manages many different kinds of data — appointments, tasks, and contact information — it does so in a strikingly similar way regardless of what module you're working in. This means it won't be long before you can perform most functions in Outlook without asking for help. The other 700-plus pages in this book are for those rare times when you attempt something new and strange or just want a friendly guide to help you along the way.

Wow! There's a New button!

You might have already met one element that unites all Outlook items: the New button. You'll see him always hanging out on the Standard toolbar. Click the New button whenever you want to create something new in the current module. If you're in Mail, it starts a new message; if you're in Notes, it creates a new note.

To create a new something that belongs in a module other than the one you're in, click the arrow on the New button and select that something from the list that appears, as shown in Figure 2-1. For example, if you've been browsing through some incoming messages, you can create a new appointment without giving up your cozy spot in Mail. Instead of jumping over to Calendar, just click the arrow on the New button and choose Appointment from the list. The Appointment form appears (more on that in a minute), but you stay put in Mail.

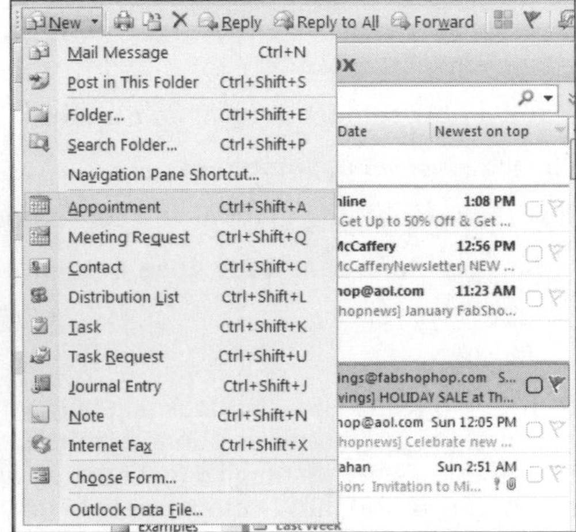

Figure 2-1: The New button helps you create new Outlook items.

Using forms to create items

In order to create a new Outlook item, you obviously have to enter some details. You enter these details into a form, like the Appointment form shown in Figure 2-2. Later, if you want to make changes to an item, you make changes to the information on the form. The form simply corrals all the details about a particular item into something that's manageable.

Although — for obvious reasons — the fields (text boxes) on a form change depending on the type of item you're trying to create or make changes to, some parts of a form remain the same for all items. Here's a look at the standard elements in the form window:

- **Quick Access toolbar:** At the top of the form window, you see the Quick Access toolbar, or QAT, in the abbreviated language favored by people on the go (POGs). The Quick Access toolbar is like a Standard toolbar just for forms; here you find buttons for common form tasks such as saving, undoing, and viewing the next item.
- **Microsoft Office Button:** At the front of the Quick Access toolbar, you find the Microsoft Office Button, or MOB (okay, just kidding). The Microsoft Office Button is located where you might normally expect a File menu, and it basically replaces the menu. The button provides

File-menu-like commands you might use on a form such as saving, printing, and closing. The Microsoft Office Button menu also provides a list of other forms that you can use to create an item such as a Meeting Request or a Contact entry.

✦ **Ribbon:** Below the Quick Access toolbar, you find the Ribbon. This special toolbar contains buttons for commands, such as commands for setting a reminder or spell checking your text, which you might use when creating or changing an item. These buttons appear in groups, with the group name below. For example, in Figure 2-2, you might notice that the Appointment and Scheduling buttons appear in the Show group. Dialog boxes aren't gone completely; occasionally one might pop up, especially if you click the dialog box launcher button, as shown in Figure 2-2.

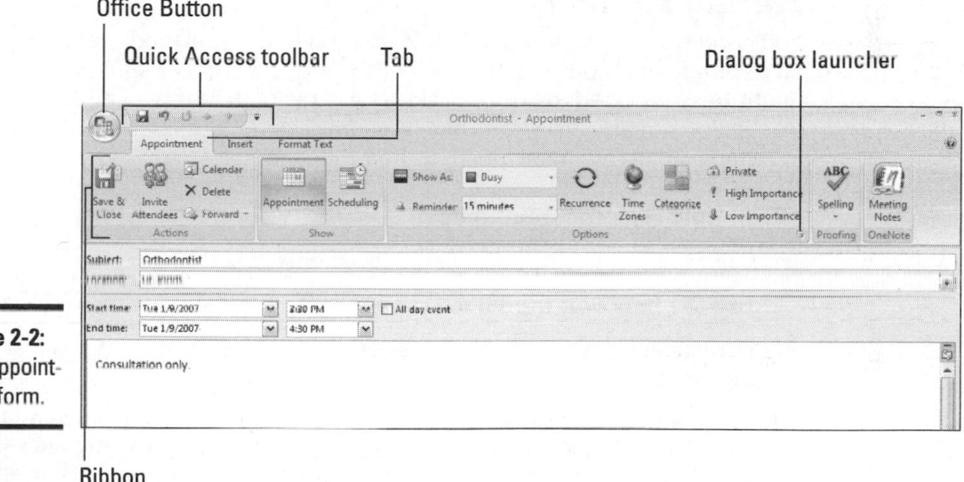

Figure 2-2: The Appointment form.

You can minimize the Ribbon temporarily, moving it out of your way so you can work with the form data more easily. To minimize the Ribbon, double-click the active tab. Restore the Ribbon by double-clicking the tab again.

Notice also that the Ribbon has tabs; in Figure 2-2, the Appointment tab is selected. You use the Appointment tab in the Appointment form to enter the bulk of your information about a particular appointment. As you might guess, you switch to different tabs to enter other specific kinds of data. For example, go to the Format Text tab to add formatting to your text. When you switch tabs, the buttons on the Ribbon change as well. If you click the Format Text tab for example, the Ribbon displays formatting buttons such as Bold or Italics. You see how to use the Ribbon buttons in later chapters, as we get into the nitty-gritty details of creating various Outlook items.

One button I want to mention before moving on is the Save & Close button. You find it on the main tab for a form. For the Appointment form shown in Figure 2-2, the Save & Close button is the first button on the Ribbon of the Appointment tab. After you enter data for a new item or make changes to an existing one, click the Save & Close button to save that data. The one exception to this Save & Close rule is e-mail; if you want to send the completed message, click Send instead of Save & Close. Clicking Save & Close on a message saves the message to the Drafts folder, where you can return and make further changes to the message at a later date.

To close a form and not save changes, press Esc or click the form's Close button. Then click No when asked to save changes.

Editing an item

You sometimes need to change information you've entered previously about an appointment, contact, or task. For example, a contact's phone number might have changed, or the due date for a task might have been accelerated (lucky you). In any case, it's easy to go back to an item after you've created it and make adjustments as needed. Just follow these steps:

1. **Double-click the item to open it.**

   For example, in the Tasks list, double-click a task.

2. **Use the fields on the form that appears to make your changes.**

   For example, set a new due date or change the amount of progress made on the task.

3. **Click the Save & Close button on the Ribbon to save the changes you've made; or press Esc to abort your changes and close the form.**

   You'll find the Save & Close button on the main tab for the form. On the Task form, for example, the Save & Close button is on the Ribbon for the Task tab.

Changing an e-mail message after you've created it is possible, assuming you haven't sent that message yet. If you create a message and click Save & Close instead of Send, the message is saved in the Drafts folder. Go there to double-click the message and make changes. If you clicked Send but the message is still awaiting delivery in the Outbox folder (which happens if you work offline and aren't permanently connected to the Internet), go there and open the message. Make your changes and click Send to put the revised message in the Outbox for delivery. See Book II, Chapter 1 for more information on the Outbox and the Drafts folder.

Deleting an item

If you're through with an item such as a competed task or outdated contact, there's no reason you can't get rid of it. Just click the item to select it, and then click the Delete button you'll find lurking on the Standard toolbar. You can also press the Delete key if that's more convenient for you. Even if the item's open, you can get rid of it. Simply click the Delete button on the Ribbon of the main tab for that form. For example, click the Delete button on the Appointment tab of an Appointment form to remove that appointment from your calendar for good.

Emptying the trash

Items that are deleted aren't really removed; you can always get them back, at least until you take out the trash. When you delete an item, the item is simply moved to Outlook's Deleted Items folder. And there it sits until you empty the trash. You take out the trash by following these steps:

1. **Click the Mail button on the Navigation pane to jump over to Mail.**

   For more on the Navigation pane, check out the preceding chapter.

2. **Right-click the Deleted Items folder.**
3. **Choose Empty "Deleted Items" Folder.**

   Remember, now, choosing this command permanently removes any item that's sitting in the Deleted Items folder.

4. **Click Yes to confirm the deletion.**

If the Folder List is showing on the Navigation pane, you don't have to change over to Mail to take out the trash because the Deleted Items folder appears in the list.

Automating trash emptying

If you have more on your mind than trash collection, you can automate the process of taking out the trash. If you follow these steps, Outlook empties the Deleted Items folder every time you exit the program:

1. **Choose Tools⇨Options.**

   The Options dialog box opens.

2. **On the Other tab, select Empty the Deleted Items Folder upon Exiting and then click OK.**

If you don't want Outlook to warn you — every time you exit — that it's about to take out the trash, you can disable the warning box and save yourself the time it takes to click Yes. To disable the warning box, click the Advanced Options button. Deselect the Warn before Permanently Deleting Items check box, and then click OK twice.

Restoring an item

If you want to restore an item after deleting it, you must act before the trash man comes (before the Deleted Items folder is emptied). To restore an item:

1. **On the Navigation pane, click the Folder List button.**
2. **At the top of the pane, click the Deleted Items folder.**
3. **Drag any item you want to restore back onto its original folder and drop it there.**

   For example, to restore a deleted appointment, drag the appointment onto the Calendar folder.

For help in permanently deleting IMAP mail messages or restoring messages marked for deletion, see Book X, Chapter 2. IMAP, or Internet Message Access Protocol, is a kind of e-mail account — so if you don't have that kind of account, don't worry about it. Not sure? See Book I, Chapter 3 for the low-down.

Adding a Quick Contact

Who knows how many people you might meet in any given day? Most of them are completely forgettable, but for those you shouldn't forget, add them quickly to the Contacts list before you do. Follow these steps:

1. **Click the arrow on the New button from any module and select Contact.**
2. **When the Contact form appears, just fill it with any information you have about the new contact, as shown in Figure 2-3.**

   Skip over any fields you don't know, such as Job Title or Home phone. (For more information about what some of these fields mean, see Book V, Chapter 1.)
3. **Click Save & Close to save the contact.**

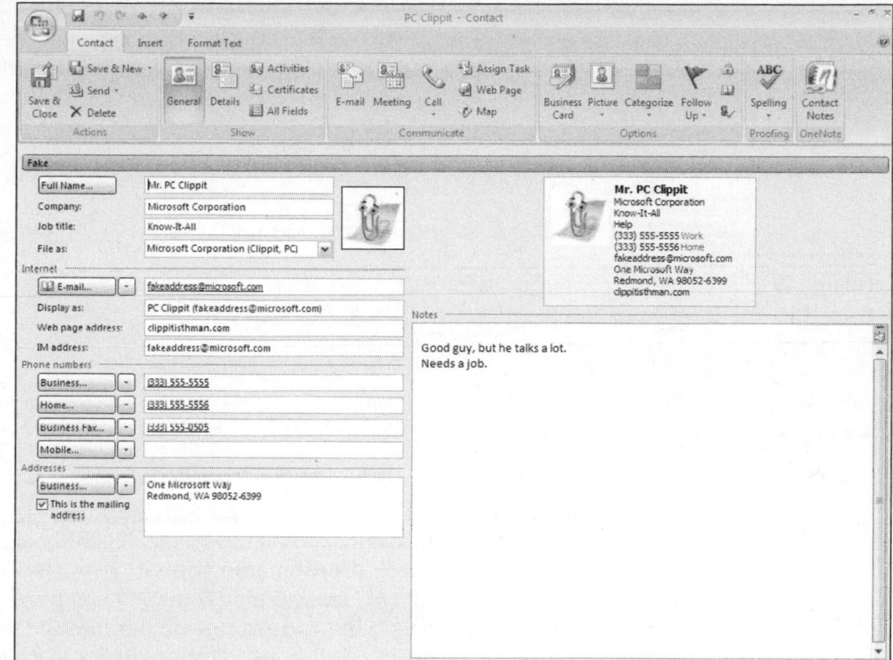

Figure 2-3: Remember even forgettable people with Contacts.

Sending a Fast E-Mail

Gotta get the word out? No problem; sending a basic e-mail message is pretty simple, as you see in a minute. It helps if the person you want to send the message to is already set up in your Contacts list, but it's not necessary.

Follow these steps to send a quick message:

1. **From any module, click the arrow on the New button and select Mail Message. If you're in the Mail module, you can just click the New button.**

   The Message form pops up, as shown in Figure 2-4.

2. **Click in the To text box and type the e-mail address of the person to whom you want to send the message.**

   If the person is already set up in your Contacts list, you can just type his name and let Outlook look up the address.

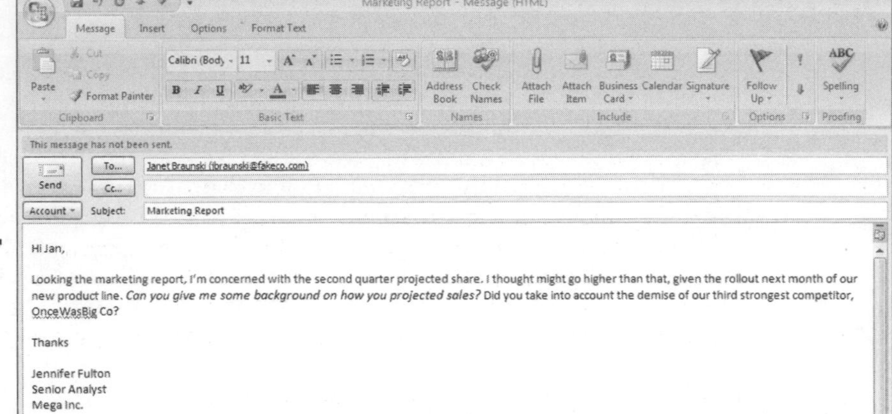

Figure 2-4: Complete the form to send a message.

The process of having Outlook look up an e-mail address based on a name you type is called *resolving*. If Outlook successfully identifies the person you mean, it underlines the name you've typed. If it can't guess who you're talking about (for example, if you spell the person's name incorrectly), Outlook puts a red, wavy underline beneath the name. If the name you type isn't in the Contacts list, Outlook does nothing (you won't see an underline). In such a case, you should type that person's e-mail address instead of his name.

By the way, e-mail addresses are assumed to be valid, even if they aren't in Contacts — thus they're always underlined. If an e-mail address matches someone in Contacts, not only is it underlined, but the person's name also appears next to the e-mail address. See Book II, Chapter 1 for more help in addressing e-mails.

3. **Type the topic of your message in the Subject text box; then click in the big text box at the bottom of the form and type your message.**
4. **Click Send.**

Obviously, you can do more than this when you send a message, or I wouldn't have devoted two minibooks to the process. For example, you might want to mark a message as urgent, format your text to make it easier to read, or include a recent photo of your kids. You discover how to do all that and more in Books II and III.

Reading and Replying to Incoming Messages

In the preceding chapter, I introduce you to the Reading pane and how to use it to review incoming messages. The Reading pane is convenient because it allows you to view the contents of messages without actually "getting out of your chair," as it were, and going through the lengthy business of opening, reading, and then closing them. The downside is that the Reading pane is notoriously small, and with some messages, you end up scrolling up and down and right and left to view the message contents. You might as well have "gotten up" and left the comfort of the main Mail window for the Mail form, which at least displays the message text in its entirety. (And hey, if you're heading to the kitchen, could you get me a soda?)

Follow these steps to open and read a series of e-mails:

1. **Click the Mail button on the Navigation pane and then, in the folder listing, click the folder where the messages you want to review are stored.**

   This is probably the default mail folder, Inbox, although it might be a different folder if you've created others.

   To find out how to create and use e-mail folders to organize your messages, see Book IX, Chapter 1.

2. **Double-click the first message you want to read.**

   The message opens in its own window, as shown in Figure 2-5. Use the vertical scroll bar or the Page Down key to scroll through long messages. If a message contains pictures, they're typically blocked (not shown). See Book II, Chapter 2 for help in viewing them.

   Don't open an e-mail message unless you know the sender and you're sure it doesn't contain any viruses, macros, or scripts. See the preceding chapter for help in previewing a message's contents without unleashing any monsters.

   Looking at the buttons on the Ribbon, obviously you can perform a lot of tasks while viewing a message, such as instantly deleting it, flagging it for follow-up, or adding the sender to your "stop annoying me" list. You can also reply to a message, which is something I get to in a minute; the other tasks I cover in Books II and III.

3. **To view the contents of the next message in the list, click the Next Item button on the Quick Access toolbar at the top of the message window.**

   To view a previous message, click the Previous Item button instead.

4. **When you're done reviewing messages, you can click the Close button on the message window to close it.**

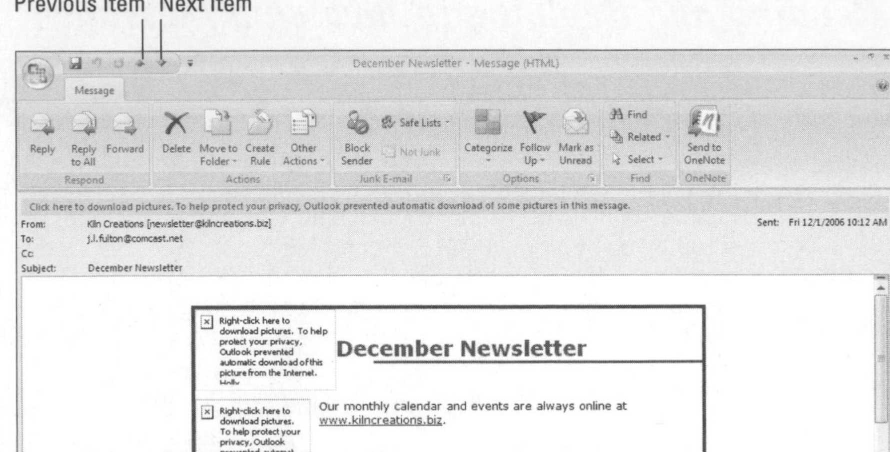

Figure 2-5: Open long messages to read them more easily.

If you're looking through a series of e-mails and you happen upon one that requires a reply, choose Message⇨Respond⇨Reply, and a new message form appears, conveniently addressed to the sender. The content of the original message is copied to the new message, so if your sender has sent out more e-mails than she can remember, she can at least identify what you're referring to. Type your reply above the copied text and click Send to send your reply on its way.

You don't have to have the original text copied to your replies; see Book II, Chapter 2.

You might notice a Reply to All button sitting coyly next to the Reply button. Cute as it is, that button is one dangerous sucker. If you click that button instead of Reply, in some instances what you thought was a private conversation gets shared with *thousands* of your nearest and dearest. See Book II, Chapter 2 for tips on how to use Reply to All safely.

Creating a Simple Appointment

Client meetings, dates with the sales rep, doctor appointments, dentist appointments, parent-teacher meetings — the list goes on. To keep track of all these demands on your time, you enter these various appointments in Outlook. After you've entered them, you can quickly browse your daily, weekly, or monthly calendar to review how many appointments you have for that time period and then decide on the best time to head out of town. Luckily, the process of entering a new appointment is much less stressful.

Outlook keeps track of all your appointments, meetings, and events in the Calendar. *Appointments* are meetings you have with people outside your company; *meetings* are appointments with your colleagues. By setting up a meeting in Outlook, you can use the company's shared network to invite attendees, book resources, and manage the whole meeting process. Events by the way, are day-long happenings such as birthdays, seminars, anniversaries, and such. You learn to add events in Book IV, Chapter 1l you find out how to add meetings to the Calendar in Book IV, Chapter 4.

Appointments can be fairly detailed when you need them to be, but — so you won't forget to meet with someone important — create one quickly and easily by following these steps:

1. **Click the Calendar button on the Navigation pane.**
2. **On the Date Navigator at the top of the Navigation pane, click the day on which you want to schedule the appointment.**

   If need be, you can switch over to a different month by clicking the left or right arrows on either side of the month name.

   The day you selected appears, sliced and diced into handy, half-hour segments. Appointments, meetings, and events appear as rectangles on this day grid, blocking out the time they take up.
3. **To create an appointment, hover the mouse over the half-hour time slot in which the appointment is scheduled to begin. Click when you see these words: *Click to Add Appointment.***

   For example, hover over the 11:30 time slot and then click. After you click a time slot, a white bubble appears, like the one shown in Figure 2-6.
4. **Type the appointment description and press Enter.**

   Type a brief name or description for the appointment, such as **Lunch with Khyla**. Press Enter and you've got a half-hour appointment. To find out how to lengthen the appointment or enter additional details, see Book IV, Chapters 1 and 2.

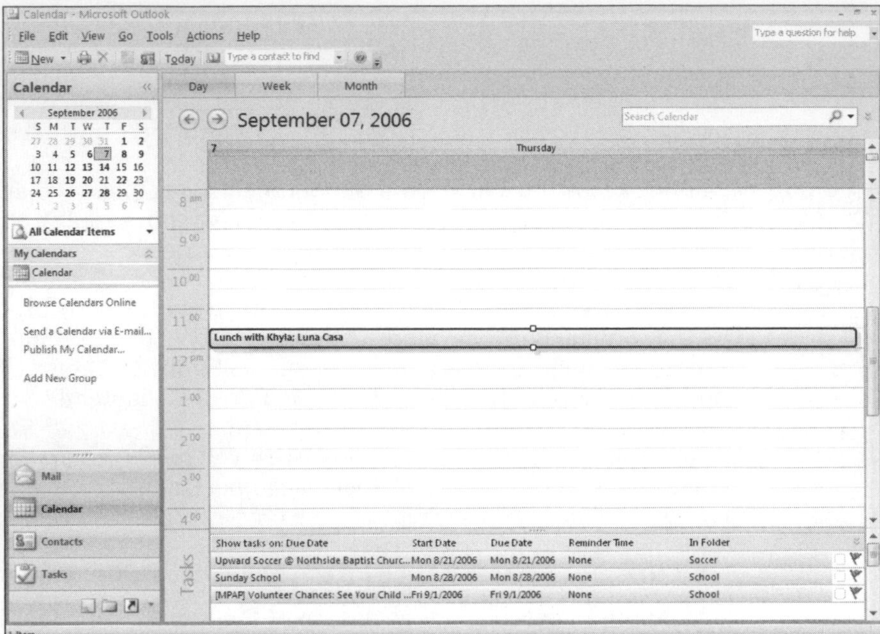

Figure 2-6: Create an appointment with a single click.

Adding a Quick Task

We all have things to do — some are quick, easy, just-do-it things, whereas others are long, drawn-out, complicated affairs. Outlook can easily help you track both types of tasks. It's left to you to find the time to get them all done or assign them to some other poor sap.

Enter your quick, easy, just-get-it-done things on the To-Do bar:

1. **Click the Type a New Task box on the To-Do bar.**

   In the bottom half of the To-Do bar, just above the list of tasks, you see a text box that says *Type a New Task.* Click this text box to add a task, as shown in Figure 2-7.

2. **Type the task description and press Enter.**

   Type a brief description of the task, such as **Project X status report** or **Pick up laundry**, and then press Enter to create the task. That's it! Now if only it were as easy to get the task done.

The task you just created appears in the task list, grouped with other things you need to get done today. If you want to change the task due date or add other task details, see Book VI, Chapters 1 and 2.

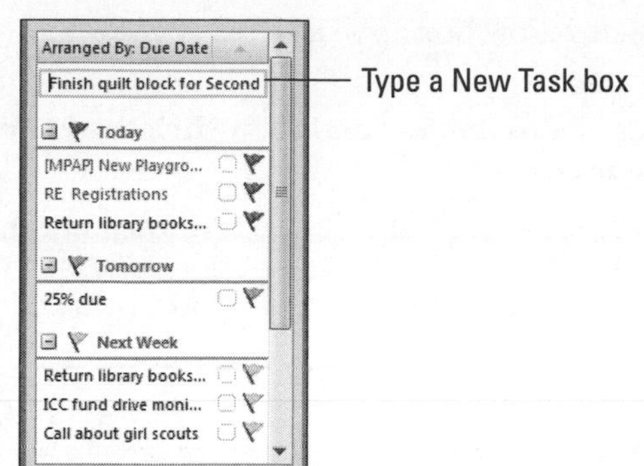

Figure 2-7: The To-Do bar provides an easy way to add a task.

Actually, a new task you create on the To-Do bar is assigned a start date based on your current Quick Click setting — which, by default, is set to Today. If you typically create tasks that are due tomorrow or next week, you can change the Quick Click setting so that the tasks you create have the correct due date starting out. See Book VI, Chapter 1.

If you put off completing a task you originally assigned to be due Today, it continues to appear under the Today heading on tomorrow's task list. It changes, however, from calm, non-threatening black text to pay-attention-to-me red text. Any new task you add appears below any red tasks for today.

A couple of things you might want to know about tasks — first, you can complete them! Yes indeedy, if you finish a task and want to strike it off your list, you can do that pretty easily. Also, you can add tasks while looking at your Calendar by jotting them down on the Daily Task List (assuming it's visible, which it is in the normal Calendar view). So if you happen to be in Calendar view, you can create a task without having to display the To-Do bar or jumping over to Mail, where the To-Do bar normally appears. I show you how to do all this stuff in Book VI, Chapter 1.

Taking a Note

Notes aren't given a high priority in Outlook, and darn if I know why. Creating a note in Outlook couldn't be simpler, and most people I know (myself included) are constantly jotting down notes all over any conceivable surface, including palms and inner arms. Follow these steps to create a note:

1. **Click the arrow on the New button and choose Note.**

   Or, you can switch to the Notes module and click the New button, assuming you can find its teeny-tiny icon, lying low at the bottom of the Navigation pane.

After you click New, a yellow box appears; this is your note. (See Figure 2-8.)

2. **Type whatever you like in the box and then click the window's Close button to close the note.**

   You can keep the note on-screen and add to it throughout the day. Whatever you type is automatically saved periodically, so you shouldn't lose anything even if your computer is taken down by a sudden power outage.

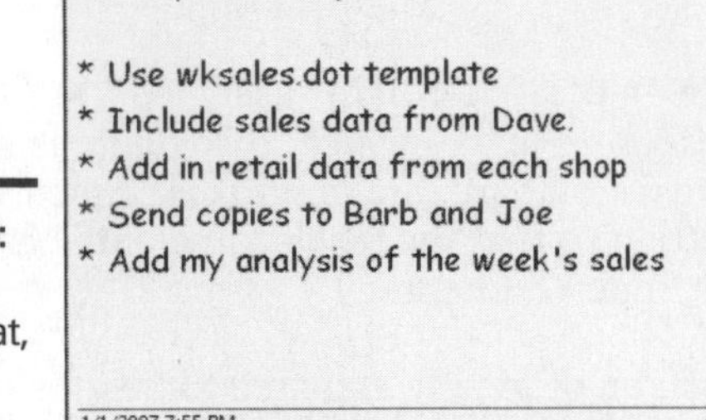

Figure 2-8: Make a note of that, will ya?

As you discover in Book VI, Chapter 4, you can do some pretty cool things with notes, such as

- **Categorize them** so that notes about the same project, client, or meeting are grouped together.
- **Put them on the Desktop** so you can't lose or forget them.
- **Resize big notes** so they're easier to read.

Constant note-takers might appreciate OneNote, an accessory program that comes with Office. OneNote allows you to create entire notebooks of notes, complete with drawings, images, charts, and even audio or video. You can link the notes you take in OneNote to items in Outlook, such as client meetings, company seminars, important contacts, or tasks. See Book VI, Chapter 5 for help.

Drag and Drop and How It Saved My Life

Before drag and drop, I used to climb mountains of menus, clicking away until finally I got something done. Now, frankly, whenever I'm working in a program, I try dragging and dropping all sorts of things just to see what happens. And in a Microsoft program such as Outlook, chances are you'll discover a handy shortcut to a common task.

Understanding how it works

For those of you who are, perhaps, a bit new to dragging and dropping, this is how it works:

1. **Select something that you want to do something with.**

   To select something, you typically click it. For example, you can click a contact in your Contacts list.

2. **Drag that sucker somewhere.**

   To drag, you click and hold the mouse button down as you move the mouse somewhere. For example, you can click a contact and hold the mouse button down as you drag that puppy over to the Mail button on the Navigation pane.

3. **Now drop it and see what happens.**

   To drop, you simply release that mouse button you've been holding down. For example, once you drag the contact over to the Mail button, you can drop it right there by simply letting go of the mouse button. Next, just pop a cold one and watch what happens as a result of your little drag-and-drop experiment. In this case, the contact you dropped on the unsuspecting Mail button is used to instantly create a new mail message, already addressed to the contact you chose. Pretty cool, eh?

To quickly send the same message to a bunch of people, just select all those folks in the Contact list (by pressing Ctrl and clicking each one), and then drag the whole kit and kaboodle to the Mail button and let go. Poof! Up pops an e-mail addressed to all the contacts you selected.

Creating Outlook items with drag and drop

Here are some of the ways to use drag and drop to save time when creating messages, appointments, and the like.

If your aim isn't to create a new Outlook item by using another as its basis, but rather to link two similar Outlook items (such as a contact name and a task), you might want to use OneNote instead. OneNote can gather lots of separate parts, text, drawings, charts, and various Outlook items into a single container called a *notebook*. Using OneNote, for example, you might create a notebook for each project or special client and keep related information in it. See Book VI, Chapter 5 for help.

Messages

To create a message using drag and drop, use one of these methods:

- **Drag a contact name onto the Mail button.** (Been there, done that, as described in the previous section.)
- **Drag an appointment onto the Mail button.** Essentially, this forwards the appointment details to someone else. But if your intention is to invite someone to a meeting, there's a better way to do that than using drag and drop. See Book IV, Chapter 4.
- **Drag a task onto the Mail button.** If you want to send a short status report to a supervisor, this is a good way to go. But if you're looking to reassign the task, there's a better way to do that so you can continue to track its progress. See Book VI, Chapter 3.
- **Drag a note onto the Mail button.** This forwards a note to someone else.

Appointments

To create an appointment with drag and drop, use one of these techniques:

- **Drag a message onto the Calendar button.** The text of the message is copied to the notes area of the appointment, so you can refer to it as needed, as shown in Figure 2-9. This trick is especially useful if the message has the appointment details or other details about the person you need to remember, such as her address and phone number.

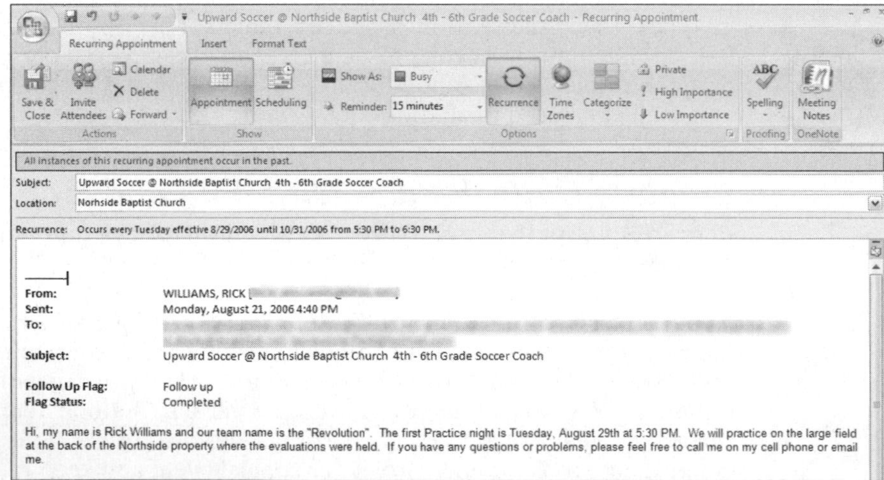

Figure 2-9: Use a message to create an appointment.

- **Drag a contact onto the Calendar button.** This actually creates a meeting and not an appointment, which means that an e-mail message is sent inviting the contact to the meeting. If you want to create an appointment from a contact, you can't do it with drag and drop. However, I do use this one a lot. I start selecting multiple contacts I want to invite to the meeting (by pressing Ctrl and clicking each name) and then dragging the motley crew over to the Calendar button.

If you want to create an appointment and copy a contact's information into the notes area of the appointment, *right-drag* (drag with the right mouse button down) the contact onto the Calendar. From the menu that appears, choose Copy Here as Appointment with Text. You can copy a shortcut to the contact information so you can quickly display it from the Appointment window by double-clicking the shortcut, or add the contact information as an attachment to the Appointment form.

✦ **Drag a task onto the Calendar button.** This seems backwards to me because I typically create an appointment first, and doing *that* creates a thousand things to do. But if you start out with a task, such as Project Status Report, and then finally schedule a time to meet with a client to go over it, this might be a handy way to add the appointment to your Calendar. The details of the task are copied to the notes area of the appointment.

✦ **Drag a note onto the Calendar button.** I don't use this one much, but if you just jot down some key ideas for a product launch in a note, you can use the note to create the appointment for the launch meeting.

Contacts

To create a contact using drag and drop, use one of these methods:

✦ **Drag a message onto the Contacts button**. This is a great way to create a contact because it takes the contact's e-mail address right out of the message for you. If the message contains other contact information, such as a phone number or address, you can refer to it without switching between the Contacts form and the message window.

✦ **Drag an appointment onto the Contacts button.** This is a strange one because the details of your first appointment become part of the contact's permanent record, but I must admit I've used it, especially if I've already typed contact details such as address and phone number into the notes area of the appointment.

✦ **Drag a task or a note onto the Contacts button.** The details of the task or note are copied into the notes area of the Contact form. Using a note to create a contact is useful when you have a note that pertains to a new contact. However, you probably won't want to use a task this way because the Contact is created using the owner of the task, which is typically you. But if you've been assigned a task by someone who's not already in the Contacts list, you could use drag and drop to get the name in there fast.

As useful as dragging and dropping is, *right-dragging* (dragging with the right mouse button instead of the left) provides a bit more control over the result. As you've gathered by now, when you drag and drop something, such as an appointment, onto a button on the Navigation pane, the details of that something (the appointment) are copied into the notes area of the new item that's created. By right-dragging, you get a menu with more choices; instead of copying the text of the item you dropped, you can create a shortcut to the item or add it as an attachment, leaving the notes area of the new item free for additional notes.

Tasks

To create tasks with drag and drop, use one of the following methods:

- **Drag a message onto the Tasks button.** The message text appears in the notes area of the task. This is useful when a message contains a lot of information related to the thing you need to do.
- **Drag an appointment onto the Tasks button.** This is a handy trick to use if you have to get several things done prior to the appointment because the details of the appointment appear in the notes area of the task.
- **Drag a contact name onto the Tasks button.** Do this only if you're trying to reassign a task to someone else. See Book VI, Chapter 4. If you'd like to associate a task with a client, use the Business Contact Manager. See Book VII, Chapter 2.
- **Drag a note onto the Tasks button.** Use this trick to quickly copy a note into a task, so you can refer to it as you work on the task. Keep in mind that a notes area is located in the Task form, so you can create a task first and add notes as you go along.

Notes

To create a note with drag and drop, use one of these methods:

- **Drag a message onto the Notes button.** The text of the message is copied into the notes window, where you can make your own additions.
- **Drag an appointment onto the Notes button.** I typically choose OneNote to link Outlook items such as appointments to notes, but you might use this if the appointment contains notes you refer to often.
- **Drag a contact name onto the Notes button.** This copies all contact information into the note, where you can add more information.
- **Drag a task onto the Notes button.** This copies task details into the note, where you can add your own comments or notes about a task. This one seems pretty silly to me because the Tasks form has a place for taking notes.

Reorganizing Outlook items with drag and drop

You can use drag-and-drop techniques for other things besides creating Outlook items. I mean, after you create all those items, you have to deal with them, and what better way than with drag and drop?

Here are some things you might want to try:

- **Delete old items** such as old tasks or contacts you'll never need again by dropping them onto the Deleted Items folder. See "Creating Outlook Items: The Common Factors" earlier in this chapter for more help in removing unwanted items from Outlook.
- **Shuffle appointments** from one day to the next by dropping them on the appropriate day on the Date Navigator.
- **Rearrange the order of tasks** for any given day by dragging and dropping them where you want them in the list. If you drag and drop a task into a group of tasks you've set for another day, you change the due date for that task as well.

Chapter 3: Setting Up Your E-Mail Accounts

In This Chapter

- Understanding the various types of e-mail accounts
- Automating the e-mail setup process
- Configuring e-mail manually
- Setting up an e-mail connection

Some people are content to use Outlook as a fancy address book and calendar, but most folks rely on Outlook as their source of e-mail. If you're lucky enough to have a full-time IT person on staff — or have a geeky friend who is easily bribed with chocolate chip cookies — you may not have to read this chapter, which is about setting up your e-mail account(s). Those of you who are forced to wear the IT hat, however — or are lousy cookie bakers — can use this chapter to help get your e-mail up and running.

This chapter covers the various types of e-mail accounts and shows you how to coax Outlook into setting them up automatically. After you're up and running, you need to know how you can change your settings or add new ones. Finally, you see how to change the type of connection you're using to access the Internet.

Understanding the E-Mail Process

Just in case you didn't know, the *e* in e-mail stands for electronic. It's no coincidence that e-mail includes the word *mail* — e-mail and its more traditional counterpoint share a lot of similarities. Understanding these similarities helps you better understand the overall concept of e-mail. As simple as the process of mailing a letter, you must take several steps in order to ensure its success:

- You must drop it into mailbox.
- You generally pay a fee.
- At your discretion, you can pay a surcharge to ensure that your message arrives to your destination faster.

- In general, there is a surcharge to send large packages or amounts of mail.
- You must choose from one of several mail service providers.
- You must check your mailbox to receive your mail.
- At times, things still "get lost in the mail" for no apparent reason.

Obtaining an e-mail account

The first thing you need for e-mail is an e-mail account. Outlook doesn't create or issue e-mail accounts; it merely provides you with a way to use one. You can get an e-mail account from your Internet service provider (ISP), your employer, an online service such as AOL, or from Web services such as Yahoo! Mail, Google Gmail, and Windows Live Mail. You generally must pay for the service by paying cold cash or putting up with annoying advertising.

When you obtain an e-mail account, you receive a user name and password. If you forget them, you need to contact your e-mail provider for this information; even the savviest of Outlook gurus can't get this information for you. You probably also received setup instructions that include cryptic words such as account, POP3, or SMTP. Hold on to those because you might just need them later.

Do not discard your e-mail setup instructions. This way, rather than waiting for other people to help solve problems with your account, you can take a shot at solving the issues yourself. If that fails, then you can suffer through automated telephone services and wait times.

Knowing the e-mail flavors

Most things you purchase — from ice cream to ovens — come with a variety of flavors and options. E-mail accounts are no different. Just like you'll probably do a bit of research before you buy your next car, you might want to do a little homework before obtaining — or trying to configure — your e-mail account so that you're familiar with all the options. Before you sign on the dotted line you might want to ask your e-mail provider exactly what flavors of service it offers; many providers can provide you with a number of methods, such as these:

- **POP3:** Post Office Protocol 3 (POP3) is the most common e-mail account type on the Internet. A POP3 account works just like traditional mail. Your e-mail messages arrive at the mail server (post office) and then are downloaded to your computer (mailbox). In general, once you receive your mail, it is no longer available on the mail server — or at the post office. POP3 accounts are prevalent in the business world because you can associate multiple POP3 e-mail addresses with a Web site. For example, a business might have the `www.mycompany.com` Web site and various related e-mail addresses including `info@mycompany.com`, `myname@mycompany.com`, and `yourname@mycompany.com`.

POP3 accounts have one disadvantage. POP3 e-mail is a good option if you don't travel very often and generally access your e-mail from the same location. Users with multiple computers, for example someone who wants to check e-mail from both office and home, find that some of mail is on one computer and some of it is on another. Or alternatively, you may find that a message that you already responded to is now reappearing on your other computer.

- **IMAP:** With an Internet Message Access Protocol (IMAP) account, your e-mail is stored on your ISP's mail server. This way, you can store and process mail and optionally download it to the computer you are working on. You can use a different computer to read your messages wherever you are. As an added bonus, because your mail is saved on the mail server, it is backed up by your ISP. You are also somewhat safer from viruses because you can view the *headers* (the sender and subject) of your e-mail messages before you download them. However, not all IMAP accounts work with software designed to manage business e-mail such as Outlook.
- **MAPI:** Messaging Application Programming Interface (MAPI) is used in Outlook with a mail server that is running Microsoft Exchange Server. MAPI is a lot like IMAP, but it allows you to combine all of Outlook's functionality with the security of an IMAP account. You commonly find this type of account in a medium or large business environment.

  If you use Microsoft Exchange Server, your e-mail messages, calendar, contacts, and other items are delivered to and stored in your mailbox on the server. When you configure Outlook to work with your Exchange Server account, all the items on the server are available to you from your computer as well.
- **HTTP:** These accounts use a Web protocol to view and send e-mail. HTTP accounts include services like Windows Live Mail. Although you can't use HTTP accounts with Outlook, you can get around this by using add-ons with certain providers.

In general, your ISP provides you with one or more e-mail accounts. You may also use an e-mail account that is provided by your Web host. The most common types of accounts are POP3 and IMAP accounts. Your ISP can tell you which protocol you use to access your e-mail account, but POP3 is by far the most common.

How e-mail accounts work

Still confused about the way that e-mail accounts work? Don't be. Just like snail mail, your e-mail originates with a sender, ends up at a post office or *server* where someone sorts lots of incoming mail, and then finally lands in your mailbox.

The trip that a POP3 e-mail takes from the sender to your mailbox is actually a very short one:

1. The new e-mail message arrives on the POP3 mail server and is placed in your mailbox.
2. Outlook connects to the POP3 mail server.
3. Outlook downloads the contents of your mail server mailbox.
4. The new items are saved to a Personal Folders file (`.pst`) on your computer. If you have an Exchange Server account, your new messages are saved to the Exchange server as well.
5. Outlook issues a command to delete the items on the mail server that were downloaded.

IMAP or HTTP e-mail follows a somewhat different route:

1. New e-mail messages arrive in your IMAP or HTTP mail server and are placed in your mailbox.
2. Outlook connects to the IMAP or HTTP mail server.
3. There can be multiple folders in your mail server mailbox. Outlook checks the folders and downloads a count of and the headers of messages.
4. When you open a message header, Outlook downloads the full item from the mail server.
5. When you delete an item, the message appears with a strikethrough in the message list. When you use the Purge Deleted Items command, all messages marked for deletion are deleted from both the server and Outlook.

Configuring Your E-Mail Accounts

In order to send and receive e-mail messages using Outlook, you need to add your e-mail account information to it. For most accounts, Outlook can automatically detect and configure the account with a name, e-mail address, and password. Alternatively, your Internet service provider (ISP) or mail administrator can provide you with configuration information if you need to manually set up your e-mail account in Outlook. Users of Exchange Server accounts may not have to do anything because Outlook can identify the network credentials that are used to connect to the Exchange Server account.

An Outlook profile is created automatically when you run Outlook for the first time. E-mail profiles are what Outlook uses to remember which e-mail accounts you use and where the data for each account is stored. A profile includes your user name, e-mail server name, and account password.

When you set up your e-mail accounts, they are added to your profiles. Your profile can contain multiple e-mail accounts. Most people need only one profile even if they have multiple e-mail addresses; if you want to have your e-mail from a specific e-mail address delivered to a corresponding folder, you can set up a rule to do it for you automatically. You may decide that you'd like to work with multiple profiles. For example, you may want one profile for work-related e-mail messages and another profile for personal messages. Or, if several family members are sharing the same computer, you can separate their e-mail accounts into separate profiles.

Having Outlook do the heavy lifting

Often you'll find that there are both easy and hard ways to accomplish the same goal. And, if you're like I am, you opt for the easiest method whenever possible. Here's how you can let Outlook automatically detect your e-mail account setting.

1. **Choose Tools⇨Account Settings from Outlook's main menu bar.**

   The Account Settings dialog box, shown in Figure 3-1.

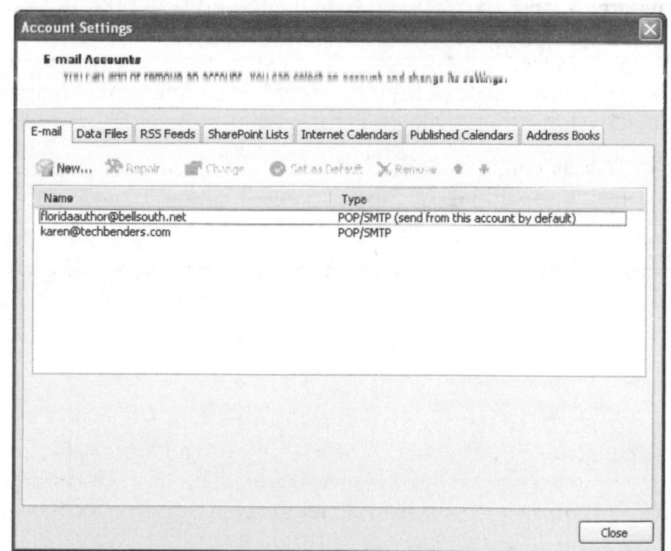

Figure 3-1: The Account Settings dialog box.

2. **Click New.**

   You will be delighted — or perhaps slightly happy — to see the Add New E-Mail Account Wizard (see Figure 3-2).

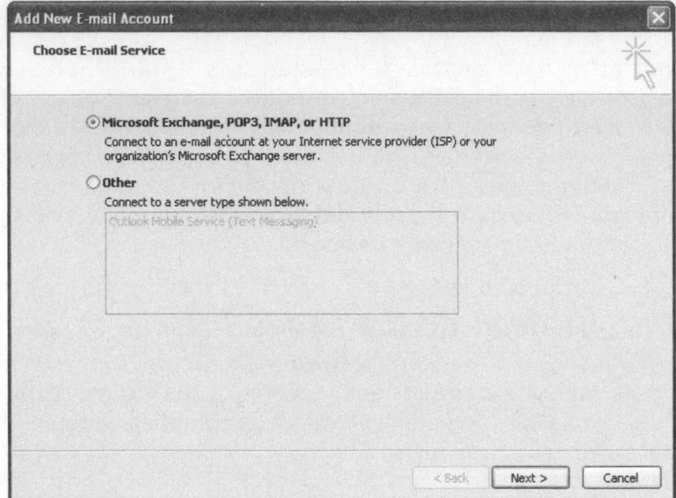

Figure 3-2: The Add New E-Mail Account Wizard.

3. **Select the E-Mail account type.**

   You can choose to set up an e-mail account or a text message account.

4. **Click Next to continue.**

   The second window of the Add New E-Mail Account Wizard opens. You can see what it looks like in Figure 3-3.

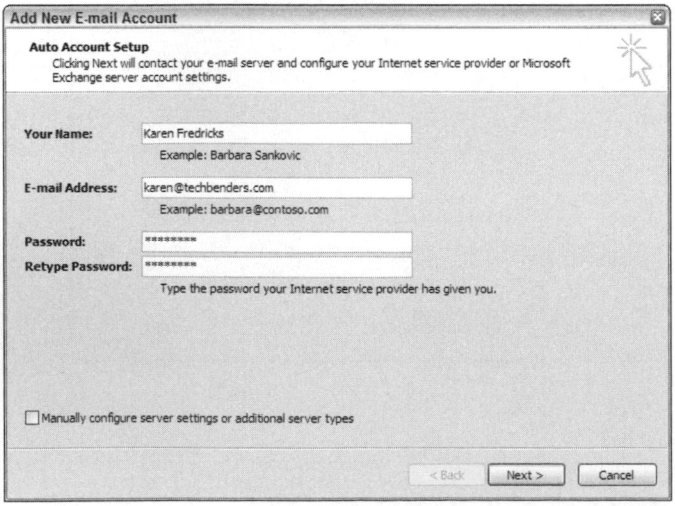

Figure 3-3: The second screen of the Add New E-Mail Account Wizard.

5. **Fill in your basic e-mail information and then click Next to continue.**

   There are three tidbits of information you need to provide:

   - **Name** as you want it to appear to all your recipients; hopefully you remember that one without prompting of any sort.
   - **E-mail address** that was provided to you by your ISP.
   - **Password** that was provided to you by your ISP; just for good measure you need to type it twice.

6. **Hold your breath as Outlook tries to connect to your e-mail account.**

   To make the time go faster, you can look at the search screen that appears.

7. **Do a congratulatory dance if you receive a message telling you that your e-mail account is now set up.**

8. **(Optional) Curse up a storm if you receive the message shown in Figure 3-4 and then read the next section.**

   Sometimes, try as it might, Outlook won't be able to detect your settings. There are a number of reasons why this might happen:

   - Your ISP uses special encryption.
   - You're using an e-mail account that's tied in to your Web site.
   - You typed your e-mail address or password incorrectly.

   Not to worry — if at first you don't succeed, you'll just have to try again!

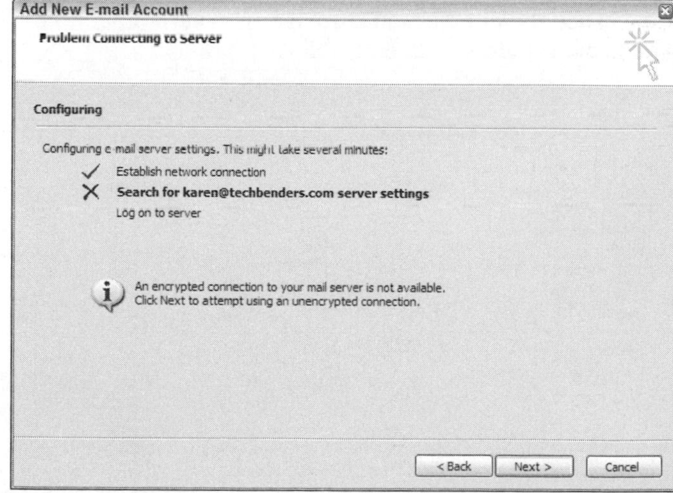

Figure 3-4: Cause for annoyance: Outlook couldn't detect your e-mail settings.

Configuring your e-mail account manually

If Outlook can't configure your e-mail account for you, you just have to bite the bullet and do it yourself.

1. **Open the Add New E-Mail Account Wizard (refer to Figure 3-2).**

   You can get there by doing the following:

   - Click the Back button when you're prompted that Outlook can't configure your e-mail account.
   - Choose Tools⇨Account Settings from the main Outlook menu bar, and then click New and then Next.
   - Choose Tools⇨Options⇨Mail Setup. Click the E-Mail Accounts button, and then click New and then Next.

2. **(Optional) Fill in your name, e-mail address, and password.**

   If you had already filled in this information when trying to have Outlook automatically configure your e-mail account, then your information is already sitting there waiting for you.

3. **Select the Manually Configure Server Settings or Additional Server Types check box and click Next to continue.**

   If you feel like someone turned the lights out, it's because the input screen becomes grayed out. Even though you are doing the things the "hard" way, you'll find that it is actually pretty easy because Outlook steps you through the procedure with a handy dandy Wizard.

4. **Choose your e-mail service type and click Next.**

   You can see the choices in Figure 3-5. The earlier section, "Knowing the e-mail flavors," covers these choices in detail.

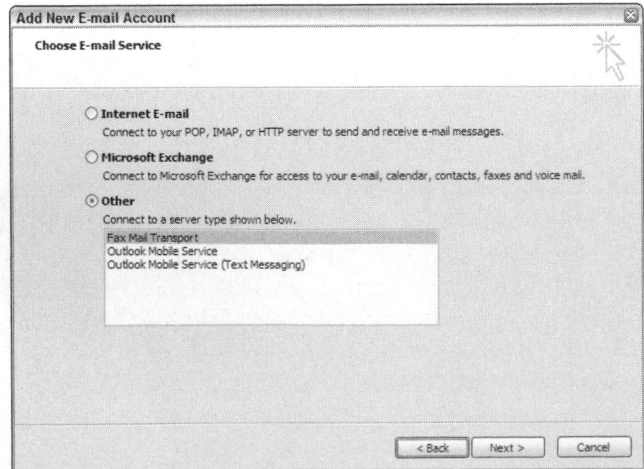

Figure 3-5: Choosing your e-mail account type.

5. **Fill in your vital statistics in the next screen of the Add New E-Mail Account Wizard, shown in Figure 3-6.**

   This is where you're going to need all that confusing information about POP, SMTP, and passwords that your ISP gave you that you (I hope) wrote down legibly and stored in a safe spot. If you didn't save this information, you have to contact your ISP to get it.

   - **User Information:** Fill in your name and e-mail address.
   - **Server Information:** Select your account type and fill in your incoming (POP3) and outgoing (SMTP) information for your ISP.
   - **Logon information:** Fill in your e-mail user name and password. Your user name is generally the portion of your e-mail address that comes before the @ sign.
   - **Remember password:** If you are working in a reasonably safe, spy-free environment, you want to check this option so that you don't have to reenter your password each and every time you want to send or receive e-mail.

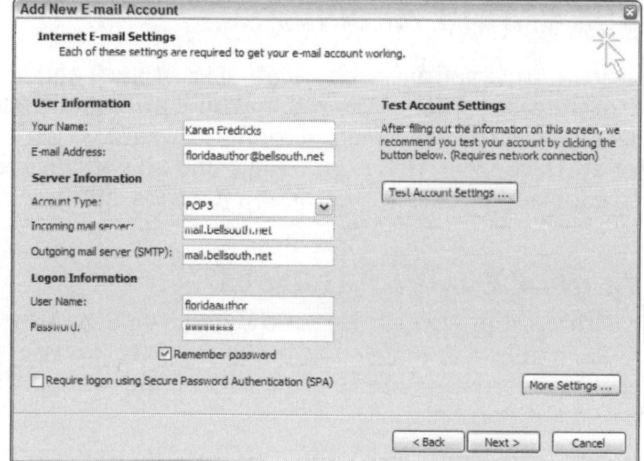

Figure 3-6: Configuring your e-mail account.

6. **(Optional) Click the Test Account Settings button.**

   It's always nice to make sure that things work now rather than to find out later that they don't. Outlook actually sends a test message to you — and makes sure that you can receive it. If all systems are go, the Test Account Settings dialog box opens and gives you a high five (see Figure 3-7). For additional excitement you can race over to your Inbox and read the test message that Microsoft sent you.

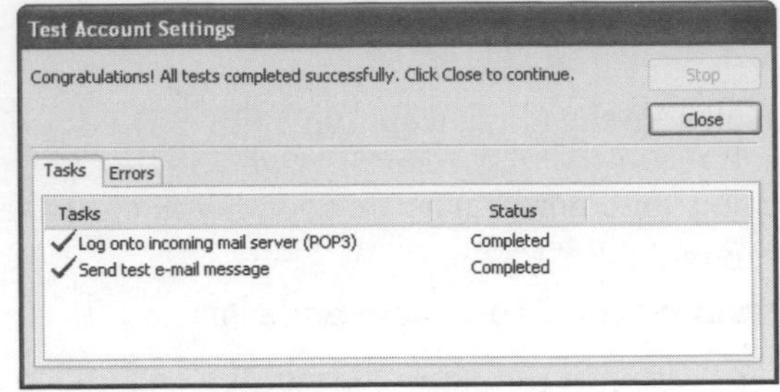

Figure 3-7: Testing your e-mail account settings.

7. **Click Close to exit the Test Account Settings dialog box, and then click Next to advance your way to the last page of the Wizard.**

   A very large congratulatory message opens. Outlook realizes the importance of positive feedback — particularly if it let you down when you tried to configure your e-mail account manually.

8. **Click Finish to close the congratulatory message.**

Maintaining Your E-Mail Accounts

After you create your e-mail account(s), you can sit back and let the good times roll — or at least let the e-mail roll in. You'll probably seldom if ever have to make changes to your e-mail account. However, as with the best laid plans of mice and IT people, things go wrong, and so you have to be ready to don your red cape and pocket protector at a moment's notice.

Changing your e-mail password

The trouble with most passwords is that they are so darn picky. Unlike in horseshoes, close doesn't count — passwords have to be letter perfect when you use them. Passwords are often case-sensitive and require that capital letters appear in the correct spot.

You may start to be bothered by the message you see in Figure 3-8.

Figure 3-8: Annoying Outlook message.

You may see that message continuously pop up for a number of reasons.

- ✦ You entered an incorrect password — or left the password blank — when you set up your e-mail account.
- ✦ You failed to check the Remember Password check box when you set up your e-mail account.
- ✦ Your ISP has assigned you a new password.

Even more annoying is the fact that the message in Figure 3-8 is often accompanied by the one shown in Figure 3-9, which is telling you that Outlook is having trouble sending and/or receiving your e-mail.

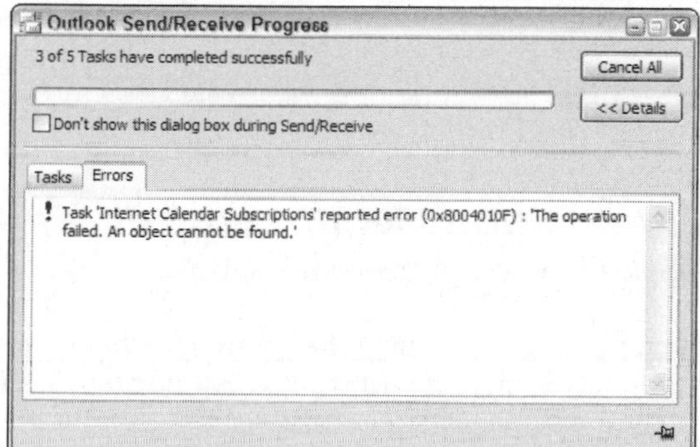

Figure 3-9: Message warning you that Outlook can't send or receive your e-mail.

At this point you're going to want to take a look at your password and correct it if necessary. Here's how you can do that:

1. **Choose Tools⇨Account Settings from Outlook's main menu bar.**
2. **Select the e-mail account you want to change and then click the Change button.**

   The Change E-Mail Account window of the Change E-Mail Account Wizard opens.
3. **Type your password in the Password box in the Logon Information area of the Change E-Mail Account window.**
4. **Select the Remember password check box.**
5. **Click Next to advance to the next window, and then click Finish to close the wizard.**

Choosing a good password

To help keep your e-mail safe, you should regularly change your password. One of the current trends in Internet security is to make use of *strong passwords.* Strong passwords generally include a combination of uppercase and lowercase letters, numbers, and symbols. Weak passwords don't mix these elements. An example of a strong password is a variation on the word Internet: !nT3rneT. An example of a weak password: Apple52. An example of a terrible password is Mary0305, particularly if your name is Mary and your birthday is March 5.

Passwords should be at least 8 or more characters in length; a password that uses 14 or more characters is better. It is critical that you remember your password. If you forget your password, your ISP has to reset them. Store the passwords in a secure place away from the information that they help to protect.

Changing your e-mail account name or reply info

Outlook buries two small tweaks in the e-mail settings:

- **The name of your e-mail account:** When you create an e-mail account, Outlook automatically names it with the e-mail address it contains. You might prefer to give your e-mail accounts names like "Business," "Personal," or even "Most Often Used Address."
- **Your reply address:** When you send e-mail through snail mail, you can use a return address that differs from the location from which you're sending your mail. For example, you might mail a postcard while on vacation and use your home address for the return address, or perhaps you mailed some work correspondence from your home but used the office address.

  Outlook provides the option of using a reply address that is different from the e-mail address that you used to send the message. For example, you might send out lots of e-mail but want all the replies to go to a specific mailbox so that someone else can follow-up on them.

Although these settings are not critical for the transmittal of e-mail, that can be helpful to your sense of organization. Here's all you need to know to change them:

1. **Choose Tools⇨Account Settings from the Outlook's main menu bar.**

   The Account Settings dialog box opens.

2. **Select the e-mail account you want to change, and then click the Change button.**

   The Change E-Mail Account window appears.

3. **Click the More Settings button.**

   The Internet E-Mail Settings dialog box opens, as shown in Figure 3-10.

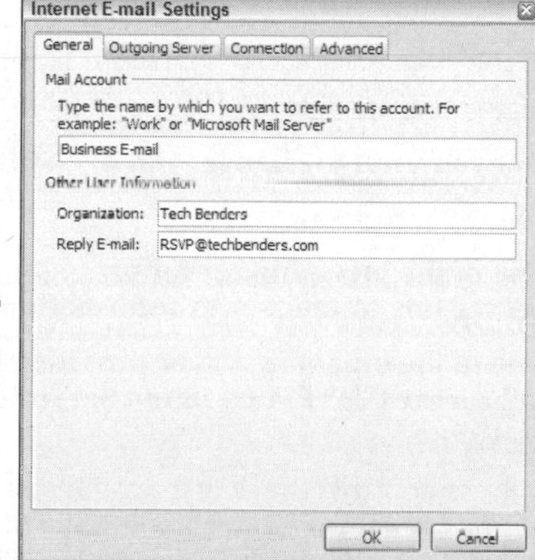

Figure 3-10: Changing the account name and reply e-mail address.

4. **Fill in the name you want to use for your e-mail account and the reply e-mail address that you want to use.**

   If you leave the Reply E-Mail box empty, any e-mail responses you receive automatically arrive at the default e-mail address location, which is usually the first e-mail address that you set up.

   If you've set up multiple e-mail addresses and you're not sure which one is the default, return to the Account Settings dialog box by choosing File➪Account Settings from the main Outlook menu. One of the e-mail addresses is the designated default. If you'd like to change it, select the new address and then click the Set as Default button.

5. **Click OK to close the Internet E-Mail Settings dialog box, and then click Next and Finish.**

Changing Your ISP Information

Outlook may require that you change a few settings from time to time. For example, you must change settings if you change your ISP or switch from dialup to a broadband connection, or if your ISP has made some changes to its servers.

Changing your account information

Once in a while, the mail server that you connect to in order to receive and send e-mail might change. For example, the cable company in your area may change from Adelphia to Comcast. Or you might receive a notice from your ISP telling you that they have upgraded their servers and your POP3 has changed from mail.isp.com to incoming.isp.com.

Here's how to change your account information:

1. **Choose Tools➪Account Settings from Outlook's main menu bar.**

   The Account Settings dialog box appears.

2. **Select the e-mail account you want to change, and click Change.**

   The Change E-Mail Account Wizard appears.

3. **Enter the complete name of the incoming server provided by your ISP in the Incoming mail server box in the Server Information section.**

4. **Enter the complete name of the outgoing server provided by your ISP in the Outgoing mail server (SMTP) box in the Server Information section.**

   The incoming server address controls the way in which you receive e-mail. Conversely, the outgoing server controls the way you send your e-mail. Theoretically your ISP supplies both server addresses. However, there are situations in which the outgoing server may come from a different source. If you are traveling, for example, you may need to connect to a different network than the one you normally use. If this is the case, you may be able to receive new mail, but none of your outgoing messages leave your Outbox.

   If changes have been made to your mail server address, your e-mail address may have changes, as well. If so, you can make the appropriate change in the wizard.

5. **Click Next and then Finish to close the Change E-Mail Account Wizard.**

6. **Click Close to close the Account Settings dialog box.**

Changing your connection type

You can connect to the Internet in two ways: through a network connection or through a phone line. When you first purchased your computer, you were probably prompted to reveal the type of Internet connection you have. However, if you're having trouble connecting to the Internet — or you change the type of connection that you have — you have to pass that information along to Outlook. Here's how to do it:

1. **Choose Tools⇨Account Settings from Outlook's main menu bar.**

   The Account Settings dialog box opens.

2. **Select the e-mail account you want to change, and then click Change from the Account Settings dialog box.**

   The Internet E-Mail Settings dialog box appears (see Figure 3-11).

3. **Click the Connection tab of the Internet E-Mail Settings dialog box.**

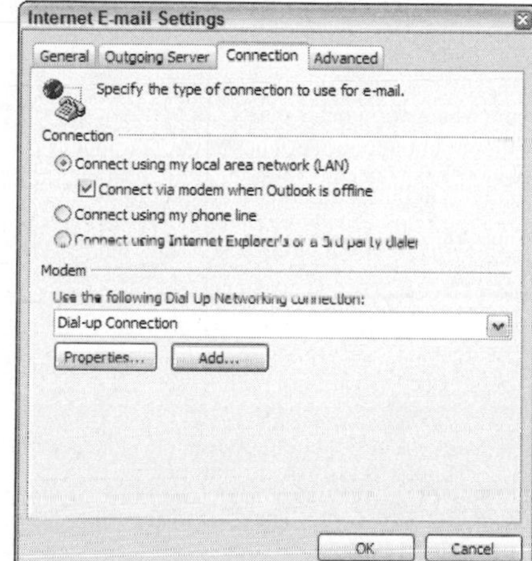

Figure 3-11: Changing Outlook's connection type.

4. **Select the correct Connection option.**

   You have three connection options:

   - **Connect Using My Local Area Network (LAN):** Use this option if your Internet connectivity is provided to you courtesy of a network. Optionally, you can select the Connect Via Modem When Outlook Is Offline check box if you want to use a dialup connection when you're not connected to your network.
   - **Connect Using My Phone Line:** This option is for instances when you need to plug a phone cord into your computer. With this type of connection, you hear all kinds of strange noises emanating from your computer when you connect to the Internet.
   - **Connect Using Internet Explorer's or a 3rd Party Dialer:** Use this option if you use an Internet dialer such as a VPN or one of the long-distance carriers.

5. **Click Add if you are using a dialup connection, and then complete the information provided to you by your service provider.**
6. **Click OK to close the Internet E-Mail Settings dialog box.**
7. **Click Next and then Finish.**

Chapter 4: Importing Data into Outlook

In This Chapter

- **Importing old e-mail account information**
- **Importing old e-mail**
- **Grabbing old names and addresses**
- **Knowing what else you can import**

After you install Microsoft Outlook and set up your e-mail account, you're ready to send and receive e-mail. If you've been using a different e-mail program in the past, though, you may not have set up any e-mail accounts yet, in hopes that maybe somehow you can get them out of that lousy e-mail program you've decided never to use again. As it turns out, you may be able to do just that.

But even if you already set up your e-mail accounts in Outlook, you may want to take one more step and import that old e-mail data into Outlook. You might import old messages so that you can still refer to them from time to time, for example. Or you might import your old contact data so that you can avoid having to retype e-mail addresses. You can import e-mail data from a variety of sources, including other popular e-mail programs and database files, such as Access or Excel files.

Importing E-Mail from Outlook Express/Windows Mail or Eudora

Chances are, when you installed Outlook, it asked you whether you wanted to import data from your old e-mail account, and you clicked Oh, Yeah!, and now that's all done. But if you weren't sure at the time whether you wanted to import that stuff until you had tried out Outlook and decided it wouldn't bite, you're stuck with a problem: You want that data and you hope it's not too late to get it.

As you see in the following sections, the process for both Microsoft Outlook Express/Windows Mail and Eudora is remarkably similar, unless you have Outlook Express/Windows Mail on a different computer than Outlook. I present the steps you need to follow here, in two conveniently marked sections.

Importing e-mail from Outlook Express or Windows Mail

First, a little background: Outlook Express is an e-mail program that comes free with Windows, and so it's a pretty popular solution for handling e-mail. Windows Mail is basically Outlook Express from a different planet (Windows Vista).The difference between Outlook Express/Windows Mail (free) and Outlook (not free) is more than just money — Outlook Express/Windows Mail includes the Mail module and a pared down Contacts list. Outlook Express/Windows Mail doesn't include a Calendar, Tasks, Notes, or Journal, or anything even close to all the features and functionality of Outlook. So it's not surprising that when Santa puts Outlook under your tree, you soon want to leave its clunky cousin far behind. Outlook, not too surprisingly, makes the transition from Express/Mail fairly painless.

If Outlook and Outlook Express/Windows Mail are on the same computer, follow these steps to import Outlook Express/Windows Mail e-mail and account information into Outlook:

1. **In Outlook, choose File⇨Import and Export.**

   The Import and Export Wizard appears, as shown in Figure 4-1.

Figure 4-1: The Import and Export Wizard.

2. **Choose Import Internet Mail and Addresses and click Next.**

   The Outlook Import Tool dialog box makes its appearance. See Figure 4-2.

3. **Choose Outlook Express 4.x, 5.x, 6.x or Windows Mail from the Select the Internet Mail Application to Import From list.**

4. **Choose the Import Mail option, and click Next.**

   You can import contacts at the same time by choosing the Import Address Book option. See the upcoming section, "Importing Contacts," for help.

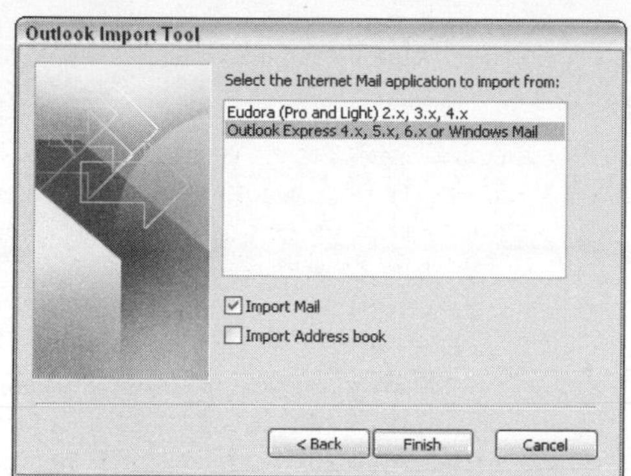

Figure 4-2: Import Outlook Express or Windows Mail e-mail.

5. **Click Finish.**

   A summary of what was imported and what wasn't appears. If you want to save this summary, click Save in Inbox. Otherwise, just click OK.

Grabbing Outlook Express/Windows Mail account information

E-mail is only one part of Outlook Express/Windows Mail you might want to grab. Another part is your e-mail account info. After all, who wants to sit there and manually type in POP3 and SMTP addresses? I know I don't.

If Outlook is on the same computer as Outlook Express/Windows Mail

To grab your e-mail account stuff out of Outlook Express/Windows Mail:

1. **In Outlook, choose File⇨Import and Export.**

   The Import and Export Wizard appears (refer to Figure 4-1).

2. **Choose Import Internet Mail Account Settings, and click Next.**

   The Internet Connection Wizard appears (see Figure 4-3).

3. **Choose Outlook Express or Microsoft Windows Mail from the Select the E-Mail Client to Import list. Click Next to move to the next screen in the Wizard where you begin to import account information.**

4. **Confirm the Display Name and click Next.**

   Outlook pulls your old account info from Outlook Express/Windows Mail and displays it for you, one screen at a time, so that you can verify it and make changes. See Figure 4-4.

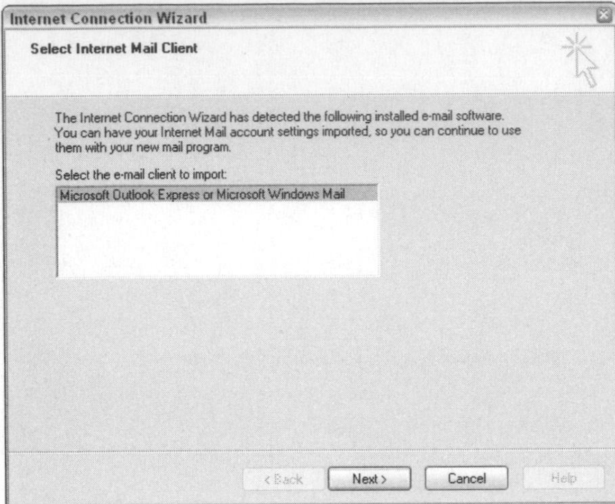

Figure 4-3: Grab that e-mail account info.

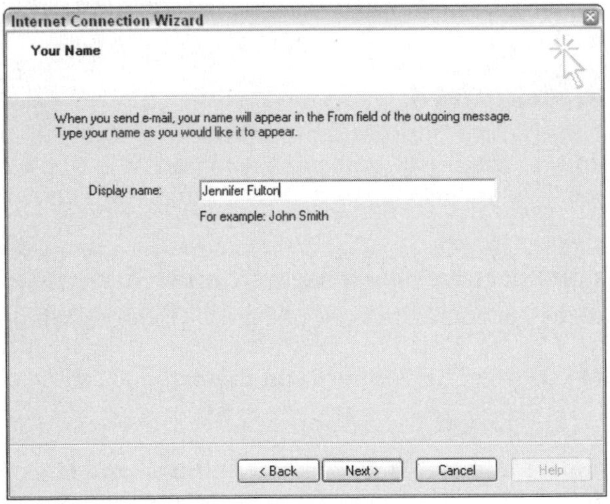

Internet Connection Wizard
Your Name
When you send e-mail, your name will appear in the From field of the outgoing message. Type your name as you would like it to appear.
Display name: Jennifer Fulton
For example: John Smith
< Back
Next >
Cancel
Help

Figure 4-4: Verify the name you want to be known as.

5. **Confirm your e-mail address and click Next.**
6. **Confirm your account info. Click Next to confirm more account information.**
7. **Confirm your login info. Click Next when you're done.**

   You need to confirm the Account Name (user name) and Password you use to log into your e-mail account. Choose the Remember Password option if you don't want to enter that data each time you check mail.

If you need to use SPA (Secure Password Authentication) with this account, be sure to select the Log In Using Secure Password Authentication (SPA).

8. **Confirm how you connect to the e-mail server: through a modem, network, or over the Internet. Click Next.**
9. **Click Finish.**

   The account is imported into Outlook. If you want to verify it for some reason, choose Tools➪Account Settings.

If Outlook is on a different computer than Outlook Express/Windows Mail

If Outlook and Outlook Express/Windows Mail are located on different computers, you must basically move Outlook Express/Windows Mail, then import your mail and account settings:

1. **Start Outlook Express or Windows Mail and then open the Store Folder dialog box.**

   Start up Outlook Express, and in Outlook Express, choose Tools➪Options to display the Options dialog box. Then choose Maintenance➪Store Folder. The location of the Outlook Express data files is displayed in the Store Location dialog box, shown here in Figure 4-5.

   For Windows Mail, you follow this same basic procedure, start it up, and display the Options dialog box. Next, click the Advanced tab in the Options dialog box, click the Maintenance button, and then click the Store Folder button to find where Windows Mail keeps its data.

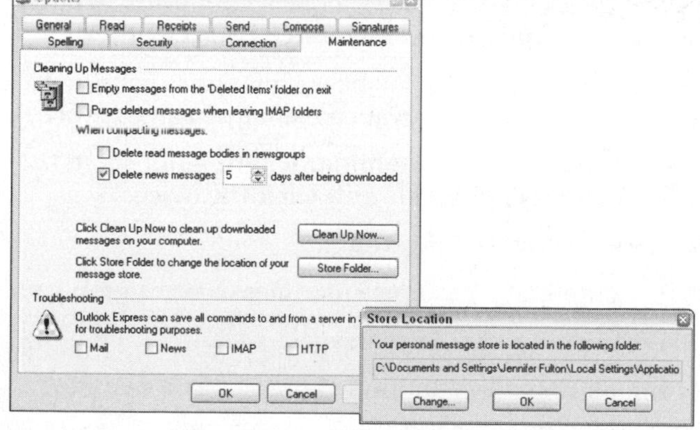

Figure 4-5: Now where is Express or Windows Mail?

2. **Copy the path.**

   You're gonna need to know the path to the Outlook Express/Windows Mail folder, so you can navigate to it using Windows Explorer or Computer. You can select the path and press Ctrl+C to copy it to the Clipboard, or just get out an old pencil and paper and copy that path down.

3. **Click Cancel to close all dialog boxes.**

4. **Browse to the Outlook Express/Windows Mail folder.**

   Open Windows Explorer or Computer and browse to the path you saw in Step 2. You can paste the path (if you copied it) into the Address box by clicking there and pressing Ctrl+V.

5. **Copy Outlook Express/Windows Mail to the Outlook computer.**

   What you're trying to do now that you've found where Outlook Express/Windows Mail hides its data, is to copy that data to the computer that contains Outlook. If the two computers are connected over a network, you can use Windows Explorer or Computer to copy the files; otherwise, copy the entire contents of the folder to a disc, and then copy that to the Outlook computer.

   You can copy the Outlook Express/Windows Mail files basically anywhere on the Outlook computer, because in the next step, you tell Outlook Express/Windows Mail where to find its stuff. So just copy the data to a location that you can remember for at least a few minutes. For obvious reasons, this should not be the same location in which you keep your car keys, cell phone, or the TV remote.

6. **Tell Outlook Express/Windows Mail where to find its stuff.**

   On the computer where Outlook (and now Outlook Express/Windows Mail) is both located, start Outlook Express/Windows Mail. If it asks you to create an e-mail account, tell it to go away by clicking Cancel.

7. **Choose Tools⇨Options⇨Maintenance⇨Store Folder.**

   The Store Location dialog box peeks out again. For Windows Mail, choose Tools⇨Options⇨Advanced⇨Maintenance⇨Store Folder.

8. **Click Change and select the folder where you copied the Outlook Express/Windows Mail data, and click OK twice.**

9. **Copy messages by clicking Yes.**

   You are prompted to either use new messages or grab your old ones.

10. **Click Yes to grab your old messages.**

11. **Exit Outlook Express/Windows Mail.**

    Now that everything's in its rightful place, you can follow the previous set of steps to import Outlook Express/Windows Mail data into Outlook when they are located on the same computer, which they now are.

Grabbing Eudora Pro or Eudora Light e-mail and account info

If you've used Eudora for a while, you have probably accumulated more than a few contacts and messages that you just don't feel like losing, at least not yet. Moving from Eudora Pro or Eudora Light (versions 2–4) is fairly straightforward, as shown in the following steps:

1. **In Outlook, choose File⇨Import and Export.**

   The Import and Export Wizard appears (see Figure 4-6).

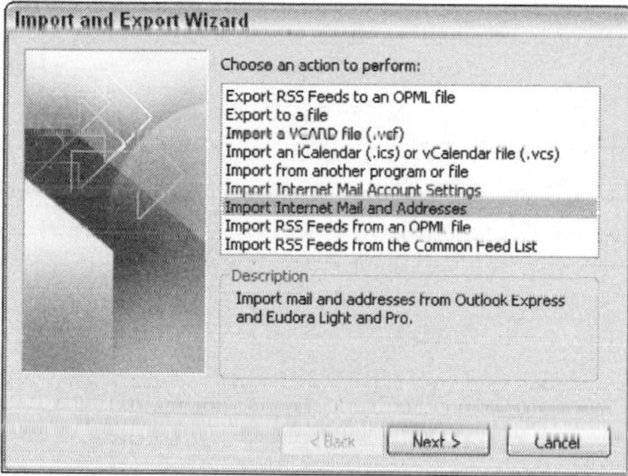

Figure 4-6: Go get those Eudora messages and addresses.

2. **Choose Import Internet Mail and Addresses, and click Next.**

   The Outlook Import Tool dialog box appears (refer to Figure 4-2).

3. **Choose Eudora (Pro and Light) 2.x, 3.x, 4.x from the Select the Internet Mail Application to Import From list.**

4. **Choose the Import Mail option and click Next.**

   You can, if you want, import contact info from Eudora when you grab old messages by choosing the Import Address Book option. See the section, "Importing Contacts," for help.

5. **Click Finish.**

   A summary of what got imported and what didn't appears. If you want to save this summary, click Save in Inbox. Otherwise, just click OK.

Grabbing Eudora 5.0–6.0 e-mail and account info

I guess Microsoft doesn't like the newer versions of Eudora much, because it doesn't make it easy for you to leave it behind and start using Outlook. But you can, after a rather tedious process, grab that stuff from Eudora 5.0–6.0 and dump it into Outlook. Basically, you import the data into Outlook Express and then import the Outlook Express data into Outlook.

Step 1: Importing Eudora data into Outlook Express

Outlook Express is not included with Windows Vista, so you'll need to move your Eudora data to a computer that includes Outlook Express (such as a Windows XP computer) if you want to follow this procedure.

To import messages and the address book from Eudora, you start in Outlook Express, as strange as that sounds:

1. **Choose File⇨Import⇨Messages.**

   The Outlook Express Import dialog box appears (see Figure 4-7).

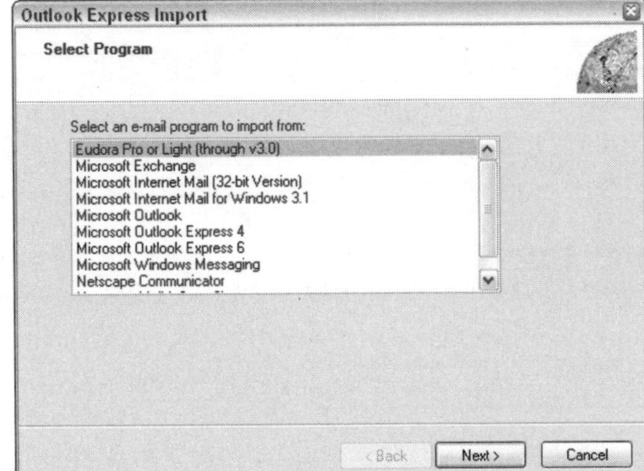

Figure 4-7: Take a message, will ya?

2. **From the Select an E-Mail Program to Import From list, choose Eudora Pro or Light (through v3.0). Click Next.**

   The next step in the Outlook Express Import Wizard, Location of Messages, appears.

3. **Locate the Eudora data file, and click Next.**

   Outlook Express may find the data file for you, but if not, click Browse to hunt down the Eudora data file and select it.

4. **Choose All Folders and click Next.**

   Eudora messages are imported into Outlook Express. Now, onto your Eudora contacts.

5. **In Outlook Express, choose File⇨Import⇨Other Address Book.**

   The Address Book Import Tool dialog box appears, as shown in Figure 4-8.

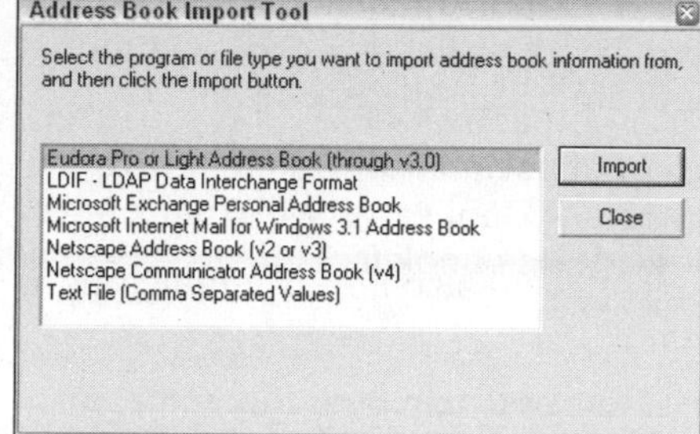

Figure 4-8: Importing a Eudora address book into Outlook Express.

6. **Choose Eudora Pro or Light Address Book (through v.3.0) and click Import.**

   Eudora contacts are imported into Outlook Express.

Step 2: Importing data from Outlook Express into Outlook

Now that everything's in Outlook Junior, you need to get the stuff into Outlook Senior. Here's how:

1. **In Outlook, choose File⇨Import and Export.**

   The Import and Export Wizard appears (see Figure 4-9).

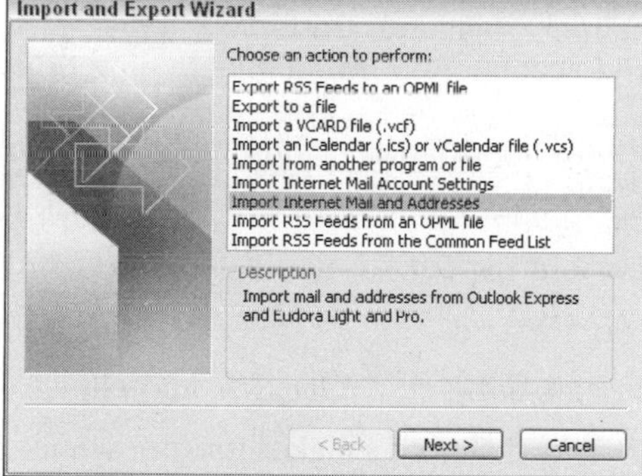

Figure 4-9: Now you can import your Eudora data into Outlook.

2. **Choose Import Internet Mail and Addresses, and click Next.**
3. **Choose Outlook Express 4.x, 5.x, 6.x or Windows Mail. Make sure the Import Mail and the Import Address Book options are selected. Click Next.**
4. **Decide what you want to do with duplicates.**

During the import process, Outlook may find a contact that matches one you already have in your Contacts list. If it does, Outlook wants to know how you want that duplicate handled. Choose one:

- To remove existing contacts and replace them with the ones you're importing, choose Replace Duplicates With Items Imported.
- To keep existing contacts and also import duplicates, choose Allow Duplicates to be Created.
- To keep existing contacts and skip over duplicate entries in the import file, choose Do Not Import Duplicate Items.

5. **Click Finish.**

   The Eudora messages and contacts stored in Outlook Express are imported into Outlook.

Importing Contacts

Importing requires more than just grabbing ancient e-mail messages from your old e-mail client. For me, at least, it's more important to get my contact data and not have to type them back in, then to be able to peruse dusty old messages. Regardless, you can easily import your old addresses from Outlook Express, Eudora Light, or Eudora Pro (2.0–4.0).

If you have Eudora 5.0–6.0, you need to import your addresses into Outlook Express first, and then import them into Outlook. See the section, "Grabbing Eudora 5.0–6.0 e-mail and account info" for complete directions.

To import addresses from Outlook Express, Eudora Light/Pro (versions 2.0–4.0), follow these steps:

1. **Choose File⇨Import and Export.**

   The Import and Export Wizard appears (refer to Figure 4-9).

2. **Choose Import Internet Mail and Addresses, and click Next.**

   The Outlook Import Tool dialog box makes its appearance (refer to Figure 4-2).

3. **Choose Outlook Express 4.x, 5.x, 6.x or Windows Mail, or Eudora (Pro and Light) 2.x, 3.x, 4.x from the Select the Internet Mail Application to Import From list.**
4. **Choose the Import Address Book option, and click Next.**
5. **Decide what to do with duplicates.**

Whenever you import contacts, chances are there are several people with the same name. These might be unique contacts that just so happen to share the same name, or they might be duplicate entries. In any case, in the Import Addresses dialog box (shown in Figure 4-10), you get to decide what you want Outlook to do if it finds duplicate contacts during the import process:

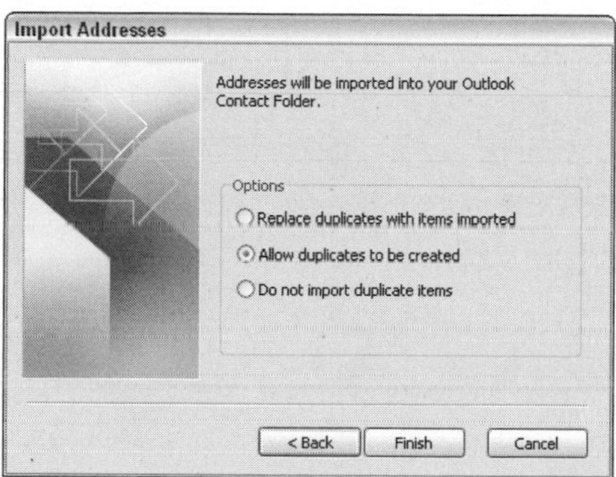

Figure 4-10: Copy cats.

- To remove existing contacts and replace them with the ones you're importing, choose Replace Duplicates With Items Imported.
- To keep existing contacts and also import duplicates, choose Allow Duplicates to be Created.
- To keep existing contacts and skip over duplicate entries in the import file, choose Do Not Import Duplicate Items.

6. **Click Finish.**

   A summary of what got imported and what didn't appears.

7. **If you want to save the summary, click Save in Inbox. Otherwise, just click OK.**

Importing Other Data

There are all sorts of data you might want to import into Outlook, such as names and addresses stored in Excel or Access. You might have an Act! client list you want to grab, or a Lotus Organizer contacts list. The process, as you'll learn here, is similar for various types of data files.

You can't import an Excel 2007 file directly into Outlook 2007, as silly as that sounds. But you can save your Excel 2007 workbook in Excel 2003 format and then import that. Before you do anything, though, you need to name the range of Excel data you want to grab.

Here's how to import other data into Outlook:

1. **Choose File➪Import and Export.**

   The Import and Export Wizard appears (see Figure 4-11).

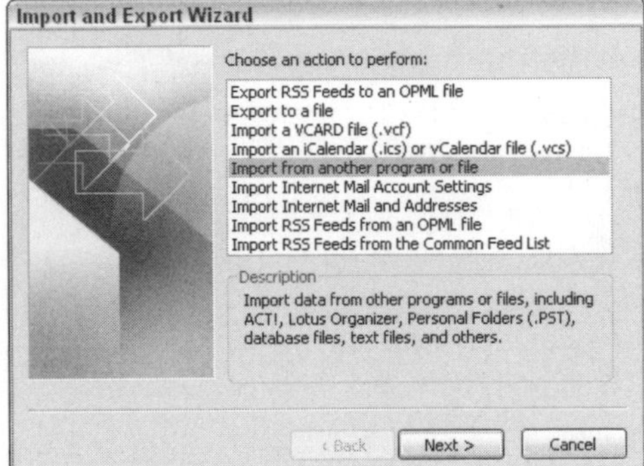

Figure 4-11: The Import and Export Wizard.

2. **Choose Import From Another Program or File and click Next.**

   The Import a File Wizard makes its appearance (see Figure 4-12).

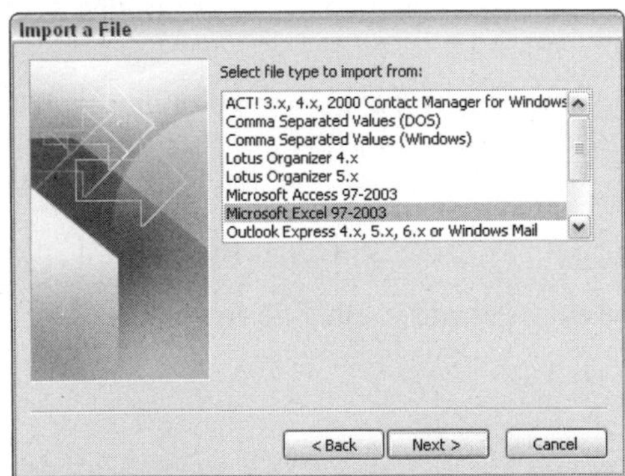

Figure 4-12: Pick a program.

3. **From the Select File Type to Import From list, choose the type of file you need to import, and click Next.**

If you don't find the file type you're looking for in the list, don't despair. You should be able to go back to your original program and save the data in either CSV (comma-separated values) or tab-separated values format. You can then import the CSV or tabbed file into Outlook.

4. **Locate the file and click Next.**

   If necessary, click Browse to find the file and click OK.

5. **Decide what to do with duplicates, and click Next.**

   As Outlook imports these new items, it may discover that one of them has the same information as an existing item. Here's where you tell Outlook what to do in such cases:

   - To remove existing items and replace them with the ones you're importing, choose Replace Duplicates with Items Imported.
   - To keep existing items and also import duplicates, choose Allow Duplicates to be Created.
   - To keep existing items and skip over duplicate entries in the import file, choose Do Not Import Duplicate Items.

6. **Choose which folder in Outlook you want the data to go, and click Next.**

   For example, if you're importing a name and address list, choose the Contacts folder. See Figure 4-13.

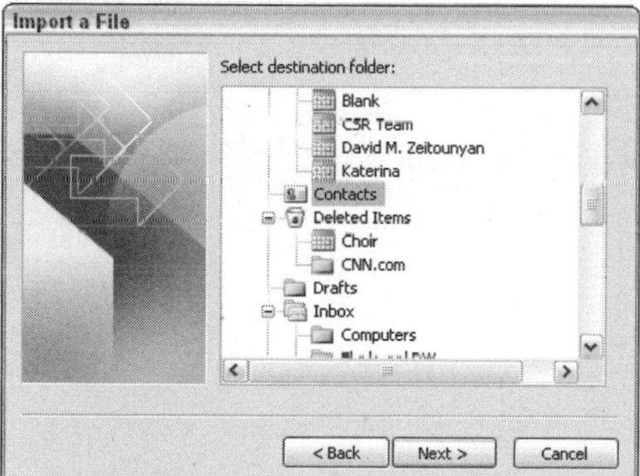

Figure 4-13: So where should this stuff go?

7. **Click the Map Custom Fields button.**

   The Map Custom Fields dialog box appears. See Figure 4-14.

8. **Match up fields.**

   For database-like files, such as Excel, Access, or CSV files, you need to select a table or worksheet, and then map the fields, a process that involves selecting a field (such as Name) in the import file, and telling

Outlook the field (such as Last Name) in Contacts (or whatever folder you're importing data into) where you want that data to go.

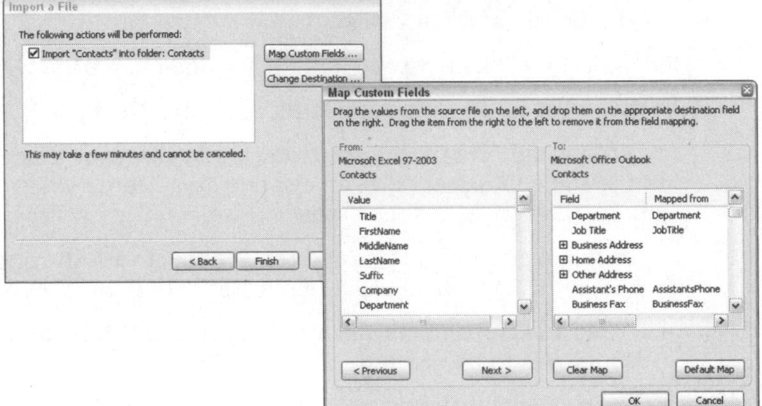

Figure 4-14: Map your data.

Basically, you select a field from the list on the left, which represents the import file, and then drag that field onto an Outlook Contacts field, listed on the right. This dragging from the left over to the right thing is called mapping, and it's basically sophisticated finger-pointing. You're pointing the way from the import file to Contacts for all of its data fields.

9. **When you're done making your map, click OK to close the Map Custom Fields dialog box and return to the wizard.**

10. **Click Finish.**

    The data is imported into Outlook.

Book II

E-Mail Basics

"Your mail program looks fine. I don't know why you're not receiving any personal e-mails. Have you explored the possibility that you may not have any friends?"

Contents at a Glance

Chapter 1: Creating New Messages: Beyond the Basics 85

Chapter 2: Reading and Replying to E-Mail....................113

Chapter 3: Making Your E-Mail Look Professional and Cool 127

Chapter 4: Repeating Yourself Easily with Signatures and Templates 161

Chapter 1: Creating New Messages: Beyond the Basics

In This Chapter

- **Understanding the steps involved in sending e-mail**
- **Dealing with multiple address books**
- **Searching for an address in your address book**
- **Sending copies and blind copies of messages**
- **Making message text beautiful**
- **Enclosing a file with a message**
- **Saving a draft of a message for later**

Sending a simple, "Hey, how are you? Where's the ten bucks you owe me?" type of message is fairly straightforward (although I review that process in this chapter, just in case you missed something in the whirlwind tour in Book I, Chapter 2). It takes a little more work to make your text look distinctive enough to stand out from the crowd of other messages most people receive in a day. And perhaps even a little more effort to include an image or a file with the message. And maybe some actual thinking is required when you need to fish for an address hidden deep inside one of your address books. No matter — you find out how to deal with all these things and more in this chapter.

Creating a Message, Step by Step

In Book I, Chapter 2, you discover a lot of quick and dirty tricks, including how to send a quick e-mail message. Sending a message isn't all that complex, but if you've never done it before, you might appreciate a little more info.

Step 1: Display the message form

This step is probably no mystery; the New button, located on the Standard toolbar, can be used from anywhere in Outlook to create a new *something*. To create a New message, here's the drill:

1. **Click the arrow on the New button.**

   A long list of options appears.

2. **Choose Mail Message from the long list that appears.**

   If you're in the Mail module, just click the New button instead, and a new message form appears.

You might have noticed that the icon on the New button changes as you move from module to module; that's to let you know it's ready to create a new item just for the current module. For example, if you're in Calendar, the New button shows a small calendar, and if you click it, you'll create a new appointment.

You can create e-mails with fancy colorful backgrounds, using templates you can get from Microsoft's Web site. See Book II, Chapter 4 for more information.

Step 2: Address the e-mail

You have to address the message so Outlook and all those e-mail servers on the Internet know who to pass the message on to. You see, there are special computers, located throughout the Internet, whose purpose is to handle incoming and outgoing e-mail for a group of people — such as all the people who work for your company. An *e-mail server* is kind of like a local post office; using the e-mail address attached to a message, the server sorts e-mails and passes them on. If a message comes in for someone working at your company, then the message is transferred to that person's computer whenever he or she logs on and requests e-mail. If a message arrives addressed to someone who uses a different e-mail server, then it's passed along the Internet chain till it gets to its destination.

Basically, an e-mail address is broken down into two parts, separated by an @ sign: The first part identifies the person to whom the message is being sent, and the second part identifies the e-mail server. For example, the e-mail address: `joebrown@fakeco.com` tells an e-mail server that the message is meant for Joe Brown, who gets his e-mail from a server at fakeco.com. Likewise, `tenesha.j.ruiz@aol.com` identifies an e-mail for Tenesha J. Ruiz who gets her mail from AOL.

After you're armed with an e-mail address, you simply type that address in the Address box of the Message form, as shown in Figure 1-1. If this person is somebody you think you'll be writing often, you might want to enter the e-mail address in your Contacts list (see Book V, Chapter 1 for the how-to). Entering the address in Contacts makes it much easier to address e-mails; all you have to do is type a contact's name in the Address box, like this:

Scott Thompson

if there's only one Scott in your Contacts list, or only one to whom you send e-mail on a frequent basis, try typing just this:

Scott

Outlook then checks the Contacts list for a match and assuming it finds one, it displays a list of matches — in this case, all the Scotts. Just click a name in the list that appears to select it. If you typed the whole name, such as **Scott Thompson**, and then moved on to typing the message or subject or whatever, Outlook won't mind. It looks up the contact name you typed as you continue to work, and (assuming it finds a match) it underlines the name you typed. This is called *resolving* the e-mail address, and I discuss this topic in more detail later in this chapter. For now, just know that the magic works, assuming you type the name in a way that's similar to how it's entered in Contacts.

Notice in the figure that Outlook underlined, or resolved, the e-mail address I manually typed in. That's because Outlook underlines all manual addresses, working under the assumption that if you took the time to type it in, you did so *carefully*. In other words, the underline here is meaningless and doesn't reassure you that the e-mail address you typed in is valid. So be careful when you're typing in e-mail addresses.

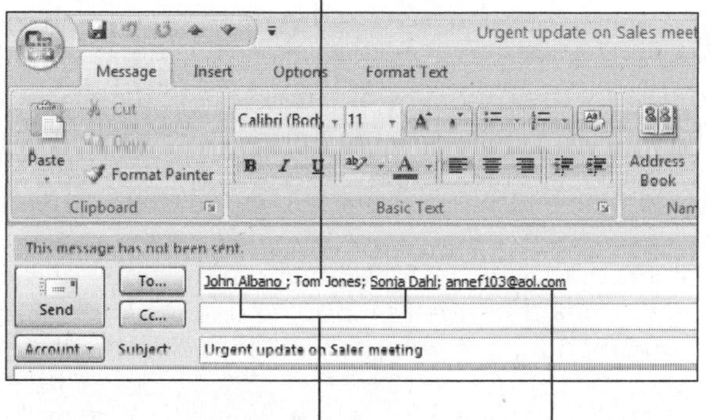

Figure 1-1: Type the e-mail address in the Address box.

If, somehow, the name you typed doesn't get matched with something in Contacts, you can go searching for the name by clicking the To button. What happens next depends a lot on your e-mail setup, and requires a broader understanding of the Contacts list and something called an address book. So, for the time being, I'll leave the clicking the To button business and let you read up on it in the next section.

Step 3: Send extra copies of the message

If you need to get the word out to multiple people, you can go about that in several ways:

- **Type ; (semicolon) after the first e-mail address in the Address box, and then type another e-mail address.** For example, the Address box might look like this:

```
scott.thompson@fakeco.com;tenesha.j.ruiz@aol.com
```

- **Type an address in the Cc or Bcc fields.** The Cc stands for *carbon copy,* and it literally sends a copy of the message to the people you designate. Bcc stands for *blind carbon copy,* and it's used to secretly send a copy of a message to someone without letting the others in the Address or Cc fields know you've done that. (See the section, "Sending Carbon Copies (Ccs) and Blind Carbon Copies (Bccs)" for help.)

Step 4: Enter a subject and a message

Before you type the message, you should enter a subject or description of that message's content. Just click in the Subject box and type a brief description. Your recipient can then glance at the subject when the e-mail comes in, and decide whether to ignore you now or later.

You don't actually need to type a subject, but most people do — and the right subject can make all the difference in whether your message gets read. You might type **Update on Sales Meeting Today** or **What you been up to?.** Both subjects identify the content of the message and help the reader identify the e-mails that need to be read right now.

After entering a subject, click in the big box at the bottom of the Mail form and type your message. (See Figure 1-2.) Even when I'm just sending a file, I always type something about the attachment in the body of the message so the reader doesn't think the e-mail's empty and some kind of strange prank. (You find out how to add file attachments later in this chapter.)

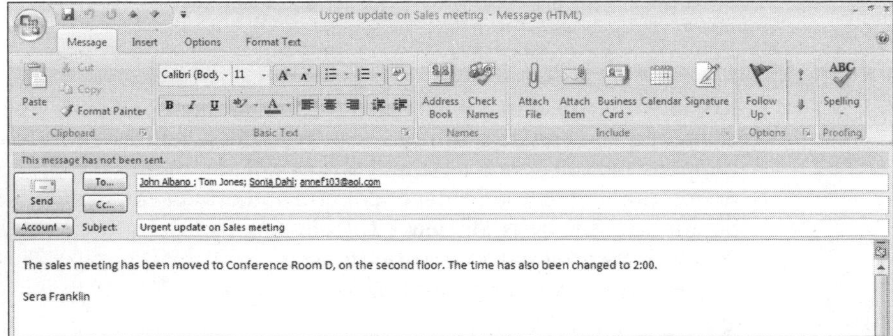

Figure 1-2: Type your message in the big box.

You can follow the normal word-processing procedures for typing your message: Just type, and the words flow automatically between margins. Follow these other tips for entering text:

- **Press Enter to begin a new paragraph.**
- **Press Backspace to back up and erase characters to the left of the cursor; press Delete to erase characters to the right.** To delete a large section of text, drag over it to select it and then press Delete.
- **Select text and drag and drop it to move it.**
- **Press Home to move to the beginning of a line; press End to move to the end of a line.** Press Ctrl+Home to jump to the top of the message, or Ctrl+End to move to the end of the message.
- **In most cases, you can add formatting** to the text before or after you type (see the "Formatting Text to Make Your Messages Stand Out" section, later in this chapter, for help).

If you're wondering what to say, you might begin as if you're typing a regular letter, with a *Hi, Hello,* or *Hey there.* For a closing, you can add *Sincerely* or *Thanks,* and then your name. A lot of people include e-mail address, postal address, Web address, and phone number after the name to make it easy for the reader to contact them. If you want to get fancy, you can save your basic contact information in a file called a *signature* that gets added to your outgoing e-mails automatically. (For the word on how to create a signature, see Book II, Chapter 4.)

Step 5: Send it off

When you're through creating the perfect message, click the Send button to send it off. If you haven't yet sent the message, you'll know because the InfoBar (located just below the Ribbon) tells you so (refer to Figure 1-2). After you click Send, the message is placed in your Outbox, where it is immediately sent up to your e-mail server for processing, assuming you're connected to the Internet or your company network.

If, for some reason, the e-mail is not sent immediately, you can press F9 or click the Send/Receive button on the Standard toolbar to coax it along. Both the F9 key and the Send/Receive button start a send-and-receive cycle that sends e-mail, checks for new e-mail on the mail server, and downloads any new messages. If you only want to send e-mail right now, click the arrow on the Send/Receive button and choose Send All.

It's probably a good idea to check your spelling and grammar before you send off a message, if for no other reason than to prevent embarrassment over a simple mistake. See Book II, Chapter 3 before clicking Send.

If you're not ready to send the message right now, you can save it in the Drafts folder, make changes later on, and then send it. (See the section, "Saving a Message So You Can Send It Later," in this chapter for help.)

After sending an e-mail message, if for some reason your mail server or one of the mail servers along the path to your recipient can't find the e-mail address you used, an e-mail server will send you a message telling you that it didn't actually deliver the e-mail. At that point, check the address carefully and resend the message.

Retrieving Your Mail

Periodically, Outlook checks your mail server for new mail. Typically this is done every ten minutes, assuming you're connected to the Internet all the time (or to your company's network). If you're not always connected to the Internet, then e-mail is probably checked when you ask Outlook to do it — whenever you click the Send/Receive button on the toolbar.

You can make Outlook get your mail at any time, by clicking the Send/Receive button. To change how often e-mail is checked, choose Tools⇨Send/Receive⇨Send/Receive Settings⇨Define Send/Receive Groups. Choose the All Accounts group from the Group Name list, and then select the Schedule an automatic send/receive every XX minutes option. Set XX to the number of minutes you want to wait between send/receive cycles. (See Book III, Chapter 1 for more information.)

In any case, at some point Outlook contacts your e-mail server — which looks to see if you've got any new messages. You can watch the process of downloading e-mail by staring intently at the status bar, where you can view a series of messages such as `Send/Receive Status 40%` and `Send/Receive Complete`.

As e-mails come in, Outlook does everything it can to gain your attention, short of bopping you in the head. First off, for each e-mail (unless they're coming in too fast), Outlook flashes a Desktop Alert. This alert briefly displays the sender's name, the subject, and the first few lines of the incoming message so you can see instantly see whether this is a message you need to read now. There are lots of things you can do with these alerts:

- **Need a longer look at the Desktop Alert?** Just hover the mouse pointer over it.
- **Want to read the message?** Simply move the mouse pointer over the bubble and click the message header, as shown in Figure 1-3.

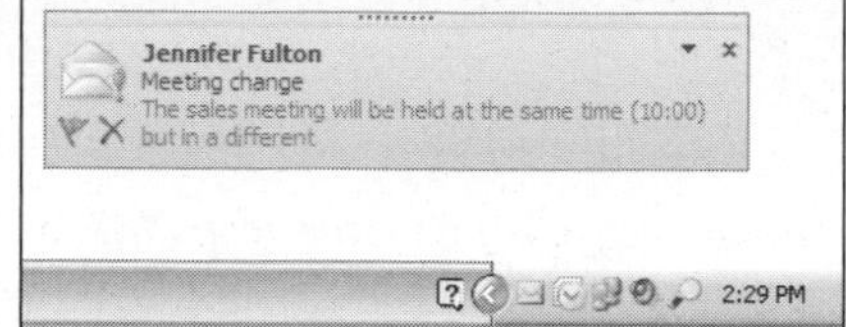

Figure 1-3: When new mail arrives, you're alerted.

- **Click the X to delete the e-mail without reading it.**
- **Click the flag to create an instant to-do item.** See Book VI, Chapter 1 for help with to-do items.

If you do nothing when a Desktop Alert appears, it fades away slowly on its own, to be replaced by the next alert if there's more mail. If you're slow on the uptake like me (without coffee, at least), you can lengthen the time that alerts stay on-screen; see Book III, Chapter 1.

In addition to displaying a series of Desktop Alerts, Outlook plays a sound to let you know you have mail, and also places a closed-envelope icon in the Windows System Tray, as shown in Figure 1-3. Those new messages are then placed in your Inbox, which is the main e-mail folder.

Actually, the Inbox is the only e-mail folder you have, until you create other folders to organize your messages. I highly recommend creating folders to keep similar messages together, such as personal e-mail. See Book IX, Chapter 1 for help.

Going through the mail

To read these new messages, you need to switch to Mail by clicking the Mail button on the Navigation pane and then click a message header to view its contents in the Reading pane, as shown in Figure 1-4. If (like me) you've created various e-mail folders, then click the folder first in the Navigation pane to see its list of messages, and then click a message header.

Messages that have not been read appear with a bold message header. In addition, e-mail folders that contain unread messages appear in bold as well, so you'll know that you need to check those folders too and not just your Inbox. Outlook also kindly lists how many unread items are in each folder.

Sometimes I click a message header to read an e-mail, only to find that my attention span is shorter than I thought. I then mark the e-mail as unread so I'll know to go back and actually read it (with full attention) later on. To mark a message as unread, select it and then choose Edit⇨Mark as Unread.

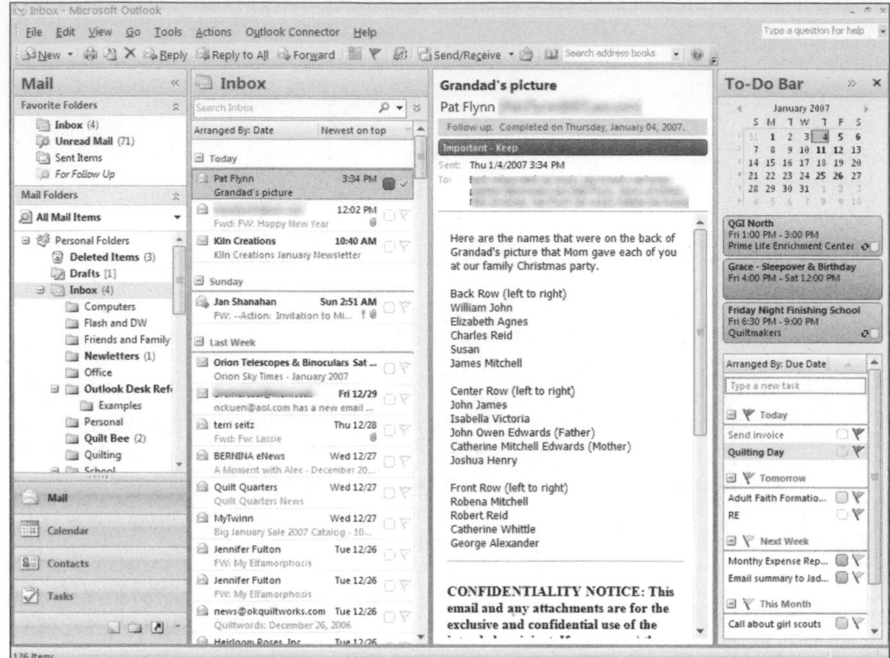

Figure 1-4: Reading the mail.

Fast ways to review mail

Obviously, clicking a header here or there and then reading the message in a tiny Reading pane may not be a very fast way to review a lot of messages — but it *is* selective. If you want to review messages faster, here are a few tips:

1. **Choose View➪Current View➪Unread Messages in This Folder.**

   This changes the view and displays only unread message headers in a long list. The Reading pane disappears, however, so you'll have to turn it back on.

2. **Choose View➪Reading Pane➪Bottom.**

   This displays the Reading pane along the bottom of the window, as shown in Figure 1-5.

3. **Click the first message header.**

   The contents of the message appear in the Reading pane.

4. **To read the next message, press the down arrow key.**

   The contents of the next unread message appear in the Reading pane.

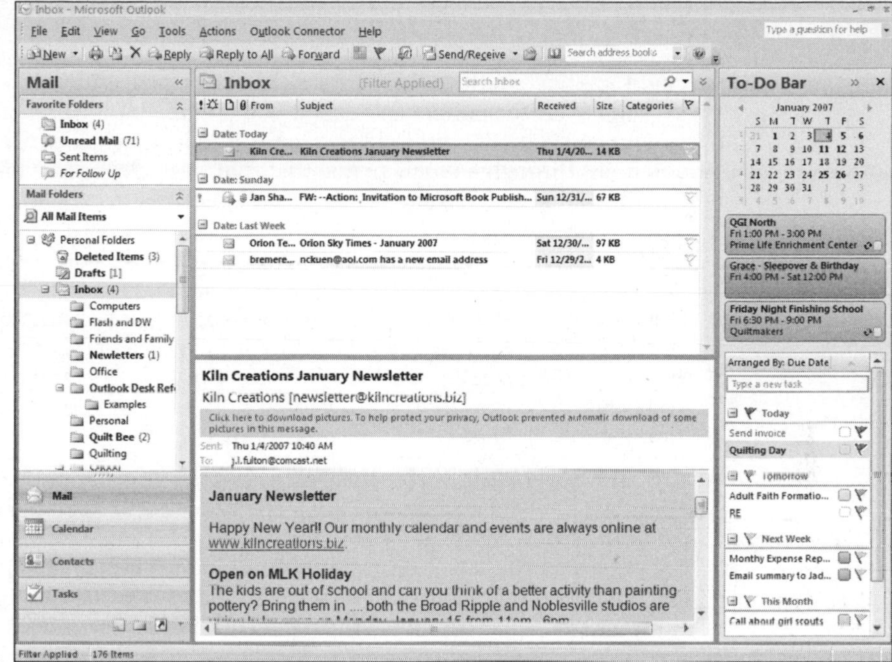

Figure 1-5: Quickly read your unread messages.

If you'd rather review your mail in a window so you can see its contents more easily, then follow these steps instead:

1. **Choose View⇨Current View⇨Unread Messages in This Folder.**

   This changes the view and displays only unread message headers in a long list.

2. **Double-click the first e-mail to view it in a full window.**

   This displays the Reading pane along the bottom of the window (refer to Figure 1-5).

3. **To view the next item, click the Next Item button.**

   You'll find the Next Item button on the Quick Access Toolbar. To review a previously viewed e-mail message, click the Previous Item button instead.

See Book II, Chapter 2 for more help in reviewing and replying to incoming e-mail.

Working with Address Books

You might not have noticed, but Outlook checks e-mail addresses to see if they're valid prior to sending any e-mail you create. Rather than glum through all the data you keep in your Contacts list to see if an e-mail address is okay, Outlook looks through a much smaller list that basically contains only names and e-mail addresses. This smaller list is called the Outlook *Address Book.*

As it so happens, you might actually have multiple address books:

- **Outlook Address Book:** The names of people you personally add to Outlook, along with their e-mail addresses, are stored in the Contacts list and also in the smaller Outlook Address Book. This is the case even if your Outlook is set up to use a Global Address List (described next), in which case you'd have two address books.
- **Global Address List:** If you work with Outlook at a company that uses Microsoft Exchange (an e-mail and groupware server program), Outlook is probably set up to use the company's *Global Address List,* which contains the names and e-mail addresses of all company employees. If you're a college student, you might've been given access to the university's Global Address List, which contains the e-mail addresses of professors and staff.
- **Other address books:** Regardless of whether you use only the Outlook Address Book (and Contacts), or you use a Global Address List as well, you might want to mix it up a little by adding other address books. For example, you could add an Internet address listing that uses LDAP (Lightweight Directory Access Protocol). Basically, such a listing can be accessed through the Internet to obtain directory information such as e-mail addresses; you might be given access to an LDAP through your college or university, for example. You might also add a mobile address book to Outlook, through Outlook Mobile Service, for example. A mobile address book keeps track of cell phone numbers and allows you to send and receive text messages through the service.

When Outlook is set up to use multiple address books, one is designated as the main one, which means that it's searched first when Outlook is verifying names. The main address book is also the one that appears first when you click the Address Book button on the Standard toolbar or click the To button in a message form to look up someone's e-mail address manually. (For more on verifying e-mail addresses and looking up names, see the upcoming section, "Resolving to Find the Right E-Mail Address.") If you tend to search for names in the Contacts list rather than in a Global Address List, you might want to change which address book is searched first. You find out how to do so in the section, "Choosing which address book is the boss," later in this chapter.

Attaching a new address book to Outlook

Companies typically set up their employees' computers, so if your company uses Exchange, your Outlook at work is probably already connected to the company's Global Address List. However, if you need to attach a university's Global Address List or some kind of Internet list to Outlook, here's what you do:

1. **Choose Tools⇨Account Settings.**

   The Account Settings dialog box pops up.

2. **On the Address Books tab, click New.**

   The Add New E-Mail Account dialog box, shown in Figure 1-6, appears.

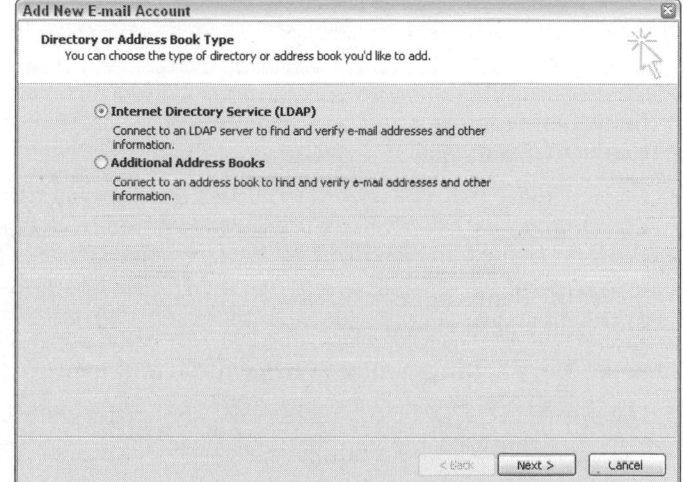

Figure 1-6: What's one more address book between friends?

3. **Choose the address book type:**

   - **To add an Internet directory list, choose Internet Directory Service (LDAP) and click Next.** The Add New E-mail Account dialog box opens, as shown in Figure 1-7. Continue to Step 4.
   - **To add a Global Address List or similar address book, select Additional Address Books and click Next.** Select the type of list you want to add and click Next. Click Finish. You're done (so skip the remaining steps here)!

4. **Enter the server and logon information:**

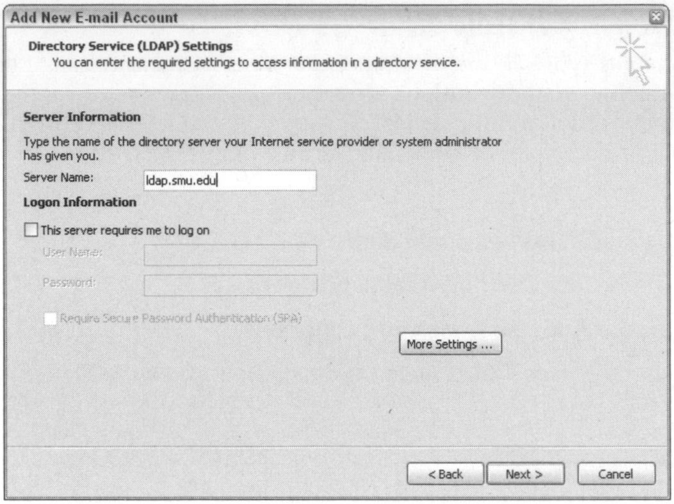

Figure 1-7: Enter LDAP settings.

- In the Server Information box, type the server name of the computer that contains the list.
- If you need to use a password to access the list (you usually do), choose the This Server Requires Me to Log on Check box, and type the User Name and Password you've been given.
- Select the Require Secure Password Authentication (SPA) option if you've been asked to do so.

5. **Click the More Settings button. Click OK to continue.**

   The Microsoft LDAP Directory dialog box, shown in Figure 1-8, magically appears, begging for more information.

Figure 1-8: Tell Outlook how to find the LDAP directory.

6. **Type the port number for the connection in the Port box.**

   Select the Use Secure Sockets Layer option if you've been asked to do so.

7. **Click the Search tab, shown in Figure 1-9.**

Figure 1-9: Just a little more info, please.

8. **Change the following options as needed:**

   - **Search Timeout in Seconds:** Change this value if you want to extend the amount of time Outlook will search for the list.
   - **Specify the Maximum Number of Entries You Want to Return After a Successful Search:** Change this value if you want to limit the number of address books Outlook lists after searching.
   - **Choose either Use Default or Custom:** If you select Custom, type the name you were given by the owner of the list.
   - **Enable Browsing:** Select this check box if you want to try searching for the list manually.

9. **Click OK to close the Microsoft LDAP Directory dialog box.**

10. **Click Next and then click Finish to find the list.**

After adding an address book, you must exit Outlook and restart it in order to make the new address book available.

Importing personal address books into Outlook 2007

In previous versions of Outlook, you could create multiple personal address books (for separating personal and business e-mail addresses, for example), but in Outlook 2007, you can only have one Outlook Address Book. You can (and should) import the addresses from these extra personal address books into the one Outlook Address Book. Just follow these steps:

1. **Choose File⇨Import and Export.**

   The Import and Export Wizard appears.

2. **Select Import from Another Program or File, and click Next.**
3. **Select Personal Address Book and click Next.**
4. **Click Browse and then select the file to import. Click Next.**
5. **Choose the Contacts folder to import into (if you have more than one).**
6. **Click Finish.**

Choosing which address book is the boss

If you have more than one address book such as a Global Address List and an Outlook Address Book where you keep your personal contacts, you can boss Outlook around and tell it which address book you prefer to have searched first when it is verifying e-mail addresses:

1. **Click the Address Book button on the Standard toolbar.**

   The Address Book dialog box snaps open.

2. **Choose Tools⇨Options.**

   The Addressing dialog box appears, as shown in Figure 1-10.

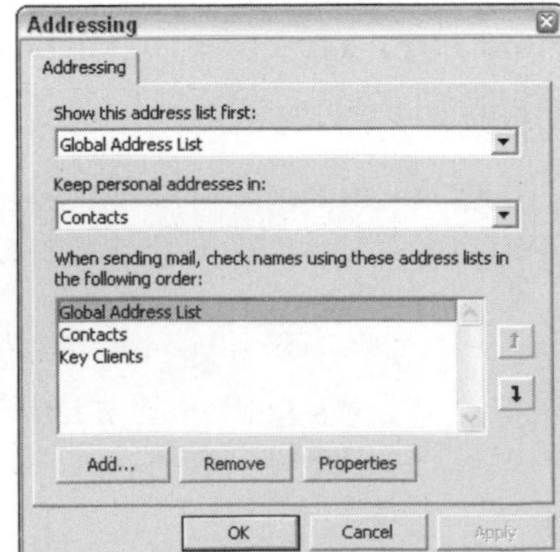

Figure 1-10: Choose which address book you want Outlook to search first when resolving e-mail addresses.

3. **To change the order in which address books are searched to resolve an e-mail address, select the address book you want to search first (in the large box at the bottom of the dialog box).**
4. **Use the up or down arrows (to the right of this large box) to move the address book up or down in the list until the books are in the order you want.**

Notice that you can change which one of your address books is shown first when you click the Address Book button. Just select the one you prefer from the Show This Address List First list box. You can even choose which address book you want to use to collect the contacts you add by selecting one from the Keep Personal Addresses in List.

You can't save new contacts in the Global Address Book, no matter what setting you use in Outlook, unless you've been given permission to do so.

5. **Click OK to finalize your choices and then close the Address Book.**

Resolving to Find the Right E-Mail Address

Ever have a problem trying to find the e-mail address for someone you've just gotta send a message to *right now?* It can be especially frustrating if you know that darn e-mail address is right there, if only you could find where it's hiding in Outlook. In this section, I explain how Outlook verifies e-mail addresses prior to sending a new message and what to do if Outlook simply hasn't got any idea to whom you're trying to send a message.

Understanding how Outlook verifies addresses

To explain how Outlook verifies e-mail addresses, I need to remind you how to properly address an e-mail. Contrary to what you might think, you don't actually need to type an e-mail address to send a message. Nope. As I explained earlier, in the section, "Creating a Message, Step by Step," you can just type a name and let Outlook do all the work of finding the matching e-mail address for you. Of course, Outlook can't find what isn't there, so this magic assumes you've added the name (and a matching e-mail address) to your Contacts list. (See Book V, Chapter 1 for help on that one.)

Assuming you know someone well enough to remember his or her name, I'm guessing you'll find this process pretty easy. Here's how it works:

1. **Start by typing the name in the To text box of a message form.**

   After just a few letters, the e-mail address of the recipient should appear automatically, courtesy of the AutoComplete feature.

2. **Press Enter to accept Outlook's suggestion.**

   If a list of addresses appears, instead of just one, use the arrow keys to highlight the correct person and then press Enter (you can also click the address you want in the list).

Any feature so fancy it that all it needs for looking up an e-mail address is a few measly letters has got to have an equally fancy name, and this one is no exception. The process of matching a name to an e-mail address is called *resolving*. And guess what? You can actually misspell the name, and as long as you're close enough, Outlook should find the address for you. When a name is resolved, Outlook underlines it so you know that it's okay to go.

I say that an address "*should* automatically appear" in the To field as you type because, in fact, AutoComplete keeps track of only those people you e-mail frequently. If AutoComplete pops out an address that you no longer plan on using (or presents you with the result of some earlier typing mistake), just highlight the address by using the arrow keys and then press Delete.

AutoComplete, as great as it sounds, can't always come up with the right e-mail address. In such a case, you might have to type the complete name and wait a second or two to see if Outlook *resolves* the name for you (locates the matching e-mail address in one of your address books). If Outlook doesn't appear to be doing anything, you can force it to try to resolve the address by choosing Message⇨Names⇨Check Names. The Check Names dialog box jumps up, as shown in Figure 1-11; it probably won't have any suggestions to make about the missing name unless the problem is that several matches for the same name are in your address books — but if it does that, select the name you want from the list and click OK. Otherwise, click the Show More Names button to display your Address Book; there you can choose the name manually. There's also a New Contact button for adding the contact right then and there, if you come up empty.

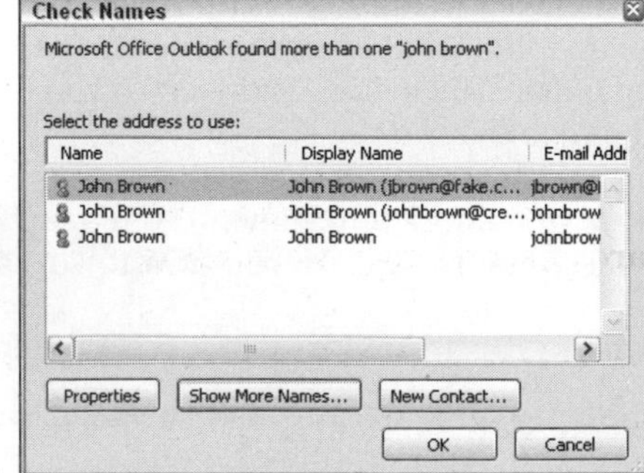

Figure 1-11: Resolve the disputed name yourself.

Sometimes you'll confound Outlook somewhat — causing it to place a red, wavy underline below the name you've typed in the To box. This means you've come close to spelling the person's name right, but not close enough for AutoComplete or AutoResolve to find a matching e-mail address. If you've stumped Outlook completely, it doesn't underline the name at all. See Figure 1-12.

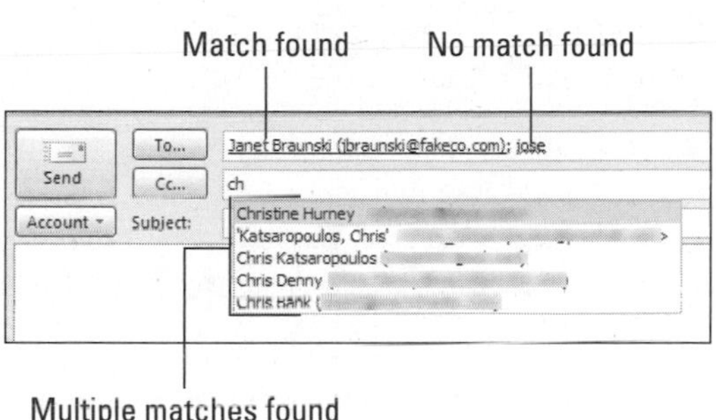

Figure 1-12: Outlook resolves e-mail addresses by checking the various Outlook address books and underlining the names it finds.

If you get tired of looking up contacts because you can't get Outlook to understand whom you're talking about when you type a name, you can try drag and drop to create a message, as described in Book I, Chapter 2.

Searching for an address in your address book

Unfortunately, if you type a name and it isn't resolved by Outlook (replaced by a matching e-mail address and then underlined), you have to address your e-mail the old-fashioned way — by searching for the e-mail address in your address book(s). Here's how:

1. **Click the To (or Cc or Bcc) button in the e-mail form.**

   The Select Names dialog box appears, as shown in Figure 1-13.

2. **From the Address Book drop-down list, choose which of your address books you want to search for a name (assuming you have more than one address book).**

3. **Type a name in the Search box.**

   As you type, Outlook obligingly highlights a matching name for you.

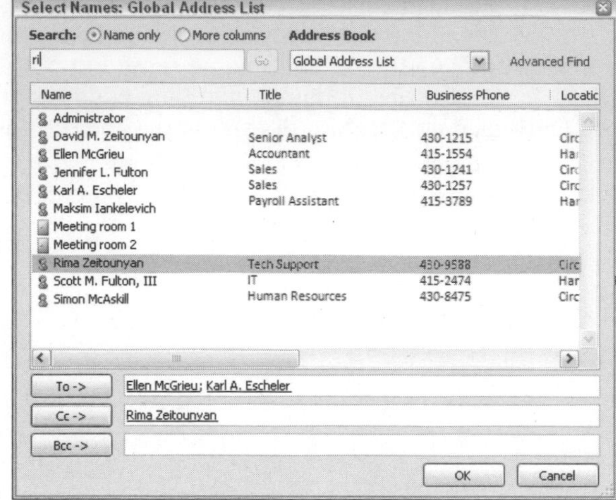

Figure 1-13: If necessary, search your address books for a name.

If you need more help to find a person's information, you can use a detail other than the name to locate it; you can search any column that appears in the Select Names dialog box. Click the Advanced Find link, located to the right of the Address Book list, and then type search clues in the appropriate boxes.

4. **Click the To (or Cc or Bcc) button.**

   This adds the highlighted name to the To/Cc/Bcc list, depending on which button you clicked. (See the next section for more on sending Ccs and Bccs.) Rinse and repeat these steps to add other e-mail addresses as needed.

5. **Click OK.**

   This closes the Address Book and returns you to the e-mail form. The recipients' addresses appear in the message form.

You can type any e-mail address you want to use into the To, Cc, or Bcc fields of an open e-mail form. You might do this to send an e-mail to someone you don't want to add permanently to your Contacts list. Outlook tries to verify that the address is valid by matching it with a name in one of your address books. Failing that, Outlook just underlines the address anyway. Underline or no underline, you can still send the e-mail. As an FYI, if you go this manual route, remember to separate addresses with a semicolon (;).

You can access any of your address books at any time (not just in a Mail form), either by clicking the Address Book button on the Standard toolbar from within any module or by choosing Message➪Names➪Address Book from within an e-mail form.

Sending Carbon Copies (Ccs) and Blind Carbon Copies (Bccs)

If you've already sent some messages, the To field should seem pretty familiar (even if you haven't finished your second cup of coffee for the day) because you use it in pretty much every e-mail. The To field of every e-mail message contains the e-mail addresses of those people you consider the message's main recipients.

In addition to the To field, the message window contains two other address fields, as shown in Figure 1-14:

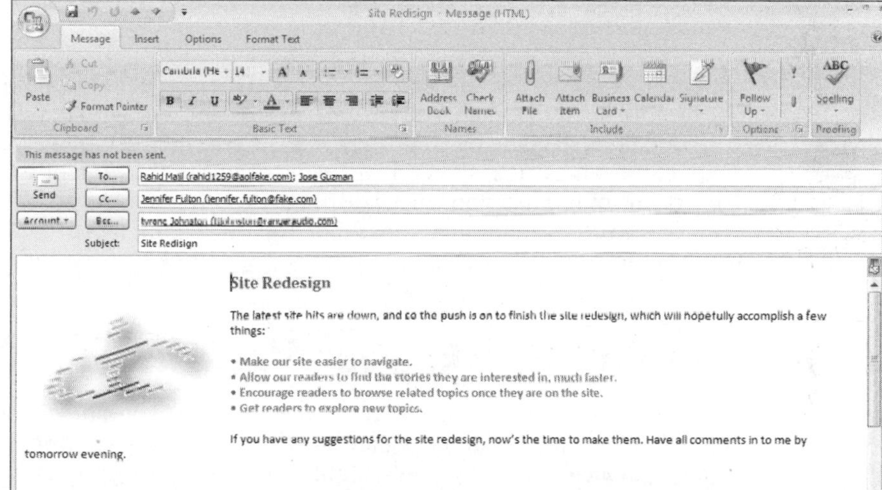

Figure 1-14: The To field, along with the Cc and Bcc fields.

✦ **Cc:** Use the Cc field (*cc* is short for *carbon copy*) when you want to send a copy of an e-mail message to someone — not so much for them to read it, study it, and maybe even reply, but more as a simple FYI.

For example, maybe you want to cc your boss on a message you're sending to a supplier who's jeopardizing a critical project because his delivery is already two weeks late. Everyone who gets the e-mail sees that it was sent to the people listed in the To field and also to those people listed in the Cc field. In other words, your supplier will soon be sweating because, when he reads your message, he'll know that your boss is aware of his failure.

✦ **Bcc:** If you type an e-mail address or a name for Outlook to resolve into the Bcc (short for *blind carbon copy*) field, that person receives a copy of the message, but no one else knows it. The people whose addresses appear in the To and Cc fields are completely unaware that you sent a copy to the person or persons listed in the Bcc field. Any address you type in the Bcc field is hidden from the other recipients of the message.

So if you want to send the same message to a bunch of people and make it look as if each and every one of them is the only one who got this special message, just type their e-mail addresses (or names) in the Bcc field.

As you might have guessed, if you type addresses in the Bcc field, you don't have to type any address in the To field if you don't want to. The Bcc field doesn't ordinarily appear on the e-mail form, so you might have to choose Options➪Fields➪Show Bcc to make it come out of hiding so you can type e-mail addresses into it.

Spammers like to use the Bcc field to send messages to tons of people. Therefore, a lot of e-mail systems are pretty unfriendly to messages that use the Bcc field, flagging them as junk mail. If your Bcc recipient knows to expect your message, she can easily fish it out of the junk pile if it lands there, but otherwise your message might go unheard. As an alternative, you can use Word to send out a mass mailing — creating lots of individually addressed e-mails from a single sample. (See Book III, Chapter 4 for details.)

Formatting Text to Make Your Messages Stand Out

Time was, communicating electronically was novel and new; nowadays, receiving an e-mail is more business as usual than an exciting event. To grab your audience's attention, you might want to employ various formatting techniques to make your text stand out. Even if you're not worried that your message will go unheard, it's kinda fun to shake things up a little and enhance a message with cool formatting.

Understanding message formats: HTML, RTF, and plain text

Outlook supports three message formats. To see what format a message is using, look at the message window's title bar. Here's a list of the formats and what distinguishes each one:

✦ **HTML (default):** What makes formatting possible in an e-mail message is HTML, the same thing used to format Web pages. Outlook can easily read HTML messages, so all you need to worry about is whether your recipients also have this capability. Unless they're using really dusty e-mail programs, chances are that anyone you want to send a message to can handle HTML. If not, what they'll see is a simple text version of your message; keep that in mind when you send out formatted e-mail.

By default, Outlook messages use HTML format, which means you can fancy them up as much as you like. You can add text formatting such as bold and italics, insert professional-looking numbered and bulleted lists, and apply paragraph formatting such as alignment, indentation, shading, line spacing, and borders. (I run through the basics of applying text formatting in this chapter. I'll show you how to fancy up text with paragraph formatting, stationery, and styles in the next chapter.)

✦ **Rich Text Format (RTF):** RTF format is like HTML in that it supports a certain amount of formatting options. The trouble with RTF format is that few e-mail programs support it — Outlook, of course, Outlook Express, Outlook Web Access, and Microsoft Exchange Client (an old Exchange e-mail program that eventually became Outlook). So you can use RTF, I suppose, if you want to send a formatted message to other people in your company over an Exchange network. I don't know why you'd want to because if you're using Outlook, chances are everyone else in your company is too, so why not just use HTML?

If you send an RTF-formatted message over the Internet, Outlook converts it to HTML format to make sure it's readable by whatever e-mail program receives it. So the bottom line is that RTF isn't worth bothering with. Suppose, for some reason, you do send an RTF message without knowing whether a recipient can read it (some people just have to try everything). You might hear that your recipient says (s)he didn't see your message, but did get an odd `winmail.dat` attachment. You have your answer — your recipient's e-mail program can't decipher RTF format. So stop using the silly thing and resend the e-mail using HTML or plain text.

✦ **Plain-text format:** True to its name, plain-text format is well, pretty plain. You won't find any formatting here, no sir — just text characters. Plain text is the format to choose if you're sending an e-mail to someone who refuses to upgrade his or her e-mail program to something from the 21st century.

By default, outgoing messages are created using HTML format. If you prefer to use another format, you can change the format you use for most of your messages by following these steps:

1. **Choose Tools⇨Options to open the Options dialog box.**
2. **On the Mail Format tab, select the format from the Compose in This Message Format list.**

   Your format choices are HTML, Rich Text, and Plain Text.
3. **When you're finished, click OK to save your changes.**

To select the format for a single message, choose Actions➪New Mail Message Using and choose the format to use. If you've already started a message, you can still change its format. Just choose Options➪Format and choose the format to use.

Applying formatting to a message

You apply text formatting to message text in the same way you format text in Word, so I won't go into too much detail. If you're unfamiliar with Word, you can look over *Word 2007 For Dummies,* by Dan Gookin (Wiley Publishing) to brush up. Basically, to format text in an Outlook e-mail, click the Format Text tab in the message form (shown in Figure 1-15) and select a formatting tool.

You can apply formatting as you type; for example, you might select a new font or font size — or apply bold format by clicking the Bold button. Anything you type after that uses the new formatting you selected. You can change the formatting back when you don't want to use it any more. For example, click the Bold button again to turn off the Bold format.

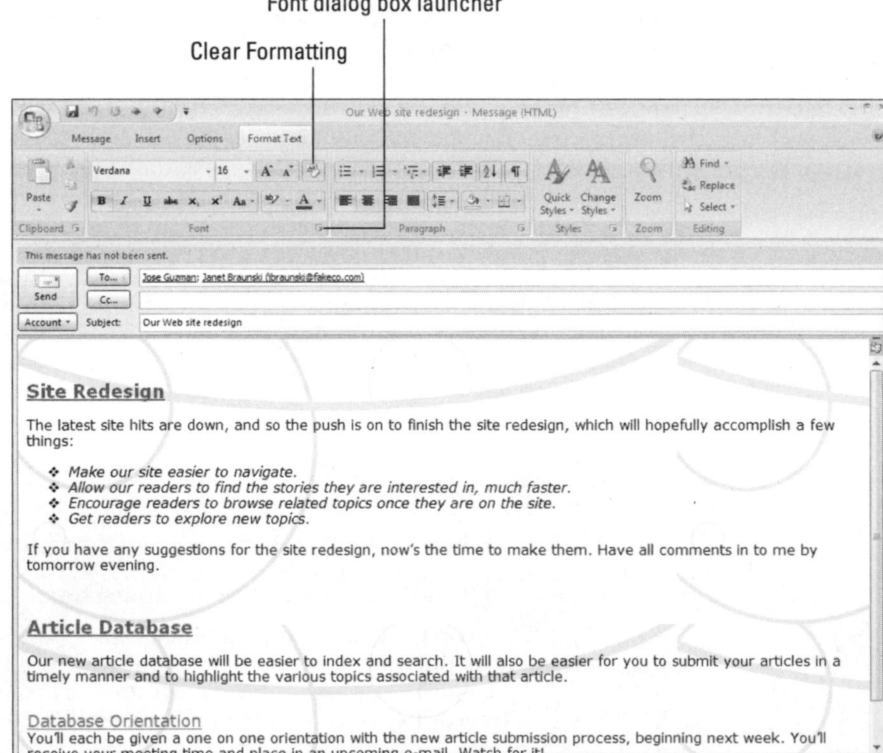

Figure 1-15: Use the tools on the Format tab to format message text.

Instead of formatting as I type, I prefer to apply most of my text formatting after the fact — by selecting text and then making selections to apply to it. Some of the advantages to using this technique might come as a surprise to those of you with previous Outlook experience. For one thing, when you format after typing, you can browse choices in any list (such as the fonts on the Fonts list) and actually preview how the selected text will look, before making your choice. For example, you might select some text and then browse the Font Color list to see how various colors look when applied to that text.

You learn the second reason for formatting after you type the first time you type some text, select it, and move the mouse pointer up just a little: A mini-toolbar appears right next to the selection (as shown in Figure 1-16), offering dessert and popular text options, such as font and font size.

One final thing you should keep in mind as you choose the method of text formatting you prefer. To use the Text Highlight Color button, you must type the text first and then select it because the highlight can be applied only to existing text.

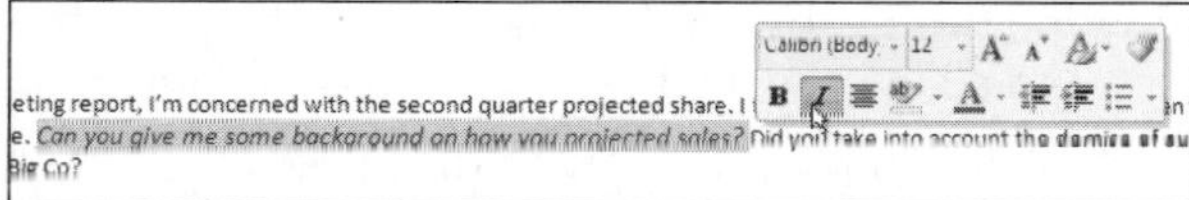

Figure 1-16: A minibar of formatting tools.

You'll probably recognize the buttons in the Font section of the Format Text tab, but if you don't, you can always hover the mouse pointer over a button to display a ScreenTip. I do want to point out the Clear Formatting button, however, because it's a bit new. Use it to remove formatting from selected text — it's a bit like using the Format Painter, only in reverse. If no text is selected, formatting is removed from the current paragraph. The Format Painter button is there, by the way; you'll find it hiding in the Clipboard group over on the left of the screen.

I have no idea why'd you want to do the following, because frankly, I prefer toolbars over dialog boxes. But if you feel more at home in a box, you can display the Font dialog box by clicking the Font Dialog Box Launcher button and then use it to apply a bunch of font changes all at once.

On the Message tab — the tab that shows up by default when you create a message — Outlook has put quite a few of the most frequently used tools for formatting text in its Basic Text group. If the tool you want to use is there, don't feel obligated to visit the Format Text tab. For example, if you want to change the font size, the Font Size list is right there on the Message tab. You'll also spy some paragraph formatting buttons, such as Left Alignment and Bullets. I go over these in the next chapter.

Attaching a File to a Message

Whenever you like, you can send along a file with a message. This file is called an e-mail *attachment.* Recipients can preview, open, and save attachments. This section explains how to send a file to a recipient. (You find out how to deal with attachments you've received in Chapter 4 of this minibook.)

Best practices for working with attachments

Here are some things you should keep in mind when sending attachments:

✦ **Compress large files.** If the file you want to send is large, you might want to compress it first (zip it) to make it as small as possible. If the recipient connects to the Internet by dialup and not by broadband, restrict yourself to sending only very small files; large files take forever to download over a dialup connection.

Need some help understanding file compression and how to go about it? Come on over to our house and read all about it:

`www.dummies.com/WileyCDA/DummiesArticle/id-3086.html`

Be sure to type this in your Web browser exactly as it appears here — initial caps and all, or you might get a message telling you the article can't be found!

✦ **Contact the recipient before sending files that might potentially exceed maximum loads.** Actually, you might not be able to send a large file to some people because a lot of companies stop the big guys at the entrance. When trying to figure out who to stop and who to let in, e-mail servers take the total of the message size plus all attachments. To add insult to injury, your message might not even get that far. It might be stopped by your own e-mail server, which sets its own message limitations. You can't guess what a company might decide is too large, so your best bet is either to ask first or to send and wait for an error-message reply. You can, however, find out what your ISP considers the maximum load and try not to go over it.

✦ **Avoid sending file types that might be flagged as potential viruses.** Some attachments are stopped at the door because they aren't welcome. These include file types that might contain nasty visitors such as viruses, macros, and scripts: Look for extensions such as `.exe`, `.vbs` (Visual Basic script), `.prg` (program file), `.ws` (Windows script), and sometimes even `.doc` and `.zip` files. You might not know what file types won't get to their destination because they're stopped by the recipient's e-mail server.

Outlook tries to protect you by warning you whenever you try to attach a file that might be stopped at the door: `.exe`, `.bat`, `.vbs` (Visual Basic source file), and `.js` (Java script). It's up to you, however, to decide whether to send the file anyway, despite the warning.

Attaching files

To send a file along with a message, follow these steps:

1. **Choose Message➪Include➪Attach File.**

   The Insert File dialog box pops up, as shown in Figure 1-17.

   You can also use the Attach File button on the Insert tab to display the Insert File dialog box. Unless you're inserting other things as well, such as pictures, tables, or hyperlinks, however, it's not really worth the trip to the Insert tab.

2. **Select the file(s) you want to tag along with the message.**

   You can select multiple files by pressing Ctrl and clicking each one, or pressing Shift and clicking the first and last files in a group.

   You can probably zip your large file prior to attaching it, right there within the Insert File dialog box because most zip utilities support this process. To see if it works for you, simply select the file(s) you want to attach and then right-click. On the shortcut menu, select the name of your zip utility. You see a submenu of choices, one of which probably allows you to zip and mail the file(s) immediately. Now that's convenient! Outlook might try to prevent the utility from working, however. (It's a control thing.) If so, choose Tools➪Trust Center➪Add-Ins➪Manage➪COM Add-Ins➪Go. From the COM Add-Ins dialog box, select your zip utility to enable its check box.

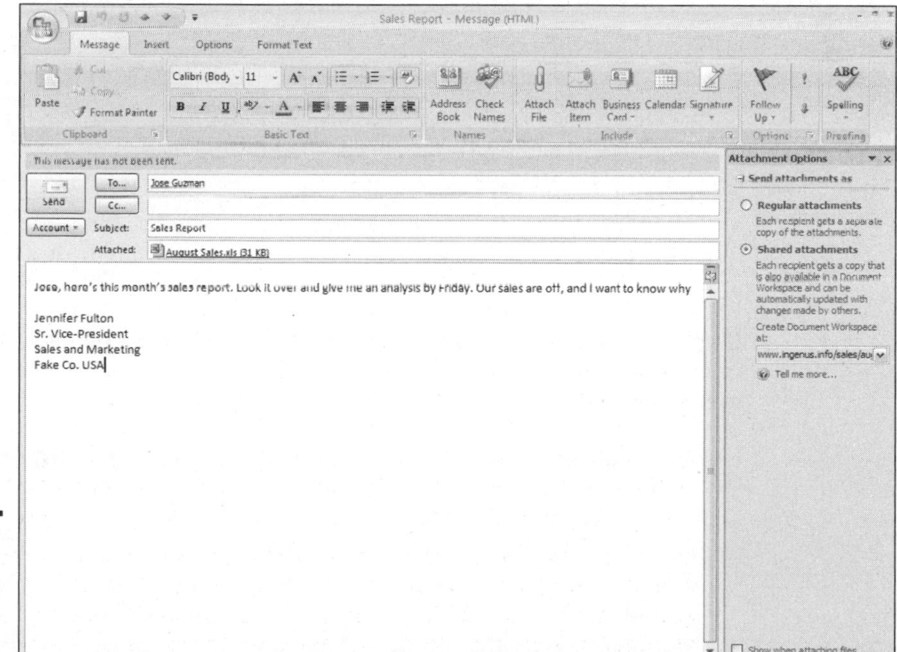

Figure 1-17: Pick out the file to attach.

3. Click Insert.

How an attached file appears within the message form depends on the message format you used:

- For HTML and plain-text messages, the name of the selected file appears in the Attach box below the Subject line, as shown in Figure 1-18.
- For RTF messages, you see a clickable icon within the body of the message. Don't let the icon fool you; the file is still attached separately from the message, and it is not embedded (inserted) into the message itself.

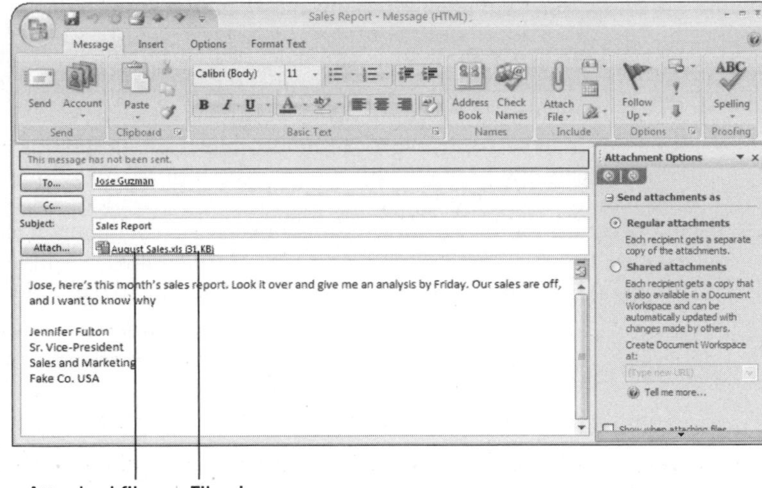

Figure 1-18: Attachments and their file sizes are listed.

Notice also that the filenames are followed by the file's approximate size. This information can prevent you from accidentally trying to send too large a file or files.

If you have access to a SharePoint site (a Web site that enables document collaboration and information sharing through Office), you can send attachments in one of two ways:

✦ **Choose Message⇨Include⇨Attach File⇨Attachment Options.** The Attachment Options pane appears on the right (refer to Figure 1-18). You can attach the file in the normal way by choosing Regular Attachments; it's sent with the message, and the user can do whatever (s)he wants with it.

✦ **Choose Shared Attachments.** This allows you to send the file in a way that informs you of changes made by the recipient(s). Here a *workspace* (shared folder) is created on your SharePoint Web site. Copies of the file are sent with the e-mail to each recipient; changes that recipients make to their individual copies are updated in the central copy in the shared folder.

You can create a document *workspace* (a shared folder) only on a SharePoint site, when sending attachments to someone else with access to that same SharePoint site.

Saving a Message So You Can Send It Later

Sometimes, in the middle of composing a missive, you discover that you don't have all the information you need to finish it. There's no need to lose all your hard work; you can easily save what you've written so far and then change or add to the message later on.

If you're looking for how to resend a message you've already sent (and not save one you haven't), just skip over to Chapter 2 of this minibook for help.

Saving a draft

To save what you've written so far, along with any files you might have attached and anything you might have inserted, follow these steps:

1. **Click the Save button on the Quick Access toolbar.**
2. **After the message is saved, you can close it by clicking its Close button.**

The saved message is placed in your Drafts folder. Here's how to open the message at a later time:

1. **Switch to Mail, if you aren't already there.**
2. **Select the Drafts folder on the Navigation pane.**
3. **Double-click the message to open it.**
4. **Make whatever changes you want, and click Send to send it on its way.**

If you repeat certain messages a lot (*Hey, sorry, but uh, you're fired. Be sure to leave the stapler on your way out.*), you can save the text in a reusable form. See Chapter 4 of this minibook for help.

Changing the Drafts folder

Actually, Outlook saves your messages every three minutes as you work on them, just in case the power goes out right when you're about to finish the "Great American Novelette." You can change the folder that's used to save unsent messages (normally it's the Drafts folder), and how often Outlook saves messages as you work. Just follow these steps:

1. **Choose Tools⇨Options to open the Options dialog box.**
2. **On the Preferences tab, click E-Mail Options.**
3. **In the E-Mail Options dialog box, click Advanced E-Mail Options.**
4. **To change which folder is used for drafts, select one from the AutoSave Items In list.**
5. **To change how often drafts are saved, type a value in the AutoSave Items Every *XX* Minutes box.**

   You can type a value from 1 to 99 minutes, although why you'd want to work over 90 minutes on an e-mail and *not* save it is beyond me.
6. **Click OK a bunch of times to close all the dialog boxes.**

Chapter 2: Reading and Replying to E-Mail

In This Chapter

- **Switching to a different view**
- **Downloading embedded images in an e-mail**
- **Opening and saving files that come with e-mail**
- **Replying to an e-mail you receive**
- **Forwarding e-mails**
- **Sending an e-mail again**

I used to think that getting messages was fun; it was nice to know that somebody cared enough to send me a special note. Alas, the fun didn't last for long, as I quickly became overwhelmed with the stack of messages that I needed to read and reply to. And those people who insisted on sending images and other files along with their notes only made the mess bigger and my life more difficult. In this chapter, you find out how to wade through it all.

Finding the Messages You Want to Read: Changing the View

When you change from Mail to Contacts to Calendar to whatever, the information in that module is displayed in a particular way. That way is called a *view.* There's no particular reason why you have to stay with Outlook's way of looking at things. You can, instead, change to a different view by choosing View⇨Current View and then selecting the view you want.

Some views, like the one shown in Figure 2-1, are table (list) views in which data is displayed in various columns. Items in a table view are typically arranged in groups like the tasks shown here, which are arranged by date on which they will never get done. To hide the items in a particular group, click the group's minus sign (–). To redisplay the items in a hidden group, click the group's plus sign (+).

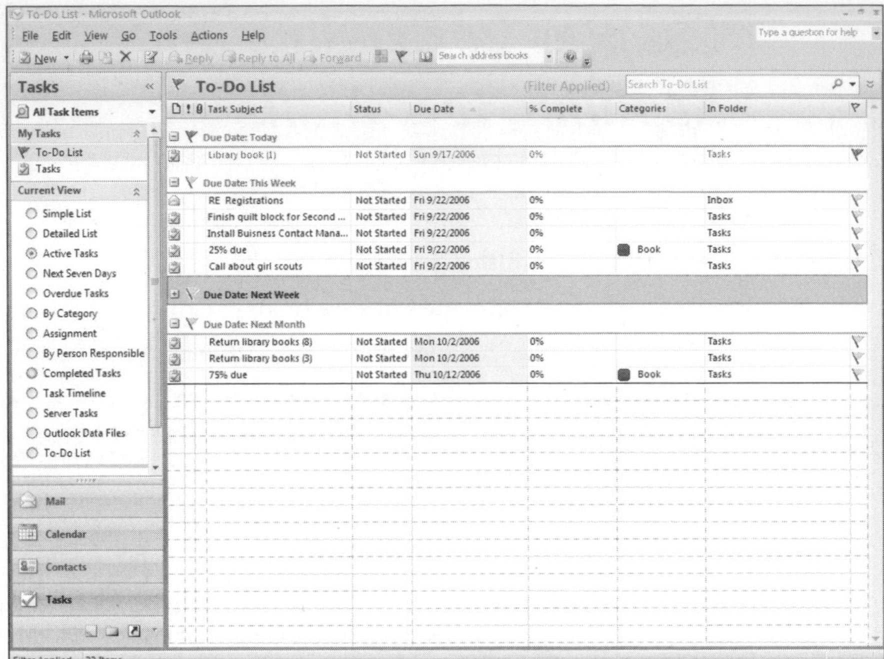

Figure 2-1: Trying out a table view.

You can do some pretty fun things with the columns in a table view, including these (see Book VIII, Chapter 2):

✦ Sort the items by one of the columns.

✦ Make a column very skinny so you can get more columns onscreen without scrolling.

✦ Add, remove, and rearrange columns to show exactly what you want.

If you're in Contacts, Tasks, Notes, or Journal, the viewing options appear on the Navigation pane where you can click them to change views quickly.

You can create custom views that display information the way you want and sort items in a folder however you like. You discover how to perform these tricks and more in Book VIII, Chapter 2.

Dealing with E-Mails That Use Pictures

It seems like everybody is slipping little pictures into their e-mail messages these days. I guess plain ol' words just don't make it anymore — at least not in newsletters, sales notices, and the like. As nice as e-mails look when they're dressed up with some photos or a few nice graphics, messages that contain downloaded images might act as a scout for spammers. And this is why Outlook stops these strangers at the door and lets you decide who to invite in.

E-mails with attached images are not a danger to you, but if a message contains a link to an image that must be downloaded to your Inbox in order for you to see it, it could be a danger. Just like a burglar who poses as a salesman, knocking at every door until he finds someone not at home, such messages might actually be searching for valid e-mail addresses. When you download images from the Internet into e-mail, you might be sending a signal that you're at home and your e-mail address is a working one — and thus open the door to tons of spam (unwanted junk e-mail). Even scarier, some e-mails contain links to files that look like they should be an image (for example, they use the `.gif` extension), but when Windows tries to display them, it discovers that they are not in proper `.gif` format. The old Windows response was to try to "run" the file — and thus a sneaky virus or other destructive program gets into your system. Beginning with Windows XP Service Pack 2 (you've installed it, haven't you?) and Windows Vista, Windows no longer tries to run the bogus "gif" file, and even begins a process to get the file out of memory so it can't be triggered by a script embedded in the e-mail. So listen when I say that you should download images from only people you know or sources you trust. An innocent-looking link to an image file may turn out to be anything but innocent.

When an e-mail arrives that contains linked images, you see a message in the InfoBar telling you so. Also, the places where the images should appear are marked by a small, white square with a red X, as shown in Figure 2-2.

Figure 2-2: The Xs represent linked images.

If the image represents a link to a particular page on the Web, you don't have to download the image; just click the link to visit the page. If you do want to download the linked images in an e-mail message, click the InfoBar and then choose Download Pictures, as shown in Figure 2-2. The images are copied from the Internet and appear in the message where the empty boxes were. If you open the message in another window, you can click the Save button on the Quick Access toolbar to save the images in the message. Otherwise, you need to download them again the next time you view the message. (If you're viewing the message in the Reading pane, you don't need to do a thing; the downloaded images are automatically saved in the message.)

If you regularly get e-mail that includes linked images from a source you trust, you can add that person or source to your list of safe senders. That way, the images won't be blocked, and you won't have to waste time downloading them. On the InfoBar menu, just click either Add Sender to Safe Senders List or Add the Domain *xxxx* to Safe Senders List (refer to Figure 2-2). See Book IX, Chapter 3 for more help.

Although I advise against it, you can stop Outlook from preventing linked images from automatically downloading. Choose Tools⇨Trust Center. Then in the Trust Center window, click Automatic Download and disable the Don't Download Pictures Automatically in HTML E-Mail Messages or RSS Items check box.

Opening E-Mail Attachments

An *attachment* is a file that's sent along with an e-mail message. If someone sends you an attachment, Outlook definitely lets you know: You see both a paper clip icon in the message header and the name of the attachment listed just above the message text.

Opening a message from someone you don't know might unleash a pack of brats (macros, scripts, and ActiveX controls) that might cause damage to the files on your computer. Previewing a file allows you to view a file's contents without danger. (See Book I, Chapter 1 for details.) However, Outlook can't preview all file types, and you can't make changes to a file you're only previewing. So, if you decide you must open a file from someone you aren't sure you can trust, my advice is to save it to your computer first and then run an antivirus program before opening it. See the next section for help in saving an attachment to your hard drive.

To protect you, Outlook blocks some file types at your front door — file types that might contain macros, viruses, scripts, or commands with mayhem on their minds. Common file types that Outlook blocks include `.exe`, `.vbs`, `.prg`, `.ws`, `.asp`, `.cmd`, `.com`, and `.js`, among others. If an attachment is blocked, a message telling you so appears on the InfoBar.

If you don't want Outlook to block a particular file with one of these extensions, you can have the sender resend the file, possibly renaming the file's extension to something that Outlook won't block. For example, if somebody tries to send you a JavaScript file, `2muchfun.js`, you could have them rename it *`2muchfun.ok`*. After you get the file attachment, you must rename it again (`2muchfun.js`), or you won't be able to use the file properly.

If a person you trust sends you a file, do either of these things to open the file for viewing:

✦ Double-click the attachment's name in the Reading pane or open message window.

✦ Right-click a message appearing in the message list and choose View Attachments⇨*attachment to open.*

To quickly locate all the e-mails with attachments, use a Search folder. See Book IX, Chapter 4 for details.

Saving E-Mail Attachments

Because you have the capability to easily preview or open attached files, you might wonder: Why would I want to save an attachment to my already crowded hard drive? Well, the answer isn't so you can while away half of a work day searching for the file later on. (I mean, when would you be able to shop on the Internet and play online poker?) No, you do so in order to check the attachments for viruses, open them, and then make changes to the files if you want.

If an e-mail contains multiple attachments, you can either save all the attachments in a single step (provided you want to save all of them to the same folder) or save just one attachment at a time.

To save all the files at once, follow these steps:

1. **Open the message with the attachment(s) you want to save and then choose Message⇨Actions⇨Other Actions⇨Save Attachments.**

   Or if you're looking at a message in the message list and spy that paper clip icon, choose File⇨Save Attachments⇨All Attachments. If you want to save a single attachment only, choose File⇨Save Attachments, and then choose that one attachment from the list. Skip Step 2 and jump over to Step 3 to save the attachment.

   The Save All Attachments dialog box opens.

2. **Select the file(s) to save and then click OK.**

   In the Save All Attachments dialog box, all the files are selected. If you want to save only a few, press Ctrl and click the ones you want.

Files you select to save are saved to the same folder. To save attachments to different folders from an open message, repeat all these steps for each attachment.

After you click OK, the Save Attachment dialog box opens.

3. **Choose a folder where you want to save the file(s) and click Save.**

   If you selected a smaller group of files in Step 2, you return to the Save All Attachments dialog box where you can select the remaining file(s) and save them as well. If you're done, click Close instead of choosing more files.

You can save a single attachment from a message by right-clicking the file's name (which appears above the message text) and choosing Save As.

After you've saved an attachment to the hard drive, it's probably best to scan it with your antivirus program even if you know the person who sent you the file. Even your best friend can accidentally pass on a file that contains a virus, so it's best to be more safe than sorry.

Replying versus Replying to All

This topic is a big one for me. I have to confess that I just hate it when somebody clicks Reply to All and sends an e-mail to the original 200 recipients of a message, when all he wanted to do was pass on a comment to the sender.

True story: I'm on a parents list for my daughter's school, and last year the president of the parents group sent an e-mail to everybody letting them know that the parent social was coming up. One parent sent a reply to everyone, asking if anyone knew of a good baby sitter. Next, various parents used Reply to All to answer that message, and before I knew it, my Inbox was filled with chatty e-mails on the trials and tribulations of finding a good baby sitter, tips on baby care, recipes, and other trivia.

So let me say this loud and clear: If you want your comments to go to everyone — count 'em, everyone — who got the original e-mail, click *Reply to All.* If you want to send a comment to just the original sender of the e-mail (and to no one else), click *Reply.* Basically, before clicking Reply to All, stop, look both ways, and then cross the street.

Okay, class, lecture's over. Now I move on to the details of replying:

- **If you're viewing the message in the Reading pane,** click the Reply or Reply to All button you find on the Standard toolbar.
- **If you're viewing the message in a message window,** choose Message⇨Respond⇨Reply *or* Reply to All.

When you click Reply or Reply to All, the text of the original message is copied to the new message, as shown in Figure 2-3. The message is also automatically addressed — either to the original sender or to everybody in the known universe (the sender and the original recipients). Outlook keeps the original subject, but adds an *RE:* to the beginning so the recipient(s) can easily see that your message is a reply. Type your response above the copied text and click Send.

Messages that you've already replied to appear in the messages list with a special icon — an envelope with a left-pointing arrow. Also, when you view such a message, the InfoBar displays a reminder that you've already replied to this message — along with the date and time when you replied.

In the following sections, I show you how to control whether text from the original message is copied to the reply, as well as how to change the font, font size, and color of your reply text. In addition, you discover how to prefix the comments you type within the reply with your name. Doing so allows you to easily type your annotated comments within the original message, just as if you were having a conversation with the sender.

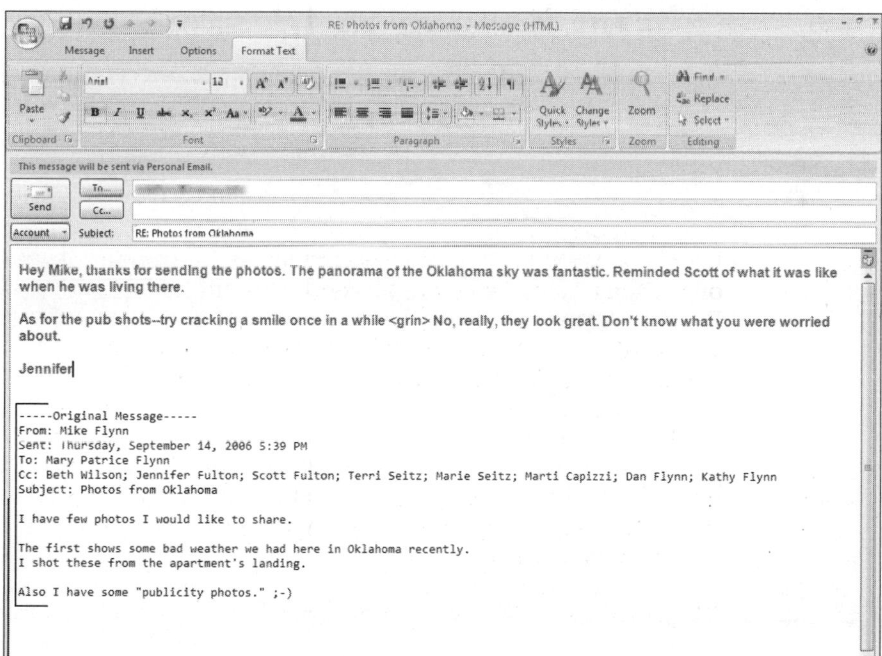

Figure 2-3: The favor of a reply is requested.

If you use Outlook on an Exchange network (it'll say `Connected to Microsoft Exchange` on the status bar), a colleague can reply to messages when you're on vacation. See Book X, Chapter 1 for details.

Controlling how text is quoted in a reply

Copying the text of the original message in a reply helps everybody involved remember what they were talking about. (After all, it's probably been at least a minute ago, and you might have gotten another 50 messages in the meantime.) For this reason, Outlook normally copies the original text when it creates your reply, but you don't have to do that.

Changing the formatting of the copied text

If you agree with me that copying the text into a reply is probably a good idea, you can still change how that copied text is formatted so that it suits your taste:

1. **Choose Tools⇨Options.**

   The Options dialog box opens.

2. **On the Preferences tab, click the E-Mail Options button.**

   The E-Mail Options dialog box opens, as shown in Figure 2-4.

Figure 2-4: How should you reply?

3. **From the When Replying to a Message drop-down list, choose an option for quoting the original message text. Here are your choices:**
   - *Include Original Message Text:* This is the default, which copies the text to the bottom of the reply.
   - *Do Not Include Original Message:* This creates the reply without copying any of the original text.
   - *Attach Original Message:* Sends the original message, along with your reply, in the form of an attachment. This keeps the text out of the way but available should the recipient need to refer to it.
   - *Include and Indent Original Message Text:* Copies the original text but indents it so that it's easier to identify the original text.
   - *Prefix Each Line of the Original Message:* Copies the original text and indents it, putting a little character in front of the text. Your reply is automatically made blue to further distinguish it from the original text. If you choose this option, in the Prefix Each Line with text box, type the character you want to precede each line of the original text.
4. **Click OK to save your changes.**

Changing the color of your reply text

If you have Outlook copy the original text in a reply, you might want to distinguish it from your text by changing its color. You can do this manually, by applying an alternative color as you type your reply, but why not let Outlook do it for you? Just follow these steps:

1. **Choose Tools⇨Options.**
2. **On the Mail Format tab of the Options dialog box, click Stationery and Fonts.**

   The Signatures and Stationery dialog box opens, as shown in Figure 2-5.
3. **On the Personal Stationery tab, select the Pick a New Color When Replying or Forwarding check box and then click OK.**

   Of course, this works only if the reply is in HTML or RTF format and not in plain text. Notice also that you can change the font and font size of the text you use in a reply, regardless of whether you decide to have Outlook automatically change its color. (See Book II, Chapter 1 for more on message formats.)

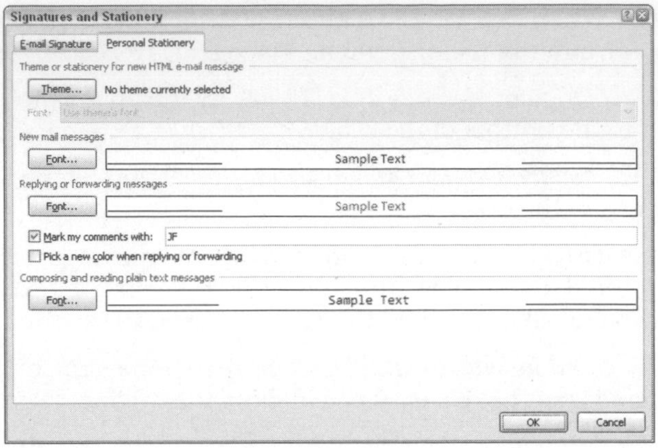

Figure 2-5: Choose a font and other text styles to use when replying.

Adding your name to a reply

Sometimes it's easier to type your reply within the original text of a message, as if you were directly responding to a question or concern. If you've ever done that, however, it can be a bit of a pain because when you type your text next to the original stuff, it's kinda hard to distinguish it from what the sender said. So, if you're like me, you probably go to the trouble of formatting your reply text a bit differently so it's easier to distinguish both sides of the conversation.

Outlook can help you accomplish this with a whole lot less sweat equity. Here's all you have to do:

1. **Choose Tools⇨Options.**

   The Options dialog box opens.

2. **On the Preferences tab, click the E-Mail Options button.**

   The E-Mail Options dialog box opens. (Refer to Figure 2-4.)

3. **Select the Mark My Comments With check box, change the name shown in the text box to your initials if you like, and then click OK.**

   When you create a reply and type any text within the original message text, your text is preceded by whatever appears in the box just below the check box, which is usually your name. You can, however, change it to something else if you want, such as your initials. Figure 2-6 shows an example of a reply with inline comments.

   By the way, if you type your reply above (rather than below) the copied text, it won't be preceded by your name.

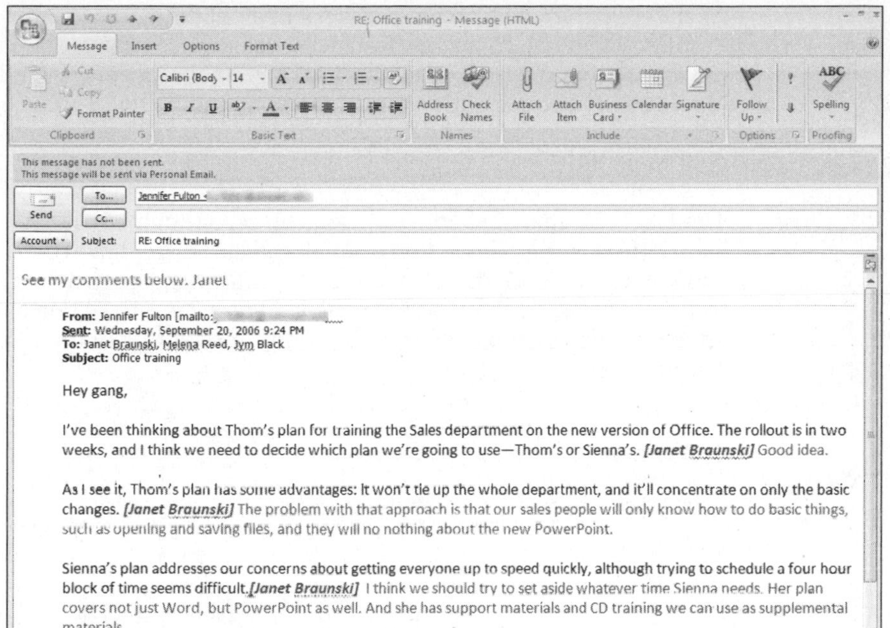

Figure 2-6: Inline comments are included in this reply.

You can easily change how your reply text is formatted, including changing its color automatically. Open the Signatures and Stationery dialog box (refer to Figure 2-5) by following Steps 1 and 2 in the previous section ("Changing the color of your reply text"). Then click the Font button in the Replying or Forwarding Messages section and make a selection.

Viewing a conversation

Outlook keeps track of messages you've replied to, and even reminds you when you've already replied to a message by displaying a reminder on the message's InfoBar. The original message and your reply form kind of back and forth conversation, and should your reply cause a reply, well, the chain just goes on and on, as shown in Figure 2-7. To arrange your messages by conversation, do either of the following:

- ✦ Choose View⇨Arrange By⇨Conversation.
- ✦ Click the Arrange By button at the top of the message list, and choose Conversation from its drop-down menu.

All messages are displayed; messages in a conversation, however, are grouped together. To display the messages in the conversation, click the down arrow to the left of the conversation header, as shown in Figure 2-7. Messages in a conversation group are arranged by date, with the latest reply appearing at the top of the list. Just click a message header to display its contents in the Reading pane.

The last reply in a long conversation can be difficult to read, because it typically contains the copied text from all the earlier replies. To help you read such an e-mail, click the "speed reading" buttons, like the Next and Last buttons shown within the Reading pane in Figure 2-7. These buttons magically appear when you move your mouse pointer over one of the headings in a section of copied text.

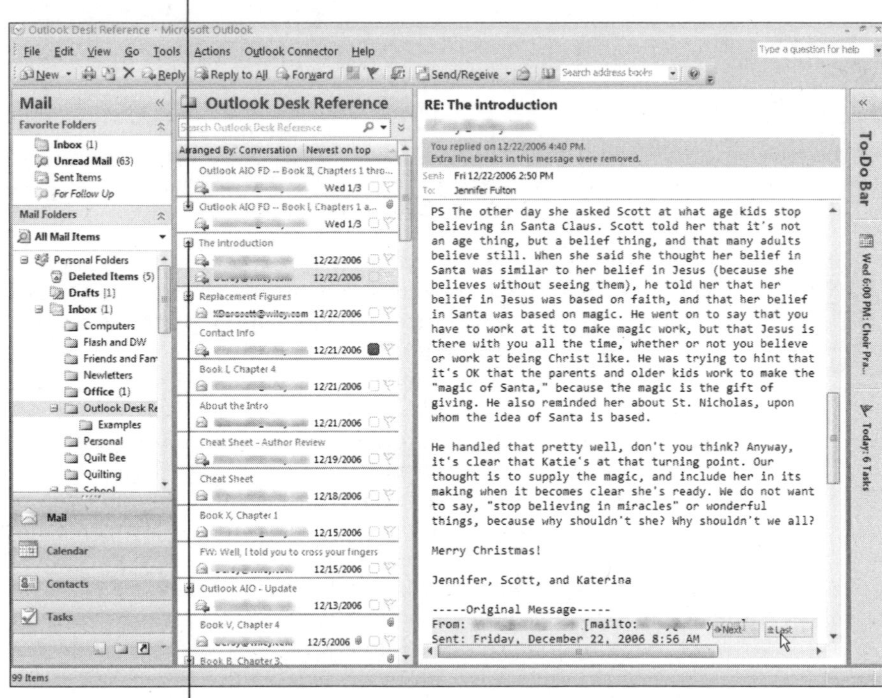

Figure 2-7: Let's have a conversation.

Forwarding an E-Mail

If you get a message that you think other people should see, you can forward the message to them. Forwarding saves you the trouble of running to a copy machine; instead, when you forward a message, Outlook copies the original message text into a new message and doesn't even charge you a quarter. Outlook keeps the original subject line as well, adding a quick *FW:* to the beginning of it to let the recipient know that you're forwarding a message you got from someone else.

To forward a message you're viewing in the Reading pane, click the Forward button on the Standard toolbar. If you're viewing the message in a message window, choose Message⇨Respond⇨Forward. After the message is copied for you, just address it normally and click Send. You can, prior to sending the message, add a quick note above the copied text (perhaps to explain what the forwarded message is about or why you're sending it on).

You can control how text appears in a forwarded message; just follow the same procedure for changing reply text. See the earlier section, "Controlling how text is quoted in a reply."

Resending an E-Mail Message

Yes, I'll admit it. Not only do I send messages once, but I sometimes send them twice. The main reason I send messages twice isn't because I like to overwhelm people with lots of notes from *moi,* but because I sometimes forget to add the attachment.

So when I click Send and discover that oops, the attachment's missing again, I just jump over to the Sent folder, open the message, and choose Message⇨Actions⇨Other Actions⇨Resend This Message. Contrary to what you might think, the message isn't just resent. Instead, Outlook copies the message, including its text, subject, recipients, and yes, attachments, if any.

This basically means that you get a Get Out of Jail Free card. You can add recipients (in case you forgot someone), change your text however you want, add attachments, and do basically anything you could have done originally, before your trigger finger clicked Send. When you're satisfied that this time you haven't forgotten anything or anyone, click Send to resend the message in its new form.

If you actually need to retrieve a sent message and replace it, you might be able to, provided you work on an Exchange network. Anyway, it's worth a try! See Book III, Chapter 1.

Chapter 3: Making Your E-Mail Look Professional and Cool

In This Chapter

- **Removing misspelled words from your messages and the egg from your face**
- **Dressing up e-mail with stationery**
- **Putting an image, shape, or SmartArt in a message**
- **Inserting a text box, table, chart, or hyperlink**
- **Creating headings in a message**
- **Adding bulleted or numbered lists, text boxes, hyperlinks, horizontal lines, and just about anything else you can think of**

Frankly, there's nothing more embarrassing than revealing your ignorance. Perhaps you've hemmed and hawed your way through a conversation whose subject was only roughly familiar to you. You nodded at the right times and added vague comments that simply repeated what was already said. If so, then I say: Good for you, you faker! One thing you can't fake, however, is Spelling Champion. If you send messages with misspelled words, people soon catch on that the spelling trophy on your desk is your brother's. You have no reason to get caught, however, because in Outlook you can automatically spell check messages before you send them.

If your goal is to look smart, cool, and professional, in this chapter I show you several ways to easily convince everyone that you are. For example, you might use decorative stationery or a Quick Style to dress up a message. I show you how to add just about any kind of doodad you can think of: images, shapes, SmartArt (pre-drawn diagrams), horizontal lines, the current date and time, charts, tables, numbered and bulleted lists, hyperlinks, and bookmarks.

You can add images, charts, tables, shapes, hyperlinks, SmartArt, and just about anything that's fun, to messages that are in HTML format only. By default, messages are already in HTML format, but if you've set Outlook to send plain text or RTF messages, you can change a single message to HTML by choosing Options➪Format➪HTML.

Checking Your Ignorance at the Door with Spelling and Grammar Checking

Outlook, like Word, automatically checks the spelling of words as you type. You can, if you want, have it step out of the way and stop hitting you over the head with its dictionary. Follow these steps to stop Outlook from checking spelling as you type an e-mail message:

1. **Choose Tools⇨Options.**

   The Options dialog box appears.
2. **Click the Spelling tab.**
3. **Click the Spelling and AutoCorrection button.**

   The Editor Options dialog box appears.
4. **Click the Proofing tab.**
5. **In the When Correcting Spelling in Outlook area, deselect the Check Spelling when You Type check box and click OK to save your changes and close the Editor Options dialog box.**
6. **Click OK to close the Options dialog box.**

   Now, you can check the spelling of a message right before you send it by pressing F7.

Because it's so easy to just type and click Send, I like the check-as-you-go option, followed by a healthy dose of the automatically-check-this-again-before-sending option. Here's how you set that up:

1. **Choose Tools⇨Options.**

   The Options dialog box opens.
2. **Click the Spelling tab.**
3. **Select the Always Check Spelling before Sending check box and click OK to save your changes and close the Options dialog box.**

You can also have Outlook check your grammar as you type, but this option can be a bit annoying, in my opinion. (However, if you want Outlook to check grammar with spelling as your composing a message, see the "Checking grammar" section for help.) English is a fairly flexible language, and I tend to be a bit colloquial in my usage, so the grammar checker and I sometimes find ourselves at odds. If you decide not to check grammar as you type, you can check grammar, along with spelling, right before sending a message. Again, see the "Checking grammar" section for help in setting this option.

The Outlook grammar and spelling checker works within all Outlook items except notes. It's obvious that Outlook might check a message, but how and why might it check a contact, appointment, or task? Well, what's checked isn't the data you entered for each item, but the *notes* — anything you type in the big, notes area of an item. If you make a typo while typing in a notes section, just follow the steps in the next section to correct it.

Checking spelling

The automatic spelling check occurs as you type. (If you've turned that option off, you can start the spelling checker with a press of the F7 key.) When you misspell a word, Outlook quickly underlines it with a red, wavy underline. You can right-click the word and instantly correct it by choosing a suggestion from the list that appears, as shown in Figure 3-1.

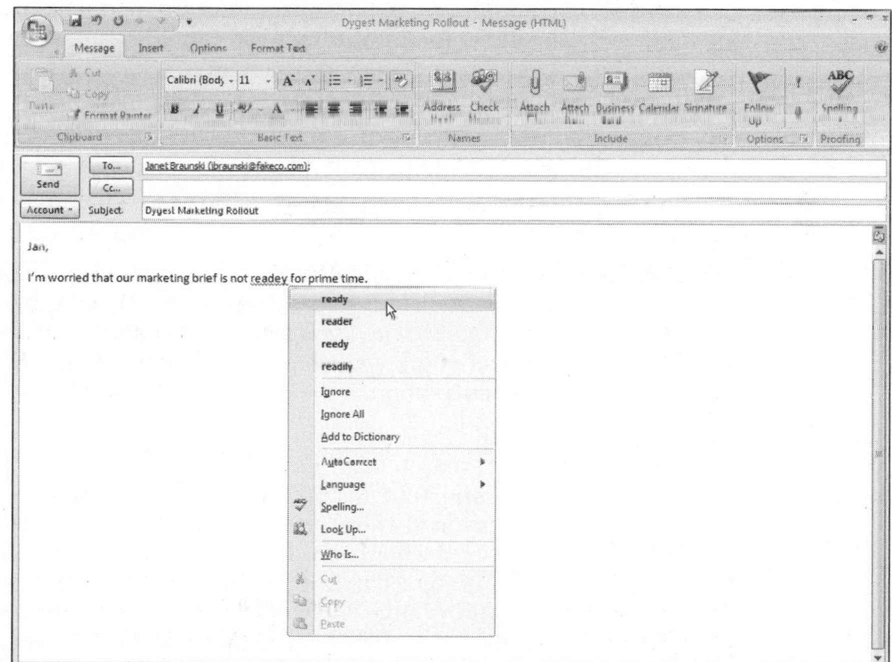

Figure 3-1: Correct spelling as you type.

Here are the other options Outlook gives you to deal with potential misspellings when you right-click a word with a red, wavy underline:

- **Ignore and Ignore All:** If the word isn't misspelled at all (so there, smartypants!) you can click Ignore to ignore this instance only; click Ignore All to ignore this word throughout the text.
- **Add to Dictionary:** Use this option when the selected word is simply one that Outlook doesn't know (like *your name*). If you click this option, the word is added to the dictionary, and you're never bothered with it again.
- **AutoCorrect:** Choose a correction from this submenu to add the misspelling and its correction to the AutoCorrect list. Or choose AutoCorrect Options to open the AutoCorrect in E-Mail dialog box. Type the misspelling in the Replace box and the correction in the With box and then click Add. Click OK to close the dialog box.

AutoCorrect is another way in which you can correct what you type. It works like this: You type a misspelled word, and if that word is in the AutoCorrect list, Outlook looks up the correction — and ZIP, POW, BANG! — Outlook replaces the misspelled word automatically. Outlook has a lot of common misspellings and their corrections (such as *thier* and *their)* already in its AutoCorrect list. But you can use the AutoCorrect Option on the shortcut menu to add to this list so that it includes the types of spelling errors you often make.

- **Language:** Allows you to select the language that the word is in. If you've set up Office to operate in more than one language, than the spelling checker will use the language you select from this menu to check the spelling of the selected word.
- **Spelling:** This is the option to choose if you agree that the word is misspelled, but Outlook fails to provide a correction. In the Spelling dialog box that appears when you select this option, you see a longer list of suggestions (where you might find the correction). Failing that, you can type the correction in the large text box provided.

- **Look Up:** Opens the Research pane and allows you to look up a term within Outlook's research materials and the Internet. When you choose Look Up from the shortcut menu, Outlook automatically searches its research materials for the term and displays the result in the Research pane. If you don't find what you want, you can open the Can't Find It? section on the pane (by clicking its plus sign) and choose an option there such as an Alternative Spelling or All Research Sites. You can also look up the word in the thesaurus (by opening the Thesaurus section) or translate the chosen word into a different language (by choosing the one you want in the Translation section of the pane). See Figure 3-2.
- **Who Is:** Opens the Check Names dialog box and looks up a misspelled Contact name. See Chapter 1 in this minibook.

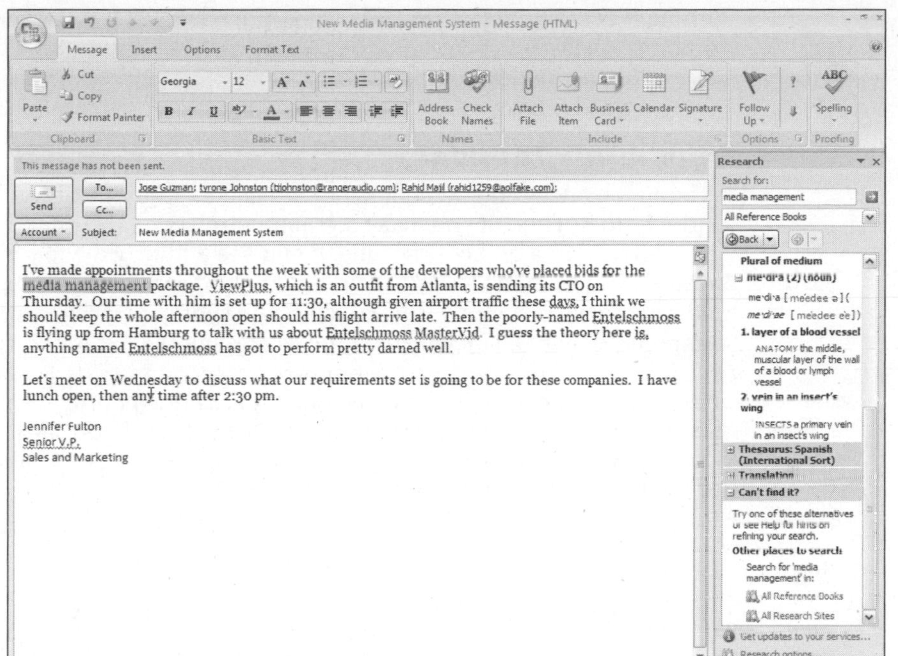

Figure 3-2: Do a little research.

The spell checker doesn't normally catch mistakes that aren't misspellings, although there are times when you might want it to. For example, if you type **This is you're responsibility,** the spelling checker won't flag the mistake. You can, however, turn on an option that allows the spelling checker to check for errors in context. This causes it to flag the use of a wrong, but similar-sounding, word. Follow these steps to have Outlook check the context when looking for spelling errors:

1. **Choose Tools⇨Options.**

   The Options dialog box appears.

2. **Click the Spelling tab.**
3. **Click the Spelling and AutoCorrection button.**

   The Editor Options dialog box appears.

4. **Click the Proofing tab.**
5. **In the When Correcting Spelling in Outlook area, select the Use Contextual Spelling check box and click OK to save your changes and close the Editor Options dialog box.**
6. **Click OK to close the Options dialog box.**

Although contextual checking is cool — gosh knows, it would catch a lot of common mistakes I make — it does slow down the computer, especially if you're running under 1GB of RAM.

Checking grammar

Although, by default, grammar is not checked automatically, you can have Outlook do it. Then, if you make a grammar mistake, the offending passage is underlined with a green, wavy line. If you see a blue, wavy underline, it's because you've made a mistake in punctuation or capitalization. If you understand what's wrong (for example, the sentence is a fragment and not a complete thought), you can just type a correction.

Otherwise, you can right-click the wavy underlined text to see a shortcut menu that tells you why the grammar police stopped you, as shown in Figure 3-3. Or you can choose one of the following options from the shortcut menu for further assistance.

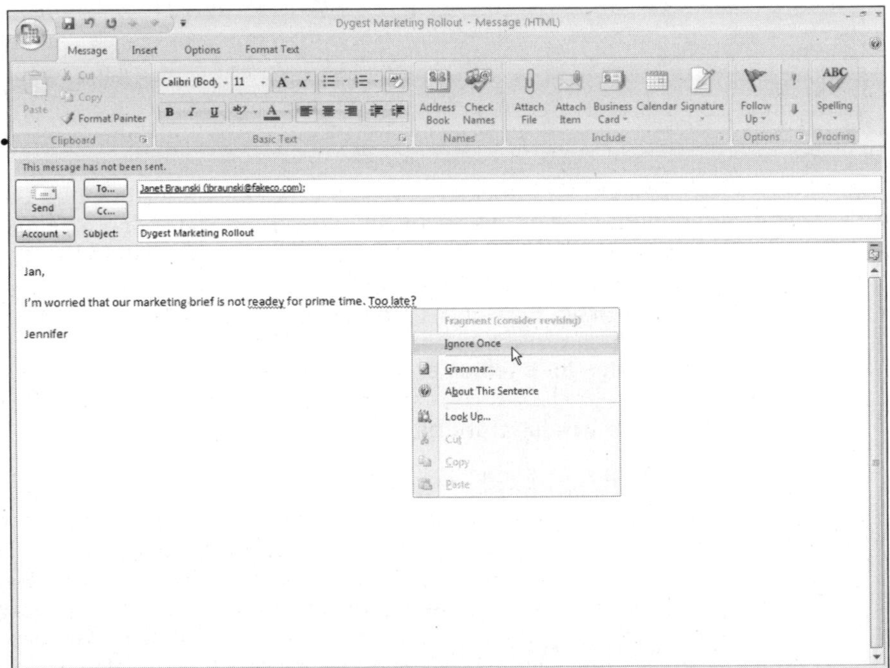

Figure 3-3: Don't know nuttin' about grammar.

✦ **Ignore Once:** Choose this option when the grammar checker puts its nose where it doesn't belong. This option ignores the "error" in this instance only.

✦ **Grammar:** If you don't like the way the grammar checker is pointing out your mistakes, you can display the Grammar dialog box, where you can promptly tell it to ignore this rule just this one instance (Ignore Once) or throughout the text (Ignore Rule). (See Figure 3-4.) To understand the "rule" more thoroughly before you decide what to do, click Explain. If you like one of the suggested fixes, select it and click Change to apply. If you're doing a full grammar check on the whole message and there's another grammatical error, you can jump to that error by clicking Next Sentence. You can also change the Grammar options from this dialog box by clicking Options; see the next section for help in understanding them.

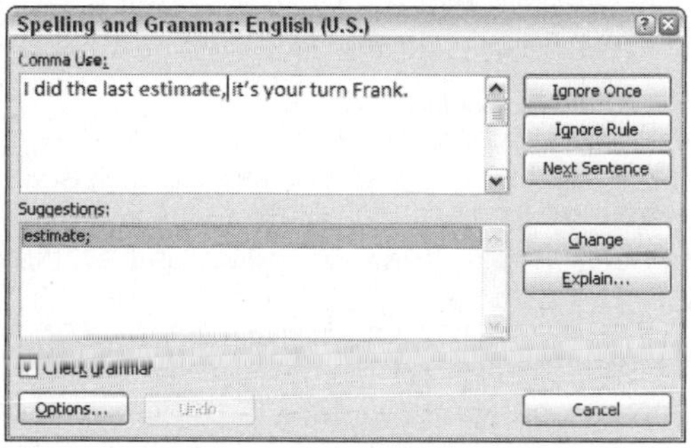

Figure 3-4: Get better at grammar.

✦ **About This Sentence:** Opens the Outlook Help window, which helps you understand your error by providing examples of that type of error.

✦ **Look Up:** Opens the Research pane and allows you to look up the grammatical phrase within Outlook's research materials and the Internet. See the earlier section, "Checking spelling," for help.

You can turn off automatic spell and grammar checking. If you do, check your Outlook message, contact, appointment, or task right before you save it or send it off. Just press F7. Or you can choose Message (or other item tab)⇨Proofing⇨Spelling⇨Spelling & Grammar. Just keep in mind that the Spelling & Grammar command, despite its name, checks spelling only unless you've set the option to check grammar and spelling at the same time (shhhh . . . I show you how in just a minute). You can also, while checking spelling, choose the option to Check Grammar, too (in the Spelling and Grammar dialog box).

To control how and when Outlook checks grammar, make the following changes to your Spelling settings:

1. **Choose Tools⇨Options.**

   The Options dialog box appears.

2. **Click the Spelling tab.**
3. **Click the Spelling and AutoCorrection button.**

   The Editor Options dialog box appears.

4. **Click the Proofing button.**
5. **Select the grammar options you want:**
   - *To have Outlook check grammar as you type:* In the When Correcting Spelling in Outlook area, select the Mark Grammar Errors as You Type check box.
   - *To check grammar any time you check spelling (when you press F7 to start the spell checker or when you click Send and Outlook automatically checks your spelling):* Select the Check Grammar with Spelling check box.
   - *To have Outlook give you some idea of how easy your text is to read:* Select the Show Readability Statistics check box. Readability statistics, should you choose to use them, appear only after a manual spelling and grammar check. This option isn't the automatic, check-as-you-go kind.
6. **Click OK to save your changes and close the Editor Options dialog box.**
7. **Click OK to close the Options dialog box.**

Using Stationery to Add Flair

To dress up your messages and add some fun, you can choose from a variety of Outlook *stationery* that provides a colorful background or pattern on which to rest your words. If you're looking for something more high-tech and professional, you can choose an Outlook *theme,* which not only provides a background but also a matching set of bullets, fonts, text colors, china, and stemware.

Outlook provides its stationery and themes through a dialog box that you use at the start of a new message. If you find an Outlook stationery or theme that you want to use most of the time, you can set it up as the message default. Word provides some extra themes to Outlook through the Ribbon on a message form, making those themes available even after you've started creating a message. (See the section, "Applying a Word Theme" for help.)

Stationery and themes are available for HTML messages only, not for plain text or RTF-formatted messages. Also, you can't add stationery or a theme to a reply or a forwarded message. See Chapter 1 of this minibook for help with message formats.

Taking a stationery out for a test run

To select an Outlook stationery or theme for a new message, follow these steps:

1. **Choose Actions➪New Mail Message Using➪More Stationery.**

   The Theme or Stationery dialog box, shown in Figure 3-5, appears.

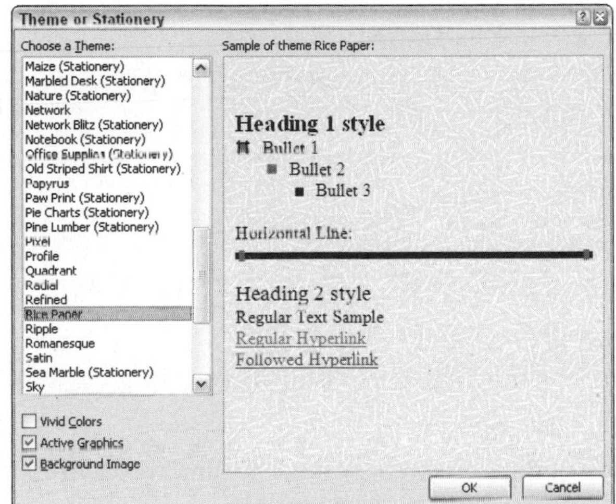

Figure 3-5: Stationery that makes your text look good.

   By the way, if you want to use the same stationery you've used before, just select it from the New Mail Message Using menu, and skip the rest of this stuff.

2. **Choose a stationery or theme, select other options, and click OK.**

   When you make a selection from the Choose a Theme list, a sample appears on the right. You'll notice that some selections are marked as stationery; the others are themes. Basically, themes provide consistent styles for various kinds of text such as headings or bulleted lists, and stationery provides a background. (More about stationery and themes in a minute.) If you select a theme, you have three more options to choose from:

   - *Vivid Colors:* Select this option to brighten up your messages.
   - *Active Graphics:* Omit animated `.gif` files by disabling this option.
   - *Background Image:* Select this option to bypass a graphic background.

If you choose an Outlook theme, the text you type in the message is automatically formatted using the body text style. If you format your text as a bulleted list, hypertext link, heading, or you add a horizontal line (as explained later in this chapter), those elements will look like the sample you saw in the

Theme or Stationery dialog box. If you choose an Outlook stationery instead, the text is formatted in the default style, which is probably Arial, 10 point. If the stationery has a graphic you want to type below, just double-click where you want to start the message and then start typing.

Stationery provides you with a graphic background, whereas a theme provides a set that includes heading, bullet, and link styles, along with a background color (in most cases).

Selecting your everyday stationery

After you've test-driven a few Outlook stationery choices and themes, you might come across one that fits you perfectly. If so, you can set that stationery or theme as your default.

1. **Choose Tools⇨Options.**

   The Options dialog box opens.

2. **Click the Mail Format tab.**

3. **Click the Stationery and Fonts button.**

   The Signatures and Stationery dialog box appears.

4. **Click the Theme button.**

   The Theme or Stationery dialog box appears. See Figure 3-6.

5. **Choose your favorite and click OK several times to close all dialog boxes.**

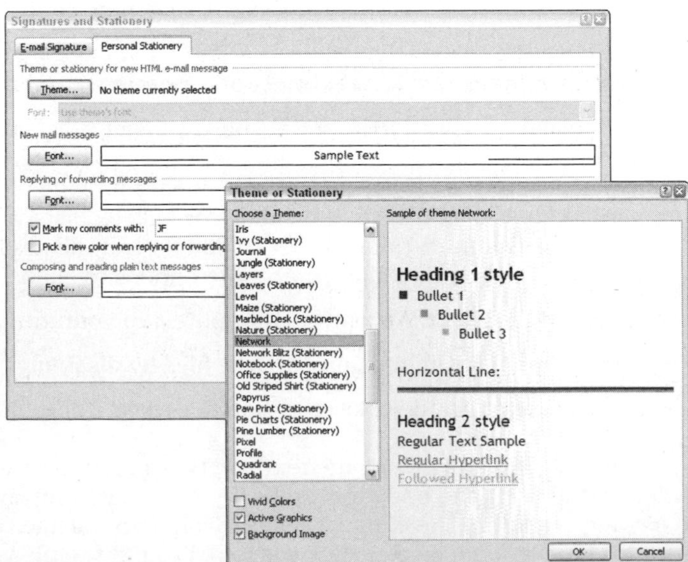

Figure 3-6: Select your favorite stationery or theme.

Even after setting a default, you can still pick and choose whatever stationery you want to use for an individual e-mail by following the steps so carefully outlined by *moi* in the previous "Taking a stationery out for a test run" section. To go without, choose Actions⇨New Mail Message Using⇨HTML (No Stationery).

Applying a Word Theme

So as not to be left out, Word provides its own set of themes to Outlook, available only after you start a message. You can add a Word theme on top of an Outlook stationery or theme, although the result is often a rather surprising mix of colors and fonts.

In a Word theme, you get custom-colored and styled fonts for body text, headings, bulleted lists, hyperlinks, and other text elements. You even get a style for horizontal lines. In addition, you get a set of colors: four text/background colors and six accent colors. After you select a theme, you see the first two text/backgrounds and the first two accent colors on the Theme Colors button. You see the entire color palette anytime you try to colorize text, shapes, and other objects.

Anyway, to use a Word theme, start out with a plain-looking HTML message. Then choose Options⇨Themes⇨Themes. A fat palette of Word themes appears, as shown in Figure 3-7. As you hover the mouse pointer over a theme, you can audition it, assuming you have some text in the message to use for the audition. If you can't see how the text is affected, you can choose a theme based on its thumbnail — and, if it turns out badly, simply repeat these steps to choose a different theme. Click a theme to select it.

If your text doesn't seem to change much when you preview a theme, don't worry — nothing's wrong with your monitor. The theme colors, for example, are applied to text that is already using a color from a different theme. (You'll see how to apply text colors in the section, "Applying a Color, Font, or Effects Set.") So if you haven't colored any text, then you won't see much of a change as you're previewing other than the font, which typically changes from theme to theme.

At the bottom of the Themes menu, click More Themes on Microsoft Office Online to search the Office Web site for more themes. Hey, you can never have enough, right? Choose Browse for Themes to search for saved theme sets on your computer. Choose Reset to Theme from Template to reapply the original message theme, which was probably the standard Office theme.

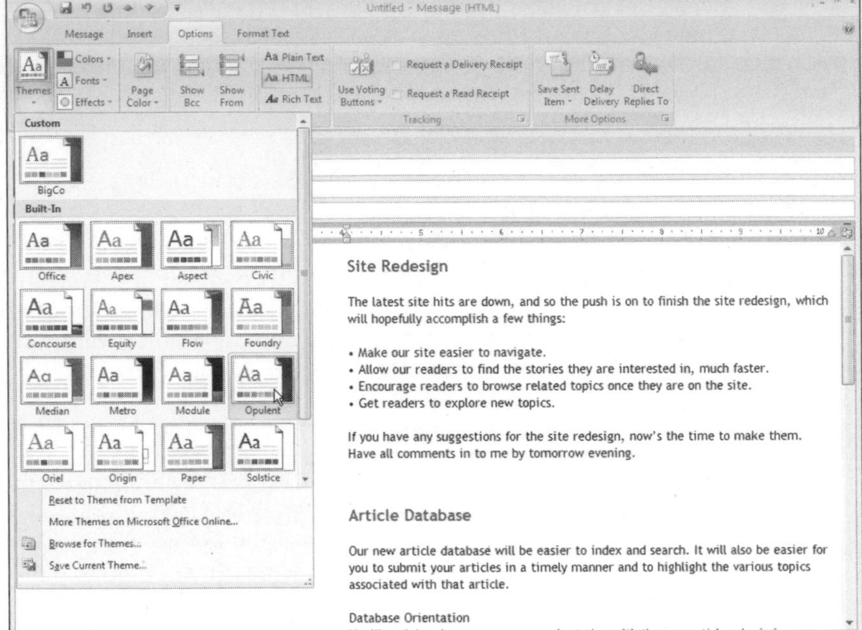

Figure 3-7: Outlook, move over for Word themes.

After selecting a theme, just type. The font, size, and color of the theme's body text style are applied to what you type (and existing text as well). The theme's heading style is applied to headings, the bullet style to bullets, and so on. (For the word on how to format text as a heading, a bulleted list, or whatever, see "Playing with Text" later in this chapter.) The fun doesn't stop there: If you create shapes, charts, tables, and the like, they're programmed by default to use the various colors built in to the theme. That way, if you change to a different Word theme, your entire message is still color-coordinated.

You can create a custom theme, if you like, and assemble a set of preferred colors, fonts, and effects. See the upcoming section, "Customizing your look," for help.

Applying a Color, Font, or Effects Set

Okay, is a theme too much decorating for you? No problem. If you want to keep the fonts you've used in a message and apply a different set of colors to bullets, headings, and the like, you can just choose a color set. No guilt, no commitment, no phone calls you have to avoid. You can do the same thing with font types — switch them out without switching the colors you might have already used in the message. If you've got lines and shapes that you've added to your message, you can pick out a set of fills and effects to apply to them.

Follow these quick steps to select a color, font, or effects set:

1. **Choose Options⇨Themes and click the arrow on the Colors, Fonts, or Effects buttons (depending on the element you'd like to change).**

   A menu of choices pops up. Briefly, here's what each button is for:

   - *Colors:* The set of colors you select can be applied to a variety of objects in your message, including the text, headings, bulleted or numbered lists, shapes, SmartArt, charts, hyperlinks, text boxes, and horizontal lines. Most of these items are inserted with buttons you find on the Insert tab (not surprisingly), which you'll learn to do later in this chapter.
   - *Fonts:* Each set includes two fonts — one for regular body text, and the other for headings, although you can apply the fonts in the set to text however you want.
   - *Effects:* Each set includes a shape style, color fill, shadow effects, and 3-D effects that provide a coordinated look to objects in your message. What objects, you ask? Good question. Here I'm talking about things like arrows, rectangles, stars, and such, inserted using the Shapes button on the Insert tab. (See the section, "Illustrating Your Point.") Effects are also applied to SmartArt, Charts, text boxes, and horizontal lines, which are also discussed in various sections throughout this chapter.

2. **Click the color, font, or effects set you want to use.**

   As you slide the mouse down the list, the elements in your message change accordingly. For example, as you slide down the Fonts list, your text changes styles so you can preview the option before you choose it. If you have a drawn object in your message (such as a star), then it'll change as you sweep down the Effects list. Colors you've applied to text or objects change as you preview the choices on the Colors list.

Creating a custom set of colors or fonts

Normally, the sets of colors, fonts, and effects that come with Outlook would satisfy most people. And hey, these fonts, colors, and effects sets are easy to select and apply. What else could you want? Well, maybe you're wishing that one of the colors was a bit lighter or darker. Then it would be just perfect. Or maybe you like the heading font, but you want to use something else for your body text. Or maybe you've been instructed by your boss to use only company colors in e-mails to clients. (Yippee.)

In any case, you can easily create your own set of custom colors and fonts. Can't do anything about creating your own set of effects, so your boss is just gonna have to live with that.

To create your own set of colors, you start by modifying the set you're currently using. Haven't selected a set? Well, then you're using the Office default set of colors. But unless that generic set of colors represents all you want in the world, I'd recommend jumping back a few paragraphs and learning how to select a color set that's at least close to what you want to end up with. Then I'd follow these steps to change it:

1. **Choose Options➪Themes➪Colors➪Create New Theme Colors.**

   The Create New Theme Colors dialog box peeks out, like the one shown in Figure 3-8.

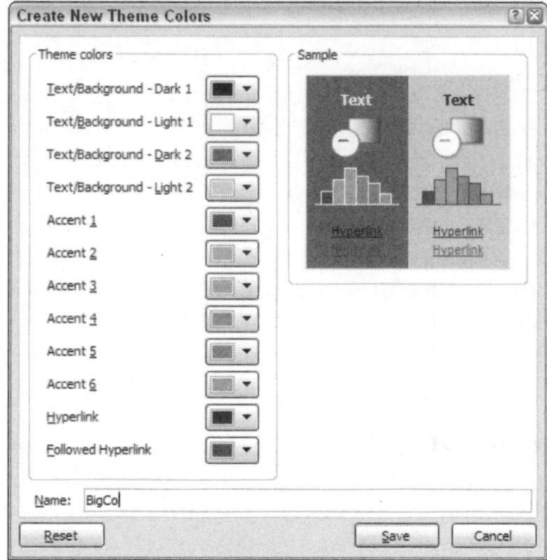

Figure 3-8: Why settle for ordinary?

2. **Select the color to change.**

   Click the button for the color you want to change and choose a new color. You can easily lighten or darken the color from the palette that appears or choose one of the standard colors.

   To select a color that isn't on that palette, click the More Colors link and choose one from the color palette that pops up. If you need help figuring out how to use the More Colors dialog box, you find it in the upcoming section, "Simply Colorizing the Background."

3. **Rinse and repeat to change other colors and click Save to save your changes.**

   Repeat Step 2 to change any other color in the theme. You can look at the sample provided to decide whether the new color works with the existing colors or if you need to select something different.

If you decide you don't like the colors you've chosen, before you click Save, you can click the Reset button to return to all the original colors in the theme.

4. **Type a name for the theme in the Name text box.**

   If you can't think of a name, you can just add a number to the existing theme name and call it quits.

5. **Click Save.**

   The colors you selected are applied automatically. For example, if a blue color was in the original color set, and you changed it to a nice green, then any text using the blue is changed to green. The set is added to the Colors list so you can choose it again for a different message.

To create your own set of fonts, you basically follow this same set of steps, but replace Step 1 with Choose Options⇨Themes⇨Fonts⇨Create New Theme Fonts and go from there. And no, you don't have to select a font set for your message first, although you're using one (even if you didn't choose one): the Office font set, which features Cambria for heading text and Calibri for body text. Anyway, after clicking the Fonts button and choosing Create New Theme Fonts, you see a simple dialog box that allows you to choose the Heading Font and Body Text font you want. There's a Sample area where you can see how your selections look together. When you're done looking in the mirror, type a name for your set and click OK.

Customizing your look

After selecting a Word theme, you can just let it go and type your message. The fonts and colors defined by the theme are applied automatically, and what could be easier than that? Still, sometimes you just need to express your own style. Luckily, even Word themes allow room for individuality.

Although you can't actually change the colors, fonts, or effects used in a theme, you can use the theme as your starting point and create a new theme to reuse as you like.

1. **Start with a Word theme and make it look the way you want it to look.**

   You start by selecting a Word theme that contains at least some of the elements you like, such as a rough set of colors and fonts. Then, you modify the color or font set (as described in the previous section), and select a set of effects you like.

   When everything is formatted the way you prefer, save your formats and reuse them whenever you want.

2. **Choose Options⇨Themes⇨Themes⇨Save Current Theme.**
3. **Type a name for the theme and click Save.**

The theme is now available for use in other messages. When you click the Themes button, you find your theme at the top, in the Custom section. Just click it to apply the custom theme to the current message.

Simply Colorizing the Background

If the thought of selecting a theme and using its heading, body text, and bullet styles seems like overkill for a simple message to a friend or colleague, you can opt for something simpler but equally as impressive: a colorful background. You can choose a solid color, gradient, texture, pattern, or image.

Keep in mind that if you select a dark-colored background, the normal body text (which is black) won't show up well on it. You should probably change your text to a lighter color to provide some contrast and make it easier to read. A sans-serif font such as Arial is probably a good idea as well, because its simple structure looks less fuzzy, even in a small size and with little contrast against the message background.

Color is a solid choice

To select a background color, choose Options➪Themes➪Page Color. A palette associated with the current theme (and yes, a theme is associated with your message even if you didn't choose one, and it's called Office) appears. You can select any of those ten basic colors listed across the top of the palette or their associated tints (white added to the basic theme color) or shades (black added). Below this color group at the bottom of the palette, you see the set of ten standard colors from which you can choose instead.

If you overdo your choices and would rather return to a plain message with a white background, choose No Color from the Page Color menu.

If you don't see a color you want to try, click the More Colors option and choose from the colors of the rainbow. (If you're overwhelmingly curious about that Fill Effects option on the shortcut menu, jump to the next section, "Why not try a gradient, texture, pattern, or image?" for help.) The Colors dialog box that appears when you choose the More Colors option has two tabs for choosing colors:

- **Standard:** Click a color from the large hexagon to select it. If you like black, gray, or white, you can click a color from the small group of hexagons that appear below the color hexagon.
- **Custom:** Click the Custom tab as shown in Figure 3-9 to custom blend your own color. Follow these steps:

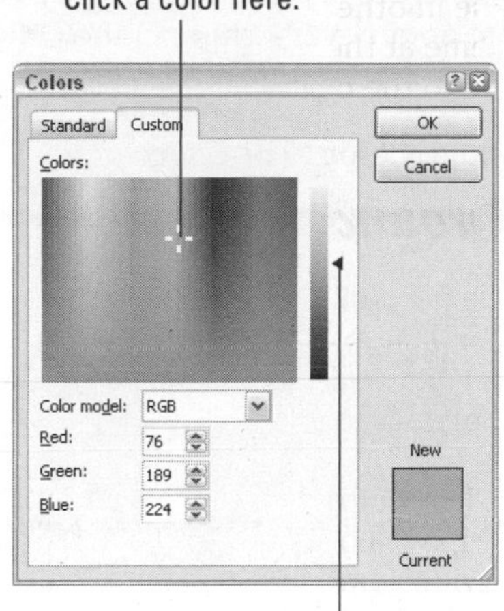

Figure 3-9: Mix your own color.

1. **Drag the four-pointed white marker within the Colors palette.**

   This selects a general color. In the figure, I selected a nice teal blue by dragging the white pointy thing to the teal blue area in the Colors palette on the left. The band to the right changes to show a range of this color from tints to shades.

2. **Drag the tint/shade marker to the color you want and click OK.**

   To the right of the Colors palette, you see a vertical band of the current color. Refine that color by dragging the marker up or down.

You can mix a color by the numbers if you want. Select the color model you're using, either RGB or HSL; then enter the appropriate values from 0 to 255. RGB is short for red, green, blue, and it's one approach to creating color on a computer monitor. If you set all values to zero, you get pure black; if you set all to 255, you get white. Another approach to mixing color is HSL, or hue, saturation, luminance. The hue value represents the color's position on the color wheel; the saturation value controls the amount of gray that's added to muddy the pure color; the luminance value controls the amount of white added. Here, 0, 0, 0, gets you pure black; 0, 0, 255, gets you pure white; and 0, 0, 127 gets you a perfect middle-gray.

Why not try a gradient, texture, pattern, or image?

If you don't want to use a pure color as your background, you can use a fill instead. Here you have several choices, such as a gradient (a slow blending from one color to another), texture, pattern (an ordered pattern of two colors), or picture (such as a company logo). You're probably familiar with this process because it's used just about everywhere in the Office universe, so I cover it at warp speed.

1. **Choose Options⇨Themes⇨Page Color⇨Fill Effects.**

   The Fill Effects dialog box appears, as shown in Figure 3-10.

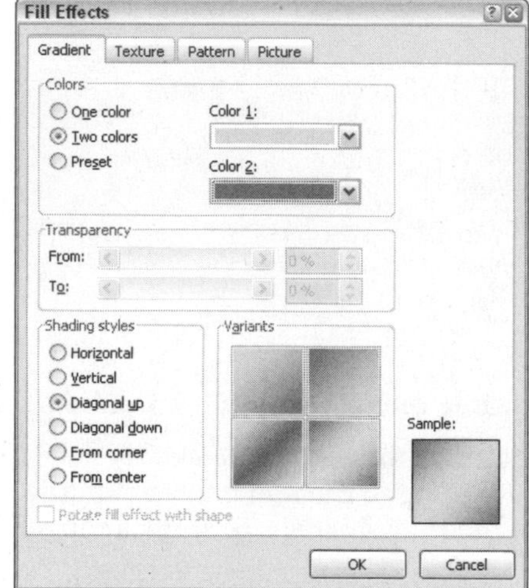

Figure 3-10: Fill a message's background.

2. **Select a gradient.**

   Click the Gradient tab and select a Colors option: One-Color, Two-Color, or Preset. Choose the one, two, or preset color(s) you want to work with. Adjust the amount of transparency in the gradient (if this option is available). Then choose a direction in the Shading Styles area.

3. **OR Select a Texture.**

   Click the Texture tab, and then select a texture. Pretty brainless.

4. **OR Select a Pattern.**

   Click the Pattern tab, choose a Foreground and a Background color, and then click the Pattern you want. Brain surgery it's not.

5. **OR Select an Image.**

   Click the Picture tab. Click Select Picture, choose the picture to use, and click Insert. Images are tiled to fit the message form. They are not adjustable in Outlook, so do your resizing, cropping, and lightening (if you want to make it easier to see your text on the image) in a photo editor before you import the image into a message.

If you're looking for more control over an image used as a message background, you might be happier just inserting the image as explained in the next section. You could then format the image to allow text to flow over top of it (if that's what you're looking for), rather than around it. You could also crop, lighten, and adjust the level of contrast in Outlook as needed to make the image a proper background.

Inserting an Image

When it comes to adding pictures to an e-mail message, you have several choices: You can use an image as a message background (as explained in the last section), you can insert one of your own images and wrap text around it, or you can use one of Microsoft's images from its Microsoft Clip Organizer. You can also attach an image file, but that's different from actually placing an image within a message, which is what this section is about; see Book II, Chapter 1 for help on attaching a file.

To insert an image, choose Insert⇨Illustrations⇨Picture, select the image and click Insert. To insert a clip, choose Insert⇨Illustrations⇨Clip Art, type something to Search for, and click Go. You can limit the results by selecting a collection from the Search In list. Further limit the results by selecting particular file types from the Results Should Be list. Click an image to insert it.

You can select, resize, move, and rotate an image the same way you manipulate objects. See the upcoming section, "Manipulating Objects," for help.

One of the coolest things about the new Office programs is that they really make formatting fun. Take images, for instance: Select one and up pops more buttons (on the Ribbon) than you find on a home theatre remote control. (See Figure 3-11.) If you've "lost the remote," as it were, click the Format tab to display the buttons.

✦ **Brightness/Contrast:** These buttons adjust the lightness (brightness) and contrast of an image. Just click a value on the menu that pops up. Plus values mean very light or high contrast; low values mean dark or low contrast.

To adjust the brightness or contrast more precisely, click the Dialog Box Launcher button in the lower-right corner of the Picture Styles group. In the dialog box that appears, you can drag to adjust the brightness/contrast or enter precise values.

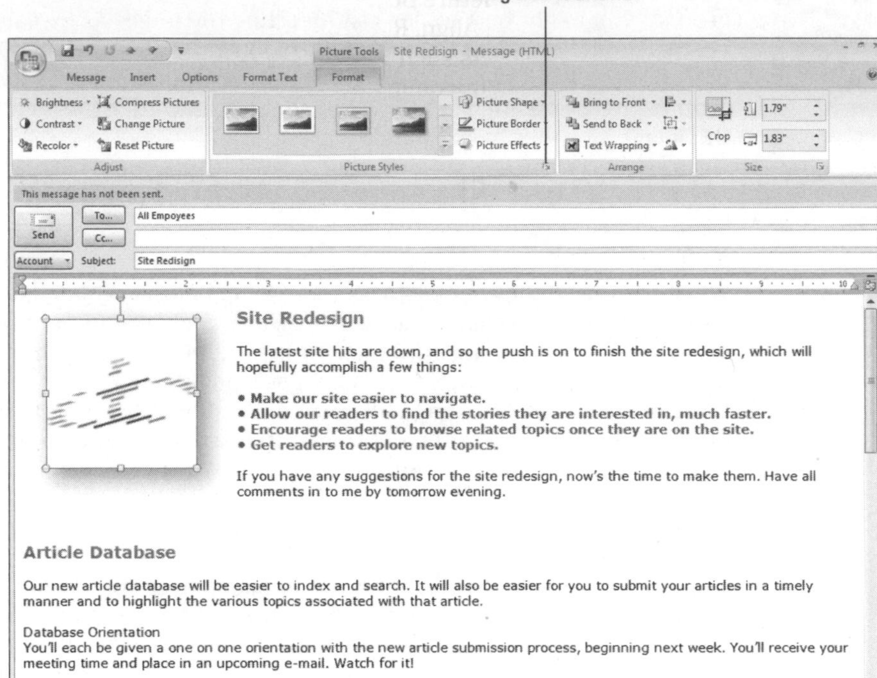

Figure 3-11: Make any image look the way you want.

- **Recolor:** Select a variation to recolor the image to those shades. Notice that the variations are all based on the current template colors; this helps you create a unified look easily. The Color Modes options allow you to quickly create a black and white, grayscale, sepia, or washed-out image. The Set Transparent Color button on the menu is interesting; after clicking the button, click in the image to change all pixels that same color to transparent pixels so text can be seen through that part of the image. Use this remove the background around the subject, assuming that background is basically one color.
- **Compress Pictures:** This compresses (reduces the file size) of all images in the document so the thing isn't too big to send. It also, however, reduces the quality of the images as well. The only option in this box is to apply the compression to selected images (rather than all images in the message), so you can do that if you want.
- **Change Picture:** Allows you to swap the current selected image with one of your own (and not one from Microsoft Clip Organizer), without losing the formatting you might have applied to that image.
- **Reset Picture:** Resets the image to normal (removing all formatting).

The Picture Shape, Picture Border, Picture Effects, Bring to Front, Send to Back, Text Wrapping, Align, Rotate, Crop, and Size buttons also apply to a variety of other objects such as shapes and text boxes. You'll find descriptions for them in the upcoming "Manipulate Objects" section.

Illustrating Your Point

They say that pictures are worth a thousand words, and when you're trying to make a point, I guess that's true. Outlook methods, which you'd probably employ most often in Word, Excel, or PowerPoint, provide several ways in which you can put the money, so to speak, where your mouth is: tables, charts, shapes, and SmartArt graphics.

SmartArt is a special graphic that you can use to illustrate a set of related data, such as a list of items or a series of steps. You can find graphics that illustrate a cycle (such as a monthly process), hierarchy (such as an organization chart), relationship between items, matrix (parts that relate to a whole), or pyramid (proportionate relationships).

This is not a book on Word, Excel, or PowerPoint, however; so I'll just be touching on the basic how-tos here. For the money, as it were, check out *Microsoft Office 2007 All-in-One Desk Reference For Dummies*, by Peter Weverka (Wiley Publishing).

To insert a symbol such as £ or ¥ or ©, choose Insert⇨Symbols⇨Symbol. In the dialog box that appears, select a character set and then click a symbol to insert it in the text.

Tabling the notion

A table is a collection of related data, presented in rows and columns. The rows and columns intersect to form *cells.* You might use a table to show your wife how you'll be able to pay for a new multimedia room in three months, using the extra income you'll save by packing both of your lunches every day, not eating out for dinner during the week, and limiting her clothing allowance. (Okay, maybe even a table won't help. . . .)

Here's the quick and easy way to insert a table: Choose Insert⇨Tables⇨Table. Drag over the grid to select the number of rows and columns you want. To enter data, click in the first cell on the left, type something, and then press Tab to move to the next cell in a row. Press Tab at the end of a row to move down a row. If you press tab in the last cell in a table, you automatically add a new row. Format the table quickly by choosing Design⇨Table Styles.

The check boxes to the far left of the Design tab control which Table Styles you see. For example, if you enable the Header Row, Total Row, and Banded Rows options, you see formatting tailored to make the headings in the first row of your table and the totals in the last row, stand out. Because of the Banded Rows option, the colors for the body of the table alternate rows.

Use the Layout tab to select table elements such as a row, and then format it using the Shading and Borders buttons on the Design tab. The Layout tab also includes buttons for adding and removing rows and columns, merging two cells together, and changing text alignment.

Charting the way

A chart is a graphical representation of a table. Rather than expecting your boss to pour over the latest boring sales data, why not show him graphically why he pays you the big bucks? And if he doesn't pay you the big bucks, maybe a chart that clearly shows how you consistently outsell everyone in the department will convince him why he should.

To insert a chart, choose Insert⇨Illustrations⇨Chart. The Insert Chart dialog box pops up; choose a column type on the left, and a sample on the right, and then click OK. A chart appears in the message, based on the fake table data that appears in a separate worksheet. Change this worksheet data to change the chart (see Figure 3-12). (See the previous section for some help with that.) When you're done, close the worksheet window.

You can't create a chart based on a table already in a message, at least, not automatically. You can, however, select the table and then paste its data into the worksheet after you create the chart.

Choose Design⇨Chart Styles to quickly format the chart. On the Design tab, you can also change the chart type and apply a Quick Layout to rearrange the various chart elements such as the chart key. On the Layout tab, you can add chart elements such as a legend, title, and labels. You can also change how often the gridlines appear and rearrange the vertical and horizontal axes of the chart.

The elements of a chart (the bars, key, title, and so on) are objects that can be formatted separately. For help with most of the buttons on the Format tab, see the section, "Manipulating Objects."

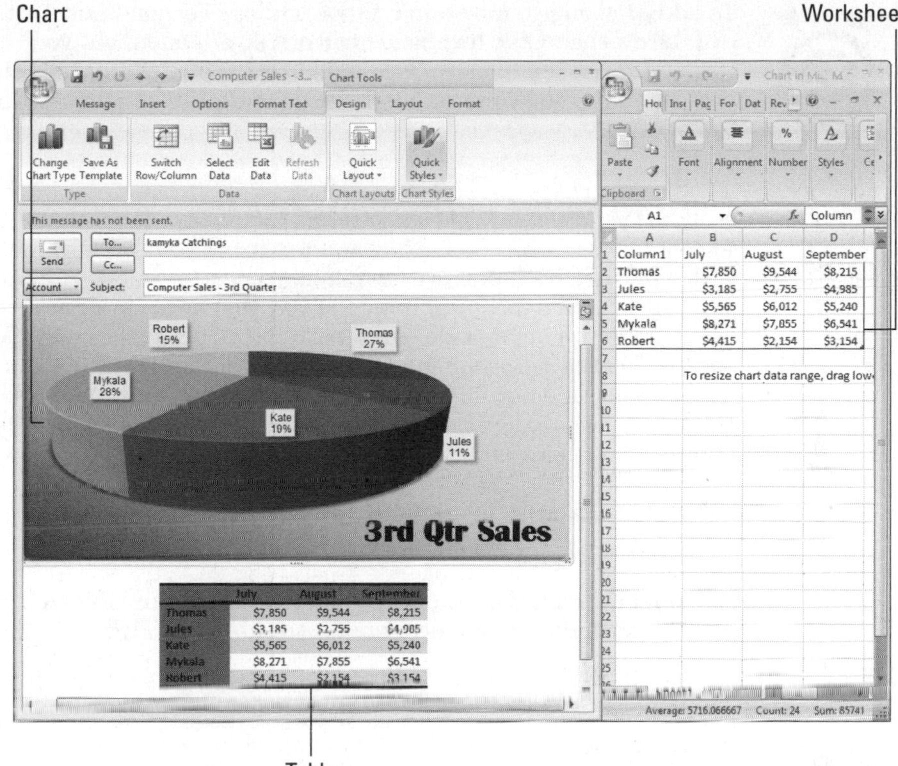

Figure 3-12: Sales are up.

Getting your message to take shape

There's no better way to call attention to critical information than to draw a big fat arrow pointing to it. Using the Shapes tool, you can insert not only arrows, but rectangles, circles, lines, stars, flowchart symbols, and other interesting shapes. The process is the same as within any other Office program; just choose Insert⇨Illustrations⇨Shapes, click a shape, and then drag from the upper-left corner down to the lower-right corner to draw the shape.

You can insert more shapes by choosing Format⇨Insert Shapes. After a shape is inserted, you can resize, move, and format it. See the section, "Manipulating Objects," for help.

To add or change text within a shape, choose Format⇨Edit Text. If you resize or rotate a shape, the text inside will not be adjusted, but you can select the text and resize it manually. You cannot rotate the text inside a shape, however (actually, you can't rotate the text inside a text box either, so don't feel too bad.)

Getting smart with SmartArt

Another way in which you might want to make your point is to illustrate it with SmartArt, a set of graphics similar to charts. SmartArt helps to tell the story of a set of data in a graphic fun way that keeps your audience interested while you bamboozle 'em. Need to keep up department morale during another senseless reshuffling of company personnel? Hide the news with a cool-looking Organization chart. Want to convince your boss that a big project will still get done on time despite several critical setbacks? Illustrate your ideas with a step-by-step plan and a process graph.

1. **Choose Insert⇨Illustrations⇨SmartArt.**

   The Choose a SmartArt Graphic dialog box jumps out.

2. **Select a SmartArt category from the list on the left (such as Process), and then choose a type from those shown on right.**

   As you click each type, a description explaining the intended use of that type appears on the far right.

3. **Click OK.**

Some SmartArt graphics are better suited for illustrating particular ideas, processes, or other data. Choose List for items that can appear in any particular order, like a grocery list. Choose Process to show the steps in a task; choose Cycle to show the steps in a task that repeats itself. Choose Hierarchy when you want to do an organization chart or illustrate a series of decisions and where they might lead. Choose Relationship when the most important point is the connections between items; choose Matrix to highlight the how various components relate to the whole unit. Choose Pyramid to show how items relate proportionately, with the biggest or most important item in the largest part of the pyramid.

The SmartArt graphic appears in the message, as shown in Figure 3-13. Click each bullet and type the appropriate text in the Text pane that appears. For example, type each item in a list or each step in a process. Notice that it's only a bulleted list; just press enter at the end of a line to add another bullet, or press Tab to create a subbullet. To remove a bullet, select the text and press Delete.

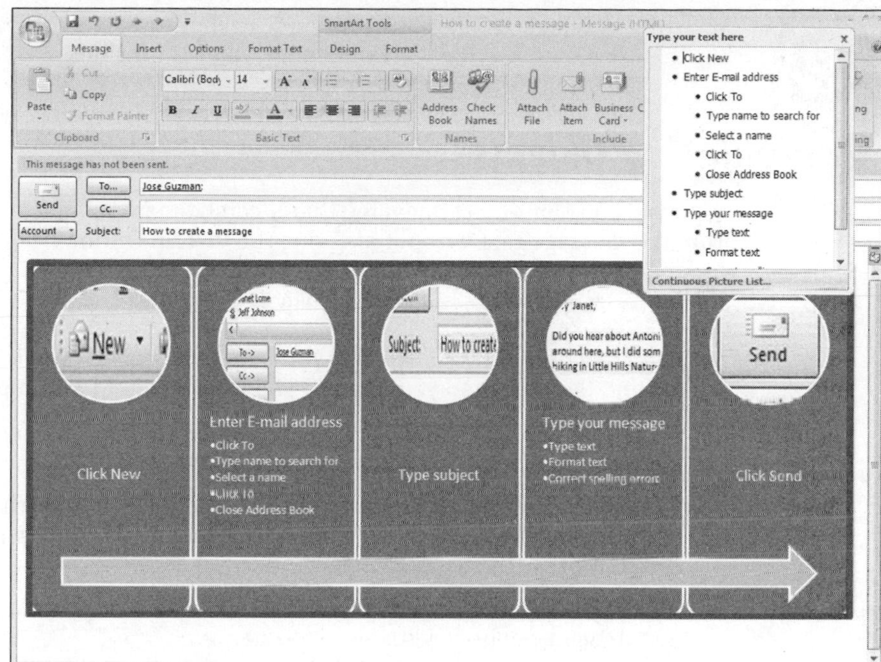

Figure 3-13: Get smart.

If you see items marked with a red X in the Text pane, you can't type data there. But you might be able to add text to those items if you switch to a different layout.

You can format the text in the Text pane; although the formatting doesn't appear there. It appears in the SmartArt graphic. Close the Text pane when you're done; if you need it to stick its head back up, choose Design⇨Create Graphic⇨Text Pane. Now that you have a SmartArt graphic, you can do lots of things to it.

- ✦ **Colorize:** At the start, your SmartArt is as blue as a suede shoe. But you don't have to leave it like that; choose a SmartArt Style on the Design tab to dress up the blue look, or click Change Colors to uh, change colors.
- ✦ **Add images:** Some SmartArt graphics contain a picture holder, which you can use to illustrate a step or process or to provide some icon to help the reader to remember what you said, even after ten seconds. Click the picture holder, search around for a graphic, and then click Insert.
- ✦ **Change the order of things:** You can flip the order of shapes in the graphic by choosing Design⇨Create Graphic⇨Right to Left.

SmartArt is similar to other objects such as shapes, text boxes, and images. See the upcoming section, "Manipulating Objects," for help.

Manipulating Objects

A shape is just an object, meaning that it can be manipulated separately from the message text without affecting the text. In Outlook, you can insert and manipulate several types of objects such as images, clipart, shapes, SmartArt, or text boxes. Use these basic techniques:

✦ **Select an object** by clicking it. White squares, called handles, appear around the object so you can get a handle on what to do next.

✦ **Resize an object** by dragging it by a handle. Drag by a corner handle to keep the object in proportion and not distort it.

✦ **Move an object** by clicking in its center and dragging. Be careful; you can only move the object as you might a selected word, by dragging and dropping it within a paragraph.

✦ **Rotate an object** by clicking the green dot connected to the top handle, and dragging right or left.

When the object is selected, you can use any of the tools that appear on the Ribbon to pretty it up. Buttons that are grayed out can't be used with the current object:

✦ **Format an object:** Apply a style by clicking it; click the More button below the scrollbar to display all the styles. Fill the object with color, gradient, texture, or pattern by selecting one from the Shape Fill palette. (See the section, "Simply Colorizing the Background," for help.) As with any other formatting palette, just hover your mouse pointer over a style or color to preview it before you buy. Change the object's outline (its color, width, and style) by choosing one from the Shape Outline (Picture Border) palette. Click No Outline to remove the border.

When sending a message to someone who does not use Outlook 2007, keep in mind that some of your formatting may not appear as you see it. For the most part, your formatting should arrive intact, but if you format shapes, they will appear in a light blue rectangle.

✦ **Change the object's shape:** Choose a one other than the Change Shape (Picture Shape) palette. For a shape in a SmartArt graphic, you can click the Larger or Smaller buttons located nearby to make that shape slightly larger or smaller. For an image, it's cropped to fit within the shape; the cropping can be undone by clicking Reset Picture.

- **Add a shadow:** Choose the effect you want from the Shadow Effects palette. The shadow color is based on the shape's fill color; change the shadow color by choosing Shadow Color from this menu. Nudge the shadow up, down, left, or right by clicking the buttons to the right of the Shadow Effects button.
- **Shape Effects/Picture Effects:** Add shadows, reflections, glows, soft edges, and 3-D effects.
- **3-D Effects:** Make the object appear three-dimensional. You can also select the color of the 3-D effect (the sides of the 3-D object), its depth, direction, and surface texture, and the direction and brightness of the light falling on the 3-D object. Tilt the 3-D object slightly, using the buttons located to the right of the 3-D Effects button when the menu is opened.
- **Text wrapping:** Controls how text runs alongside or over the object. In-line With Text causes text to flow beside the bottom edge of the object as if it were one really big word; this also causes the object to move as text is added or deleted from the paragraph. The other options allow text to flow around all sides of the object, top and bottom only, or through the object.

TIP

If you change the Text Wrap to anything other than In-Line With Text, you can stack the object with other objects in the message (such as another shape, image, or text box) so the object is either partially obscured by the other objects or partially obscures them.

Think of a stack of pancakes: You can move the object in the stack so it's above certain "pancakes" and below others. To move the object to the top of the stack (so it moves in front of all other objects), choose Format⇨Arrange⇨Bring to Front. To move the object up in the stack one "pancake" at a time, choose Format⇨Arrange⇨Bring to Front⇨Bring Forward, as many times as needed. To move the shape behind all objects, just click the Send to Back button. To move an object down the stack one object at a time, choose Format⇨Arrange⇨Send to Back⇨Send Backward. By the way, the Bring in Front of Text and Send Behind Text commands on these buttons are the same as the In Front of Text and Behind Text commands on the Text-Wrapping button.

- **Align:** First, choose whether to align the object to the page or the page border (margin). Then choose a vertical (left, center, right) or horizontal (top, middle, bottom) alignment. You can press Ctrl and click multiple objects to align them relative to each other, the page, or the margin, or to distribute them evenly between the page or margin borders.
- **Group:** Allows you to group multiple selected shapes and/or text boxes together in order to move, resize, and format them in one step. Press Ctrl and click each object to select it. Choose Ungroup from this menu to ungroup objects and treat them separately.

- **Rotate:** Rotate your shape 90 degrees left or right, or flip it (mirroring). Choose More Rotation Options to rotate by the exact amount you enter.
- **Crop:** Available only for images. Click the crop button, and crop handles (thick dashes) appear around the image's border. Drag a handle inward to crop off that part of the image (to prevent that portion from showing). You're not actually doing anything to the real image, and you can undo whatever you crop, so don't worry. When you're done, click outside the image.
- **Size:** Enter the exact vertical and horizontal dimensions you want.

Making an image significantly larger reduces its quality.

Linking to the Outside World

Yes, there is a world outside your computer, and Outlook attempts to keep you connected to it, mostly by dumping a lot of messages on your desktop. It's a bit ironic, because if you weren't tied to your computer reading tons of e-mail, you'd be able to actually experience the world outside. Anyway, if you're on the Internet and you find an interesting Web page, you can provide a clickable link to the page within an e-mail message. You can also insert a link to any file on your computer or your company's network, assuming that the file is in a shared folder and that your recipient has access to the shared folder as well. In addition, you can link to another spot in this same message, which is a really neat way to allow someone to jump around a lengthy communiqué. And if that's not enough, you can link to an e-mail address. This kind of link creates an automatically addressed e-mail message when the user clicks it.

To insert a link, select the text in your message that the user must click to activate the link. Next, follow these steps:

1. **Choose Insert⇨Links⇨Hyperlink.**

   The Insert Hyperlink dialog box, shown in Figure 3-14, appears.

2. **Create the link.**

   From the Link To pane, click the button that best describes where the page or file you want to link to is located. The list on the right changes depending on what you choose.

The text you selected appears in the Text to Display box. You can change this text if you want, and even add a ScreenTip that appears when the user hovers the mouse pointer over the link.

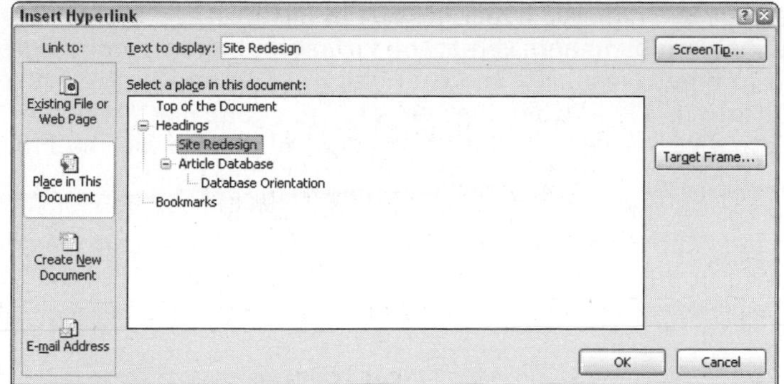

Figure 3-14: Add a link to a Web page or file.

Here are your choices:

- **Existing File or Web Page:** Select the file or Web page to link to. You can browse files in the current folder, those you've recently used, or go searching for a file located elsewhere. If linking to a Web page, you can look through a list of recently browsed pages or type the Web page Address.
- **Place in This Document:** This option assumes that you've premarked the places within the message you want the reader to navigate to, by either bookmarking them, or formatting them as headings. (See the "Adding headings and other QuickStyles" section for more info.) Anyway, just select the bookmark or heading to link to from the Select a Place in This Document list.

  To create a bookmark in a message, select the text to bookmark and then choose Insert➪Links➪Bookmark. Type a Bookmark Name (no spaces) and click Add.

- **Create New Document:** Type the Name Of New Document. Click the Change button to change the folder in which this new file will be stored. Select when you want to actually edit this file.
- **E-Mail Address:** Type the E-Mail Address to link to or select from the list of Recently Used E-Mail Addresses. Type a Subject for the e-mail message this link creates; use something that helps you remember what your message is about.

After you click OK, the hyperlink is created. The text for the link is formatted according to the current template you're using. See the sections, "Using Stationery to Add Flair" and "Applying a Word Theme" for help. To test the link, press Ctrl and click it.

You can also type the hyperlink text in the message, rather than inserting it. The only problem here is that the format for most hyperlinks is pretty difficult to type in manually and get right. Get it wrong and you send your recipients into la-la land when they click the resulting link. I will, however, copy a link to a Web page from the Address box of my browser, and then paste it into a message when needed. Anyway, whether you type a link or paste it, as soon as you press the Spacebar, Outlook recognizes that what you've typed is a link, and formats it appropriately. If (for some reason) the magic doesn't work, put the link text in between < and > and then press the Spacebar or hit Enter.

Inserting an Outlook Item

You might want to share a certain contact or the details of an appointment with someone without actually sharing your full Calendar or Contacts list. Of course, you learn how to share parts of Outlook (such as the Calendar) later in this book, but if the person you want to pass the information on to isn't a part of your shared network, well, then you might think you're out of luck. As it turns out, your luck is about to turn: You can, when needed, send along any Outlook item with an e-mail message to just about anyone.

Attached Outlook items come out as gibberish to anyone who does not have Outlook, so don't bother. You can, however, send part of your calendar to even a non-Outlook user. See Book IV, Chapter 3.

To attach an Outlook item to a message:

1. **Choose Message⇨Include⇨Attach File⇨Item.**

   The Insert Item dialog box jumps out.

2. **Select the item's folder.**

   Open the folder that contains the item you want to send from the Look In list on the left. The list of items in that folder appears in the Items box at the bottom of the dialog box.

3. **Attach the item.**

   Click the item you want to send, make sure that the Attachment option is enabled, and click OK to insert that item. The subject of the item becomes its name, and the item appears in the Attach list at the top of the message form.

When a recipient receives a message with an Outlook item attached, she can just open the attachment normally to view it. The attachment is displayed just like any other Outlook item.

You can send along a part of your calendar in an e-mail message, rather than directly sharing it with someone. This process allows you to control exactly how much detail you share about each appointment or meeting, and which days you send along in the message. See Book IV, Chapter 3.

Playing with Text

You can do a lot more with text in Outlook messages than simply typing it. You might have already played with formatting; if not, skip over to Book II, Chapter 1 for help. You have, I hope, discovered the spell-checking feature; it's saved me from embarrassment more times than I care to admit. If not, skip back to "Checking Your Ignorance at the Door with Spelling and Grammar Checking," at the beginning of this chapter. Anyway, this section is kind of a catchall for other things you can do with text such as formatting it with Word styles and creating bulleted and numbered lists.

From time to time, you might want to insert the date and/or time into a message, if for no other reason than to remind your recipient just how long she's sat on it without responding. You can insert the date as text or as a field; you can update a field to reflect the current date or time as needed, such as after creating a long, detailed message that took several days or weeks to finish. To insert the date or time, choose Insert⇨Text⇨Date & Time. Choose the format you want; select Update Automatically to enter it as a field, and then click OK. To update a date/time field, hover the mouse pointer over it and a button magically appears. Click the button to update the field.

Adding headings and other QuickStyles

You can use themes to quickly dress up an e-mail so that it actually looks like you know what you're doing. In a theme, you instantly get a package of formats that apply to body text, bulleted lists, headings, horizontal lines, hyperlinks, and a variety of other elements. (See the earlier section, "Applying a Word Theme," for help.)

For the formats in a selected theme to work, you have to identify the elements of a message, such as the headings and hyperlinks. Some elements, such as hyperlinks, are identified by the way you insert them. Other elements, such as headings, are just ordinary text until you apply a QuickStyle. Chances are, you won't use headings in most e-mail messages; but if you're composing a longer message, you might want to break up the text with headings that help your reader jump to important information. Look at me; I add headings in this book to break up the text and to allow you to find your place again after you're rudely interrupted by the people stuck behind you at the stoplight, honking for you to move. Can't they see you're trying to learn something here?

To apply a QuickStyle, follow these steps:

1. **Select the text to format.**

   Just drag over the text to select it.

2. **Choose Format Text➪Styles➪Quick Styles.**

   A palette of styles appears, as shown in Figure 3-15.

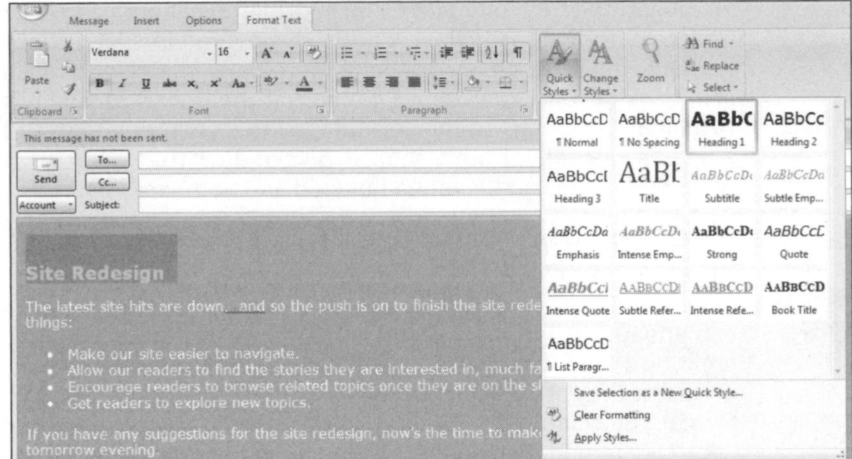

Figure 3-15: Identify yourself, please.

3. **Click a style.**

   As you hover the mouse pointer over a style type, the selected text changes to that style. For example, select Heading 1 or Heading 2 (a subheading in a Heading 1 section.)

As you switch from theme to theme, various elements (such as headings) change to match the formats in the theme. Obviously, other text elements change as well, including many that you identify with a style, such as Title, Subtitle, Book Title, and the other elements you see listed in the Styles pane and on the Quick Styles palette.

You can quickly apply styles to text using the Styles pane (refer to Figure 3-15). To display it, click the Dialog Box Launcher in the Styles group on the Format Text tab. Then, to apply a style, select text as you did before and click a style in the Styles pane.

You can break up text into sections by adding horizontal lines. These lines are formatted by the current theme, and change when the theme is changed. To insert a line, choose Insert⇨Symbols⇨Horizontal Line. To change line's size, click and drag its handle. To change a line's alignment, width, height (thickness), or color, right-click it and choose Format Horizontal Line.

Dealing with bulleted and numbered lists

A bulleted list contains items that can appear in random order, such as a list of things to bring to the quarterly sales meeting or a stuff you've got to get done before you leave on vacation. A numbered list must appear in a specific order; typically it's used to take you through the steps in a procedure. (I use a lot of both these list types in this book if you want to see some examples.)

To create a bulleted or numbered list, follow these steps:

1. **Choose Format Text⇨Paragraph⇨Bullets or Numbering.**

   If you click either of these buttons, you get the standard bullet/numbering style. Click the arrow on either button instead to select the bullet/numbering style you prefer.

2. **Create the list.**

   To create your bulleted/numbered list, just type the first item and then press Enter to create the next item. Stop the list by pressing Enter twice.

Placing text exactly where you want it with a text box

Outlook's basically an e-mail program, and so it shouldn't surprise you that its editor treats text just as Word does, wrapping text as you type between the borders of the message form. Sure, you remove a word or two or add a sentence, and everything moves over in a nice orderly fashion. But what do you do if you want text to appear in a specific spot? Do you add a bunch of spaces to move it over from the margin? That works up to a point, but when you add or remove text elsewhere after adding those spaces, the perfect alignment of that special text might be affected.

An easy way to solve the problem is to add your text within a text box. To Outlook, a text box is just an object, subject to its own rules, and easily resized or moved at will. Here's how to create a text box:

1. **Choose Insert⇨Text⇨Text Box⇨Draw Text Box.**
2. **Draw the box.**

   Click to establish the upper-left corner of the box and drag downward and to the right, creating it.
3. **Type your text.**

   The cursor automatically appears within the text box; just type your text and click outside the box to finish.

You can format your new text box using the buttons on the Format tab; see the earlier section, "Manipulating Objects," for help.

Chapter 4: Repeating Yourself Easily with Signatures and Templates

In This Chapter

- Designing an e-mail signoff
- Adding your new signature to a message
- Saving reusable content for messages
- Inserting your reusable content
- Creating a message template

It's so easy to send e-mail messages, that you might be surprised just how many you send in a single day. If you're anything like me, you probably repeat a lot of the same information at the end of each message, such as your name, e-mail address, and other contact information. You can save such text in a reusable signature that's applied to all out-going messages (or just the ones you choose). Or maybe you're in regular contact with new clients or sales prospects, sending along the same new client tips or sales pitch. In any case, if you find yourself repeating the same text in lots of messages, you can save that text and pop it into a new message whenever you need to. You can also take your recycling to the next level by creating a message template, which not only saves text but formatting and other elements such as images, shapes, SmartArt, and so on. In this chapter, I show you how to do as much recycling as you want — minus that annoying kitchen odor.

Adding Your Signature

E-mails aren't letters, so they don't often contain the elements of a formal letter, such as a salutation or a date. But even if you start all your e-mails with "blah, blah, blah" and leave out even a measly "Hey, you!" greeting, you probably still sign your messages with at least your name. You might even conclude all your business e-mails with detailed contact information, such as your address, phone number, cell number, IM address, and so on.

Rather than type all that stuff at the end of every business e-mail, you can create a reusable signature that Outlook automatically appends to your messages. Want to include some of that stuff in personal e-mails too? No problem; Outlook lets you create as many different signatures as you like and choose which signature to use when.

Signatures can contain text (formatted however you like), images, and electronic business cards. (See Book V, Chapter 3.) You might even include a hyperlink to a personal or company Web site or to your own e-mail address. If needed, you can include a privacy notice stating that the material in the e-mail is confidential. You're pretty much free to add whatever you want to a signature; the idea is that a signature is added at the end of whatever e-mails you want.

If you have other stuff you like to repeat often, such as directions to your office or an off-site meeting room you use frequently, you can type the text once and save it in a reusable format called a Quick Part. You can save images for reuse as well; see the section, "Repeating the Same Stuff Over and Over," for help.

Creating a signature

To create a signature, start out in a message and then do the following:

1. **Choose Message⇨Include⇨Signature⇨Signatures.**

   The Signatures and Stationery dialog box appears, as shown in Figure 4-1.

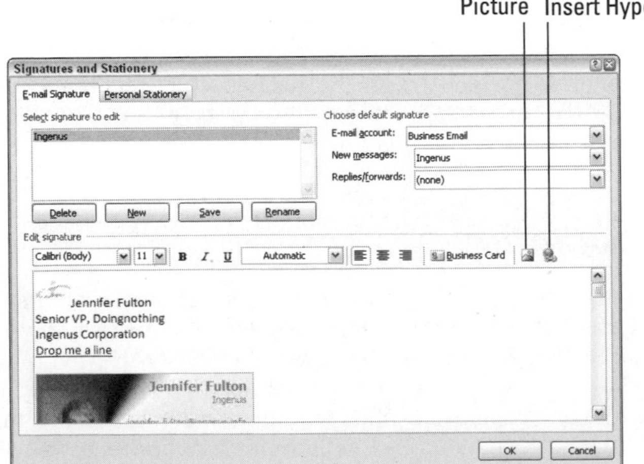

Figure 4-1: Create your own signature e-mails!

2. **Click the E-Mail Signature tab and click the New button.**

   The New Signature dialog box pops up.

3. **Type a name for the new signature and click OK.**

4. **Type your signature text.**

   In the Edit Signature text box, type the text you want to reuse in your e-mails. Use the formatting tools just above this box to format the text so it's nice and pretty. For example, change the font, font size, or color.

5. **Add a business card if you want.**

   Assuming you've created an electronic business card for yourself (see Book V, Chapter 3), you can insert that card in your signature. Recipients can use the card to create a contact record for you in their Contacts list.

   Here's how you can include the business card:

   a. *Click the Business Card button located just above the Edit Signature text box.*

      The Insert Business Card dialog box appears as shown in Figure 4-2.

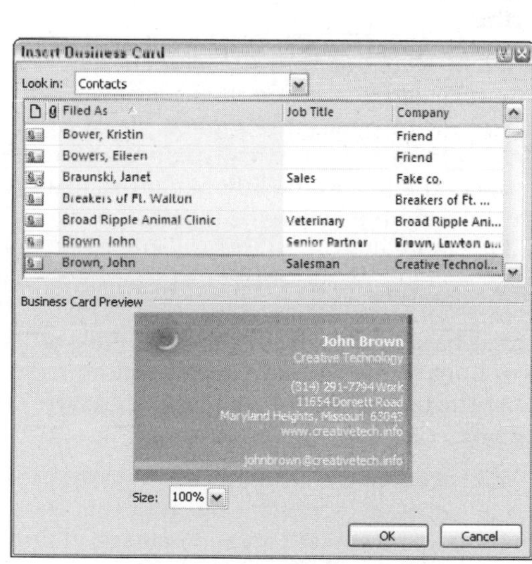

Figure 4-2: Add your card to the signature.

   b. *Scroll through the list and select the contact whose card you want to use. (Uh, that would be you.)*

      A preview of the card appears in actual size.

   c. *If you want, choose a different size from the Size list to make the card appear in your e-mail at less than 100 percent of its normal size. Click OK.*

      The card appears in the Edit Signature box, along with the text you typed in Step 4.

6. **Add a picture if desired.**

   a. *Back in the Signatures and Stationery dialog box, click at the spot in the Edit Signature text box where you want the picture to go.*

   b. *Click the Picture button (located to the right of the Business Card button), select the image to insert, and click Insert.*

      Surprisingly, you don't have to limit yourself to only Web-friendly graphics: JPEG, GIF, and PNG.

   You don't have any tools in the Edit Signature dialog box for resizing or correcting the image you choose, so use a graphics editor to make any adjustments prior to inserting the image. Also, you can't change how text wraps around the image, but you can make that small adjustment after the signature is inserted in a message, if you wish. See Book II, Chapter 3 for help.

7. **Insert any hyperlinks.**

   You might insert a hyperlink to a Web site, a document in a shared folder, or to your e-mail address. When the user clicks the link, one of three things happens: (s)he opens a Web page, views a document, or creates a new message that's automatically addressed to you. To create a hyperlink, you select the text in the Edit Signature text box that you want to use as the link and then click the Insert Hyperlink button. See Book II, Chapter 3 for more help.

8. **Set options for the signature.**

   Now that you have a basic signature, you need to tell Outlook when to use it by setting options in the Choose Default Signature section, which you'll find sitting in the upper-left corner of the Signatures and Stationery dialog box.

   First, select an e-mail account from the E-Mail Account list. You might have only one e-mail account, in which case, hey, this choice is pretty easy. (For information on how to set up and manage multiple e-mail accounts in Outlook, see Book III, Chapter 5.)

   After choosing the e-mail account with which you want to associate the new signature, choose how and when you want the signature added to outgoing e-mails for the chosen account.

   - *To attach a signature automatically to all new messages* generated by the e-mail account that you selected earlier, choose the signature to use from the New Messages list. If you don't want to add a signature to all new e-mails from this account, choose `<none>`.

- *To attach a signature automatically to replies and forwarded messages* sent from the account you chose earlier, select the signature to use from the Replies/Forwards list. Again, if you don't want to add a signature when sending replies or forwarding messages from this account, choose `<none>`.

9. **Click OK to save the signature.**

Well, now that you have a signature, you might as well use it. Jump to the next section to find out how.

Adding the signature to e-mail messages

After you've created a signature or two, you can add them to e-mail messages. You have two choices: You can add your signature yourself to each message, or you can tell Outlook to add your signature for you to all messages.

✦ **Manually add a signature to a message:** Click in the message where you want the signature to appear and then choose Message⇨Include⇨Signature. Choose a signature from those listed. The signature instantly appears within your message, as shown in Figure 4-3.

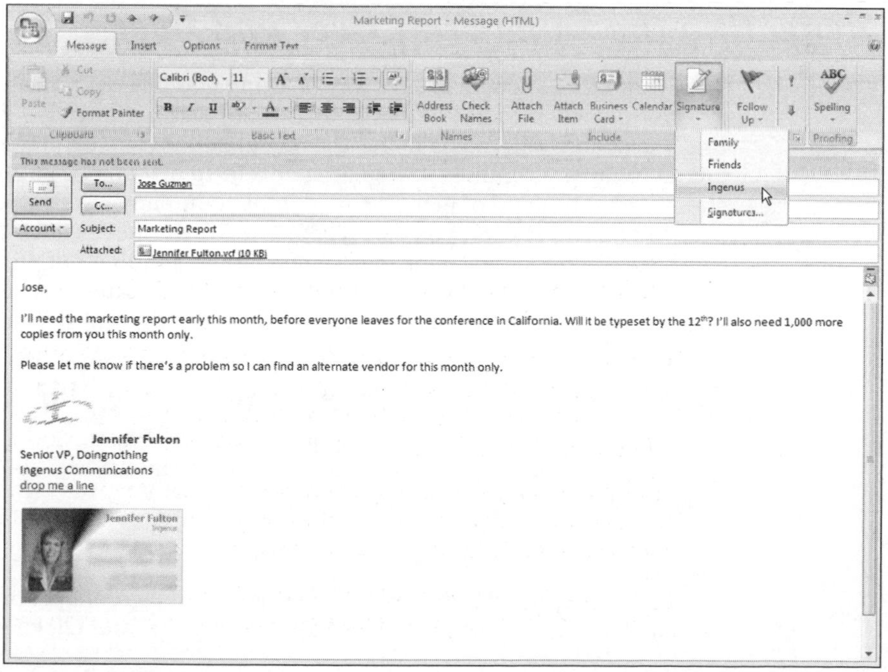

Figure 4-3: Add your John Hancock.

✦ **Have Outlook automatically add a signature to messages:** Use the options that appear in the Edit Signature dialog box, as explained in the previous section. If you select to automatically add a signature to new messages or to your replies/forwards, that change won't happen until the next e-mail you send. For example, if you just created a new signature and designated that it should be added to all new messages, that signature is added to the next new message you create (not the current message).

If you've added formatting to signature text and you insert the signature into a plain text message, you keep the signature text but lose the formatting. Other things get dropped if you insert a signature into a plain text message, including images, hyperlinks, and business cards. The business card still appears as an attachment, but it just isn't included in the message itself. So, when using signatures, it's best to use HTML or RTF format for your messages. See Book II, Chapter 1 for more information on message formats.

I've shown you how to add signatures, but what if you want to remove one for a single message? Well, after a signature's been inserted into a message, it's just like any other text and/or graphic. That means you can edit it, remove stuff you don't want to send this time (like your phone number or address). To remove text, drag your cursor over it to select the text and then press Delete. To remove an image or a business card, click it and then press Delete.

Repeating the Same Stuff Over and Over

With Quick Parts, you can save any ol' thing you use over and over, and insert it quickly into any Outlook item — not just messages — although that's probably where you'll find the most use for this feature. For example, if your company requires you to include a little disclaimer or confidentiality statement at the end of e-mails that contain company information and are sent to non-employees, you can type the text just once, select it, and save that text as a reusable Quick Part. When you're sending out an e-mail that contains company info, you can quickly insert the statement. If you're just swapping recipes with your sister, you can leave out the statement.

Saving reusable text and images as a Quick Part

Quick Parts can include images, hyperlinks, text, shapes, and anything else you might ordinarily use in an item. To create a Quick Part, open any item that contains the content you want to save.

1. **Select the reusable content.**

   To select text, just drag over it. To select an image, shape, or other object, click it. Select multiple objects by pressing Ctrl and clicking each one.

2. **Choose Insert➪Text➪Quick Parts➪Save Selection to Quick Part Gallery.**

   The Create New Building Block dialog box appears, as shown here in Figure 4-4.

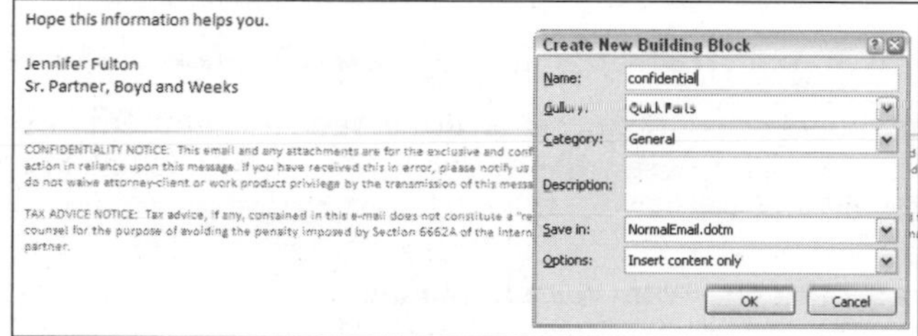

Figure 4-4: Why type the same stuff over and over?

3. **Type a name for the Quick Part.**
4. **Select a category.**

   You can save the Quick Part in the General category, or you can create a different category in which to store it. For example, if you use a series of different texts to explain company policies to new employees, you can save each text as a Quick Part in a category called New Employees. Then later, when you're searching for some text you normally send to new employees, you can look under the New Employees category.

   Here's how you can create a category:

   a. *Select Create New Category from the Category list.*

   b. *Type a Name for the new category and click OK.*

5. **Type a description.**

   Your description should be something that helps you remember what it contains and why you might reuse the Quick Part.

6. **(Optional) Choose a place to save the Quick Part.**

   From the Save In drop-down list, you can select a template in which to save the Quick Part. Normally, all new messages are created based on a simple, generic message template called `NormalEmail.dotm`. You can design your own templates to make it easy to create messages with a custom look. If you do, you might want to save your Quick Parts in specific templates so that you can use them within the items you create using those templates. If you want to know how to create a template, see the upcoming section, "Using a template to create a reusable message."

7. **Select an insert option.**

   From the Options list, select the way you want the Quick Part to be inserted when it's used. You can have the contents inserted at the cursor, within its own paragraph, or on its own page.

8. **Click OK to save the Quick Part.**

Inserting a Quick Part into an Outlook item

Now that you've created and saved some reusable content, it's time to put this baby in drive and see what it can do. To insert a Quick Part into any Outlook item:

1. **Click where you want the data to go.**

   In a message, you can pretty much click anywhere; in other items, you can only insert Quick Part into the Notes section.

2. **Choose Insert⇨Text⇨Quick Parts.**

3. **Select the Quick Part.**

   A gallery of saved Quick Parts appears, organized by category; just click one and it magically appears within your Outlook item. Pretty painless.

To make changes to a Quick Part, right-click it in the gallery and choose Edit Properties from the menu that appears. To get rid of a Quick Part, right-click it and choose Organize and Delete from the shortcut menu. In the Organizer dialog box, select the Quick Part you want to delete and click Delete.

Using a Template to Create a Reusable Message

As a parent, it seems that I'm always repeating myself. Too bad I can't save what I'm always saying and then resend it to my kid whenever necessary. Actually, I suppose I could do that, but she's only three and doesn't have an e-mail address yet. I guess Outlook can't solve every problem.

If you find yourself repeating the same thing in several messages, you can save it in a template that you can use to repeat yourself as often as you like. You can save repeatable content in other ways, but with a template, you can save not only text, but formatting, graphics, and anything else that happens to be in the message.

Here's how to create a template for e-mail:

1. **Start with a new message.**

   If you want to start your template out with some style, use Outlook stationery. (See Book II, Chapter 3 for help.)

Well, okay, if you have an old message you want to use as a template, you can start there, too, by simply opening it and then making whatever changes you want before saving the message as a template. Just double-click the message you sent to open it, then choose Message⇨Actions⇨Other Actions⇨Edit Message to make the message editable so you can make changes.

If you want to save the message as a template without making changes, then skip the Edit Message part and simply open the message and continue to Step 2.

2. **Add the reusable text.**

   Don't add anything you wouldn't use in each version of this kind of message. Add graphics, formatting, a subject line, whatever. Apply a theme or colorize the background. Go all out because, hey, you only have to do this once! (See Figure 4-5.)

If you find yourself stuck for words, why not turn to the word expert, Microsoft Word? There you'll find a plethora of templates with text, designed to help you compose letters, memos, and the like, for specific situations such as a rent increase, approving customer credit, collecting an overdue amount, and sales and marketing offers. After using a Word template to generate the reusable text you want for e-mail, just select and copy it to an Outlook message.

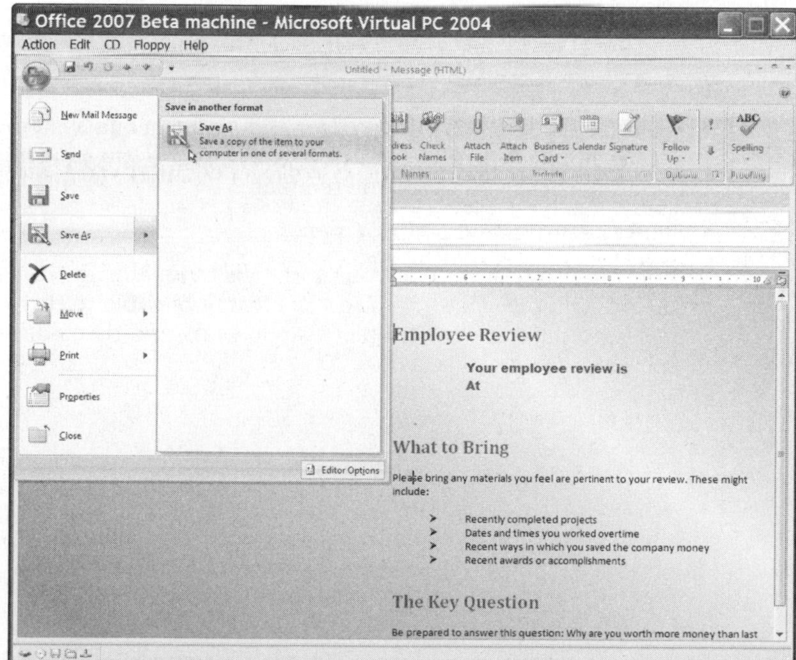

Figure 4-5: Create a reusable message.

3. **Click the Microsoft Office button and choose Save As⇨Save As.**
4. **In the Save As dialog box that appears, type a name for the message template in the File Name box, such as** New Product Release. **Choose Outlook Template (*oft) from the Save As Type list. Click OK.**

To use the template to create a message, follow these steps:

1. **Choose File⇨New⇨Choose Form.**

   The Choose Form dialog box appears, as shown in Figure 4-6.

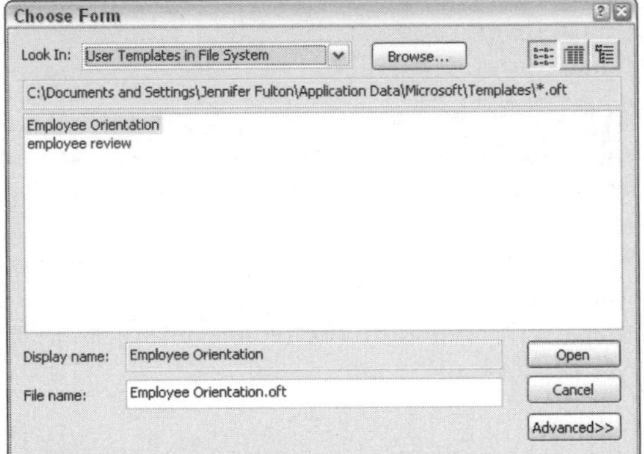

Figure 4-6: Find your template.

2. **Find your templates.**

   From the Look In list, choose User Templates in File System. Your templates should appear in the list; if not, click Browse and travel to the folder in which you saved the template.
3. **Select a template and click Open.**

   A new message, based on your gorgeous template, appears in a message form. You know what to do; add the text applicable to this version of the message, make any other changes you want, and then address and send the message on.

Book III

Über E-Mail

"Hold on, Barbara. Let me launch Outlook and see if I can find a newsgroup on this."

Contents at a Glance

Chapter 1: Controlling the Sending and Receiving of Messages 173

Chapter 2: When You Have to Know Now: Instant Messaging..189

Chapter 3: Getting the Latest News Delivered Right to Your Inbox 195

Chapter 4: Sending Mass Mailings 205

Chapter 5: Managing Multiple E-Mail Accounts 213

Chapter 1: Controlling the Sending and Receiving of Messages

In This Chapter

- **Finding out whether someone actually reads your e-mails**
- **Conducting a poll via e-mail**
- **Delaying messages until you're ready to send them**
- **Recalling and replacing a message**
- **Stopping a long e-mail download**

By now you're probably feeling pretty confident about using e-mail, and rightly so. E-mail in and of itself is not a terribly complicated affair, although it can be. For example, you may have started a new job, and now you have to e-mail everyone in several departments about an upcoming meeting you're hosting. You've managed to gather all the addresses you need, but even though you're new, you're already aware of how many e-mails people get each day. How will you know everyone got the e-mail and read it? Can you make sure they see your e-mail as important and not just ignore it? Can you delay delivery of the message until you get the exact meeting location and other details nailed down? Can you discover who's been stealing your lunch out of the refrigerator?

You'll probably never get to sleep worrying about all the things that could go wrong with a simple e-mail. Well, because you'll be up anyway, I invite you to read this chapter because all these questions and more are answered for you right here.

How Can I Tell If You Read This?

Sometimes, after you send an e-mail message, you find yourself checking the Inbox frequently, wondering when you'll get a response. After a few hours of this nonsense, you may even find yourself wondering if the recipient got the e-mail at all. Well, there's no reason why you need to sit there and worry that your e-mail dropped into the Twilight Zone. Instead, you can flag important messages so that they won't be so easily ignored by their recipients. You can also track when messages have been successfully delivered, and when they've been opened and read.

Making what you send look really important

Tired of having e-mail ignored? Worried that your message will land in the Inbox with hundreds of other messages, in a hopeless battle to be read? You can easily make an important message stand out by flagging it as such, prior to sending it off. In addition to a flag, you can add a reminder that will appear above the message text on the message's InfoBar, reminding recipients to take action.

To add a flag and a reminder to an outgoing message, follow these steps:

1. **Choose Message⇨Options⇨Follow Up⇨Flag for Recipients.**

   The Custom dialog box pops up, with the Flag for Recipients check box already selected, as shown in Figure 1-1.

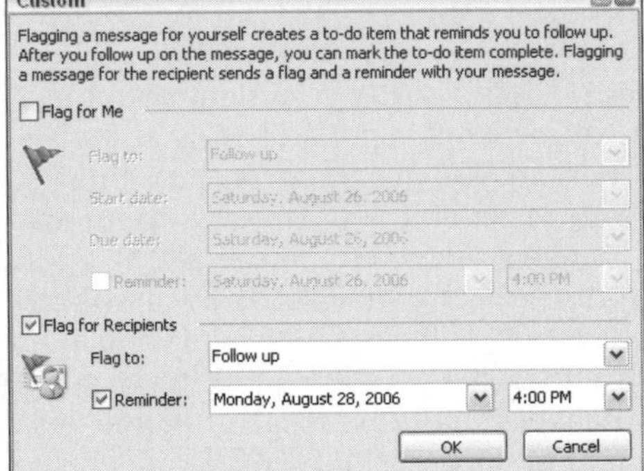

Figure 1-1: Add a reminder to an outgoing message.

2. **Select a flag.**

   From the Flag To list, select the type of flag you want to use, such as Follow-up or No Response Necessary. You can also replace the text by typing something more specific of your own.

3. **Set a reminder date and time.**

   You don't have to add a reminder to the message, but if you want to, select the Reminder check box and set a date and time for the reminder to go off. Click OK to close the dialog box, finish your message, and then click Send to send it along.

Because a message that's flagged only for the recipient shows up as any ol' message in your Sent folder, you may want to flag the message for yourself as well, if for no other reason than to make it easier to locate it again should you ever need to. See the next section for help.

Using your time zone as a basis, the reminder time you select is adjusted accordingly after the message arrives at its destination. For example, if you live in the Eastern time zone and you choose 2:00 p.m., then the time is adjusted to 1:00 p.m. when the message arrives in the mailbox of someone in the Central time zone.

When the recipient gets a message from you that's been flagged, the flag appears in Outlook next to the message header, as shown in Figure 1-2. Notice that in the InfoBar for the message, the reader can view the text of the flag (in this case, the words, Follow up) and the date and time of the reminder (assuming you set one). Notice also that a recipient flag doesn't create a To-Do item on that person's To-Do bar. If you did indeed set a reminder, then at the appropriate time, the message header changes from its ordinary black text, to a much more urgent red text. No, a reminder window doesn't appear, and a buzzer doesn't go off. Hopefully this gentle red nudge is all that's needed to spur your recipient into action. (If not, a club that pops out of the screen and hits the recipient over the head is available for a small additional fee.)

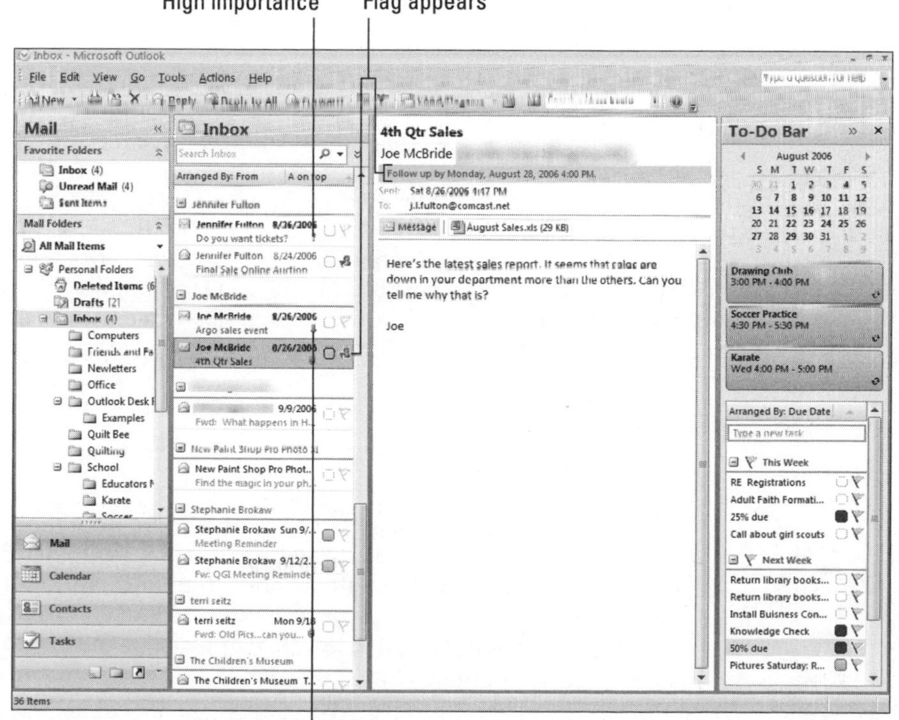

Figure 1-2: You can flag messages you send to other people so they act on them.

Another way in which you can make your messages look important to a recipient is to simply mark them that way. Messages marked as important appear with an exclamation icon next to them (refer to Figure 1-2). To send a message and mark it as important, just choose Message⇨Options⇨High Importance. When you turn on the High Importance flag for a message, it's highlighted on the Ribbon so you can easily see if you've set the flag or not, as shown in Figure 1-3. If you want to let your boss know that this message contains a routine report that she can safely put off reading until later, click the Low Importance button instead. Low importance messages appear in the Inbox with a down arrow next to them (refer to Figure 1-2).

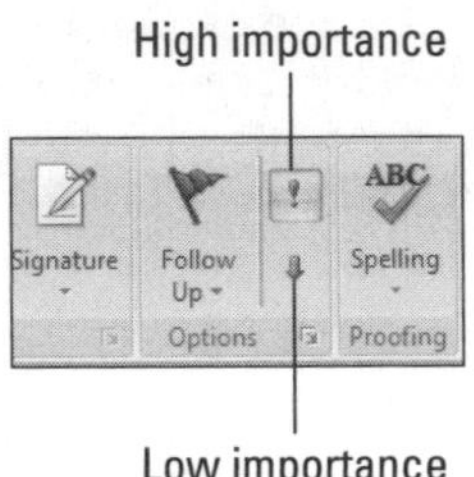

Figure 1-3: The High Importance button makes an outgoing e-mail look urgent.

Flagging messages for yourself

If you're sending a message that corresponds with something you need to do, you can flag it before you send it, so that it creates a To-Do item in the To-Do bar. If your list of things to do is long, you may want to set a reminder that makes a lot of noise until you remember to do that something. For example, if you're sending a reply that promises your boss you'll pick up an important client at the airport tomorrow, you may want to flag the message and create a reminder so you don't accidentally leave the client feeling terminal at the terminal. Follow these steps:

1. **Choose Message⇨Options⇨Follow Up⇨Custom.**

   The Custom dialog box, shown in Figure 1-4, appears, with the option, Flag for Me, already set.

   If all you want to set is a flag that creates a To-Do item (and not a flag and a reminder), just choose a flag from the Follow Up list, such as Tomorrow. If the message contains important information that you don't want to lose, but nothing you need to do, you can choose No Date from the Follow Up list to set a flag that still appears in the To-Do bar, but without a date that bugs you. Then see Book VI, Chapter 1 for ways to deal with all these flags you keep setting!

2. **Select flag type.**

   Choose the type of flag you want from the Flag To list, such as Read or Reply.

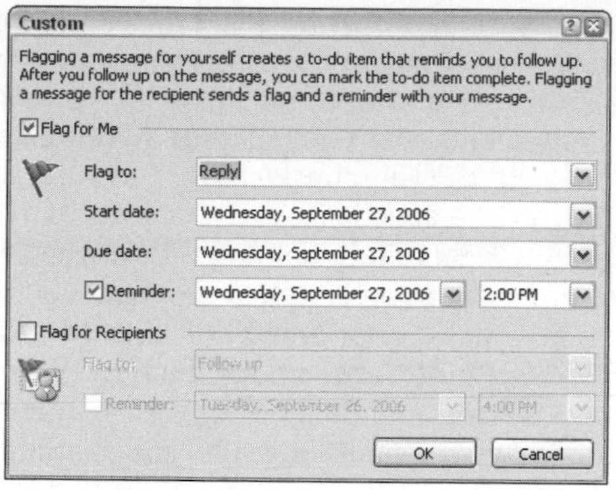

Figure 1-4: Flag me.

3. Set a date.

Choose a Start Date and a Due Date for the task. If you're planning on starting and finishing the task on the same day, you can use the same date for both.

4. Set a reminder, if you want.

Wanna have Outlook buzz you when this is due? Then set a reminder by selecting Reminder, and choosing a date and time when you want to be clubbed over the head. Click Close, and the details of the flag you just set appear in the message's InfoBar. Finish the e-mail and click Send to send it. The subject for the message is used to create a To-Do item, which appears on the To-Do bar under its due date.

Tracking when messages are delivered and read

Have you ever wasted time checking e-mail every five minutes wondering why you haven't gotten a response to an urgent message? Well, wonder no more. Outlook provides a simple way in which you can find out if a particular message got to its intended destination, and if your recipient has opened and read that message:

- ✦ To track when a message gets delivered, choose Options⇨Tracking⇨Request a Delivery Receipt in an open e-mail form.
- ✦ To track when a message is read, choose Options⇨Tracking⇨Request a Read Receipt. You can turn on both the delivery and read options for a message, if you like.

Assuming that you choose both options, after your message is delivered, an e-mail is sent back to you to let you know that it got there. After the message is opened, another e-mail is sent, as well.

No system is perfect, however. Before the outgoing messages are sent from the recipient's system, he or she is asked if Outlook can generate the delivery or read receipts. If the recipient refuses permission, Outlook doesn't create the outgoing messages, and you may still end up not knowing if your message got there or not.

If you need to, you can quickly scan your incoming mail to see if you've gotten a delivery or a read receipt. Just open the original message you sent (it's in the Sent Items folder), and choose Message⇨Show⇨Tracking. (The Tracking button doesn't show up on the Ribbon until you actually get a read or a delivery receipt, so if the button is not there, then either your recipient didn't get your message or blocked his or her e-mail program from sending a response.)

Wanna automate the process of dealing with delivery and read receipts? Then choose Tools⇨Options⇨Preferences⇨E-Mail Options⇨Tracking Options, and after all that effort, the Tracking Options dialog box appears. (See Figure 1-5.) Select the options you want:

Figure 1-5: Set options to control how Outlook tracks your outgoing messages.

- **To automatically delete receipts after you get them,** choose Process Receipts on Arrival.
- **To move receipts to some other folder after you read them,** choose After Processing, Move Receipts To, and then select a folder.
- **To add a read and/or delivery receipt for all messages you send,** choose Read Receipt and/or Delivery Receipt.
- **To automatically send a read receipt when it's requested,** choose Always Send a Response. If you never want to send a receipt, choose Never Send a Response.

After selecting whatever options you want to use to automatically track outgoing messages, click OK a bunch of times to close all those dialog boxes.

Getting Out the Vote

Voting is one of the most important rights granted to a democratic society. After voting, people can leave the voting booth knowing that their voices are being heard and that their opinions matter, even though the government will just do what it wants anyway. With Outlook, you can gather opinions from coworkers and automatically tally their votes (and then do what *you* want anyway).

The Voting feature can only be used with Microsoft Exchange, which is typically supported by corporations and not home systems.

To use Outlook to ask for a vote, follow these steps:

1. **Choose Options⇨Tracking⇨Use Voting Buttons.**
2. **Select a button type.**

   Choose a button type from those listed on the menu, such as Yes;No. If you choose Custom, you can create your own button types. For example, you can create buttons marked The Palomino, La Hacienda, and Saturn Grill if you're asking recipients to choose a restaurant for the quarterly staff meeting. When you click Custom, the Message Options dialog box rears its head, as shown in Figure 1-6. Replace the text in the Use Voting Buttons box with the button text you want to use, such as **The Palomino; La Hacienda; Saturn Grill**. Notice that button names are separated by a semicolon. Click Close to get rid of the dialog box and return to your message form.

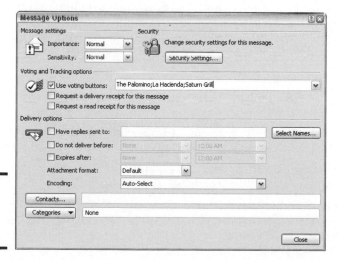

Figure 1-6: Setting up the voting "booth."

After your special voting message is received, the recipient simply needs to click the message's InfoBar, as shown in Figure 1-7, to display the menu of voting options. After making a choice from the list, a dialog box appears, asking the recipient whether it's okay to send the response now. She can choose instead to edit the response first, which she might do if she wants to add a comment or explain her choice.

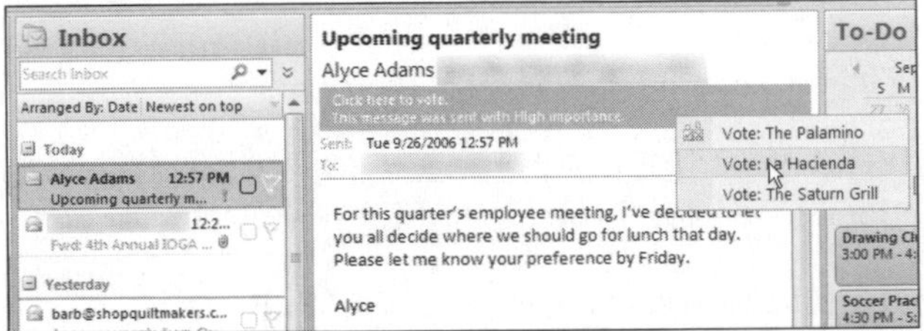

Figure 1-7: Click the InfoBar to cast your vote.

The recipient can also cast a vote by opening the message and choosing Message➪Respond➪Vote.

After several people have exercised their civil right to have their choices ignored by you, you start getting e-mail responses in your Inbox. To tally the votes, you can simply look at each individual response (the user's choice appears in the InfoBar of the response message) and add the votes manually, or you can use your computer (imagine that!) to tally them up for you. Open the original voting message (you find it lurking in the Sent folder), and choose Message➪Show➪Tracking. The names of the people to whom you sent a voting message appear in a list; their responses appear in the Response column. (See Figure 1-8.) The Response column is blank for people who haven't responded yet. Voting totals appear in the InfoBar.

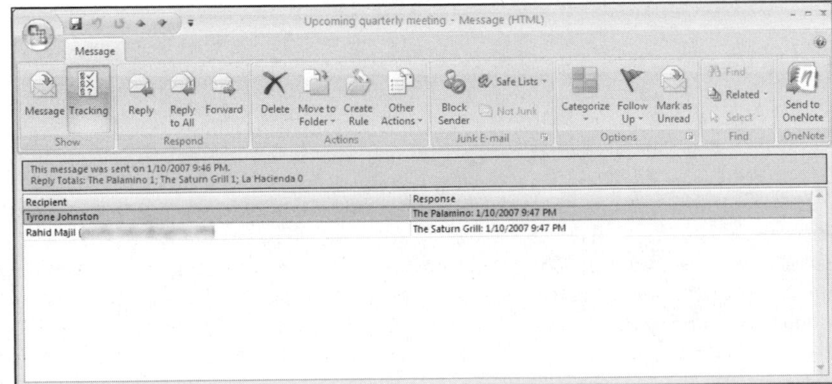

Figure 1-8: Tally the votes.

You can select and copy the voting response list and paste it into an Excel worksheet if you need to play with the totals a bit more. For example, you can analyze responses by department or office location by adding department/office data to the list and then sorting it.

Just like the reading and delivery receipts I talk about in the last section, you can't have all those voting receipts cluttering up your Inbox. To have Outlook handle those receipts automatically, choose Tools⇨Options⇨Preferences⇨E-Mail Options⇨Tracking Options. The Tracking Options dialog box appears. (Refer to Figure 1-5.) Select the options you want:

- **To automatically record the voting responses in the original message,** select Process Requests and Responses on Arrival.
- **To move receipts to some other folder after you read them,** select After Processing, Move Receipts To, and then select a folder. If you want receipts automatically deleted, you can leave the folder set to the default, which is the Deleted Items folder.
- **To delete blank voting responses (responses that do not contain any additional comments),** select Delete Blank Voting and Meeting Responses After Processing.

Controlling Message Delivery

One of the best reasons for using Outlook is that it puts you in complete control over your e-mail. Wanna hold messages until the end of the day because sending them over your dialup connection ties up your computer? Can do. Wanna set messages to expire after their content no longer applies? No problemo. Wanna take back what you said and say something else? No worries, be happy. Wanna change that annoying sound that alerts you to new mail? No big deal.

Yes you can, sort of!

If you're not an Exchange student (a user of Outlook on an Exchange network), then you can't really delay the delivery of a single message. You can, however, use Outlook to create a rule that does that for you. Rules and their creation are discussed in detail in Book IX, Chapter 2, but I'll give you a hint here so you'll know how to set the rule up right. To create a rule that delays delivery of all messages, apply the rule so that messages are checked by Outlook after sending (after you click Send), then choose the Defer Delivery by a Number of Minutes action. You can delay delivery for up to 2 hours (120 minutes) after you click Send.

Delaying when messages are sent

Sometimes you just can't gather all the information you need to put into a message at the time you're thinking about sending it. If you've already created a message, only to realize that you can't really let everyone know about Brad's new promotion just yet, you don't have to scrap the message. And you don't have to save it to the Drafts folder and hope you remember to send it later. Instead, you can just delay sending it.

If you use Outlook on a corporate Exchange server, then to delay the delivery of a single message, choose Options➪More Options➪Delay Delivery. The Message Option dialog box appears, as shown in Figure 1-9. Because the Do Not Deliver Before check box is already selected, all you have to do is enter the date and time you want the message to be delivered and click Close. The Delay Delivery button is highlighted on the Ribbon, not just because it looks cool that way, but to remind you that you've chosen to delay delivery of this message, and thus Outlook won't do anything with it when you click Send.

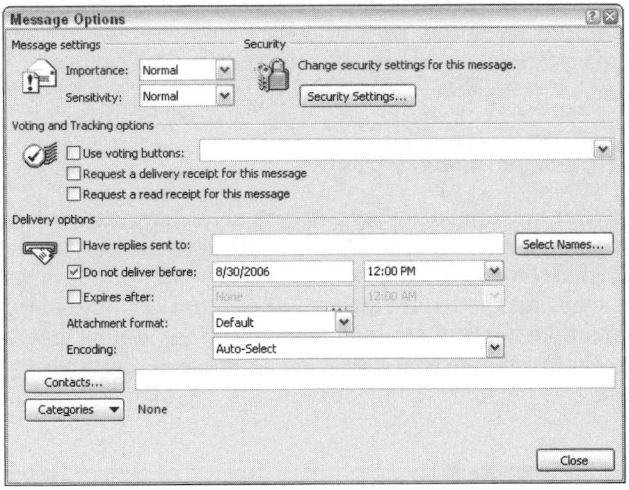

Figure 1-9: Choose when you want e-mail delivered.

Setting messages to expire after a certain date

Lots of things expire — driver's licenses, coupons, milk. After something expires, you have to first notice that it has expired (Sorry, officer, I forgot my birthday was this month, honest!), and then throw it away and get a new one. Well, messages can expire too — for example, you might receive a voting message that must be replied to by Friday. When a message expires, nothing particularly bad happens; the message header simply changes to strikethrough text. The message itself is not deleted and can still be read. Message expiration just makes it a bit more evident to your reader that he or she has missed the boat.

To set a message to expire, follow these steps:

1. **Choose Options⇨More Options⇨Message Options dialog box launcher.**

   The launcher, by the way, is that right arrow thingie located at the right end of the More Options group.

   The Message Options dialog box appears, as shown in Figure 1-10.

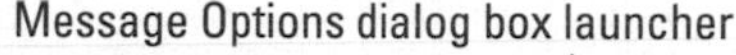

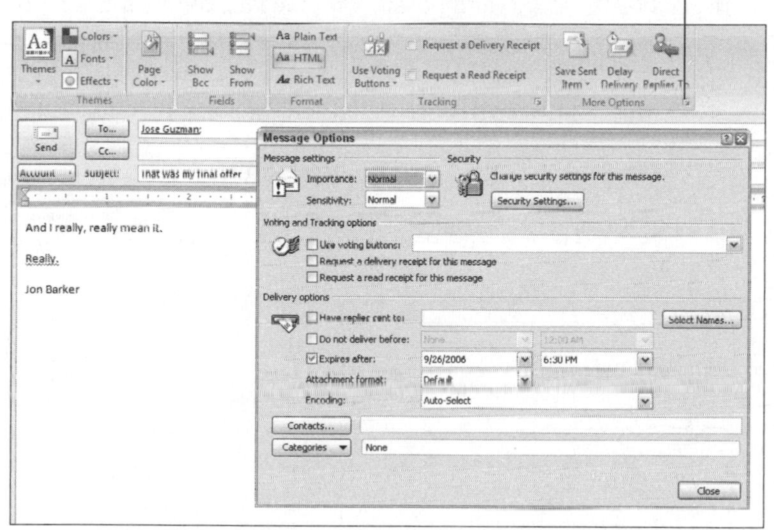

Figure 1-10: Even messages can expire.

2. **Set an expiration date.**

   Select the Expires After check box, then choose a date and time for the message to expire. Click Close to return to the message form.

Recalling and replacing messages

Have you ever sat there after clicking Send, watching as a message is being prepared and sent, and then realized, "Oops, I shouldn't have sent that!" or "Darn, I forgot to attach the file and now I'm going to look like I shouldn't have refused that fourth cup of coffee this morning." Well, if you e-mail through a Microsoft Exchange network, then lucky you, because Outlook provides a way in which you can take your words back — literally.

In order for Outlook to recall or replace an e-mail message, both you and your recipient must use a Microsoft Exchange network. How you will know whether or not your recipient uses Exchange, I haven't a clue, so my advice is to simply attempt to recall or replace messages as needed, and then see if it works. One thing I can tell you, and that's that home e-mail addresses typically don't use Microsoft Exchange. Exchange is mostly used only by large corporations and universities to handle e-mail.

When it becomes necessary to chase down an e-mail message and stop it at the door, Outlook provides you with two choices: You can recall the message, which essentially deletes it from the server so that it's not actually delivered or you can replace the message, which removes the original e-mail from the server and replaces it with the new one.

To recall a message (and possibly replace it), follow these steps:

1. **Open the message you sent.**

   Change to the Sent Items folder and double-click the message you want to recall.

2. **Choose Message⇨Actions⇨Other Actions⇨Recall This Message.**

   The Recall This Message dialog box appears (see Figure 1-11).

Figure 1-11: This you can recall.

3. **Select a delete option.**

   To simply recall the message and not replace it, select Delete Unread Copies of This Message. To recall the message and replace its text or add attachments, select Delete Unread Copies and Replace with a New Message.

4. **Ask to be notified.**

   If you want to know if the recall works or not, make sure the Tell Me if Recall Succeeds or Fails for Each Recipient check box is also selected. However, if you're recalling a message sent to everyone in your company, then you might want to turn this option *off* and avoid flooding your Inbox with thousands of return receipts.

   Click OK to close the dialog box, and the message is automatically recalled. If you are replacing the message, make changes as needed to the copy of the message that appears, and then click Send.

If the recall fails, you can always resend the message (with changes), and beg the recipient to ignore the original transmission. See Book II, Chapter 2 for info.

Changing how Outlook tells you e-mail has arrived

When a new message arrives, Outlook lets you know by sounding its "You've got mail!" chime, and briefly displaying the e-mail's header on the Windows taskbar. If you get a lot of e-mail (and who doesn't nowadays?) it's easy to become immune to the constant chiming of the Outlook postman. If you need something really annoying to draw your attention (or something less annoying so you can ignore all those messages and get some work done), why not change the sound Outlook plays on message arrival?

For this one, you have to exit Outlook and have a suitable `.wav` file prepared. After exiting Outlook, open the Control Panel and double-click the Sounds and Audio Devices icon to open the Sounds and Audio Device Properties dialog box (see Figure 1-12). Click the Sounds tab, and select New Mail Notification in the Program Events area. Click Browse, select a `.wav` file, and click OK. As soon as new mail arrives in Outlook, the new sound you choose plays.

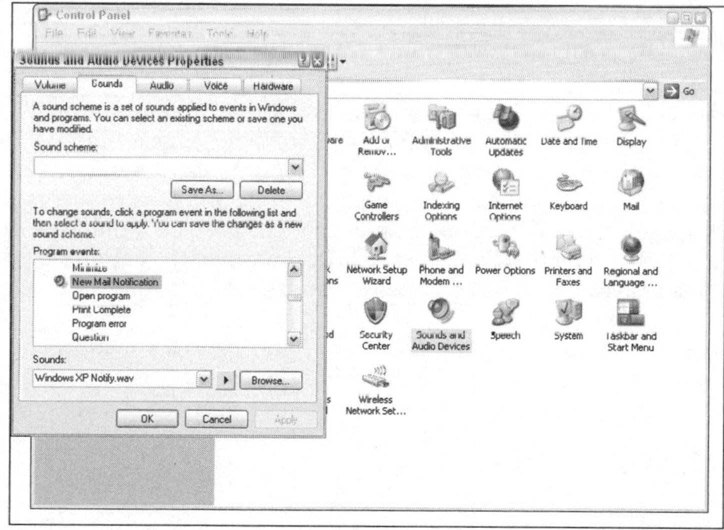

Figure 1-12: Change how Outlook sounds.

To turn off the sound alerts completely, choose Tools➪Options➪Preferences➪E-Mail Options➪Advanced E-Mail Options. The Advanced E-Mail Options dialog box appears, as shown in Figure 1-13. Disable the Play a Sound option in the When New Items Arrive in My Inbox section to turn off the sound alerts. Notice that in that section, you can also disable the mouse wiggle, and prevent the envelope icon from crowding your Windows system tray when new mail comes in. While we're on the topic, you can remove the Outlook icon from the system tray as well, and only permit its presence when new mail arrives. See Book I, Chapter 1 for more info.

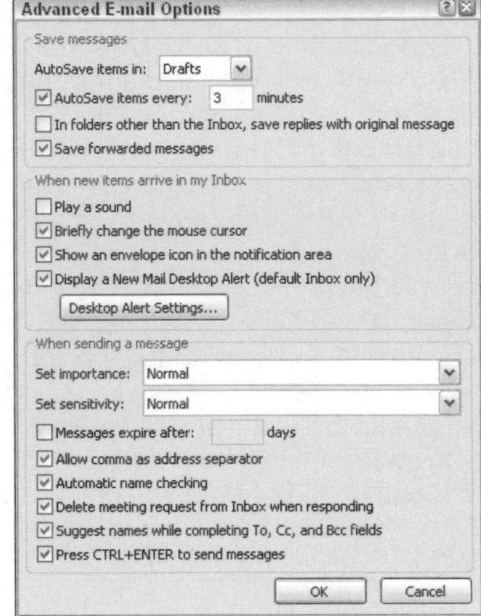

Figure 1-13: Control how Outlook tells you e-mail is "in the house."

Another way in which Outlook lets you know "You've got mail!" is through its Desktop Alerts — the quick flash of e-mail message on the Windows taskbar as it arrives in the Inbox, as shown in Figure 1-14. A similar alert occurs to let you know when you have incoming meeting and task requests. If several messages arrive at the same time, chances are you'll only see one or two message summaries. In any case, if you happen to "catch the flash" for a particular message, click it to open the message (or request).

The alerts go by real quick, so don't be surprised if you miss one. If you need more than a second to decide whether the message is important enough to read right now, just hold the mouse pointer over the alert to keep it on-screen.

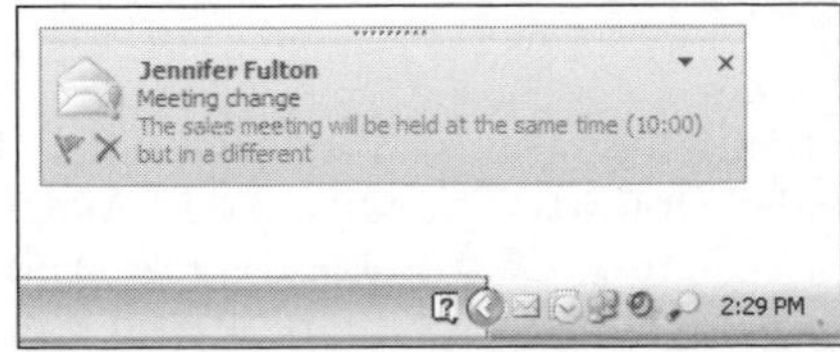

Figure 1-14: Summaries of incoming messages appear on the taskbar as they arrive.

If you're just too busy to deal with incoming e-mail, you can still process it with a single click. To flag the message without opening it, click the flag icon that appears on the alert. To delete the message without opening it, click the Delete icon (the X in the lower-left corner of the alert).

Desktop Alerts only notify you of e-mail incoming to Exchange or POP3 accounts. In addition, the alerts only appear for e-mail coming into your default Inbox, and not some other folder. You can, however, set up a rule to alert you of messages incoming to other folders, or meeting other conditions such as "sent by my boss." If you use an IMAP account, you can get alerts too; just set up a rule that handles that condition. See Book IX, Chapter 2, for more information on setting up rules.

To turn alerts on or off, or change their appearance to suit your style, follow these steps:

1. **Choose Tools⇨Options.**

   The Options dialog box appears.

2. **Choose Preferences⇨E-Mail Options⇨Advanced E-Mail Options.**

   The Advanced E-Mail Options dialog box appears (refer to Figure 1-13).

3. **Turn alerts on or off.**

   To display Desktop Alerts, select the Display a New Mail Desktop Alert option. To turn them off, disable the option.

4. **Click the Desktop Alert Settings button.**

   The Desktop Alert Settings dialog box appears, as shown in Figure 1-15.

5. **Adjust the amount of time the alerts appear on-screen by dragging the How Long Should the Desktop Alert Appear? slider.**

   You can make the alerts more or less transparent by dragging the How Transparent Should the Desktop Alert Be? slider. Click Preview to view your choices; click OK to accept them.

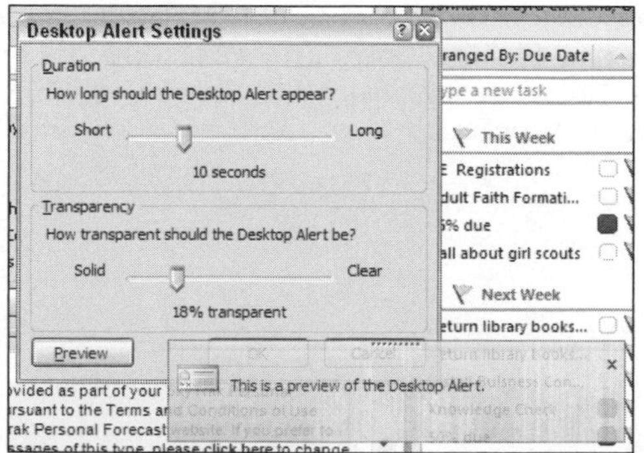

Figure 1-15: Test your new Desktop alert.

Stopping a Long E-Mail Download

Nothing is more interesting than watching the progress of an e-mail download, than possibly um, watching grass grow. So frankly, I don't bother to watch the progress of Outlook getting my mail from its electronic mailbox out in Cyberspace, even though it shows up right there on the Outlook status bar. But if you notice that it's taking an extra-ordinarily long time for Outlook to complete a particular Send/Receive, you may want to figure out why Outlook's acting so sluggish.

To view the progress of a Send/Receive, choose Tools⇨Send/Receive⇨Send/Receive Settings⇨Show Progress. The Send/Receive Progress box appears, as shown in Figure 1-16.

You can also display the Send/Receive Progress box by clicking the words *Send/Receive Status* on the Outlook status bar, and selecting Details.

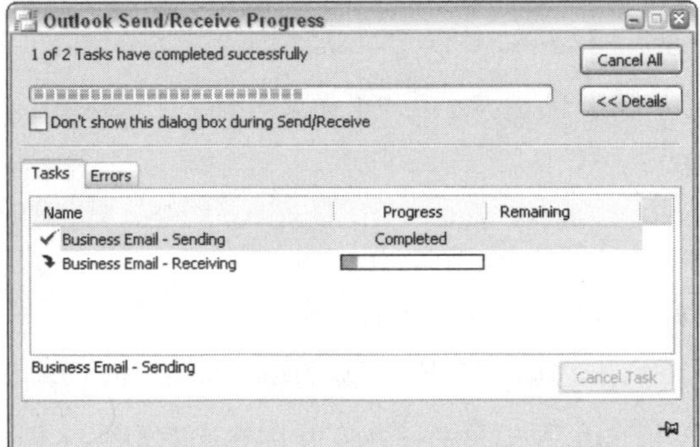

Figure 1-16: Now that's progress.

If you want to stop the download because maybe Outlook's stuck on a large file attachment, or maybe the mail server's stuck in some endless loop, click the Cancel All button.

You can always cancel a Send/Receive without first displaying the Send/Receive Progress box; just click the down arrow that appears on the status bar next to the words *Send/Receive Status,* and then select Cancel Send/Receive from the menu that pops up.

Chapter 2: When You Have to Know Now: Instant Messaging

In This Chapter

- **IMing someone when Outlook e-mail isn't fast enough**
- **Finding an IM service that Outlook likes**
- **Sending instant messages**
- **Keeping up with everybody's online status**

Sometimes it feels like e-mail is so old school. When you want to carry on a real back-and-forth conversation with someone, it can seem like forever as you wait for your e-mail to upload to the server and then be downloaded by your recipient and finally read. Wouldn't it be great if you had a way to communicate instantly — hear the other person's voice and judge her mood, share information, debate, confer, argue, and deliberate in real time? Besides using the telephone, I mean. (Talk about old school!)

Understanding the Magic

With instant messaging, you can communicate instantly — assuming the person you want to communicate with is also online and "receiving visitors." After someone "picks up" your call, you can exchange instant text messages and, depending on the instant messaging service you use, utilize real-time audio and video, file sharing, and remote help (a help desk situation where you can take over someone else's computer and guide him through a solution or simply fix a problem).

Outlook is basically about sending e-mail, but it can also send instant messages — in fact, Outlook enables you to "initiate" instant messages. It basically wakes up your instant message program. This is how it works: When you receive an e-mail from someone, Outlook alerts you that the person is also online (receiving visitors), so you can stop the e-mailing madness and talk live via instant messaging. Outlook lets you know the message sender is online by putting a green circle icon in front of his or her name in the message header, as shown in Figure 2-1. If you rest the mouse pointer over the name of any others who got this same message, you see their online status as well. Depending on the IM service you use, additional status icons you might see include a red dash (for Busy) and a pinkish circle (for Offline).

Figure 2-1: Is anybody there?

You must add a person to your instant-messaging contacts list before you can view her status. Adding someone basically entails knowing her IM address, or grabbing that address from an invitation to converse sent from her instant messaging program to you. You find out how to add people to your IM list in the section, "Sending an Instant Message."

Instant messaging is by no means secure, despite the attempts by many services to make it so. At this time, instant messaging is much less secure than regular e-mail, allowing any kind of content, whether malicious or not. In theory, using Windows Live Messenger, you should only receive messages from people you've added to your allow list, but a determined hacker could bypass that and send you messages anyway. To protect your privacy, keep the list of allowed IM contacts small, and do not view or respond to instant messages from people you know are not on your IM list. Also, when setting yourself up in your instant-messaging service, choose a user name that's not cute or famous like imapreetygirl or windsurferdude or donaldtrump, because hackers choose those at random to steal IM identities and send messages in your name.

Compatible IM Services

Lots of instant-messaging services out there offer pretty much the same things, but you should be aware of a few differences. For openers, does the service work with Outlook? If a particular instant messenger doesn't, you can certainly still use it, but you won't have the convenience of being able to check a person's online status while working in Outlook. These services (all Microsoft) are compatible with Outlook:

- **Microsoft Windows Live Messenger:** Allows you to chat via text and also talk and use live video. It also supports help-desk tasks such as taking over a computer. It supports communication with Yahoo! Messenger as well.

You can download Microsoft Windows Live Messenger from Microsoft's Web site: `http://ideas.live.com`. After installing, you supply an e-mail address and sign up for a Windows password (.NET Passport). A wizard leads you through all the steps, I promise. Note that the address you supply to Windows Live Messenger for login doesn't have to be a Microsoft e-mail address (hotmail, msn.com, live.com, or any others Microsoft may invent) — you can use any e-mail address you like, and it becomes your IM address channeled through Windows Live Messenger.

- **Microsoft Office Communicator:** Installed in some offices in order to connect Microsoft Windows Live Messenger with the phone service so that if you pick up your office phone, your status changes to Busy automatically.
- **Microsoft MSN Messenger:** Supports text chatting, live audio and video chatting, and help desk.
- **Microsoft Windows Messenger:** Included with Windows XP so you don't have to do much to set it up. It supports text chat, live audio and video chatting, and help desk. It also allows you to block certain users and to control who can add you to an online list of chatters.

Sending an Instant Message

To begin instant messaging, sign up for the same instant-messaging service used by the people you want to contact. How you sign up varies (obviously), but no money changes hands. If you want to sign up for Microsoft Windows Live Messenger, go to `ideas.live.com`. After downloading the instant messaging software, you install it and then create an IM address for yourself. After that, you just log in to the IM software to send instant messages within Outlook.

If you want to view the online status of other people but don't want to be bothered right now with instant messages, log in to your instant-messaging program and change your status to Busy.

After installing some instant-messaging software and creating your IM address, you're ready to add some contacts. Again, how you do that varies by instant messenger — but look for a button somewhere in the IM program called Add a Contact (or something similar). Adding contacts in your IM program allows you to send instant messages using that program and also to initiate instant messages within Outlook. You can, if you want, keep your IM addresses in Outlook as well, which might be handy if you often share contact information with other people (and you want the contact info to be complete) or if you sync your Outlook with your PIM or mobile phone and you also want that contact information to be complete.

To add IM addresses to Outlook contacts, follow these steps:

1. **Open a contact you want to IM with.**

   In the Contacts list, locate a person you want to exchange instant messages with and then open the contact.

2. **Type the person's IM address.**

   In the Contacts form, type the person's IM address in the IM Address field. See Figure 2-2. Click Save & Close to save the change.

If you get an e-mail message from anyone you have set up in your IM program as a contact, the sender's online status is automatically checked. You can view it yourself in the message header, assuming you've turned on the Online Status option, by choosing Tools⇨Options⇨Other⇨Display Online Status Next to a Person's Name. You can also view the online status of others who also received the message. Again, to view someone's status, just hover the mouse pointer over his name in the message header, as shown in Figure 2-1.

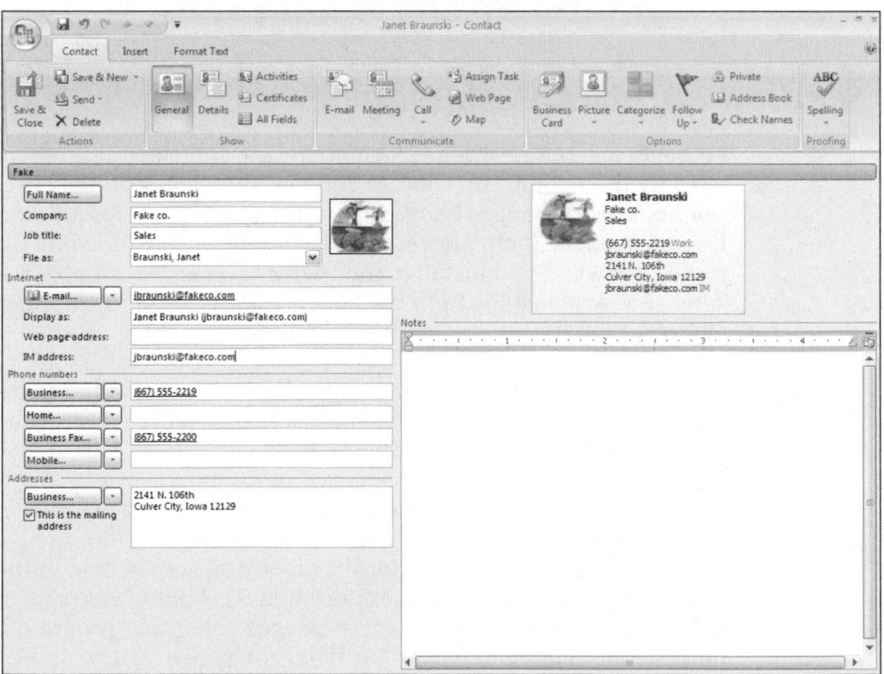

Figure 2-2: Add IM addresses.

After adding contacts to your IM program, when you get an e-mail message from someone, you can instantly view his online status by simply looking for the icon to the left of his name. If someone is online (if there's a green dot icon) and you want to reply with an instant message instead of an e-mail, follow these steps:

1. **Click the online status indicator.**

   It lurks next to the person's name in the message header. When you click the indicator, a menu appears.

2. **Choose Reply with Instant Message.**

   If you want your instant message to go out to all recipients of the original message, choose Reply All with Instant Message instead. You're switched to your Instant Messaging program, and a conversation window appears. See Figure 2-3.

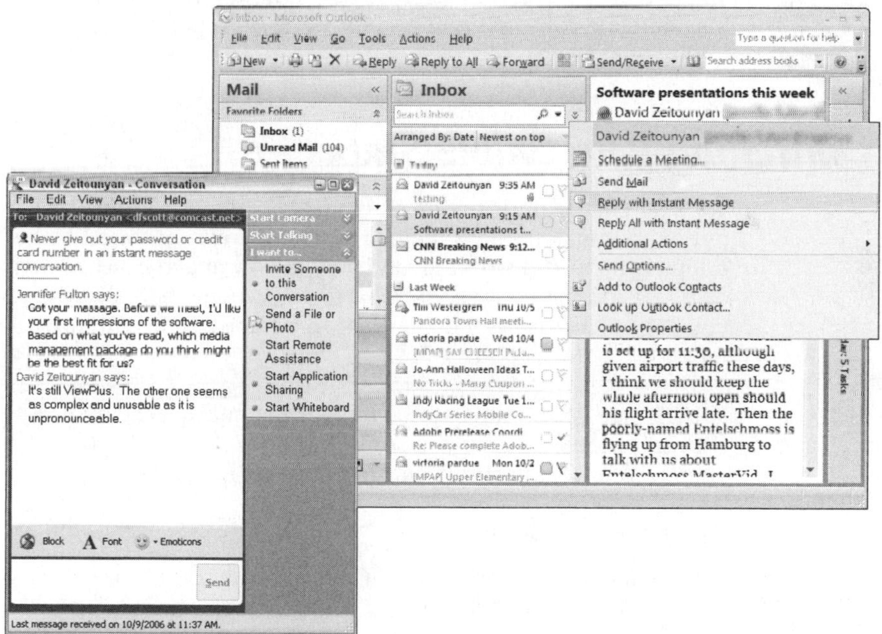

Figure 2-3: Yet another way to bother people instantly.

3. **Type your message and click Send.**

   The window you see at this point varies depending on the IM program you use; the one shown here is for Windows Live Messenger. Type what you want to say in the box at the bottom of the conversation window and click Send. What you type appears in the upper window; when the user replies, you see the reply just below your text in the upper window.

   I caution that this is the Internet. You cannot guarantee a secure conversation by any means. Don't share confidential information just in case someone is hacking into your online connection.

   Eventually, your conversation may scroll off the screen, but you can use the scroll bars to revisit anything you said earlier. Carry on your instant-messaging conversation, and when you're through, click the Close button to close the conversation window and end it.

Notice that Windows Live Messenger provides *Emoticons* (small icons you can use to express your feelings throughout a message), along with buttons for changing your text font and for blocking a particular contact from contacting you again.

Controlling Your Online Status

You can change your online status from Online to Offline by simply logging out of your instant-messaging program. If you don't want to be completely offline (you're still working, and may even want to send an instant message or two), you can change your status to Busy instead. Busy means just that; you are online, but you don't want to be bothered right now with instant messages.

You change your online status in your instant-messaging program and not within Outlook. To give you some idea how this works, here are the steps to change your online status within Windows Live Messenger:

1. **Display status options.**

   Click the arrow next to your name at the top of the Windows Messenger window. A list of status options appears.

2. **Select the status you want to display.**

   Notice that Windows Messenger gives you plenty of options here, not just Offline or Busy. Hey, if you're on the phone, why not tell everyone that so they'll stop trying to get you involved in two conversations at the same time?

Chapter 3: Getting the Latest News Delivered Right to Your Inbox

In This Chapter

- **Getting the lowdown on RSS, weblogs, podcasting, and syndicated content**
- **Getting coffee and the latest news**
- **Reviewing headlines and retrieving articles**
- **Sharing the news**
- **Canceling your news "subscription"**

In this electronics-driven world, news is all around us — on our cell phones and Blackberries, on TVs in our homes, grocery carts, shopping malls, and sports stadiums, and oh yeah, in actual newspapers. So it shouldn't surprise you to learn that you can also get your news within Outlook using something called RSS.

RSS is short for Really Simple Syndication, and it's a way for news content providers and *bloggers* (people who run online Web journals) to keep their readers updated on the latest goings-on. After you subscribe to an RSS *feed* (channel), news articles from that source arrive in your Inbox in a special folder. You view these articles just as you would any other e-mail. Typically, these articles contain only headlines that, when clicked, take you to a particular Web page where you can "read all about it."

Sometimes, instead of just links, the articles themselves arrive in the message. An article might also contain links or attachments for audio (or even video) versions of news articles. A *podcast* is an RSS feed that contains MP3 audio and sometimes video files, which you download and then play on an iPod or compatible multimedia player. You might hear news feeds referred to as RSS feeds, Web feeds, or XML feeds (because XML is the format used). Among its other capabilities, Outlook serves as an *RSS aggregator* — a program that receives and displays your feeds and the links or attachments they contain. Outlook supports all the most popular RSS feed types, including RSS, RDF, and Atom.

Adding News Feeds

You can add RSS feeds (news feeds) to Outlook either by manually or by using your Web browser and clicking a bright orange button called a *chicklet*, which appears on a Web page (for examples, see Figure 3-1). Friends can also share RSS feeds if you e-mail the feeds or export them to an RSS file (which you can identify by its `.opml` extension). See the "Sharing News Feeds" section, later in this chapter, for help with these last two options.

Figure 3-1: Want a chicklet?

You'll notice right away that when you subscribe to an RSS feed, you're not asked to give a lot of personal data like your name, Social Security number, or e-mail address. That's because the RSS provider isn't sending stuff *to* you or your computer; instead, your computer is collecting articles from the RSS provider when you tell it to. So the process is pretty anonymous, and thus a bit more secure than signing up for an e-mail newsletter. Also, most RSS feeds are free, although sometimes you have to pony up for their content. If you have to pay for something, you're given a chance to decide whether it's worth the fee.

Manually adding a news feed

Probably the simplest way to add a news feed to Outlook is automatically through Internet Explorer 7, as discussed in the next section. Sometimes, however, RSS feeds that you find using a Web browser are provided only for online RSS readers and not for Outlook. In such a case, a generic link to the feed is usually shown. Use this URL to add the news feed:

1. **Choose Tools⇨Account Settings⇨RSS Feeds⇨New.**

   The New RSS Feed dialog box appears.

2. **Type the URL and click the Add button.**

   The RSS Feed Options dialog box opens, as shown in Figure 3-2.

3. **Type a name for your feed in the Feed Name box.**

4. **Set your options.**

   You have several ways to go here:

   - **Change Folder:** If you want to change where the feed articles are stored, choose this option and select a different Outlook folder.

- **Automatically Download Enclosures for the Feed:** Choose this option to download media files (enclosures) within the feed.
- **Download the Full Article as an .HTML Attachment to Each Item:** Choose this option if you want to download full articles rather than just links to articles. (Before you choose this option, make sure you have enough free space on your hard drive to accommodate all those articles.)
- **Update the Feed with the Publisher's Recommendation:** Leave this option turned on. It prevents you from trying to get articles too frequently — which might lead to you getting dumped by the RSS provider.

When you're done selecting options, click OK and then click Close. The feed is added to Outlook. See the upcoming section, "Reading News Feeds," for help in slogging through the news articles for the new feed.

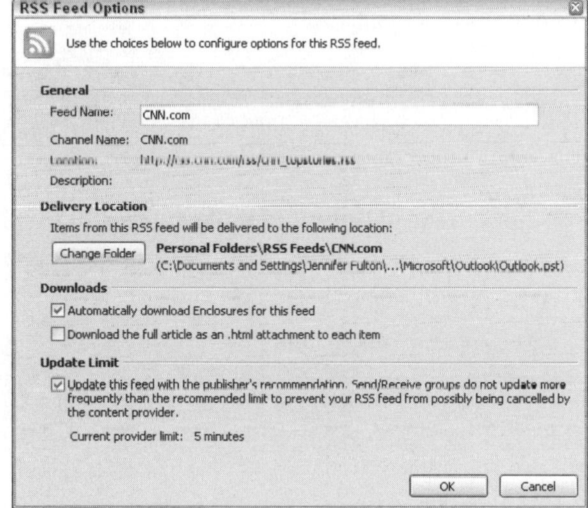

Figure 3-2: Add a feed manually if necessary.

Adding a recommended feed

You can also add a news feed to Outlook by browsing its list of recommended feeds. Here's how:

1. **Click the RSS Feeds folder in the Navigation pane.**

   A list of news feeds appears on the right. See Figure 3-3.

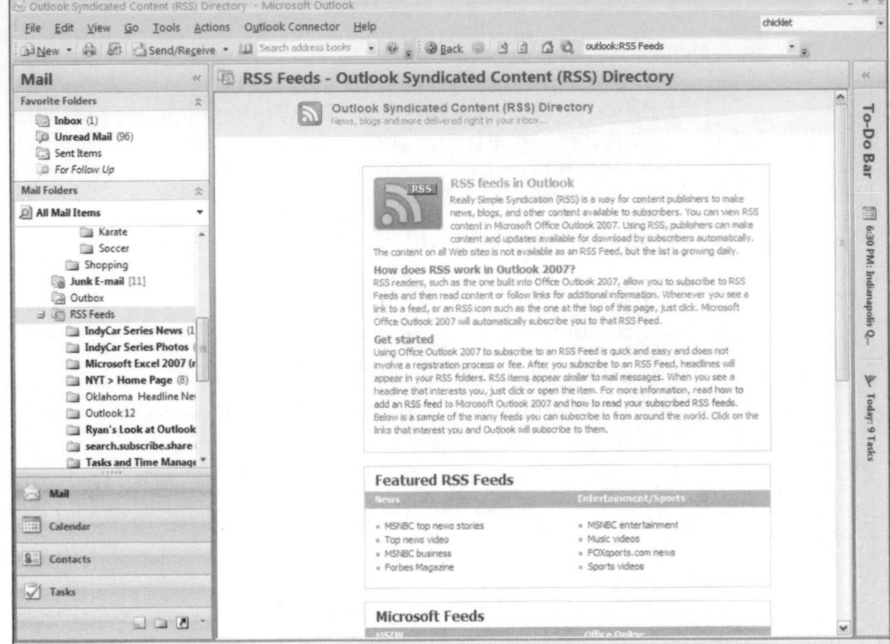

Figure 3-3: Add one of the recommended feeds.

2. **Click one of the news-feed links that looks interesting.**

   The Microsoft Office Outlook dialog box appears. See Figure 3-4.

Microsoft Office Outlook

Add this RSS Feed to Outlook?

You should only add subscriptions from sources you know and trust.

http://rss.video.msn.com/s/us/rss.aspx?t=Living&c=NBC Today&title= MSN Video - Today show features&p=05

To configure this RSS Feed, click Advanced.

Advanced... Yes No

Figure 3-4: Choose to add a feed to Outlook.

3. **(Optional) If you want to change any of the default news-feed options, click Advanced.**

   If you click Advanced, the RSS Feed Options dialog box appears (refer to Figure 3-2). Select the options you want for this feed and click OK to return to the Microsoft Office Outlook dialog box.

4. **Click Yes to add the feed.**

Keeping your RSS feeds in sync

First off, you can indeed add RSS feeds through most browsers, *to that browser's RSS feed list.* But to add an RSS feed to Outlook using a browser, you must use Internet Explorer 7. This process, by the way, also adds the feed to Internet Explorer, making it easy to view the feed articles in either place.

The first time you add a feed to Outlook using Internet Explorer, you may be asked if you want to synchronize Internet Explorer's list of RSS feeds with those in Outlook. Click Yes to make sure that the feeds you add through IE7 are added to Outlook automatically (and vice versa). If (for some goofy reason) you're never asked — or if you change your mind and want to keep separate feeds in both IE7 and Outlook — then choose Tools➪Options➪Other➪Advanced Options➪Sync RSS Feeds to the Common Feed List.

If the Sync RSS Feeds to the Common Feed List option is turned on, the feeds in both programs are kept in sync — if you add a feed to Outlook, it's added to IE7's list of feeds. Likewise, remove a feed from Internet Explorer, and it's removed from Outlook as well. Turn off this option to prevent changes in Outlook from affecting IE7 and vice-versa.

Adding a news feed through Internet Explorer

Assuming you're using Internet Explorer 7 (and if you're a Microsoft fan, why wouldn't you be?), you can click a chicklet when you see one on a Web page and instantly add a news feed automatically to Outlook.

So, if you've decided to add news feeds to Outlook automatically through your IE7 browser, do the following:

1. **Navigate to a Web page that has a news feed.**

   When you're browsing a page that contains a link to a news feed, the chicklet button (okay, Microsoft calls it the RSS Feeds button) magically appears next to the Home button at the top of the Internet Explorer window.

   You can find RSS feeds at most news sources such as `www.cnn.com` and `www.msnbc.com`. You can also find them at RSS source sites such as `syndic8.com`, `www.feedster.com`, `w.moreover.com`, `dmoz.org`, `www.newsisfree.com`, `www.rssfeeds.com`, and `www.masternewmedia.org/rss/top55`.

2. **Click the chicklet.**

   Click the arrow on the RSS Feeds button and select the particular feed on that page that you want to add, as shown in Figure 3-5. If there's no arrow, there's only one feed, so just click the button. You can also click the RSS, XML, or whatever they're calling it button located on the Web page.

   You're taken to another Web page that displays a sample of some of the articles associated with this feed.

Figure 3-5: Add a feed from IE7.

3. **Click Subscribe to This Feed.**

   The Internet Explorer dialog box appears. See Figure 3-6.

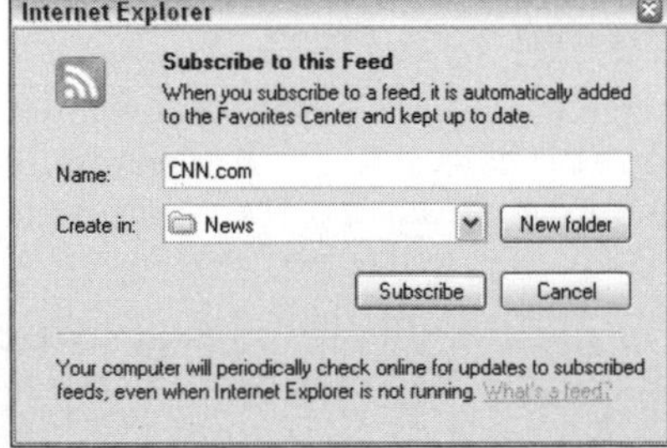

Figure 3-6: Subscribe to the feed.

4. **Type a name for the feed in the Name field.**
5. **Choose which Internet Explorer folder you want the feed saved in.**

   You can choose one from the Create In list, or click the New Folder button to create a new folder if you want.

6. **Click Subscribe.**

   You see a message telling you that you have successfully subscribed. Click the View My Feeds link to review your news feeds in Internet Explorer. Switch over to Outlook to read articles from your new feed. See the section, "Reading News Feeds," for help.

Changing or removing a feed

After adding a feed, you can change its options in just three steps:

1. **Choose Tools⇨Account Settings⇨RSS Feeds.**

   A list of your current RSS feeds appears in the Account Settings dialog box. See Figure 3-7.

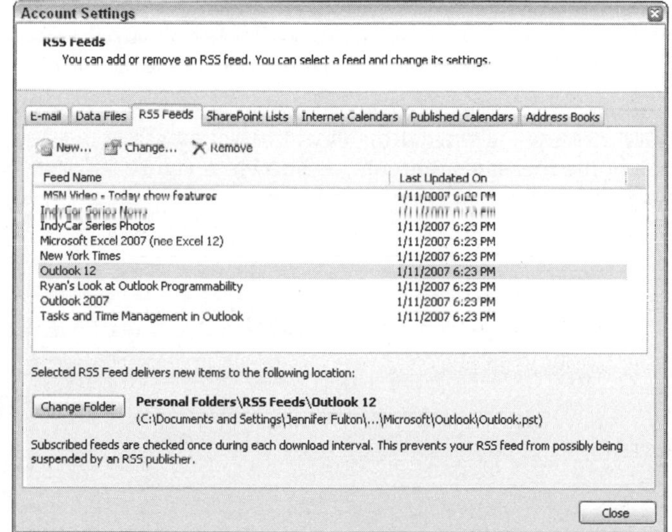

Figure 3-7: Manage your feeds.

2. **Select the feed you want to modify, and click Change.**

   That RSS Feed Options dialog box opens (refer to Figure 3-2).

3. **Make your changes, click OK in the RSS Feed Options dialog box, and then click Close in the Account Settings dialog box.**

   If a news feed proves annoying with its frequent articles (or just proves uninteresting), you can remove it altogether: Just select the feed in the Account Settings dialog box and click Remove.

Reading News Feeds

Reading news feeds is actually nothing *new.* You simply do what you already know how to do, which is reading messages. All the news feeds are typically collected in one spot for you, the RSS Feeds folder. To view a news feed, open the RSS Feeds folder in the Navigation Pane and then click the folder for that news feed.

The articles for the feed appear as ordinary e-mail messages; you have several ways to view them:

- ✦ If you have the Reading pane open, you can click a news article and view its contents on the right.
- ✦ Double-click the article to open it in a separate window.
- ✦ If the article contains a link, you can click it to view the entire article.
- ✦ If the feed didn't automatically download enclosures, and you want to see them, click the InfoBar and select Download/Update All Content.
- ✦ If you have a long list of articles to scan, you may prefer the Messages with AutoPreview view; it displays the full message header and a few lines of the message contents, as shown in Figure 3-8. (See Book VIII, Chapter 2 for help in changing views.)

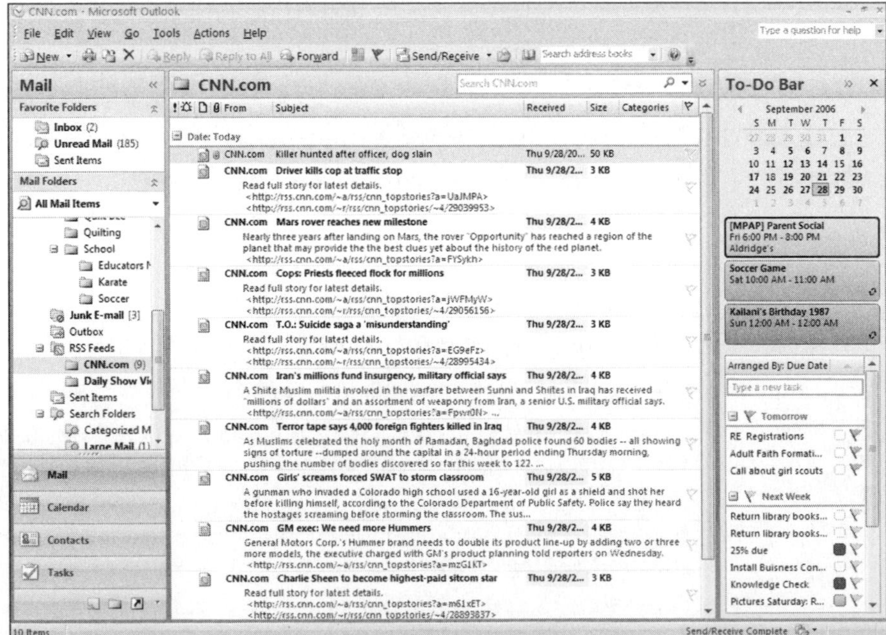

Figure 3-8: View news feeds using Messages with Auto-Preview.

Sharing News Feeds

You can share your news feeds in one of two ways: by sending an invitation via e-mail to subscribe to the news feed or by exporting your feeds in a file. If you choose to export, you can select which feeds you want to share. The upcoming sections detail these different approaches.

Sharing a feed by e-mail

After you've added a news feed to Outlook, if you find that you like its articles, you can forward the URL for the news feed in the form of an invitation:

1. **Open any article within the feed you want to share.**
2. **Choose RSS Article➪Respond➪Share This Feed.**

   A new message is created. Just under the Subject, in the header area, the RSS feed is listed, along with the URL to the feed.
3. **Address the message, add any comments you want in the text area, and click Send to send the invitation.**

TIP

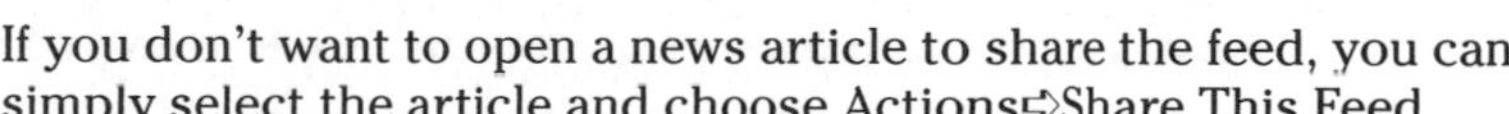

If you don't want to open a news article to share the feed, you can simply select the article and choose Actions➪Share This Feed.

If someone sends you an invitation to subscribe to a news feed, you can add the feed to Outlook by following these steps:

1. **Click Add This RSS Feed.**

   Click the Add This RSS Feed button at the top of the Reading pane when previewing the message, as shown in Figure 3-9. If you've opened the message, you can choose Share➪Open➪Add This RSS Feed instead.

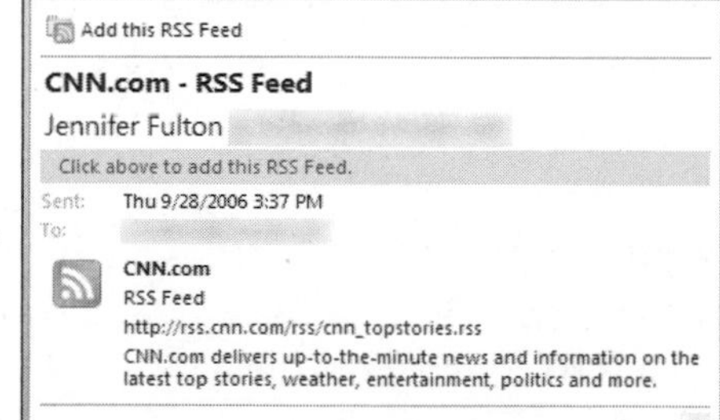

Figure 3-9: Feeding frenzy.

2. **Accept the invitation.**

   The Microsoft Office Outlook dialog box appears (see Figure 3-4); click Advanced if you want to change any of the default news feed options using the RSS Feed Options dialog box.

3. **When you're done setting options, click Yes to add the feed.**

   See the previous section, "Reading News Feeds," for help in reading the articles in the feed you've just added.

Importing/exporting a news feed list

You can export your list of news feeds into a file, and then send that file as an attachment in an e-mail message to anyone you wish to share the feeds with. To create an export file, follow these steps:

1. **Choose File⇨Import and Export.**

   The Import and Export Wizard appears.

2. **Select Export RSS Feeds to an OPML File and click Next.**
3. **Select which feeds to export.**

   From the list, select the feeds you want to share. They are all checked off initially, so you can just uncheck those you don't want to share. Click Next.

4. **Click Browse and choose a folder in which to save the file. Click Save.**
5. **Type a name for the file and click Next to save it.**

   To send the list onto someone else, create a new message and attach the file. (See Book II, Chapter 1.)

If you receive an e-mail with an RSS feed list attached, save the file and then import the list into Outlook. Here's how:

1. **Choose File⇨Import and Export.**

   The Import and Export Wizard dialog box appears.

2. **Select Import RSS Feeds from an OPML File and click Next.**
3. **Click Browse, select an RSS feed file to import, click Open, and then click Next.**

   RSS feed files have the `.opml` file extension.

4. **Select the feeds you want to import.**

   All the feeds in the file are listed; just select the ones you want to import into your Outlook, and click Next to import them.

5. **When you get a confirmation; click Finish.**

   The feed is added to the RSS Feeds folder, and articles are downloaded to it.

Chapter 4: Sending Mass Mailings

In This Chapter

- Grouping contacts in a distribution list
- Using a list to send one e-mail to lots of people
- Pulling contacts into Word to create a massive snail mailing
- Pulling contacts into Word to create a massive e-mailing

Since the invention of electronic messaging, getting the word out has never been easier. Using distribution lists, you can easily send the same message to a group of your friends or colleagues. You have a list of personal and business contacts. Why not use it? Well, Outlook lets you leverage your Outlook Contacts names and addresses to personalize a letter or other document you create in Word. You can also leverage your Contacts list to create printed envelopes or labels for mass paper mailings. And if that lever isn't high enough yet, you can leverage your Contacts again to create a professional-looking mass e-mailing that's born in Word templates and sent using Outlook.

Another way to get the word out is to use Business Contact Manager, a program that comes with Outlook, but that's not routinely installed. Basically, Business Contact Manager can be used to track the mass mailing and the responses you get from your customers or potential sales contacts. (In a not-so-strange coincidence, you can find about Business Contact Manager in Book VII.)

Creating a Distribution List

Do you often find yourself sending messages to the same group of people? Do you find yourself wandering aimlessly around the office trying to remember what it was you got up for? Well, I can't help you with the last one, but I can make sending group messages easier. If you have a group of people you like to bother regularly with meaningless correspondence (uh, I mean *really important messages*) — such as your departmental colleagues, best clients, brothers and sisters, or the members of your Mommies and Me group — you can create a distribution list. You can create as many distribution lists as you like, and bother people easily with a single click. You can even attach a distribution list to an e-mail message so others can use the list to bother people (uh, send really important messages).

To create a distribution list, follow these steps:

1. **Choose File➪New➪Distribution List.**

   The Distribution List form appears, as shown in Figure 4-1.

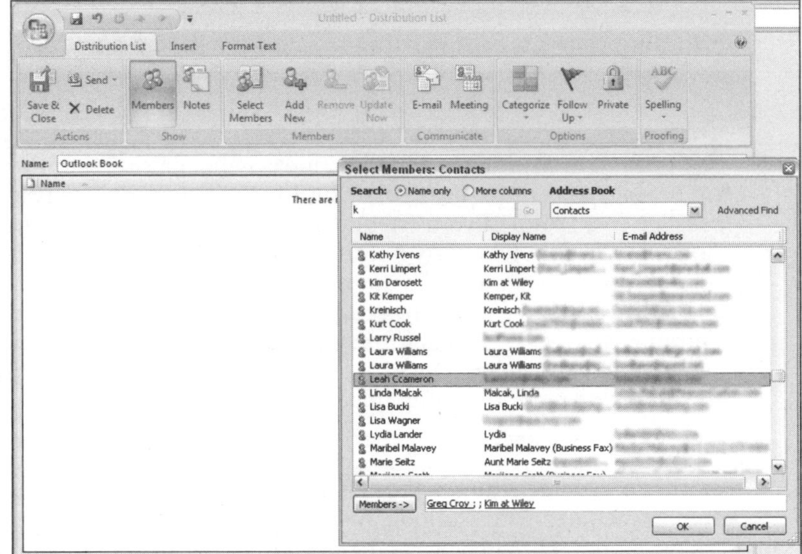

Figure 4-1: Bother people with a single click.

2. **Type a name for the list in the Name box.**

   You have to give your distribution list a name so Outlook can keep track of it. Use a name that helps you to identify the purpose of the list, such as My Department, Family, or Soccer Moms.

3. **Choose Distribution List➪Members➪Select Members.**

   The Select Members dialog box appears. The contacts in your default address book appear in a large list. If needed, change to a different address book.

4. **Add members to the distribution list by double-clicking each member's name or by selecting a name and clicking the Members button.**

   The members you select appear in the Members box at the bottom of the dialog box.

To search for someone in the large list, type a few letters of the person's name into the Search box.

5. **When you're done adding names, click OK.**

   The Select Members dialog box disappears. The names you selected appear in the Distribution List form.

6. **If you want to add someone to the list who's not already in Contacts, follow these steps:**

   a. *Choose Distribution List⇨Members⇨Add New.*

      The Add New Member dialog box appears. See Figure 4-2.

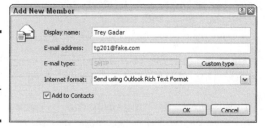

Add New Member

Display name: Trey Gadar

E-mail address: tg201@fake.com

E-mail type: SMTP | Custom type

Internet format: Send using Outlook Rich Text Format

Add to Contacts

OK | Cancel

Figure 4-2: The Contact list always has room for one more.

   b. *Type the person's name in the Display Name box.*

   c. *Type the new person's E-Mail Address.*

   d. *From the Internet Format list, select the e-mail format (plain text or HTML) you prefer to use when sending email to this person.*

      You can also let Outlook choose the format to use.

   e. *Put a check in the Add to Contacts check box to add this name to your Contacts list.*

      Notice that this option means you can add people manually to a distribution list while keeping them off your Contacts list (although why you'd want to do that is a mystery to me).

   f. *Click OK to add the new member.*

      You return to the Distribution List dialog box.

7. **Save the list by choosing Distribution List⇨Actions⇨Save & Close.**

   Distribution lists appear within the Contacts list, but with a special icon that helps to identify them, as shown in Figure 4-3.

Distribution List icon

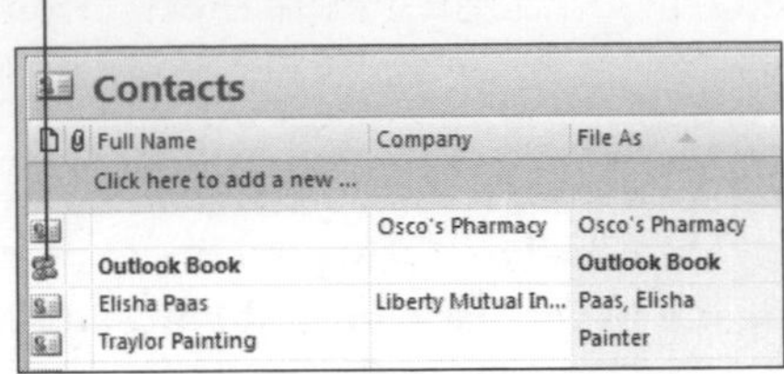

Figure 4-3: Look for this distribution list icon.

If you're having trouble finding a distribution list (maybe because you forgot what name you used to create it), keep this in mind: Distribution lists can easily appear at the top of the listing when you use Phone List view if you click the Sort by Icon button at the top of the first column on the left. For more help in sorting a list, see Book VIII, Chapter 2.

Using a distribution list to send e-mails

Distribution lists give you a lot of options for efficient e-mailing:

- **To send an e-mail message or meeting invitation to everyone on the list**, follow the same steps as you would to send any other message — just type the name of the list in the To box of an e-mail/meeting invitation form.
- **To send an e-mail to each member without the other members knowing,** type the list name in the Bcc box.

If the distribution list is open, you can click the E-mail or Meeting buttons in the Communicate group on the Ribbon to send a message or a meeting invitation.

Making changes to a distribution list

Sadly, the members of a list may leave the department, change e-mail addresses, or simply fall off your "favored friends" roster. To change a distribution list, jump over to Contacts and double-click the list name. When the Distribution List form appears, there are a range of changes you might make:

- **Add someone.** Just do what you did before:
  - To add someone from the Contacts list, choose Distribution List⇨Members⇨Select Members.
  - To add someone who isn't in the Contact list, choose Distribution List⇨Members⇨Add New.
- **Remove someone.** Select the name in the list and choose Distribution List⇨Members⇨Remove.

- **Update old e-mail addresses.** If you know you've changed the e-mail address of someone in the list, you can update the list with the new e-mail address. Choose Distribution List⇨Members⇨Update Now. Outlook searches your address books for the new address.
- **Make the list private.** To prevent others who have permission to see your Contacts list from viewing or changing this distribution list, choose Distribution List⇨Options⇨Private button.
- **Send the list to someone.** To share your list with someone, choose Distribution List⇨Actions⇨Send and then choose a format: vCard (which should be compatible with most e-mail programs) or Outlook format.
- **Annotate the list.** Having trouble remembering who all is on the list and why? Choose Distribution List⇨Show⇨Notes and type a reminder for yourself. Your note appears in the Contacts list when you use Detailed Address Cards view. You can also redisplay the note by clicking the Notes button again when the distribution list is open.

  To remind yourself about something you want to do with the list, use the Follow Up button instead of a note.
- **Group the list.** Group the list together with similar items by adding it to a specific category. Choose Distribution List⇨Options⇨Categorize. Then choose the category to which you want to add the list. (See Book VIII, Chapter 1 for help in creating categories.)

Creating a Mass Mailing in Word Using Your Contacts

One way you can get the same message to a lot of people is to create a single Word document, print it a bunch of times, and then print matching labels or envelopes for everyone you want to reach. Okay, you know this isn't a book on Word, so you may be wondering what this has to do with Outlook. Well, first off, you can use the names, addresses, and other information you keep in Outlook Contacts to create hundreds of "personalized" printed letters in Word — in a matter of minutes. You can then reuse that same Contacts information to create labels or envelopes so you can send your "personalized" letter to all your nearest and dearest. You can also use the power of Word — and its templates, if you want — to create a mass e-mailing that's professionally formatted and personalized with information you pull from Contacts (for example, each person's first name).

Again, this isn't a book on Word. For the juicy details of *mail merge* (the Word term for this magic) and other advanced Word techniques, see

Word 2007 All-in-One Desk Reference For Dummies by Doug Lowe (Wiley Publishing, Inc.). Here are the basic steps:

1. **Start a document.**

   If you have a document ready to use, open it in Word. If you want to use a Word template (and maybe check out the templates online), choose Microsoft Office Button➪New.

   Although you can postpone choosing a template to use, you can choose only from those you've already installed if you wait till later in this process. And because the templates online change often and there's a good chance that there's something out there designed to do exactly what you want (maybe a newsletter or sales brochure), why not check them out? Just keep in mind that if you want to check for templates online, do that here, in Step 1.

2. **Start the merge.**

   Choose Mailings➪Start Mail Merge➪Start Mail Merge➪Step by Step Mail Merge Wizard. The Mail Merge Wizard task pane appears on the right. Select a Document Type such as letters or e-mail messages and click Next: Starting Document.

3. **Choose the document to use.**

   Choose Use the Current Document. If you have an existing document you want to use, and you haven't opened it already, choose Start from Existing Document instead. Click Next: Select Recipients.

   If you're creating labels, you may want to make sure Word knows which type you're using so it formats everything correctly. After choosing to use a new document, click Label Options to select the label type.

4. **Select the Contacts list.**

   Choose Select From Outlook Contacts. Click the Choose Contacts Folder link, choose the Contacts list you want to use, and then click OK. The Mail Merge Recipients dialog box appears, similar to the one shown in Figure 4-4.

5. **Refine the list.**

   Use The Mail Merge Recipients dialog box to narrow your Contacts list to the people you actually want to send the Word document to. You can simply select recipients manually, sort the list, or filter the list to narrow it down. To sort, click a column heading; to filter, click the arrow on a column heading and choose an option. Click OK when the list is right. Then click Next: Write Your Letter.

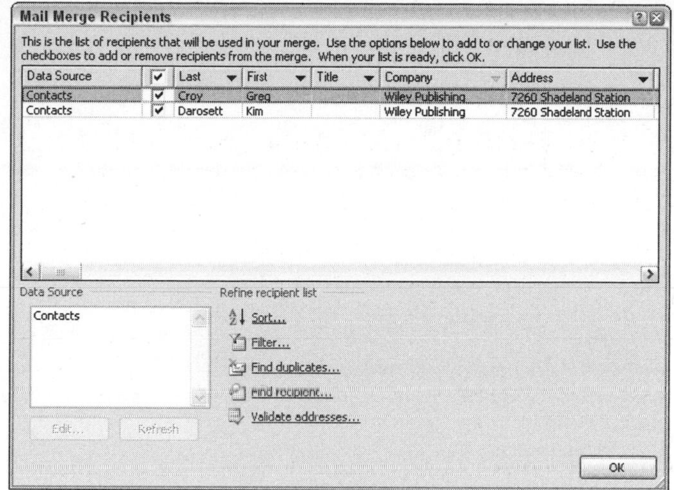

Figure 4-4: So who do you want?

6. **Create the letter, label, or envelope sample.**

   Create your sample letter, label, envelope, or e-mail message. Add fields that represent Contacts list info (such as a person's first name, or his address) by clicking that item in the task pane. If you don't see a field you want to add, click More Items. Then select a field and click Insert.

   If you're creating labels, after inserting the fields you want on the first label, click Update All Labels to copy the information to each label on your sample label sheet.

7. **Finish up and merge.**

   a. *Click Next: Preview.* Here's where you can view how your letter, labels, envelopes, or e-mail message will look when merged with the Contact information you inserted.

   b. *Click Next: Complete The Merge.* If you're creating a form letter, each letter starts on its own page, but they are all contained in the one Word document. Click Print to print all the letters, labels, or envelopes. Choose Finish⇨Finish & Merge⇨Send E-Mail Messages on the Ribbon to e-mail your messages.

   c. *Close the task pane.* You can save your merged document if you think you'll reuse it again as is.

Chapter 5: Managing Multiple E-Mail Accounts

In This Chapter

- Controlling e-mail coming and going
- Weeding out the junk mail before you actually download it
- Controlling how often Internet calendars and news feeds are updated
- Choosing which e-mail account to use when sending e-mail
- Getting Outlook to organize mail coming and going
- Directing replies to a different e-mail address
- Setting up Outlook for multiple people and multiple e-mail accounts

Nowadays it's not unusual for someone to have multiple e-mail addresses. Even though I work from home, I still have multiple e-mail addresses for personal versus business mail. I even have one address I use strictly for those Web sites that require my address — I find it helps me deal with the inevitable junk mail that often results. This chapter shows how to deal with the issues that crop up when you're using several e-mail accounts. For example, maybe you don't want to get your personal e-mail as often as your work mail. Or maybe you want the opportunity to review e-mail headers and weed out the junk before you take the time to download it all. Maybe you want to select the e-mail account you use for sending a specific message, so that replies go back to that address. Maybe your issue is organization — some easy way of directing e-mail for a particular account into a special folder. If you have multiple people using the same computer, the problems seem to multiply — how do you keep your contacts, calendar info, and e-mail separate from those of your kids? In this chapter, I tackle all these issues and more to boot.

If you need to set up a second (or third) e-mail account and you're wondering where I cover that, see Book I, Chapter 3.

Controlling Sending and Receiving

If you have only one e-mail account — and you're not interested in downloading news feeds into Outlook or displaying Internet calendars — then controlling the sending and receiving of e-mail is pretty straightforward. If you have multiple e-mail accounts, one or more news feeds, and some Internet calendars that need updating every once in a while, well, it gets a bit more complicated. Still, if you use Send/Receive groups, you can soon have things under control.

You find out how to set up news feeds in Outlook in Book III, Chapter 3. For pointers on adding Internet calendars to Outlook, see Book IV, Chapter 5.

Creating Send/Receive groups

You start Outlook life with a single Send/Receive group called All Accounts. As you might expect, even if you have multiple e-mail accounts, a bunch of news feeds, and several Internet calendars, the All Accounts group controls them all. You use the All Accounts group to send and receive *everything.* So if you want to use the same schedule to send and receive all your messages and update your news and calendar subscriptions, then hey, skip the stuff in this subsection; you don't need it. But if you'd like to send and receive messages for each e-mail account at different intervals — or want to update your news feeds more often (or your Internet calendars less often) than you get e-mail — then setting up multiple Send/Receive groups help you establish separate schedules.

You can't remove the All Accounts group, but you can remove e-mail, news, and Internet calendar accounts from it if you want, and then include those accounts in some other Send/Receive group you create. By the way, accounts can be included in multiple Send/Receive groups, so you don't actually have to edit the All Accounts group if you don't want to. And by accounts, remember that I mean not only e-mail accounts, but also news feeds and Internet calendars.

Some news feeds and Internet calendars can't be updated more frequently than at specific intervals, so even if you try to Send/Receive them, you might not see any new messages.

Send/Receive groups are a pretty useful way to control a lot of stuff:

- **Sending and receiving:** This one's a *duh.* Using Send/Receive groups, you can control when mail, news updates, or calendar changes coming to a particular account are received. You can also control the sending of messages created with a particular account. (See the section, "Sending from a Specific E-Mail Account," for help.)
- **Frequency:** Control how often sending and receiving for this group actually occurs.
- **Limitations:** Limit the size of messages that are downloaded. This option prevents you from downloading messages with really large attachments.

- ✦ **Folders:** Update specific folders on your corporate Exchange account as frequently as you desire.
- ✦ **What you get:** You can download only headers from the mail server so you can mark the ones you want, or get everything without reviewing.
- ✦ **Offline:** Control what Outlook does when you're offline (not connected to the Internet).

To create a new Send/Receive group, follow these steps:

1. **Choose Tools⇨Send/Receive⇨Send/Receive Settings⇨Define Send/Receive Groups.**

   The Send/Receive Groups dialog box appears.

2. **Click New.**

   Type a name for your new group, such as Personal. Click OK. The Send/Receive Settings dialog box jumps up (see Figure 5-1).

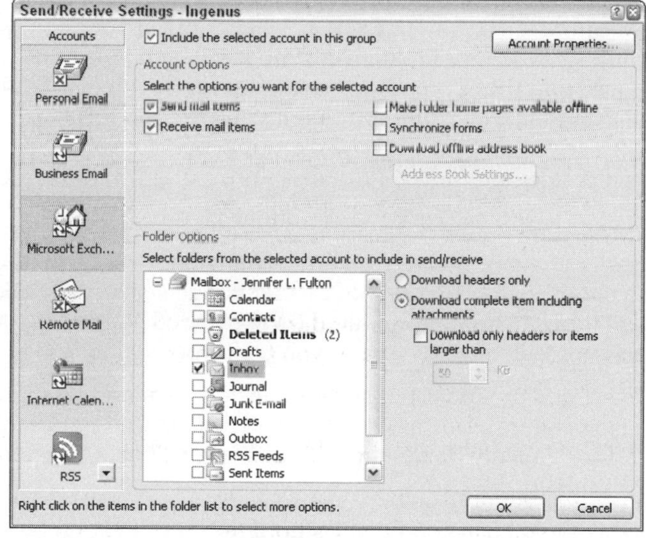

Figure 5-1: Who belongs in this group?

3. **Choose the accounts for this group.**

   The Accounts list on the left shows all the accounts you have set up: e-mail, news, and Internet calendars. From the Accounts list, select an account to include in this new group; then check the Include the Selected Account in This Group option. The icon for that account changes: instead of a red X, it now includes a blue double-arrow send/receive thingie. So if you glance down the Accounts list, you can quickly see which accounts are associated with this group.

4. **Set the account options.**

   Select the options you want for this account and click OK (the options you see vary, depending on the type of account):

   - *Send Mail Items:* Do you want e-mails created for this account to be sent when this Send/Receive group is activated?
   - *Receive Mail Items:* Do you want to receive e-mails sent to this e-mail account?
   - *Make Folder Home Page Available Offline:* For Exchange accounts, a home page can be created for each Outlook folder (such as Inbox, Calendar, and so on) to help users navigate the contents of the folder quickly (get to subfolders). Assuming the owner of the folder (typically, the system administrator) has created a home page for a folder (which you see when you click the folder's name in the Folder list), you can have Outlook copy the home page to your computer so you can use it to navigate folders when you're offline.
   - *Synchronize Forms:* For Exchange accounts, if your company provides Outlook forms for creating certain items and you want to access them from the server even when you're offline, you can use this option to update your computer's copy of the forms.
   - *Download Offline Address Book:* For Exchange accounts, this allows you to pull up e-mail addresses and such even when you're not connected to the network (you're offline).
   - *Folder Options:* If you're on an Exchange network, use the folder list to choose which folders on the Exchange server (such as Calendar and Inbox) you want updated (downloaded) during the send/receive action.
   - *Download options:* Choose whether to Download Headers Only (message headers), Download Complete Item Including Attachments, or Download Only Headers for Items Larger Than *XX* (where you set the *XX* limit).

   This last option is a good one to use if you routinely receive e-mails with large file attachments, and you're tired of them slogging up your machine. With this option set, you still get all your regular, slender e-mail. For larger e-mails with bulky attachments, you get headers only. You can then pick and choose which of these large-attachment e-mails you want now and which ones can wait until you've nothing better to do than twiddle your thumbs while they download.

5. **Set send/receive options for this group.**

   After clicking OK, you return to the Send/Receive Groups dialog box (see Figure 5-2). There, you can set options that control the automatic sending and receiving of e-mail for this account:

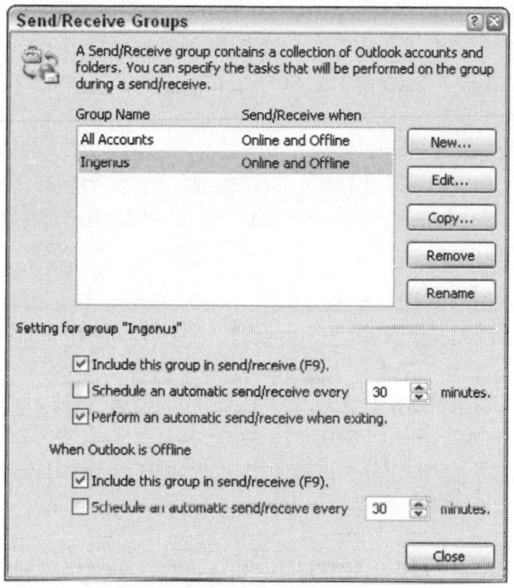

Figure 5-2: Set other options.

- *Include the Group in Send/Receive (F9):* Tells Outlook to send and receive e-mail for the accounts in this group whenever you say "Go get 'em, boy!" by pressing F9.
- *Schedule an Automatic Send/Receive Every XX Minutes:* Tells Outlook to automatically send and receive messages for this account at regular intervals every *XX* minutes. Normally, the interval for automatic send/receives is set to 30 minutes, but you can change the interval.
- *Perform an Automatic Send/Receive When Exiting:* Tells Outlook to do one last send/receive for this account right before you shut down the program.

  You can also choose options to control what happens when you're offline.

- *Include This Group in Send/Receive (F9):* When you press F9 while working offline, Outlook reconnects you, gets the messages for your account, and disconnects you again. For an extra $50, it'll pick up your laundry and order take-out.
- *Schedule an Automatic Send/Receive Every XX Minutes:* Outlook automatically reconnects you every so many minutes, and then it disconnects you after it gets the messages for this group.

The heady business of message headers

If you download message headers only, you can mark the ones you want to get, and then use the Download Marked Headers command to get them. To mark a header for download, choose Send/Receive➪Mark to Download Message(s). To get a copy of the message and leave it on the server, choose Send/Receive➪Mark to Download Message Copy. Unmark headers by selecting them first and choosing Send/Receive➪Unmark Selected Headers. Unmark all headers by choosing Send/Receive➪Unmark All Headers. To mark a header so its message is removed from the server the next time you connect, click the message header and press Delete. A red X appears on the header to remind you that it's a goner the next time you process headers.

You can edit a group to add or remove accounts from it. For example, you can remove accounts from the All Accounts group if you don't want them controlled by its settings, or you can make changes to a group you created. To edit a group, follow these steps:

1. **Choose Tools➪Send/Receive➪Send/Receive Settings➪Define Send/Receive Groups.**

   The Send/Receive Groups dialog box appears. (Refer to Figure 5-2.)

2. **Select the group you want to change.**
3. **Click Edit.**

   The Send/Receive Settings dialog box appears (Refer Figure 5-1.)

4. **Make your changes and click OK to save them.**

Now, let's go get that mail!

Even if you don't create new Send/Receive groups, you've the good ol' All Accounts group. And it has settings (which you can change, using the steps in the previous section) that control how often it does a Send/Receive. Other Send/Receive groups have their own settings that control when they do their thing. So — one way or the other — you get e-mails, updated news feeds, and online calendars whenever those groups are scheduled to go off.

If you're waiting anxiously for an important e-mail, you aren't at the mercy of the various Send/Receive groups because you can poke 'em to make them do a Send/Receive whenever you feel like it. Your options look like this:

✦ **Send/Receive everything:** To do a Send/Receive for all groups, press F9 or choose Tools➪Send/Receive➪Send/Receive All.

If you go back to the previous section, you see a setting in the Send/Receive Groups dialog box that can *prevent* Outlook from doing a send/receive when you press F9. If you've activated this setting for a particular group, then that group has "opted out" of the F9 business; it won't go get mail when you press F9, but it does if you select the Send/Receive All command.

✦ **Send and receive e-mail for one folder only:** Choose that folder in the Folder List first, and then choose Send/Receive➪This Folder (Microsoft Exchange) or press Shift+F9. This command applies to Exchange users only, and it allows you to send/receive updates for a particular folder only, such as the Inbox or Calendar.

✦ **Send but don't get:** To send messages for all groups without receiving anything, choose Tools➪Send/Receive➪Send All.

✦ **Send/Receive all the accounts in one group:** Choose Tools➪Send/Receive➪*group*. For example, if you created a Work send/receive group, you could choose Tools➪Send/Receive➪Work.

✦ **Send/Receive for a particular e-mail account only:** Choose Tools➪Send/Receive➪*e-mail account*➪*action*. After you choose the account you want to play with, you choose the specific Send/Receive action. Your choices include Inbox (which gets everything), Download Inbox Headers (which gets message headers only), and Process Marked Headers (which downloads or deletes messages from the server, depending on how you've marked the headers on your end). You can process the headers in a single folder by selecting that folder first and then choosing Process Marked Headers in This Folder.

✦ **Get headers for a particular folder:** Select that folder in the Folder List first, and then choose Send/Receive➪Download Headers in This Folder. This option applies only to Exchange users, and it allows you to download headers for a particular folder.

✦ **Download the Exchange Address Book:** If you want to make sure that your Global Address Book is updated with the most recent contacts on your Exchange network, choose Send/Receive➪Download Address Book.

✦ **Update free/busy time:** Update the free/busy time for any calendar a colleague has shared with you by choosing Send/Receive➪Free/Busy Information.

You can cancel all regular Send/Receives temporarily by choosing Tools➪Send/Receive➪Send/Receive Settings➪Disable Scheduled Send/Receive. You can then send/receive messages on-demand, by account, or by Send/Receive group. Just follow the steps given here. Resume your regularly scheduled program by choosing the Disable Scheduled Send/Receive command again.

Selecting Your Default E-Mail Account

If you've ever worked on a team, you're used to the concept of team leader, otherwise known as the "person to blame if something goes wrong." If you have multiple e-mail accounts, one of them has to be the boss. Outlook basically needs to know which account to treat as the *default* (the one used if no other account is specified).

When you reply to or forward an e-mail you've received, Outlook doesn't send that message using the default e-mail account, but instead uses the account to which that e-mail was sent originally (although you can override this option when needed). Your default account is used whenever you create a new e-mail; your default account is the one that a return e-mail is automatically sent to if the recipient clicks that ol' Reply button. So you should take pains to make sure that the default account is the one you want people to address you by most often. When needed, you can always send a new e-mail from any one of your accounts, instead of from the one you have crowned as king. To set the default account, follow these steps:

1. **Choose Tools⇨Account Settings.**

   The Account Settings dialog box appears, as shown in Figure 5-3.

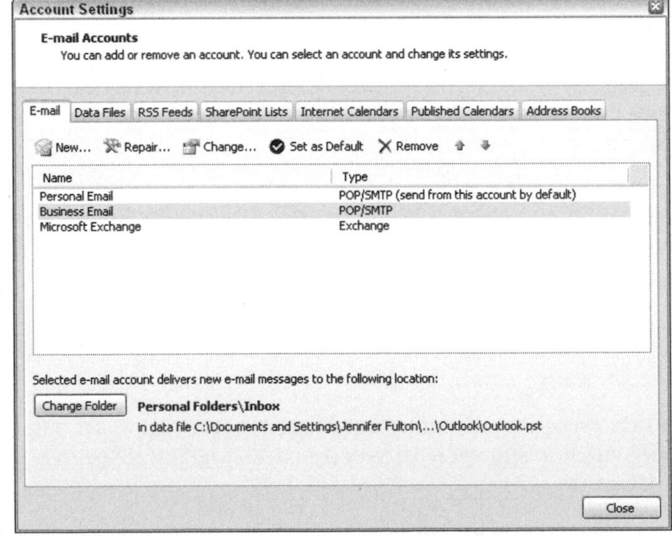

Figure 5-3: Here's where you crown the king of Outlook accounts.

2. **Select an account.**

   On the E-Mail tab, select the account you want to act as your default e-mail account.

3. **Click Set as Default and then click Close.**

   This sets the selected account as your default and completes the procedure.

Changing the Order in Which Accounts Are Checked

When multiple accounts are lumped together in a group (such as All Accounts or a Send/Receive group you've created), e-mail for each account is sent and received in a specific order. If you happen to display the Send/Receive Progress screen during a Send/Receive, you see this order on-screen as Outlook checks each account in that group one by one.

If you want, you can change the order in which accounts are checked — not within a specific group, but in general. The change affects all groups. Here's how:

1. **Choose Tools⇨Account Settings.**

   The Account Settings dialog box pops up. (See Figure 5-4.)

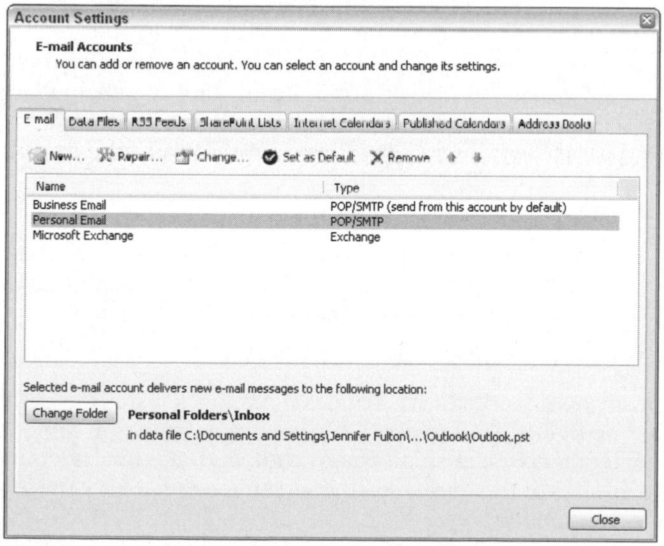

Figure 5-4: Change your order.

2. **Select an account.**

   When multiple accounts are placed in the same group, accounts are sent and received in the order in which you see them listed here.

   To move an account up in the listing, select it and then click the Up button. To move a selected account down in the listing, click the Down button instead. Click Close.

Sending from a Specific E-Mail Account

When you set up multiple e-mail accounts in Outlook, one of them acts as the default, meaning that all messages you send from Outlook are sent from that account (see the previous section for help in setting the default account). Because e-mail providers don't limit the number of e-mails you can send and receive (if only I could talk my cell phone provider into that kind of plan!), it probably doesn't matter to you which of your accounts is used to send a particular e-mail. But it does make a difference. When a user replies to your message, the reply is sent to the e-mail address that was used to send the initial message — and that may cause problems for you. For example, if you send an e-mail using your personal account and a reply comes back while you're at work, you might not know it until you get home and check the personal account again.

Even if the user doesn't reply to a particular message, the e-mail address you used to send that message is the one that appears in the message header. Ordinarily, this is perfectly fine. However, this might be a problem if you accidentally sent the message to your kid brother using your business account, he sends it on to a few hundred of his closest friends (and their closest friends), and you mysteriously start getting a lot of junk mail at work.

To send a message from an e-mail account that's not the default:

1. **Click Message⇨Send⇨Account.**

   As long as more than one e-mail account has been set up in Outlook, the Account button appears near the Send button in an open message form. Click it to reveal a list of your accounts, as shown in Figure 5-5.

2. **Select the account to use.**

   The account marked with a check mark in the list is the default account — the one that is used to send this message if you don't choose anything else. If you do make an alternate choice, that e-mail account appears in the InfoBar of the message so you can make sure it's the right account before you click Send.

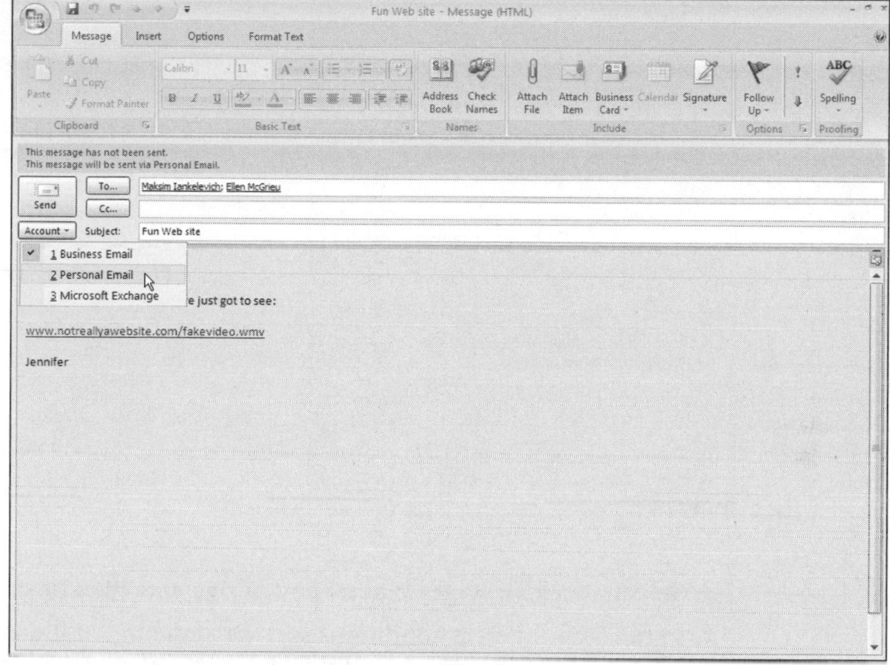

Figure 5-5: Select which account you want to use for sending a message.

Directing Incoming Mail to a Specific Folder

For anyone, keeping e-mail organized is an ongoing job. But when you add multiple e-mail accounts and the tons of e-mail they generate to the mix, the problem increases dramatically. That's because when you add multiple e-mail accounts to Outlook, the e-mail for each account is unceremoniously dumped in the Inbox folder. To redirect incoming mail to a different folder, you create a rule.

I cover rules in detail in Book IX, Chapter 2, so here I go over things pretty quickly. For example, if you want all your personal e-mail to go into a folder called *Personal* or *Family*, create a rule like this one:

1. **Choose Tools⇨Rules and Alerts.**

   If necessary, change to Mail first and then choose the Rules and Alerts command. The Rules and Alerts dialog box appears.

2. **Click New Rule.**

   The Rules Wizard appears. (See Figure 5-6.)

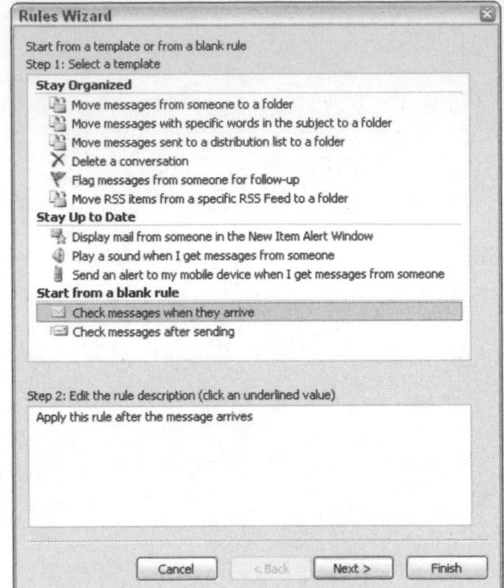

Figure 5-6: I make the rules around here.

3. **Select Check Messages When They Arrive and click Next.**
4. **In the Step 1: Select Conditions section at the top of the window, select Through the Specified Account (see Figure 5-7).**
5. **In the Step 2: Edit the Rule Description section at the bottom of the window, click the Specified link and select the account whose incoming mail you want to reroute in the Account dialog box. Click OK in the dialog box and then click Next in the wizard.**

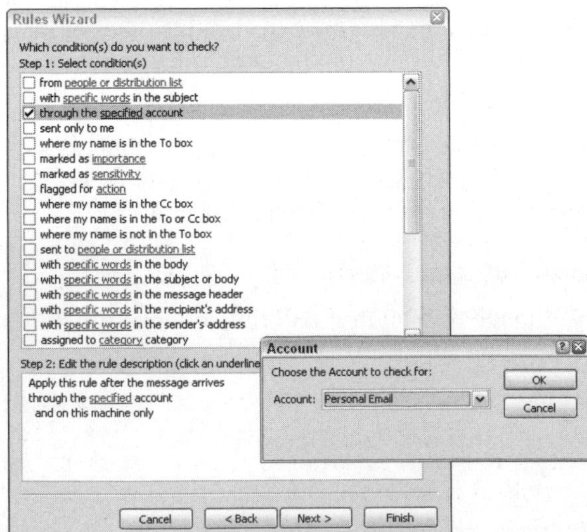

Figure 5-7: Select an account.

6. **In the Step 1: Select Action section at the top of the window, select Move It to the Specified Folder.**

7. **In the Step 2: Edit the Rule Description section at the bottom, click the Specified link and select the folder in which you want all incoming mail from this account placed. (See Figure 5-8.) Click OK and then click Next.**

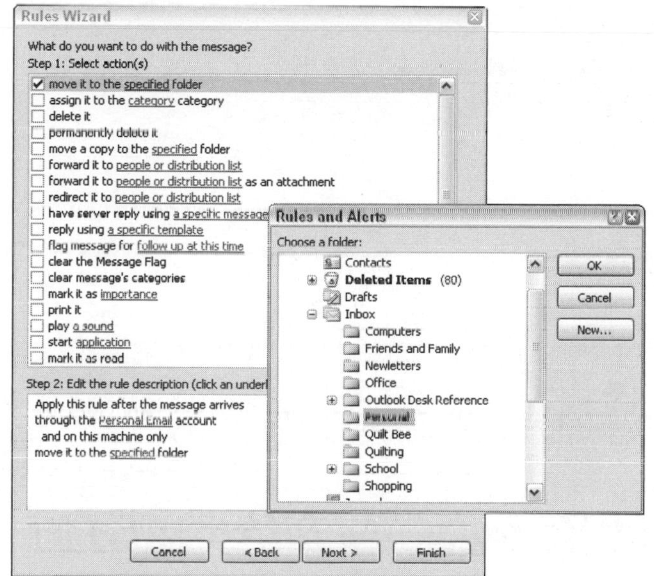

Figure 5-8: Select a folder.

8. **Create any exceptions. When you're through making your exception, click Next.**

   If you don't want all mail from this account dumped in the folder you selected, here's your opportunity to create an exception. Choose the exception from the Step 1 panel, and then refine it using the Step 2 panel. For example, maybe you want all your personal mail rerouted except stuff from your spouse.

   You can create multiple exceptions by repeating this step. (For more help with Rules, see Book IX, Chapter 2.)

9. **Review the rule.**

   In the final panel of the Rules Wizard, you can review the rule you've created. Type a name for the new rule in the Step 1 box. (See Figure 5-9.) In Step 2, decide if you want this rule run now on existing e-mails. In Step 3, review the details. Click Finish. You return to the Rules and Alerts dialog box; click OK.

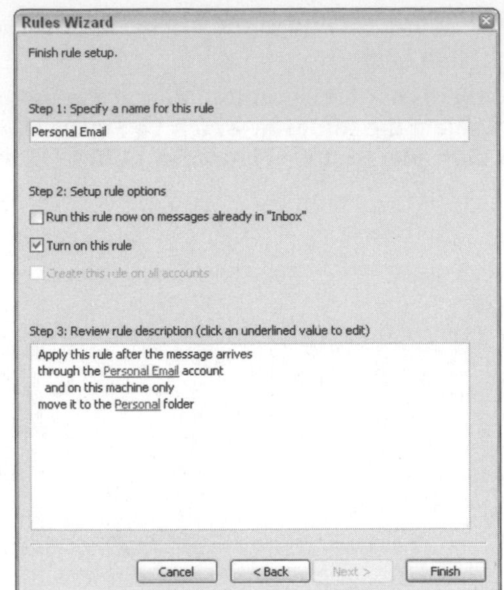

Figure 5-9: Finishing touches.

If you ask for the rule to be run right now, the appropriate e-mail is moved to the folder you selected.

Directing Sent Messages to a Different Folder

As you've probably figured out by now, when you send an e-mail to someone, a copy of that e-mail is placed in the Sent Items folder. That enables you to go back and check what you sent and to whom. You can also easily locate a message you've sent and resend the e-mail when needed. (See Book II, Chapter 2 for details.)

If you use an Exchange or an IMAP account, you can redirect where your sent messages are saved. You might be thinking, "Why? If they are all in the Sent Items folder, I can find them." That's true, but wouldn't it be more convenient to save sent e-mails in the same folder as related messages? For example, I keep all e-mails related to this book in a special folder. The e-mails I send to the people working on this book are also placed in that folder automatically. That way, I can locate any message related to the book quickly.

Exchange accounts are typically used within large corporations or universities. If you use an Exchange account, replies and forwards of messages in the Inbox are saved to the Sent Items folder, and you can't do anything about that. You can, however, keep replies and forwards of e-mail messages saved in any folder other than the Inbox in the same folder as the original message. To redirect sent messages on an Exchange account:

1. **Choose Tools➪Options➪Preferences➪E-Mail Options.**

   The E-Mail Options dialog box appears.

2. **Select Save Copies of Messages in Sent Items Folder.**
3. **Click Advanced E-Mail Options.**

   The Advanced E-Mail Options dialog box pops up. (See Figure 5-10.)

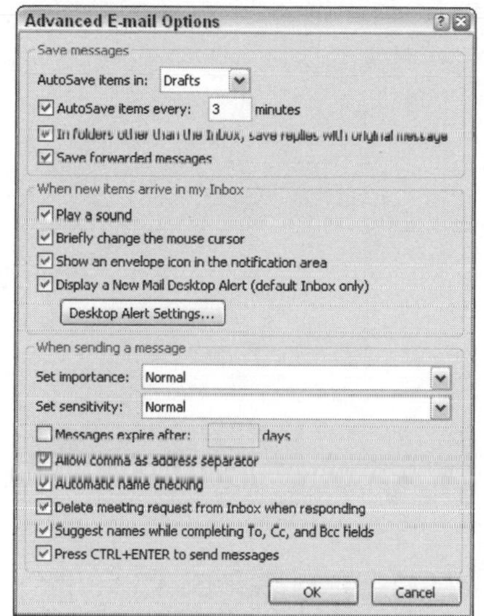

Figure 5-10: Redirecting traffic.

4. **Select In Folders Other Than the Inbox, Save Replies With Original Message. Then click OK.**

An IMAP account stores your messages on its server — making it a great account to have when you must have access to your e-mail from any computer. When you use an IMAP account for the first time, you choose where you want sent items saved. To redirect sent messages on an IMAP account to a different folder, follow these steps:

1. **Choose Tools➪Account Settings.**

   The Account Settings dialog box opens.

2. **Select the IMAP account you want to change from those listed on The E-Mail tab, and then click Change.**

   The Change E-Mail Account dialog box appears.

3. **Click More Settings.**

   The Internet E-Mail Settings dialog box appears.

4. **Select the folder in which to save sent messages.**

   Click the Folders tab and then enable the Choose an Existing Folder or Create a New Folder to Save Your Sent Items for This Account In option. Select the folder you want to use, or click New Folder and create a new one. (See Figure 5-11.)

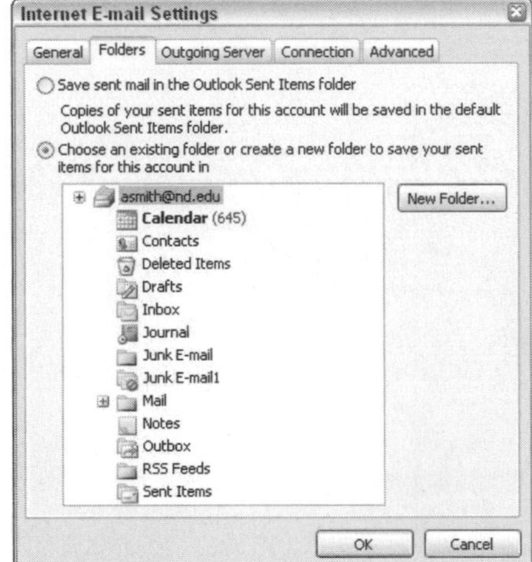

Figure 5-11: Change IMAP folders.

Having Replies Sent to Another Address

Sometimes you want replies to go to an e-mail address other than the one you're using to send a message. For example, you might want replies to a company training invitation to go to your assistant, so he can keep track of the number of people expected and order enough food and party hats.

To have replies for a message sent to a different e-mail address, then create a message and in the Message form:

1. **Choose Options⇨More Options⇨Direct Replies To.**

   The Message Options dialog box appears.

2. **Enter the reply address.**

   Remove the address already appearing in the Have Replies Sent To box, and replace it with the e-mail address you want replies sent to. If the address you want to use is in Contacts, click Select Names, choose a name, and click Reply To. You can choose several addresses from this list if you want replies sent to more than one address; when you're through picking names, click OK.

3. **Click Close.**

   You return to the Message form. The Direct Replies To button remains highlighted on the Ribbon so you won't forget you've redirected the replies for this message.

4. **Finish your e-mail message as usual and click Send to send it along.**

Dealing with Multiple People, Multiple Accounts, and One Little Ol' Computer

If you have kids fighting over the one computer in your household — or if you and the sales team are duking it out over the one laptop for your department — you might be able to end the arguments by setting up e-mail profiles. Basically, a *profile* contains the one or more e-mail accounts used by a single person. Set up multiple profiles, and everyone in your family/department/group can instantly live in peace and harmony while sharing the one lousy computer. (Or get a start on it, anyway.)

Even if you're the only person using your computer, you might still find e-mail profiles useful — they not only keep track of e-mail accounts, but also record where the incoming mail is stored (on the server or locally in an Outlook `.pst` file), Contacts, Calendar, Notes, Tasks, Journal, rules, search folders, and so on. For example, if you want to keep your personal contacts and calendar separate from your business ones, you can create two e-mail profiles. When Outlook starts, you choose which profile to use (such as your Home profile), and you see only that e-mail, Calendar, Contacts, and such. To change to a different profile, you make a hasty exit and then restart Outlook.

An e-mail profile can contain information for multiple e-mail accounts, but all data is stored in a single `.pst` file. In addition, although a single e-mail profile might contain both an Exchange e-mail account and a POP3, IMAP, or HTTP account, it cannot contain two different Exchange accounts.

You start out with one e-mail profile. To create another e-mail profile, follow these steps:

1. **Open the Control Panel.**

   Exit Outlook and open the Windows Control Panel by clicking the Start button and choosing Control Panel.

2. **Start Mail.**

   Double-click the Mail icon. The Mail Setup dialog box peeks out.

3. **Click Show Profiles.**

   The Mail dialog box pops up. See Figure 5-12.

Figure 5-12: Create a new profile.

4. **Click Add.**

   The New Profiles dialog box appears.

5. **Type a name for your profile. Click OK to create the profile.**

   A wizard appears to step you through the process of setting up an e-mail account for this profile. See Book I, Chapter 3 for help.

6 **Get Outlook to use the new profile.**

   By default, Outlook uses the first profile that was set up when you initially installed the program. To get Outlook to prompt you for the new profile, you select the Prompt For a Profile to Be Used option in the Mail dialog box. (See Figure 5-12.) Click OK.

The next time you start Outlook, it asks you which profile you want to use, as shown in Figure 5-13. Choose one from the Profile Name list and click OK. The Mail, Contacts, Calendar, and other modules associated with that profile appear. Having multiple accounts is all about choices.

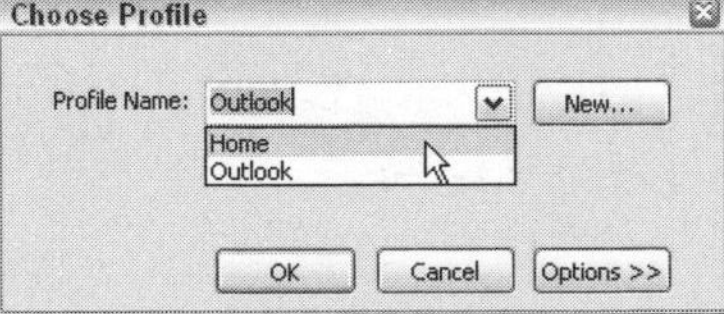

Figure 5-13: Nice to have a choice — so select a profile to use.

Book IV

Working with the Calendar

The 5th Wave By Rich Tennant

"It's your wife Mr. Dinker. Shall I have her take a seat in the closet, or do you want to schedule a meeting in the kitchen for later this afternoon?"

Contents at a Glance

Chapter 1: Getting Familiar with the Calendar 233

Chapter 2: Going Further with the Calendar 251

Chapter 3: Calendar Collaboration 263

Chapter 4: All About Meetings 301

Chapter 5: Making the Calendar Your Own..........327

Chapter 1: Getting Familiar with the Calendar

In This Chapter

- **Getting the lowdown on appointments, meetings, and events**
- **Displaying daily, weekly, or monthly calendars**
- **Changing to a different day, week, or month**
- **Keeping an appointment**
- **Setting reminders and then dealing with them**
- **Entering all-day events**

When people think of Outlook, mostly they think of e-mail and, maybe, Contacts because the two are so closely tied together. Me, I think of Calendar. Without something to help me keep track of all the lunch meetings, doctor appointments, soccer games, choir practices, hair appointments, and special school events I have to attend, I would literally lose my mind. Now if I can only find a way for Outlook to keep my appointments while I take a nap.

Appointments, Meetings, and Events — What's the Difference?

Because we tend to use the word *appointment* to describe "any ol' thing that interrupts my day," how does Outlook differentiate among *three* ol' things — appointments, meetings, and events?

- **An appointment** is set up between yourself and someone whose calendar you cannot access, such as friends and family or service people such as doctors, plumbers, roofers, carpenters, and so on.
- **A meeting** is set up with someone in your company, assuming that your company uses Microsoft Exchange and that you want to hold this meeting with people who have shared their calendars with you. When you create a meeting, you can check people's schedules and find the best time for everyone to get together. For more information on meetings, including how to create them in Outlook, see Book IV, Chapter IV.

Okay, technically speaking, you can set up a meeting with anyone whose e-mail address you've entered in Contacts, because that's all the information Outlook needs to send invitations to the meeting. However, if you're on an Exchange network, not only can you send invitations but you can view other participants' schedules and suggest a time that's free for most people. Also if you use an Exchange network, Outlook helps you schedule meeting resources such as meeting rooms, multimedia equipment, and so on. In addition, you can create a Meeting Workspace where files can be shared (such as the meeting agenda and handouts) and meeting details (such as attendees and location) can be kept current. So all in all, I personally consider meetings useful for Exchange users only although, as I said, you can technically create a meeting for anyone whose e-mail address you have, even if you don't share an Exchange network.

- **An event** is an all-day happening that may or may not interfere with your attending appointments or meetings that day. Typical events include birthdays, holidays, and seminars.

You find out how to create detailed appointments and to set up all-day events in this chapter. (For help with meetings — scheduling them, anyway — jump over to Book IV, Chapter IV.)

Understanding Day/Week/Month View

A *view* is simply the way in which Outlook decides to lay out the data in a particular module. The normal view for Mail is Messages view, which simply lists the messages in the order in which they were received. Also, the Reading Pane is normally shown on the right in Mail, but that's an ON/OFF thing and not really part of the view.

For Calendar, the normal view is Day/Week/Month, meaning that appointments are displayed graphically on the right, by day, week, or month, rather than in a long list. Figure 1-1 shows Week view; I explain each view — Day, Week, and Month — in a moment. Here are some things you should notice right away:

- Notice that appointments and meetings are shown as rectangles that graphically depict the amount of your day they consume.
- Events appear in that little gray area at the top of each day in Day and Week view, or at the top of the list of items for a given day in Month view. In Figure 1-1, if you look at that gray area that runs across the top of each day in the week, you might notice lots of different events, such as Tall Stacks and Picture Day at school.
- To view the details of an appointment, meeting, or event, hover the mouse pointer over its rectangle.

The Daily Task List typically appears at the bottom of the view window in Calendar, although again, that's an ON/OFF thing and not part of any view you might select. Notice also that, by default, the To-Do bar does not appear in Calendar, although you can make it show up if you want. You can also turn on the Reading pane and use it to view the details of any selected appointment, meeting, or event, but frankly I think it takes up too much space so I leave it off.

The Navigation pane, To-Do bar, Reading pane, and Daily Task List are all On/Off elements you control separately from the view. Use the View menu to turn these screen elements on or off as desired.

If you display the Navigation pane or the To-Do bar, keep in mind that you can easily minimize them by clicking their Minimize buttons.

Day view

You change from view to view by selecting the view to use from the Current View menu. (See Book I, Chapter 1.) Assuming you're using Day/Week/Month view (as shown in Figure 1-2), you still have a bunch of options left for customizing the view. To display a single day's worth of appointments, meetings, and events, click the Day tab at the top of the viewing window. While in Day view, keep the following in mind:

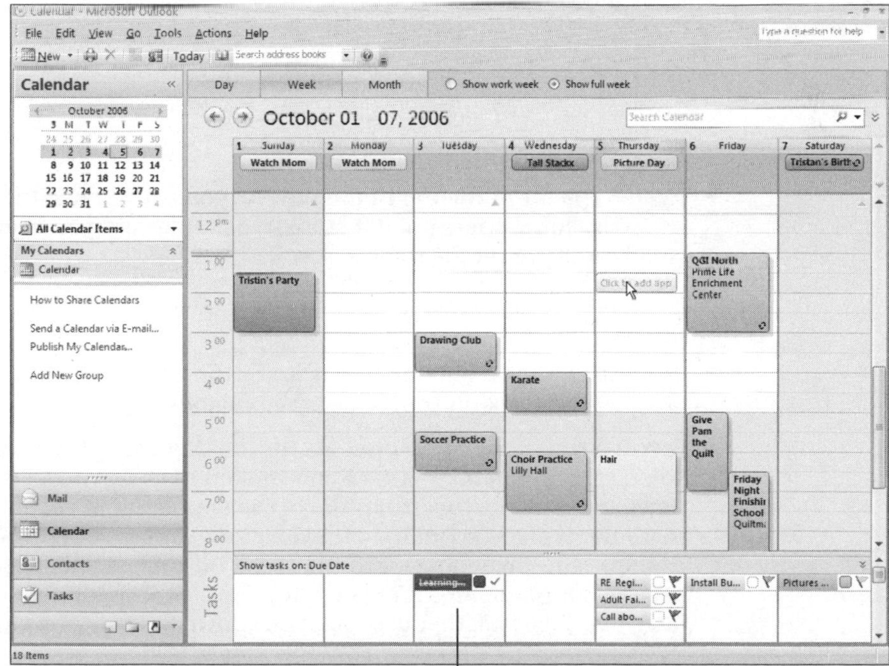

Daily Task List

Figure 1-1: The Calendar is full of information about what you have to do today, this week, or this month.

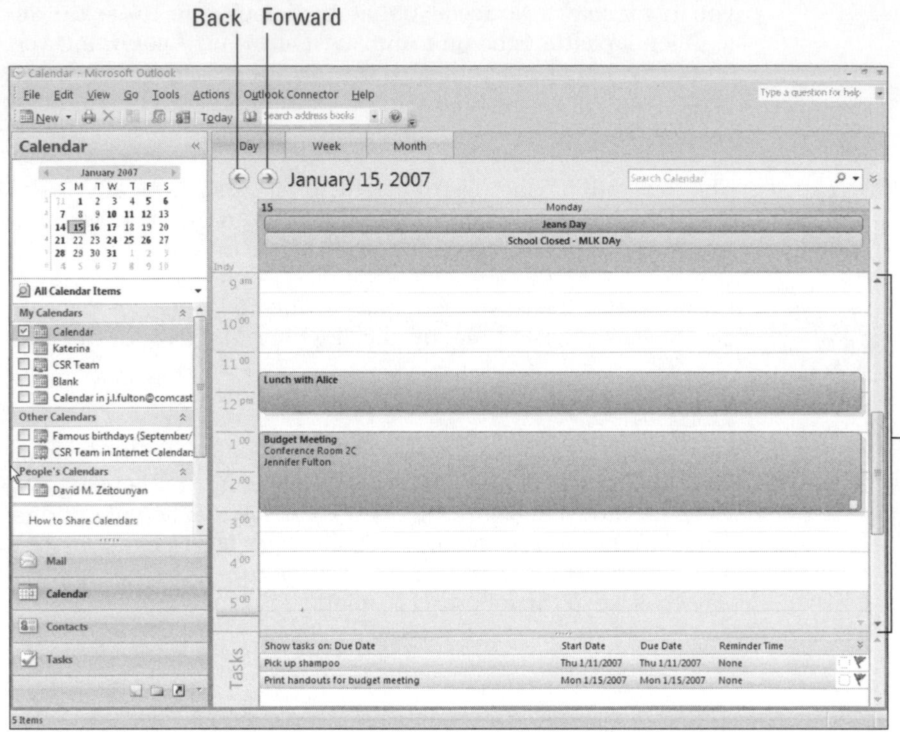

Figure 1-2: Day view.

- **Events appear at the top of the day.** As you add events, the events area expands, but at some point it stops expanding, and you need to use the small scroll bar on the right to scroll.
- **The current time is marked.** It shows up with a yellow band on the left, on the time bar.
- **You can change from day to day.** Click the Forward button (to see the next day) or Back button (to see the previous day).
- **Scroll through the appointments for the day using the scroll bar.** If some appointments or other items are out of view, you see a gray up or down arrow at the top or bottom of the appointment section. Click the up or down arrow to jump to the next item for that day. In Figure 1-2, for example, the small down arrow is at the bottom right of the appointment section. This indicates that you have another appointment or meeting later than 5:00 P.M. that day. Click this down arrow to view that item.

✦ **If you have no appointments, events, or meetings for the current day, you see two blue tabs on either side of the current day.** Click either the Previous Appointment or Next Appointment tabs to jump to the previous or next day that contains an appointment, meeting, or event (see Figure 1-3).

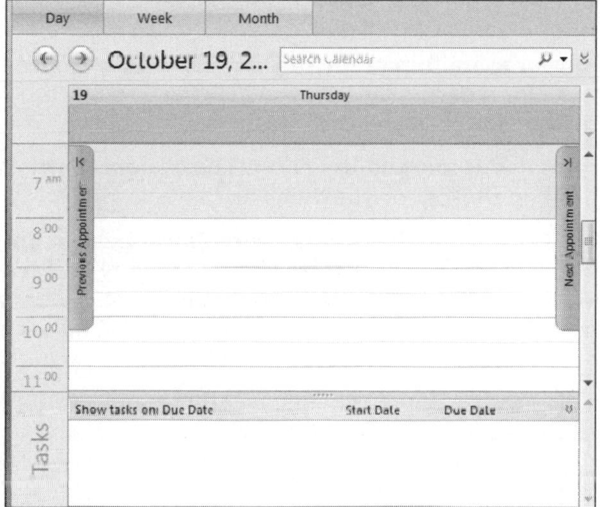

Figure 1-3: Jump to the next appointment.

✦ **Hours that fall outside the normal work day appear in gray.** You can change the start and end time for your day if you want — for help, see the upcoming "Displaying just the days you work" sidebar.

To change to Day view quickly while in Week or Month view, click that day's header (the gray bar with the date on it). For example, in Figure 1-1, which shows Week view, you can jump to Day view and display the appointments for October 4th by clicking the 4 Wednesday header.

Displaying just the days you work

Not everybody's work week is Monday to Friday; if needed, you can select other days to show in the Work Week view. Choose Tools⇨Options⇨Calendar Options. Then, in the Calendar Work Week area, select the days to show in the Work Week view. These do not have to be consecutive days, by the way. Notice also that you can change the month that starts out your year and the time you start and end each day. Hours and days outside these normal work times are shown in gray when you use Day or Week view. (See Figures 1-2 and 1-4.) Click OK.

Week view

To display a week's worth of appointments, meetings, and events, change to Week view by clicking the Week tab at the top of the window (assuming you're using Day/Week/Month view in Calendar — if not, choose View➪Current View➪Day/Month/Day). See Figure 1-4 for a glimpse at Week view.

While in Week view, make a note of the following:

- **Events appear at the top of the day on which they occur.** If you have a lot of events for a particular day, you may need to use the scroll bar on the far right to scroll so you can see them all.
- **The current day is marked in yellow.** The current time is marked with a yellow band on the left, on the time bar.
- **Hours that fall outside the normal work day appear in gray.** That's why you're seeing Sunday and Saturday show up in gray in Figure 1-4. You might notice in the figure that the hours after 5 P.M. each weekday also show up in gray. You can change the start and end time for your day if you want — for help, see the "Displaying just the days you work" sidebar.
- **You can display the appointments, meetings, and events for the entire week.** Select the Show Full Week option.

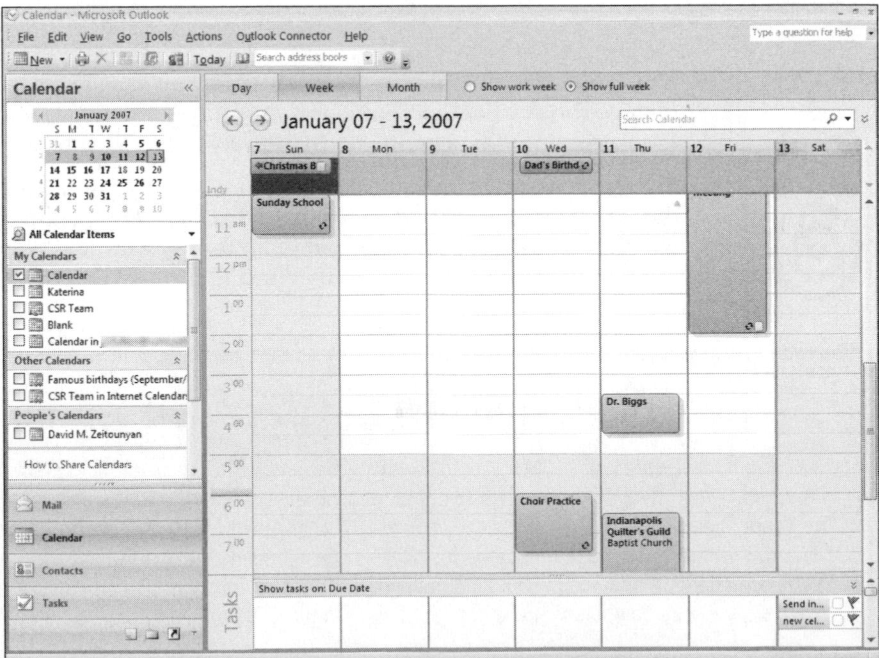

Figure 1-4: Week view.

✦ **You can display just Monday – Friday appointments.** Select the Show Work Week option instead.

✦ **You can change from week to week.** Click the Forward button (to see the next week) or Back button (to see the previous week).

✦ **Scroll through the appointments for the weekday using the scroll bar.** If some appointments or other items are out of view for a particular day, you see a gray up or down arrow at the top or bottom of the appointment section for that day. Click the up or down arrow to jump to the next item for that day. For example, in Figure 1-4, an up arrow is at the top of the appointment section on Thursday the 11th. Click the up arrow to view whatever's hidden at the moment.

✦ **If you have no appointments, events, or meetings for the entire week, you see two blue tabs on either side of the view window.** These tabs are marked Previous Appointment and Next Appointment. Click either one of these tabs to jump to the previous or next week that contains an appointment, meeting, or event.

Month view

To display a month's worth of appointments, meetings, and events, click the Month tab while in Day/Week/Month view. Change to Day/Week/Month view by choosing View➪Current View➪Day/Week/Month. See Figure 1-5.

Figure 1-5: Month view.

- **Appointments, meetings, and events appear on the day on which they occur.** Events appear first in the listing. It's a little hard to tell events from appointments and meetings, but if you look closely, you might notice that the events are outlined in black. For example, in Figure 1-5, notice that the event, Tall Stacks on October 4th, is outlined and that the appointments Karate and Choir Practice, are not.
- **The current day is marked in yellow.** In Figure 1-5, Thursday the 5th is the current day.
- **You can display only events.** Select the Low option at the top of the window. (See Figure 1-5.)
- **You can display the event headings, and only bands of color for each appointment or meeting.** Select the Medium option. The colors chosen for each appointment or meeting are based on the categories you've assigned to each item, so this option lets you gauge the type of activities you have going on each day. Also, the width of each color band helps you to judge the time involved in each activity, as shown in Figure 1-6. You might notice a thin blue line that divides each day in half; that helps you gauge where in your day a particular appointment or meeting falls — items appearing above the blue line fall within your work hours; below the line indicates an item that follows after work.

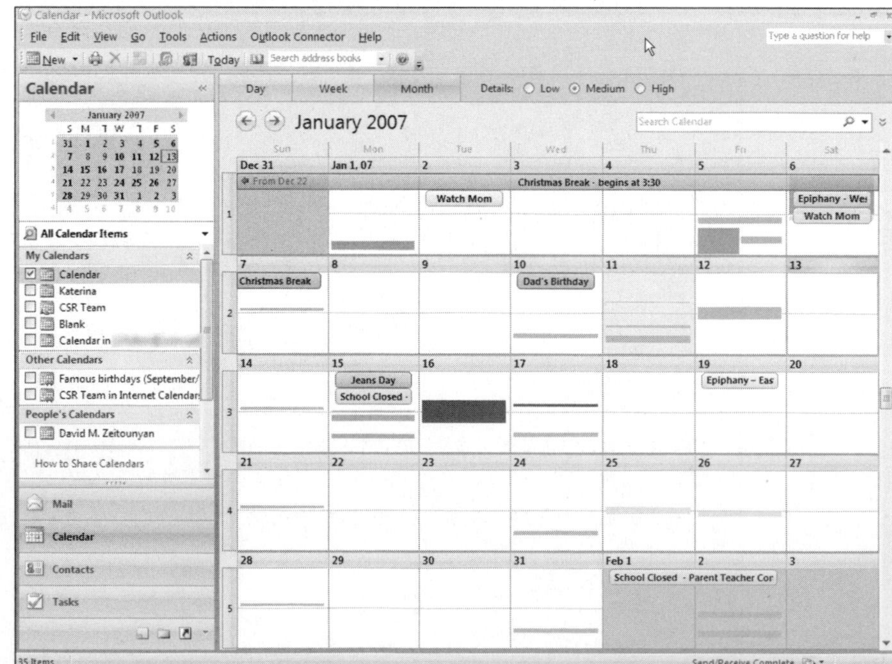

Figure 1-6: Bands of color let you get a quick sense of how busy your month looks.

- **You can display a heading for each event, appointment, or meeting.** Select the High option. See Figure 1-5.
- **You can change from week to week.** Click the Forward button (to see the next week) or Back button (to see the previous week).
- **Scroll through the items for a particular day if needed.** If some appointments or other items are out of view for a particular day, you see a gray down arrow on that day's square. Click the down arrow to scroll through the hidden items. For example, in Figure 1-5, there's a down arrow on October 18th and 31st that you can click to view whatever's hiding.
- **If you have no appointments, events, or meetings for the entire month, you see two blue tabs on either side of the view window.** Click either the Previous Appointment and Next Appointment tabs to jump to the previous or next month that contains an appointment, meeting, or event.

To discover how to change to a different day, week, or month, see the next section, "Navigating around the Calendar."

If you're on an Exchange network, you can view other people's calendars within Calendar, should they choose to share them with you. See Book IV, Chapter 3 for information on how to get sharing.

Navigating around the Calendar

After you choose Day, Week, or Month view, you aren't stuck. You can quickly change to a different day, week, or well, month. First off, the day, week, or month currently being shown is listed at the top of the viewing window, as shown in Figure 1-7. Here, you're looking at the meetings, appointments, and events for the week of December 10th - 16th. In views that show more than one day, the current day is highlighted in orange. The day of the week is also shown at the top of each day so you won't confuse Tuesday with Wednesday (if you're prone to that kind of thing). Here's how to browse through your calendar:

- **To change to the next day, week, or month**, click the left or right Back or Forward navigation arrows at the top of the viewing window.
- **To jump back to today**, click the Today button on the Standard toolbar.

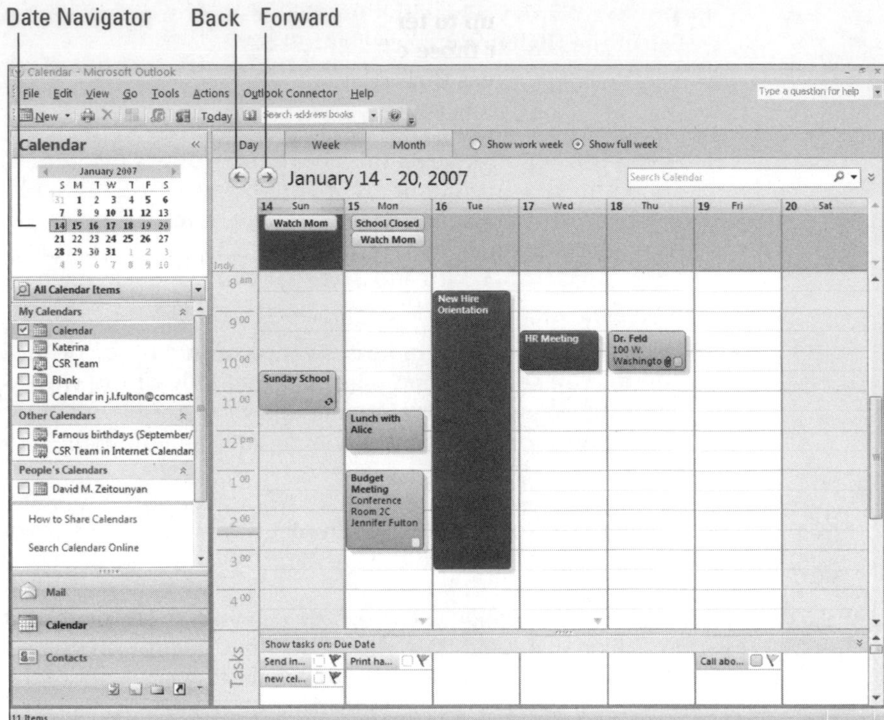

Figure 1-7: Your typical calendar view.

The Date Navigator (that calendar thing at the top of the Navigation pane) is where Outlook highlights the current day, week, or month being shown. For example, in Figure 1-7, the current week, December 14–20, is highlighted in orange in the Date Navigator. Today is marked on the Date Navigator with a red outline.

Here are some techniques for using the Date Navigator to browse your calendar:

- **If you're using Day or Week view, you can click any day in the Date Navigator and get a quick display of the appointments, meetings, or events for that day — without changing the view.** If you're in Week view for example, and you click a particular day, you're changed to the week that contains that day. So you remain in Week view, but the week that contains the day you want to see is displayed.
- **If you're in Month view and you click a day in the Date Navigator, you see that day displayed in Day view.** So in this example, the view is changed from Month to Day view in order to show the items for the selected day.

- **You can display up to ten consecutive days in a modified Week view by dragging over those days in the Date Navigator.** To display nonconsecutive days, press Ctrl and click those days in the Navigator. For a quick display of consecutive days beginning with the current day, press Alt plus any number from 0 (the current day plus nine more days) to 9 (the current day plus eight more days). For example, if the currently displayed day is October 10th, if you press Alt+9, you see October 10–19 in a crowded Week view.
- **If the day you want to review isn't displayed in the Date Navigator, you can change to a different month.** Click the left or right arrows on either side of the month name, at the top of the Date Navigator.
- **You can also click the month name and select a month from those that appear in the list to change months in the Date Navigator.** If you're in Month view and you change to a different month, all the items for that month appear on-screen. If you're in Day or Week view, the corresponding day or week for that month (respectively) is instantly displayed. For example, if you're currently looking at October 16 and you change to August, August 16 is shown.

Jump to a specific day quickly by using Go To. Choose Go➪Go To Date or press Ctrl+G, type the date you want to view in the Date box, and click OK.

Creating a Complete Appointment

It's easy to create a quick appointment (as discussed in Book I, Chapter 2): Change to the day on which you want to create the appointment, hover the mouse pointer over the time for the appointment, and click when you see the words `Click to Add Appointment`. Type the description (and optionally, the location, separated by a semicolon) for the appointment in the white bubble that appears and then click outside the bubble to create a half-hour appointment. To lengthen the appointment, drag its bottom edge. See Figure 1-8.

I should probably mention here that sometimes appointments appear in your Calendar without you actually creating them. For example, someone may forward an appointment to you in an e-mail message (basically, sending a copy of the appointment to you). You can then easily add that appointment to your calendar, essentially copying it from the e-mail. Also, if you work on an Exchange network, a colleague might invite you to a meeting, and if you accept, that meeting is added to the Calendar automatically. See Book IV, Chapter 3 for more info.

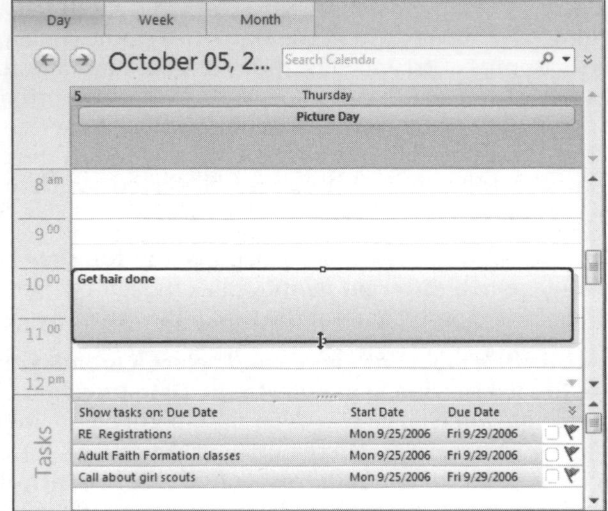

Figure 1-8: Drag to expand an appointment's time.

To create a more detailed appointment, you should use the Appointment form:

1. **Choose New⇨Appointment.**

   Actually, it saves time if you go to the date for the appointment and click the appointment time *before* you click the New button, but you don't have to do it that way.

   If you want to create appointments from other Outlook items, you can do so quickly by using drag and drop. For example, you can create an appointment from an incoming e-mail — or copy related contact information into an appointment using drag and drop. (See Book I, Chapter 2 for more drag-and-drop tips.)

2. **Type a subject and a location.**

   The Subject field is where you enter a basic description for the appointment, such as **Dr. Feld**. See Figure 1-9. The Location field is optional; but sometimes it's handy to make a note where something is taking place, such as **100 W. Washington, Suite 202**.

3. **Enter the start and end times.**

   Select the date of the appointment and then set a Start time. If the appointment ends on the same day, you then need only set the End time by choosing a time from the list. Otherwise, you need to select an End date first, then an End time. Notice that appointments are all set at half-hour intervals; you can type an exact start or end time in the boxes if you can't find what you want on the lists.

You can type words in the date boxes instead of selecting an actual date. For example, you could type **today** or **tomorrow**, or **three days from now**. Some holidays are recognized as well, such as **Fourth of July**, **New Year's Day**, or **Christmas**.

Outlook lets you schedule overlapping appointments; I guess the folks at Microsoft have worked out how to be in two places at the same time. Anyway, if you select a time that overlaps another appointment, you see a warning on the InfoBar. That gives you an opportunity to select a different time before you click Save & Close. If you want to preview this appointment within your current Calendar before you decide to adjust the time for this appointment, choose Appointment⇨Actions⇨Calendar. This unfinished appointment appears in the preview, identified by a dark blue rectangle.

4. **Set a reminder.**

   By default, the reminder goes off 15 minutes before the appointment start time. If you need longer than that to get to the appointment, open the Appointment⇨Options⇨Reminder list and choose an interval. You can also type something, such as **25 minutes**, **2.5 hours**, or **5 days**. Don't want to be reminded? Just choose None from the Reminder list. (The next section offers details of what the reminder does when it goes off, and what you should do about it.)

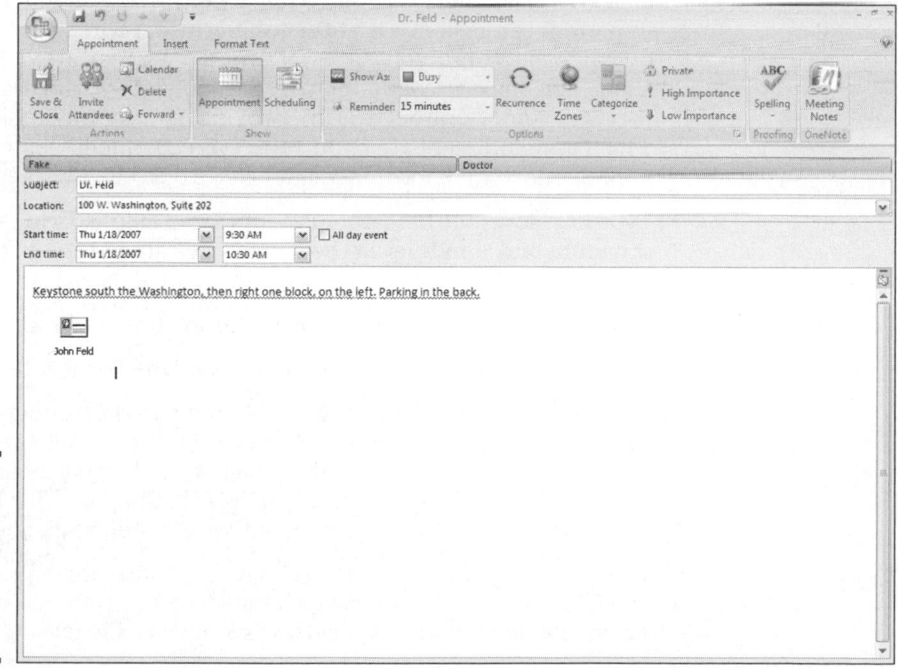

Figure 1-9: Create an appointment with the Appointment form.

5. **Select a category.**

   One of the easiest ways to keep things organized and easy to identify and locate within Outlook is to use categories. (See Book VIII, Chapter 1.) If you've set up some categories, select as many as you like for this appointment by choosing them one at a time from the Categorize list (Appointment⇨Options⇨Categorize).

6. **Set other options.**

   A lot of the other options have to do with creating a meeting (covered in Book IV, Chapter 4). You can, however, set a few options for appointments — these, for example:

   - Mark an appointment as "gotta keep" by choosing Appointment⇨Options⇨High Importance.
   - Choose Appointment⇨Options⇨Low Importance to mark appointments you can blow off if you have to (such as your gym time, right?).

     When you mark an appointment as High Importance or Low Importance, it doesn't change how they appear in Day/Week/Month view. If, however, you change to a list view such as Active Appointments or By Category, you can then arrange items by importance by choosing View⇨Arrange By⇨Importance. Arranging items by importance works, but it doesn't help much because none of the calendar views show the Importance field. In other words, High importance items appear at the top of the list when you arrange it by importance, but you can't tell which ones they are. To keep you from going insane wondering why Outlook lets you mark appointments as important but doesn't provide an easy way to let you see which appointments are important, I'd recommend customizing a view to show the Importance field. See Book VIII, Chapter 2.

   - Type any notes for the appointment (for example, **Bring new project schedule and timeline**) in the large Notes area at the bottom of the form.
   - Spell-check your notes by choosing Appointment⇨Proofing⇨Spelling.
   - Format the note text using the buttons on the Format Text tab.
   - Insert related files or attach Outlook items to the appointment using the buttons on the Insert tab. (For example, you might attach a related e-mail, contact, or task to make that item easily accessible from within the appointment.) See Book II, Chapter 3 for help with inserting files or items. Granted, in that chapter, I talk about inserting items into an e-mail message, but the process is the same for all Outlook forms. Trust me.

7. **When you're done setting options, click Save & Close.**

   The appointment appears in your Calendar.

Wanna make a change already? No problem; appointments by their nature are flexible. (For the word on how to make changes, see Book IV, Chapter 2.)

Dealing with a Reminder When It Rears Its Ugly Head

When you create an appointment, you have an option to set a reminder. Actually, if you do nothing when you create an appointment, a reminder is automatically set that goes off 15 minutes before the appointment. Of course, you can change this interval (or remove the reminder altogether) when you create the appointment. Assuming you set a reminder, then, at the right time, Outlook bops you on the head. Figure 1-10 shows what the bop looks like.

You can set reminders when creating meetings, events, tasks, and To-Do items as well; those reminders work exactly as described here.

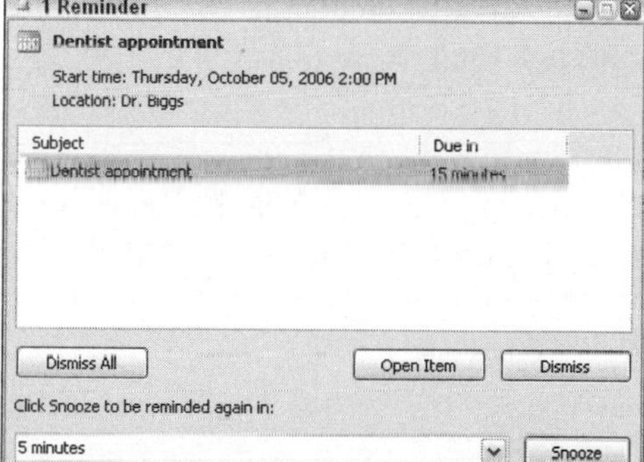

Figure 1-10: A nice little reminder to get going.

At the top of the Reminder window, you see the date and time of the original appointment. If you need to review the rest of the appointment details, click Open Item. You can click Dismiss to simply get rid of the reminder — after that, you are on your own to get to the appointment on time. If you want to be reminded again before the appointment, choose an interval from the Snooze list and click Snooze.

Planning an All-Day Event

An event takes up the whole day and includes things like birthdays, anniversaries, conferences, vacations, and Saturday naps. The idea behind scheduling an event in Calendar is that you're reminded about a special day, but you can still schedule appointments and meetings on that day if you want. For some events, such as conferences, vacations, and all-day meetings, you might not want to schedule other things to occur at that same time. Well, okay, maybe your boss wants you to keep appointments during your vacation, but that's not Outlook's problem. Based on what you manage to work out with your boss, Outlook can mark your time during the event as busy or not (you see how in a minute).

You can actually schedule as many appointments or meetings as you like during an event day, regardless of how you mark your time within Outlook (that is, whether you mark it as busy or not). The only reason for taking care to mark your time as busy during an event is to prevent people who might also have access to your Calendar (such as an overeager assistant) from scheduling appointments or meetings you can't actually attend.

To add an event to your Calendar, follow these steps:

1. **Choose New➪Event.**

   In Day or Week view, you can also change to the date on which the event will occur and double-click the gray area at the top of that day to create an event.

2. **Type a subject and a location.**

   The Subject field is where you enter a basic description for the event, such as **Tall Stacks**. See Figure 1-11. The Location field is optional; but might be needed for events that actually occur in a different place, such as conferences or seminars.

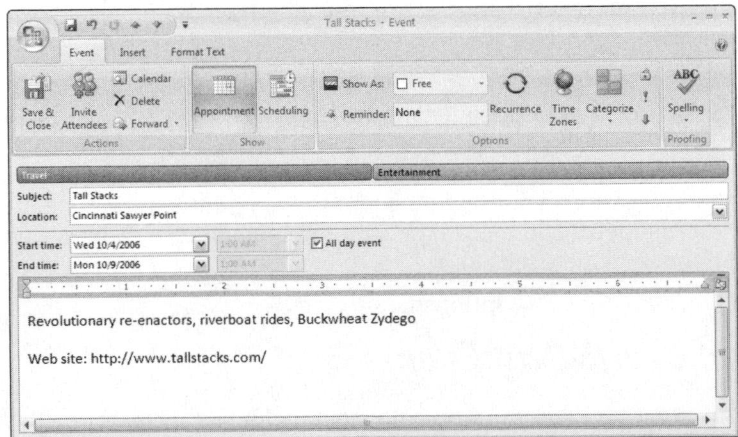

Figure 1-11: Add an event.

Outlook lets you schedule events even if you already have appointments or meetings on that day; it assumes that most events are just holidays and such — not something you actually have to attend. (Book IV, Chapter 3 explains how to designate your time as "busy" during an event and not "free.") Anyway, if you change the event time to Busy and you have a conflict in your Calendar, you see a warning on the InfoBar. That gives you an opportunity to select a different day for the event before you click Save & Close. If you want to take a look at what's causing the conflict in your Calendar, choose Appointment➪Actions➪Calendar.

3. **Enter the start and end dates.**

   If needed, select the start date for the event. Events sometimes take more than a single day. When they do, set an end date for the event as well. You don't enter any times when setting up an event because events take all day. If this event doesn't and you want to show that part of your day is free, you can change this into an appointment by unchecking the All-Day Event option.

   You can type words in the date boxes instead of selecting an actual date. For example, you could type **today** or **tomorrow**, or **three months from now**. Some holidays are recognized as well, such as **Fourth of July**, **New Year's Day,** or **Christmas**.

   A lot of events recur. For example, birthdays and anniversaries occur on the same day each year. For help in setting up recurring events, see Book IV, Chapter 2.

4. **Set a reminder.**

   By default, the reminder goes off 18 hours before the event's start date. If you need longer than that to get to prepare, open the Appointment➪Options➪Reminder List and choose an interval. You can also type a specific amount of time, such as **25 minutes**, **2.5 hours**, or **5 days**. Don't need to be reminded about your brother's birthday because you're not getting him anything? Just choose None from the Reminder list. To find out how to deal with reminders, see the previous section.

5. **Select a category.**

   You can keep your Outlook items organized with categories; see Book VIII, Chapter 1 for details. After setting up some categories, choose the ones that apply to this event by selecting them, one at a time, from the Appointment➪Options➪Categorize List.

6. **Set other options.**

   Most of the other options on the Ribbon have to do with creating a meeting, which you find out about in Book IV, Chapter 4; however, you can set a few more options for an event. For example . . .

   • Mark this event as "better not forget" by choosing Event➪Options➪High Importance.

- Choose Event➪Options➪Low Importance to mark events that don't require your presence and that you can even forget about if you get too busy — such as your anniversary (kidding, kidding . . .)

Events marked as either High or Low importance appear as ordinary events in any calendar view because the Importance field is not normally shown. You can add the Importance field to any list view; see Book VIII, Chapter 2 for help.

- Type any notes for the event, such as **Flight #2047**, **leaving at 10:02 a.m.**, **arriving 12:37 p.m. Shuttle to conference on lower level**., in the large notes area at the bottom of the form. You can spell check your notes by choosing Appointment➪Proofing➪Spelling. Format the note text using the buttons on the Format Text tab.
- Insert related files or attach Outlook items to the event using the buttons on the Insert tab. For example, you might attach an e-mail that details the conference schedule, the contact who made your hotel arrangements, or the tasks you need to finish before the event. (See Book II, Chapter 3 for help with inserting files or items.)

7. **When you're done setting options, click Save & Close.**

   The event appears in your Calendar at the top of the selected day(s).

Events often happen anywhere but at work. If you type some critical information in the Event form that you want to take with you (such as your flight info, conference agenda, or emergency phone numbers), you can print the Event form and take it with you to the event. See Book X, Chapter 3.

You can change an event later if needed; see Book IV, Chapter 2 for the steps that do the job.

Chapter 2: Going Further with the Calendar

In This Chapter

- Making appointments, meetings, and events repeat
- Changing an existing appointment or event
- Reorganizing your schedule
- Getting rid of appointments or events
- Adding holidays to the calendar

I wish I could tell you that after adding an appointment, meeting, or event to your Calendar, that would be it. But life doesn't work that way; all too often, you have to make adjustments. In this chapter, you find out how to navigate those changing waters with ease — copying, moving, and deleting appointments or events, changing appointment times, or making appointments, meetings, or events occur multiple times automatically. You find out other things as well, but I won't spoil the suspense. Read on!

Scheduling a Recurring Appointment, Meeting, or Event

Let's face it: Some appointments, meetings, and even events just won't go away. Like a stubborn stain, they keep coming back, even after repeated washings. Well, there's no reason that you have to manually copy an item repeatedly just to get it to appear on your Calendar multiple times. If an item's recurrence has a pattern, you can get Outlook to do the hard work for you and copy the item throughout your Calendar.

To make an appointment, meeting, or event recur on a regular basis (such as every Wednesday, for example), open the item first if needed and then follow these steps:

1. **Click the Recurrence button.**

   In the open form, you'll find the Recurrence button in the Options group on the main tab: Appointment, Event, or Meeting, depending on what type of Calendar item you're scheduling.

   The Recurrence dialog box appears, as shown in Figure 2-1.

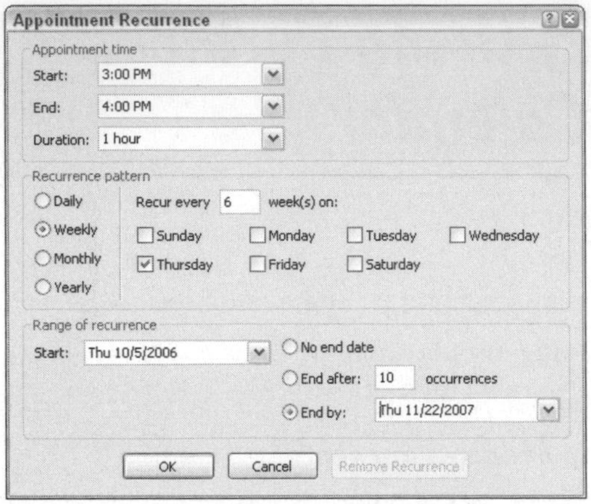

Figure 2-1: Rinse and repeat.

2. **Select the recurrence frequency.**

   Select the basic interval at which you want the appointment, meeting, or event to repeat: Daily, Weekly, Monthly, or Yearly.

3. **Set recurrence options.**

   Depending on the frequency you selected in Step 2, a set of options appears on the right. Set those options to match the pattern of repetition:

   - *Daily:* Choose to repeat Every Day, Every 2 Days, and so on. Or if it's something that happens only during the work week, you have the option of setting it to repeat Every Weekday and skipping weekends.
   - *Weekly:* First, choose how often the item recurs: Recur Every Week, Every 2 Weeks, or whatever. Then choose the day on which that happens, such as Monday, Tuesday, and so on.
   - *Monthly:* Here you have two choices. You might choose a particular day of the month or every so many months, such as the 10th of every third month. Or you might choose the first, second, third, fourth, or last weekday of every month, such as the second Thursday of every other month.
   - *Yearly:* Like the Monthly option, you can select either a particular date to repeat each year, such as October 16th, or a particular day within a certain month, such as the last Friday of November.

If you can't find a pattern in the Recurrence dialog box that fits the actual pattern for the appointment, meeting, or event, you might have to create multiple items, select a pattern for each one that when combined, create the pattern for the actual appointment or event. For example, if your garden club meets on the last Friday of every month except during January–April, when it meets on the second Tuesday, you need to create two recurring items: one that recurs every last Friday, and another that recurs on the second Tuesday. You can set limits for the number of recurrences to fit January–April.

4. **Set limits to the recurrence and click OK.**

   After setting the pattern of recurrence, set its limit. Will the appointment repeat forever? Will it recur a certain number of times (say, five) and then stop? Or will it repeat until the end of November and then no more? Set the limit of recurrence by using the options in the Range of Recurrence area at the bottom of the dialog box.

After you make an appointment, meeting, or event recur, the pattern you establish appears in the InfoBar of the item's form. The Recurrence button is also highlighted on the Ribbon as kind of a visual reminder that this item repeats. Click Save & Close to save the item and its repeating pattern. The item is automatically copied throughout your Calendar, using the recurrence pattern you set. Recurring appointments, events, or meetings appear with a special Recurrence icon (as shown in Figure 2-2).

Figure 2-2: Recurrent items use a special icon.

Making Changes to a Recurring Item

After you create a recurring appointment, meeting, or event, Outlook treats the repeating items as a series. Basically, if you make a change to one of the recurring items, Outlook expects that you'll want to make the same change to all of them. For example, if you lengthen one appointment (as explained in the section, "Changing Appointments or Events"), Outlook figures chances are pretty good that all similar appointments should also be lengthened.

When you double-click a recurring appointment, meeting, or event, Outlook asks you whether you want to affect the related items as well (see Figure 2-3). To affect only this particular appointment, meeting, or event, select Open This Occurrence. To affect all items in a recurring series, select Open the Series.

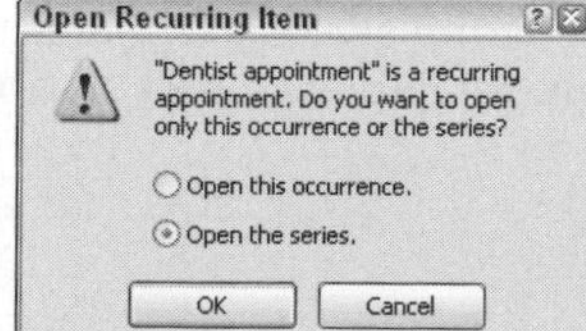

Figure 2-3: Repeating yourself?

Either way, the appointment, meeting, or event form opens as usual — but the Recurrence button appears only if you're making changes to all items in the series (if you chose Open the Series). Click the Recurrence button if you want to change not only the pattern of recurrence, but also the start or end date for the series, or the time for the appointment. If you chose Open This Occurrence, then you can't change the recurrence pattern, but you can change the date or time for this occurrence. You do that, by the way, by making changes to the Start date/time or End date/time just like you might to any appointment or event.

Make your changes and save them by clicking Save & Close. If you choose Open This Occurrence, your changes affect only that item. If you choose Open the Series, your changes are copied to all items in the series.

If you delete an item that's part of a series, you're asked the question again: Do you want to remove just this occurrence or the entire series? (Not sure how to delete an appointment or event? See the upcoming section, "Removing an Appointment or Event." Meetings are a whole different animal; for help in removing them, see Book IV, Chapter 4.)

Changing Appointments or Events

It seems that the only thing constant in life is change. So if you've made an appointment and later on the doctor's office calls asking if you can come an hour earlier because Mrs. Hoover was a no-show, here's what you can do to make that change, and others, in Outlook:

1. **Open the appointment or event.**

   Double-click the appointment or event you want to change. If the appointment or event is part of a recurring series of appointments/events, choose one of these options:

   - Open this Occurrence (to change this appointment or event only)
   - Open the Series (to change the entire series)

   The Appointment/Event form opens.

2. **Make any changes you want.**

   You can change anything you like; for example, you might change the description (Subject), Location, or add some notes.

   To change the date or time for a recurring series of appointments or events, make sure you choose Open the Series when you open the item, and then click the Recurrence button.

To shorten or lengthen an appointment without opening it, change to Day view and drag the appointment's lower border. To change an appointment or event's Subject without opening it, click it twice — slowly — within Day, Week, or Month view to position the cursor in the text, and then simply edit it.

- *To remove a reminder:* Change the Reminder to None.
- *To change the recurrence pattern:* Choose Appointment/Event⇨Options⇨Recurrence. (See the previous section, "Scheduling a Recurring Appointment, Meeting, or Event," for help.)
- *To change an appointment into an event:* Select the All Day Event option. The Start and End times disappear, but you can still change the End Date.
- *To change an event into an appointment:* Simply deselect the All Day Event option. When you do, the Start and End Times appear so you can change them.
- *To change an appointment into a meeting:* Choose Appointment⇨Actions⇨Invite Attendees. To find out more about creating meetings, see Book IV, Chapter 4.

3. **Choose Appointment/Event⇨Actions⇨Save & Close.**

Removing an Appointment or Event

Sometimes, an appointment or event gets cancelled; sometimes, you just get uninvited. Okay, that never happens to me, but I've heard it happens to other people. If it happens to you, you can easily remove the unneeded appointment or event from your Calendar:

✦ **To remove a nonrecurring appointment or event,** click it once to select it. You can remove multiple appointments or events at one time by pressing Ctrl and clicking each one to select it. After selecting what you want to remove, click the Delete button on the Standard toolbar or press Delete. See Figure 2-4.

✦ **To remove a recurring appointment or event,** click it to select it, and then click the Delete button on the Standard toolbar or press Delete. A dialog box appears; to delete all occurrences of the recurring appointment or event, select Delete the Series. To delete this occurrence only, select Delete This Occurrence.

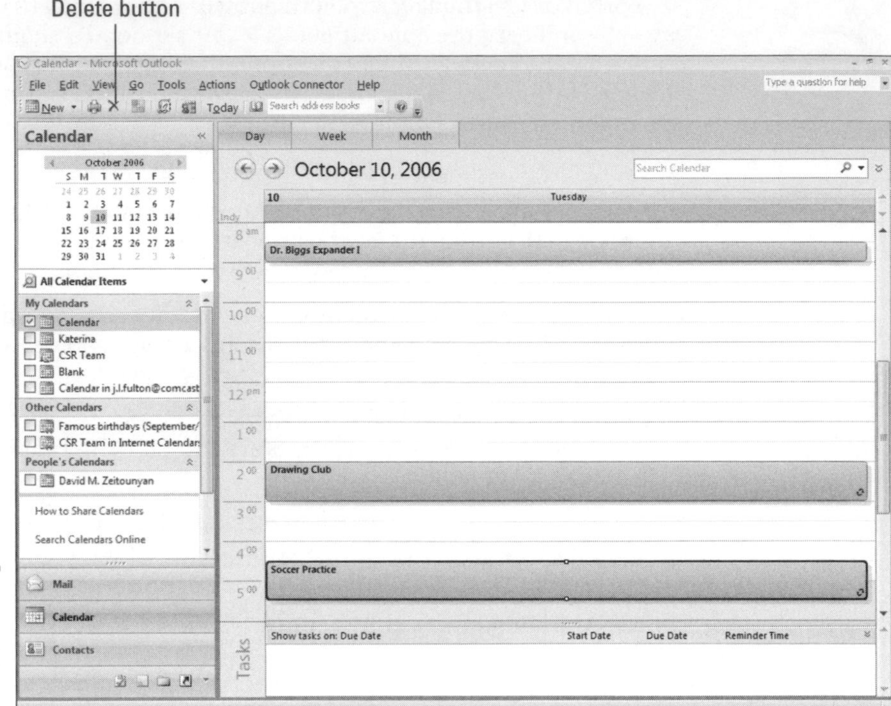

Figure 2-4: Remove the appointment or event.

You don't have to delete a recurring appointment or event to get it to stop. Instead, you can simply change the date the recurrence ends. See the previous section, "Scheduling a Recurring Appointment, Meeting, or Event," for help in making changes to an item.

Archiving is a process of backing up (saving) older items, such as appointments and events, and then removing them from Outlook. Archiving allows you to reduce the size of your Outlook data file without losing important data; you can always search for, view, and even restore any archived item. (See Book IX, Chapter 1 for details.)

Reorganizing Your Time

Everybody's schedule changes — some more than others. Luckily, Outlook makes it pretty easy to keep up with the changing times.

- **To move an appointment's time,** just drag and drop the appointment within the Calendar. For example, to change a 1:00 appointment to 3:00, change to Day or Week view, drag the appointment to the 3:00 time slot, and then drop it.

✦ **To move an appointment or event's date,** change to Week or Month view, drag the appointment or event onto a different day, and drop it. For example, you might move an appointment or event from Monday to Wednesday. You can also drag and drop an appointment or event on any day in the Date Navigator to change its date. (See Figure 2-5.) As you drag an item onto the Date Navigator and hover the mouse pointer over a date, the Calendar changes to display that date for you. This allows you to change the start time for the item as well, because you can then move back into the viewing window and drop the item on the appropriate time slot.

✦ **If you need to move an appointment or event pretty far**, you can use the Edit, Cut and Edit, Paste commands to move it. First click the appointment or event to select it, and then choose Edit⇨Cut to temporarily delete it. Change to the day on which you want to move the item, and click the time slot where you want the appointment or event to appear. (Do not click when it says Click to Create Appointment or you'll end up moving the appointment inside the small white bubble that results.) Choose Edit⇨Paste to complete the move and make the item appear at the slot where you clicked.

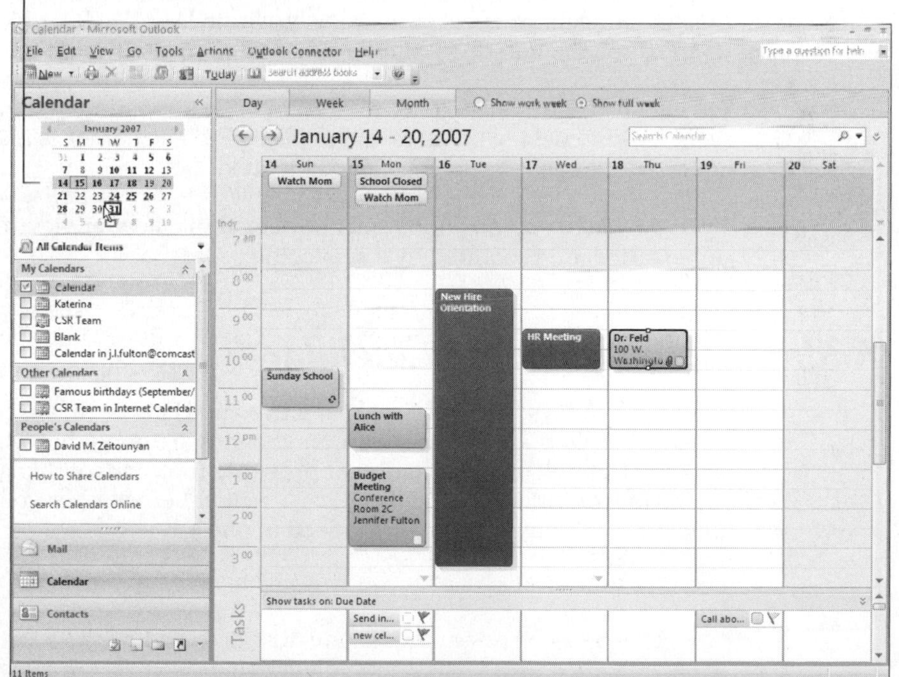

Figure 2-5: Drag items to the Date Navigator to change their date.

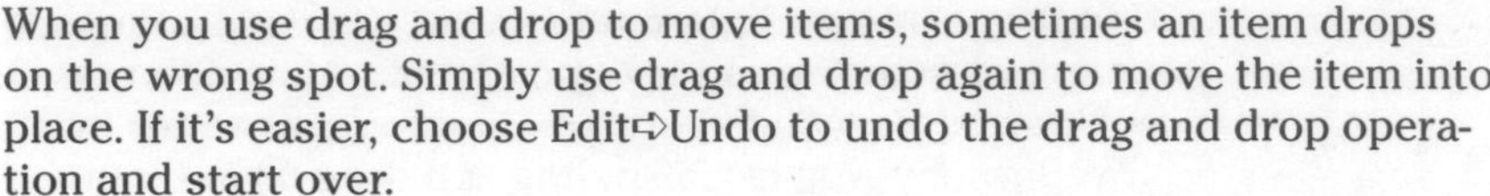

When you use drag and drop to move items, sometimes an item drops on the wrong spot. Simply use drag and drop again to move the item into place. If it's easier, choose Edit⇨Undo to undo the drag and drop operation and start over.

If you move an appointment from one day to another in Month view, or if you drag and drop an appointment on another day within the Date Navigator, the appointment time isn't changed unless you display that day, and drop the appointment on a new time slot.

✦ **To copy an appointment or event,** click it to select the item, and then press and hold Ctrl as you drag the copy where you want it. Also, you can use the Edit, Copy and Edit, and/or Paste commands to copy an item. Click the appointment or event to select it, and then choose Edit⇨Copy to make a copy. Change to the day on which you want to place the copy of the item, and click the time slot where you want the appointment or event to appear. (Do not click when it says Click to Create Appointment or you'll end up copying the appointment inside the small white bubble that results.) Choose Edit⇨Paste to complete the copy process and make the copied item appear at the slot where you clicked.

✦ **To shorten or lengthen an appointment,** change to Day view and drag the appointment's lower border.

✦ **To change an appointment or event's subject or location,** click the appointment or event twice, slowly, within Day, Week, or Month view to position the cursor within the text, and then simply edit it.

You can also edit the Subject or Location of an appointment, meeting, or event by just clicking the item and pressing F2. The cursor is instantly positioned within the item so you can edit its text.

If you decide to edit an appointment or event in calendar view, the subject and location are separated by a semicolon.

Adding Holidays to the Calendar

Common holidays, such as New Year's Eve and Halloween, are typically added when Outlook is first set up. So chances are good that whoever installed Outlook on your computer probably took care of this next step. (If you installed Outlook yourself and can't remember whether you added the holidays, you're probably in great need of one.)

Outlook has a set of holidays common to various countries or religions, and you can add as many holiday sets as apply to you. To check if you already have holidays installed, do this:

1. **Choose View⇨Current View⇨Events.**

   Only the events on your Calendar are listed.

2. **Sort by Location.**

   To do that, click the header at the top of the Location column. Holidays for your country are listed together. If you add religious holidays, they're listed under that religion in the Location column. In addition, Outlook holidays appear with the word *Holiday* in the Categories column.

After following the previous steps, if you see that your holidays haven't been added, you can add them to the Calendar now.

1. **Choose Tools⇨Options⇨Calendar Options⇨Add Holidays.**

   The Add Holidays to Calendar dialog box opens, as shown in Figure 2-6.

Figure 2-6: Add a holiday set.

2. **Select holidays to add.**

   Select any holiday set you want to add. The check boxes for the holiday sets that are already installed are selected, so you want to deselect them to prevent installing them all over again.

3. **Click OK.**

   The holidays you selected are added to the Calendar. Holidays are the gifts that keep on giving; once added, they appear year after year automatically — at least from 2006 to 2011 (which is all Outlook has installed).

If, despite carefully checking, somehow you still manage to select a holiday set that's already installed in Outlook, you see a warning telling you so — and asking whether you really want to install the holidays again. Click No to prevent creating duplicate holidays on your Calendar.

Creating Your Own Holiday List

I love holidays. I mean, what's not to love? You get the day off (assuming you turn off the phones so your boss can't reach you), you get to sleep in (the kids can reach the cereal boxes if they just stand on the countertops), and you have a great excuse to eat too much. (Woo hoo, Columbus Day! Let's eat!)

If you're in human resources and you'd like to issue a list of official company holidays so all the employees can update their Outlook calendars easily, Microsoft provides a way for you to do that. Remember, holidays are simply events, so if you don't happen to work in human resources, you can still create a list of family birthdays, school holidays and events, or club meetings and outings — and easily distribute the whole set. Follow these steps:

1. **Open the `outlook.hoi` file.**

   To create this list, you edit a file Microsoft provides for this purpose. To do the editing, you need a simple text editor, such as Notepad. (Using Word is a bit of overkill here.)

   Exit Outlook and start My Computer (or just Computer, as Microsoft's now calling it). You'll find the file carefully hidden in the `C:\Program Files\Microsoft Office\Office 12\`*`LCID`* folder, where *LCID* is actually your local identification number, which identifies the language you speak. The United States version of English (in which we do *color* and not *colour*) is LCID #1033.

2. **After locating the file, make a copy of it. Then, right-click the copy and choose Open With➪Notepad.**

   Make a copy of the `outlook.hol` file before you edit it. Microsoft doesn't say what can happen if you mess up the file and don't have an original copy to go back to, but I'm sure it's ugly. So just back up the file before you do anything. Personally, I copied the file and named the copy `orig outlook.hol` (so I could remember that it contained the original data and none of my edits) and then opened `outlook.hol` to edit.

3. **Press Ctrl+End.**

   The cursor moves to the end of the file.

4. **Type a heading.**

   Press Enter to begin a new line. Then, type a heading for your holiday list, like this: **[*Marketing Department Events*] *6***. Note that the name of your holiday list appears in square brackets, and that there's a space, followed by a number. This number represents the total number of holidays on your list.

5. **Enter the holidays and press Enter one last time to add a blank line at the end of the file.**

   Press Enter to begin a new line, and then type the first holiday, like this: **AdCon 2007, 2007/03/10** (for March 10, 2007). (Figure 2-7 shows how that looks.) Notice that there's a comma separating the holiday/event name from its date and that the date is in *yyyy/mm/dd* format (where *yyyy* is the four-digit year, *mm* is the two-digit month, and *dd* is the two-digit day). Press Enter and add the next holiday, and so on.

Figure 2-7: Create your own holidays.

6. **Save the file by choosing File⇨Save and exit Notepad.**

   A sample holiday list might look like this:

```
[Marketing Department Events] 6
AdCon 2007, 2007/03/09
Market Watch III, 2007/05/21
Market Watch III, 2007/05/22
Market Watch III, 2007/05/23
Market Watch III, 2007/05/24
Year-End Market Review, 2007/12/07
```

7. **Restart Outlook.**

8. **Import the dates by choosing Tools➪Options➪Calendar Options➪Add Holidays.**

   The Add Holidays to Calendar dialog box opens.

9. **Select the special event group and click OK to add those holidays/events to your Calendar, as shown in Figure 2-8.**

   When adding your custom holiday set, be sure to uncheck the holiday sets you've already added; otherwise you add them again.

Figure 2-8: Add custom holidays.

To share the list with friends or colleagues, simply attach the file to an e-mail message or place the file in a shared folder. Save the file in your Outlook folder, perhaps first making a copy of your original `outlook.hol` file.

You can also share events and holidays by creating a special calendar just for the holidays and then placing that calendar in a shared folder. (See Book IV, Chapter 5 for details.)

Chapter 3: Calendar Collaboration

In This Chapter

- Sharing what's on your calendar
- Taking a peek at someone else's calendar
- Playing well with a group's schedule
- Controlling your available time
- Preventing access to certain appointments
- Sharing appointments via e-mail
- Publishing your calendar online

If you're a fairly private person, it may come as a shock that of all the data you keep in Outlook, the Calendar is probably the least private thing. At least, it should be. As much as you might prefer letting everyone in the office guess whether or not you'll be in today, letting other people have access to your Calendar has some advantages. If you're lucky enough to have an assistant, for example, you can instantly delegate the responsibility of looking up your schedule and then explaining to Mr. Please-give-me-that-product-demo-again-even-though-there's-no-chance-I'm-ever-going-to-buy-it-I'm-just-no-good-at-making-decisions that you simply have no room in your schedule this week for another appointment, sorry. It's also much easier to corner Kenny and Joe and schedule that group project meeting if you can see their calendars and they can see yours.

So this sharing calendar thing is not all that bad, and being able to view your calendar may just convince your boss that you are way, way, underpaid. Even so, there's no reason that you have to share everything. I mean Joe, Kenny, and Nora your boss don't need to know that you're skipping out early on Thursday to get your nails done, or that you're seeing Hairspray for the third time this month on Saturday. When needed, you can keep certain appointments private.

Live, let-me-see-what-you're-doing kind of sharing happens over a Microsoft Exchange network. So, if your company uses Exchange, you can share your calendar with your colleagues and they can share theirs with you. For those of you that aren't on an Exchange network, you can share your calendar in other ways: through e-mail or over the Internet. You find all the fascinating ways to share in this chapter.

Sharing Your Calendar via Exchange

If you're on an Exchange network, you can share your calendar, live and up-to-date, with everybody you know, or just the select people on your team. Likewise, they can share their calendars with you, and you can view those calendars in Outlook just as easily as you can view your own. While sharing a calendar, you can designate whether users can only view your calendar, or make changes to it as well.

Even when sharing, you can mark particular meetings, appointments, or events private so they cannot be seen. You can also create a separate calendar for sharing, and only keep the kinds of appointments you want to share in it. For example, you could create a team calendar and keep all your team-related appointments in it. Or you could create a personal calendar, keep all your private appointments in it, and share only the default Calendar.

To make an appointment, meeting or event private, open the item and choose Appointment/Meeting/Events⇨Options⇨Private.

When you share a calendar, other people can view the appointments, meetings, and events in it (at least, those that you don't mark as private). Other people, however, can't update your calendar for you or accidentally delete an appointment. If you want to grant them that kind of freedom, you need to delegate your supreme and magnificent authority. See Book X, Chapter 1 for the lowdown.

When it comes to sharing your calendar over an Exchange network, you have two choices. You can either

- **Share the main calendar with basically everyone on the network**, while also designating what they are allowed to do, such as view only or view and edit. See "Sharing a calendar with everyone," later in this chapter.
- **Share either the main or a custom calendar completely,** but with only the specific people you select. See "Sharing a calendar with specific people," later in this chapter.

If you decide that it's a good idea to create a new Calendar folder and put either the private or the not-so-private appointments, meetings, and events in it, then flip to Book IV, Chapter 5 for the necessary help.

Sharing a calendar with everyone

You can't share a custom calendar you've created by following the steps in this section, even if you'd like to share it with "everyone." Basically, you can share the custom calendar with only the people you send an e-mail to — a *sharing invitation.* The invitation e-mail is used by the recipient to access your custom calendar — there's no way around it. So if you want to share your custom calendar with everybody on your network, you're gonna have to figure out how to send out the multitude of e-mails. See the section, "Sharing a calendar with specific people," for help.

To share the main calendar folder with everyone on the network, follow these steps:

1. **In the Navigation pane, right-click the main Calendar folder.**
2. **Choose Change Sharing Permissions from the menu.**

   The Calendar Properties dialog box pops up.
3. **Click the Permissions tab, and then in the Name list, click Default (see Figure 3-1).**

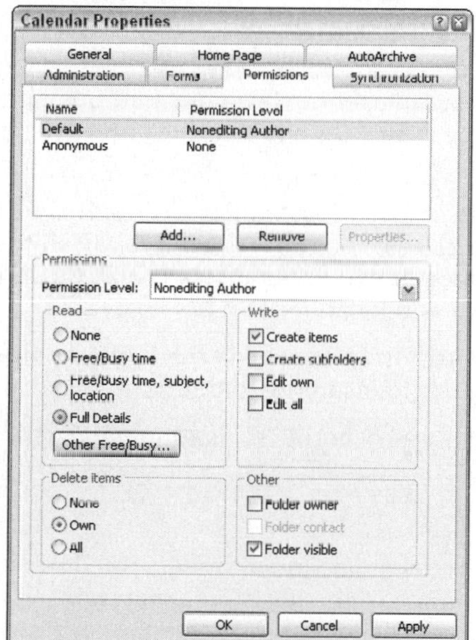

Figure 3-1: Why not share?

4. **From the options that appear in the Permissions Level list, choose the one that describes the kind of things you want visitors to be able to do, and then click OK.**

   Here are the options you can choose from:

   - *Publishing Editor:* Create, edit, delete, and view calendar items. Publishing Editors can also create subfolders within the shared folder.
   - *Editor:* Same as Publishing Editor except the user can't create subfolders.

- *Publishing Author:* Create and view calendar items, create folders, and edit or delete calendar items they have created themselves.
- *Author:* Same as Publishing Author except that the user can't create subfolders.
- *Nonediting Author:* Same as Publishing Author, except that the user can't edit existing calendar items, even if he created them. Also, the user can't create folders. The user can delete calendar items he creates himself, however.
- *Reviewer:* View calendar items only.
- *Contributor:* Create and edit new calendar items, but the user can't view existing ones unless she created them.

I do not recommend that you use Contributor access, because it prevents users from scheduling meetings with you (because they can't view items — existing meetings and appointments that might interfere with the meeting they're trying to set up).

- *Free/Busy Time:* Allows a user to view your free/busy time so they can determine the best time for a meeting. This is the initial setting for Calendar.
- *Free/Busy Time, Subject Location:* Similar to Free/Busy Time, except that it allows a user to view not only the free/busy status of an appointment, meeting, or event, but also a few more details, such as the items' subject and location.
- *None:* Prevents the user from accessing the folder at all — he can't even view the calendar items in the folder.

The folder you choose appears in the Navigation pane with a special "Welcome, welcome" icon (a hand holding a business card), showing that it's now shared.

Anyway, you've shared your Calendar, and although you don't need to send everybody an invitation to come to the party, you may want to do so, so that they know they can access your Calendar. All someone on your Exchange network needs to know right now, however, is your name in order to gain access to your shared Calendar. See the section, "Viewing Someone Else's Calendar," later in this chapter, for more info on how your recipient gains access to your main Calendar folder.

Sharing a calendar with specific people

When it comes to sharing, I'm probably like most people. I don't mind sharing as long as I can be selective. There's just no sense sharing a piece of pie with Aunt Minnie, for example, because she'll just smile and then turn around and give the pie to someone else. It's not that Aunt Minnie doesn't like pie, she just has a problem accepting presents. This makes our family Christmas a fairly strange event, because we all have to check our boxes before we head out, just in case we have any presents that were originally tagged "Aunt Minnie."

Anyway, if you have a calendar to share but you want to be selective about who has access to it, you can share your calendar with only with certain people.

The following steps show you how to share either the main Calendar or a custom one, and send a sharing invitation to the specific people you choose. For custom folders, you have only two access levels you can select from:

- **Reviewer:** Users can view calendar items only.
- **Editor:** Users can create, edit, delete, and view calendar items, even ones they don't create themselves.

If you're sharing your main Calendar in this way, you can only provide visitors with Reviewer status using this procedure, at least initially. Once the sharing invitation goes out, you can always change a particular person's access level as you see fit — see "Changing permissions or stopping sharing," later in this chapter.

To share a calendar with a select few, follow these steps:

1. **Click the calendar you want to share.**

   Jump over to Calendar and select the calendar you want to share. You should find your calendars lurking in the My Calendars group on the Navigation pane. You can share your main Calendar or a custom calendar with this procedure.

2. **Share the calendar.**

   If you're sharing the main Calendar, then just click the Share My Calendar link on the Navigation pane. To share a custom calendar, right-click it instead and choose Share *calendarname,* where *calendarname* is the actual name of the calendar such as Client Services Team. A message form appears, as shown in Figure 3-2.

3. **Address the message.**

   In the To box, type the addresses of the people with whom you want to share your calendar. Type a subject, and a short message explaining the invitation.

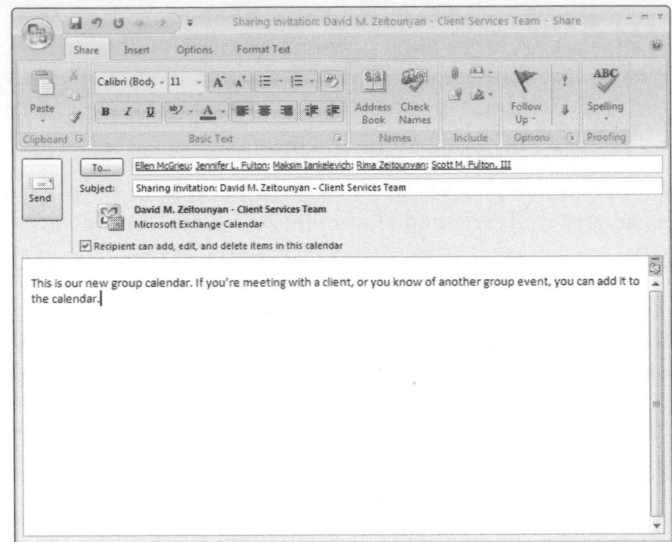

Figure 3-2: Message sent, sir!

4. **Set sharing options.**

   If you're sharing your main Calendar, you can request permission to view each addressee's Calendar in return. Again, you're only granting them Reviewer status (look only), so you're asking them to grant you that same access in return. To do that, choose the Request Permission to View Recipient's Calendar option.

   If you'd like to request access to somebody's created calendar, and not their default Calendar, you have to send your own separate message making that request. Don't expect Outlook to do it for you.

   If you're sharing a calendar you created and not your main Calendar, you can control what users can do. If you want users to only view appointments, meetings, and events (Reviewer access), disable the Recipient Can Add, Edit, And Delete Items In This Calendar Folder option. If you want them to be able to make changes and additions (Editor access), turn on the option instead.

5. **Finish the message and click Send.**

   Outlook asks whether you really want to grant access to your calendar to those silly people you work with; if so, click Yes. Next, you'll be told your calendar is shared.

6. **Click OK.**

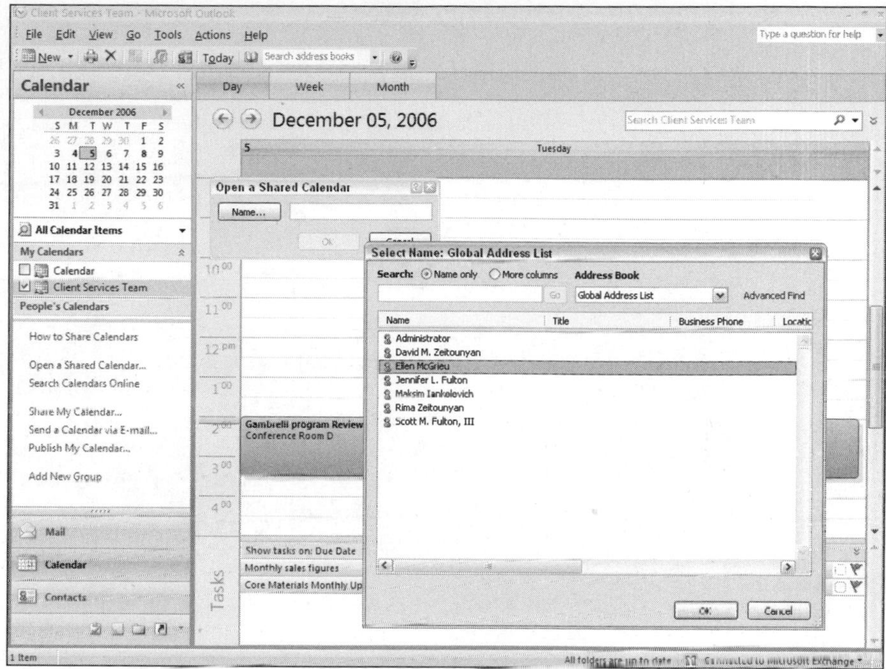

Figure 3-4: Open sesame.

When you gain access to someone's Calendar, you can simply click that calendar in the Navigation pane at any time to display the appointments, meetings, and events within.

Assuming you've been granted permission to open the calendar, it's added to the People's Calendars list on the Navigation pane, and then the calendar is tucked in next to your open calendars, as shown in Figure 3-5. The next time you start Outlook, you can click the calendar's name in the People's Calendars listing to view it again — you don't have to go through all this business again just to open it back up.

Notice that in Figure 3-5, although you can view someone's calendar, you can't view their tasks, unless they also grant you access to their Tasks folder. Even so, those tasks will not show up in Calendar like yours will.

You can view up to 30 calendars side-by-side although unless you have a really big monitor and a very high resolution, you'll just end up with a bunch of too skinny to read calendars full of mish-mash if you try. There are other ways to view a calendar; see Book IV, Chapter 5 for tips.

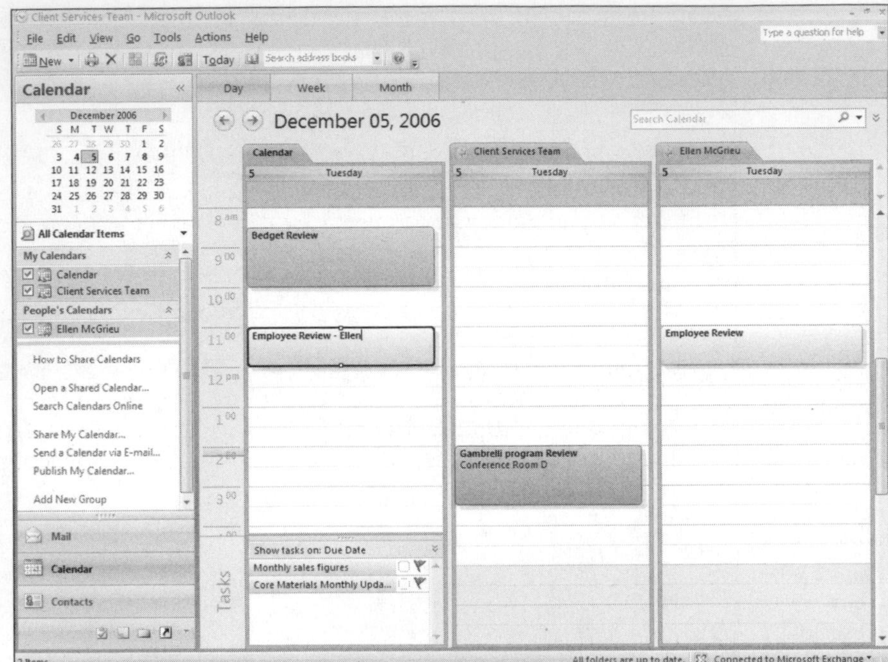

Figure 3-5: Snug as some bugs in a rug.

If you're viewing your own calendar using some kind of customized view, then you need to go about opening a shared calendar in a different way in order not to lose that view. Just right-click the shared calendar in the People's Calendars list, and choose Open from the shortcut menu. Any calendars you already have open automatically close, and the shared calendar you chose opens, utilizing the custom view you were just using. You can then reopen the calendars that were closed, and even in side-by-side view, the calendars will now use the custom view settings you're so fond of.

If you haven't been given permission to view the calendar yet, it won't open. Instead, you see a message asking whether you'd like to request permission from its owner to view the calendar; click Yes to send a sharing request message. Notice that there's an option for you to share your default Calendar. Click Send to send the request.

You can remove a shared calendar from the People's Calendars list if you don't think you'll need to open it again. Simply right-click the shared calendar you want to remove, and choose Remove from People's Calendars from the menu that appears.

If the folder is shared but you haven't been given access to it just yet, you'll be asked if you want to beg permission. Click Yes, and a message form appears, asking for permission to use the folder. Make sure to select the

Request Permission to View Recipient's Calendar option. If you would like to offer access to your main Calendar in return, choose the Allow Recipient to View Your Calendar. Click Send to send the request.

Accessing someone's custom calendar

When someone shares a calendar he's created, he sends special e-mail invitations. If you get one, you can use it to gain access to the special calendar. By the way, you probably are granted either Reviewer (view only) or Editor (create, edit, delete tasks) access to the calendar. In any case, after you gain access to the calendar, you can easily view its contents any time you want.

To access someone's shared, custom calendar, follow these steps:

1. **Change over to Mail and either select the sharing invitation to view it in the Reading pane, or double-click it to view it in a separate window (see Figure 3-6).**

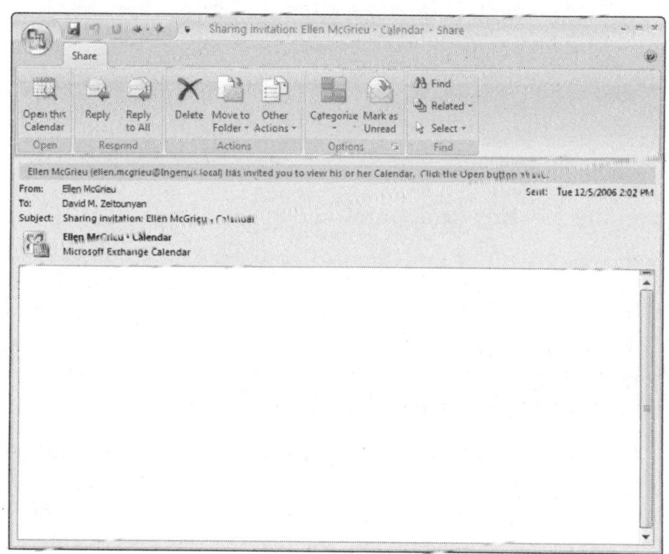

Figure 3-6: Accessing a custom calendar.

2. **Click Open This Calendar at the top of the Reading pane.**

   A new Outlook window is opened up for some goofy reason, and the folder is added to the People's Calendars group on the Navigation pane. You can close this window and view the contents of this calendar in your previous window.

Managing Your Time

After you begin sharing your calendar, it becomes pretty important that people learn to respect what you have scheduled. For example, if you add a New Employee Interview to your schedule, your colleagues need to understand that although you're in the office, you are not to be disturbed. Or maybe you want people to interrupt if it's important, and you'd like to indicate that on your calendar instead.

The trouble, my friend, begins with you. You see, when you create an appointment, Outlook automatically lists you as Busy. That probably fits most appointments, but sometimes, it just doesn't. For example, maybe you've listed your son's football practice on your calendar, and it takes place at 4:00 every Thursday. You want to go, but you may not be able to make it each time. And if you do go, people at the office can certainly reach you by cell phone if something really important comes up, so you're not exactly Busy. If you change the appointment to show that you're Tentative, or Out of the Office, at least people know more about the nature of the appointment. Although you can't create a label that says, Busy but Reachable, you could add that to the appointment notes, or you could create a special color category to indicate that.

To indicate whether you're still available while at an appointment or meeting, follow these steps:

1. **Open the meeting or appointment.**

   The appointment or meeting form appears, as shown in Figure 3-7.

2. **Adjust your availability.**

   To change your availability from the default Busy to something else, open the Show As list in the Options group on the Meeting or Appointment tab. You can choose from these options:

   - *Free:* You are still available, despite the appointment or meeting. For example, maybe you've scheduled some time to go over the employee reviews. It's important, which is why you scheduled time to get it done. But you can be interrupted if need be.
   - *Tentative:* The appointment or meeting is not firm yet, and may very well change.

     Be sure to return to a tentative appointment or meeting and mark it as Busy once the time gets firmed up.

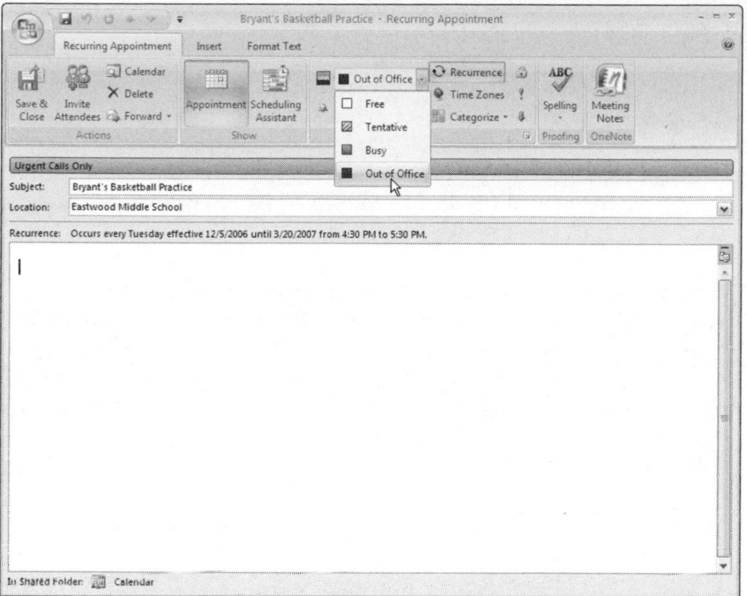

Figure 3-7: Why hide your availability?

- *Busy:* This indicates that you are busy and should not be interrupted with questions and concerns.
- *Out of the Office:* This indicates that you, like Elvis, have left the building and should not be paged. You may want to either set a standard that says, Out of the Office means Don't Call, or add something in the notes of such appointments/meetings to indicate whether your coworkers can contact you by cell during this time.

The Free, Busy, Out of Office, and Tentative markers may not tell the whole story. For example, you might be out of the office in a private meeting and wish not to be disturbed. Or you might be at a conference in which you can discretely accept calls of an urgent nature by putting your cell phone on vibrate. To help you and your coworkers sort out this mess, I recommend creating at two categories, Do Not Disturb and Urgent Calls Only, and assigning the appropriate category to related appointments or meetings.

3. **Save your changes by choosing Meeting or Appointment⇨Action⇨Save & Close.**

After you mark an appointment or meeting as anything other than Busy, a special marker appears in the Calendar to help you identify an item's Show As status, as shown in Figure 3-8.

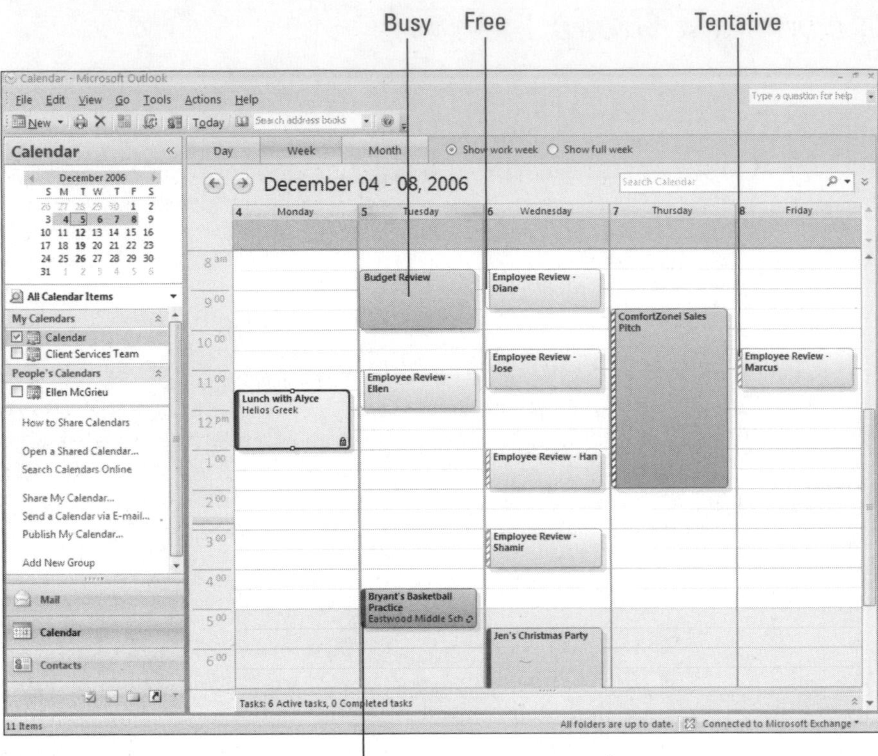

Figure 3-8: Free or busy?

The markers, by the way, show up only in Day or Week view, on the left side of each item's rectangle. Here's how things shake out:

- **Busy:** These items appear as normal, without a marker.
- **Free:** These items appear with a white banner along the left side of the appointment or meeting rectangle.
- **Tentative:** These items appear with a diagonal striped banner along the left side of the appointment or meeting rectangle.
- **Out of Office:** These items appear with a solid blue banner along the left side of the appointment or meeting rectangle.

Another important aspect in determining whether you are free or busy is your normal work schedule. For example, if you normally work on Tuesday, Wednesday, and Thursday, you need to set up Outlook so that it shows Mondays and Fridays as non-work days to anyone who views your calendar. For help setting up your actual work days and hours, see Book IV, Chapter 5.

Creating a Group Schedule

After you start sharing, it's hard to stop. Loan your hedge clippers to a neighbor, and he'll be back, this time for your ladder. Still, it's hard to complain because he still hasn't remembered that three months ago, you borrowed his snow blower, chipper/shredder, and tiller. In any case, when you get accustomed to the give and take of calendar sharing, you may want to try group schedules. You have to be on an Exchange network for this to work, though.

A *group schedule* is simply a collection of the combined appointments, meetings, and events in a series of shared calendars. These calendars do not have to represent just people. On an Exchange network, resources such as multimedia equipment and conference rooms can also have "calendars" that display when those resources are being used. So, for example, your group schedule might help you quickly identify not only the available time slots for all the members of your team, but also the available meeting rooms and equipment.

To create a group schedule, follow these steps:

1. **Choose Actions⇨View Group Schedules from in Calendar.**

   The Group Schedules dialog box appears, listing any existing group schedules. See Figure 3-9.

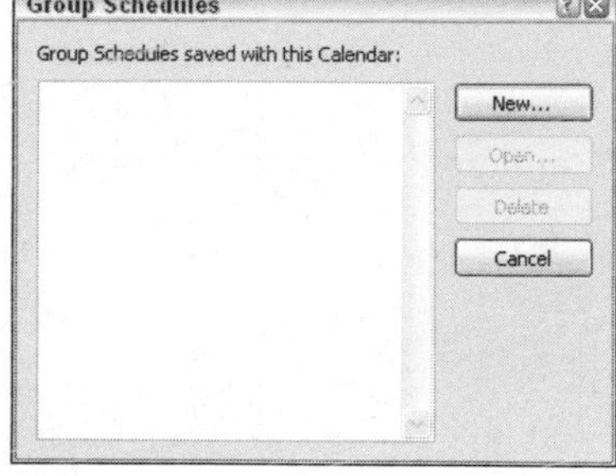

Figure 3-9: Create a schedule for your whole group to share.

2. **Click New.**

   The Create New Group Schedule dialog box appears.

3. **Type a name for the new group schedule in the Name box and click OK.**

   A scheduling box appears. See Figure 3-10.

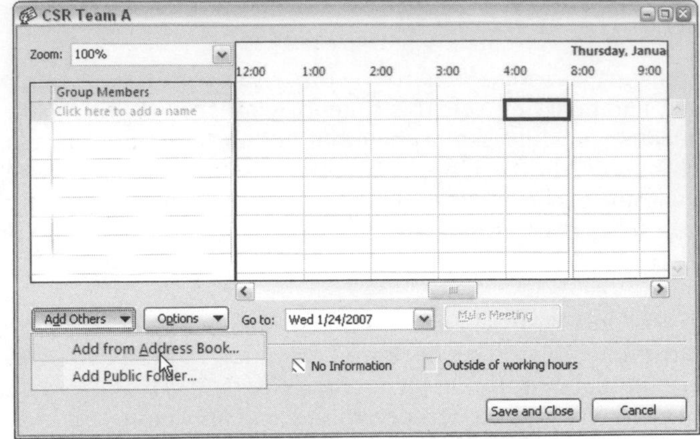

Figure 3-10: Group together the schedules you reference often.

4. **Add calendars or resources to the schedule.**

   Click Add Others, and make a choice from the menu that appears:

   - *To add someone's calendar,* click Add from Address Book. The Select Members: Global Address List dialog box jumps out. Select the name of someone you want to add to the group schedule, and then click To. Repeat to add other names, and then click OK to close the dialog box.
   - *To add a resource,* click Add Public Folder. The Select Folder dialog box jumps up. Choose a folder for each resource you want to add, then click OK.

5. **Click Save and Close.**

   The group schedule is saved, and you return to Outlook.

To view a group schedule at any time, follow these steps:

1. **Choose Actions⇨View Group Schedule.**

   Once again, the ol' Group Schedules dialog box jumps up (refer to Figure 3-9).

2. **Select the group schedule to view.**

   In the list, click the schedule you want to peek at.

3. **Click Open.**

   The schedule you selected is displayed. See Figure 3-11.

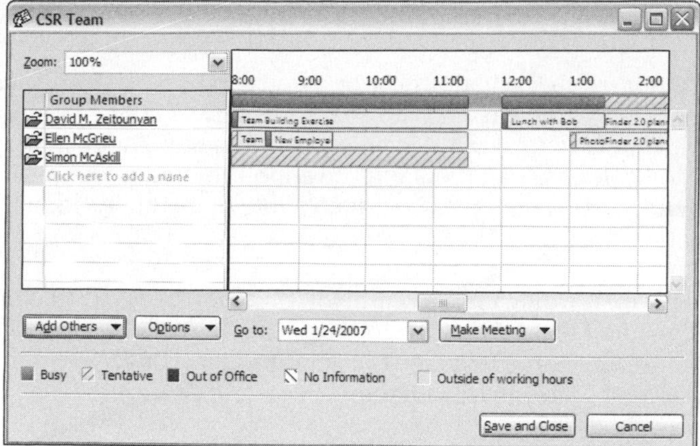

Figure 3-11: Here's your group schedule.

4. Perform some kind of action.

Thanks to your new group schedule, you can easily poke around someone's schedule, create a group meeting, or simply send a mass e-mail.

- *To view someone's schedule (assuming you have permission),* click the open folder icon in front of that person's name.
- *To send a meeting request to one member of the group,* select that member and then choose Make Meeting➪New Meeting. For more help with meetings, see Book IV, Chapter 4.
- *To send a message to one member,* select that member and choose Make Meeting➪New Mail Message.
- *To send a meeting request to all the members of the group,* choose Make Meeting➪New Meeting with All. For more help with meetings, see Book IV, Chapter 4.
- *To send a message to everyone in the group,* choose Make Meeting➪New Mail Message with All.
- *To schedule a resource* (for example, to schedule a conference room), select the resource from those listed, and click New Meeting as Resource.

If you suspect that maybe the schedule isn't updated for someone, you can choose Options➪Refresh Free/Busy.

TIP

To remove someone's schedule from the group schedule, from the group schedule box, choose Add Others➪Add From Address Book. In the Select Members: Global Address List dialog box that appears, select that person's name in the To list and press Delete. Click OK to finalize the change.

Forwarding Appointments to Others

If you're not on an Exchange network, you can't share your calendars in the traditional way. One easy way to share the details of an appointment, meeting, or event, is to forward it in an e-mail message. The recipient of your forwarded calendar can then add the appointment, meeting, or event to her calendar list. This saves her the trouble of manually adding the same information.

Of course, forwarding an appointment, meeting, or event to someone only does him some good if he has Outlook 2007. If he doesn't, send him the same information as simple text. See the section, "Inserting Calendar Information into an E-Mail," later in this chapter.

To forward an appointment, meeting, or event to someone, follow these steps:

1. **Double-click the appointment, meeting, or event to open it.**

   You can even forward a recurring appointment, meeting, or event if you want.

2. **Click the Forward button on the Appointment, Meeting, or Event tab in the Actions group.**

   A new message form is created, showing the calendar item as an attachment. See Figure 3-12.

3. **Complete the message.**

   In the To box, type the address of the person you want to forward the appointment, meeting, or event to. The subject has been neatly typed in for you; it's based on the item name. Still, you can change the subject if you want.

4. **Click Send.**

When your friend receives your package, she has a few options:

- **To simply view the calendar item**, she just needs to open the attachment, and she'll see the familiar appointment, meeting, or event form.
- **To add the appointment, meeting, or event to her calendar**, she should not open the e-mail, but instead, simply drag the attachment from the Reading pane and drop it on the Calendar button sitting on the Navigation pane.

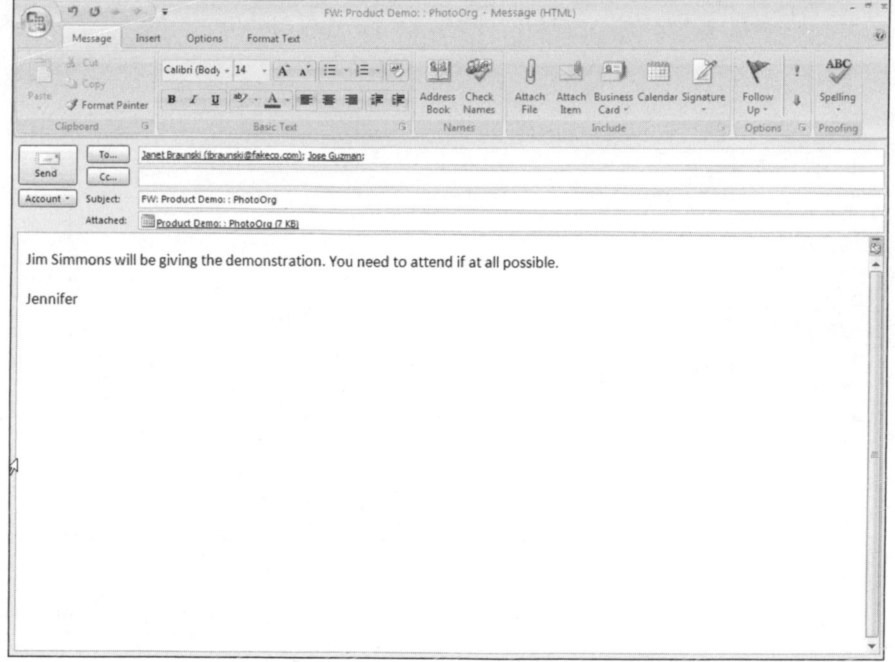

Figure 3-12: Hold the salt, pass the calendar item.

Sharing a Calendar in iCalendar Format

If you need to share your calendar, you're not necessarily stuck if the person or persons you want to share it with don't happen to be on your company network, or your company simply doesn't use Exchange. You can, as explained in the section, "Forwarding Appointments to Others," share an appointment, meeting, or event in Outlook format, which can then be directly applied to the recipient's Calendar. But if someone doesn't use Outlook 2007, you're still not out of luck. You can instead share an entire calendar or a smaller portion of it (your choice) through a pretty universal format called iCalendar. The iCalendar format is supported by a lot of programs, including Apple's iCal, Google Calendar, Lotus Notes, and Windows Calendar (the calendar built into Windows Vista).

To save a calendar in iCalendar format, follow these steps:

1. **Choose File⇨Save As.**

   Jump over to Calendar and make the calendar you want to save the active one. If it's the only one showing, it is the active calendar. If more than one calendar is showing, click the tab of the calendar you want to save.

   The Save As dialog box appears, as shown in Figure 3-13.

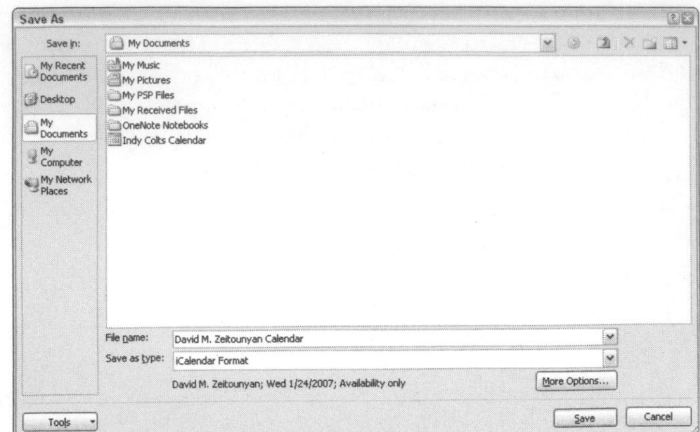

Figure 3-13: Save your calendar in a sharable iCalendar format.

2. **In the File Name box, type a name for the file.**
3. **Using the Save In list, change to the folder where you want to save the file.**
4. **If you don't want to share the entire calendar, click the More Options button hiding just below the Save As Type box.**

   Another Save As dialog box appears (call it the Save As wanna-be), as shown in Figure 3-14. You can choose from the following options:

   - *Select the portion of the calendar you want to share from the Date Range list.*

     If you want, you can specify a unique portion of the calendar to share by selecting Specify Dates from the Date Range list, and then entering a Start and End date.

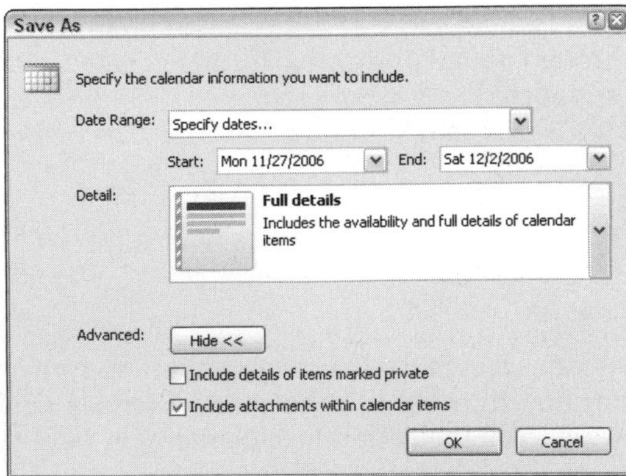

Figure 3-14: Set the portion of the calendar to share.

- *Specify the amount of Detail you want to show:* Availability Only, which only shows your Free/Busy status; Limited Details, which shows Free/Busy and Subject information; or Full Details, which includes basically everything. In addition, if you choose Availability Only, you can limit the detail to your working hours by selecting the Show Time Within My Working Hours Only option.

5. **To set any of the Advanced options, click Show and then select the options you want:**

   - *To include details from private appointments, meetings, or events,* set the Detail to either Limited Details or Full Details, and then choose Include Details of Items Marked Private.
   - *To include any attachments to the included items,* set Detail to Full Details, and choose Include Attachments Within Calendar Items.

6. **Click OK to close the Save As wanna-be dialog box, and then click Save.**

   Now that the file's been created, you can e-mail it to whoever you want to share this calendar with by simply attaching the file. See Book II, Chapter 1.

Inserting Calendar Information into an E-Mail

You can share your calendar using Outlook in so many ways, that after a while, you start to think there can't be anybody anywhere who doesn't know you have a doctor's appointment tomorrow and that your boss is giving you a performance review on Friday. However, if you're not on an Exchange network, or if your friends or colleagues do not use Outlook, this may not be the case.

Even so, you're not out of options yet. You can share your calendar using regular e-mail. The calendar data is included within the e-mail message, in HTML format, so it's important that your recipient be able to handle HTML (almost every e-mail program today handles HTML easily, it's just that some people turn that option off). In addition, the calendar data is also attached to the e-mail, in iCalendar format, which is recognized by a lot of programs (see the previous section, "Sharing a Calendar in iCalendar Format" for more info).

To e-mail somebody a portion of your calendar, follow these steps:

1. **In the Navigation pane in Calendar, click Send Calendar via E-mail.**

   When you click this command, an e-mail message is created, and the Send a Calendar via E-Mail dialog box appears (see Figure 3-15).

2. **Select the calendar to share.**

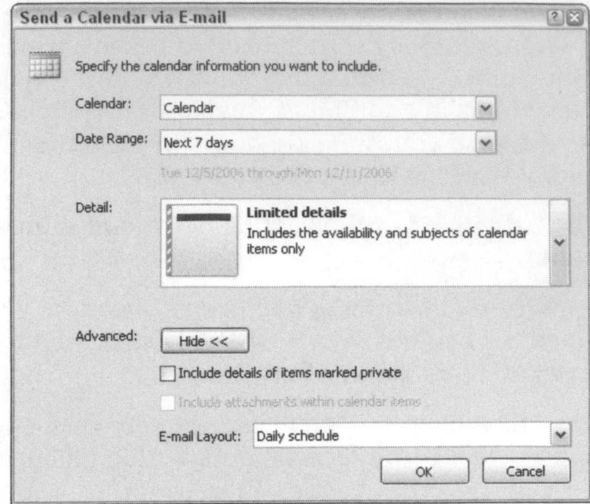

Figure 3-15: Select the part of your calendar you want to e-mail.

By default, Outlook assumes that you want to share a portion of your main Calendar. If you think differently, there's no need to get into a huff; just select the calendar you want to share from the Calendar list.

3. **Select the portion of the calendar you want to share from the Date Range list.**

If you want, you can specify a unique portion of the calendar to share by selecting Specify Dates from the Date Range list, and then entering a Start and End date.

If you select a large portion of your calendar to include, the e-mail message you create may be so large it'll be difficult to send. Another way in which you might want to share a calendar is online. See the upcoming sections, "Publishing a Calendar to Microsoft Office Online," "Publishing a Calendar to Any Web Server," and "Sharing a Calendar through Google."

4. **Specify the amount of detail you want to show.**

From the Detail list, choose the amount of detail to include in the e-mail:

- *Availability Only:* Shows only your Free/Busy status. In addition, to limit the detail to your working hours only, select the Show Time Within My Working Hours Only option.
- *Limited Details:* Shows Free/Busy and Subject information.
- *Full Details:* Includes basically everything.

5. **To set any of the Advanced options, click Show, then select the option you want:**

- *To include details from private appointments, meetings, or events,* set the Detail to either Limited Details or Full Details, then choose Include Details of Items Marked Private.

- *To include any attachments to the included items,* set Detail to Full Details, and choose Include Attachments within Calendar Items.

6. From the E-Mail Layout list, choose a format for your calendar:

- *Daily Schedule:* Includes a mini calendar at the top, with links to each day's details. Each day includes the entire schedule, including free periods, which are marked as such.
- *List of Events:* Includes a mini calendar at the top, with links to each day's details. Each day includes only the time periods in which some item is scheduled.

7. Click OK.

The detail for the portion of the calendar you selected appears in the e-mail message, as shown in Figure 3-16. In addition, an iCalendar format file is created and attached to the e-mail.

8. Address and send the e-mail.

Enter the addresses of the people you want to send your calendar in the To box. You can type a message above the calendar text. Click Send to send the e-mail.

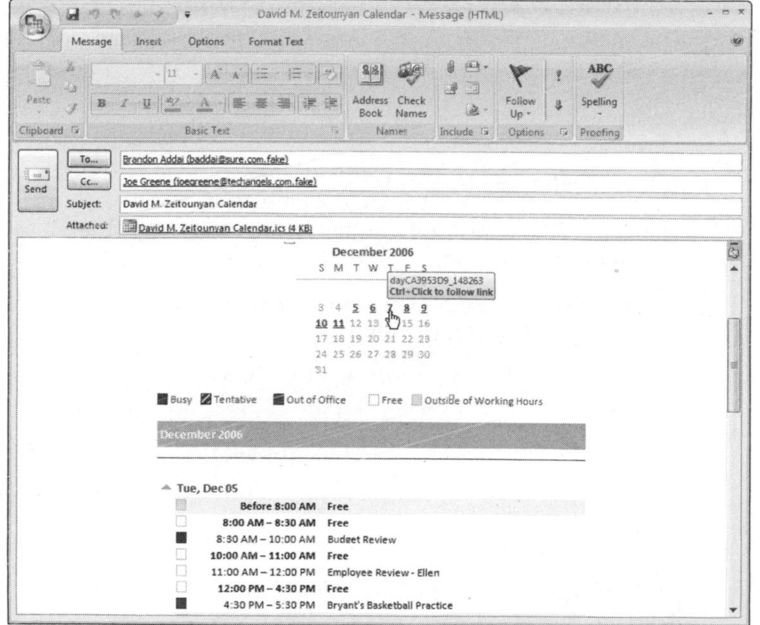

Figure 3-16: Here's my calendar.

Okay, you're still not out of options if your friend uses only text-based e-mail and not HTML. Instead of sending the calendar information in HTML format, you can send the details of individual appointments as text: Start an e-mail message and choose Insert⇨Include⇨Attach Item. Choose Calendar from the Look In list, and then select the calendar item you want to share. Before you click OK, however, be sure to choose the Text Only option. The calendar item's details are copied into the message as text.

Publishing a Calendar to Microsoft Office Online

The Internet is pretty easily accessible to just about everyone, making it a good place to share a calendar with a large group of diverse people. The only thing that might give you pause is the idea that although you want to be able to share your calendar with a big group of people, you don't want to share it with the world. With Microsoft Office Online, you don't have to make your calendar public — you can keep it private if you want.

Another thing that might give you pause is how to keep your online calendar up-to-date. Again, there's no problem there since Outlook will synchronize the online calendar with any changes you make, and all without bothering you.

To complete this procedure, you need to sign up for a free Windows Live account in Step 2. If you already have one, great — pass Go! and collect your $200.

To publish your calendar online, follow these steps:

1. **Select a calendar to publish.**
   - *To publish your main Calendar,* click the Publish My Calendar link in the Navigation pane.
   - *To publish a custom calendar,* right-click it and choose Publish to Internet⇨Publish to Office Online.
2. **To log on to Windows Online, click Next. Type your Windows Online E-Mail Address and Password and click Sign In.**

   If you've never used Windows Online before, click the Sign Up For A Free Account and follow the on-screen instructions.
3. **Determine what to include.**

   After you log on to Windows Online, the Publish Calendar to Microsoft Office Online dialog box pops up, as shown in Figure 3-17. Select options that determine how much you want to share:
   - *To set the date range that's included,* choose either Whole Calendar or Previous, and then set the date range from the two lists supplied. For example, choose Previous 30 Days Through Next 60 Days.

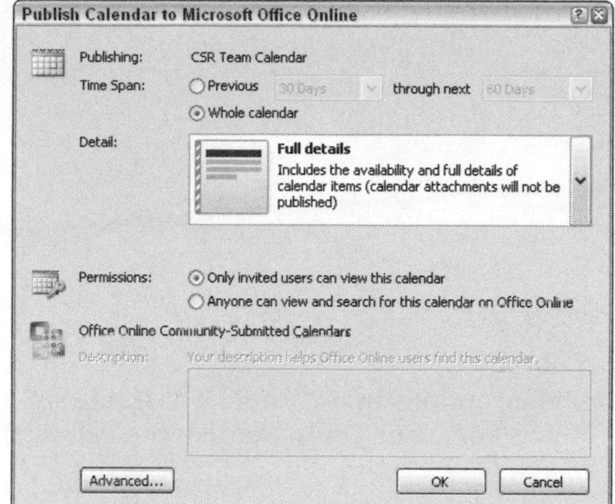

Figure 3-17: How much detail do you want to share?

- *To set the level of detail,* select an option from the Detail list: Availability Only, which only shows your Free/Busy status; Limited Details, which shows Free/Busy and Subject information; or Full Details, which includes basically everything. In addition, if you choose Availability Only, to limit the detail to your working hours only, select the Show Time Within My Working Hours Only option.

4. **Determine who can see your calendar by choosing an option from the Permissions section:**

   - *To allow only selected users to view the calendar,* choose Only Invited Users Can View This Calendar.
   - *To allow anyone who searches for your calendar to view it,* choose Anyone Can View and Search for This Calendar on Office Online. Type a description for the calendar in the box provided; it'll be used by other Office Online users to search for your calendar.

5. **To set advanced options, click Advanced.**

   The Published Calendar Settings dialog box appears, as shown in Figure 3-18.

6. **Set the options you want:**

   - *To have the online calendar updated automatically* if you change the copy on your computer, choose Automatic Uploads. Then select the Update the Calendar with the Server's Recommended Frequency to let Microsoft determine how often to update the calendar.
   - *To never update the calendar,* choose Single Upload.
   - *To include details for any private items,* choose Include Details of Items Marked Private.

Published Calendar Settings

Upload Method:
- (•) Automatic Uploads: Upload updates periodically
- ( ) Single Upload: Updates will not be uploaded

Private Items:
- [ ] Include details of items marked private

Update Frequency:
- [x] Update this calendar with the server's recommended frequency. Send/Receive groups do not update more frequently than the recommended frequency. This helps to prevent your ability to publish a calendar from possibly being canceled by the server.

OK | Cancel

Figure 3-18: Set some advanced options.

7. **After you set all your options in the Publish Calendar to Microsoft Office Online dialog box, click OK to publish the calendar.**

   You'll see a confirmation that the calendar was published correctly; click Yes to continue.

8. **Send Invitations.**

   If you choose to share calendars with only selected people, you're asked if you want to send the invitations to visit the calendar right now. Click Yes, and a special e-mail message appears, as shown in Figure 3-19.

9. **In the To box, type the addresses of the people you want to invite. Type a message while you're at it.**

10. **Click Send to send the sharing invitation.**

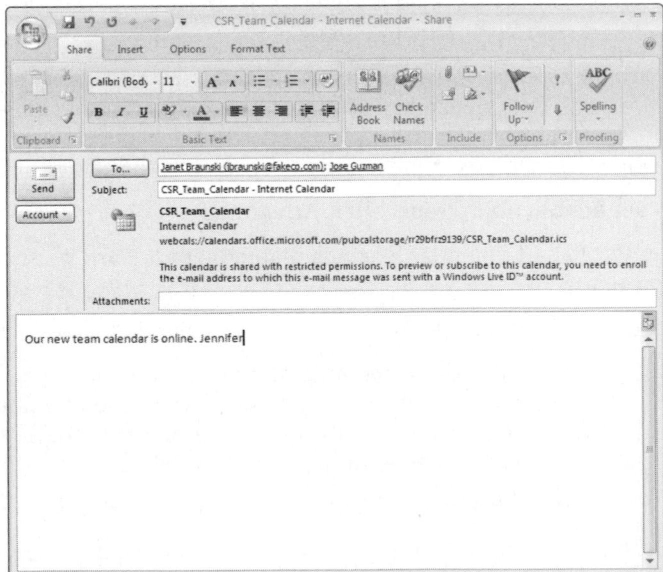

Figure 3-19: Be sure to mail the invitations.

When you send a sharing invitation, users have two options upon receiving it:

- *To preview the calendar online,* click the Preview This Calendar button, located at the top of the Reading pane when they view the message, or choose Share➪Open➪Preview This Calendar. You might be asked to confirm that you want to start the Web browser; if so, click Yes. The calendar appears in a Web browser, as shown in Figure 3-20.
- *To subscribe to your calendar,* click the Subscribe to This Calendar button, located at the top of the Reading pane, or choose Share➪Open➪Subscribe to This Calendar. The calendar is added to the Other Calendars list, and updated along with other subscriptions such as RSS news feeds and Internet calendars. With this option, the calendar can be viewed right in the user's Outlook. See Book III, Chapter 3 and Book IV, Chapter 4 for more information on RSS feeds and Internet calendars.

Your recipients need to log on to the Windows Online to preview or subscribe to your calendar.

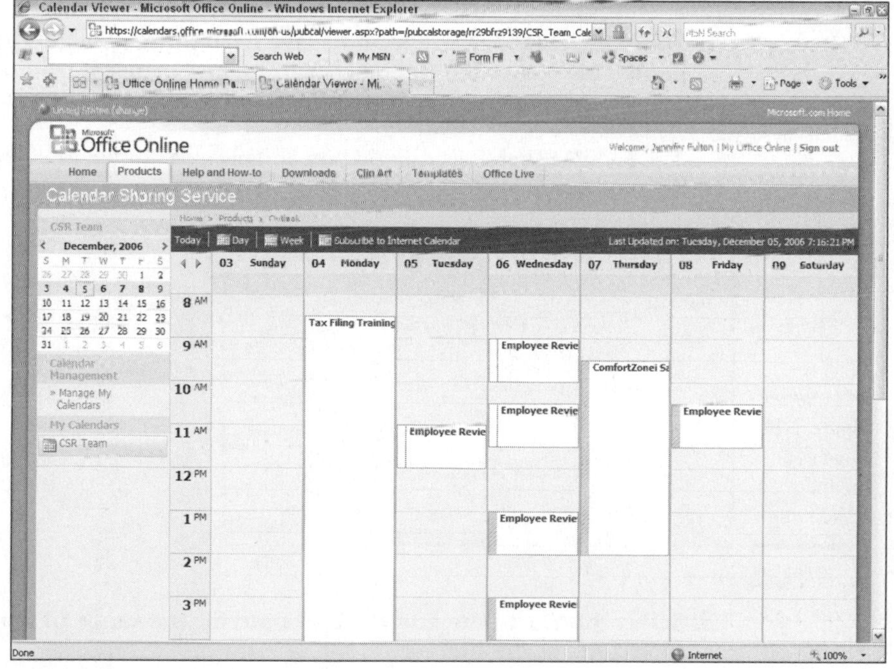

Figure 3-20: View the shared calendar online.

Publishing a Calendar to Any Web Server

There are a ton of reasons why you might have decided to convert your calendar to Web page format. You may like the idea of creating an Internet calendar, but perhaps not oh-so-public places like Microsoft Office Online and Google. If your company has a Web site, you can save your calendar in Web format and post it as a page, which might be a little more private. You could instead go "more public" and convert your calendar to Web format and post it to a free Web site. In any case, Web format is pretty universal, given that it only takes a Web browser to view, so you could decide to bypass the whole posting to the Web thing and simply convert your calendar to Web format as a brilliantly inspired no-fail way to share a calendar via e-mail.

The only downside that I can see in this particular method of sharing a calendar is that, should you make a change to the calendar, you need to resave it in Web page format again and repost or resend it. In other words, the calendar does not get automatically updated if you should change it later on. To learn how you can share a calendar online and keep it current, see "Publishing a Calendar to Microsoft Office Online" and "Sharing a Calendar through Google."

Converting a calendar to Web page format is easy:

1. **Select the calendar you want to save from those listed in the Navigation pane. This makes the calendar current, and brings it front and center.**
2. **Choose File⇨Save as Web Page.**

   The Save As Web Page dialog box appears, as shown in Figure 3-21.

Save as Web Page
Duration
Start date: Fri 12/1/2006 End date: Wed 1/31/2007
Options
Include appointment details
Use background graphic: C:\Documents and Settings\All Users\Doc Browse...
Save as
Calendar title: David's Busy, Busy, Calendar
File name: \\Blue-diamond\jen's docs\Outlook Desk Reference\Wil Browse...
Open saved web page in browser Save Cancel

Figure 3-21: Save your calendar as a Web page.

3. **Select the Start Date and the End Date for the range of dates you want to include in the file.**
4. **Select the options you want:**
   - *To include more than just the calendar item date and subject,* select the Include Appointment Details.

- *To add a background to the Web page,* select the Use Background Graphic option and then click Browse and choose a suitable graphic file.

5. **Choose file-saving options.**

- *To change the Web page title* (which appears in the browser's title bar, and at the top of the Web page), change the text in the Calendar Title box.
- *To change the Web page filename* and where the file is saved, click Browse and select a folder. Then type the filename you want to use in the File Name box; otherwise, the Web page is saved in your my Documents folder using the name of the calendar.

6. **Save the page.**

To preview the page before you post it on a Web site, or e-mail the file to someone, select the Open Saved Web Page in Browser. When you're ready, click Save.

If you choose to display the Web page in a browser, you may see a message warning you not to open files from untrustworthy sources. Assuming that you yourself are trustworthy, click Open to continue. The page appears in a browser, as shown in Figure 3-22. To view the details for an appointment, just click it. The details, such as they are, appear on the right.

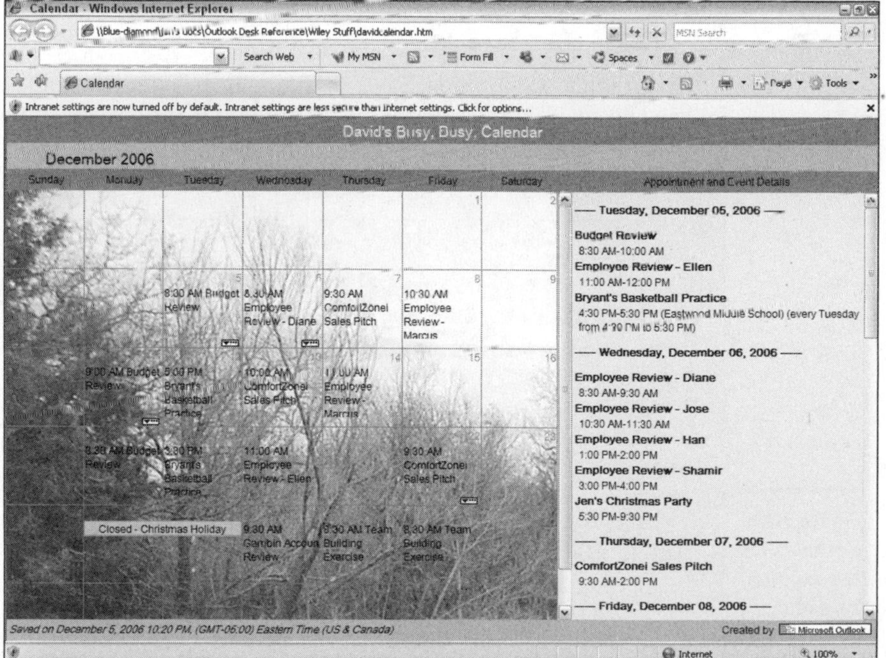

Figure 3-22: You can share your calendar as a simple Web page.

Sharing a Calendar through Google

For a lot of people, the Internet is synonymous with Google. If you've seen something interesting on the Internet lately, chances are, you Googled it. So, if you have a calendar that you'd like to share with the general Internet community, Google seems as good a place as any. For example, maybe you've compiled a calendar listing the football and basketball games for your old high school. Put it online and update it with final scores every once in a while, and your old alums can easily keep up with the Fighting Tigers.

Using Outlook, you can export a calendar to Google and share it on Google Calendar. You can also import somebody else's Google Calendar and have it automatically updated or not — your choice. (You can also find a bit about this part of the process in Book IV, Chapter 5, but I'll throw it in here for free.) One thing to keep in mind — you have to be a member to view and share Google Calendars, but the registration is free and painless.

Exporting one of your calendars to Google Calendar

If you've designed a calendar you'd like to share with other Google Calendar users, you can easily upload it from Outlook. Along the way, you'll get to choose whether or not to include certain details.

1. **Change over to Calendar and select the calendar you want to share so that it's the active one.**
2. **Choose File⇨Save As.**

   Your standard-looking, Save As dialog box appears, as shown on the left in Figure 3-23. You're creating an iCalendar format file so that's already selected for you from the Save As Type box.

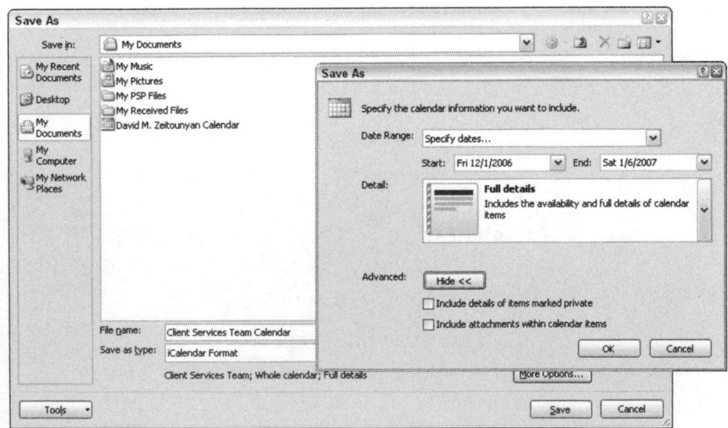

Figure 3-23: Set limits for the exported calendar.

3. **Type a name for the file in the File Name box.**
4. **Click More Options and determine what to include.**

   Another Save As dialog box pops up (I'll call it Save As Jr.), as shown in Figure 3-23.
5. **Select options that determine how much you want to share:**
   - *To set the date range that's included,* choose either Whole Calendar or Previous, and then set the date range from the two lists supplied. For example, choose Previous 30 Days Through Next 60 Days.
   - *To set the level of detail,* select an option from the Detail list: Availability Only, which only shows your Free/Busy status; Limited Details, which shows Free/Busy and Subject information; or Full Details, which includes basically everything. In addition, if you choose Availability Only, you can limit the detail to your working hours only by selecting the Show Time Within My Working Hours Only option.
6. **Click Show.**

   The Advanced settings appear, as shown in Figure 3-23.
7. **Set the options you want:**
   - *To include details for any private items,* set Detail to either Limited Details or Full Details, and then choose Include Details of Items Marked Private.
   - *To include attachments,* set Detail to Full Details, and then choose Include Attachments within Calendar Items.
8. **After you've set all your options in the Save As Jr. dialog box, click OK to return to the Save As Sr. dialog box. Click Save to save the calendar is saved in iCalendar format.**
9. **Log on to Google Calendar using your account info.**

   If you haven't signed up yet for Google Calendar, you'll find a link that guides you through the process.
10. **Create a new calendar.**

    Yep, you heard right. Your iCalendar file is going to be imported into an existing Google calendar. So, if you want to create a new Google calendar to act as the receiver of all that iCalendar data, click the plus button to the right of My Calendars over there on the left. A Calendar Details tab appears, like the one shown in Figure 3-24.

    Type a Calendar Name and Description. Add the Location, and select the Country and time zone that applies, or choose Display All Timezones.

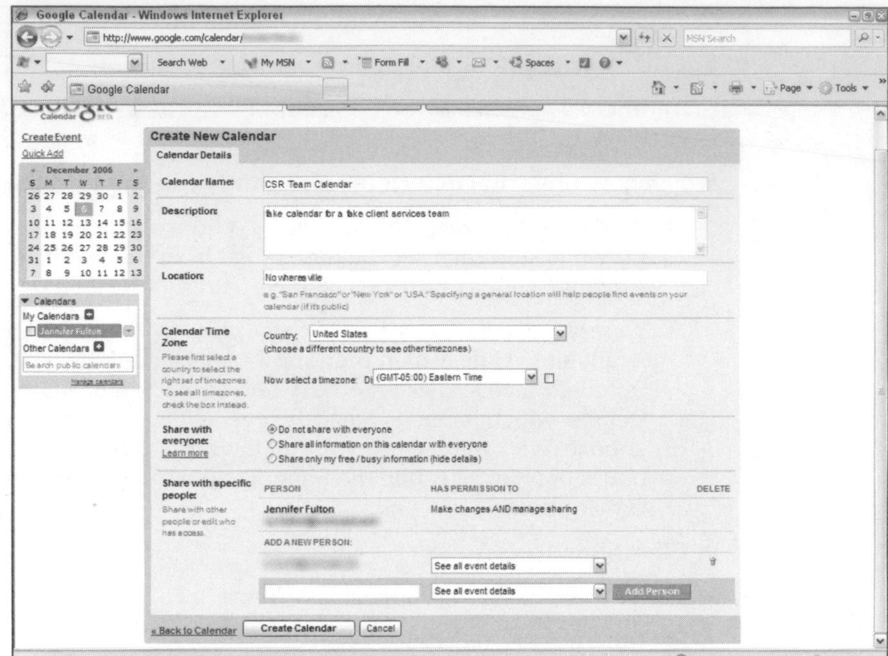

Figure 3-24: Create a new Google calendar.

11. **You can allow any Google Calendar user to view your calendar, or you can restrict access to specific people, as follows:**

    - *To allow anyone to see your calendar and all its details,* choose Share all Information in This Calendar with Everyone.
    - *To allow anyone to see your calendar but only the free/busy information,* choose Share Only My Free/Busy Information.
    - *To restrict access to the calendar to a select few,* type someone's e-mail address in the Add a New Person box, and select a level of access from the second list. Click Add Person to add the user. Repeat this process to add each person you want to share the calendar with.

12. **Click Create Calendar.**

    The calendar is created and added to your list of calendars on the left.

    If you added a specific user to your permissions list, and that user does not currently have a Google Calendar account, you are prompted to send her an invitation. Click Invite.

13. **Now that you have a Google calendar to import the iCalendar file into, click the Settings link at the top of the page. On the Calendar Settings page, select the Import Calendar tab.**

    The Import Calendar options are displayed, as shown in Figure 3-25.

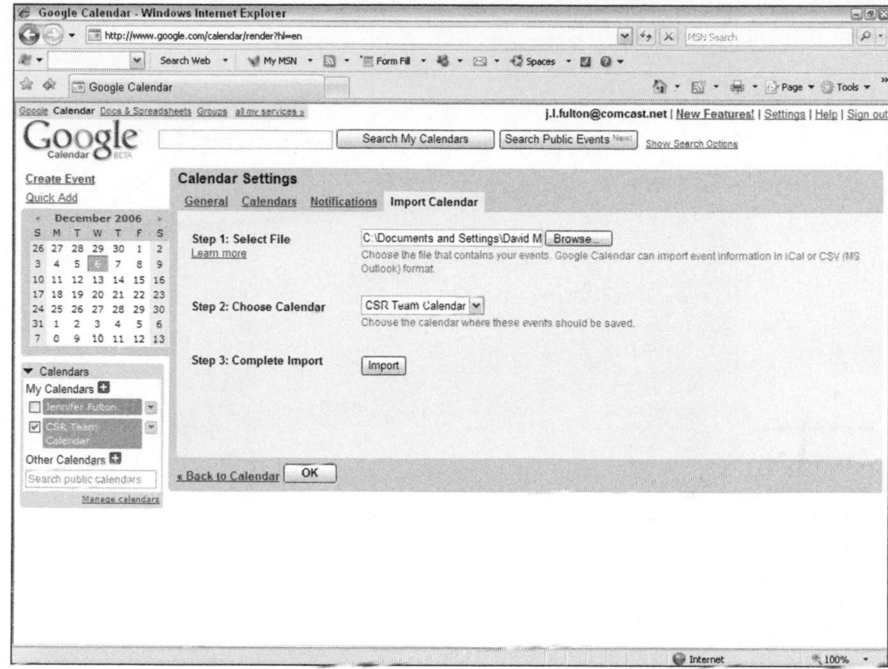

Figure 3-25: Import your calendar into Google Calendars.

14. Find your iCalendar file.

In Step 1, you need to locate your iCalendar file. Click Browse, and navigate to the folder that holds it. Select the file and click Open.

15. Choose a calendar category.

In Step 2, from the drop-down list box that's provided, choose the Google calendar into which you want this calendar data imported.

16. Import the calendar.

In Step 3, click Import to import your calendar into Google Calendar. You'll see a message telling you how many events (items) were imported successfully. Click OK to return to your calendar.

You should keep in mind that your Google calendar is static; if you make changes to the one in Outlook, those changes aren't updated automatically to Google. Instead, you need to repeat these steps to create an updated iCalendar file and upload it.

The calendar appears in Google calendar in a fashion that's similar to Outlook; appointments appear as rectangles that block out the time associated with that item; daily events appear in a band across the top, as shown in Figure 3-26.

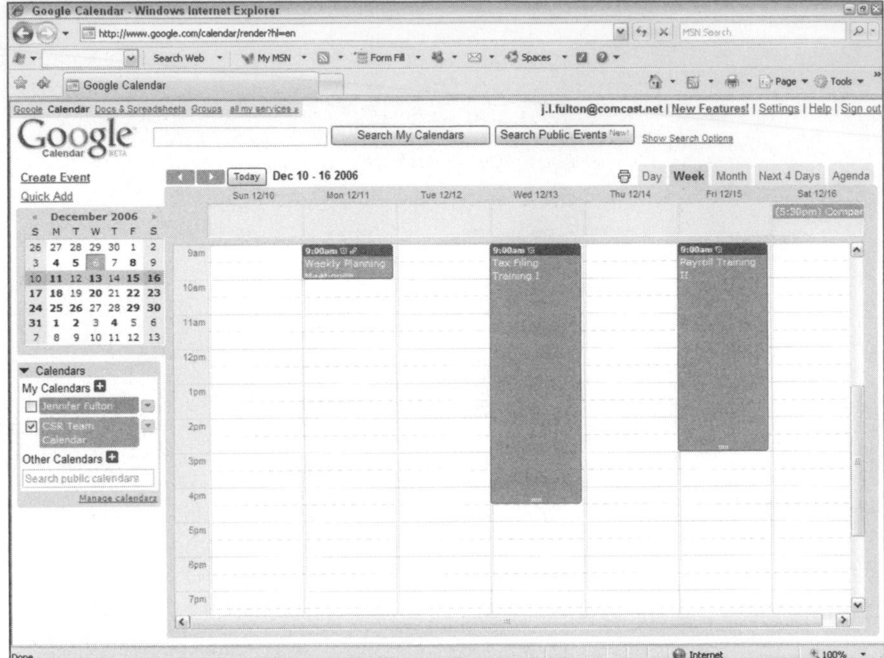

Figure 3-26: Here's your new calendar, for all the world to see (or not).

Importing a Google calendar

When inviting a Google calendar into your Outlook home, you can choose to let it sit quietly and never get updated, or let it jump up and down, run around, and change itself as often as the online copy gets changed.

To import a Google Calendar so that it is updated whenever its online copy is changed, you need to subscribe to it. See "Subscribing to a Google calendar."

To copy a static, non-changing Google calendar to Outlook, follow these steps:

1. **Log on to Google Calendar using your account info.**

   If you haven't signed up yet for Google Calendar, you'll find a link that guides you through the process.

2. **Select the calendar you want to import into Outlook.**

   The calendar appears on the right in Google.

   Yep, in order to import a calendar from Google to Outlook, it has to be one that you have already added to your Calendars or Other Calendars list. So, if there's a shared Google calendar online that you want to import into Outlook, add it to your Other Calendars list first.

3. **Locate the calendar's address.**

   Click the Calendar Settings link at the top of the Web page, and then click the Calendars tab. A list of all your calendars appears. Click the link to the calendar you want to import into Outlook.

4. **Click the calendar's address.**

   The Calendar Details tab appears for the chosen calendar, as shown in Figure 3-27.

5. **Click the ICAL button. When the Calendar Address dialog box jumps out at you, click the Internet address for the calendar that appears as a link.**

6. **Click Save to save the calendar.**

   The iCalendar file is located, and a dialog box appears, asking what you want to do with it. Click Open to import the calendar into Outlook. The calendar is snuggled next to the currently open calendar, in a side-by-side view. The Google calendar is added to the Other Calendars list, where you can switch back to it anytime you want.

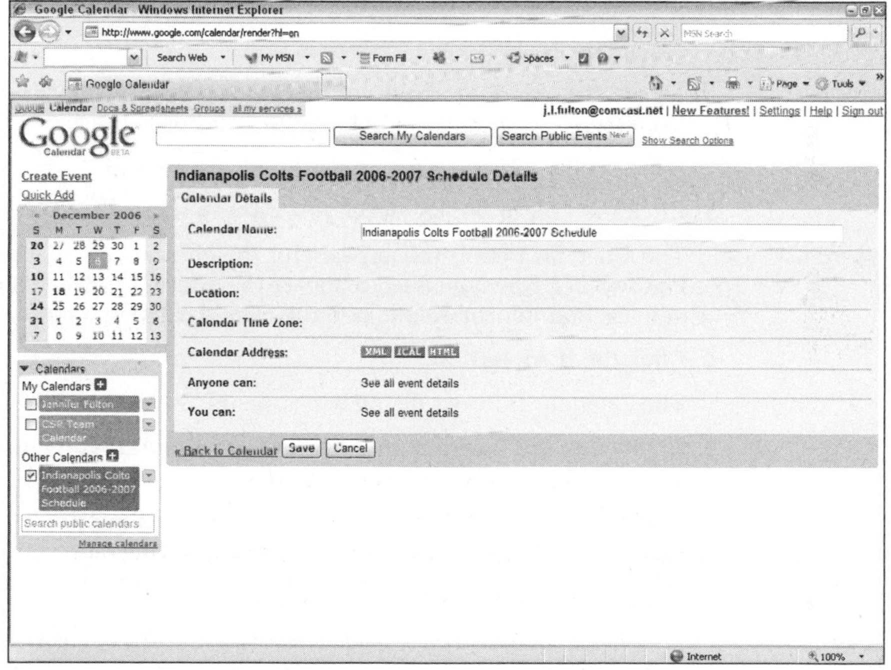

Figure 3-27: Fill me in on all the details.

If you want to update your calendar at some later time, you need to repeat these steps.

Subscribing to a Google calendar

Sometimes, the people who create calendars they wish to share come back and actually update them. Of course, you have no idea going in whether or not the guy who posted the Bergersville Cloggers dance schedule is ever going to return and add more dates, but that's a chance a true fan has to take.

To subscribe to a Google calendar so that it's updated as you go:

1. **Log on to Google Calendar using your account info.**

   If you haven't signed up yet for Google Calendar, don't worry; just navigate to `www.google.com/calendar` and click Create a New Google Account.

   Yes indeedy, in order to import a calendar from Google to Outlook, it has to be one that you have already added to your My Calendars or Other Calendars list in Google. So, if there's a shared Google calendar online that you want to import into Outlook, be sure to add it to your Other Calendars list in Google Calendars first.

2. **Locate the calendar's address by clicking the Settings link at the top of the Web page, and then clicking the Calendars tab.**

   A list of all your calendars appears. See Figure 3-28.

3. **Click the link to the calendar you want to import into Outlook.**

   The Calendar Details tab appears for the chosen calendar (refer to Figure 3-27). Now you need to locate the address for the calendar so you can use that information to add the calendar to Outlook.

4. **Click the ICAL button.**

   The Calendar Address dialog box appears. See Figure 3-29.

5. **Right-click the Internet address for the calendar, and choose Copy Shortcut to copy it to the Clipboard.**

   Don't go clicking that calendar address link, as tempting as it might seem. If you do, you create a static, non-changing calendar in Outlook rather than the self-basting-and-automatically-updating one you're hoping to create.

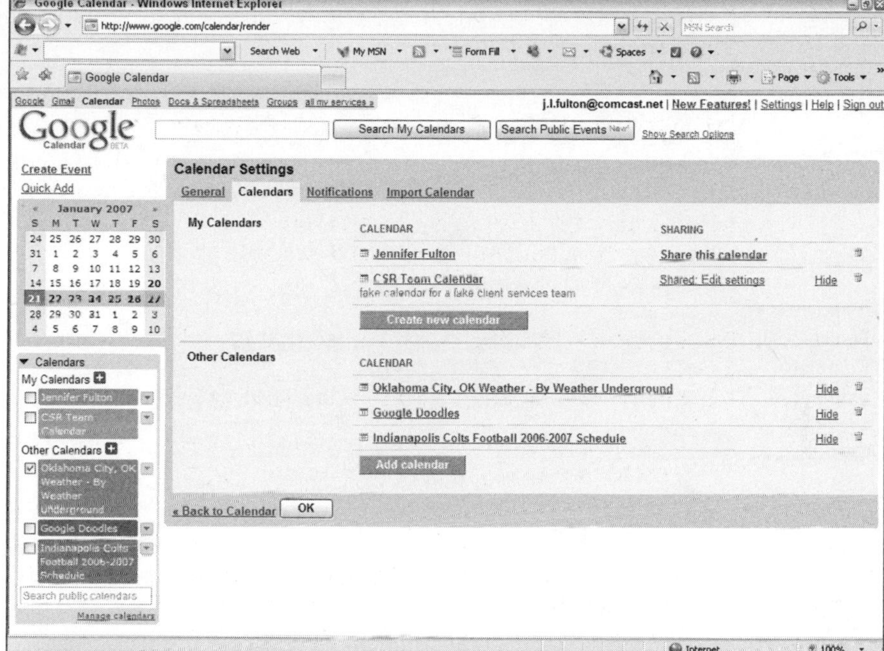

Figure 3-28: Which of your Google calendars would be great in Outlook?

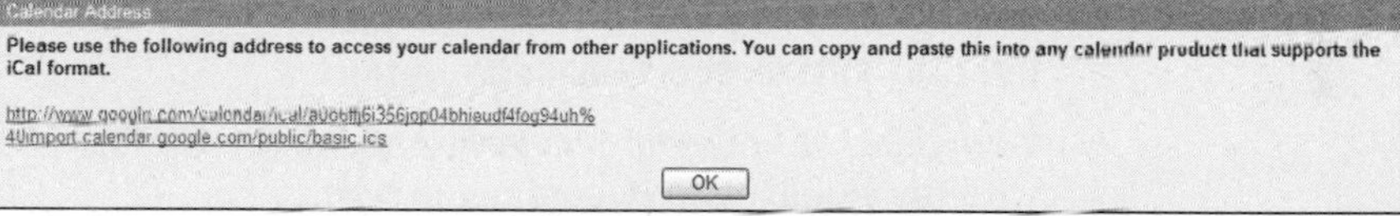

Figure 3-29: Copy the calendar's address.

6. **In Outlook, choose Tools➪Account Settings➪Internet Calendars➪New.**

   The New Internet Calendar Subscription dialog box pops up.

7. **Click in the text box that's provided, and press Ctrl+V to paste that calendar address you copied to the Clipboard.**

8. **Click Add.**

   The Subscription Options dialog box, shown in Figure 3-30, jumps out.

9. **Type a name for the calendar.**

   In the Folder Name box, type a name for the Google calendar as you want it to appear in Outlook.

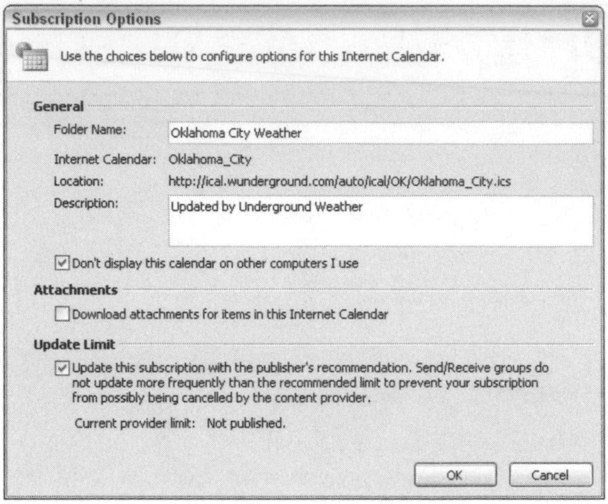

Subscription Options

Use the choices below to configure options for this Internet Calendar.

General

Folder Name: Oklahoma City Weather

Internet Calendar: Oklahoma_City

Location: http://ical.wunderground.com/auto/ical/OK/Oklahoma_City.ics

Description: Updated by Underground Weather

☑ Don't display this calendar on other computers I use

Attachments

☐ Download attachments for items in this Internet Calendar

Update Limit

☑ Update this subscription with the publisher's recommendation. Send/Receive groups do not update more frequently than the recommended limit to prevent your subscription from possibly being cancelled by the content provider.

Current provider limit: Not published.

OK Cancel

Figure 3-30: Complete your subscription.

10. **Set other options.**

    Type a description for the calendar if you want. Set other options as desired:

    - *If you use Outlook on multiple computers,* you can prevent this calendar from appearing everywhere by choosing Don't Display This Calendar on Other Computers I Use.
    - *To download any attachments,* choose the Download Attachments for Items in This Internet Calendar option.
    - *To update the calendar regularly,* choose the Update the Subscription with the Publisher's Recommendation.

11. **Click OK to import the calendar.**

    The subscription is added to those listed on the Internet Calendars tab.

12. **Click Close to close the Account Settings dialog box.**

    The calendar is added to the Other Calendars list, where you can switch to it anytime you want. At periodic intervals, to view the calendar, click its check box.

    Periodically, Outlook checks the calendar online to see if any changes have been made, and then import those changes into your copy of the calendar, automatically.

Chapter 4: All About Meetings

In This Chapter

- Finding the best time for a meeting
- Inviting people to a meeting
- Scheduling resources for a meeting
- Dealing with meeting requests when they come in
- Proposing a different meeting time
- Handling meeting requests painlessly

In Outlook, a meeting is an appointment that takes place between you and somebody else at your company, at least most of the time. The main difference in Outlook between creating an appointment and creating a meeting is that with a meeting, e-mail requests to attend the meeting automatically go out when you create it. With Outlook, you can schedule meetings with people within and outside your organization. However, the power of creating meetings with Outlook only comes alive when you involve only the people in your company.

Assuming you work on an Exchange network, prior to creating a meeting and sending the invitations to attend, you can quickly scan people's free/busy time on their calendars and select a meeting time you already know is open. That way, Rene can't claim that she has an appointment she can't cancel, just so she can get out of that boring planning meeting on Friday. And Marcus can't slide out of the quarterly budget meeting on the flimsy excuse of being too busy with that new Hardwick account, when his calendar actually shows the exact opposite. In addition, on an Exchange network, you can schedule company resources needed for the meeting at the same time that you enter meeting details — resources such as the meeting room or any multimedia equipment. So, if you're on an Exchange network, you can be sure that the meeting is pretty well set up before you even send the meeting invitations. For non-Exchange users, you can use the meeting feature to easily send invitations for the meeting to everyone who's invited, and also track the replies. This chapter gives you the rundown on how to get it all done.

Scheduling a Meeting

There are all sorts of benefits in creating a meeting when you work on an Exchange network. You can peek at your colleague's schedules and find the perfect time when most people can attend. You can also grab a meeting room, cool new data projector, and digital whiteboard. If you're not on an Exchange network, you can still schedule a meeting, because meeting invitations are sent using regular e-mail. You won't know in advance, however, whether the time you've selected works for everyone involved. And you have to let your legs, rather than your fingers, do the walking down to the receptionist's desk to schedule that meeting room you need.

If you want to quickly schedule a meeting with someone's calendar you are currently viewing (because she's shared it with you, as covered in Book IV, Chapter 3), change to the Calendar module and choose Actions⇨New Meeting Request With. Then either choose a name from the menu that appears, or choose All to set up a meeting with everyone whose calendar you are currently viewing. Keep in mind that to use this command, it's not enough that someone has shared her calendar with you, and that you have it loaded into Outlook; nope, you have to also be displaying that calendar.

If you're sharing several of your colleague's calendars, you can collect them together in a group schedule. With a group schedule, you can quickly create a meeting and invite the members of the group. See Book IV, Chapter 3 for more info.

Scheduling a meeting on an Exchange network

To schedule a meeting, follow these steps:

1. **Choose File⇨New⇨Meeting Request.**

   You can also click the arrow on the New button on the Standard toolbar, and choose Meeting Request. In either case, the same thing results: A new Meeting form appears, as shown in Figure 4-1.

   A few things you need to note here. First, when you start creating a meeting, the form says Appointment on the title bar. It continues to do that until you actually invite people to the meeting, which you do in Step 6.

   You might notice that the Appointment button is highlighted on the Ribbon. So what's up? Is this a meeting or not? Well, the information for a meeting in Outlook is divided into two sections: the general appointment-like info, such as date, time, and location, and the meeting info, such as invitees and meeting resources. To access the general appointment info for a meeting, you click the Appointment button on the Ribbon and you see the data that's shown in Figure 4-1. To view meeting info such as who's been invited to a particular meeting, click the Scheduling Assistant button on the Ribbon. You do that in Step 6 here, after typing all the general appointment-like information for your meeting.

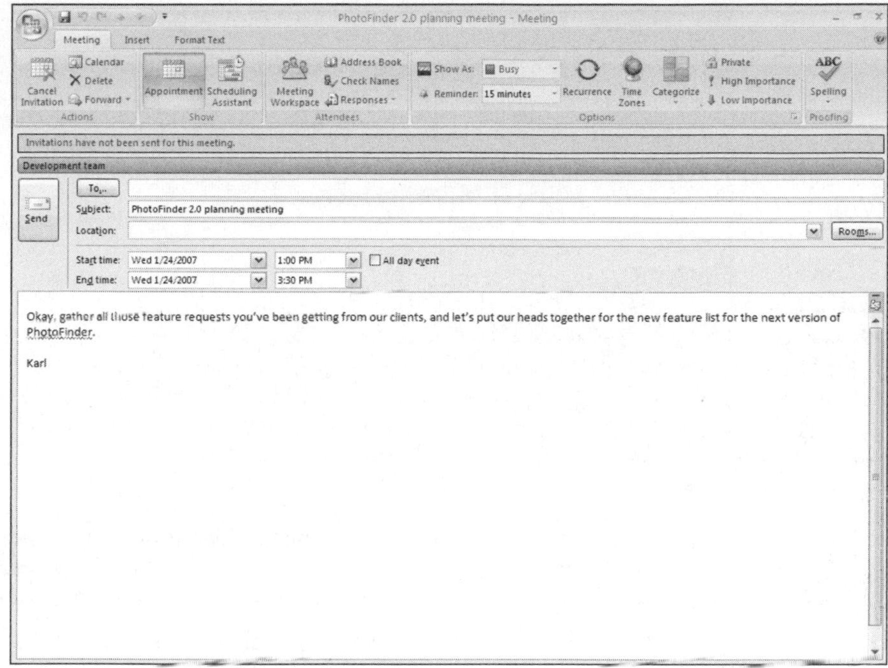

Figure 4-1: Let's take a meeting.

2. **Click in the Subject box and type a description for the meeting, such as** PhotoFinder 2.0 Planning Meeting.

3. **Set other options.**

   Type a message or maybe describe the meeting further using the large notes section. Attach an agenda, select a category, set a reminder, and select other options as desired.

   You can set an option to prevent attendees from proposing a time change for the meeting. See the later section, "Preventing time change proposals for a meeting request." You can also prevent them from responding at all and overwhelming you with too many e-mails. Of course doing that prevents you from viewing a summary of who's coming and who's not, but if it's a really big meeting, that may be one detail you don't want to deal with. See "Preventing replies for a meeting request," later in this chapter.

4. **Choose Meeting⇨Show⇨Scheduling Assistant.**

   The Scheduling Assistant peeks out.

5. **To enter the people you want to invite, click Add Attendees.**

   The Select Attendees and Resources dialog box jumps up, as shown in Figure 4-2.

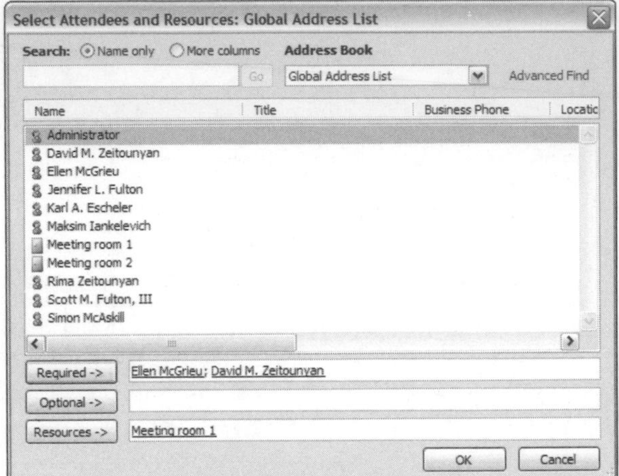

Figure 4-2: So, who do you want to attend?

6. **Choose the address book you want to pull names from (such as the Global Address List), select someone, and click either Required or Optional, depending on whether that person must attend or not.**

   Repeat this step to add more invitees. You can search for someone in a long list by typing a name in the Search box.

7. **Select a meeting location.**

   On an Exchange network, you can schedule resources just like you schedule people, by sending an e-mail and waiting for an acceptance. Assuming this feature has been set up by the system administrator, you also see meeting resources in the listing, such as meeting rooms and projectors. To schedule a local meeting location, select it from the list and click Resources. To schedule a resource such as a projector screen, select that resource from the list and click the Resource button.

   If you don't see any rooms listed, then your system administrator hasn't set up meeting resources you can schedule. In such a case, click OK to close the Select Attendees and Resources dialog box, choose Meeting⇨Show⇨Appointment to redisplay the appointment-like information for the meeting (refer to Figure 4-1), and type a location in the Location box.

It may seem silly to "invite" a meeting room to your party, but on Exchange, meeting rooms and other resources such as projectors, sound equipment, screens, and so on are set up with an e-mail address and calendar just like you. This allows you to check their "schedule" and then book the room or resource for your meeting. The meeting request gets sent to the resource just as it gets sent to each invitee, and it's automatically processed and added to the calendar. Pretty cool, don't you think? Now if only all your employees would greet your meeting requests so cheerfully.

8. **When you're finished adding names, click OK.**

   Outlook returns you to the Scheduling Assistant, shown in Figure 4-3. The assistant looks up the schedules of everyone you invited, and displays them in horizontal bands. This enables you to review everyone's schedule before selecting a meeting time.

9. **Set a meeting time.**

   Enter a Start date and time, and an End date and time. Here's how to decipher what the assistant's trying to tell you, and to use that information to adjust your meeting time:

   - *The green and red vertical bars* mark the starting and ending times for the meeting. You can drag these bars in either direction to adjust the start or end time, or the length of the meeting.
   - *Each attendee's schedule is marked with colored rectangles* that denote appointments, meetings, or events. Using the attendee's calendar and its free/busy time, each rectangle has a particular pattern that lets you know whether a particular block of time is marked as Busy, Tentative, Out of the Office, or Free. (See the key at the bottom of the dialog box.)

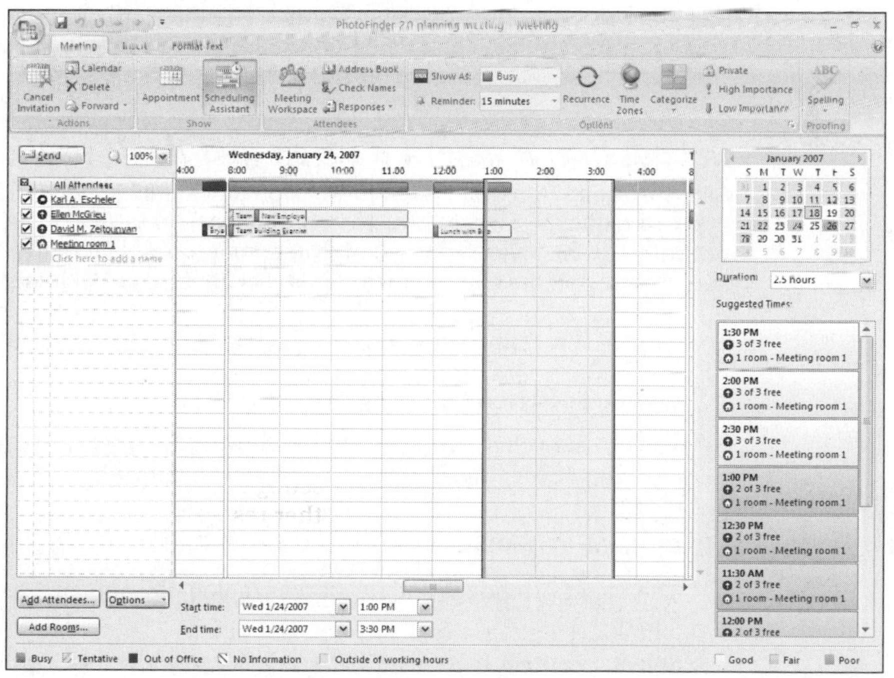

Figure 4-3: May I assist you with your scheduling needs?

- *Alternate times in which you might hold the meeting* appear in the Suggestions pane over there on the right; to choose one of these alternates, simply click it.
- *To change to a different day,* select that day from the calendar that appears above the Suggestions pane. The yellow square marks the current date you've selected; the other colors indicate your chances of finding a good meeting time on that day: white (Good), light blue (Fair), and dark blue (Poor).

10. **Click Send to send the invitations.**

    Outlook calls these *meeting requests,* but I like *invitations* better. No matter what you call them, they are essentially e-mail messages. If you need to set some additional options before you finalize the meeting, choose Meeting⇨Show⇨Appointment to display the meeting's appointment-like information.

If you use OneNote, you can create an instant page where you can gather information about the meeting by choosing Meeting⇨OneNote⇨Meeting Notes. See Book VI, Chapter 5 for help.

The meeting is added to your calendar. Once each attendee receives the meeting request, they can either accept, decline, or propose a different meeting time. (See the upcoming section, "Dealing with Meeting Requests.") You, in the meantime, can't do much except catch a movie, do some Internet surfing, and oh yeah, prepare for the meeting.

Scheduling a meeting when you don't use Exchange

As it turns out, you don't need to work on an Exchange network to send meeting requests. The process is very similar to creating an appointment, but with a twist: When you're done, meeting requests go out to each invitee, and your recipients can then respond by accepting or declining.

To schedule a meeting without using Exchange, follow these steps:

1. **Choose File⇨New⇨Meeting Request.**

   You can also click the arrow on the New button on the Standard toolbar, and choose Meeting Request. A new Meeting form appears, as shown in Figure 4-4.

2. **Click the To button.**

   The Select Attendees and Resources dialog box appears, as shown in Figure 4-5.

3. **Select a contact from your list and click Required or Optional, depending on whether his presence is required. Repeat this process to add more invitees. When you're through, click OK.**

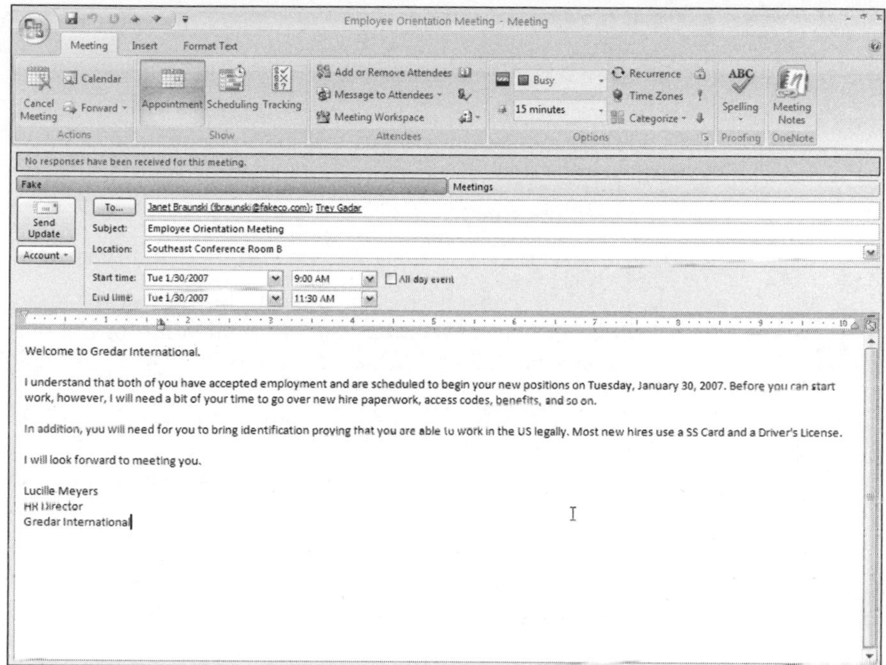

Figure 4-4: Hey everybody, let's get together!

You can search for a contact name by entering some text in the Search box.

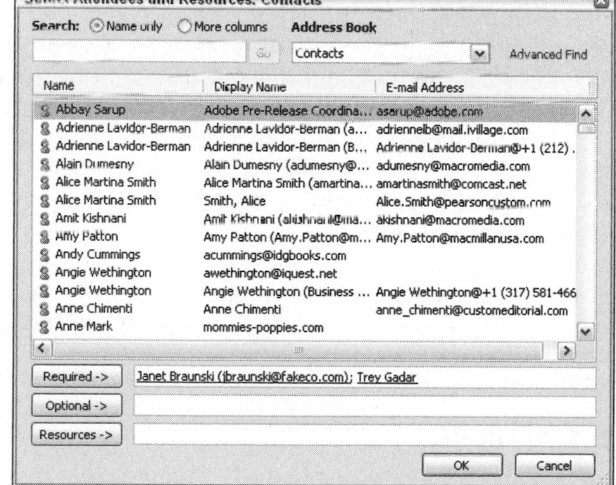

Figure 4-5: Select who you want to invite.

4. **Click in the Subject box and type a description for the meeting, such as** Employee Orientation Meeting.

5. **Type a location.**

   To choose a location you've used before, open the Location list and make a selection.

6. **Set a meeting time.**

   Enter a Start date and time, and an End date and time.

   If you want to consult your calendar before selecting a time, choose Meeting⇨Actions⇨Calendar, and your calendar for the date you've chosen appears in a separate window.

7. **Set other options.**

   Type a message or describe the meeting further using the large notes section. Attach an agenda, select a category, set a reminder, and select other options as desired.

   You can prevent attendees from proposing a time change for the meeting. See "Preventing time change proposals for a meeting request." You can also prevent them from responding at all and overwhelming you with too many e-mails. Of course doing that prevents you from viewing a summary of whose coming and whose not, but if it's a really big meeting, that may be one detail you don't want to deal with. See "Preventing replies for a meeting request," later in this chapter.

8. **Click Send to send the invitations.**

The meeting requests are sent as e-mail messages to each attendee, and the meeting is added to your calendar. After each attendee receives the meeting request, they can either accept, decline, or tentatively accept (assuming the recipient uses Outlook). If the recipient doesn't use Outlook, he gets the message, but he won't see the Accept, Decline, or Tentative buttons. Outlook users, on the other hand, can even propose a different meeting time. (See the upcoming section, "Dealing with Meeting Requests.") You, in the meantime, have the wonderful job of simply waiting and snacking on chocolate, although the chocolate is optional.

If you use OneNote, you can create a new page on which you can keep all your meeting related information. Choose Meeting⇨OneNote⇨Meeting Notes. See Book VI, Chapter 5 for help.

Changing a meeting

Even before you get any replies, you can make changes to a meeting, and Outlook kindly lets everyone know how forgetful you are. For example, you may have forgotten to set a reminder, invite a particular attendee, mark the meeting private so it doesn't show up on your shared calendar (only the people you invited know about it), or make a meeting recurring. No matter what you need to change, it's no problem; you can easily make the necessary changes and leave the updating thing to Outlook. After all, you're busy planning meetings. . . .

To change a meeting, follow these steps:

1. **Double-click the meeting to open it.**

   If the meeting recurs, you see a message asking whether you want to change only this occurrence or the whole series. Select whether to edit this item only, or the series of meetings and click OK to continue.

   Eventually, the Meeting form opens, as shown in Figure 4-6.

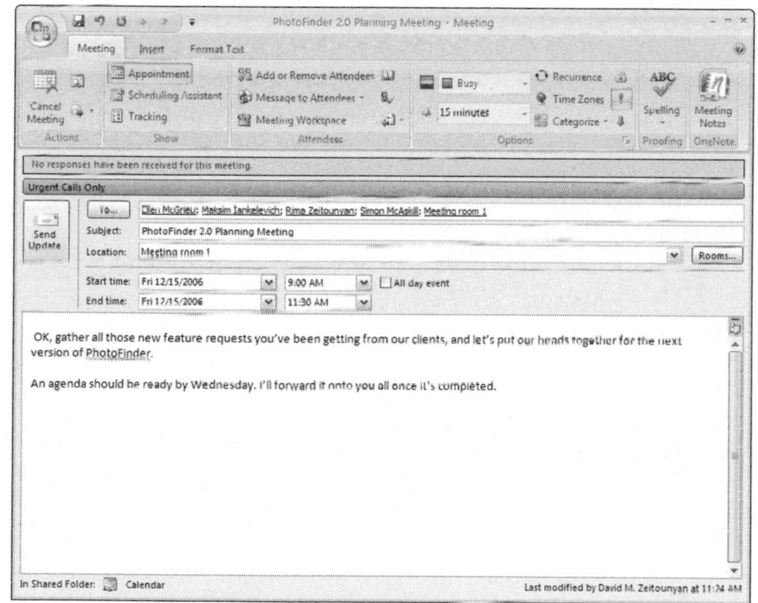

Figure 4-6: You can change a meeting without messing things up.

2. **Make your changes.**

   For example:

   - *To make a meeting recur, or to change its recurrence,* choose Meeting⇨Options⇨Recurrence. Make the changes you want in the Recurrence dialog box; see Book IV, Chapter 2.
   - *To set a reminder,* choose one from the Reminder list, located in the Options group.
   - *To mark a meeting as private,* choose Meeting⇨Options⇨Private.

- *To invite (or uninvite) someone,* choose Meeting⇨Add or Remove Attendees. The Select Attendees and Resources dialog box pops back up; see Figure 4-7. Select someone and click Required or Optional to add him to the attendee's list. To remove someone, select his name in the Required or Optional list, and press Delete. Click OK.
- *To change the date or time for the meeting,* just change the Start date or time, or the End date or time. You can also choose Meeting⇨Show⇨Scheduling Assistant to have it search for a suitable time.

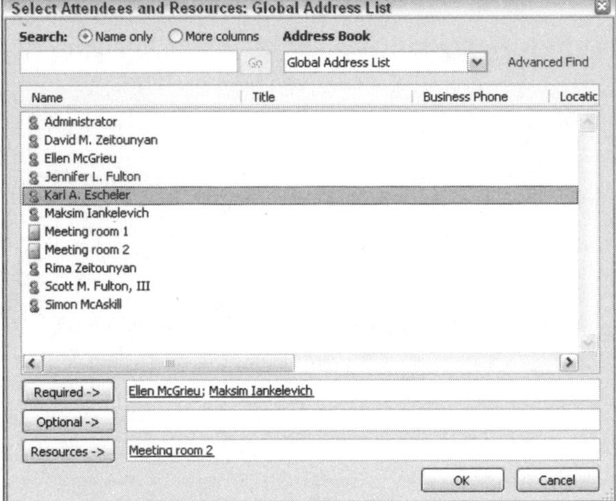

Figure 4-7: You can invite someone to a meeting and uninvite him just as easily.

You can also simply drag the meeting in your calendar to change its date and time. After you drag and drop, you see a message asking whether you want to save the changes and send updates, or undo your change. If you choose to save the change, the Meeting form opens again; review the change and click Send Update.

3. **When you're done making changes, click Send Update.**

   The Send Update to Attendees dialog box appears, as shown in Figure 4-8.

4. **Select who to notify:**

   - *Choose Send Updates Only to Added or Deleted Attendees* to send e-mail notices only to new attendees you've just added, and to people you may have uninvited.
   - *Choose Send Updates to All Attendees* to notify everyone of the change, regardless of whether they are original attendees, just added attendees, or uninvited attendees.

Send Update to Attendees

You have made changes to the list of attendees. Choose one of the following:

Send updates only to added or deleted attendees.

Send updates to all attendees.

OK Cancel

Figure 4-8: Who needs to know now?

5. **Click OK.**

   New meeting invitations are sent, explaining the change.

Canceling a meeting

It's hard to imagine right now, what with all that hard work you've put in creating the meeting, sending meeting invitations, and sharpening all those pencils, but there may come a time when you might actually have to cancel a meeting. Sigh. Maybe you can still get a refund on the uneaten donuts (you know — the ones you kind of bought for the meeting, but somehow gobbled down while preparing for the silly thing). One problem you don't have to worry about at least, and that's the problem of letting everyone know the meeting's been cancelled.

To cancel a meeting, follow these steps:

1. **Double-click the meeting to open it.**

   If the meeting recurs, you see a message asking if you want to change only this occurrence, or the whole series. Select the option you want and click OK to continue.

   The Meeting form appears (refer to Figure 4-4).

2. **Choose Meeting⇨Actions⇨Cancel Meeting.**
3. **Click Send Cancellation.**

   A new e-mail is readied so that you can notify everyone that the meeting has been cancelled. (See Figure 4-9.) You can use the message section to provide an explanation for the cancellation, if necessary.

The meeting is removed from your calendar. Meeting cancellation notices are sent to each attendee. When the attendee views the notice, she sees a Remove From Calendar button at the top of the Reading pane that she can use to remove the meeting from her calendar. (See Figure 4-10.) If she opens the meeting, she can choose Meeting⇨Respond⇨Remove From Calendar instead.

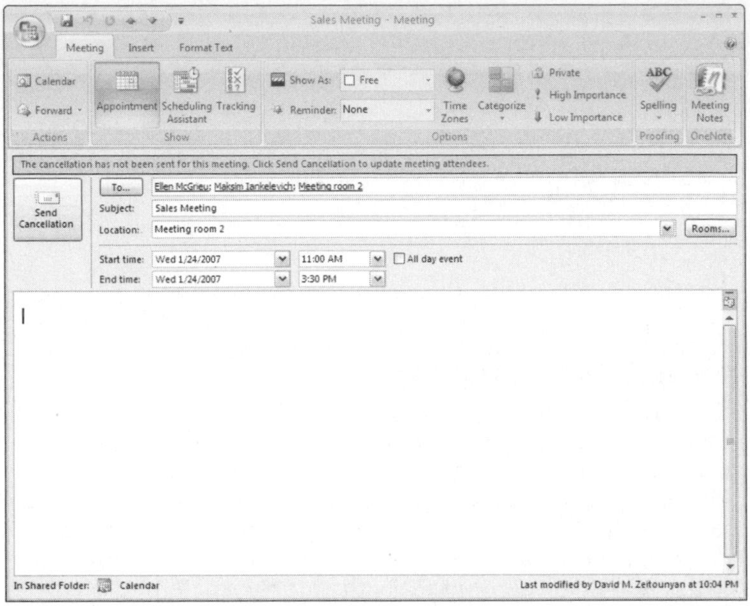

Figure 4-9: Cancel that.

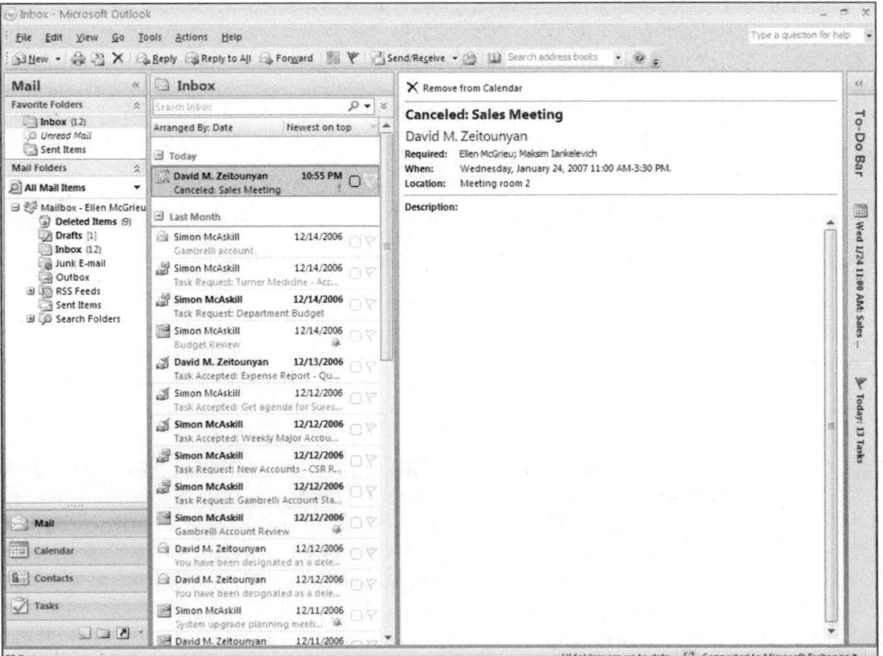

Figure 4-10: Remove a meeting from your calendar.

Sending a Message to All Attendees

Even if you haven't changed the meeting time or place, there may be an occasion when you need to get a message to all attendees. For example, maybe you want to forward the meeting agenda so they can review it before attending. Or perhaps you want to send directions to an out of office meeting venue. Because Outlook keeps track of who you've invited, it's a simple matter to get it to send out a message for you.

To send out a message to people attending one of your meetings, follow these steps:

1. **Open the meeting.**

   Change to Calendar and double-click that old meeting to open it right up. The Meeting form appears, displaying all the current meeting information.

2. **Choose Meeting➪Message to Attendees➪New Message to Attendees.**

   A new message form appears, already self-addressed and stamped for you, as shown in Figure 4-11. People who have declined the meeting are still included for some odd reason. Guess Outlook just doesn't feel good about leaving anyone out.

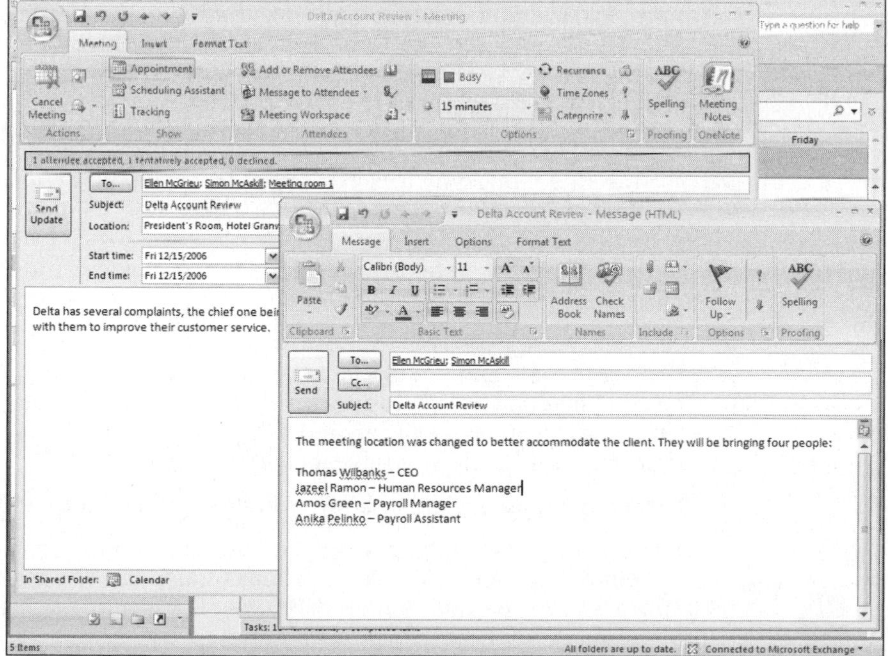

Figure 4-11: Get the message out.

The Subject shows the name of the meeting; you can change the subject if you want.

3. **Type your message in the big notes area, and add any attachments you like.**
4. **Click Send.**
5. **Close the meeting window.**

   After sending your meeting message, return to the message window and close it by clicking its Close button. Outlook asks whether you want to save changes, which is kinda dumb if you didn't make any. Just shake your head, make sure that ol' Don't Save Changes option is selected and click OK. Of course, if you did make changes, that's fine. Just click Save Changes and Send Update instead.

Dealing with Meeting Requests

Just because you're busy, that doesn't mean that your colleagues will stop asking for your help and advice. In fact, I venture to guess that your good work is one reason why you are so busy in the first place. In any case, given your busy schedule, the simple fact is that you can't accept every request to attend a meeting. Luckily, you can choose whether to attend or decline a meeting request when it comes in. You can even propose a different meeting time that works better for you. And if you're really busy, you can automate your responses to meeting requests, rather than deal with them one at a time.

Accepting, tentatively accepting, or declining a meeting

When a meeting request arrives in your Inbox, you have a choice: You can accept, decline, or accept kinda, at least for now.

To deal with a meeting request when it arrives, follow these steps:

1. **Open the meeting request.**

   Change to Mail, and double-click the meeting request to open it. The name of meeting organizer appears on the InfoBar. You also see the names of the other people invited to the meeting, its location, date, and time. Figure 4-12 shows a typical meeting request.

2. **Let the meeting organizer know whether you can attend the meeting.**

   If you want to consult your calendar before accepting or declining an appointment, choose Meeting➪Actions➪Calendar. Your calendar appears in a separate window, displaying the meeting along side any other items you have scheduled that day.

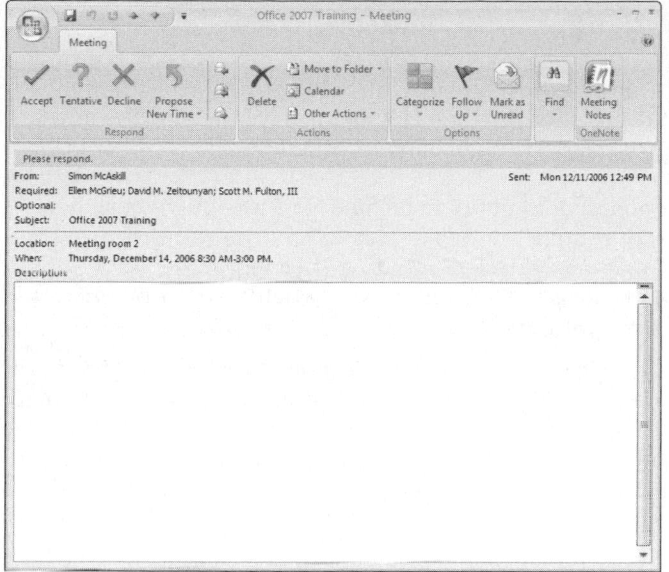

Figure 4-12: Reviewing a request for a meeting.

- *To accept the invitation and attend the meeting,* choose Meeting➪Respond➪Accept.
- *To respectfully decline the meeting,* choose Meeting➪Respond➪Decline.
- *To indicate that you might be able to attend but that you're not sure right now,* choose Meeting➪Respond➪Tentative.

If you'd like to suggest a different meeting time, see the next section, "Proposing a new meeting time," for help.

If you replied that you are tentatively accepting the meeting request, you can later reopen the request and send a more definite answer, such as Accept or Decline.

A dialog box appears, asking if you'd like to add a comment to the reply.

3. **Choose whether to say more.**

   Select an option and click OK:

   - *To add a comment,* choose Edit the Response Before Sending. A message form appears, addressed to the meeting organizer; add your comment and click Send.
   - *To simply send the response,* choose Send the Response Now. The e-mail response is sent immediately to the meeting organizer.
   - *To cancel your choice and not send a response right now,* choose Don't Send a Response.

Proposing a new meeting time

If a meeting request arrives and you'd like to accept, but the meeting time simply isn't the best one for you, you can propose a new meeting time. With your proposal for the time change, you can decline the current time or tentatively accept, depending on your schedule.

To propose a different date or time for a meeting you've been invited to, follow these steps:

1. **Open the meeting request by switching to Mail and double-clicking the meeting request.**

   Although you can click the Propose New Time button in the Reading pane after selecting a message request, without going to the trouble of actually opening the e-mail, if you do, you can tentatively accept the current meeting time while proposing a new one. To definitely decline the current meeting time and propose a new one, you need to follow the steps given here.

   To select the default setting for the Propose New Time button in the Reading pane, choose Tools⇨Options⇨Calendar Options. Then select either Tentative, Accept, or Decline from the Use This Response When You Propose New Meeting Times list. Click OK twice to save the change.

2. **Choose Meeting⇨Respond⇨Propose New Time.**
3. **From the drop-down menu that appears, choose a command (see Figure 4-13):**
   - *To tentatively accept the current time, while also proposing a change,* choose Tentative and Propose New Time.
   - *To decline the current meeting time and propose a different time,* choose Decline and Propose New Time.

   The Propose New Time dialog box peeks out, as shown in Figure 4-14.
4. **Propose a new time.**

   The dialog box displays the schedule for all attendees. A time block's color tells you whether the item is marked as Busy, Tentative, or Out of the Office. The current meeting time is marked with a yellow vertical band.

   - *To manually select a time,* click in your row, on any time slot that's open. The proposed time is flanked by green and red bars. You can also select a new Meeting Start and Meeting End date and time from the lists provided.
   - *To have Outlook propose a new time,* click the AutoPick Next >> button. Outlook finds the first available free time slot for all attendees.

Click the << button to locate the first free time slot available in the other direction. The suggested meeting time is flanked by green and red bars.

- *To reset the suggested time to the current meeting time,* click Current Meeting Time.

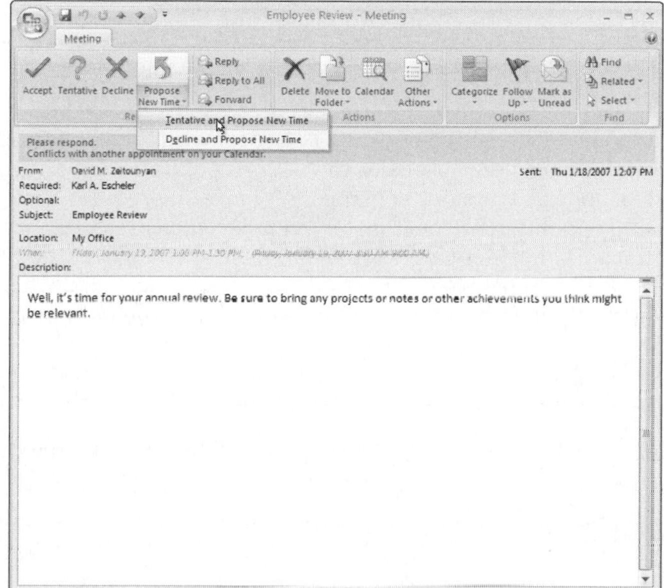

Figure 4-13: Pick one, only one.

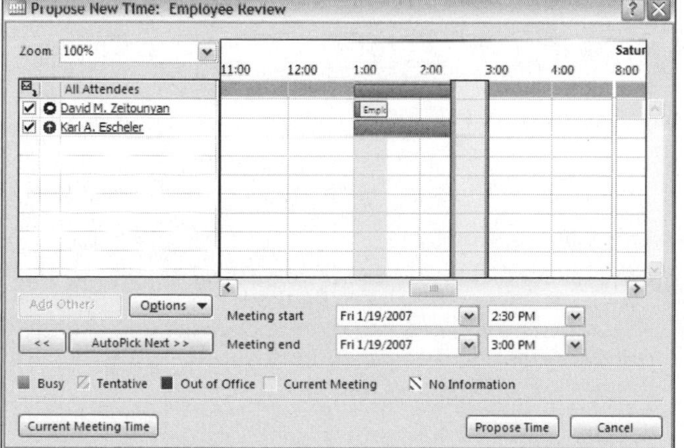

Figure 4-14: Hmmmmm. Now what time works best for me?

5. **Click Propose Time.**

   A meeting reply is created. The InfoBar displays the current meeting time and the one you're proposing. Add any message you want in the notes area.

6. **Click Send.**

   The message is sent to the meeting organizer. The meeting is changed in your Calendar, using your proposed time.

Automatically handling meeting requests

One way to handle meeting requests is to deal with them automatically, without any input from you. Typically, the majority of us accept any meeting request, as long as it fits our schedule. Any meeting request that conflicts with an existing appointment, meeting, or event is usually rejected. So it makes sense that we simply let Outlook handle these seemingly automatic responses.

To set up Outlook to handle meeting requests for you as they come in, follow these steps:

1. **Choose Tools⇨Options⇨Calendar Options⇨Resource Scheduling.**

   The Resource Scheduling dialog box appears, as shown in Figure 4-15.

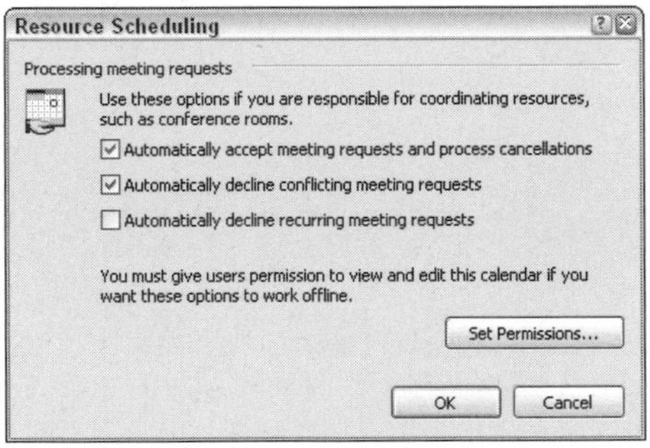

Figure 4-15: Let Outlook handle those replies.

2. **Set automatic options.**

   Select how you want Outlook to handle meeting requests:

   - *To just accept any meeting requests you get and deal with any meeting cancellations you receive,* choose Automatically Accept Meeting Requests and Process Cancellations.

- *To simply reject any meeting requests that conflict with items already in your calendar,* choose Automatically Decline Conflicting Meeting Requests.
- *To always decline requests to attend recurring meetings,* choose Automatically Decline Recurring Meeting Requests.

3. **Click OK three times.**

None of these options work if you're working offline, unless the people sending the meeting requests have view and edit access to your Calendar. To provide access, click Set Permissions. See Book IV, Chapter 4 for help in sharing your Calendar.

Checking on Meeting Responses

Well, the fun doesn't end with you sending a meeting invitation or request; no, there are tons of things to do to get ready for the meeting, such as creating and copying the agenda, programming the PowerPoint presentation, and locating that silly laser pointer you keep misplacing. The last thing you need to be doing is constantly nagging attendees to find out who's really coming or not so that you can have enough agendas and color copies of your slides printed, and order enough donuts and coffee. Luckily, Outlook's there to do all the nagging for you. Whenever the need arises, you can easily check on each attendee's response to your invitation, and get a quick head count.

To check on responses to your meeting request, follow these steps:

1. **Open the meeting.**

   Jump over to Calendar and double-click the meeting to open it right up. You can also open any of the e-mail replies you've gotten to your meeting request, if that's more convenient for you.

   The InfoBar at the top of the Message form displays the total number of responses, divided into three categories: accepted, tentatively accepted, and declined. You can view these responses in more detail.

2. **Choose Meeting⇨Show⇨Tracking.**

   A list showing each attendee's name, her status (as a required attendee or an optional one), and her response (if any). See Figure 4-16.

If someone has not accepted but has instead proposed a new time for the meeting, his response doesn't appear in the listing. An attendee must either accept the meeting, decline the meeting, or accept tentatively to have a response appear in this listing.

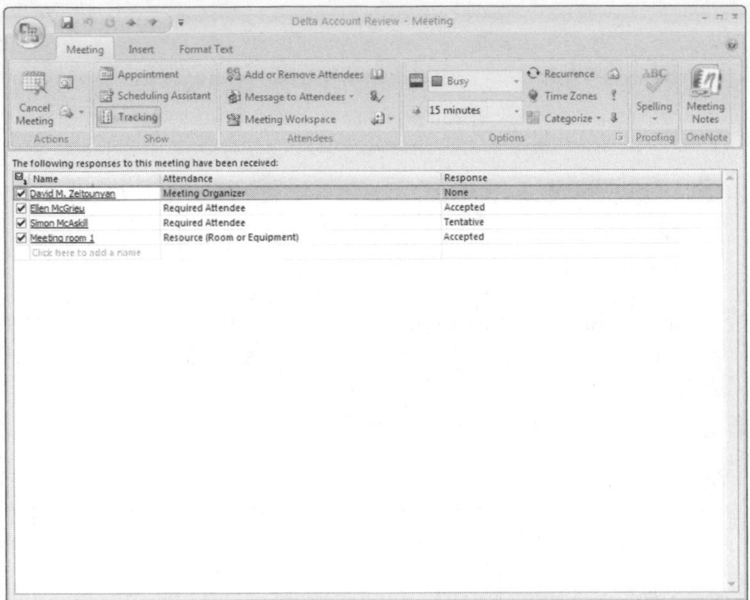

Figure 4-16: So who all's coming?

3. **When you're done viewing the meeting responses, close the meeting form by clicking the window's Close button.**

   You're asked if you want to save changes, which is kinda dumb because you didn't make any. This is just Outlook's way of over-parenting. You can:

   - Choose Save Changes and Send Updates to save any changes you made but forgot about, and also send out an update to all attendees to let them know you made some mysterious, forgotten change.
   - Choose Save Changes but Don't Send if you made a change to the meeting but really didn't mean it.
   - Choose Don't Save Changes if you, like most people, only came here to look at the responses and didn't actually make any changes, thank you very much.

4. **Click OK.**

Accepting or declining a time proposed by others

Well, it's bound to happen. Even though you've checked everybody's schedule twice (and made a note of who's naughty or nice), someone somewhere is gonna have a problem with the time or the date you picked for your meeting. And that somebody is going to ask, "Hey, could we change that perfectly good time to one that's harder for everyone to make?"

In reality, one of your attendee's may actually suggest a time that is better for everyone, so it pays to at least listen to suggestions. Even while reviewing time change proposals, you still reserve the right to stick with the original time, of course.

To review time change proposals for a meeting you created, and accept or decline any of them:

1. **Change over to the Mail, and double-click the meeting response that contains the proposed change.**

   It's easy to identify such messages because the message header says something like **New Time Proposed: XX** where XX is the name of the meeting.

2. **View all the proposals.**

   At the top of the Meeting form, in the InfoBar, you see the current time of the meeting, and the proposed new time. You also see a summary of responses to the meeting.

   You might have gotten more than one proposal to change the meeting time, so to be sure that you check them all out by choosing Meeting Respond➪View All Proposals. The proposed times appear in a list, as shown in Figure 4-17.

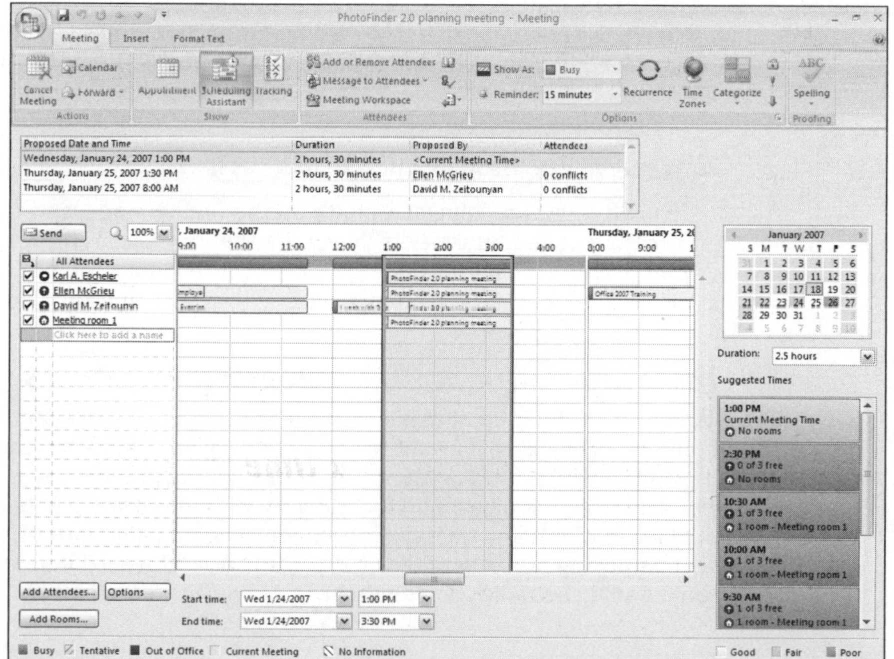

Figure 4-17: View the proposed time changes for a meeting.

For some goofy reason, you won't see all of the proposed time changes unless you've at least viewed each proposal in the Reading pane. You don't need to go so far as to open each response, but you do need to view them so they are marked "read" in your Inbox. Then you can gather all the proposed time changes together and view them as described here.

If you don't want to view all the responses first, you can accept or reject an individual proposal from within the message reply. To accept the proposal, choose Meeting Response➪Respond➪Accept Proposal. A new message appears so you can let everyone know about the meeting change; click Send Updates. The meeting is changed in your Calendar. To reject the proposal, choose Meeting Response➪Respond➪Reply. Type a message explaining why you still like the guy but it's just not working out, and click Send.

3. **Accept or reject the new time.**

   Choose what you want to do. If you want to view your calendar first, Meeting➪Actions➪Calendar button.

   - *To accept a proposed time,* select that proposal in the listing, and then choose Send. The meeting is automatically moved to the new time in your Calendar.

     By the way, accepting a proposed time automatically notifies anyone else who may have sent time proposals that their time changes were rejected.

   - *To reject a proposed time,* select a proposal, and then choose Meeting➪Attendees➪Message to Attendees➪Reply With Message. A message form appears so you can explain a bit about why you're rejecting the time.

4. **When you're through, click Send.**

   The attendees receive an update on the time change, and then need to accept, decline, or tentatively accept the new time. This applies even to the person whose time change you accepted; yep, she needs to wait until she gets the time change notice from you, and then accept it.

Automatically handling meeting responses

By my way of thinking, it makes little sense to have a computer if it makes life harder. Well, okay, if I want to be truthful, Windows does sometimes make me wonder why I use a computer at all, but on most days when Windows is behaving itself, I look around for ways to keep life running smoothly and peacefully, and the other day I found one: a way to get Outlook to handle all those annoying meeting replies for me, so I don't have to interrupt my harmonic day by actually reading them.

Here's how you do it:

1. **Choose Tools⇨Options⇨E-Mail Options⇨Tracking Options.**

   The Tracking Options dialog box, shown in Figure 4-18, pops up.

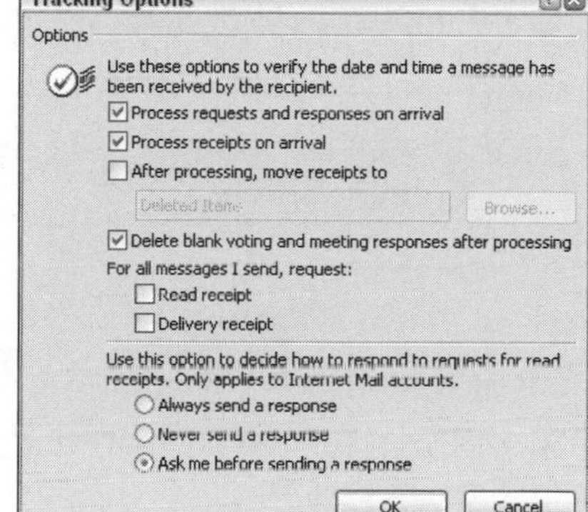

Figure 4-18: Let Outlook handle those replies.

2. **Set tracking options.**

   Select how you want Outlook to handle meeting replies as they arrive in your Inbox:

   - *To just record somebody's response to your meeting request without waiting for you to read it* (if someone accepts your meeting request, for example, record that in the meeting form without waiting for you to read the message reply), choose Process Requests and Responses on Arrival.
   - *To automatic delete meeting responses after you read them,* choose Delete Blank Voting and Meeting Responses After Processing.

3. **Click OK three times.**

Preventing replies for a meeting request

If you're planning a meeting for 50 people and you don't want to keep track of who can come and who can't (you just want to notify everyone), you can prevent attendees from bothering you with too many replies.

Whether or not you choose to track meeting replies, you can prevent people from trying to propose alternate meeting times. See the upcoming section, "Preventing time change proposals for a meeting request."

You can set up Outlook to handle meeting replies automatically, if doing it manually is too tiring for you. See "Automatically handling meeting responses," earlier in this chapter.

Follow these steps to request a meeting, but your attendees from sending you a reply:

1. **Create the meeting request by choosing File⇨New⇨Meeting Request.**

   The Meeting form appears.

2. **Use the Meeting form to select attendees, enter a start and end date/ time, choose a location, and set other options.**

3. **Choose Meeting⇨Attendees⇨Responses.**

   A drop-down menu appears, as shown in Figure 4-19.

4. **Choose the Request Responses option to deselect it.**

   Turning off Request Responses also turns off the ability for the recipient to bother you with alternate time proposals.

   When you turn off the Request Responses option, you can't check whether attendees can come to the meeting, or who won't attend.

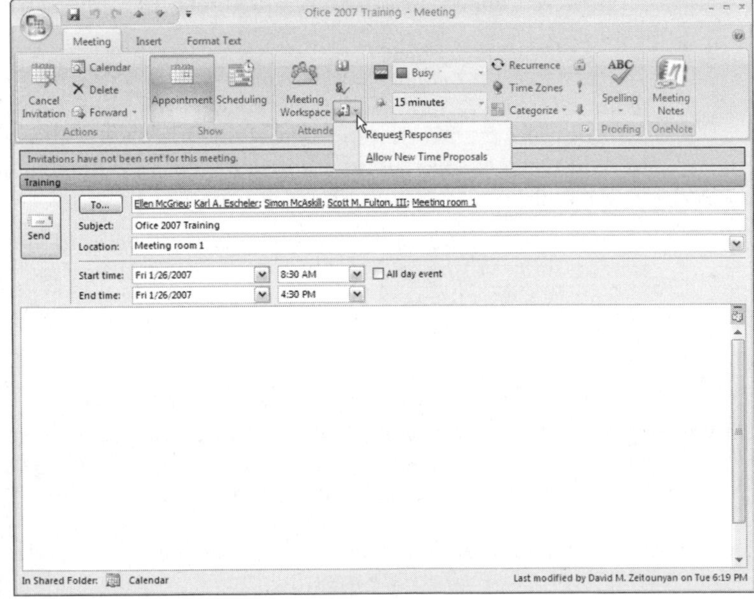

Figure 4-19: Prevent meeting attendees from bothering you.

5. **Complete the meeting request.**

   Set any other options you want, and then click Send to send out the meeting invitations.

Preventing time change proposals for a meeting request

When creating a meeting, you don't have to listen to endless gripes about the meeting time or date. Nope, you can just put the kabash on the idea that everybody can just push you around and propose different times for your meeting. What do they think you are anyway, a great big pushover? Just because you gave your Employee of the Year parking space to Rianna because she suffers from tenderfeetiatius and yet can still wear those expensive Jimmy Chou spike heels doesn't mean you're gullible. This time you're gonna really put your foot down and not even accept time change suggestions. That'll show them who's not the boss.

Just because you've prevented them from proposing a different time for your meeting, attendees can still accept, decline, or tentatively accept your original time, and you can still track their responses. See the section, "Checking on Meeting Responses."

To prevent your recipients from proposing time changes, follow these steps:

1. **Create the meeting request.**

   Choose File➪New➪Meeting Request. Use the Meeting form to select attendees, enter a start and end date/time, choose a location, and set other options.

2. **Choose Meeting➪Attendees➪Responses.**

   A drop-down menu appears. (Refer to Figure 4-19.)

3. **Choose the Allow New Time Proposals option to deselect it.**
4. **Complete the meeting request.**

   Set any other options you want, and then click Send to send out the meeting invitations.

Chapter 5: Making the Calendar Your Own

In This Chapter

- **Creating calendars for each of your kids, departments, whatever**
- **Adding Internet calendars to the mix**
- **Changing how Calendar looks and acts**
- **Waking up in two different time zones**

As a busy working mother, I frankly do not know where I'd be without Calendar to prod me into being where I should be. Add my busy schedule of deadlines, club meetings, social obligations, and regular hair, dental, and doctor's visits to my kids' busy schedules and you have one fat mess. If your kids are old enough to get themselves around town, perhaps things become a bit easier; but still, you need to know where everyone is and when they'll be home for dinner. One way to solve this problem is to create a calendar for each child and display the calendars in Calendar whenever you need to refer to them.

Okay, say you're not a mom. Instead, you're a busy manager left to cope with not only your impossible schedule but the department's as well. As much as you'd like to attend *every* marketing rollout, training session, and group hug, you can't. Yet, you still need to be aware of when all these things occur. One way to do so is, once again, to create a separate calendar for the department that you can review whenever you like. You can even copy the appointments, meetings, and events that you intend to actually keep from the department calendar into your own calendar. In case I haven't given you enough reasons to add another calendar to Outlook, say you're not a mom or a manager, but you still have a life (sorta), and you want to create a second calendar for personal appointments to keep them away from prying eyes at work.

You can share any calendar you create. Not sharing a calendar keeps it private (for your eyes only). One reason for creating a separate calendar for personal appointments for example, is so when you share your work calendar (assuming you do, that is), your personal appointments aren't visible. See Book IV, Chapter 3 for help in sharing.

You can add other calendars to Outlook as well — such as published company, family, or school calendars, and specialty calendars such as horoscopes and lunar calendars. You can customize Calendar in other ways — for example, changing the number of days in your work week, the length of a work day, and the time intervals throughout a day (for example, showing each hour broken into 15-minute intervals rather than 30-minute intervals). You can display multiple months on the Date Navigator rather than just one, change the default reminder time so you don't have to keep changing it yourself every time you make an appointment, and adjust the size of the Calendar text for those tired eyes of yours. If you travel a lot — or if you deal with people in other times zones throughout the day — you can easily adjust your Calendar view to suit the time zone you're in.

Creating Multiple Calendars

Earlier, I spouted off several reasons why you might want to create multiple calendars in Outlook. They include these:

- It's an easy way to keep track of your kids without getting their schedules mixed up with yours.
- It's a simple way to manage the schedule for a department and keep it separate from your own.
- It's a manageable way to keep your personal appointments separate from your work ones.

You might have other reasons of your own for creating lots of calendars, and it may be nothing more complicated than *hey, it's easy to do.* Here's how to create a new calendar:

1. **Change to Calendar and choose File⇨New⇨Calendar.**

   The Create New Folder dialog box appears, as shown in Figure 5-1.

2. **Type a calendar name and click OK.**

   Make sure that Calendar Items is selected in the Folder Contains list. The new calendar is listed in the Navigation pane. To find out how to display and work with this new calendar, see the section, "Displaying Multiple Calendars."

You can share your calendar with other people in one of two ways: You can essentially send a *snapshot* — a graphic that looks like your calendar — embedded in an e-mail message. This kind of calendar can be viewed within the e-mail but not within Calendar; because it's basically a picture graphic and not an Outlook file. You can also send along a piece of your actual calendar that can be viewed within Outlook just like any other calendar. (See Book IV, Chapter 3 for more info.)

Figure 5-1: Create your own calendar.

Adding Internet Calendars

Internet calendars are huge. Without even trying, you can find tons of programs to help you publish an Internet calendar to your Web site. Not much of a self-publisher? No problem, because many Web sites can publish your calendar for you, also providing the software you use to create it. But this section isn't about publishing your Internet calendar; a quick look at the heading tells me that it's about adding other people's Internet calendars. So here you discover how to subscribe to an already published Internet calendar so you can view it in Calendar and receive automatic updates. For example, suppose someone has been kind enough to publish the game schedule for the Indianapolis Colts on the Internet, with plans to update it with the scores from each game as the season progresses. You can subscribe to the Internet calendar and keep up with your favorite football team, even if you live in California (go Colts!).

Outlook allows you to publish any of your calendars online, using an Internet calendar (iCalendar) format that allows others to subscribe to it. So after subscribing to an Internet calendar or two, you can jump on the bandwagon and publish your own Internet calendar to share. You can also share your calendar with your colleagues on an Exchange network. See Book IV, Chapter 3 for help in publishing or sharing your calendar.

So, where to find these gems? Well, I'd pay a visit to Google Calendar (`www.google.com/calendar`), which not only offers to host your own Internet calendar, but makes calendars other people designate as public available to you and me (provided we sign up for Google Calendar). As popular as Google is, think of how many Internet calendars you might be able to find there — for instance, the entire schedule for the South Flagston Amateur Sledding Association, the Junior Frog Comics Collectors Club meeting dates, and the Recent Elvis Sightings Calendar.

These calendars were created for use with Google Calendar, but after you add a calendar to Google, you can click the Manage Public Calendars link, click the calendar you want to add to Outlook, and click the ICAL button to get the calendar's `webcal://` address. Occasionally, when searching through the calendars, you find the `webcal://` link to the calendar in its description, so you won't even need to add it to Google Calendar first. Anyway, after you discover a Google calendar's address, you can enter it manually in Outlook to create a subscription, as I explain in a minute. You might also enjoy these sites:

- **Internet Calendar Directory** has a nice listing of online calendars at `www.icalshare.com`.
- **Microsoft's Web site** is at `http://office.microsoft.com/en-us/outlook/FX011933421033.aspx?pid=CL100794051033`; you can find calendars published by Microsoft and its partners, and calendars shared by Microsoft users like you.

A link to an Internet calendar begins with `webcal://` (instead of `http://`); the filename for the calendar ends in `.icf` (for *Internet calendar format*).

After you locate an Internet calendar, follow these steps to subscribe to it:

1. **Click the link to the Internet calendar.**

   You might have received a link to an Internet calendar in an e-mail, or you might find a link on a Web page. After you click the link, the Microsoft Office Outlook dialog box jumps out. See Figure 5-2.

   You can add an Internet calendar manually, if you know its address. Choose Tools⇨Account Settings⇨Internet Calendars⇨New. Type the calendar's address in the box provided and click OK.

2. **Click Yes to subscribe or Advanced to set additional options first.**
   - After you click Yes, the Internet calendar is added to Outlook.
   - If you click Advanced, you see the Subscription Options dialog box (see Figure 5-3). Here, you can add a description, change the folder in which the calendar is stored, choose whether to automatically download attachments, and permit automatic updates to the calendar. After making selections, click OK. You return to the Microsoft Office Outlook dialog box where you click Yes to subscribe to the calendar.

After you subscribe to an Internet calendar, that calendar is added to the calendar list on the Navigation pane in the Other Calendars section. In addition, the Internet calendar automatically opens and displays beside your private calendar(s). Outlook checks for updates to the calendar periodically and adds them for you automatically. The items in the calendar can be copied to your private calendar if you like; see the "Displaying Multiple Calendars" section (up next) for help.

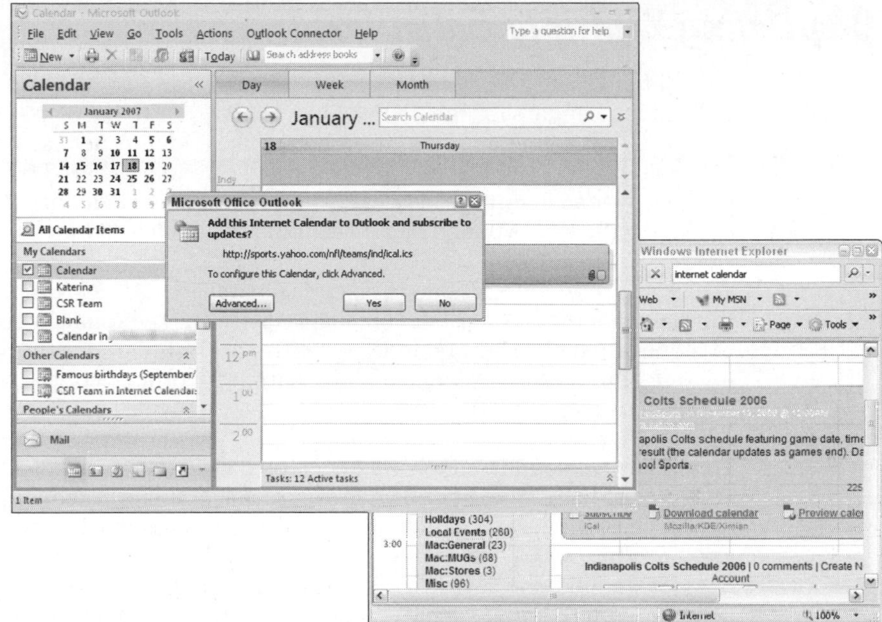

Figure 5-2: Our best subscriber.

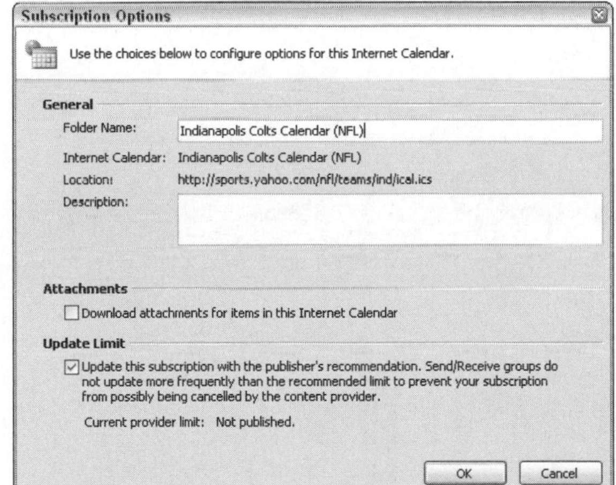

Figure 5-3: Modify a sub-scription.

To remove an Internet calendar, right-click it in the Navigation pane and choose Delete *calendar name* (where *calendar name* identifies your selection).

Displaying Multiple Calendars

It's not hard to add extra calendars to Calendar; for example, you can easily add extra calendars for the people in your family or to keep your personal and business appointments separate. You can also add Internet calendars that are automatically updated by the publisher and calendars shared by your colleagues over an Exchange network. After adding a few calendars to Calendar, managing the whole bunch might seem overwhelming. Turns out it's not.

When you have more than one calendar installed, each calendar appears in the Navigation pane, as shown in Figure 5-4. Your personal calendars — and extra calendars you've created yourself — are listed under the My Calendars heading; Internet calendars and calendars from other people are located in the Other Calendars list.

To display a calendar, enable its check box. Calendars are automatically snuggled side-by-side, as shown in Figure 5-4. You can display up to 30 calendars side-by-side, but I'm not sure you'd want to (they'd be awfully skinny and hard to read). Each calendar is given a color that matches its color in the Navigation pane listing. This color coding helps you keep track of which calendar you're looking at. The main calendar is normally color-coded blue, but you can change the color assigned to it (see the upcoming "Customizing the Calendar" section for more info).

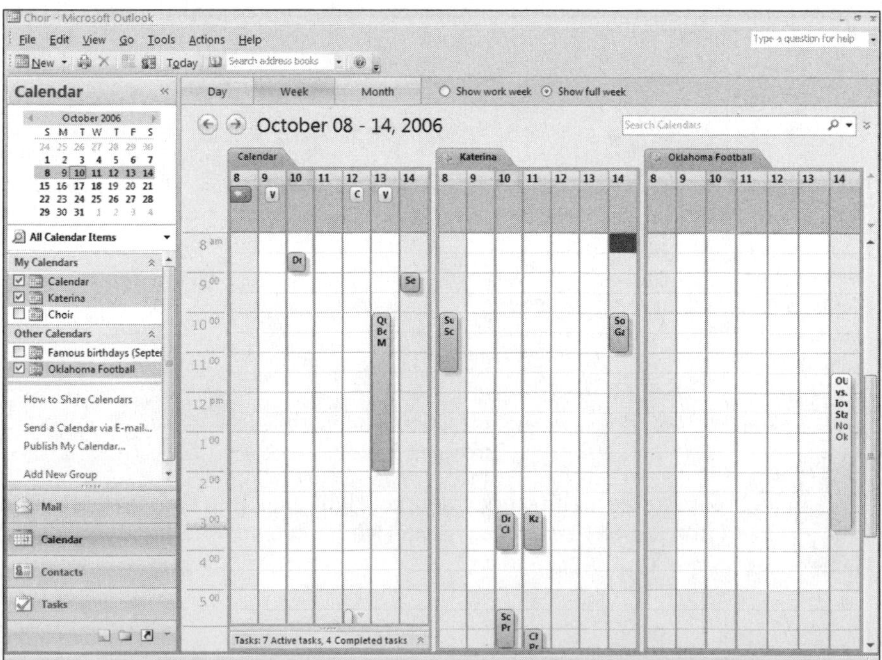

Figure 5-4: Side-by-side calendar view.

To reposition the order in which calendars are shown in side-by-side view, drag the calendar name up or down in the Navigation pane list.

The trouble with side-by-side view is that if you want to view more than two or three calendars, it's really hard to make out the details because they are so crammed together. Instead of displaying calendars side by side, you can display each one in its own window and then simply switch from window to window to view the calendar you want to work with. Just right-click the calendar and choose Open in New Window. The calendar displays in a new Outlook window, separate from the main window. You can arrange the two windows on-screen however you like; that's the beauty of well, Windows. And the fun doesn't end there; you can open as many Outlook windows as you like to display several calendars in separate windows. When you're done with one of them, click its Close button just as you would for any other window.

Outlook offers you a final alternative for viewing calendars, and it involves only one Outlook window. The alternative is called Overlay view, in which the appointments, meetings, and events in one calendar are overlaid (like a clear sheet of film) on top of the other calendar. You can overlay as many calendars as you like, although overlaying more than a few may create a mess that's impossible to decipher. Overlaying the calendars allows you to see right away where free time exists — so you can quickly eliminate it with a new appointment, meeting, or event.

To overlay a calendar, follow these steps:

1. **Display the calendars you want to overlay.**

   If needed, enable the check mark in front of any calendars you want to overlay. You don't need to hide any calendars you don't want to overlay, but you may want to reposition them because of the way overlay works. When you tell Outlook to overlay a calendar, that calendar is overlaid onto the first calendar shown on the left. You might want to reposition your calendars to display the main calendar on the left.

2. **Click the left arrow on the tab of any calendar you want to overlay.**

   The calendar you selected is overlaid on top of the calendar on the far left. To get the configuration shown in Figure 5-5, I positioned my main calendar on the left, and the calendar for Katerina on the right. Then I clicked the left arrow on Katerina's calendar to overlay it on top of the main calendar. If I wanted to overlay these two calendars with the information in the Oklahoma Football calendar (go OU!), I'd click the left arrow on its tab.

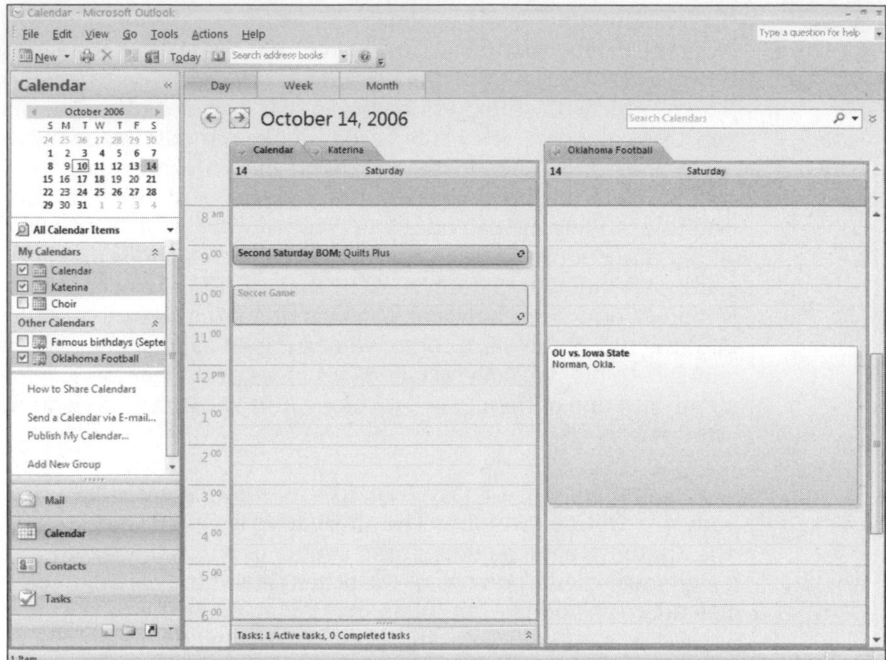

Figure 5-5: Overlay calendar view.

The appointments, meetings, and events of the lead calendar (the one whose tab is currently selected, and which appears in front of the other tab) appear in full color; items in calendars that overlay the lead calendar are semitransparent. So in the figure, an appointment from the main calendar (Second Saturday BOM) appears in full color, while the appointment from Katerina's calendar (Soccer Game) appear in semi-transparent color.

Repeat these steps to overlay more calendars. To remove a calendar so it's no longer laid over another, click the calendar's right arrow, located on the calendar's tab.

Grouping Calendars by Type or Purpose

Using something called the Outlook 2007 Calendar Views add-in and super-extravaganza, you can create custom views that display appointments, meetings, and events based on the categories you've assigned them. For example, if you have a category called New Client, and you apply it to every new client meeting, appointment, or event, you can use Calendar Views to quickly see how much hand-holding you'll have to do this week by displaying all your New Client items.

Haven't assigned any categories yet? See Book VIII, Chapter 1.

You can do a lot of things with a customized calendar view, as you can find out in Book VIII, Chapter 2. For example, you might create a view that displays only calendar items that contain particular bits of text, such as "sales" or "Big Important Company." Or you might want a view that displays only meetings organized by a particular person or with a particular person attending.

To create a custom calendar view that displays only items marked with a certain set of categories:

1. **Change to Calendar and choose View⇨Current View⇨Define Views.**

   The Custom View Organizer dialog box opens.

2. **Click New.**

   The Create a New View dialog box opens, as shown in Figure 5-6.

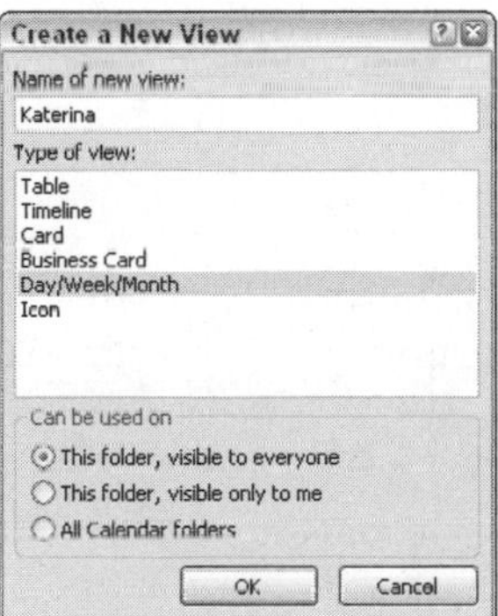

Figure 5-6: Here you'll find all the calendar views and the ones you've created yourself.

3. **Type a name for this custom view in the Name of New View box.**

4. **In the Type of View box, select the view type that you want.**

   Your new view displays items using a particular standard viewing format such as Table, Timeline, Card, Business Card, Day/Week/Month or Icon view.

5. **Select an option in the Can Be Used On area:**

   * *This Folder, Visible to Everyone:* Make this view available within the current calendar only, and to anyone with access to this calendar.

- *This Folder, Visible Only To Me:* Make this view available within the current calendar only, but only by you, and not anyone else with whom you may have shared this calendar.
- *All Calendar Folders:* Make this view available within all your calendars, even other people's calendars that you happen to have access to.

6. **Click OK.**

   You return to the Customize View Organizer dialog box. You can do a lot in this dialog box, as explained in Book VIII, Chapter 2. Here, I show you how to set up a view that displays items with particular category or categories.

7. **Click the Filter button to display the Filter dialog box, and click the More Choices tab. (See Figure 5-7.) To choose the categories that apply to the items you want to show in this view, click the Categories button.**

   The Color Categories dialog box pops up. (See Figure 5-7.)

8. **Select the categories that apply to the items you want to display and click OK three times.**

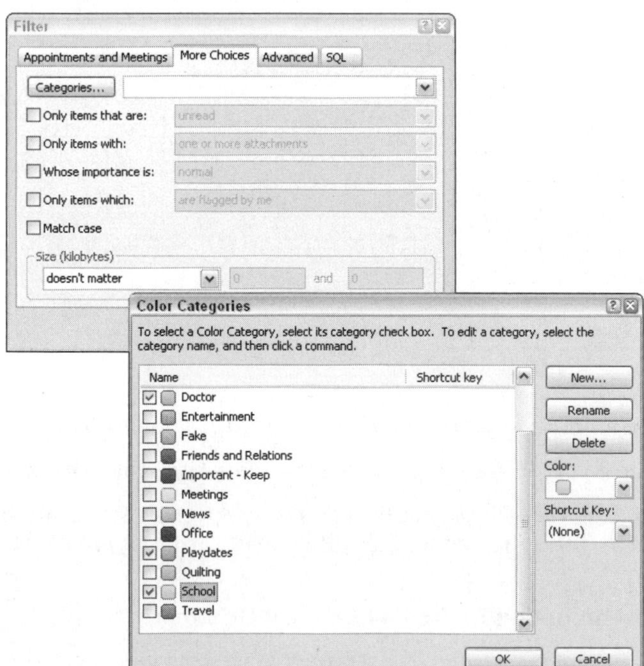

Figure 5-7: Define the view you want.

The view you created is highlighted in the Custom View Organizer dialog box.

9. **Click the Apply View button if you want the new view applied immediately, if not sooner.**

10. **Click Close to close the Custom View Organizer dialog box.**

To change from view to view in Calendar more easily, you can display the list of views on the Navigation pane; see the section, "Displaying the View List on the Navigation Pane," for help. You can also display the Advanced toolbar, and use it to change from view to view. Here's what you can do:

1. **Choose View⇨Toolbars⇨Advanced.**

   The Advanced toolbar appears at the top of the window. See Figure 5-8.

2. **Open the Current View list on the toolbar, and choose the view you want to apply.**

   Your custom views, and the regular Calendar views are listed. After you make a choice, the Calendar is changed to that view.

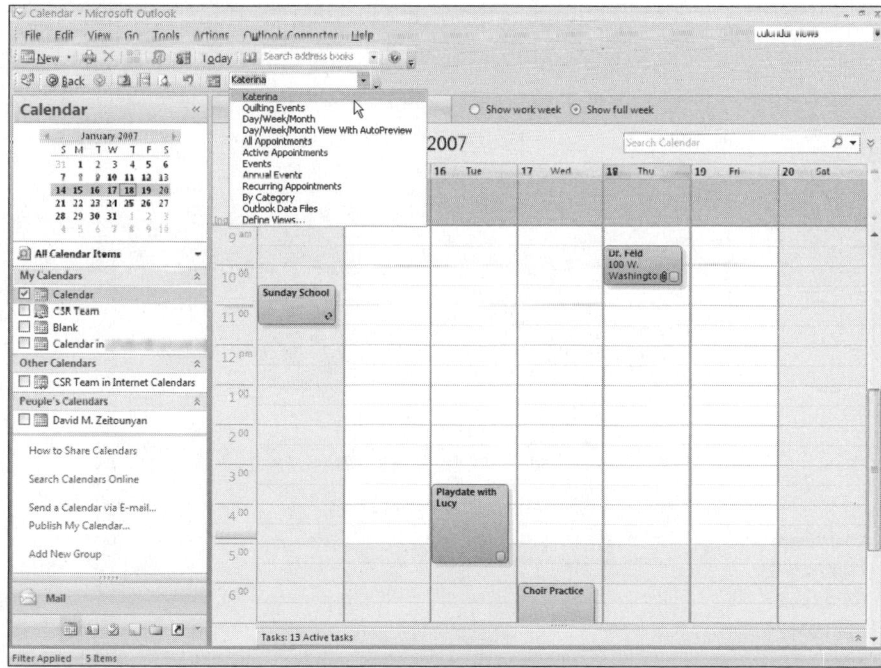

Figure 5-8: Use the Advanced toolbar to change Calendar views.

Customizing the Calendar

For some people, vanilla ice cream works just fine; hamburgers with mustard, ketchup, and pickle work just fine. The last seat in the stadium, right up by the ceiling ("Hey, I can almost see Sting, and at least I can say I was there") works just fine. I guess I'm not a "just fine" girl, at least not when it comes to Outlook. I figure, if I'm going to use something every day, I'm gonna get comfortable and make it work the way I do. So this section shows you how to make Calendar more comfortable for you.

Establishing the work week and work days

When you choose Week view in the Calendar (actually the Week option in Day/Week/Month view), Outlook displays a single week from your calendar. You can choose to show the full week or just the work week. If you choose work week only, Outlook shows just Monday through Friday. In addition, it assumes that the work day lasts from 8:00 a.m. to 5:00 p.m. Now, this probably works for most people, but it may not mirror your actual work schedule.

To change the work week, follow these steps:

1. **Choose Tools⇨Options⇨Calendar Options.**

   The Calendar Options dialog box jumps up. (See Figure 5-9.)

2. **Select the days in your work week.**

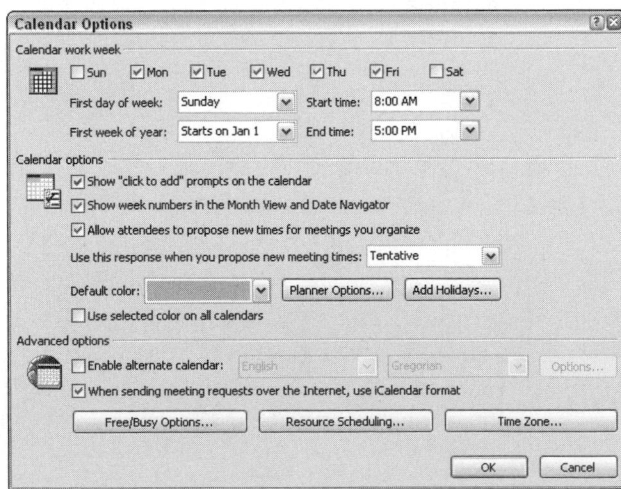

Figure 5-9: Calendar options.

In the Calendar Work Week section, check the days you want to include in the display when you choose Work Week view. Uncheck any days you don't want included.

3. **Change the start of the week.**

   Normally, Sunday starts the full week and Monday starts the work week. If you want to change the day that starts your week (work week and full week), make a selection from the First Day of Week list.

4. **Change your work hours.**

   To change your normal work hours from 8:00 to 5:00 to something else, enter a new Start Time and/or End Time. Hours of the day outside this range are shown in a light blue in Day and Week view; they're ignored when Outlook displays your free/busy times to people with whom you've shared your calendar.

5. **Click OK when you're done making changes.**

Changing the time grid

A single day in your calendar is divided into 48 half-hour time slots. Half-hour time intervals work for most people, because most people schedule appointments and meetings at either the top of the hour or at the half-hour mark, and not at (say) 1:45. However, if you're a regular 1:45 or 2:15 scheduler, the half-hour time slots may drive you crazy because to enter an appointment that starts at 1:45 or 2:15, you have to enter the start time manually. You may also have to enter the end time if, for example, the appointment lasts an hour and 15 minutes. Multiply this manual business by the number of appointments or meetings you create each day and you see what I mean when I say it'll drive you crazy — until you change the default time interval, anyway.

To change the time interval, follow these steps:

1. **Change to Day or Week view.**

   Choose View➪Current View➪Day/Week/Month. Then click the Day or Week tab to change to Day or Week view.

   This grid runs along the left side of each day in the calendar in Day or Week view (in Month view, the day isn't divided into segments, so the grid shows the range of dates for each week). Vertical bands mark each hour on the grid; thin lines divide each hour into equal intervals. Normally you see only one line each hour, dividing the hour into two equal half-hour parts.

2. **Right-click the time-interval grid.**

   A menu appears, as shown in Figure 5-10.

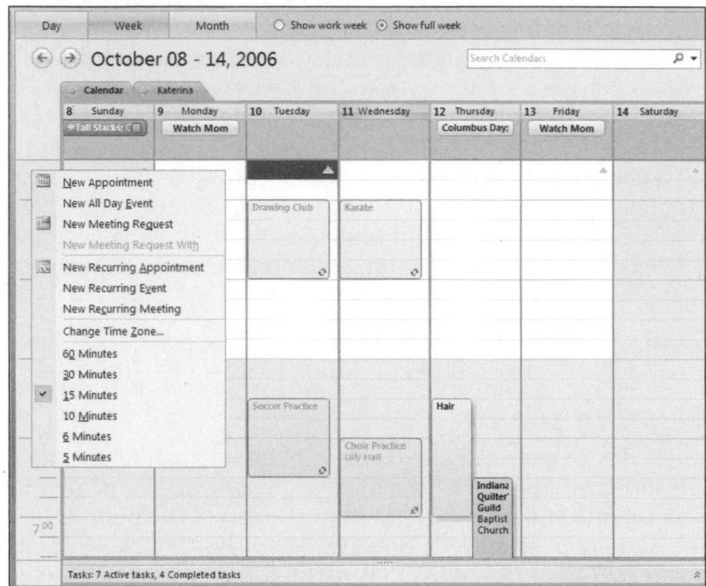

Figure 5-10: Change the time interval.

3. **Choose the interval you want.**

   For example, choose **15 Minutes**. The grid changes to divide each hour into the interval you choose. (Refer to Figure 5-10.)

Days with appointments or meetings scheduled appear in the Date Navigator in bold so you can quickly identify them. Days with events appear normally, without the bold accent. Anyway, if you'd like all the dates to appear unbolded, you can turn that off by customizing the view. You get further into customizing views in Book VIII, Chapter 2, but here are the basics:

1. **Choose View⇨Current View⇨Customize Current View.**
2. **Click the Other Settings button and then disable the Bolded Dates in Date Navigator Represent Days Containing Items option.**
3. **Click OK.**

You would think that this option would affect only the current view, but because both the Day/Week/Month and Day/Week/Month with AutoPreview views display the Date Navigator, this option affects them also.

The time grid shows the range of dates for each week when you display the calendar in Month view. A lot of companies use week numbers to control when particular events happen — most notably, payday. I don't know about you, but I've always had a special place in my heart for payday. If you do, too, you can display the week numbers in Month view:

1. **Choose Tools➪Options➪Calendar Options.**

   The Calendar Options dialog box pops out.

2. **Select Show Week Numbers in the Month View and Date Navigator.**
3. **Click OK.**

   The week numbers, instead of a range of dates, appear along the left side of each week in Month view, as shown in Figure 5-11. And as a special bonus to you, for this week only, the week numbers appear along the left side of the Date Navigator as well.

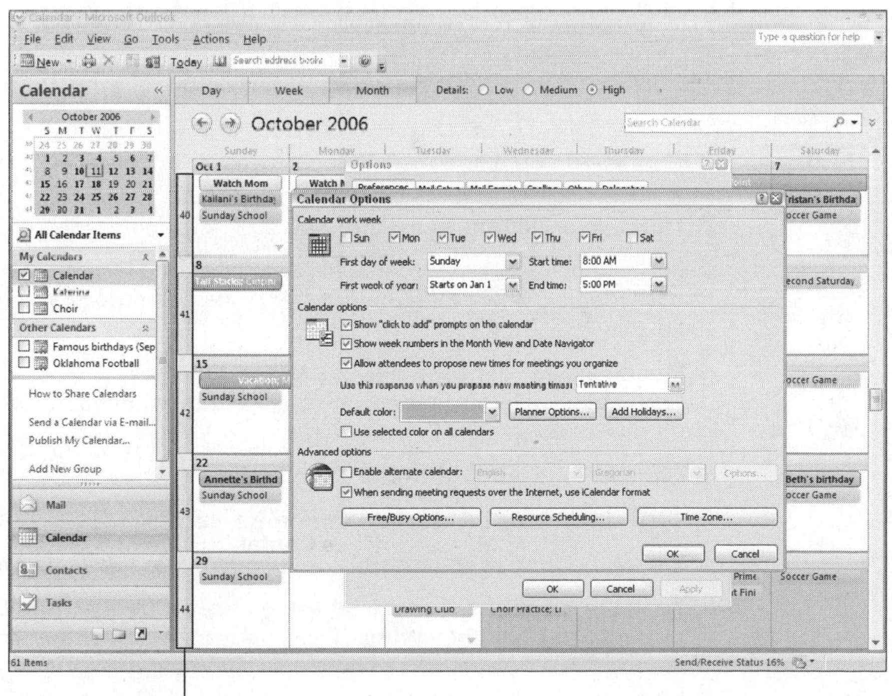

Figure 5-11: Let's get paid!

There's a final change you might want to make to the time grid, and it involves travel — at least, cyber-travel. If your work involves dealing with people in different time zones or traveling between time zones with a laptop computer, you may want to display another time zone next to the main time zone on the time grid. Adding a time zone display does not affect the main calendar, which normally bases the time for appointments and meetings on the current time zone only.

1. **Choose Tools⇨Options⇨Calendar Options⇨Time Zone.**

   The Time Zone dialog box appears, as shown in Figure 5-12.

Figure 5-12: You're in the Time Zone.

2. **Label your current time zone.**

   In the Label box, type a name for this time zone (it'll be used at the top of the time grid). For example, type the name of the city in which you live, such as New York.

   If you change your base time zone (the Windows time zone), it may be changed back by the server on your Exchange network (assuming you're on one, of course).

3. **Choose Show an Additional Time Zone.**
4. **Type a label for this second time zone, such as** LA.
5. **Select the time zone you want to display from the Time Zone list.**
6. **To make sure the times are adjusted appropriately when the country switches to Daylight Savings Time, select the Adjust for Daylight Saving Time option. Click OK.**

   The current time zone is displayed next to the calendar, and the second time zone you added is displayed to its left, as shown in Figure 5-13. The current time, based on your normal time zone, is highlighted by a small gold line on the current time zone grid. Appointments and meetings you create are still based on your current time zone, but can easily convert that time to the second time zone simply by looking at the time listed on the second time grid.

Second time zone

Your time zone

LA New York

8 am 11 am

Group meeting - teleconference

Figure 5-13: Get in the zone!

If you've recently moved into a new time zone, you can have Outlook move your future appointments and meetings to the right time in that new zone by clicking the Change Calendar Time Zone button in the Time Zone dialog box (refer to Figure 5-12). If you simply travel a lot between two zones, you can flip the times in Calendar just as you might adjust your watch. Click the Swap Time Zones button in the Time Zones dialog box. This changes your Windows time zone, however temporarily. This makes it easy for you to schedule new appointments or meetings in that new time zone, knowing that if you schedule something to happen at (say) 1:00 p.m., you want to use local time and not your own time zone.

By the way, when you're setting up meetings with people who live in a different time zone, when the meeting request arrives in their Inbox, the time for the meeting is automatically adjusted to their local time without your doing a thing.

Setting the default reminder time

When you create an appointment, meeting, event, an automatic reminder is created. For appointments or meetings, this reminder beeps about 15 minutes before it's gonna happen. For events, the reminder comes about 18 hours beforehand. You can't change the default for events, but you can change the reminder time for a particular event when you create it. You can also change the reminder time for a particular appointment or meeting, but this assumes you know in advance that you're going to need more time. But if you find, on a regular basis, that 15 minutes just isn't enough time to get to an appointment or meeting on time, you can change the default reminder to give you more time to break into a run.

To change the default reminder time for appointments and meetings, follow these steps:

1. **Choose Tools➪Options➪Preferences.**

   The Options dialog box jumps up, as shown in Figure 5-14.

Figure 5-14: Wanna see a reminder?

2. **Set the default reminder time.**

   Make sure the Default Reminder option is selected; then select when you want the reminder to appear.

3. **Click OK.**

You may be thinking, "Hey what about tasks? I get reminded about tasks all the time." Well, I can't stop your boss from nagging you, but if you're getting reminded about tasks *by Outlook,* it's because you set up a reminder when you created the task. It's not an automatic thing, so if you don't want to be bugged all the time about the stuff you haven't gotten around to yet, then well, don't set a reminder when you create the task. (Maybe you could set a reminder to remind yourself not to do that.)

Changing the calendar color

By default, your main calendar is blue. The normal working hours are shown in white, while hours outside the work day appear in a lighter shade of blue, at least in Day and Week view. See Figure 5-15. (In Month view, where the day isn't broken down into intervals, the entire day appears in white.) Maybe blue just isn't your color; or maybe you've added other calendars and it would help if they were assigned colors that make sense to you. Although you can only change the color of the main calendar, the colors of any other calendars are typically shifted when you change the main calendar.

1. **Choose Tools⇨Options⇨Calendar Options.**

   The Calendar Options dialog box, as shown in Figure 5-15.

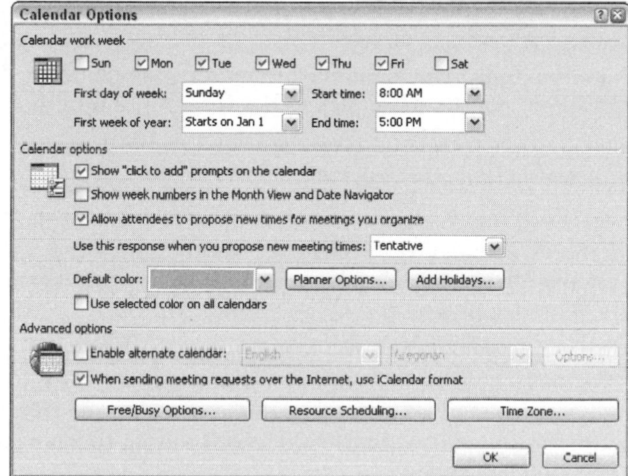

Figure 5-15: Calendar colors.

2. **Choose a calendar color.**

   Choose the color you want assigned to the main calendar from those that appear in the Default Color list. If you want all calendars to use this same color, choose Use Selected Color on All Calendars.

3. **Click OK.**

   The main calendar is displayed in the color you chose, and (assuming you did not select the Use Selected Color on All Calendars option) other calendars are changed so each calendar appears in a different color.

Customizing the Date Navigator

You can use the Date Navigator to jump to any date in your calendar. The Date Navigator appears on the left in Calendar, on the Navigation pane. Initially, Outlook shows only one measly month on the Date Navigator. If you're often going back to a previous month or jumping ahead, you might approach the problem in several ways:

- **Show more than one month on the Date Navigator:** Drag the right border of the Date Navigator to the right, making the Navigator wider. When it's wide enough to show more than one month, a second month appears. Of course, this approach narrows the viewing area for your calendar, so you may not want to do this unless you're using Day or Week view.
- **Display the To-Do bar and have it show more than one month:** To display the To-Do bar in the Calendar, choose View⇨To-Do Bar⇨Normal. The Date Navigator is automatically removed from the Navigation pane because you don't need to see two of them. Now, to show more than one month on the To-Do bar, right-click it and choose Options. Then enter the number of months to display in the Number of Month Rows box.

  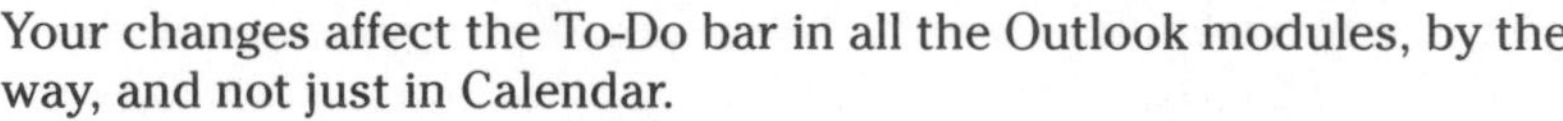

  Your changes affect the To-Do bar in all the Outlook modules, by the way, and not just in Calendar.

  Now, with both the Navigation pane and the To-Do bar displayed, you've considerably narrowed the viewing area. To remove the Navigation pane, choose View⇨Navigation Pane⇨Off. To remove it temporarily, click its Minimize button.
- **Jump from month to month without changing a thing:** This is discussed in detail in Book IV, Chapter 1, but if you want a hint, here it is: You can show a list of adjacent months by clicking the top of the Date Navigator. Assuming the month you want to jump to is a recent one, it's just a second click away.

Now that I have that "need more months on the Navigator" problem solved, I have another bone to pick. Okay, I'm getting older. I know it because I'm starting that trombone thing with the newspaper, trying to get it exactly in focus. Sure, I could get my eyes checked, but I'd rather live in denial a little bit longer, thank you very much. Still, when I'm chatting with a colleague, trying to check a particular date in my calendar to see if it's a good time for a meeting or a lunch date, and I keep fumbling around the Date Navigator because I can't see the dates clearly, it's getting harder and harder to keep my colleagues from figuring out that maybe I'm not really 29. So I've decided that two best things to do are dye my hair and change the Navigator font so I can read its text more easily. Here's how to do the latter thing:

1. **Choose Tools⇨Options⇨Other⇨Advanced Options.**

   The Advanced Options dialog box peeks out. See Figure 5-16.

2. **Choose a font.**

   In the Appearance Options section, click the Font button and choose a font and size that's easy on the eyes from the Font dialog box (see

Figure 5-17). Keep in mind that your selection is also used in the Date Navigator, so it's probably best to keep the font clean (no serifs) and relatively small (no bigger than 12-point).

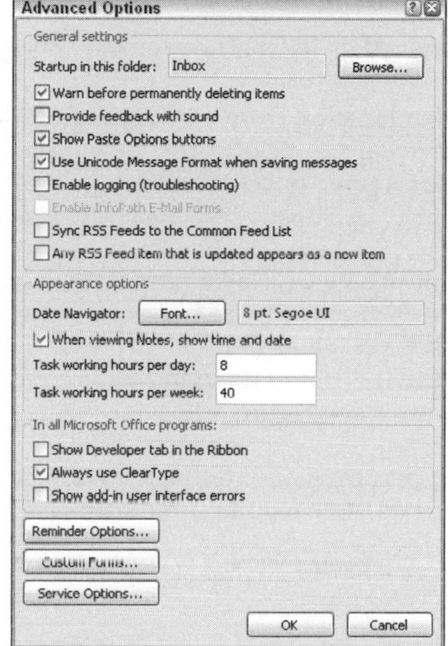

Figure 5-16: These options aren't too advanced for you!

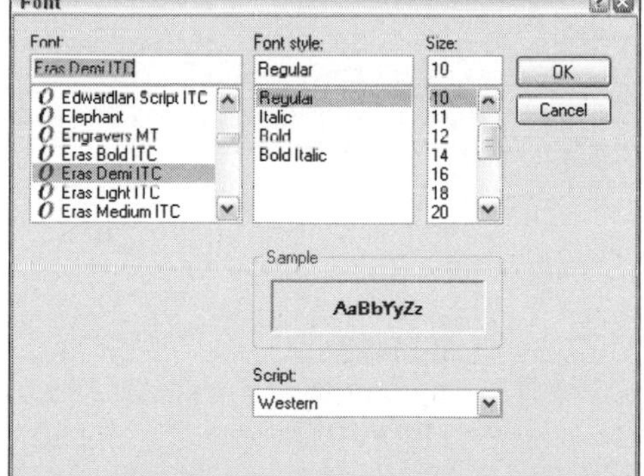

Figure 5-17: Change the Calendar font.

You can change your default message font as well, making what you type easier to read. (This does not affect the size of the text in e-mails you receive, however — but who knows, maybe you'll start a trend!) To change the font and size of the text used in outgoing messages, choose Tools⇨Options⇨Mail Format⇨Stationery and Fonts. Then, under New Mail Messages, click the Font button and select the font and size you prefer to use most of the time. (In HTML and RTF messages, you can still change the font manually.) You can change the font for replies and forwards you send — as well as the font for composing text messages — by clicking the other Font buttons.

Displaying the View List on the Navigation Pane

If you change views within Calendar a lot, from say Day/Week/Month view to Active Appointments, you might want to display the view options on the Navigation pane, just as they are shown in just about every other module but Calendar.

To display the view options, choose View➪Navigation Pane➪Current View Pane. The various Calendar views are listed just below your list of personal, shared, and Internet calendars. If you can't see the entire view list, you can shrink the module buttons at the bottom of the pane by dragging the border just above the buttons downward. (See Figure 5-18.)

With the calendar views listed, just click one to display your Calendar items in that view. For example, to list all your regular appointments, choose Recurring Appointments view.

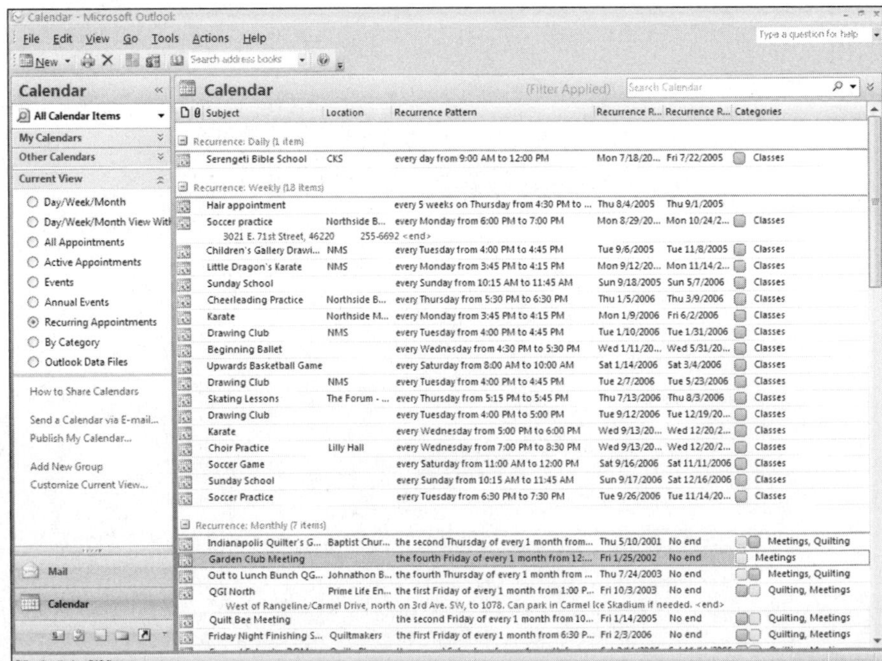

Figure 5-18: Change your view.

Book V

Managing Contacts

"Roger! Check the sewing machine's connection to the PC. I'm getting e-mails stitched across my curtains again."

Contents at a Glance

Chapter 1: Getting in Contact 351
Chapter 2: Working with Your Contacts..363
Chapter 3: Dealing with Business Cards 375
Chapter 4: Contacts Collaboration 385

Chapter 1: Getting in Contact

In This Chapter

- **Keeping track of all sorts of trivia about your friends, colleagues, and distant relations**
- **Picking new contacts out of your mail**
- **Keeping contact info current**
- **Creating more than one contact from the same company**
- **Tracking down duplicate contact entries**

If you think about it, Outlook is all about contacts — keeping in contact via e-mail, keeping in contact through appointments and meetings, and uh, keeping contacts. As you find out in this chapter, you can record whatever information you want to remember about a contact, including a photo if it's not too ugly. Outlook provides lots of timesavers for you so you can create contacts in a jiffy; if you get carried away, Outlook also makes it easy to track down duplicate contacts and get rid of them.

Malicious e-mails typically target your contact list, using it to send spam and viral messages to everyone you know. To protect yourself (and your friends, family, and colleagues), be very careful about which e-mails you open. Be especially careful about opening file attachments; as a general rule, you should run a virus scanner on such files first, prior to opening them. See Book I, Chapter 1; Book II, Chapter 2; and Book IX, Chapter 5 for more information.

Adding a Complete Contact

Contacts have no rules; you can record as little or as much information as you want. If you record an e-mail address, you can use the contact to send mail messages. Record an IM address, and you can exchange instant messages. Record a phone number and you can ring 'em up. Record a Web page address, and you can display it in your browser with a single click. Record a street address, and you can get directions to a contact's location instantly.

Create contacts in a list view

Another way to quickly add a new contact is to first select a list view in Contacts, such as By Location or Phone List. Just above the listing, you see an area marked Click Here to Add a New Contact. Go ahead, it won't hurt: Just click and type the data (such as the Full Name, Company, and Business Phone) for the contact in each field. Skip any fields you don't know or don't feel like entering. For help changing your view, see Book VIII, Chapter 2.

For tips on working with your new contact, such as calling, viewing an address, or viewing a Web site, see Book V, Chapter 3. For info on how to send an e-mail, see Book II, Chapter 1. Looking to IM someone? See Book III, Chapter 2.

You can create a contact quickly by simply pulling his name and e-mail address from a message he's sent you. See the upcoming section, "Basing a Contact on an Incoming E-Mail." You can also create a contact using other Outlook items by simply dragging the item to the Contacts icon and dropping it. For example, you can drag an appointment onto the Contacts icon. See Book I, Chapter 2. Finally, you can create an instant contact using the Electronic Business Card someone may have thoughtfully included in an e-mail to you. See Book V, Chapter 3 for help on that one.

To create a new contact, follow these steps:

1. **Choose New⇨Contact.**

   If you're already in Contacts, just click the New button to create a new contact. The Contact form pops up, as shown in Figure 1-1.

   If you have multiple contacts lists, such as your personal list and a work list or your company list and a list of key contacts, then your life is more complicated than most. Adding a new contact doesn't have to be as complicated however, but you do need to make sure you select the right Contacts list, before you choose New⇨Contact. Otherwise, you'll add the contact to the wrong list.

2. **Enter contact information.**

   Type what you know about this contact in the appropriate fields:

   - *Full name or not:* If the contact is a person, type his or her name (such as **Cameron McNichol**) in the Full Name box. If the contact is a business and not a person, skip the Full Name box and type the name of the business in the Company box instead.

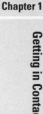

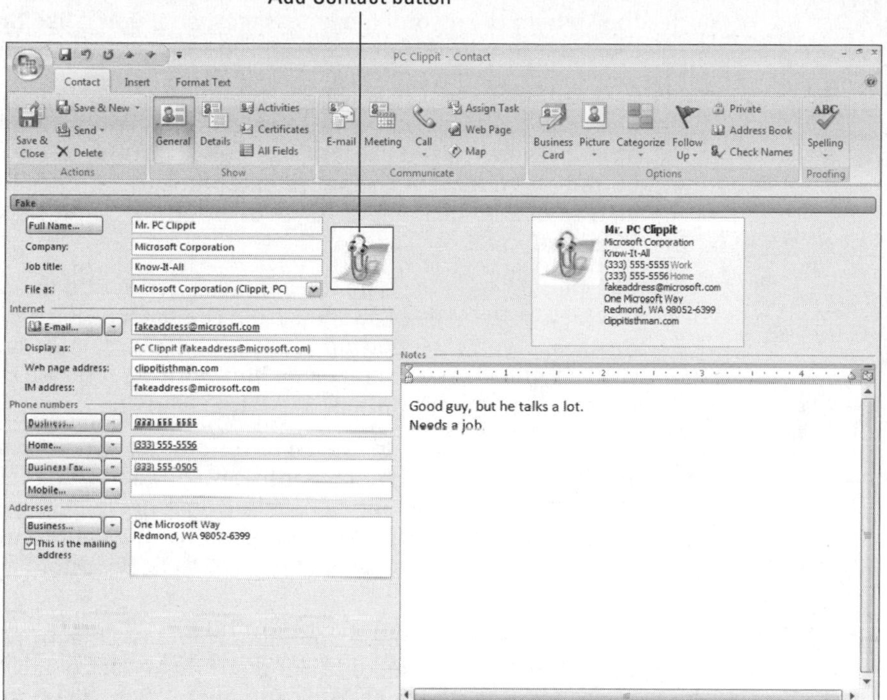

Figure 1-1: Keeping in contact.

- *Select how you want the contact sorted with other contacts:* Choose an option from the File As box. You can also type something in the File As box; whatever appears in it is used not only for sorting but also for locating a contact and resolving an e-mail address.

  Resolving, you may recall, is the process Outlook goes through to make sure an e-mail address is valid prior to sending of a message. See Book II, Chapter 1 for the lowdown.

  If you have multiple contacts from the same company, you might want to file them as Big Co., Gladys Brown and Big Co., Jorge Suento so they'll be grouped together. See the upcoming section, "Creating Another Contact from the Same Company," for help in creating multiple contacts that work for the same company.

- *You can store up to three e-mail addresses for a contact:* After entering the first one, click the arrow on the E-Mail button and choose E-Mail 2.

- *Choose how to contact your contact:* The Display As name is used in the To field of any outgoing messages, so if you'd like the name to look a bit less formal than `Tyra Jones (tjones@nowhere.com)`, you might want to type just **Tyra** or **T Jones** here.
- *The fields with an arrow:* Use these fields (Business, Home, and so on) for whatever you like. For example, click the arrow on the Home button and choose Assistant to enter an assistant's phone number instead of a home number. You can enter up to four phone numbers for a contact.
- *The mailing address:* Type the contact's address in the Address box. Select the type of address from the button (it's initially set for Business); you can enter up to three addresses. If the address you're typing is the contact's mailing address, choose the This Is the Mailing Address option.
- *Add a contact picture:* If you have a photo of the new contact, you can add it by choosing Contact⇨Options⇨Picture⇨Add Picture, or by clicking the Add Contact Picture button (shown here with the Mr. Clippit's picture on it). Choose the photo you want to use and click OK. The photo is resized and cropped to fit the photo area on the form.

  The photo appears in the Contact form on the Electronic Business Card (see Book V, Chapter 3), and on the header of any message sent to you from this contact. You can double-click the photo in a message header to open that contact.

  The photo doesn't have to be a photo of a person; if the contact works for a particular company and that's what you want to remember, you can add the company logo as the photo.
- *To add more details not shown:* Choose Contact⇨Show⇨Details. Additional fields appear, as shown in Figure 1-2. Here you can add work-related stuff like the department or specific office that the contact works for and his manager's or assistant's name. You can also add personal info such as a contact's nickname, spouse's name, birthday, and such. If the contact keeps his calendar online and wants you to access it to see when he's free or busy, you can keep that online address in the Internet Free/Busy Address field.

Even more fields are available for entering contact data if you want 'em. See the next section, "Changing Contact Information," for help.

3. **When you're through recording information on this contact, choose Contact⇨Actions⇨Save & Close.**

   The new contact is sorted with existing contacts using the name you typed in the File As box.

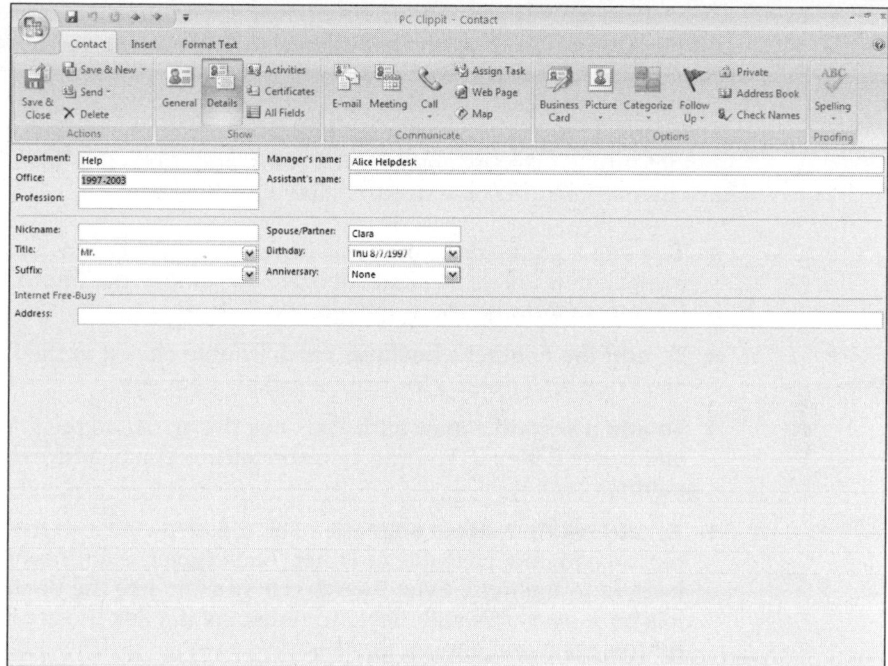

Figure 1-2: Add more detail.

For help in locating a contact, see Book V, Chapter 2.

Changing Contact Information

It's rare that you'll have a contact whose information doesn't change. People change jobs, phone numbers, home and work addresses, and e-mail addresses often. Maybe, instead of changing some bit of information, you may have new stuff you've just learned about a contact, such as a related Web site address or a cell phone number.

To change a contact, you first locate him or her. Typically, the Contacts list is displayed alphabetically, so if you're looking for Alfonso Duerre, just look in the Ds. In Book V, Chapter 2, you find lots of tips for locating a contact.

If you display contacts in a list view, such as Phone List or By Company, you can click in any field and edit the data right there. For example, in Phone List view, click in the Business Phone field for a particular contact. Then either type a new phone number (if the field is empty) or edit the one that's already there. To replace existing data (such as a phone number), click in the field, select the phone number by dragging over it, and then type the new phone number. Don't know how to change views? No problem, see Book VIII, Chapter 2 for the lowdown.

After you locate a contact, simply double-click her name to reopen the Contact form. Make any changes you want, and then click Save & Close to save them. Here are some tips to help you:

- **To swap a contact's photo for a different one:** Double-click the photo, select a new image file, and click OK. To remove the photo altogether, Contact➪Options➪Picture➪Remove Picture.
- **To edit the contact's business card:** Double-click it in the Contact form. See Book V, Chapter 3 for help in making changes.
- **To add a second e-mail address:** Click the arrow on the E-Mail button and select E-Mail 2. You can also add a third e-mail address in a similar manner.
- **To add another street address:** Click the arrow next to the Business button and choose Home or Other. Then type the address in the box located to the right. Even though it may seem like the Business address has gone away, it's still there. To redisplay it, click the arrow on the button again and choose Business.
- **Add lots and lots of detail:** Contacts can store just about anything you can think of about a contact in its own proper little place. In the previous section, you saw the general Contact page (Figure 1-1), and the Details page (Figure 1-2). But if you find that you still need to locate the proper place for a particularly interesting bit of information on a contact, check out All Fields. Choose Contact➪Show➪All Fields. Funny as it seems, you won't suddenly see all the fields that Outlook can track. Nope, you can still see only some, but at least you get to choose which *some.* Select the ones to show from the Select From list, and those fields appear, like the ones shown in Figure 1-3. To enter information, click in the box to the right of the field name and type. For example, click in the box to the right of the name, Customer ID, and type the customer's ID number.

On the Miscellaneous Fields page shown, you see four user-defined fields. *User-defined* means you're free to use 'em for whatever you want. As you change from page to page, notice that some fields are already filled in; the data for these fields was probably entered on the General or Details pages. In fact, if you find it easier, you can enter all your contact data on the All Fields page.

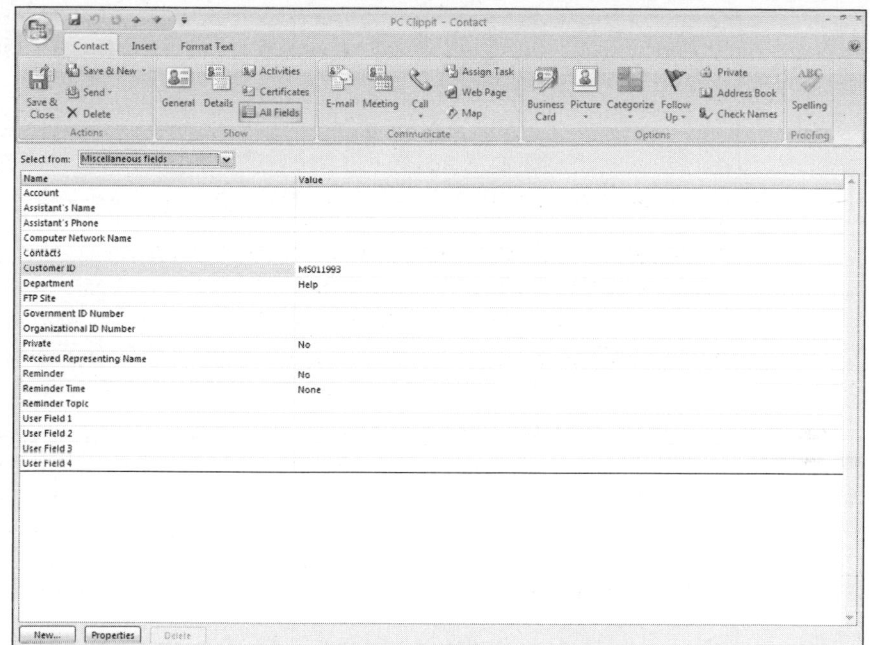

Figure 1-3: Miscel-laneous minutiae.

Basing a Contact on an Incoming E-Mail

Because you mostly use contacts to send e-mail messages, it makes sense to create new contacts using the information gleaned from messages they send you. After Outlook automatically creates a contact using what it knows, you can always fill in the missing blanks manually.

To create a new contact from an e-mail message, follow these steps:

1. **Right-click the person's name.**

   In the header of a message someone's sent to you, locate the name of the person you want to add to Contacts. The name doesn't need to appear in the From field; it can simply be the name of someone the message was also sent to.

   A menu pops up, shown in Figure 1-4.

2. **Choose Add to Outlook Contacts.**

   The Contacts form opens. Outlook creates the new contact and fills in what it knows: Full Name, File As, E-Mail, and Display As. Looks like you're off to a good start. Feel free to change any of these fields and to add other information.

3. **Choose Contact⇨Actions⇨Save & Close to save the new contact.**

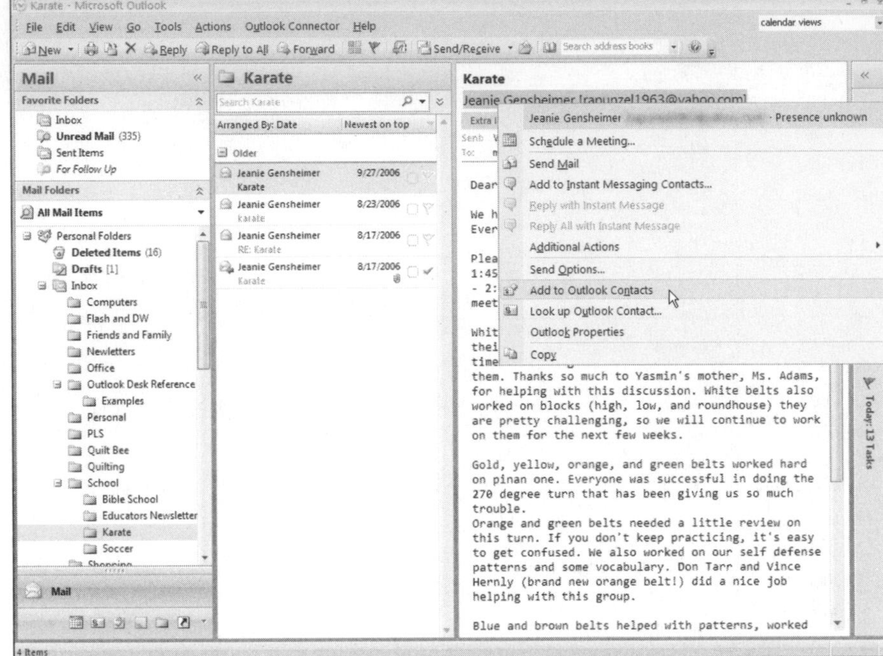

Figure 1-4: Use an e-mail message to create a contact.

Creating Another Contact from the Same Company

Quite often, you meet several people from the same company. From a Contacts point of view, there's a lot of duplication going on there — the same company name, company phone number (but different extension), same company address, and so on. You don't need to manually reenter all this duplicate stuff when setting up a series of similar contacts — I mean, this is the digital age isn't it?

To set up a new contact from the same company as an existing contact, follow these steps:

1. **Open the contact you want to base the new contact on.**

   Go to Contacts and double-click somebody from the same company as the new person you want to add.

2. **Choose Contact➪Actions➪Save & New➪New Contact from Same Company.**

   A new Contact form appears, partially completed with the company information of the original contact, as shown in Figure 1-5. Outlook copies such things as the Company, Picture, Web Page Address, Business Phone, Business Fax, and Business Address.

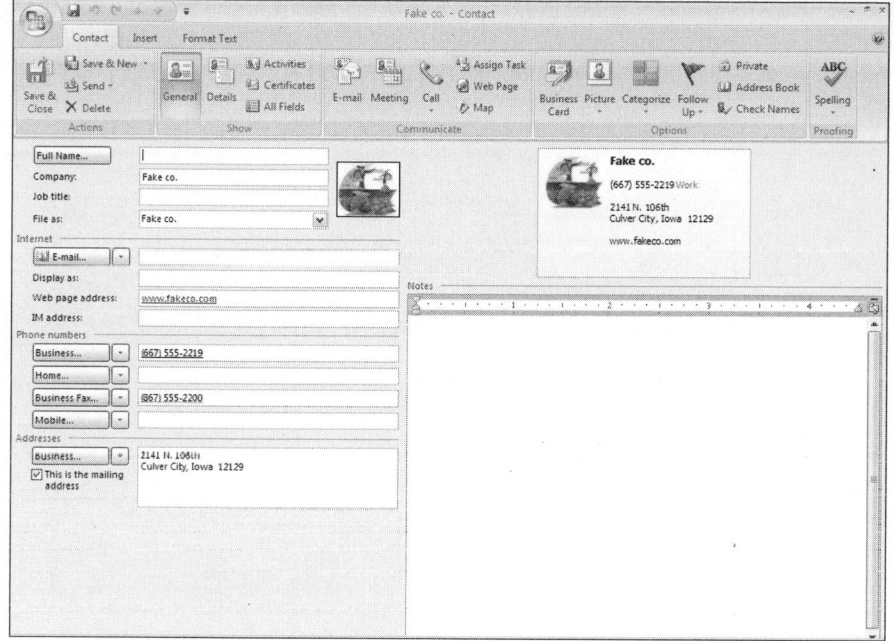

Figure 1-5: Same company, different contact.

Also notice that Outlook's taken the liberty of choosing the company name as the File As field, whether or not that's what you used on the original contact. However, as soon as you enter a Full Name, the File As field changes. You might, however, want to choose *Company Name* from the File As field to sort the similar contacts together.

3. **Add or change whatever information you want and then choose Contact⇨Actions⇨Save & Close to save the new contact.**

Getting Rid of Duplicate Contacts

Well, you gotta give it to Outlook: It tries darn hard to stop you from creating duplicate contacts. When you attempt to, it flashes a dialog box at you asking you if you really, truly want to do this. (See Figure 1-6.) This happens, by the way, whether you're creating the new contact from scratch, from an e-mail message, electronic business card, or Outlook item, or simply importing a bunch of contacts, one of which happens to be a duplicate.

Outlook stays on the look out for duplicate contacts because of its Duplicate Detection option. By default, this baby's on, but you can turn it off if it's bothering you. For example, if you're importing a bunch of contacts from some other source, you might want that process to go automatically without prompting you every minute or so about some silly duplicate. If you turn the option off, you have to hunt down and destroy the duplicates yourself manually, but it's not that bad a tradeoff for a few minutes of uninterrupted work. To turn off the Duplicate Detection option, choose Tools➪Options➪Contact Options. Then turn off the Check for Duplicate Contacts option and click OK.

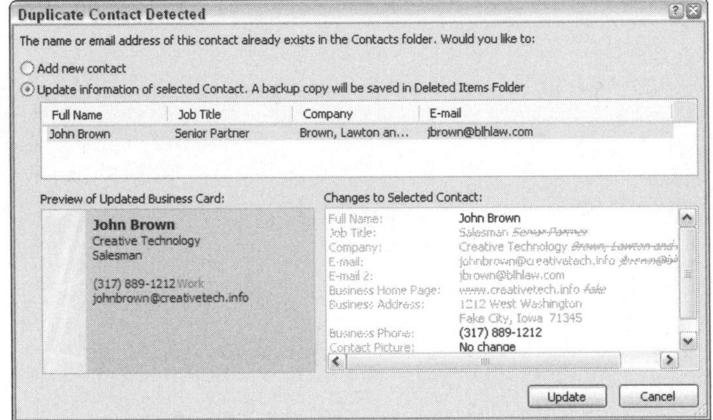

Figure 1-6: Duplicate dilemma.

As you can see, the Duplicate Contact Detected dialog box shows you which contact Outlook thinks is similar to the one you're trying to add, displaying the old contact's Electronic Business Card. On the right, you can see what's going to be changed if you continue — the stuff in orange is the new contact info, whereas the stuff that's crossed out is the old info that'll be replaced. The stuff in black is from the old contact; it won't be changed if you continue because the new contact doesn't contain this information. Anyway, you can choose Add New Contact at the top of the dialog box to add the new contact despite the warning (which you might want to do, if this contact just happens to share the same name as someone else you know). You can also choose Update Information of Selected Contact to update the information in the existing contact, using the information from the new contact.

If you choose the update option, the new contact is not added. Instead, data from the new contact that's different from the info in the existing contact is changed. A copy of the original contact before it was updated is placed in your Deleted Items folder, should you need it back.

If you choose to add the new contact, you end up with two entries. You might want to add an initial or something to one of the duplicate contacts to help distinguish the two. You can, whenever needed, search and destroy any duplicate contacts. Here's how:

1. Change views.

Change to Contacts, and then select a view that you can use to sort the records and find duplicates most easily. I tend to choose Phone List view because it's one of the list views where each contact is displayed on its own line and easily sorted, as shown in Figure 1-7. (For more on list views, see Book VIII, Chapter 2.)

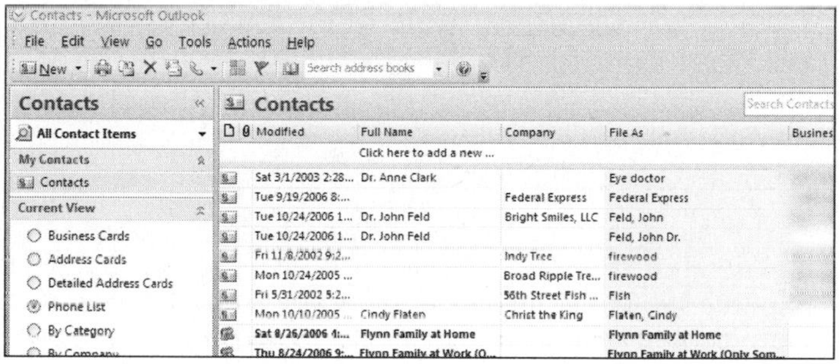

Figure 1-7: Phone List view.

2. Change the list.

When you find a set of duplicates, you might find it helpful to know which of the two duplicates is older. You can do that by customizing the view to show the Modified field, as shown in Figure 1-7. To do that, choose View➪Current View➪Customize Current View. The Customize View dialog box peeks out, as shown in Figure 1-8.

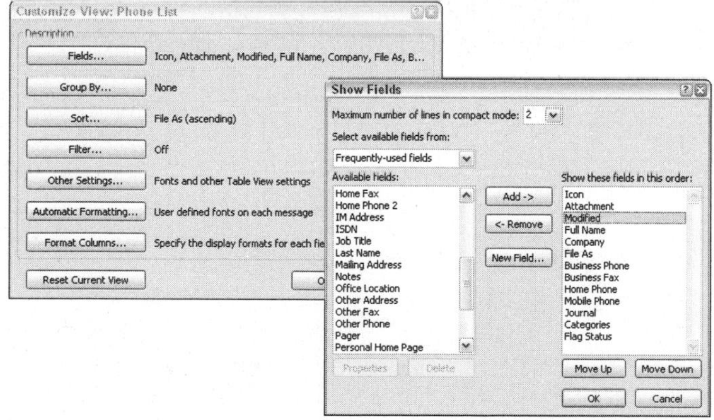

Figure 1-8: Add the Modified field.

3. **Add the Modified field.**

   Click the Fields button. The Show Fields dialog box jumps up, as shown in Figure 1-8. Choose Modified from the list on the left and click Add. Click Move Up a few times to move the Modified field up in the list where you can easily see it in the Phone List view. Click OK two times to go back to the Phone List view, where a new field has joined the rest.

4. **Sort the list.**

   To sort the list, click the header at the top of any column. For example, you might want to sort the list by Full Name or by File As. The list shown in Figure 1-7 is sorted by File As, as you can tell by the little triangle on the File As column header.

5. **Manually delete duplicates.**

   At this point, you simply scroll down the list looking for duplicates. I've apparently got two Dr. Felds in my Contact list. When you find one, compare the two modified dates to see which one is newer (and perhaps more current). Select the duplicate you want to delete and then click the Delete button on the Standard toolbar.

Chapter 2: Working with Your Contacts

In This Chapter

- **Changing your view of the Contacts list**
- **Tracking down a lost contact**
- **Locating similar contacts**
- **Locating a contact's address or Web page**
- **Ringing up a contact**
- **Reviewing all the things you've done for a contact**

Having a long list of people you know and work with can be useful for more than just sending e-mails. Sometimes it's useful to know that you have two contacts for a company. For example, if you really need some tech help and your main contact is out sick, it's helpful to have someone else you can yell at. You can use several different methods for locating the people you need to contact, such as changing the view of the Contacts list or searching for information you know is contained in a contact's data (such as a name or city). After you find a contact, you can use the information to help you locate the contact's address on a map or display a contact's Web site in your browser. Assuming your computer has a modem (most do, even now, on their motherboards), you can use your computer to automatically dial the contact. Finally, in this chapter, you discover how to review the activity associated with a contact such as recent appointments, tasks, or e-mail messages.

Picking a View That Suits Your Needs

As with all Outlook modules, the Contacts list can display its information in lots of different ways. Although I detail the views (and how to customize them) in Book VIII, Chapter 2, I thought I'd mention them here because unlike the other modules, Contacts displays its list of views rather prominently in the Navigation pane. (See Figure 2-1.)

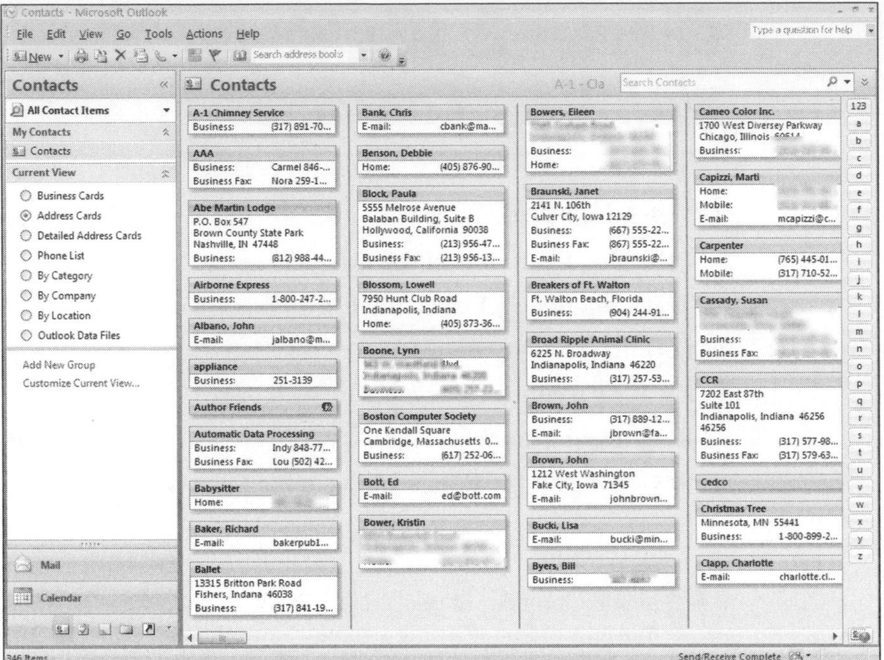

Figure 2-1: Address Cards view.

Normally, Contacts displays its information in the form of Electronic Business Cards. You can choose to view simple address cards instead, which display a bit less information on each contact, but allow you to see more contacts at once. In both views — Business Cards view and Address Cards view — buttons run along the right side of the window; click a button to jump to a contact that begins with that letter. Typically the cards are listed last name first, but it's actually sorted by the File As field for each contact. The Detailed Address Cards view offers a compromise: You can show enough information to locate a contact and displaying enough people on a single page so you're not constantly browsing.

The other views are list views; a list view displays its information in columns with each contact appearing in a separate row. The By Category list view is shown in Figure 2-2. List views group similar information together in collapsible groups. In the view shown here, you could collapse the Doctor group by clicking the minus sign in front of the Categories: Doctor heading. You could expand the group that doesn't have a category by clicking the plus sign in front of the Categories: (none) heading.

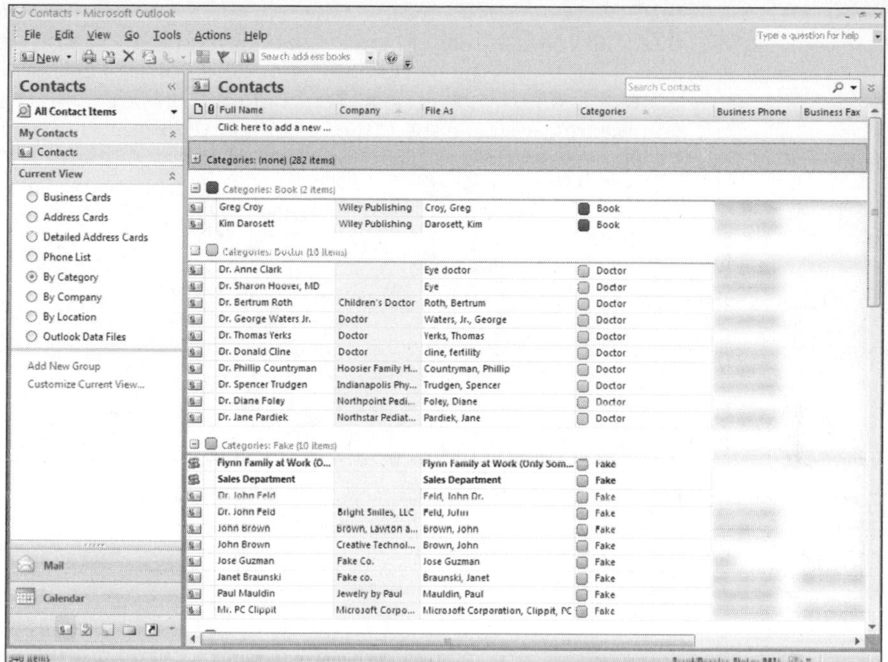

Figure 2-2: By Category view.

To change to a different view, just click its name in the Navigation pane. You can sort and customize each view, and even create your own views; see Book VIII, Chapter 2 for the lowdown.

Locating a Contact

Nothing's more frustrating than looking for something you know should be right there because, by goodness, you remember putting it there just a second ago, carefully balanced on the stack of unopened mail and lists of phone calls you need to return. Luckily Outlook makes it easier to find a lost contact than it is to find your keys, cell phone, or the remote. In fact, you have as many ways to find a contact as you have to lose your stuff:

✦ **Search for a contact by name, e-mail address, display name, or company name:** Simply typing the search criteria in the Search Address Books box that's conveniently found on the Standard toolbar, from within any Outlook module. For example, you can find that guy who's a whiz at fixing the copier even when you can't remember his name. Just type the name of the company he works for (or just his first name, if that's all you can remember) in that handy-dandy Search Address Books box at the top of the Outlook window. Then press Enter. The matching contact instantly appears. If there's more than one contact that matches your search, you see the Choose Contact dialog box. (See Figure 2-3.) Choose one of the contacts listed and click OK.

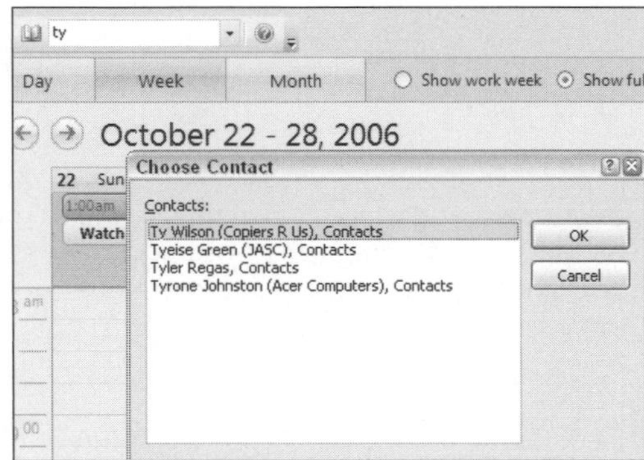

Figure 2-3: Got him!

You can type all or any part of a contact's name (first or last), e-mail address, the contact's display name (the name used to resolve e-mail names), or company name to locate a contact using the Search Address Books box. You can also type the File As name, which is typically the first and last name, but it could be anything. For example, when I add contractors to my Contacts list, I use the File As box to list what they do, such as plumber, electrician, or carpenter. That way, when I want to search for the plumber I used last time, I can just type **plumber** and press Enter.

To relocate a contact you found recently using the Search Address Books, just open the list and select from it.

✦ **Search for a contact using any of its information:** If you know a particular contact is out there but can't find that person by typing something in the Search Address Books box, you can try the Search Contacts box in the Contacts module. For example, to find the eye doctor whose name you've forgotten because you only saw him once over a year ago, you can type **eye** in the Search Contacts box, press Enter, and, I hope, find the doc (assuming you've typed the word *eye* anywhere in that contact's information). See Figure 2-4. You can enter partial information and even combine stuff to find a contact — for example, you might type **t copier** to find someone named Tom, Tyler, Tyrone, or Ty who also sells or fixes copiers.

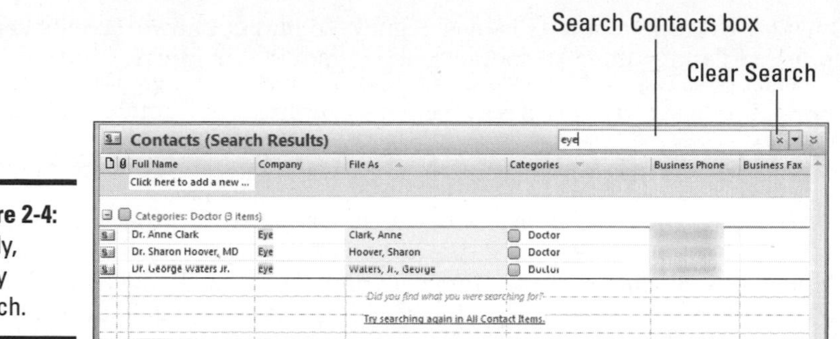

Figure 2-4: Really, really search.

After you type something in the Search Contacts box and press Enter, the display changes so that only matching contacts appear. You get the details of searching in Book IX, Chapter 4; for now, to return to displaying all contacts, click the Clear Search button.

✦ **Group, then search to find a contact:** Another way in which you might hunt down a lost contact is to group similar ones together by sorting. You find out all about sorting in Book VIII, Chapter 2, but for now, I can show you some basics.

First, you change to a list view in Contacts (such as Phone List or By Company). The Phone List view simply lists everyone alphabetically and doesn't group similar contacts together, but you can still sort the listing. For example, to find someone who works for a particular company but whose name you can't exactly remember, you can click the Company heading to sort by it, and then scan down the list until you find the person you're looking for. Other list views group similar contacts. For example, the By Location listing groups contacts by their country. You might then sort the listing by State to locate someone you know is from Arizona, as shown in Figure 2-5.

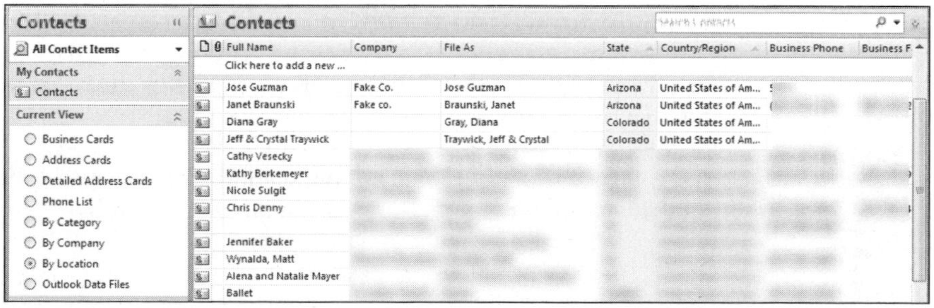

Figure 2-5: Use groups to find a contact.

One way to group contacts is by category. To find out how to create categories and assign them to contacts, see Book VIII, Chapter 1.

Viewing a Map to a Contact's Address

I do business with a lot of my contacts, so having an address is pretty important. More important than that, however, is knowing where the silly address is located! Well, not to worry; though cyberspace was almost as uncharted as an ancient sea ten years ago, Internet maps have brought accessibility to those thar-be-dragons areas.

To work this magic, you must be connected to the Internet.

To display a map of a contact's address, follow these steps:

1. **Open the contact whose address you'd like to find.**
2. **Display the address to find.**

   Because a contact can have up to three addresses, you need to display the address you want to find first so Outlook knows which address to look up. To do that, click the arrow next to the button in the Addresses area of the Contact form and select the type of address you want to locate, such as Business, Home, or Other.
3. **Choose Contact⇨Communicate⇨Map.**

   Your Web browser opens, displaying the map using Live Local, a Microsoft site. See Figure 2-6. You can change from map view to a photo view by clicking either Aerial (for a satellite view) or Hybrid (for a view that overlays the road map on top of the satellite view) from the navigation box. Use the zoom controls to zoom in and the arrows to move within the map (or just click the map and drag it up, down, left, or right to change the portion of the map you're seeing).

   To get driving directions, click the pushpin icon on the Scratch Pad next to a location and choose either Drive From or Drive To. Then type your location in the Driving Directions pane in either the Start or End box and click Get Directions.

To send a link to this map in an e-mail, click the Share button just above the map and select E-Mail.

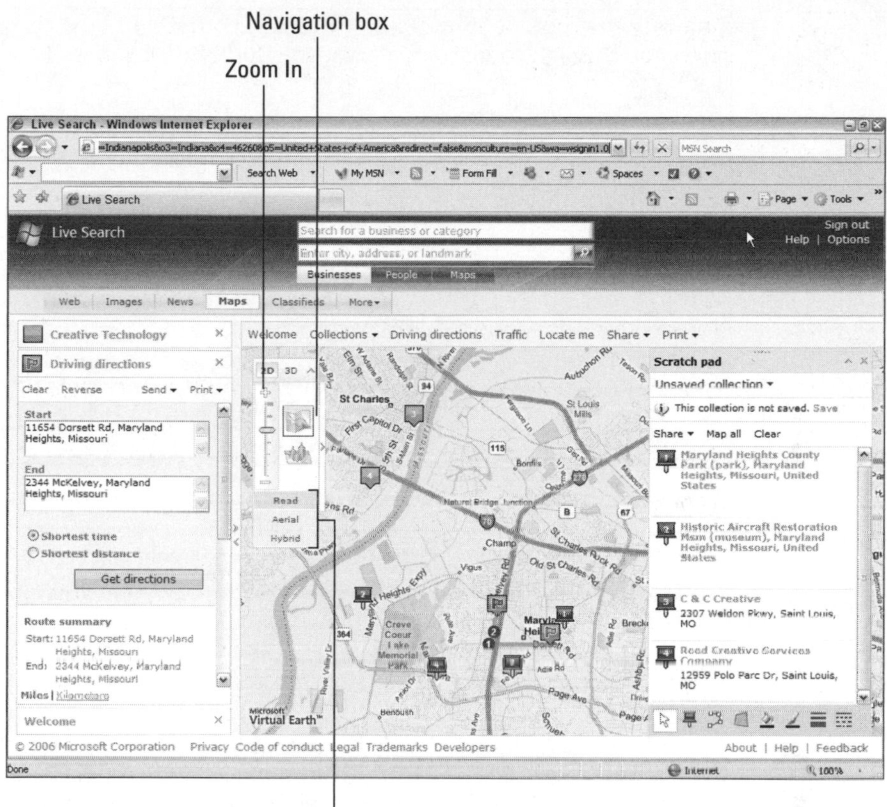

Figure 2-6: A Live Local map.

Browsing to a Contact's Web Page

It seems that just about everyone is on the Web: bookstores, groceries, government offices, car lots, dance studios, libraries, and offices such as yours. Many people even have their own personal Web sites — especially because so many sites give you the space for free. The point I'm trying to make here is that the chances are pretty good that a lot of your contacts have Web sites associated with them.

After you find the address of a contact's Web site, you can enter it in the Web Page Address box in the Contact form, as shown in Figure 2-7. To visit the contact's page, choose Contact⇨Communicate⇨Web Page or just click the Web-page link. The page is instantly displayed in your Web browser, as shown in Figure 2-7.

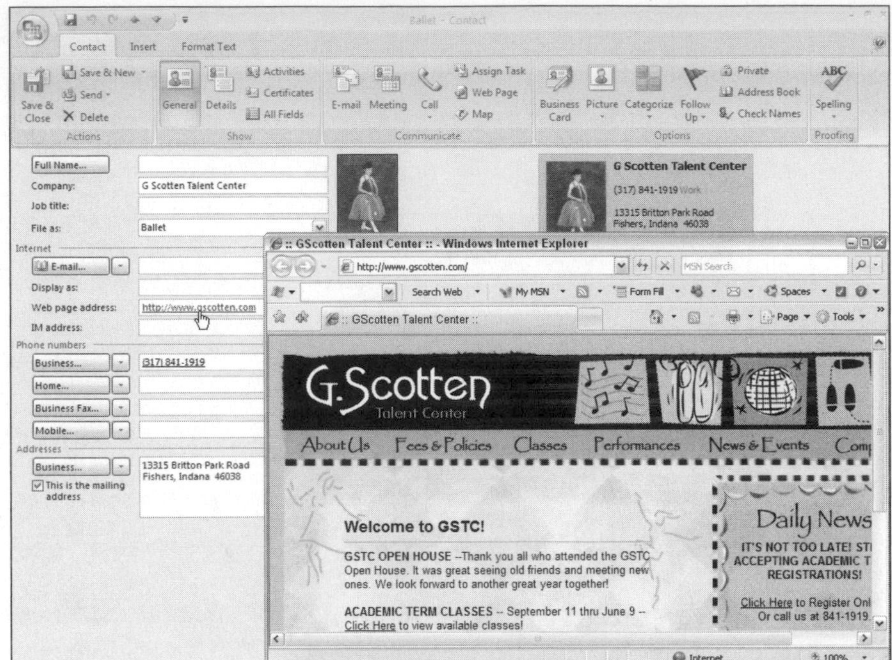

Figure 2-7: Visit a contact's page.

A lot of people include not only their contact information, but their company's Web page address at the bottom of all their e-mails. You can right-click such text, choose Copy, and then paste the address right into the Web Page Address box rather than typing it manually.

As easy as it might be to record a contact's Web site, I personally don't enter a Web site address into Outlook for someone or some company I don't know. In addition, I typically test the Web site address in my browser before I enter it in Outlook. At the same time, I always exercise restraint, and I make it a point not to visit any ol' Web site some stranger sends me in an e-mail. I look at "official" e-mails with disbelief — especially unsolicited e-mails that threaten to turn off my credit card unless I confirm my private information on what is sure to be a bogus Web site. In any case, there's nothing to fear as far as Web sites addresses and Outlook are concerned — you have to manually add a Web site into a Contact form and then click the link to display that site in your Web browser. So rest assured that there's no way for some scam e-mail to enter a Web site address into an existing contact, launch your browser, and force you to order ten tons of chocolate at double the price.

Calling a Contact

Although e-mail is convenient and we all use it (even for silly things like e-mailing a co-worker about lunch although she works in the cubicle next door). For those of you out there who e-mail too much (hey, you know who you are), let me reintroduce you to an old friend — the telephone. Using this old-fashioned-yet-sturdy device, you can call a colleague or friend, and talk *live*.

Okay, there's another way to talk with a person live, and it's a little more hip: instant messaging. Granted, by talking, I mean texting, although you can send live video and audio through an instant messenger if you want. (See Book III, Chapter 2 for more about instant messaging.)

Now, there's a small hitch — this whole thing depends on your computer having a modem (most do, these days, often on the motherboard), and also on whether the modem is connected to a phone outlet. Actually, the phone cord from the modem needs to run to your phone, and then from your phone to the wall jack. If not, Outlook may dial the number, but you won't have any way of talking to the person. After you get everything hooked up, you can initiate all your phone calls with a simple click, saving those newly manicured hands for more productive work.

Now, I know that you're probably thinking (*gee, that's a whole lot of messing around with the back of my computer for a simple task — dialing a phone*). Keep in mind that you can store a whole lot of phone numbers for a contact within Outlook — including home and work numbers, cell phone number, assistant's phone number, pager number, you name it. And because you have to open Outlook to look up the phone number anyway, why not have it do the dialing for you? If you do, you can also create a Journal entry to make a note about the call and its length — which is handy if you bill clients for your time.

To phone a contact, follow these steps:

1. **Open the contact to call.**

   The Contact form pops up, as shown in Figure 2-8.

   You don't actually need to open a contact to dial his or her phone number. After selecting a contact from the Contacts list, click the Dial button on the Standard toolbar, and you see the familiar list of phone numbers associated with that contact. Click a phone number and then skip to Step 3 to see what to do next. You can also press Ctrl+Shift+D from any module to bring up the New Call dialog box, where you can choose a contact and number to dial.

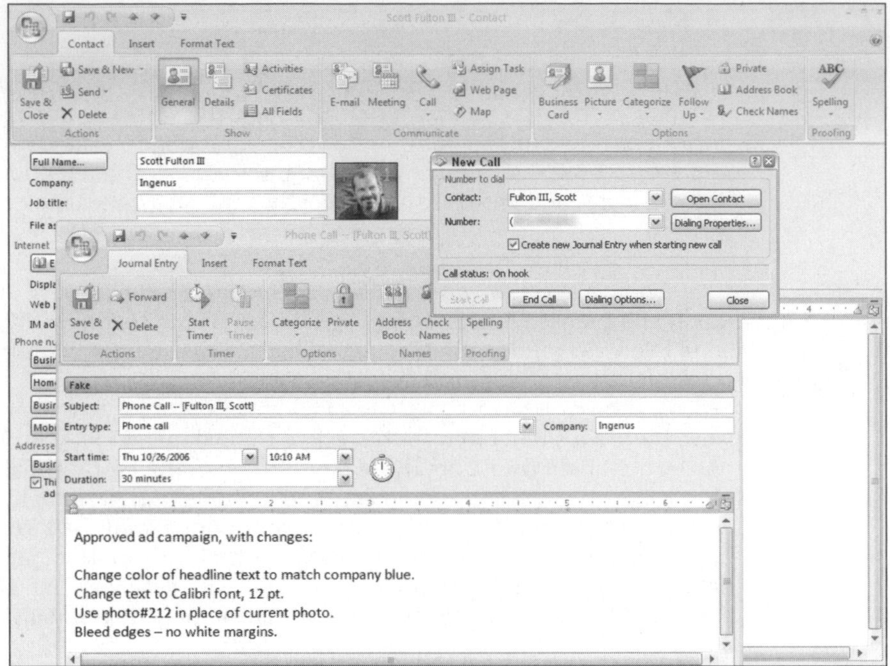

Figure 2-8: Phone a friend.

2. **Choose Contact⇨Communicate⇨Call.**

   A menu appears, listing all the phone numbers you have for that contact. Select one of the numbers on the list. The New Call dialog box jumps up. Refer to Figure 2-8.

3. **Set Options and click Start Call.**

   To create an entry in the Journal that logs this call, select the Create New Journal Entry When Starting New Call option. To check that your location has been set up correctly in Windows, click Dialing Properties. Here you can verify that Windows knows what area code you're in — and whether it has to dial a 9 or some other code to get an outside line on your phone.

   The Call Status dialog box appears.

4. **Click Talk.**

   The modem dials the number. If you started a Journal entry as well, a Journal form appears; type your notes in the notes area. See Book VI, Chapter 6 for help.

5. **When you're through with your chat, click End Call.**

6. **Click Close.**

7. **Back in the Journal form (assuming you have one), finish your notes and click Save & Close.**

   For help in viewing the Journal entry of your call, see the next section, "Viewing Activity Associated with a Contact."

If you get used to your new "phone butler," you might want to make it even more convenient to have Outlook dial for you by setting up a speed-dial list:

1. **Open the New Call dialog box.**

   You can do that in several ways, but the simplest is to press Ctrl+Shift+D from any module. If you're already in Contacts, you can click the Dial button on the Standard toolbar and choose New Call.

2. **Click Dialing Options.**

   The Dialing Options dialog box jumps out, as shown in Figure 2-9.

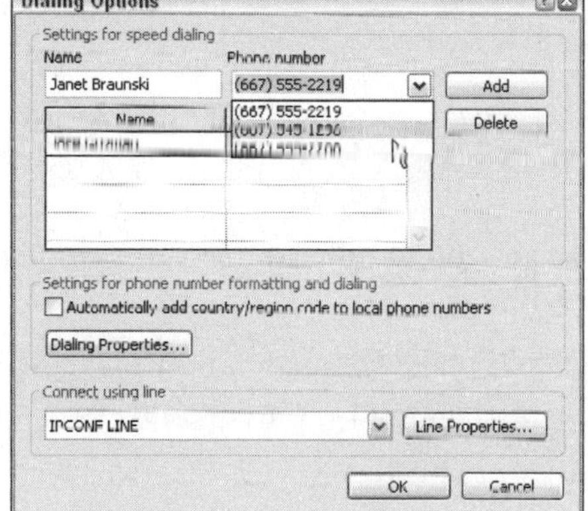

Figure 2-9: Add the favored to your speed dial list.

3. **Add a name and number.**

   Type the name of a contact in the Name box and press Tab. The contact's first phone number should appear in the Phone Number box; if you want to add a different number, click the arrow and select a phone number from the list. If, for some reason, a phone number doesn't appear at all, type the phone number you want to use and click Add to add this person to your speed dial. Repeat this step to add other speed dial contacts; click OK when you're through.

To remove a speed-dial contact from the list, redisplay the Dialing Options dialog box, select a speed-dial contact, and click Delete.

To dial one of your speed-dial numbers, change to Contacts, click the Dial button on the Standard toolbar, and choose Speed Dial. A list of speed-dial contacts appears on the submenu; select one to bring up the New Call dialog box with that phone number already selected. Opt to start a Journal entry if you want, and then click Start Call.

Viewing Activity Associated with a Contact

Outlook can track specific activity associated with selected contacts in its Journal, which you can read about in Book VI, Chapter 7. Regardless of whether you choose to use the Journal, you can have Outlook instantly scan its records for any items associated with a particular contact.

When you create an e-mail, receive one, or send or receive a meeting or task request, those items are automatically associated with a contact. You can associate a task with a contact without sending out a task request (reassigning a task). Just drag the task with the right mouse button, drop it onto the Task button on the Navigation pane, and choose Copy Here As Task with Shortcut.

To display a list of items associated with a contact, follow these steps:

1. **Open a contact.**

   Locate a contact whose activities you want to view and then double-click to open the contact.

2. **Choose Contact⇨Show⇨Activities.**

   A list of activities associated with this contact appears.

3. **Double-click an activity to view it.**

   To see the details for an item in the list, double-click it.

You can track other activity in the Journal — for example, any Word, Excel, and PowerPoint files you create or change. (See Book VI, Chapter 7 for help.) You can build a comprehensive record of activities related to business contacts by using the Business Contact Manager; see Book VII for details.

Chapter 3: Dealing with Business Cards

In This Chapter

- **Improving the look of a business card**
- **Using the business-card format to add a new contact**
- **Creating contacts from business cards you receive**
- **Sending business cards to friends and colleagues**
- **Changing the appearance of business cards**

Business cards are fairly common; even though they're still made with simple paper, they're an easy way to share contact information with another person. And, paper or not, business cards sure beat writing on your arm or the back of a napkin. Electronic business cards are a bit rarer — but even so, they're a great way to share contact information digitally.

When you create a contact, an electronic business card is automatically created as well; it's just a conglomeration of basic contact data (name, address, phone number, and so on), arranged in the familiar business-card format.

You can share basic contact information quickly by simply attaching an electronic business card to an outgoing e-mail. Likewise, others can share contact data with you by sending you electronic business cards — either theirs or someone else's. Because you can share business cards — yours, or someone in your Contacts list — it doesn't hurt to make them look pretty.

Editing a Contact's Business Card

You don't actually need to do anything to make an electronic business card; it's created automatically when you create a contact. You may want to edit the electronic-business-card portion of a new or existing contact, however — especially if it's yours, and you plan on sharing it with others.

One way in which you can share an electronic business card is to attach it to an e-mail; you find out how to do so in the section "Sharing Business Cards," later in this chapter. You can also share your electronic business card as part of your *signature file* — a bit of text that appears at the end of every outgoing e-mail message. (See Book II, Chapter 4 for the lowdown on signature files.)

To edit the look of a business card for a contact, follow these steps:

1. **Open or create the contact whose business card you want to change and then choose Contact➪Options➪Business Card.**

   The Edit Business Card dialog box appears, as shown in Figure 3-1.

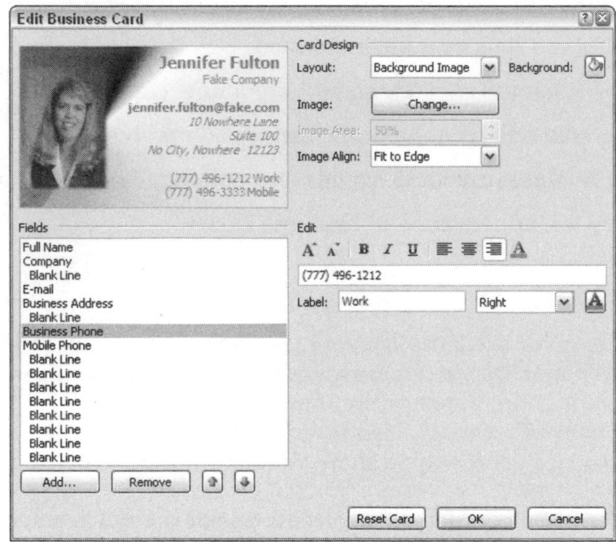

Figure 3-1: Make your card pretty.

2. **Add, remove, or reorder the fields.**

   The electronic business card appears on the upper left; on the lower left, you see the fields displayed on the card and the order in which they appear. You can add or remove fields or change their order:

   * **Add a field:** To add a new field to the card, such as E-Mail2 or Home Phone, first click in the Fields list, above where you want the new field to appear. Click Add and then choose the field you want from the shortcut menu that appears. For example, choose Phone➪Home Phone.

     The Blank Line field allows you to add a blank line between items on the card.

   * **Remove a field:** To get rid of a field you don't want to appear on the card, choose it and click Remove.

   * **Rearrange fields:** To rearrange the order in which a field appears, click it in the Fields list and then click the up or down arrow buttons.

You don't normally change contact info in the Edit Business Card dialog box; typically, you just change the appearance of information. To change contact data, use the Contact form. Simply double-click the contact whose information you want to change, make your changes, and click Save & Close. See Book V, Chapter 1.

3. **Format a field.**

   To change how the data in a particular field looks on the card, click that field in the Fields list.

   - For example, in the figure, I clicked the Business Phone field. The data in the Business Phone field appears on the lower right, in the Edit area.
   - To change the field's appearance on the card, click one of the formatting buttons — such as Increase Font Size, Decrease Font Size, Bold, Italics, Underline, Align Text Left, Center, Align Text Right, or Font Color.

   Some fields have labels that identify them, and these labels appear below each filed in the Edit area (for example, the Business Phone field has a label: `Work`). You can change a label in various ways:

   - Change its text by retyping the label.
   - Change its location relative to the data by choosing an option from the list to the right of the label (for example, Left or Right). I choose Right, so the label, Work, appears to the right of the business phone number.
   - Change its color by clicking the Font Color button.
   - Remove it altogether by selecting the label text and pressing Delete.

4. **Change designs.**

   The general layout of the electronic business card is controlled by its design. Here, too, you have some choices to make:

   - Choose the layout you want from the Layout list, such as Image Right.
   - To use the image as a background, choose Background Image from the Layout list. Even if you use a background image, you can fill the rest of the card's background with a color by clicking the Background button.
   - If the contact's card doesn't already have an image on it, you can choose one by clicking the Change button, selecting an image file, and then clicking OK. Adjust the size of the image by messing with the Image Area controls. Finally, change where the Image appears by choosing a position from the Image Align list.

5. **When you're done making changes to the card, click OK.**

   The edited business card appears in the Contact form.

6. **To save the card changes permanently, choose Contact⇨Actions⇨Save & Close.**

If you make changes to the card that you don't like, you can remove them in one step: Click the Reset Card button and then click Yes to reset the card's formatting and layout to the Outlook default.

Creating a Reusable Business Card

The electronic business card is pretty handy. Not only can you use it to share your information with somebody, but you can also use an electronic business card sent to you to effortlessly create a new contact in your Contacts list. (You get to perform this magic later in this chapter, in the section, "Creating a Contact from a Business Card Sent to You".) In addition, you can use a business card as a template to create similar business cards for a several contacts. For example, you might create a business-card template for yourself and modify it slightly to create multiple cards for different occasions — business, personal, and simply fun. Or you might create a template to apply to all your top clients, making them easier to spot in Contacts. Your company, meanwhile, might create a template so that employees present a unified appearance through their electronic business cards.

Creating a new business card template

When you create a new business card, you're really creating a new contact. So for example, if you create multiple business cards for yourself, you're listed in your Contacts list several times. Not that it matters, unless you find multiple entries for one person confusing — Outlook doesn't. Here's the drill for creating the reusable business card:

1. **Get a template or create one.**

   The respective processes look like this:

   - *Getting a Microsoft business-card template:* You can download one from Office Online, in the Outlook templates section. (Make sure that you look in the Outlook section of the online templates; otherwise, you browse templates for creating and printing paper business cards in Word.) Navigate to the right page, browse through the templates, and when you find one you like, click Download Now. Poof! The template appears in Outlook as a new contact (see Figure 3-2).

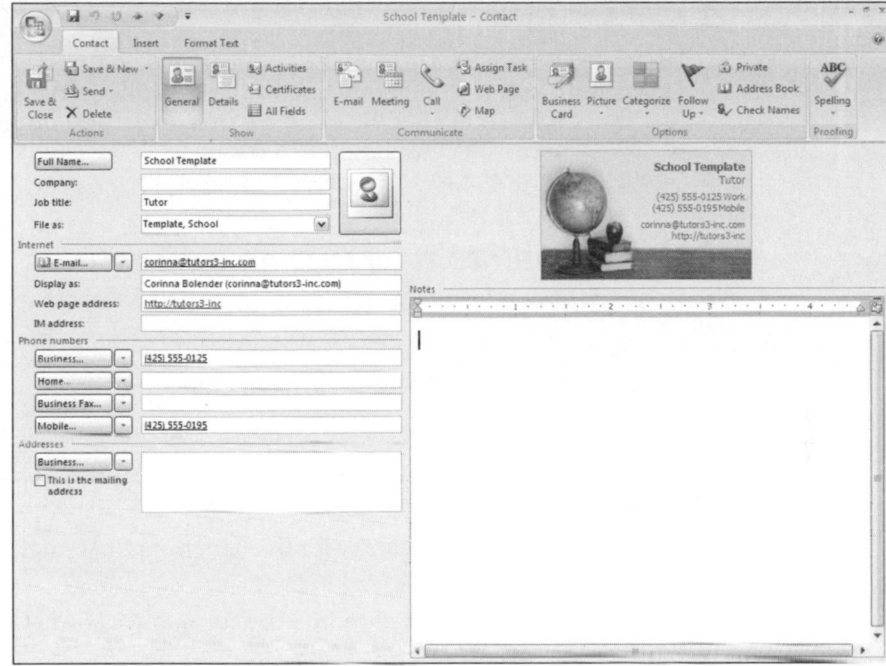

Figure 3-2: Microsoft provides some neat templates you can use.

You don't need to leave the Microsoft template the way it is; if the font used isn't your style, or you want some text bolded or a different color, follow the steps given earlier (in the "Editing a Contact's Business Card" section) to make changes.

- *Custom design your own reusable template:* Start with a new contact and then use the steps in the earlier "Editing a Contact's Business Card" section to make your design.

2. **Clean up the template.**

   Here are the tweaks:

   - If you downloaded a Microsoft template, you may want to remove the fake phone numbers, addresses, and other data, or just leave 'em there as placeholders for when you create actual contacts from this template.
   - If you created a new contact with the purpose of making a business-card template, be sure not to include any contact data you don't want to make reusable. For example, include the Company Name and Work Phone if this template is for business purposes; include your name, address, and phone number if this template is for your own use.

3. **Save the template.**

   Because business card "templates" appear as actual contacts in Outlook, I save the template/contact thingie with an obvious name (such as `Leaf Template`), whether I get the template from Microsoft or create one of my own. Then, when I want to find a template, I can simply search the Contacts list for the word **template** or look in the Ts.

Using a template to create a new contact

Now that you have a template, here's what you can do to create a new contact using it:

1. **Open the electronic business-card template.**

   Search your Contacts list for the template and double-click to open it.

2. **Choose Contact⇨Actions⇨Save & New⇨New Contact from Same Company.**

   A new Contact form appears, with the data from the template, including the business-card style.

3. **Type the contact information into the form and choose Contact⇨Actions⇨Save & Close.**

Applying a new template to an old contact

You can use a template to update an existing contact, but it's a little tricky. Follow the steps given in the previous section to create a template and open it. Then follow these steps:

1. **Choose New Contact from Same Company.**
2. **Remove all contact information.**

   Make sure that you get rid of all data in the new contact, including the placeholders; you don't want the template data to override your real contact's stuff.

3. **Enter only the Full Name.**

   The name must exactly match the Full Name for the contact you want to apply this template to.

4. **Click Save & Close.**

   A warning tells you that you're about to add two contacts with the same name.

5. **Select the Update option.**

   Your existing contact is updated with the business card template.

Sharing Business Cards

One of the chief reasons for creating electronic business cards (besides making your contacts look cool) is to share them. For people who use Outlook, you can simply send them a card for one of your contacts in an outgoing e-mail. You can also include your own card, either as part of the signature placed at the end of every e-mail, or with just a single message. (For help in adding your electronic business card to your e-mail signature, see Book II, Chapter 4.)

To include an electronic business card for one of your contacts in an e-mail message, follow these steps:

1. **Choose Message⇨Include⇨Business Card.**

   A list of contacts appears.

2. **Select a contact from the list or click Other Business Cards to view the entire listing.**

   If you choose a contact from the list, the card is inserted into the text area of the message and attached to the message as well. If you choose Other Business Cards, then the Insert Business Card dialog box appears, as shown in Figure 3-3.

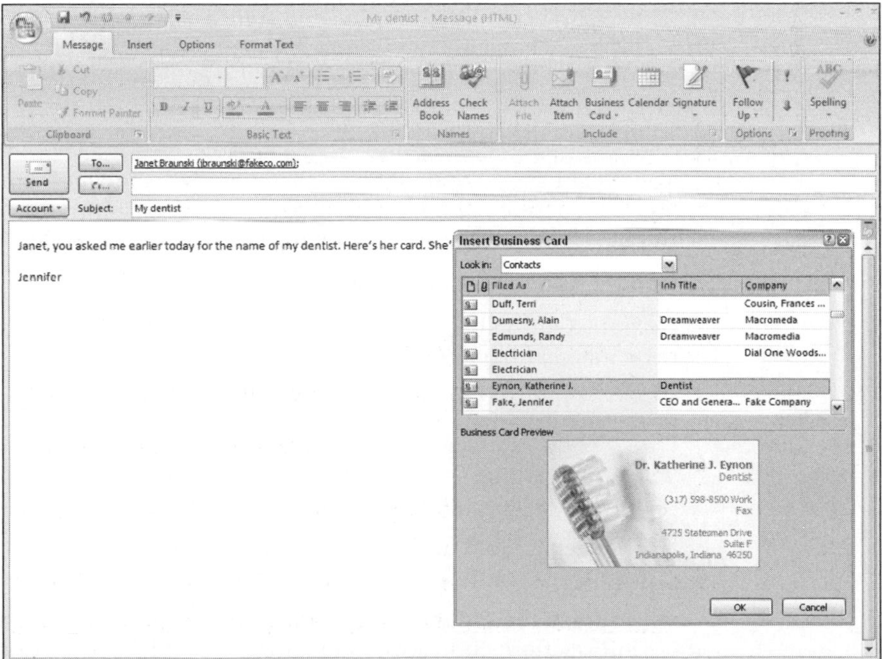

Figure 3-3: Look for other contacts.

3. **Choose the address book you want to look in from the Look In list, scroll down until you see the contact you want to send, and click that contact.**

   The contact's business card appears in the lower part of the Insert Business Card dialog box.

4. **Click OK to attach the business card.**

   The business card is inserted into the text of the message and also sent in vCard format as an attachment. *vCard* is a format that's compatible with most address book programs, so if your recipient doesn't use Outlook, they should still be able to get what they need from your e-mail.

5. **Repeat Steps 1 through 3 to attach other business cards if you want.**
6. **Click Send to send the message.**

You can quickly send a business card from within Contacts, assuming that you're using Business Cards view. Anyway, just locate the contact you want to send and choose Actions⇨Send As Business Card. Address the e-mail message that appears and click Send to send it.

Creating a Contact from a Business Card Sent to You

I discuss the details of sharing contacts in the previous section, "Sharing Business Cards." Even if you haven't gotten around to it yet, let's assume that someone else has read that section and sent you a business card in an e-mail. What's probably consuming you now is the problem of getting the contact data out of the e-mail and into Outlook. As you'll see, it's all pretty straight-forward.

1. **Right-click the business card.**

   You don't have to open the message if you don't want to; you can just view its contents in the Reading pane. In any case, when you right-click, the business card appears within the message text, and you see a menu.

2. **Choose Add to Outlook Contacts.**

   A Contact form appears, with the info taken from the business card prominently displayed (see Figure 3-4).

3. **Choose Contact⇨Actions⇨Save & Close to save the new contact.**

   If the contact's name happens to match somebody in your Contacts list, you see a warning — if you continue with the save, you'll lose that old contact. You have a couple of options:

   - To keep the old and add the new, choose the Add New Contact option to create a separate, new contact with the same name.
   - To trash the old data and update your existing contact with this new information, choose Update Information of Selected Contact instead.

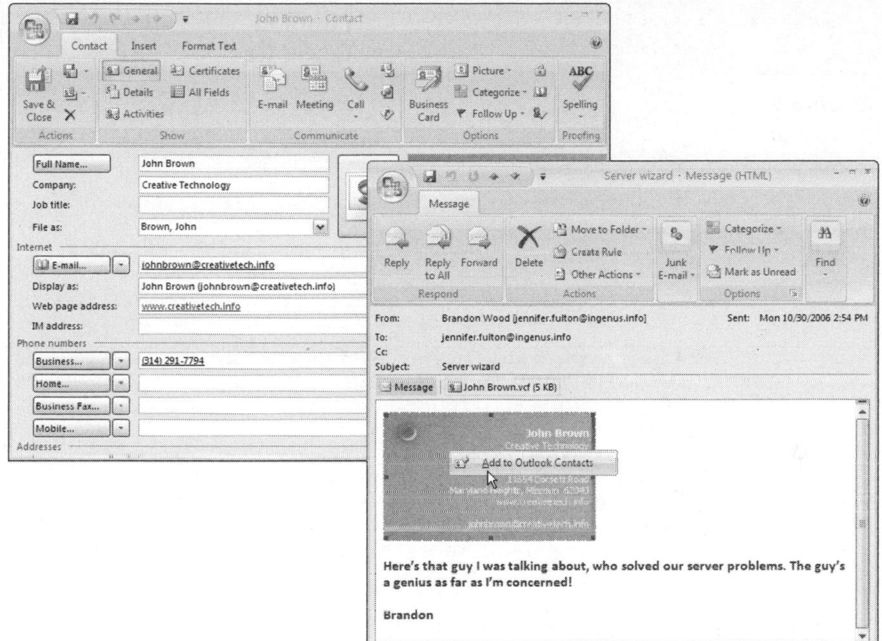

Figure 3-4: Adding a business card.

Displaying More Business Cards

When you look at Contacts, by default, each contact is displayed as an electronic business card in Business Card view. If you make the Navigation pane real skinny, you can display more business cards. But that trick makes the Navigation pane almost too thin to use. A better solution, assuming that you want to see more cards at one time, is to customize the view. For an intro to customizing Outlook views, check out Book VIII, Chapter 2; for now, I can give you the specifics you need to make such a change:

1. **Change to Contacts and choose Business Cards View from the Navigation pane.**
2. **Click Customize Current View at the bottom of the Navigation pane.**

   The Customize View: Business Cards dialog box appears, as shown in Figure 3-5.
3. **Click Other Settings.**

   The Format Business Card View dialog box opens (that's it in Figure 3-5).

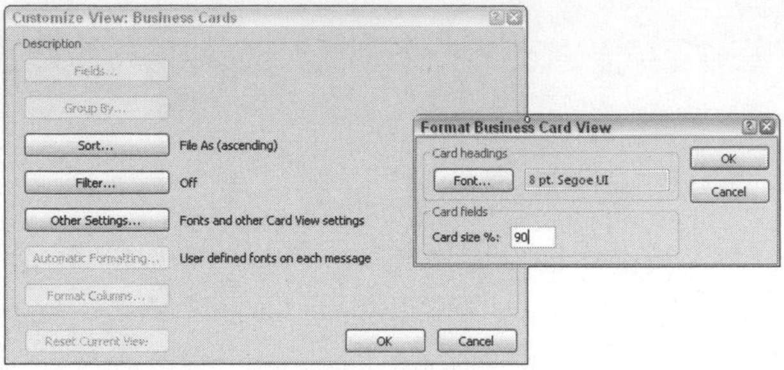

Figure 3-5: Customize the view so you can display lots of cards.

4. **Change the value in the Card Size % box.**

   Here the idea is to reduce the size of the cards and display more of them at one time.

5. **When you're done adjusting, click OK twice.**

   With any luck, you now have a view that shows as many cards as you need to see. If not, repeat these steps to change the card size even more.

Chapter 4: Contacts Collaboration

In This Chapter

- ✓ **Sharing contacts over an Exchange network**
- ✓ **Restricting access to your contacts**
- ✓ **Viewing somebody else's contacts**

In your Contacts list, you probably have quite a collection of people: friends, family, and colleagues. In addition, you may have many other contacts you may want to share, such as doctors, babysitters, plumbers, electricians, carpenters, and other resources. In addition, your co-workers might be interested in your list of new and prospective clients. So there are any number of reasons why you might want to share your Contacts list, and in this chapter, you'll learn how.

Normal sharing occurs over an Exchange network (a corporate network that uses Microsoft Exchange), between you and your co-workers. However, you can share contacts even if you're not on an Exchange network. For example, you can e-mail an electronic business card or simply share the contact in Outlook format. (See Book V, Chapter 3 for help.)

Sharing Your Contacts

Assuming that you work on an Exchange network (it'll say Connected to Microsoft Exchange on the Outlook status bar), you can share your contacts with other people on the network. Now, like me, you may have contacts in your Contacts list that you don't want to share. Unfortunately, sharing is mostly an all or nothing proposition — if you share a Contacts folder, you share pretty much everything in it. You can, however, create an additional Contacts folder, place only the contacts you want to share in that folder, and share just that folder and not your main Contacts one. For example, if you're working with a big team on a huge project, you can create a project folder and put all the contacts you need to complete the project, including client contacts, in that folder. Or, if it's easier, do the reverse: Create a folder and place your private contacts in it. Then share the main Contacts folder.

You can mark individual contacts as private so that they're not seen when someone views the other contacts in a shared folder, which may be a good method to use if you have only a few contacts you don't want to share. To make a contact private, open the contact and choose Contact⇨Options⇨Private.

Like the idea of creating a new Contacts folder and putting only the contacts you want to share in it? I do, too. (See Book IX, Chapter 1 for step-by-step pointers on how to create the folder and move contacts into it.)

Now, when I say all or nothing, I don't mean that you have to open your Contacts list to the world, or at least, the part of the world that has access to your Exchange network. Nope, you can share your list with Bryan and not with Kelly if you want. You can also define the level of sharing: for example, you can control whether people can just view contacts, or update and create them when needed as well.

So, to summarize, when sharing your contacts, you can do one of two things:

- **Share the main Contacts folder with basically everyone on the network,** while also designating what they're allowed to do, such as view only or view and edit. See "Sharing contacts with everyone."
- **Share either the main or a custom Contacts folder almost completely,** but with only the specific people you select. See "Sharing contacts with specific people."

Sharing contacts with everyone

Following the steps in this section, you can share Contacts, your main Contacts folder. You can't use these steps to share a Contacts folder you may have created. Well, okay, you might try — and it may seem to work — but it won't work right. Basically, Microsoft can't think of a reason why you might create a special Contacts folder and want to share it with *everybody.* I mean, a *special* Contacts folder, by its nature, probably appeals to a special few. Anyway, if you're determined to share the custom folder with everyone, you're gonna have to follow the steps in the section, "Sharing contacts with specific people" — and (unfortunately but literally) e-mail everyone with a sharing invitation. That's because to access a custom folder, you must use a sharing invitation. (Sorry, that's just the way it is.)

To share a main Contacts folder with everyone on the network, follow these steps:

1. **In the Navigation pane, right-click the main Contacts folder and choose Change Sharing Permissions.**

   The Contacts Properties dialog box appears, as shown in Figure 4-1.

2. **Choose Permissions⇨Default.**

   That option is on the Permissions tab, in the Name list.

3. **From the Permissions Level list, choose the option that describes what you want visitors to be able to do and then click OK.**

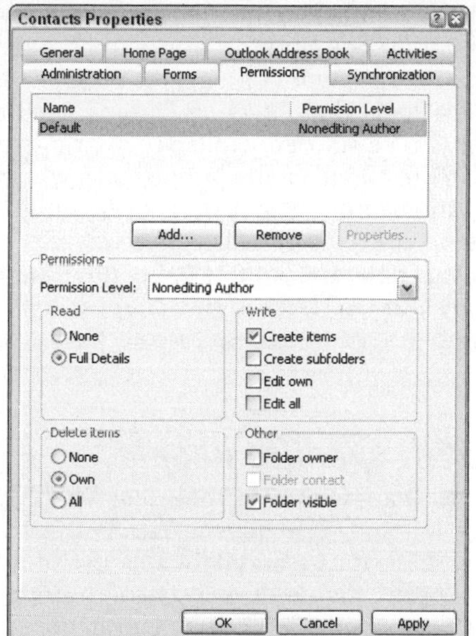

Figure 4-1: You decide how much to share.

The permissions options include:

- *Publishing Editor:* Create, edit, delete, and view contacts. The users can also create subfolders within the shared folder.
- *Editor:* Same as Publishing Editor, except the users can't create subfolders.
- *Publishing Author:* Users can create and view contacts, create folders, and edit or delete contacts they've created themselves.
- *Author:* Same as Publishing Author except the users can't create subfolders.
- *Nonediting Author:* Same as Publishing Author except the users can't edit existing contacts, even if they created them. Also, they can't create folders. They can delete contacts they create themselves.
- *Reviewer:* View contacts only.
- *Contributor:* Create and edit new contacts, but can't view existing ones unless they created them.
- *None:* Prevents the users from accessing the folder at all; they can't even view the contacts in the folder.

The folder you chose appears in the Navigation pane with a special icon that looks like a hand holding a business card. This icon shows everyone that the folder is open for visitors.

Now, as long as everyone knows you're in the sharing mood, they can access your main Contacts folder simply by choosing your name from a list. They do not need an e-mail invitation from you, or a secret codeword. All the same, unless you work at the Real Good Psychics Hotline, chances are your colleagues won't know that you've suddenly taken to sharing your Contacts list. So you may want to send an e-mail to the people with whom you want to share this folder, just to let them know. The rest of "everybody" on your network can just fend for themselves. This e-mail, by the way, isn't special, just a little note from you that your default Contacts list is now shared. Check out "Viewing Contacts Shared by Others," later in this chapter, for the lowdown on how a person on your network gains access to your Contacts folder now that you've shared it.

Sharing contacts with specific people

Sometimes you don't want to share with everyone, like when you have only three pieces of pumpkin pie left and eight guests. Yep, better to stash the pie away until they all leave and have it as a midnight snack. (No need to tell the husband either, because you can't divide three by two. Nope, better that you save everyone the bad feelings of being left out by eating the rest of the pie yourself. Oh, the things you do for your family!)

In this procedure, you share the folder and send a sharing invitation to the specific people you choose. For custom folders you've created, you only have two access cards you can hand out to visitors: *Reviewer* (which means they can view your contacts only) or *Editor* (which means they can create, edit, delete, and view contacts, even ones they don't create themselves). If you're sharing your main Contacts folder using this procedure, then you can only provide visitors with Reviewer status, at least initially. After the sharing invitation goes out, you can always change a particular person's access level as desired — see the section "Changing permissions or stopping sharing," later in this chapter.

To share a Contacts folder with a select few, follow these steps:

1. **Click the Contacts folder you want to share.**

   Change over to Contacts and locate the folder you want to share. You should find it hiding under the My Contacts category on the Navigation pane. You can share your default Contacts folder or a custom folder in this manner.

2. **Share the folder.**

   If you're sharing the main Contacts folder, simply click the Share My Contacts Folder link on the Navigation pane. Otherwise, right-click the folder and choose Share *foldername,* where *foldername* is the actual name of the folder (such as Big Group Project). A message form jumps up, as shown in Figure 4-2.

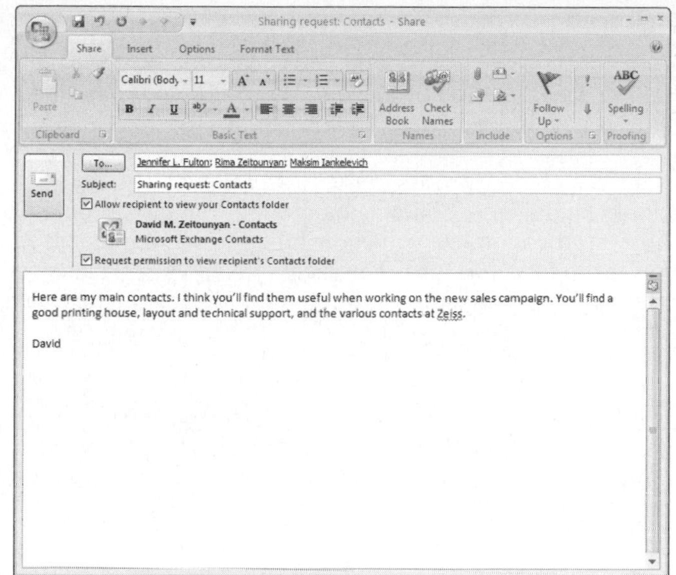

Figure 4-2: Send your sharing invitation.

3. **Address the invitation.**

   In the To box, add the addresses of the people you want to share this folder with. Change the subject to make it more clear what it is you're doing here and type a message explaining the invitation.

4. **Set some options.**

   Assuming that you're sharing your main Contacts folder, you can request permission to view each addressee's Contacts folder in return. Again, you're granting them only Reviewer status (which means they can look, but not touch), so you're asking them to grant you that same access in return. To do so, choose the Request Permission to View Recipient's Contacts Folder option.

   WARNING!

   You can't request permission to view a specific folder within an addressee's main Contacts folder, at least not in this e-mail message. You have to send your own separate message requesting permission.

   If you're sharing a folder you created — and not the main Contacts folder — you can allow users to not only view but also add, edit, and delete contacts if you feel like it (that's Editor access). To do so, choose the Recipient Can Add, Edit, And Delete Items In This Contacts Folder option. If you don't choose this option, visitors are given only Reviewer access, which means "look, but don't touch."

5. **Click Send.**

   You see a message asking whether you really want to share this folder. Confirm the invitation by clicking Yes. Next, you're notified that the folder is now indeed shared. Click OK.

The folder you chose appears in the Navigation pane with a special icon, which looks kinda like a Contacts handout — a hand holding a business card. Anyway, the icon lets you know that you've shared this folder, just in case you're the forgetful type. The recipients of your e-mails will use the link in the message to connect to the shared folder. See the upcoming section "Viewing Contacts Shared by Others" for more information.

Changing permissions or stopping sharing

After sharing a Contacts folder, you don't have to continue sharing it forever. For example, you can change a person's permissions so that he can't add or remove contacts any more, or you can remove his permission to even access the folder at all.

When you initially share the main Contacts folder with individual users, they are set up with Reviewer status, which means they can only view contacts. Reviewer status is probably best, because it's really unlikely that you'll want to grant someone the ability to add contacts to your main list or to change or delete them.

However, by following the general steps given here, you can change the access level for anyone you want and grant someone broader access to your Contacts folder. I wouldn't, however. Instead, move the contacts you want to relinquish control over into a different Contacts folder and then grant a higher level of access to that new folder. But that's just me — a control freak who doesn't like to think of someone accidentally deleting all the Contacts it took me so long to collect.

To change a user's permission to use a shared folder, follow these steps:

1. **Right-click the shared folder.**

   In the Navigation pane, right-click the shared folder whose permissions you want to change.

2. **Choose Change Sharing Permissions.**

   The Properties dialog box for your folder appears. Figure 4-3 shows the Key Clients Properties dialog box because I opened the Key Clients folder.

Figure 4-3: Change permissions to use a folder.

3. **Change permissions as desired.**

   You have a couple of options:

   - *To make a change that affects everyone*, click the Permissions tab and then in the Name list, click Default. Change the options shown in the Permissions List; to completely revoke all access, click None.
   - *To make a change to a particular user's permissions,* click the Permissions tab and choose the user's name from the Name list. Then, from the Permission Level list, remove the options you no longer want to grant this user.

If you've granted basically the same access to everyone through the Default classification, then you can add a specific user to the list and set the permission level you want for that particular person. To add someone to the Name list, click Add, select the person from the list that appears, and click Add to add her. Select more names if you want and click Add. After you gather all the names you want to add to the Name list in the Properties dialog box, click OK. The new name you added is given the Default permission level. Select a name in the Name list and choose a different Permission Level as desired.

4. **Click OK.**

   The permissions are changed right away.

If someone is viewing your Contacts folder when you change his level of access, it affects him immediately — or as soon as your change filters through the network. If you've removed access from someone, the Contacts list is soon removed from the screen, and he won't be able to see it anymore.

Viewing Contacts Shared by Others

If someone on your company's Exchange network has been nice enough to share her Contacts folder with you, or even a special Contacts subfolder, it's not hard to gain access to it. After you make the initial contact (pardon the pun), the folder appears in the Navigation pane — just like any other folder — making it really easy to retrieve those contacts when they're needed.

After you gain access to someone's Contacts folder (the main one or a custom Contacts folder), if you don't have editing permissions, you won't be able to make any changes to a contact. If you try to change a contact when you don't have permission to, you'll be asked if you want to save a copy of this contact to your Contacts folder. Click Yes to do just that.

Accessing someone's main Contacts folder

To gain access to somebody else's shared, main Contacts folder for the first time, follow these steps:

1. **Click Open Shared Contacts.**

   You can find the link on the Navigation pane. The Open Shared Contacts dialog box appears, as shown in Figure 4-4.

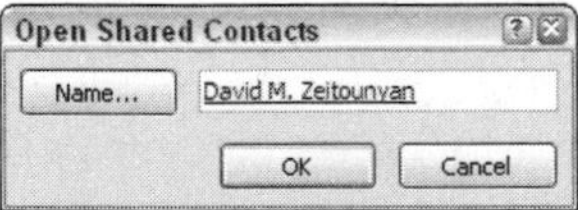

Figure 4-4: Open a shared Contacts folder.

2. **Name that folder.**

   Either type the name of the person whose folder you want to access in the Name box or click Name, select that person from those listed, and click OK.

3. **Click OK.**

   The folder, assuming that it's shared and you have permission to access it, appears in the Navigation pane, along with your other Contacts folders. The contacts in the folder appear on the right.

After you gain access to someone's Contacts folder, you need only click that folder in the Navigation pane at any time to display its contacts.

If the Contacts folder you just tried to open is shared, but not with you, you're asked whether you want to ask for permission. Click Yes, and a message form appears, with a nicely typed request to use the folder. Make sure that the Request Permission to View Recipient's Contacts Folder option is selected. If you want to allow access to your main Contacts folder in exchange, choose the Allow Recipient to View Your Contacts folder. Click Send to send the request.

You can get rid of a shared contacts folder from the People's Contacts list if you don't think you'll need to view it ever again. Just give the Contacts folder the old right-click and choose Delete *foldername* from the menu that appears. This step does not, by the way, actually delete the Contacts folder from the owner's system, so it's safe.

Accessing someone's custom Contacts folder

If someone has gone to the trouble of creating a custom group of contacts they want to share with you, then at some point, you'll get an e-mail invitation asking you to come on in. Most likely, you've been granted either Reviewer access (view only) or Editor (create, edit, delete tasks) access. Regardless of what kind of access the user decided to grant you, once you add that folder to your People's Contacts list, you can easily view its contents any time you want.

To access someone's shared, custom Contacts folder, follow these steps:

1. **View the sharing invitation.**

   Change over to Mail and either select the sharing invitation to view it in the Reading pane or double-click it to view it in a separate window. The choice is yours. See Figure 4-5.

2. **Click Open This Contacts Folder at the top of the Reading pane.**

   A new Outlook window opens (why, I can't explain), and the folder is added to the People's Contacts group on the Navigation pane. You can close this extra window and view the contents of this Contacts folder in the main window if you want, as shown in Figure 4-6.

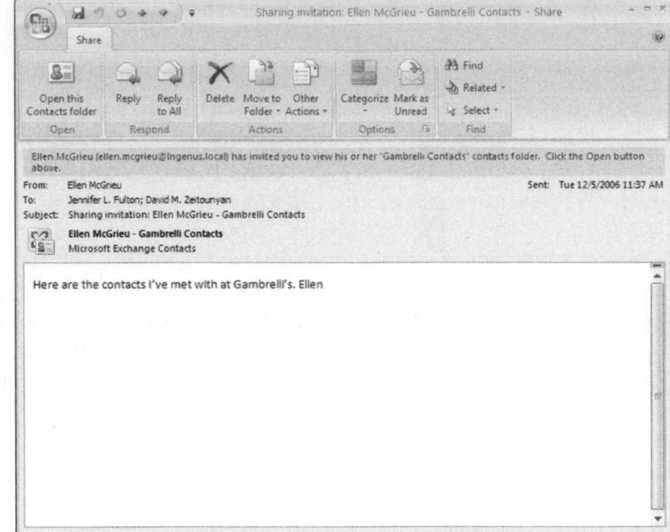

Figure 4-5: Gaining access to a custom Contacts folder.

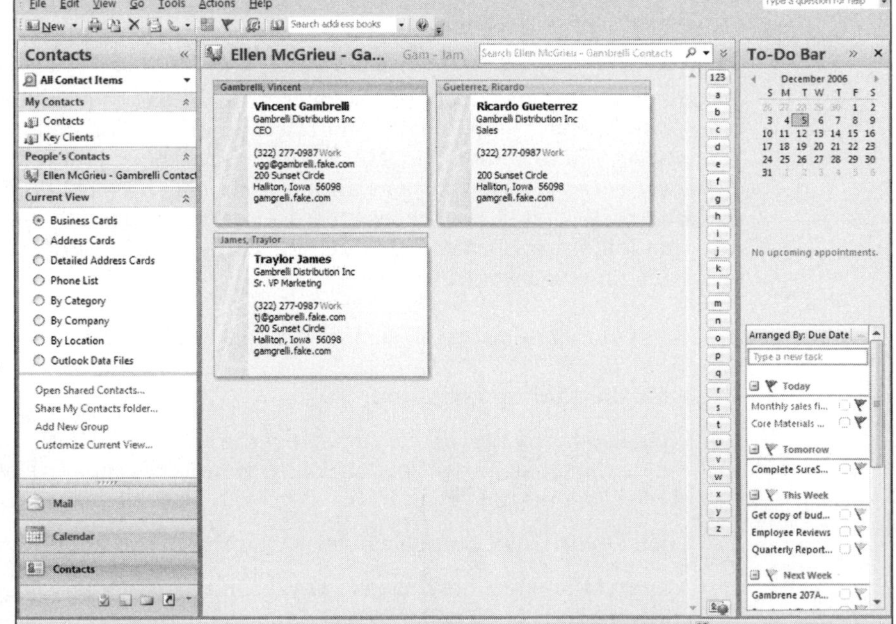

Figure 4-6: Once it's shared, just click a Contacts folder to view its contents.

Book VI

Tracking Tasks, Taking Notes, and Recording Items in the Journal

Contents at a Glance

Chapter 1: Creating Tasks with the To-Do Bar **397**

Chapter 2: Dealing with More Complex Tasks **413**

Chapter 3: Spreading the Joy: Task Assignments **425**

Chapter 4: Taking Notes **447**

Chapter 5: Taking Notes in Overdrive: OneNote **455**

Chapter 6: Maximizing the Power of OneNote **489**

Chapter 7: Making History in the Journal **521**

Chapter 1: Creating Tasks with the To-Do Bar

In This Chapter

- **Playing hide-and-seek with the To-Do bar**
- **Creating To-Do items from e-mails and contacts**
- **Checking off another To-Do item**
- **Finding stuff to do**
- **Making the To-Do bar your own**
- **Working with the Daily Task List**

It always seems like I have more than enough to do — in fact, I have so many things on my list I probably won't be taking a vacation anytime soon. Luckily, I've got my nagging buddy Outlook to remind me what to do so that I don't waste valuable time thinking about what impossible task to tackle next. Outlook presents its list of tasks in several places so that it's nearly impossible for you to say, "Sorry, I forgot to do that." You find tasks on the To-Do bar, the Daily Task List in Calendar, the Tasks module, and under the couch. It's not like I think you don't have enough to do, but if you want to find out how to deal with all those nagging tasks, I recommend one more task: reading this chapter.

The To-Do bar normally appears in every module except Calendar, where tasks and To-Do items are displayed on the Daily Tasks list. However, if the To-Do bar is not displayed, choose View⇨To-Do Bar⇨Normal to show it. To hide the To-Do bar temporarily, click its Minimize button or choose View⇨To-Do Bar⇨Minimize.

Using the To-Do Bar to Track Tasks

In Book I, Chapter 1, I introduce you to the To-Do bar, with its To-Do items and Tasks list, Date Navigator, and appointment/meeting bubbles (see Figure 1-1). That chapter also covers the difference between a To-Do item (which is created from another Outlook item, such as an e-mail) and a task (which is pretty complex, typically including a starting/ending date, status, priority code, and percentage complete). Here are some other differences of note:

- ✦ You can reassign a task to somebody else, whereas you can't reassign a To-Do item.
- ✦ A task can recur at regular intervals, whereas a To-Do item is a one-shot deal.
- ✦ Both tasks and To-Do items appear on the To-Do bar, the Tasks list, and the Daily Task List in Calendar, so you can't tell one from the other by just looking. When you open them up, however, you can tell right away — tasks open up into a conventional Task form, while To-Do items open into the Outlook item used to create them, such as an e-mail message.

In Book I, Chapter 2, you discover how to create a simple To-Do item using the Type a New Task space on the To-Do bar. In this chapter, I show you how to create To-Do items the way they were meant to be created — from other Outlook items. (For help in creating complete tasks, see Book VI, Chapter 2; for information on how to add quick tasks using the Daily Task List, see the section "Creating a Task using the Daily Task List in the Calendar," later in this chapter.)

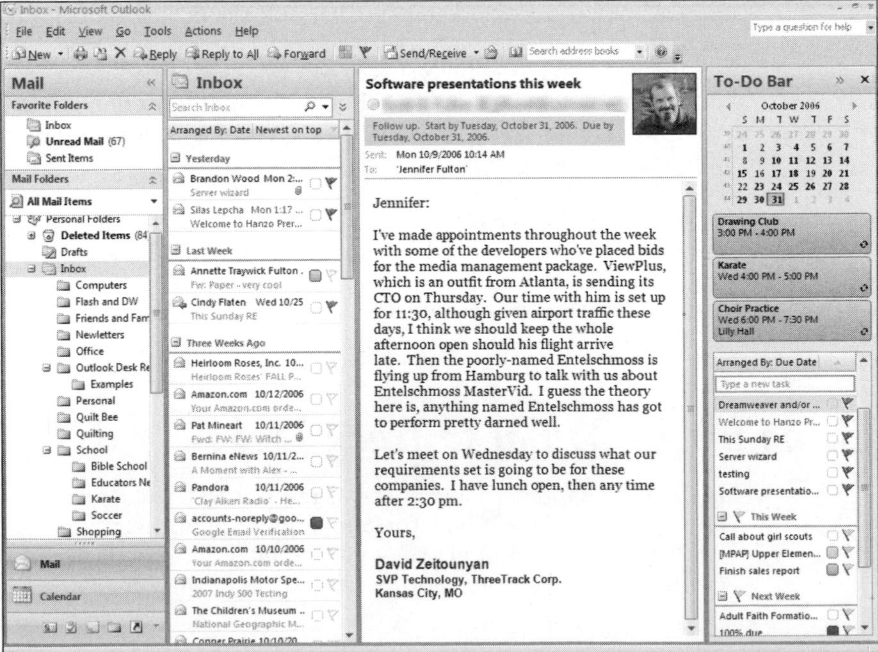

Figure 1-1: The handy dandy To-Do bar.

To automatically assign a flag to certain incoming messages, simply design a rule that describes the type of messages you want to flag. See Book IX, Chapter 2 for help.

Turning an incoming e-mail into a To-Do bar item

Because e-mails often contain requests for you to look up something, report on something, or to do some other something, Outlook makes it easy for you to turn an e-mail into a reminder to do that *something.* To flag an e-mail message for follow-up and add a reminder to the To-Do bar:

1. **Locate the e-mail you want to flag and either select it or open it (your choice).**
2. **Choose a flag associated with a particular due date.**

   If you're viewing the contents of the message in the Reading pane, right-click the flag column next to the message header and choose a due date from those listed. If the message is open, choose Message➪Options➪Follow Up and then select a flag from the list that appears. Your choices, shown in Figure 1-2, include:

   - **Today:** Sets the due date to today.
   - **Tomorrow:** Sets the due date to tomorrow.
   - **This Week:** Sets the due date to Friday of the current week (or the last day of your work week, if you've changed what you consider "work days" in Outlook — see Book IV, Chapter 5).
   - **Next Week:** Sets the due date to Friday of next week (or whatever the last day of your work week is currently set to).
   - **No Date:** Flags an item with an indefinite, get-to-it-when-you-can kind of date.

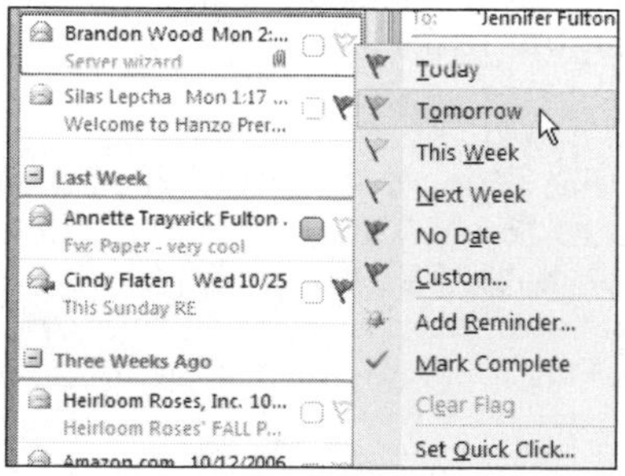

Figure 1-2: Plant your flag.

- **Custom:** Choose this option to flag the item with a unique date. When you choose Custom from the menu, the Custom dialog box appears, as shown in Figure 1-3. Normally when you flag an item such as a message, the Start Date is set to the date on which you set the flag, and the Due Date is based on the kind of flag you choose such as Tomorrow. Here you can choose any Start Date and Due Date you want. To be reminded about the task, select Reminder and set a reminder date and time. Click OK.

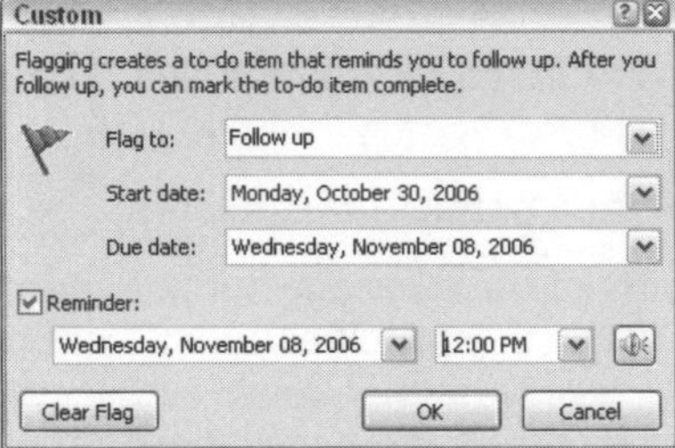

Figure 1-3: Customize the flag.

In Figure 1-2, I got a message from Brandon Wood asking me to change some network server settings, so I right-clicked the message header and chose Tomorrow from the list because I can't get to it today. As you can see in the figure, I already have two other messages flagged for some kind of follow up action, so I better get cracking on them!

After you flag a message, a colored flag appears in the flag column, next to the mail header. The flag's color is based on the due date you choose. In Figure 1-2, there are two messages with bright red flags because they represent things I need to get done today. After I choose the Tomorrow flag for the Brandon Wood message, a slightly less red flag appears next to its header. In addition, after you flag a message, a To-Do item is added to the appropriate group in the To-Do bar (for example, the Today group); the same item is added to the Daily Task List and the Tasks list.

You can flag an e-mail message quickly by clicking the flag column rather than right-clicking it. The flag that appears is controlled by the Quick Click Flag value, which is usually set to Today. Thus, if you click the flag column on a message's header, you'll probably be setting a Today flag and adding that message-task to the To-Do bar under the Today group. You can find out how to change the Quick Click Flag to some other value in the next section, "Setting the Quick Click Flag."

If you've used an older version of Outlook, then you may have noticed that something is gone. You used to be able to flag items and color the flags so that you could easily identify certain tasks. Well, don't pout — instead of coloring your flags, Outlook now gives you the ability to assign a color category (or several) to an item to identify its purpose. See Book VIII, Chapter 1 for help.

Turning a contact into a To-Do bar item

If you have a special contact you want to get in touch with, you can flag them. When you do, a To-Do item is added to the To-Do bar as a visual reminder to pick up the phone, e-mail, or stop by soon. The To-Do item also appears in the usual places — the Tasks list and the Daily Task List. The flag doesn't appear in Contacts in any view, but a textual reminder does appear in the InfoBar if you open the contact, as shown in Figure 1-4.

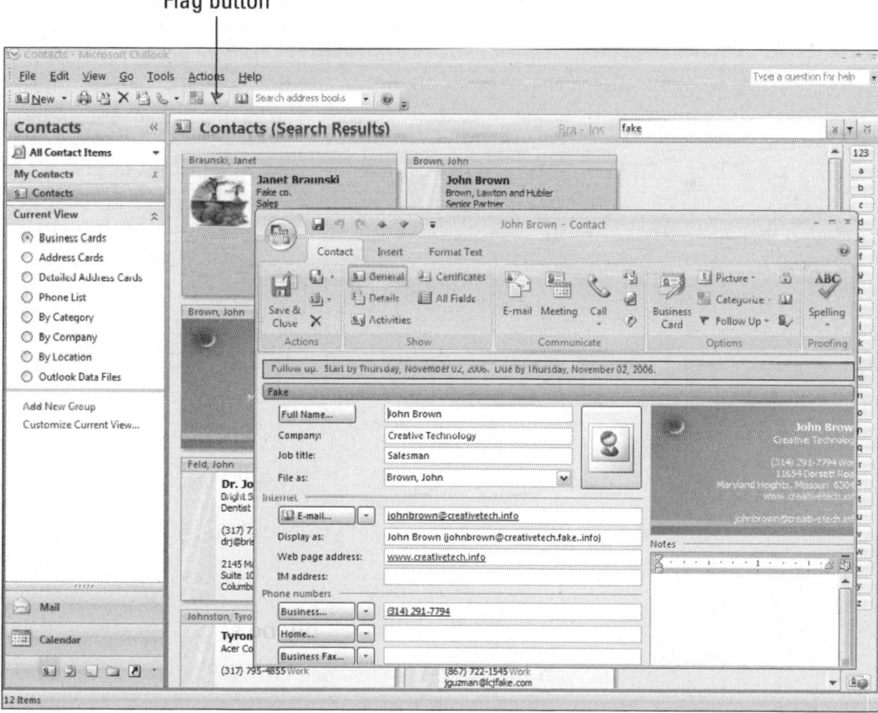

Figure 1-4: Gotta call soon.

To flag a contact and create a To-Do item:

1. **Select the contact you want to flag.**
2. **Choose a flag (due date).**

   Click the Flag button on the Standard toolbar (see Figure 1-4) and select a due date: Today, Tomorrow, This Week (actually, Friday of the current week, or the last work day), Next Week (that's Friday of the following week), or No Date (which flags the item but doesn't create a due date). Choose Custom to set your own specific date and add a reminder if you want. (See the earlier section, "Turning an incoming e-mail into a To-Do bar item," for a complete description of each due date type.)

   If the contact is open, choose Contact⇨Options⇨Follow Up and then select the flag you want to assign.

Now, a flag doesn't appear anywhere in Contacts, but you do see the flag if you double-click the contact itself — it's hiding in the InfoBar. The flag does appear in the usual places, however: the To-Do bar, Tasks list, and Daily Task List. If you contact your contact and you want to check that task off as completed, see "Marking a To-Do item as finito," later in this chapter. If you need to move the item to somewhere later in the Tasks list, change the flag: See "Changing the Flag You've Assigned."

If the To-Do bar happens to be displayed in Contacts, and it's currently sorted by either start or due date, you can just drag a contact and drop it on the To-Do list to create a To-Do item. For example, grab a contact you want to get in touch with by the end of the day, and drag the contact onto the To-Do bar and drop it in the Today group.

Setting the Quick Click Flag

You may have already discovered that in Mail, if you click the flag column next to an e-mail message rather than right-click it, you set an automatic flag for Today. That's because the Quick Click Flag, as Outlook calls it, is set to Today by default, meaning that if you want to quickly flag an item, Outlook obliges you and sets a flag for Today.

To change the Quick Click Flag value:

1. **Choose Actions⇨Follow Up⇨Set Quick Click.**

   The Set Quick Click dialog box jumps up. See Figure 1-5.
2. **Choose the value you want.**

   From the list box, choose the value you want Outlook to assign an item, should you quick click it.
3. **Click OK.**

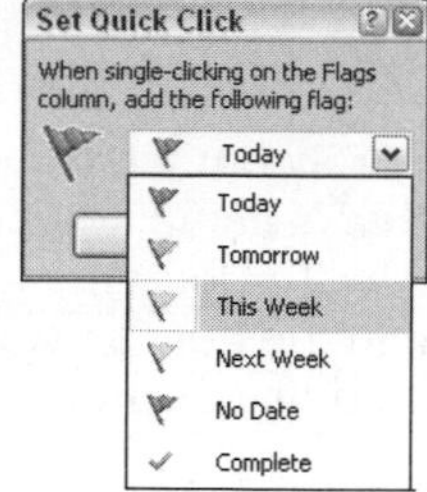

Figure 1-5: Just choose the flag you use most often.

As a reminder, to use Quick Click, you just click in the Flag column next to a message. Now, with contacts, there typically isn't a Flag column visible in any of the list styles that you can click. If you want to take advantage of Quick Click with contacts, you need to customize the view to add the Flag column. See Book VIII, Chapter 2 for help. Otherwise, you need to right-click a contact and assign a flag the old-fashioned way, as explained in the previous section.

Changing the Flag You've Assigned

If you don't happen to get your To-Do item done when you thought you would, it doesn't go away. For example, if you assigned a Today flag to an e-mail so that you'd remember to look something up and get back to a client, and you just didn't get that done, then the To-Do item continues to nag you from its place on the To-Do bar, appearing in tomorrow's Today list. It changes color, however, from ordinary black text to a more eye-catching-you-better-really-get-this-done red text. Red tasks appear above the black tasks originally scheduled for that day.

There's no need, however, to let Outlook get away with its aggressive red-texting behavior: If you know you really can't get something done on the day that flag says you need to and you want to reschedule it for another day, you can change the flag:

1. **Right-click the flag.**

   In the To-Do bar, Tasks list, or Daily Task List, right-click the flag for the To-Do item you want to change. If you're changing the flag for a message and you see the message in the message listing, you can right-click that flag instead.

2. **Choose a new flag setting.**

   Couldn't be simpler; just choose the flag you want to use from the menu that appears. For example, if you choose Next Week, the To-Do item is moved to the appropriate group in the To-Do bar (in this case, the Next Week group) and comes back to haunt you at that time.

Changing the Task Name on the To-Do Bar

When you create a To-Do item from a message or a contact, the message subject or contact name is used as the To-Do item's name. Chances are, that name may not be enough to tell you what it is the To-Do item means when you just glance at it. Fortunately, you can change the item's name in the To-Do bar, without affecting the actual message heading or contact name.

1. **Slowly click the To-Do item twice.**

   In the To-Do bar, click the item whose name you want to change and then click it again. If you double-click, you won't break anything, but you'll just open the item, which won't do a thing to help you change the item's name. So watch your trigger finger and just click the item two times slowly.

2. **Type a new name.**

   Edit the item name or simply drag over it to select it and then type a new name.

3. **Press Enter.**

   The new item's name appears in the listing.

Dealing With To-Do Items You've Finished or No Longer Want to Flag

After creating all your To-Do items, you're probably anxious to check one or two off your list. When a To-Do item is marked as complete, it's instantly removed from the To-Do bar. Check that one off! Now, if you haven't actually completed anything but you simply put the item on the To-Do list by accident, you can remove it just as easily, by simply removing the flag. You can also remove a To-Do item from the To-Do bar, but doing so also deletes the message or contact you may have used to create it.

Marking a To-Do item as finito

Marking off something on your To-Do list is somehow very satisfying. I sometimes add stupid stuff to my list such as "Get a cup of coffee" just so that I can experience the satisfaction of checking off something before 10 a.m. Anyway, if you've got something on your list done, you can easily check it off.

1. Locate the item you've completed.

You can finish off an item from the To-Do bar, the Tasks list, or the Daily Task List (which you find at the bottom of the Calendar, as shown in Figure 1-6). So change to the appropriate module and locate the item you want to mark off.

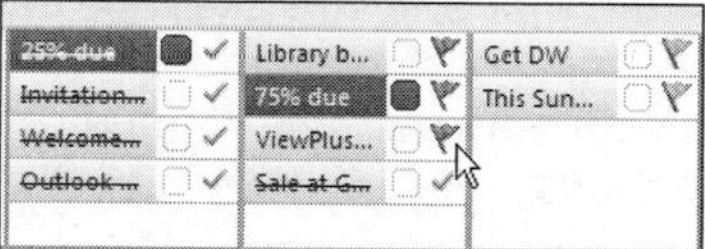

Figure 1-6: Check another one off.

2. Click the item's flag.

To mark an item as done, just click its flag. The item is immediately removed from the To-Do bar; from the Tasks list or the Daily Task List, the item is simply struck through, as shown in Figure 1-6.

If you just used the To-Do bar to check off an item, don't freak; if you created the To-Do item from a message or a contact, the message/contact doesn't go away, just the To-Do item. And to tell the truth, the To-Do item doesn't actually go away either. Nope, you can find it on the Daily Task List and the Tasks list — with a line struck through it, but still there nonetheless. To find out how to get items off the Tasks list, see Book VI, Chapter 2.

Removing a flag instead of marking it complete

Sometimes you just want to remove a flag, not because you got something done, but because the flag was set by accident or has simply lost its relevance. Or maybe you just want to remove a flag because it's become more annoying than helpful. To remove a flag:

1. Right-click the flag.

In the To-Do bar, Tasks list, or Daily Task List, right-click the flag you want to get rid of. If you happen to see the flag on a message header rather than in one of the To-Do lists, you can right-click that flag instead.

2. Choose Clear Flag.

From the menu that pops up, choose Clear Flag. The flag is removed, and the item is taken off the various To-Do lists: To-Do bar, Tasks list, and Daily Task List. The message or contact that may have been used to create the To-Do item simply returns to its normal, boring existence — it isn't deleted.

Deleting a To-Do item

Deleting a To-Do item gets rid of it permanently. This means it won't go off skulking to the Tasks list or the Daily Tasks list with simply a line struck through it — no, the item goes away permanently. Okay, maybe not exactly permanently, because it'll still be in the Deleted Items folder until you empty it, but you know what I mean. It's a goner.

In addition, if you delete a To-Do item this way, the message or contact you may have used to create the To-Do item goes away, too. Don't worry; you get a warning, so you can always talk your way out of it if you didn't actually mean to remove the message or contact, too.

To delete a To-Do item:

1. **Select the To-Do item.**

   In the To-Do bar, Tasks list, or Daily Task List, click the To-Do item you want to get rid of.

2. **Press Delete.**

   If the To-Do item was created from a message or a contact, rather than manually (as described in Book I, Chapter 2), then you see a warning asking whether you really, really, want to delete it because you'll be removing that message or contact, too.

3. **Click OK to remove the To-Do item and its associated Outlook item.**

Finding Flagged Messages

Yeah, it's easy to flag a message so that you can remember to follow it up. (If you forget how, see the earlier section, "Turning an incoming e-mail into a To-Do bar item" for help.) You can even set a flag on an e-mail you're sending to someone else, to remind you to follow up on it. (See Book III, Chapter 1 for help on that one.)

After flagging all these messages, however, you may simply want to corral them all. Want to find the incoming messages you've flagged for follow-up? No problem. Want to locate the outgoing messages you flagged before you sent them off? No worries. How about finding any responses you've sent to a flagged message? A little trickier, but still doable. Here's what you need to do:

- **To find all the messages you've flagged,** just click the For Follow Up folder, located in either the Search Folders or Favorite Folders section of the Navigation pane. Instantly, all flagged messages appear in a list, as shown in Figure 1-7. (For more on using Search Folders, see Book IX, Chapter 4.)

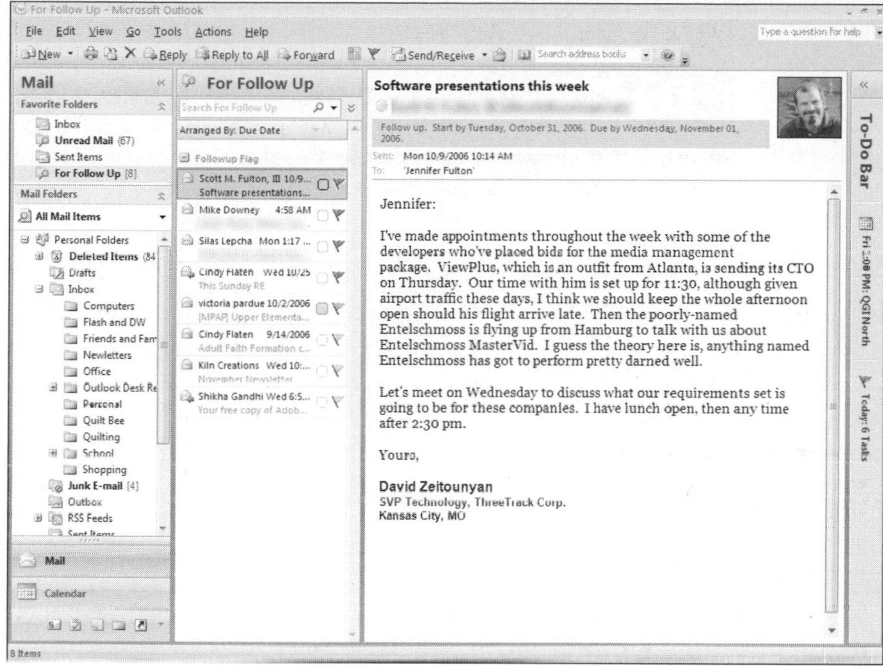

Figure 1-7: Time to follow up.

- **To find flagged messages in a specific folder,** change to that folder in Mail. Then click the Arranged By button at the top of the listing and choose either Flag: Start Date or Flag: Due Date. The messages are grouped together by the type of flag they have, including the ones that were flagged but are now completed.
- **To find messages you flagged for yourself before you sent them to other people,** change to the Sent Items folder and sort it by flags: click the Arranged By button at the top of the message list and choose either Flag: Start Date or Flag: Due Date. (Messages you sent with a flag for the recipient only is treated as an unflagged message because you didn't set a flag for yourself.)

If messages are currently being displayed in a list view such as Last Seven Days, you can sort messages by flag by just clicking the Flag column heading.

- **To find responses to messages you flagged,** first find either the message you flagged and sent or one of the responses to that message. Then click the InfoBar and choose Find Related Messages. Outlook searches for responses to the original message and displays them in its Advanced Find box, such as the one shown in Figure 1-8. To peek at one of the listed messages, simply double-click it.

Figure 1-8: Find related flags.

Customize the To-Do Bar

I don't know if you use the To-Do bar a lot, but frankly I find it almost as indispensable as coffee. For example, if I haven't had a second cup of coffee yet, I'm constantly glancing over there to see what day it is or what month. Okay, maybe I already know (despite the lack of caffeine in my system), but I do find that I refer to the To-Do bar constantly, to remind me of upcoming appointments and meetings, and things I better get done soon (especially if I want to keep my job and my ability to buy more coffee).

If you're a To-Do bar devotee like me, then you should customize it so that it works and acts exactly the way you want it to:

- **To show more or less tasks and To-Do items,** you actually hide or reduce the size of the other To-Do bar parts: the Date Navigator or the Appointments section.
- **To hide one of the To-Do bar parts,** right-click the To-Do bar title bar and select Date Navigator, Appointments, or Tasks list to remove that section. If you turn off the Tasks list, for example, more appointments/meetings appear.
- **To adjust the width of the To-Do bar,** just position the mouse pointer over its left edge and drag to the left to make the To-Do bar wider and the viewing area smaller. If you make the To-Do bar wide enough, two months appear in the Date Navigator area.

✦ **Show more than one month on the Date Navigator without making the To-Do bar fatter** by choosing View➪To-Do Bar➪Options. The To-Do Bar Options dialog box, shown in Figure 1-9, appears. Type the number of months you want displayed vertically down the To-Do bar in the Number of Month Rows box. Click OK.

Figure 1-9: Exercise your options.

✦ **Show more appointments or meetings** by choosing View➪To-Do Bar➪Options. In the To-Do Bar Options dialog box, change the value in the Number of Appointments box and click OK (refer to Figure 1-9).

✦ **Rearrange tasks and To-Do items** by dragging them up or down the Tasks list area on the To-Do bar and dropping them where you want them. For example, if you've got several To-Do items staring you in the face for Today, you can rearrange them by priority or the order in which you hope to get them done. As you drag, a red line and a small diamond on the left guide you so that you know where the item will appear if you drop it right then, as shown in Figure 1-10. By the way, if you drag an item into a different group (moving it from Today to Tomorrow, for example), the item's flag automatically changes.

✦ **Sort your tasks and To-Do items by** clicking the Arranged By button at the top of the Tasks list on the To-Do bar and choosing a sort option. Normally, items are sorted by due date, but you can choose Start Date, Categories, Folder, Type (which separates the To-Do items from the tasks), or Importance. If you click Custom, you can create your own unique sort. See Book IX, Chapter 1 for help with that one.

When you create a task (as opposed to a simple To-Do item), you can set a priority to that task, which will hopefully light a fire under you when the time comes. Anyway, assuming that you've prioritized your tasks, you can sort the To-Do bar by priority (Importance).

✦ **Show completed items on the To-Do bar.** As you know, when you check off a task or a To-Do item, it's removed from the To-Do bar, although it still appears on the Daily Task List and the Tasks list with a line struck through it to show that it's done. You can keep completed items on the To-Do bar if they provide some sense of closure for you. Start by clicking the Arranged By button at the top of the Tasks list area. Choose Custom➪Filter➪Advanced➪Clear All. Click OK twice to return to the main Outlook screen.

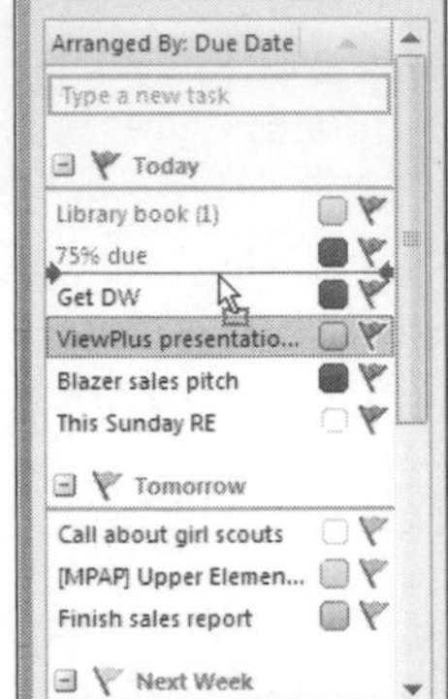

Figure 1-10: Rearrange your tasks.

Be sure you want to show completed tasks on the To-Do bar because undoing it is rather complicated. To hide completed tasks and To-Do items once again, you need to click the Arranged By button and choose Custom⇨Filter⇨Advanced⇨Field⇨All Task Fields⇨Date Completed. Set the Condition to Does Not Exist and click Add to List to add the condition. Choose Field⇨All Task Fields⇨Date Completed again and set the Condition to On or After. Set the Value to Today and then click Add to List again. Two conditions set, two more to go: Choose Field⇨All Mail Fields⇨Flag Completed Date. Set the Condition to Does Not Exist and click Add to List to add this third condition. Choose Field⇨All Mail Fields⇨Flag Completed Date. Set the Condition to On or After and set the Value to Today. Choose Add to List to add this fourth and final condition. Whew! Click OK twice and vow never to display completed items again.

✦ **Change the color of an overdue item.** When an item is past its Due Date, it appears on the To-Do bar in a red font. If you prefer some other color to alert you when an item's past due, click the Arranged By button at the top of the Tasks list area and choose Custom⇨Automatic Formatting. Choose Overdue Tasks and click the Font button. Choose the Color you want and click OK three times. This action does not, by the way, change the color of overdue items on the Daily Task List or the Tasks list.

Creating a Task Using the Daily Task List in the Calendar

If you display your appointments, meetings, and events in the Calendar using Day or Week view, a Daily Task List appears at the bottom of the viewing area. The tasks and To-Do items appear on the day on which they are due, unless of course you don't get them done. In that case, the items move to the next day and appear in frantic-get-it-done red text. You can use the Daily Task List to create a quick, non-detailed task (to learn how to create a more complete task, see Book VI, Chapter 2):

1. **Change to Day or Week view.**

   In the Calendar, change to Day or Week view by choosing View⇨Current View⇨Day/Week/Month. Then click either the Day or Month tab at the top of the viewing area.

   REMEMBER

   If the Daily Task List isn't visible for some reason, choose View⇨Daily Task List⇨Normal.

2. **Display the day on which you want to add a task.**

   You want to see the day on which the task is due, so scroll if needed until you can see it.

3. **Add the task.**

   Click an open area within the Daily Task List for the day on which you want to add the task. A little bubble appears; type a name for the task, as shown in Figure 1-11, and press Enter.

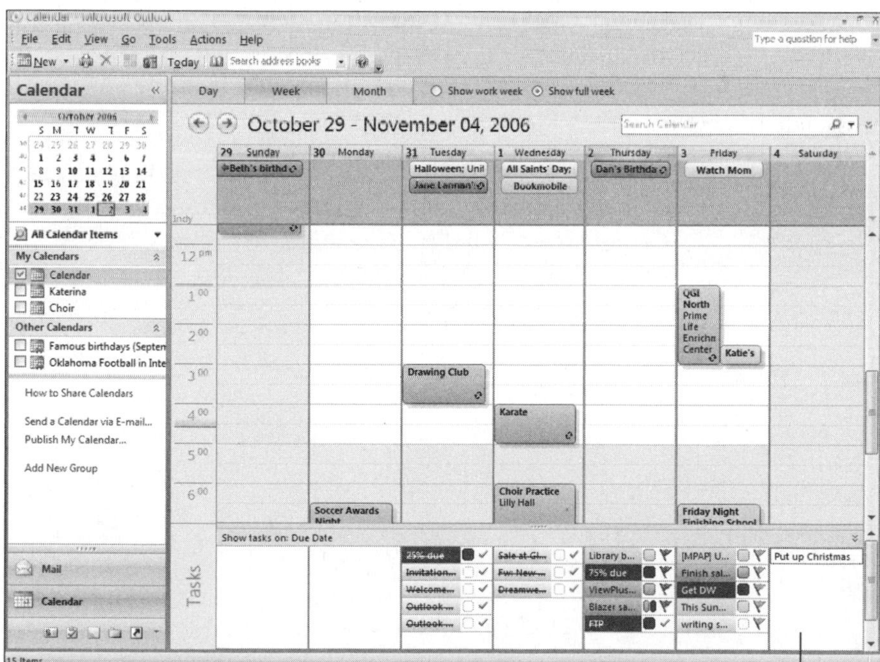

Figure 1-11: Add a new task to your Calendar.

Click and type in this area to add a new task for that day

If you need to change a task or To-Do item to a different day, you can just drag and drop it within the Daily Task List. You can also rearrange the order in which items are displayed for a single day by dragging and dropping them within that day.

You can make other changes to the Daily Task List as well. For example, you can temporarily minimize it by choosing View➪Daily Task List➪Minimized or by simply dragging the top border of the Daily Task List downward. When the Daily Task List is minimized, Outlook displays the total number of tasks and the number of completed ones on a bar at the bottom of the Outlook window so you'll still know that you have tasks due that day. To restore the list, choose View➪Daily Task List➪Normal or drag the top border of the list back up.

Now, you may find it odd, but completed tasks continue to appear on the Daily Task List, even after you check them off. Of course, they appear below the unfinished tasks so that they don't make it hard for you to continue to see the things you need to get done. If you'd rather get rid of the tasks you've completed so that they stop cluttering up the Daily Task List, choose View➪Daily Task List➪Arrange By➪Show Completed Tasks to turn that option off (uncheck it).

The tasks and To-Do items on the Daily Task List appear on the day on which they are due, unless they don't get done, in which case they appear on the next day. These items keep on moving onto the next day until you get them done. If you have multiple tasks or To-Do items on a single day, they are arranged by original due date, meaning that the things you didn't get done yesterday appear at the top of the list. To arrange items by start date, choose View➪Daily Task List➪Arrange By➪By Start Date.

Chapter 2: Dealing with More Complex Tasks

In This Chapter

- Creating tasks with detailed information
- Turning tasks into appointments and e-mails into tasks
- Linking tasks to contacts
- Making a task repeat
- Looking at your Tasks list

In Book VI, Chapter 1, you find out how to create quick-just-make-a-note-of-that To-Do items from e-mails, contacts, or scratch. To-do items are real handy and quick to make. But they aren't so hot when you have more information you need to record on a task, such as its current status, priority, and the amount of work that's complete. With a task, you can record not only all this info, but you can also do fancy stuff like make the task recur at regular intervals, or reassign the task to someone else on your staff while still maintaining some control. You can also set a reminder to complete the task on time, just like the reminders you set for appointments, meetings, and events. If you want to create tasks that have realized their full potential, read on.

Creating a Detailed Task

If you want to keep track of the little details surrounding something you've got to get done, you need to create a task and not a To-Do item. (For more on To-Do items, see the previous chapter.)

You can create a task from any module. Here's what you need to do:

1. **Choose File⇨New⇨Task.**

   If you happen to be in Tasks, you can just click that ol' New button on the Standard toolbar. The Task form appears, as shown in Figure 2-1.

2. **Type a description for the task in the Subject box and choose a Due Date.**

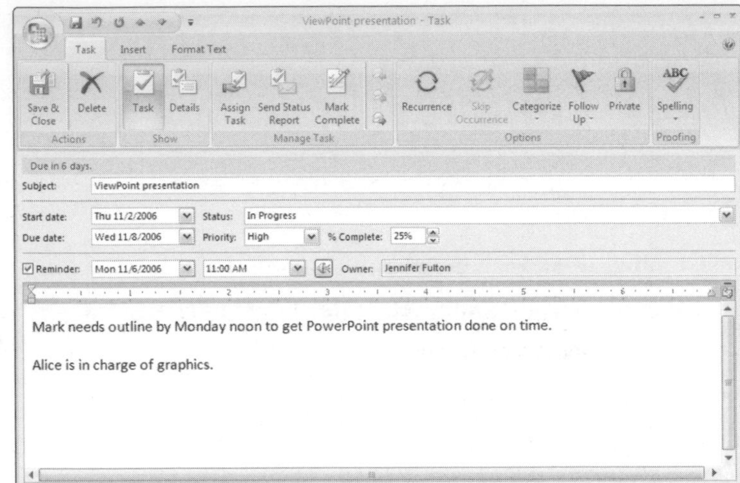

Figure 2-1: Creating a detailed task.

3. **Fill in the information you want to track:**

   - If you've started the task, choose a Start Date and change the Status. You may also want to make a note of how much you've done by changing the % Complete.

     You can't update the % Complete without changing the Status first. If you change the Status to Completed, the % Complete becomes 100 automatically. If you choose In Progress as a Status, you can enter any value below 100; if the task was Deferred or if you're Waiting on Someone Else, you can enter any value from 0 to 100.

     You can type words in the date boxes instead of selecting an actual date. For example, you can type **today** or **tomorrow**, or **three days from now**. Some holidays are recognized as well, such as **Fourth of July, New Year's Eve,** or **Christmas.**

   - **If this task is important,** you can select High from the Priority list; select Low to remind you that although this task has a due date, you may be able to let it slide a little.
   - **To prevent you from forgetting the task's due date,** choose Reminder and select a date.
   - **To group this task with similar ones,** assign it a category or two. Assuming that you've set up categories (see Book VIII, Chapter 1 for help if you haven't), select as many as you like for this task by choosing them one at a time from the Task⇨Options⇨Categorize list.
   - **To record any details,** type them in the large notes section. Flip over to the Format Text tab to format the text if you like. You can insert

related files or attach Outlook items such as a contact record. See Book II, Chapter 3 for the lowdown on inserting files and such.

4. **To record even more details about a task, choose Task⇨Show⇨Details.**

   The Details tab of the Task form, shown in Figure 2-2, appears.

   - **To track the amount of work you've done on this task so far**, enter the number of hours in general terms in the Total Work box. If you prefer to mark the time in days, weeks, or months, just type that instead, such as **3 days** or **2 weeks**.
   - **If you're keeping track of this information because it's client-related,** enter the specific billable hours in the Actual Work box. Enter any other billing info in the Billing Information box. Type the client or company name in the Company box.
   - **If you're going to be reimbursed for the number of miles you've driven** to complete this task, enter the number of miles you've driven so far in the Mileage box.

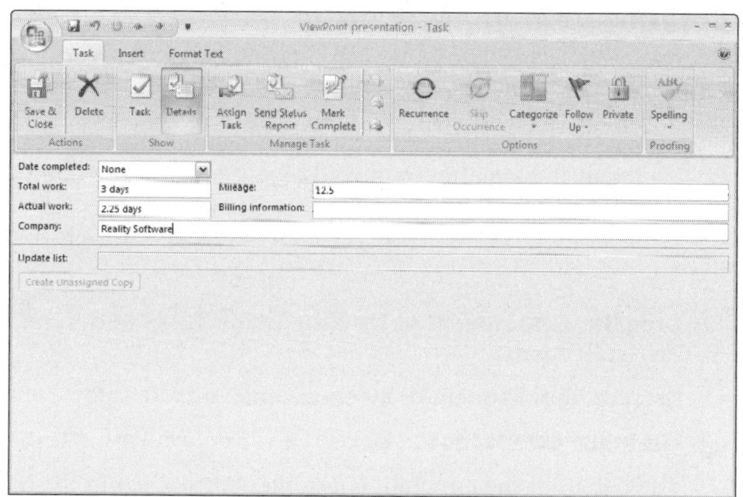

Figure 2-2: It's all in the details.

5. **If you're done, choose Task⇨Actions⇨Save & Close.**

   But if this task is one that happens again and again at some kind of regular interval, you can easily copy it. (See the upcoming section "Scheduling a Recurring Task.")

To make changes to a task you've saved, just double-click it to open it again. You can do that from the Tasks list, Daily Task List, or the To-Do bar.

Turning an e-mail into a task

You can easily turn an e-mail message into a To-Do item by simply flagging it, as explained in Book VI, Chapter 1. A To-Do item is fine if all you need is a simple reminder. But if you want something more detailed, you should create a task. You don't need to start from scratch, however — not if you have an e-mail message to provide some of the details.

To create a task from an e-mail:

1. **Drag the message to the Tasks button in the Navigation pane.**

   Drop the message, and a new Task form appears.

2. **Complete details concerning the task.**

   The text of the e-mail message appears in the Notes section; the message's subject becomes the Subject of the task. Choose a Due Date and set other options.

3. **Choose Task⇨Actions⇨Save & Close to save the task.**

Linking an appointment or meeting to a task

You may want to link a task to an appointment (or vice versa) for several reasons, although I can't think of a one. No, just kidding. Actually, I often set up appointments or meetings with clients or colleagues and then think of several things I better do before that appointment or meeting happens. So for me, it's handy to have the two linked together.

To use an existing appointment or meeting to create a task, follow these steps:

1. **Drag the appointment or meeting to the Tasks button on the Navigation pane.**

   Drop the appointment or meeting, and a new Task form appears.

2. **Fill in the details for the task.**

   The details of the appointment or meeting appear in the Notes section of the task; the subject of the appointment or meeting is used as the Subject of the task. Choose a Due Date and set other options as you like.

3. **Choose Task⇨Actions⇨Save & Close to save the task.**

Which happened first, the chicken or the egg? If you created your task first, such as creating a sales demo or a department report, only to later schedule a meeting or appointment in which to present it, you can still use the existing task to create the appointment/meeting you need:

1. **Drag the task onto the Calendars button on the Navigation pane.**

   A new Appointment form appears.

2. **Enter the details for the appointment.**

   The details of the task appear in the Notes section; the message's subject becomes the Subject of the appointment. Choose a Start Time and date, and an End Time and date. Set other options as well. To turn this appointment into a meeting, choose Appointment⇨Actions⇨Invite Attendees. (See Book IV, Chapter 4 for help in creating meetings.)

3. **When you're through adding the details of your appointment or meeting, click the Save & Close button to it.**

Scheduling a Recurring Task

Some tasks just keep on giving. You finish them once, and they return the next day, bearing gifts of multiple reports, endless notes, and recurring demands on your time. If you have a task you need to complete on a regular basis, such as reviewing a sales report and preparing a chart analyzing its data, then there's no reason you have to manually copy it over and over again in your Tasks list. Instead, you can set up the parameters that make it recur.

If you're still in the process of creating the task, fine; otherwise, open the task (by double-clicking it) so you can make changes. In the Task form, follow these steps:

1. **Choose Task⇨Options⇨Recurrence.**

   The Task Recurrence dialog box appears, as shown in Figure 2-3.

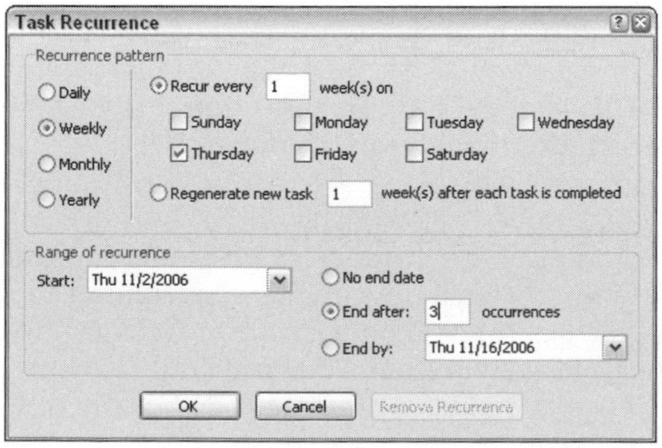

Figure 2-3: Can you repeat that?

2. **Select recurrence frequency.**

   Select the basic interval at which you want task to repeat: Daily, Weekly, Monthly, or Yearly.

3. **Set recurrence options.**

   Depending on the frequency you selected in Step 2, a set of options appears on the right. Set those options to match the pattern of repetition.

   - **Daily:** Choose between repeating every day, every other day, and so on or repeating every weekday and skipping weekends.

     There's one more choice to make after you choose the Daily pattern. Normally, you want the task to recur at whatever pattern you select, whether or not you get each task done on time. If you want Outlook to create a new copy of the task only after the previous one is completed, then select the Regenerate New Task XX Day(s) After Each Task Is Completed option and type an interval in the box provided. When you choose this option, the next recurrence is depends on the date on which you get the previous task done.

   - **Weekly:** Choose how often the item recurs: weekly, every other week, or whatever. Then choose the day on which that happens: Monday, Tuesday, or whatever. To create a new copy of the task only after the previous task is completed, choose the Regenerate New Task XX Week(s) After Each Task Is Completed option and choose the interval you want (such as 2 weeks after the previous task was completed).

   - **Monthly:** Here, you have two choices. You can choose a particular day of the month (or every so many months) such as the 10th of every third month. Or you can choose the first, second, third, fourth, or last weekday of every month or so, such as the second Thursday of every other month. Finally, you can choose to Regenerate New Task XX Month(s) After Each Task Is Completed.

   - **Yearly:** Like Monthly, you can either select a particular date such as October 16, or a particular day within a certain month, such as the last Friday of November. You can also choose to Regenerate New Task XX Year(s) After Each Task Is Completed.

4. **Set limits.**

   After setting the pattern of recurrence, set its limit. For example, does the task repeat forever? (Well, only if you're Sisyphus.) Or does it recur so many times (like five times) and then stop? Or does it repeat until the end of November and then no more? Set the limit of recurrence using the options in the Range of Recurrence area at the bottom of the dialog box.

5. **Click OK.**

After you make a task recur, the pattern you established appears in the task's InfoBar. Click Save & Close to save the task and its repeating pattern. Recurring tasks appear in the Tasks list with a special Recurrence icon. The task only appears once in the Tasks list, however. When you mark the first task complete or when its due date passes, the next occurrence of the task appears in the list, like magic, only without the black hat and white doves.

To skip one occurrence of a recurring task, open it and choose Task⇨Options⇨Skip Occurrence. To end a task recurrence, open the task and choose Task⇨Options⇨Recurrence and click Remove Recurrence.

Working with Tasks

I must confess; sometimes when I switch over to the Tasks module, it can be quite overwhelming. Not only do I see an almost endless list of things I better get done soon, but hey, what's that doing there? For reasons I can't fathom, you also see all those tasks you've already gotten done. Frankly, I don't need the list to be any longer, but maybe you like seeing all the stuff you've ever done. To each his own.

Fortunately, you can do a number of things to make your Tasks list more user-friendly. For starters, you can

✦ **Change your view:** One way to get rid of those completed tasks and yet not actually remove them is to change to the Active Tasks view by clicking that option in the Navigation pane, as shown in Figure 2-4. Here, active tasks mean things you're still working on and haven't completed yet. This step should shorten your list considerably. By the way, you can also use several other views that don't show completed tasks: Next Seven Days, Overdue Tasks, and To-Do List. (The To-Do List is a rather special view, the upcoming section, "Using To-Do List view," discusses it in depth.)

If you like one of the other views better, such as Simple List or By Category, and you don't want the completed tasks showing up, you can customize the view so that they don't appear. See Book VIII, Chapter 2 for help.

✦ **Clear the flag:** You can only do this for a To-Do item that was created from an e-mail message or a contact. Anyway, clearing the flag (removing it, basically) takes the item off the Tasks list for obvious reasons. You may not want to take this route, though, if you flagged the message or contact with the intention of being able to locate it months later.

✦ **Delete the task:** This step works pretty well, dumping those completed tasks in the trash. However, if you created a To-Do item using a message or contact, then removing the completed To-Do item from your Tasks list by deleting it also removes the associated message/contact. Probably not the best idea, but hey, you're done with it, right? So why not delete it?

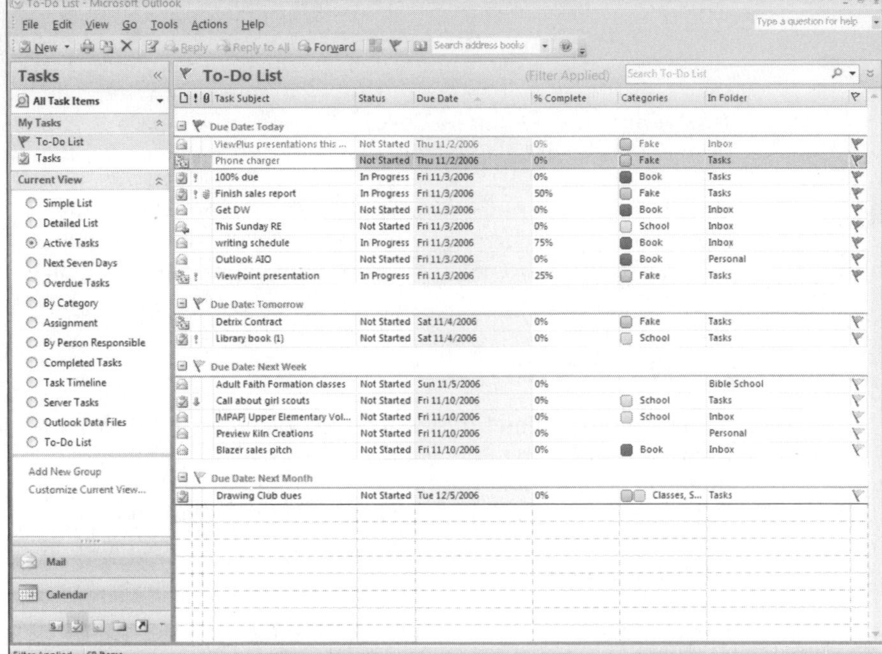

Figure 2-4: Why stare at a bunch of completed tasks?

- **Change the color of completed tasks:** Frankly, I find the gray Outlook uses for completed tasks to be quite fine and unnoticeable. But maybe you want to notice them more, or maybe your eyes are just naturally attracted to gray and won't notice blue or some other color as much. So, to change the color of completed tasks, choose Tools⇨Options⇨Task Options and then choose a color from the Completed Task Color list. Click OK twice.

Changing the color of overdue tasks

When a task isn't completed by its due date, Outlook gets real angry and changes the task text to red, in a pitiful attempt to get you to sit down, be quiet, and get the task done already. Okay, maybe it's not so pitiful, because frankly red makes me anxious and actually does make me want to do that task so it'll stop haunting me. But what if red's your favorite color? What if you wait until a task is overdue to complete it, just so that you get to see it change color first? What about that, eh, Outlook?

I guess you can continue to ignore the red color of overdue tasks, or you can change it to a color that'll prompt you to do something, like finish the silly thing. To change the color of overdue tasks on the Tasks list:

1. **Choose Tools⇨Options⇨Task Options.**

   The Task Options dialog box appears, as shown in Figure 2-5.

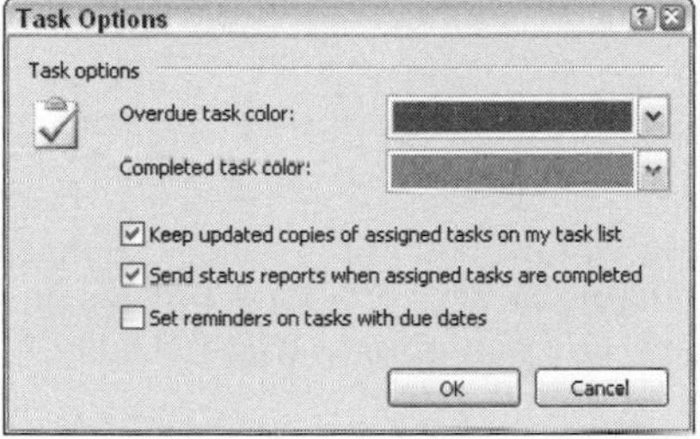

Figure 2-5: Change how overdue a task looks.

2. **Choose the overdue color.**

   Open the Overdue Task Color list and choose the color you want to use to mark tasks not completed on time.

3. **Click OK twice.**

This color change, by the way, affects only tasks and To-Do items as they appear on the Tasks list. You can't change the color of overdue tasks in the Daily Task List, which appears in the Calendar. You can, however, change the color of the tasks and To-Do items on the To-Do bar, but not in the manner shown here. See Book VI, Chapter 1.

Sorting and rearranging tasks

You can also sort and rearrange your tasks. To sort tasks in a list view, simply click the heading above the column you want to use to sort. For example, click the Status column to sort by that. For more tips on sorting a list view, see Book VIII, Chapter 1.

Tasks that have the same due date may appear in a rather random order in the listing, typically by the date on which they were created. However, there's no reason why you can't rearrange the listing, in order to show the tasks in whatever order that's useful for you. Just drag and drop tasks to rearrange their order. Doing so also rearranges those tasks on the To-Do bar and the Daily Task List so that you don't have to spend the time you should be using to complete tasks in simply rearranging them.

Wanna keep certain tasks together? One way is to give them the same category, and then use By Category view. Another way is to assign the tasks the same Priority, and then sort by the Priority column in whatever view you like.

Updating what you've done

To make changes to a task so that you can see where you stand at a glance, double-click it, make changes to the Task form that appears, and click the Save & Close button as you normally would. To update the progress you've done on a task, double-click the task and change what applies:

- **Choose Task⇨Show⇨Task,** and you can update the Status and % Complete.
- **Choose Task⇨Show⇨Details,** and you can update the amount of Total Work and Actual Work (billable hours) you've spent on the task. If you get reimbursed for Mileage, you can update that as well.

Marking a task as complete

Nothing is quite as satisfying as getting something done, except maybe checking it off your impossibly long list of things to do. And I guess the folks at Microsoft understand, because Outlook provides lots of ways in which you can mark off a task once you get it done:

- **Click in the Flag column** next to the task, in either the Tasks list, the Daily Task List, or the To-Do bar. The flag changes to a check mark to indicate that the task is done. Completed tasks are removed from the To-Do bar.
- **Click in the Complete column** next to the task in the Tasks list. The column isn't marked as Complete, but a small check box appears, as shown in Figure 2-6.

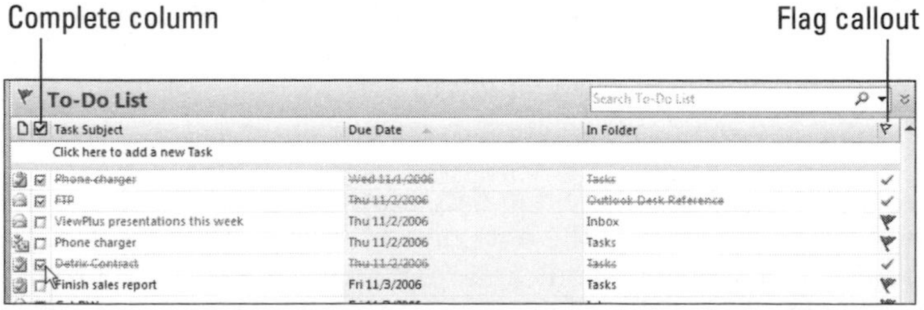

Complete column

Flag callout

Figure 2-6: Complete your task.

- **Right-click a task** and choose Mark Complete from the menu that appears. You can do this from the Tasks list, Daily Task List, or To-Do bar. Again, completed tasks are marked with a check mark.
- **Update the % Complete to 100.** You can do this from many of the list views in Tasks, or if the % Complete column isn't visible in the current view, you can just open the task and change it there.

Using To-Do List view

The Tasks list offers many different arrangements for your viewing pleasure. By and large, they're all list views that offer a particular perspective, such as organizing tasks by category, or listing only the tasks that are due in the next seven days. One view, however, is uniquely different because it looks a whole lot like the default Mail view, and that's To-Do List view, shown in Figure 2-7.

There's nothing particularly alarming about To-Do List view, but because it's the only one that's substantially different, I thought I'd talk about it. When you change to To-Do List view, a list of active (noncompleted) tasks is presented in a column, with a Reading pane on the right, just like in Messages view in Mail. Not surprisingly, the whole thing works just like Messages view; click a task or To-Do item on the left, and its details appear on the right. So if you were wondering how much work you've done on a particular task, you can click it and check out its % Complete value.

This view is also pretty nifty if you routinely create tasks and To-Do items from other Outlook items such as messages, contacts, and appointments. As you know, when you use an Outlook item as the basis for a new task or To-Do item, the contents of that Outlook item are copied to the new task or To-Do item's notes section. And that's where you can quickly scan it, if you use the To-Do List view.

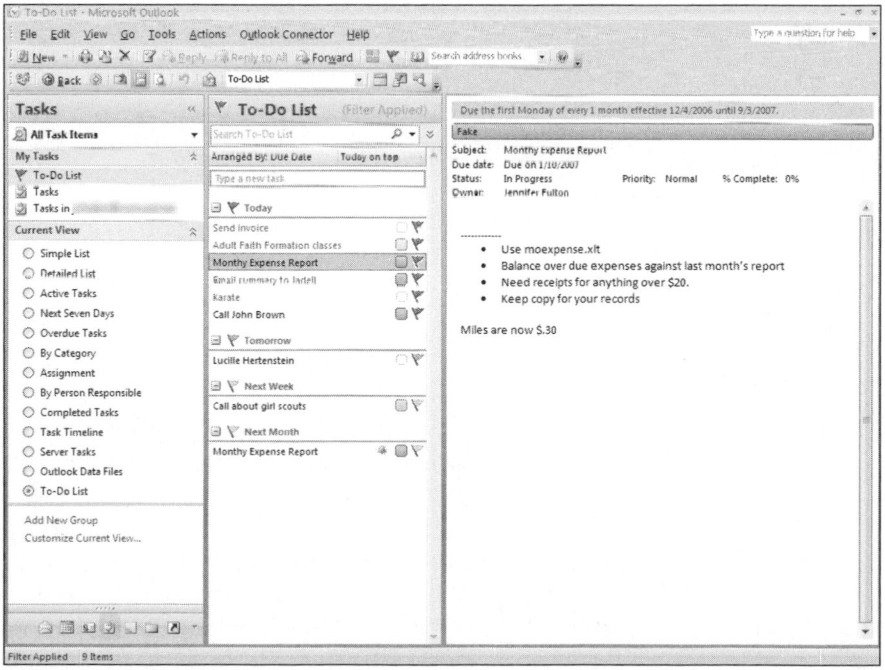

Figure 2-7: To-Do or not to do?

Chapter 3: Spreading the Joy: Task Assignments

In This Chapter

- **Assigning tasks to others**
- **Receiving progress reports on a reassigned task**
- **Dealing with tasks someone wants to reassign to you**
- **Viewing somebody else's tasks**

Lately, it seems like everybody has lots to do. Whether it's writing a report, attending a conference, viewing a new product presentation, or wooing a new client, there's always work to be done. Sometimes, no matter how good a scheduler you are, time simply gets away from you. At such times, it's nice to know that you have co-workers to help share the load, provided you come bearing a good enough bribe.

Because Outlook comes equipped with a nice task master, it should be no surprise that it also includes a nice task delegator as well. With Outlook, you can send requests to colleagues to take on a task — basically, reassigning the task to them. Of course, what goes around comes around, as they can say, "Right back at ya!" and reassign tasks to you, too. Along the way, both of you can receive regular status reports that let you know just how lousy both of you are at getting anything accomplished.

In addition, just like your other Outlook folders, you can share your Tasks list. You may want to do so if you have a micromanager boss who likes to control every minute of your day, of if you simply want to prove to her that you really are truly busy right now. In any case, this chapter shows you how to reassign tasks, accept reassignments, and share your Tasks list.

Assigning a Task to Someone Else

When needed — or hey, whenever you feel like it — you can reassign one of your tasks to someone else. At least, you can try. The way it works is this: You create a task, make little progress, and then wake up one day with the brilliant plan of passing it on to someone else before someone asks you whether you've finished working on it yet. So you send out a task reassignment, which comes in the form of an e-mail message. Here begins a game I call "Pass the Hot Potato."

You can reassign tasks to colleagues, or anyone for that matter, even if you're not on an Exchange network. The process simply happens via e-mail rather than invisibly. Even automatic updates occur, but through e-mail. That is, if you request to be kept updated on a task, and someone changes the status of a task or the amount of work completed, you get an e-mail updating you. When you open that e-mail, your copy of the task gets updated automatically.

The recipient of your joy opens the e-mail and gets the potato, which in this game is ownership of the task. Yep, whether he or she wants it, he or she is now the task's owner. And only the owner of a task can make changes to it, so watch the potato as we continue, because potato-ownership is important when it comes to task management.

As the current potato guy, the recipient can decide to either accept or decline your kindness, depending on his mood. He can also try reassigning the task to someone else, in which case that someone else becomes the potato owner. Should he accept the task, he becomes the task's permanent owner, and the task is placed on his Tasks list. Should he decline, the task gets sent back to you, and you become the potato owner once again, although you can't actually update the task until you officially reclaim it. Don't worry; reclaiming a task is simple, but if you don't want to finish the task yourself, you can boot that task over to the next poor sap on your list without reclaiming it.

Now, back to that hot potato. As I mentioned earlier, the owner of a task is the only one that can update it. When a task is updated, Outlook hunts down all previous potato owners of the task, all the way back to the task originator, and updates all copies of the task on their system. When the task is finally completed, a status report is sent to all the prior owners.

To reassign a task:

1. **Create the task request.**

   To do so:

   - **If you haven't created the task yet,** choose File⇨New⇨Task Request.
   - **If you've already created a task you want to reassign,** open the task and choose Task⇨Manage Task⇨Assign Task.

   A Task Request form appears, as shown in Figure 3-1.

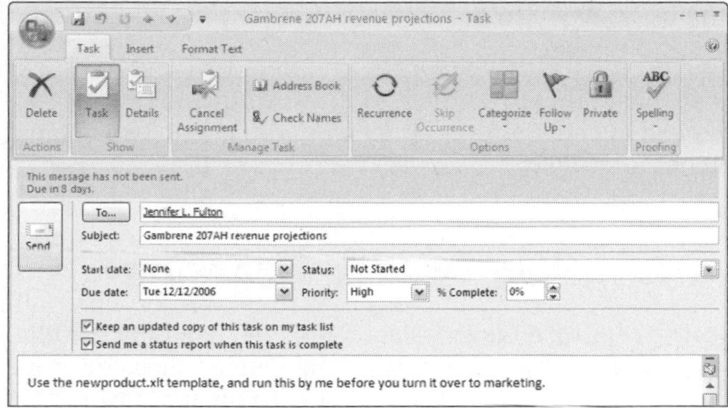

Figure 3-1: Please take this task.

2. **Address the request.**

   In the To box, enter the e-mail address of the person or persons to whom you want to assign the task. The Subject shows the name of the task; if it's a new task, type the name of the task in the Subject box.

   WARNING!

   Although you can assign the same task to more than one person, if you do, you aren't automatically updated on its status. Instead of assigning one task to several people, you may want to consider breaking up a large job into smaller, more specific, tasks and assigning those smaller tasks to different people.

3. **Set task options.**

   Set the Due Date for the task, and if the task is already underway, update its Status, % Complete, and Start Date if needed.

   If you want to stay updated on the task status, be sure to select the Keep an Updated Copy of This Task on My Task List and the Send Me a Status Report When This Task Is Complete options.

   If you don't want to be bothered so much, but you want to know when the task is finally finished, turn off the first option.

   You can make a new task recurring, prior to assigning it to someone else. See Book VI, Chapter 2 for help.

   If this is a recurring task, the task remains in your Tasks list, even if you don't select the Keep an Updated Copy of This Task on My Task List option. If you select the Send Me a Status Report When This Task Is Complete option, you get updates when each occurrence of the task is finished.

4. **Send the task request.**

   You can type a message for the recipient if you want. Click Send to send the request. There's nothing to do now but wait and see whether your recipient accepts or not. Either way, you get an e-mail message telling you her intentions.

Reclaiming a Task You Tried to Reassign

After you've sent off a task reassignment, you can only twiddle your thumbs until you hear back from the victim (recipient). Unless or until he officially rejects the task, the recipient retains potato-ownership, and there ain't nuttin' you can do abou' it. Well, okay, if needed, if the guy is unavailable, clueless, or otherwise indecisive and simply can't be coaxed into at least declining the task so that you can get the potato back, you can give up on him entirely and create a copy of the task that you can either finish yourself or attempt to reassign to someone else at the bottom of your like-list. See the sidebar "What to do when a task gets lost in Neverland" for help.

When the recipient chooses to accept or decline your kind invitation to do more work, you receive an e-mail message. If the recipient declines, the task in your Tasks list changes to bold to alert you, just like an incoming message is bold to indicate that it's unread. Open either one, and the task and the message return to normal text. The icon for the task still looks like a handout: a hand holding a task. Click the task to view the response in the Reading pane.

Again, if your task request is rejected, and you want to reassign the task to someone else, you don't have to officially reclaim it. See "Assigning a Task to Someone Else" for how-to's. If you need to update the task before passing it on, or you want to simply reclaim a task you tried reassigning that was ultimately rejected, follow these steps instead:

1. **Open the original task request.**

   You can find it hanging out in your Sent Items folder. When it opens, the task displays its information, but not in changeable form. In addition, you see extra buttons, as shown in Figure 3-2.

2. **Choose Task⇨Manage Task⇨Return to Task List.**

   The task is displayed in regular form, which means that you can update its Status, Start Date, and so on.

3. **Choose Task⇨Actions⇨Save & Close.**

   The task is added back to the Tasks list, with a normal task icon (the simple check mark).

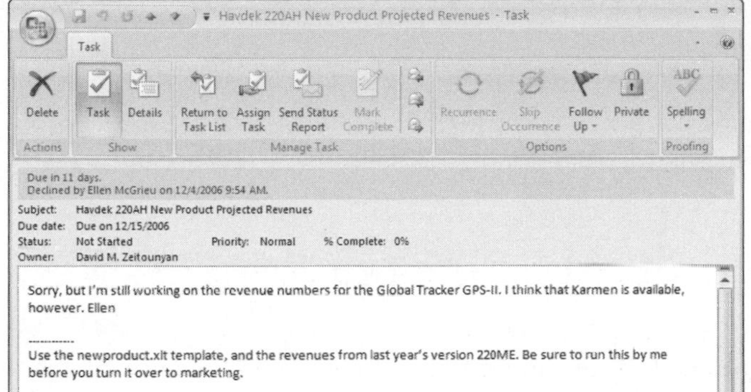

Figure 3-2: Reclaim that task.

Notice that you can reassign the rejected task without officially reclaiming it first. To do so, choose Task➪Manage Task➪Assign Task. Notice that if you do reassign the task, now or later, it retains the message reply from the first rejectee. Just a suggestion, but you may want to get rid of that before trying to coax someone else into taking on the task.

You can also reclaim a task when the rejection notice comes in without switching over to the Tasks list. Open the message and simply choose Task➪Manage Task➪Return to Task List to take that task back.

Checking the Progress of an Assigned Task

Assuming that all goes well and your victim (colleague) accepts the task reassignment request, you're still not completely out of the loop. You receive an update when the task is completed (assuming that you selected that option when you sent the task request), although you can request an update whenever you like by sending off an e-mail requesting that the task owner send you one (see the later section "Sending a status report on an assigned task" for information on how to generate a status report at any time). In addition, the task automatically updates from time to time, as the recipient makes progress on the task and updates his or her copy (assuming that you selected the Keep an Updated Copy of This Task on My Task List option when you reassigned the task).

For the I-don't-want-to-do-the-task-but-I-must-maintain-control-over-it-because-I-don't-trust-anyone types, Outlook provides several ways in which you can "check up" on your reassigned tasks. For example, you can set options that affect every task you reassign. (This setup should also satisfy the I'm-very-busy-so-let's-just-get-this-done types as well.)

1. **Choose Tools➪Options➪Task Options.**

   The Task Options dialog box presents itself, as shown in Figure 3-3.

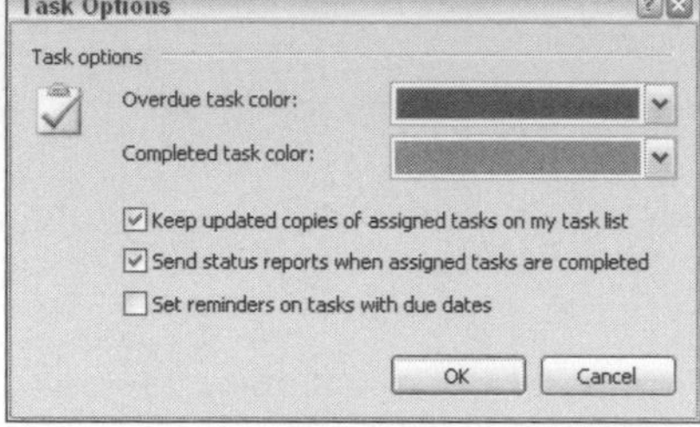

Figure 3-3: Set task reassignment options.

2. **Set the options you want.**

   To stay updated on the status of every task you reassign as it's being worked on, choose the Keep Updated Copies of Assigned Tasks on My Task List option.

   To receive a report for every task you reassign, once that task is completed, select the Send Status Reports When Assigned Tasks Are Completed option.

3. **Click OK twice.**

   From now on, any task requests you send will use the options you selected. Of course, for an individual task, you can always override the options you set as the defaults.

Besides setting the options that affect all task reassignments, you can check up on reassigned tasks periodically, as the mood hits you. For example, if you regularly reassign tasks, it may be quite easy to simply forget which ones you've reassigned and which ones you haven't.

To view a list of all the tasks you've reassigned:

1. **Change to the Tasks list by clicking the Tasks button on the Navigation pane.**

2. **Choose View⇨Current View⇨Assignment.**

   The view changes and displays only those tasks you've reassigned, in a list view, like the one shown in Figure 3-4. Another good view you may want to try is By Person Responsible, which groups the tasks by their owner and allows you to see both your tasks and any reassigned ones.

   If the Navigation pane is showing, you can also click the Assignment option to change to Assignment view.

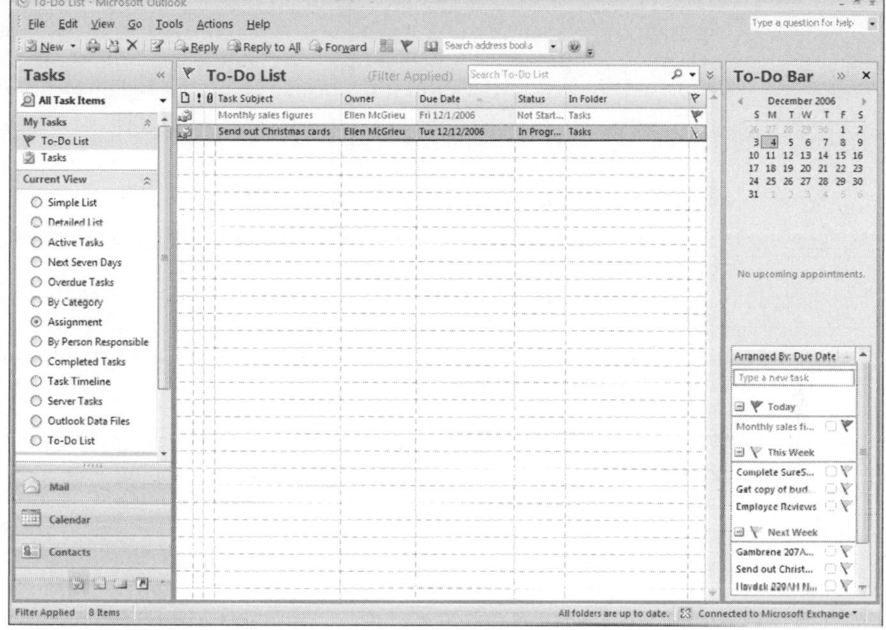

Figure 3-4: All you needed was a different point of view.

If you'd like to compare how many tasks you've reassigned to Betsy and Robyn, you can sort the Assignment list by owner by clicking the Owner heading at the top of that column. You can sort by Status to see how many tasks are nearing completion, or Due Date to see how many tasks are overdue. See Book VIII, Chapter 2 for more help on sorting and adjusting the view.

3. **View the task details.**

   Once you've located a reassigned task in the Assignment or By Person Responsible list that you'd like to check up on, simply double-click the task to open it up and view its details.

Dealing with Task Assignments Sent to You

No sense fooling yourself; sooner or later, your boss or somebody else on your team will read the Outlook manual and figure out that she can automate a job she loves to do — that is, reassigning tasks to *you.* Oh, well. At least the process makes it just as easy for you to say, "Uh, no thanks." And when you find yourself pressured to accept a task, don't despair; you can easily pester the task giver with status reports and updates. That'll show 'em.

In the rare instance where you accept a task and later discover that completing it on time is simply no longer in the cards, you can try reassigning the task to someone else. It'll feel a little like regifting a holiday fruitcake that keeps getting passed around from house to house because nobody wants to eat it, but then, someone's bound to be hungry enough to try it, right?

Accepting or declining a task

As you may know by now, a task request comes to your door disguised as a regular ol' e-mail message. When you get a task request, you have to accept it before it can be added to your Tasks list where you can track it. If you decline the invitation to take on more work, the person who sent you the task request can then reclaim the task and either do it himself or send a task request to some other patsy.

When you receive a task request, you become the task's owner, whether or not you actually accept the task. As the owner, you become the only one who can update the task. Should you decline the task request, it's up to the task giver to reclaim the task so that she can resume ownership. Again, ownership is key because only the owner of a task can change it, mark it complete, or delete it. And remember to at least accept or decline the task request; until you do, the original owner can do nothing with the task. To do so, follow these steps:

1. **Open the task request.**

   A task request comes at you as a normal e-mail message, which proves once again that you should be careful what e-mails you open. Anyway, change over to Mail and open the task request.

2. **Accept it or reject it.**

   On the Task tab, in the Respond group, are two buttons: Accept and Decline. Click either one, depending on what you've decided to do.

   In either case, the Accepting Task or the Rejecting Task dialog box appears, as shown in Figure 3-5.

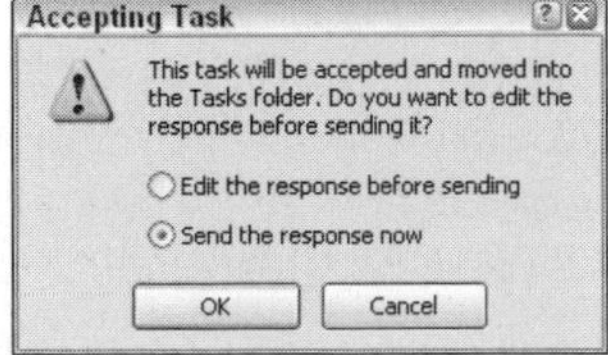

Figure 3-5: Choices, choices.

3. **Edit the reply or not.**

   Choose whether to edit the reply:

   - **To edit the reply and perhaps explain your response,** choose Edit the Response Before Sending. Then type your comments in the message form that appears. Click Send to send it along.
   - **To simply send your response to the task request,** click Send the Response Now.

Sending a status report on an assigned task

As the new owner of the task, it's up to you to keep everyone updated on your progress. Of course, some things happen automatically. For example, whenever you make changes to a task, such as updating its status or the number of hours you've spent on it, all copies of that task are automatically updated as well — at least the copies whose owners asked to be updated periodically when they sent the task request on to you. Copies of the task exist with the task originator, and any prior owners who passed the task onto you. The only problem is, all these prior owners are probably not as invested in getting the job done as you are, and so they're most likely not opening the task and looking at it for updates. Nope, they're waiting to hear from you, and the easiest way for you to make that happen is to throw a status report at them.

Don't depend on updates to keep your boss informed of your hard-earned progress on a task. If your boss originally sent the task request to more than one person (whether or not they accepted it), his task no longer is automatically updated. Also, your boss may not have selected the Keep an Updated Copy of This Task on My Task List option when he created the task request. In such a case, your boss is dependant on your status reports to keep him informed, so make sure that you send them often!

Keep in mind that a status report is automatically generated when you complete a task you've been assigned, so you don't need to follow these steps to create one manually when you finish a task.

To generate a status report on a task you've been assigned:

1. **Open the reassigned task you want to report on.**

   Reassigned tasks appear with a special icon in the Tasks list — a small task icon being held by two hands, one at the top and one at the bottom.

   As silly as it may see, you can send a status report on a task you reassigned, although you can't edit or update that task at all because you're no longer its owner. Not sure what you'd say in such a report, though? Maybe, "Hey what's going on?"

2. **Choose who to send the report to.**

   Choose an option:

   - **To send the report to the originator only,** choose Task➪Manage Task➪Send Status Report.
   - **To send the report to everyone who's requested one,** choose Task➪Manage Task➪Reply to All.

   A message form appears, as shown in Figure 3-6. In the body of the message are the pertinent details of the task, including its start date, due date, current status, percentage complete, and number of hours spent on the task so far.

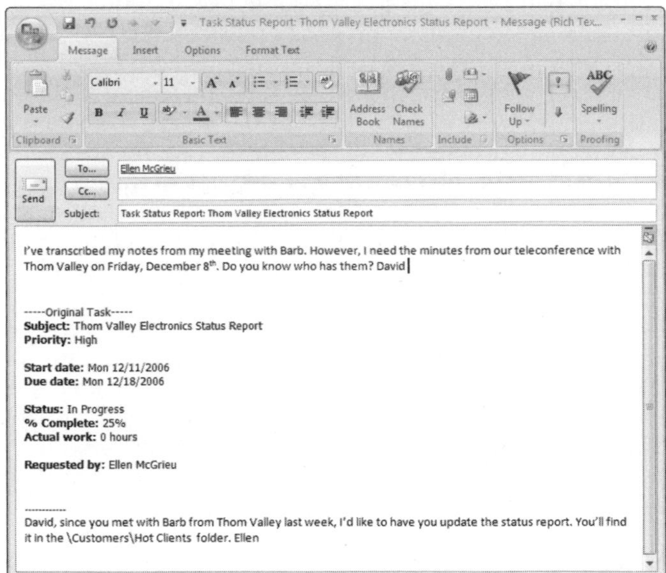

Figure 3-6: Hey, Ma, look what I've done!

3. **Address the message.**

   If the task is assigned to you, the names of everyone who needs to be updated appear automatically in the To box. If, however, you're a former owner of the task or simply an interested party, you need to enter the addresses of the people you want to update in the To box.

4. **Complete the report and click Send.**

   In the message area, type any comments you want to make about the task and its current status and then click Send to send the report.

Status reports, by the way, show up as regular messages in the Inboxes of whomever you send them to. The copy of the task the original owner may have in her Tasks list isn't changed or flagged in anyway, so hopefully, she'll see your status report in her avalanche of e-mail and appreciate the update. Regardless, assuming that she requested an updated task copy, the original owner's task is updated automatically when you change the task's details, so that's one way in which she might know you've made progress.

Reassigning a reassigned task

When a task request arrives at your door, whether or not you accept it, you're its owner, at least until the task giver decides to take the poor task back and reclaim it. As the owner, you can update the task and even send periodic status reports. You can also pass on the love, so to speak, by reassigning the task to someone else.

1. **Select the task you want to send along.**

   In Tasks, locate the task you were reassigned, that you now want to reassign to someone else.

2. **Choose Task⇨Manage Task⇨Assign Task.**

   The humble Task form transforms itself into a task request, as shown in Figure 3-7.

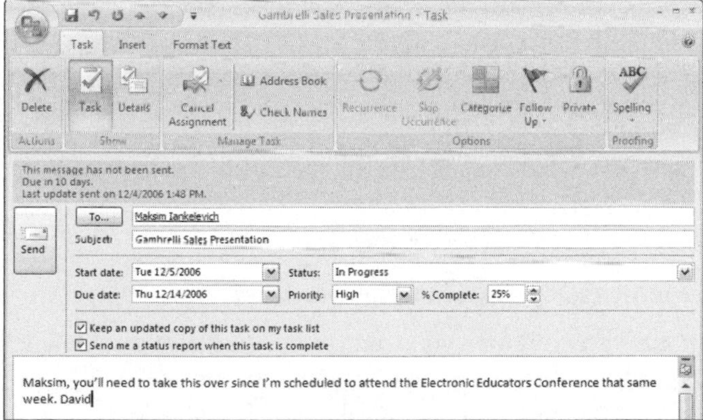

Figure 3-7: Pass the hot potato.

3. **Address the request.**

   In the To box, enter the e-mail address of the person(s) to whom you want to reassign this task.

4. **Set task options.**

   Update the task's Status and any other information. For example, you may want to change the Status to Deferred.

   Even though you're passing this task along to somebody else, you can still stay updated on the task's status by choosing the Keep an Updated Copy of This Task on My Task List and the Send Me a Status Report When This Task Is Complete options.

5. **Send the task request.**

   You can type a message for the recipient if you want — perhaps an offer of money will help. Anyway, when you're ready, click Send to send the request. You'll know in a little while if he accepts — just watch your mail box.

Forwarding a Task Instead of Reassigning It

Sometimes, what you want to do with a task is share it, which may or may not have anything to do with task reassignment, however. For example, if you've created a task that reminds you to get your monthly expense report in, and you've made it recurring and have set all the dates and even included a series of reminders to check over before you turn in the report, you may want to share your fully developed task with another colleague. You're not asking them to complete your expense report, so you're not reassigning the task. Instead, you're providing them with the details needed to create a similar task in their Tasks list.

One way you can share a task is to forward it just like you might forward a regular e-mail message. The recipient of the forwarded task can then add the task to his Tasks list, which saves him the trouble of manually adding the task.

To forward a task to someone:

1. **Open the task you want to forward.**

   Just pick any old task you want to forward and double-click that thing to open it right up.

   You can even forward a recurring task if you want.

2. **Choose Task⇨Manage Task⇨Forward.**

   A new message form is created, listing the task as an attachment, as shown in Figure 3-8.

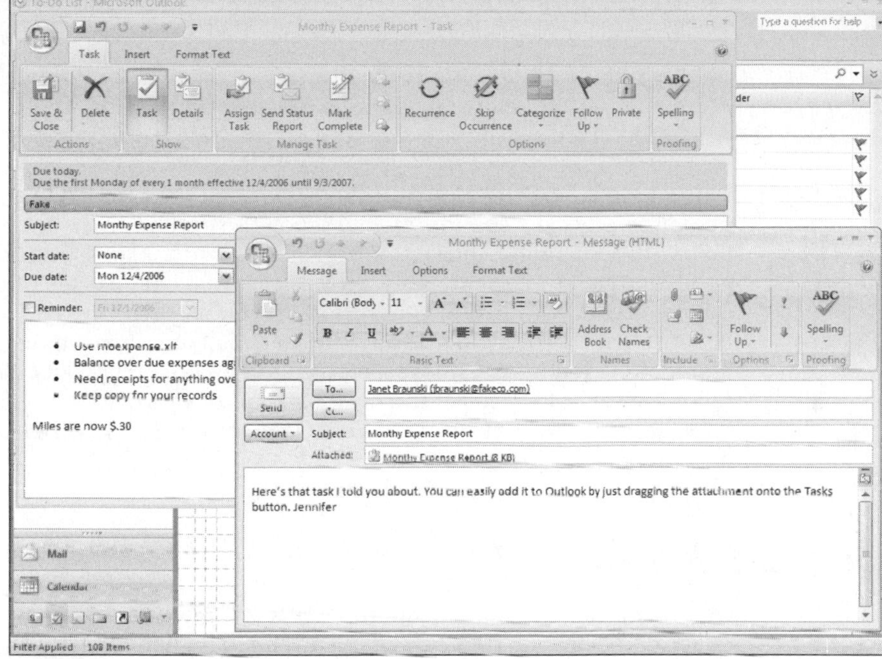

Figure 3-8: Here's that task you were looking for.

3. **Complete the message.**

   In the To box, type the address of the person you want to forward the message to. The Subject is already provided for you; it's based on the task name. You can change it if you want.

   Type a message in the message area.

4. **Click Send to forward the task and the message.**

Now, what happens when the recipient gets your little package? Well, obviously she needs to open the message first. There, she sees the task listed as an attachment, as shown in Figure 3-9.

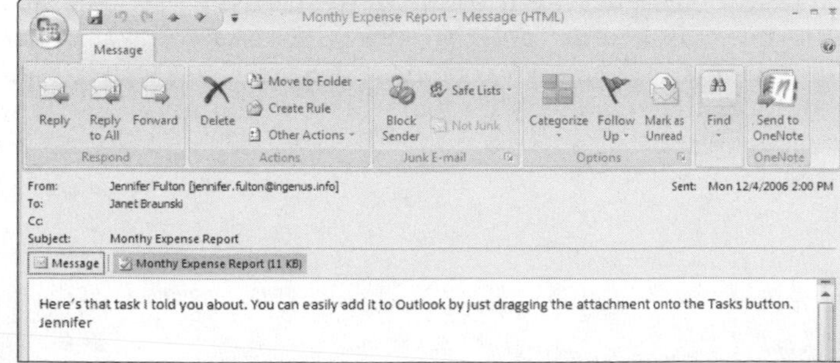

Figure 3-9: Here's something else I want you to do.

- **To simply view the task,** all the recipient needs to do is to open the attachment, and she sees the familiar Task form.
- **To add the task to his Tasks list,** the recipient does not need to open the e-mail, but instead simply drags the attachment from the Reading pane and drops it on the Tasks button on the Navigation pane.

This whole procedure of forwarding a task and then dragging and dropping it on your Tasks list depends, of course, on the person you want to share the task with actually having Outlook. True, the outlook for Outlook is pretty good, and so you can probably assume that in most cases, Outlook is what people use, but some don't, and what do you do then? In such instances, you can just send the task in text form. In an e-mail message, choose Insert⇨Include⇨Attach Item. Choose Tasks from the Look In list, and when your tasks appear below, select the one you want to share. Before you click OK, however, be sure to choose the Text Only option. The task details are copied into the message as text.

Sharing Your Tasks List

One way in which you can "share" a task is to pass it onto someone else, as described in the section "Assigning a Task to Someone Else," earlier in this chapter. When you reassign a task to a colleague, he takes over ownership, and he is the only one who can make updates to the task. You can try reassigning a task to more than one person, but that kinda leaves you out of the loop, update-wise — unless each recipient of the task request manually sends you status reports about his or her progress on the task.

Another way in which you can distribute responsibility for particular tasks is to simply share them. Sharing your Tasks folder is only possible if you work on an Exchange network. Once shared, your colleagues can view the tasks in the folder, and depending on what kind of security you establish, they can even add new tasks and update existing ones.

Now, just because you're in a sharing mood doesn't mean that you have to share everything. When needed, you can designate certain tasks as private, which means that no one can view them but you. You can also approach this problem in a different way. If you want to share only certain tasks, you can create a new Tasks folder and then drag the tasks you want to share into it. Or, if it's a smaller group, you can drag the tasks you want to hide into the new folder and then share your main Tasks folder only.

To make a task private, open the task and choose Task⇨Options⇨Private.

Want to create a new Tasks folder and put either the private or the not-so-private tasks in it? Good idea. Wish I'd thought of it. Oh, yeah, I did, and I put the details you need to create just such a folder in Book IX, Chapter 1.

Again, this sharing process lets you be a little bit more picky than just putting up a "No Trespassing" sign on a few select tasks. You can either

- **Share the main Tasks folder with basically everyone on the network,** while also designating what they're allowed to do, such as view only or view and edit. See the next section, "Sharing tasks with everyone."
- **Share either the main or a custom task folder almost completely,** but with only the specific people you select. See the upcoming section "Sharing tasks with specific people."

Sharing tasks with everyone

You can't share a custom folder in the manner described in this section, because a sharing invitation isn't sent with this method and a sharing invitation is required to share a custom folder. I know — what I just said probably doesn't make much sense right now. I mean, just what is a sharing invitation? (Hint: a special e-mail message.) Anyway, for now, you must trust me that these steps simply don't apply to you even if your intention is to share a custom folder with everyone. This section is for people who want to share their main Tasks folder. If you want to share a custom folder instead, you need to jump over to the section, "Sharing tasks with specific people," later in this chapter.

To share the main tasks folder with everyone on the network:

1. **Right-click the main Tasks folder.**

   In the Navigation pane, right-click the main Tasks folder.

2. **Click Change Sharing Permissions.**

   On the menu that appears, choose Change Sharing Permissions. The Tasks Properties dialog box appears.

3. **Choose Permissions⇨Default.**

   Change over to the Permissions tab, and then in the Name list, click Default, as shown in Figure 3-10.

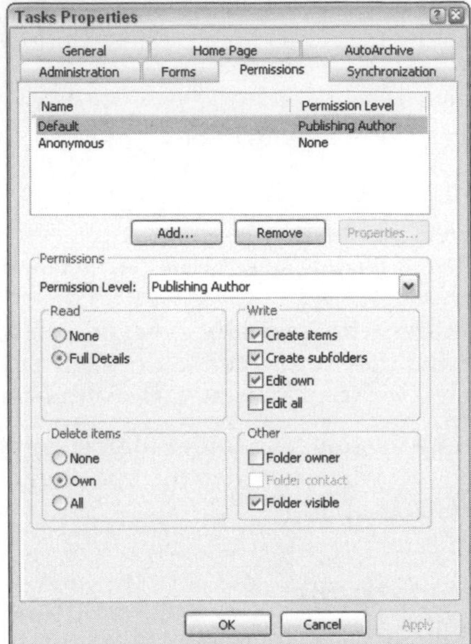

Figure 3-10: See, it's fun to share.

4. **Set sharing permissions.**

   From the options that appear in the Permissions Level list, choose the one that describes the kind of things you want visitors to be able to do:

   - **Publishing Editor:** Create, edit, delete, and view tasks. The user can also create subfolders within the shared folder.
   - **Editor:** Same as Publishing Editor except the user can't create subfolders.
   - **Publishing Author:** Create and view tasks, create folders, and edit or delete tasks they have created themselves.
   - **Author:** Same as Publishing Author except the user can't create subfolders.
   - **Nonediting Author:** Same as Publishing Author except they can't edit existing tasks, even if they created them. Also, they can't create folders. They can delete tasks they create themselves.
   - **Reviewer:** View tasks only.
   - **Contributor:** Create and edit new tasks, but can't view existing ones unless they created them.
   - **None:** Prevents the user from accessing the folder at all — they can't even view the tasks in the folder.

5. **Click OK.**

   The folder you chose appears in the Navigation pane with a special "Hey, I'm open for business" icon (a hand holding a task), showing that it's now shared.

After you share the Tasks folder, although it's not required, you may want to send the people you want to notify a general message that your folder is shared. They don't actually need an invitation as described in the next section. Nope, all someone on your Exchange network needs to know to access your folder right now is your name and the fact that you've placed a Welcome mat at the door of your main Tasks folder. See the upcoming section "Viewing Tasks Shared by Others" for more info on how your recipient gains access to your main Tasks folder now that you've granted it.

Sharing tasks with specific people

When it comes to sharing, I'm probably like most people — I mean most people who also grew up in a family of ten where if you didn't grab and grab quickly, you were eating your napkin for dinner. Anyway, if you have a Tasks folder to share but you want to be selective about who has access to it, you can share that folder with only certain privileged people.

WARNING!

In this procedure, you share the folder and send a sharing invitation to the specific people you choose. For custom folders you've created, you only have two access levels you can select from: Reviewer (which means they can view tasks only) or Editor (which means they can create, edit, delete, and view tasks, even ones they don't create themselves). If you're sharing your main Tasks folder in this way, you can only provide them with Reviewer status, at least initially. Once the sharing invitation goes out, you can always change a particular person's access level as desired — see "Changing permissions or stopping sharing," later in this chapter.

To share a Tasks folder with a select few:

1. **Click the task folder you want to share.**

   Change over to Tasks and locate the folder you want to share. You should find it hiding under the My Tasks category on the Navigation pane. You can share your main Tasks folder or a custom folder in this manner.

2. **Share the folder.**

   If you're sharing the main Tasks folder, simply click the Share My Tasks Folder link on the Navigation pane. Otherwise, right-click the folder and choose Share *foldername,* where *foldername* is the actual name of the folder such as Team Tasks. A message form appears, as shown in Figure 3-11.

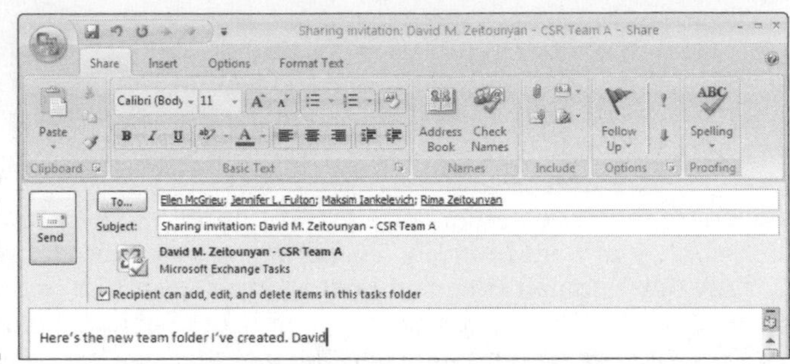

Figure 3-11: Here, please share my workload.

3. **Address the invitation.**

   In the To box, add the addresses of the people with whom you want to share this folder. Change the Subject if you want and type a message explaining the invitation.

4. **Set some options.**

   Assuming that you're sharing your main Tasks folder, you can request permission to view each addressee's Tasks folder in return. Again, you're granting them only Reviewer status (looky, but no touchy), so you're asking them to grant you that same access in return. To do so, choose the Request Permission to View Recipient's Tasks Folder option.

   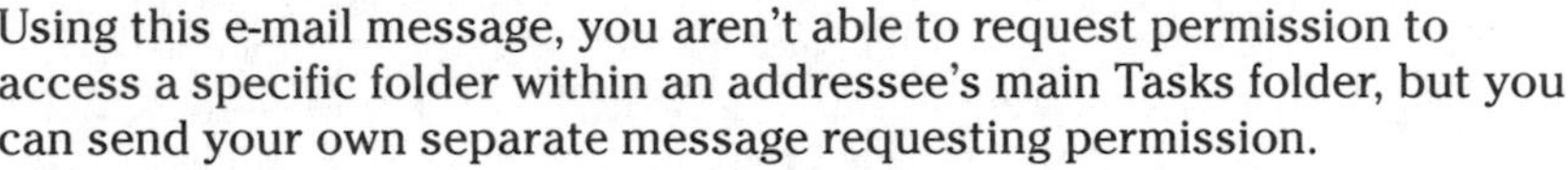
   Using this e-mail message, you aren't able to request permission to access a specific folder within an addressee's main Tasks folder, but you can send your own separate message requesting permission.

   Big IF: If you're sharing a folder you created and not your main Tasks folder, you can control what users can do. If you want users to only view tasks (Reviewer access), disable the Recipient Can Add, Edit, And Delete Items In This Tasks Folder option. If you want them to be able to muck things up (Editor access), turn on the option instead.

5. **Click Send.**

   Be sure to confirm the invitation by clicking Yes. You get a notice telling you that the folder is now shared.

6. **Click OK.**

The folder you chose appears in the Navigation pane with a special icon, showing that it's now shared — a hand holding a task. When the recipient(s) get your invitation, it's up to them to follow up and actually gain access to your Tasks folder. Luckily, that's not a complicated process, as explained in the upcoming section "Viewing Tasks Shared by Others."

Changing permissions or stopping sharing

Just because you were nice enough to share a Tasks folder, it doesn't mean you have to keep giving and giving and giving. Nope, if you're sharing the folder with select people, for example, you can change what they can do. If you're sharing the folder with basically everyone on the network, you can just stop sharing it if you want or change that basic access level.

To change an individual's permission to use a shared folder:

1. **Right-click the shared folder.**

   In the Navigation pane, right-click the shared folder whose permissions you want to change.

2. **Choose Change Sharing Permissions.**

   The name of the shared folder appears in the Properties dialog box, as shown in Figure 3-12.

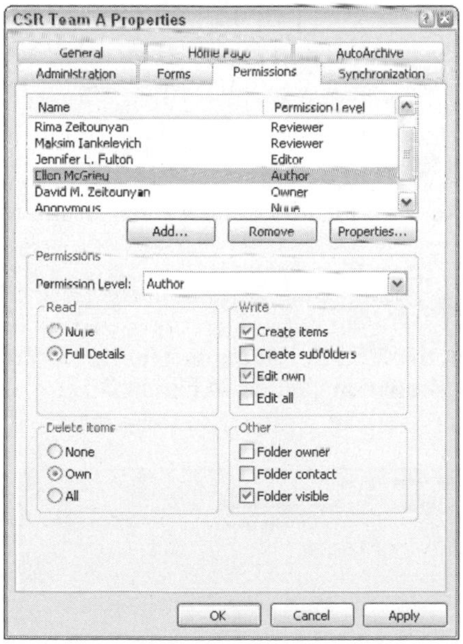

Figure 3-12: Change what a user can do to your tasks.

3. **Change permissions as desired.**

   You have two options:

   - **To make a change that affects everyone,** click the Permissions tab and in the Name list, click Default. Then change the options shown in the Permissions List; to completely revoke all access, click None.

- **To make a change to a particular user's permissions,** click the Permissions tab and choose the user's name from the Name list. Then, from the Permission Level list, remove the options you no longer want to grant this user.

4. **Click OK.**

   The permissions are changed right away.

If someone is viewing your Tasks folder right now, and you change her level of access, it affects her immediately — or, well, almost immediately, as soon as your change filters through the network. If you've removed access, the tasks she's viewing are removed from the screen, and she isn't able to see them anymore.

Viewing Tasks Shared by Others

Assuming that you've been giving access to someone's shared Tasks folder (or a special subfolder he's created just for sharing), it's not difficult to open it and view the tasks within. After you open the folder for the first time, it's added to the Navigation pane and is listed just like any other folder, making it real easy to view tasks (and edit them, if you have permission) when needed.

Accessing someone's main Tasks folder

If someone's shared her main Tasks folder, follow these steps to open it the first time:

1. **Click Open Shared Tasks.**

   You can find the link on the Navigation pane. The Open Shared Tasks dialog box appears, as shown on the left in Figure 3-13.

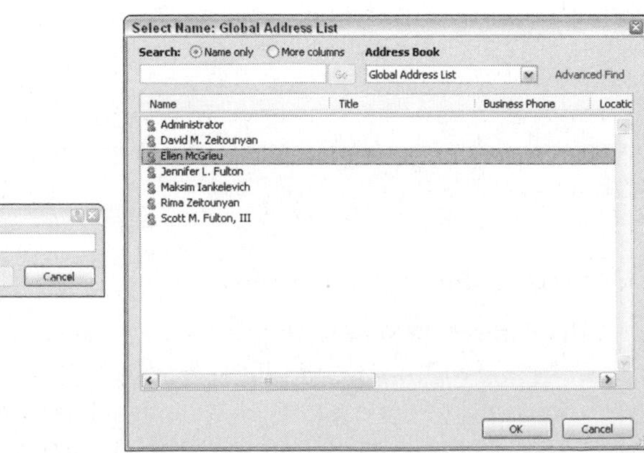

Figure 3-13: Open a shared tasks folder.

2. **Name that sharer.**

   Either type the name of the person whose folder you want to access in the Name box or click Name to display the Select Names: Global Address List dialog box, shown on the right in Figure 3-13. Select the person from those listed, and click OK to return to the Open Shared Tasks dialog box.

3. **Click OK.**

   The person's main Tasks folder, assuming that it's shared and you have permission to access it, appears in the People's Tasks group on the Navigation pane. The tasks in that folder appear on the right.

   If the folder is shared but you haven't been given access to it just yet, you're asked whether you want to beg for permission. Click Yes, and a message form appears, asking for permission to use the folder. Make sure to select the Request Permission to View Recipient's Tasks Folder option. If you'd like to offer access to your main Tasks folder in return, choose the Allow Recipient to View Your Tasks folder. Click Send to send the request.

Once you've gained access to someone's Tasks folder, you can simply click that folder in the Navigation pane at any time to display the tasks within.

You can remove a shared tasks folder from the People's Tasks list if you don't think you'll need to open it again. Simply right-click the shared task folder you want to remove and choose Delete *foldername* from the menu that appears. This action does not, by the way, actually delete the tasks folder from the owner's system, despite your level of access.

Accessing someone's custom task folder

If someone has decided to share only a special Tasks folder that he's created, you get an e-mail telling you so. You can use this e-mail to gain access to the special folder. The level of access you've been granted is determined by the user; typically, you have either Reviewer (view only) or Editor (create, edit, delete tasks) access. Regardless, once you gain access to the folder, you can easily view its contents any time you want.

To access someone's shared, custom Tasks folder:

1. **View the sharing invitation.**

   Change over to Mail and either select the sharing invitation to view it in the Reading pane or double-click it to view it in a separate window.

2. **Click Open This Tasks Folder.**

   You see a button at the top of the Reading Pane window, or on the Ribbon in the Open group, called Open This Tasks Folder. Click the button and say, "Open Sesame."

   A new Outlook window is opened for some silly reason, and the folder is added to the People's Tasks group on the Navigation pane as shown in the figure. You can close this window and view the contents of this Tasks folder in the main window if you want.

Chapter 4: Taking Notes

In This Chapter

- Creating notes with detailed information
- Organizing notes
- Changing how notes look
- Covering the Desktop with reminders
- Passing notes onto others

Seems like I keep notes everywhere — in my purse, jacket pocket, on the fridge, and all over my desktop. Despite the fact that Outlook lets you keep all your notes in one place, I don't use the feature too often, although I should. With Outlook, you can not only jot down something important, in a place where you can actually find it, but you can also group similar notes together using categories, stick them on the Desktop where you can remember to read them first thing each morning, and even share notes with friends and colleagues when needed.

Covering your desk with miscellaneous bits of papers isn't a good option, and creating notes in Outlook is at least *organized.* But to take your notes to the next level, you need OneNote. With OneNote, you can gather related notes, graphics, video, audio, Outlook items, and more in one spot. See Book VI, Chapter 5 for more info.

Creating a Complete Note

You can create notes from just about any Outlook item, and when you do, the contents of that item appear in the note where you can add additional comments. For example, you can create a note from an appointment. To do so, just drag and drop the appointment on the Notes icon on the Navigation pane. I almost never use this approach, however, because I can just open the appointment and type my notes in that large white box that's provided for just that purpose. But if you like this drag and drop stuff, see Book I, Chapter 2 for more ideas on how to use it.

Nope, when I get around to actually recording a note in Outlook, I do it the old-fashioned way, which only takes a second as it turns out:

1. **Choose File⇨New⇨Note.**

   A new, blank note window jumps out.

   If you're in Notes, you can click the New button on the Standard toolbar to create a note.

2. **Type the note.**

   That's right, just type to record your note, as shown in Figure 4-1. The first line of the note is important, however, because it acts as a kind of note title, and in some cases, may be all you see prior to reopening the note. So make that first line count. (By the way, you can copy stuff to the Clipboard and paste it into the note if you need to.)

Weekly Sales Report

* Use wksales.dot template
* Include sales data from Dave.
* Add in retail data from each shop
* Send copies to Barb and Joe
* Add my analysis of the week's sales

11/9/2006 9:21 AM

Figure 4-1: Make a note of that.

As you type, text automatically wraps within the note frame. However, if your note is really long, you may want to resize the note window so that you can see its text more easily. To resize a window, do what you'd do normally to resize an object — just drag an edge or a corner.

You can't format a note, but you can create a kind of bulleted list by preceding each item with an "o" or a "*". You can also change the text font, color, and size for all notes. See the section, "Making Notes Look the Way You Like," later in this chapter for more information.

3. **Close the note.**

   You can keep the note open as long as you like — while you keep working, adding more information as you finish that phone call, exchanging e-mails, or reviewing your meeting notes. Even if Outlook is minimized, you still can see your note because it's inside its own window.

4. **When you're done with the note, close it by clicking its Close button (X).**

After you close a note, it appears on the right in the Notes module, as a small adhesive-note type icon. To see the contents of a particular note, just double-click it, and it opens right up. You can resize the note window by dragging the note border. You can maximize the note window by double-clicking the gray title bar that runs along the top of the window.

Organizing Notes with Categories

As you probably noticed, notes by default are yellow. You can change this default color, although I don't mind the yellow myself; if you do, see the upcoming section "Making Notes Look the Way You Like." Another way to change a note's color is to assign a category to it. Categories have the advantage of allowing you to group similar notes together.

To assign a category to a note, follow these steps:

1. **Click the note's icon.**

   You can do so even if the note's still open, but don't expect the note window to help you. You need to be the able to see the note's icon to click it.

2. **Select a category.**

   Click the Categorize button on the Standard toolbar and select the category you want to assign this note from the list that appears. (Wanna know how to create categories so that you can organize notes? I know I do! See Book VIII, Chapter 1.)

After you assign a category to a note, the note's icon changes to that color That way, you can easily see which notes belong together. You can also arrange notes by category, as you can see in the upcoming section "Selecting a Notes View." In addition, when you open the note, the note's color has changed, too. You may think that assigning a dark purple category to a note would make it impossible to read, but Outlook automatically changes the text to white in such cases, so you're able to read your note text easily.

You can assign more than one category to a note, just as you can with any Outlook item. The color of the note is taken from the last category you assign.

Selecting a Notes View

Like all the Outlook modules, you can change the arrangement of items to make finding stuff easy. By default, Outlook shows you all your notes, as icons, arranged much more neatly than notes typically appear on my desk, let me tell you. To change to a different view, simply select it from those listed conveniently on the Navigation pane, as shown in Figure 4-2, which depicts the Notes List view. Here's the lowdown on the various views:

- **Notes List** view displays a long list of your notes, in a kind of AutoPreview, where the contents of each note appear below the note's title.
- **Last Seven Days** lists your notes similar to Notes List view, except that you see only the notes you've created recently.
- **By Category** groups notes by category (duh), but this view doesn't show you the contents like the other list views.
- **Outlook Data Files** groups notes by data file, assuming that you use more than one (more than one `.pst` or `.ost` file). See Book III, Chapter 5.

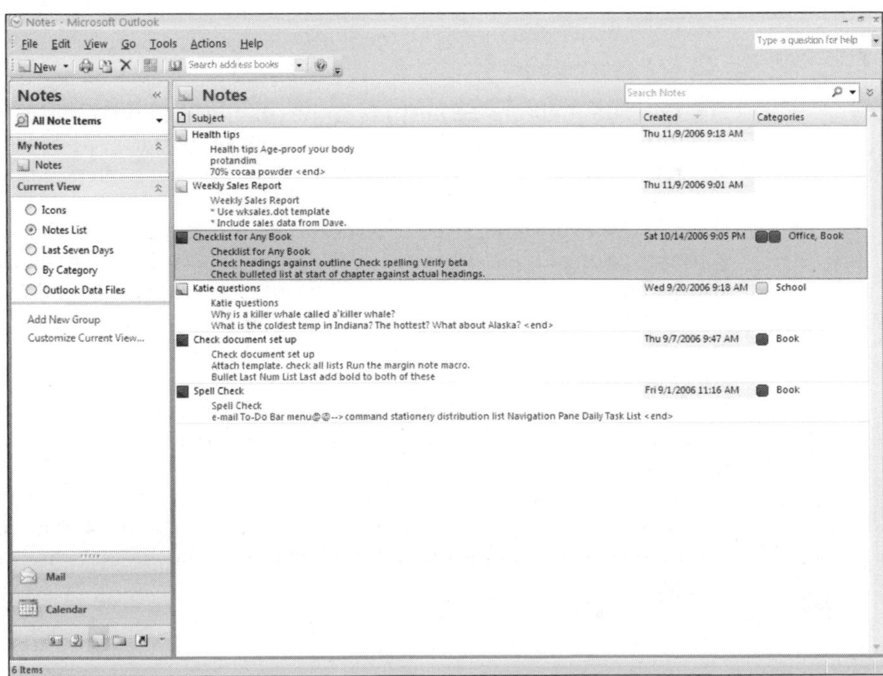

Figure 4-2: It's up to your point of view.

Regardless of which view you choose, you can quickly sort your notes so that it's easier to work with them. I wish sorting through my pile of notes jotted down on the back of envelopes, scrap paper, and napkins was as easy, but here goes:

1. **Choose View➪Arrange By.**

   A list of sort options appears.

2. **Choose a sort.**

   For example, choose Subject to arrange notes alphabetically, by the note title. Frankly, some of the sorts don't make a lot of sense with notes, such as From and To (unless you forward notes to other people, or get notes from them in return, as you can discover how to do in the upcoming section "Passing Notes"), but there are a lot of useful ones you might want to try, such as Subject, Category, and Date.

If you're using a list view, you can sort the list using a particular column by simply clicking that column's header. For example, to sort by date, click on the Created column.

Making Notes Look the Way You Like

Notes are kinda fun, and handy — when you remember to use them, that is. We all make lots of notes all day long, and if you're at your computer, you may as well put them in Outlook where they won't fall out of your pocket.

After spending some time creating notes, you'll be happy to know you can modify the way they work and look. For example, if you're bored with that dull yellow color, you can start off your notes with a jazzy blue or a calm lilac. If you're playing the ol' eye trombone thing like me (moving closer to the screen one minute and then farther back the next to keep things in focus), you can increase the default font size or select a more readable font to make notes easier to use. You can change the note's default size as well, perhaps saving you time resizing note windows.

To change the default color, size, or font for all your notes:

1. **Choose Tools➪Options➪Note Options.**

   The Notes Options dialog box appears, as shown in Figure 4-3.

Figure 4-3: Set note defaults.

2. **Choose the defaults you want:**
   - **To select a default note color,** choose one from the Color list. You may want to choose a color not associated with a category so that you can easily tell which notes do not have a category assigned to them.
   - **To change the default note size,** select a size from the Size list. You can choose from Small, Medium (the default), or Large.
   - **To change the default note text's font, size, or color,** click the Font button. In the Font dialog box that appears, choose a Font, Font Style (such as bold or italic), Size, and Color. Click OK.
3. **Click OK.**

If you changed the default note color or size, you see the change the next time you create a new note. If you changed the text font, size, or color, however, your choices affect all notes instantly.

You can make another change to all notes if you want, which is removing the date and time the note was created or changed from the bottom of the note window when the note's opened. Here's how:

1. **Choose Tools⇨Options⇨Other⇨Advanced Options.**

   The Advanced Options dialog box appears.
2. **Turn off dates.**

   In the Appearance Options section in the middle of the dialog box, turn off the When Viewing Notes, Show Time and Date option. Click OK twice, and the date and time a note was last changed no longer distract you when you open a note. The date and time still appear in list views, however.

Sticking Notes to Your Desktop

If you have a note you need to see tomorrow morning, bright and early, you can stick the note on your Desktop rather than leave it in Outlook. This handy trick also works for notes you need to see often, such as "Lay off the donuts — the reunion is this summer!"

To put a note on your Desktop, drag and drop it there. A note on your Desktop looks just like it does in Outlook — an icon that looks like a small adhesive note. To open the note, double-click the icon. You can even make changes if you like and then close the note by clicking its Close button.

The note, by the way, still appears within Outlook, so if you happen to be working in Outlook, you can still find your note there as well as the Desktop.

Passing Notes

Hopefully, you have something useful to record in a note, other than this week's grocery list, your gym locker combination, and your favorite laugh from `www.jokes.com`. If so, you can easily share your pearls of wisdom with colleagues and friends.

1. **Click the note you want to share.**

   The note is highlighted.

2. **Choose Actions⇨Forward.**

   A new mail form opens, with the note shown as an attachment (see Figure 4-4).

3. **Address the message, change the Subject if you want (it's taken from the title of your note), and then type a message in the large notes area.**

4. **When you're done with your message, click Send to send the message with its note attachment.**

The recipient, assuming that he has Outlook, can open the attachment and read it or print it. He can also drag the attachment to the Notes icon and drop it, copying the note to his system.

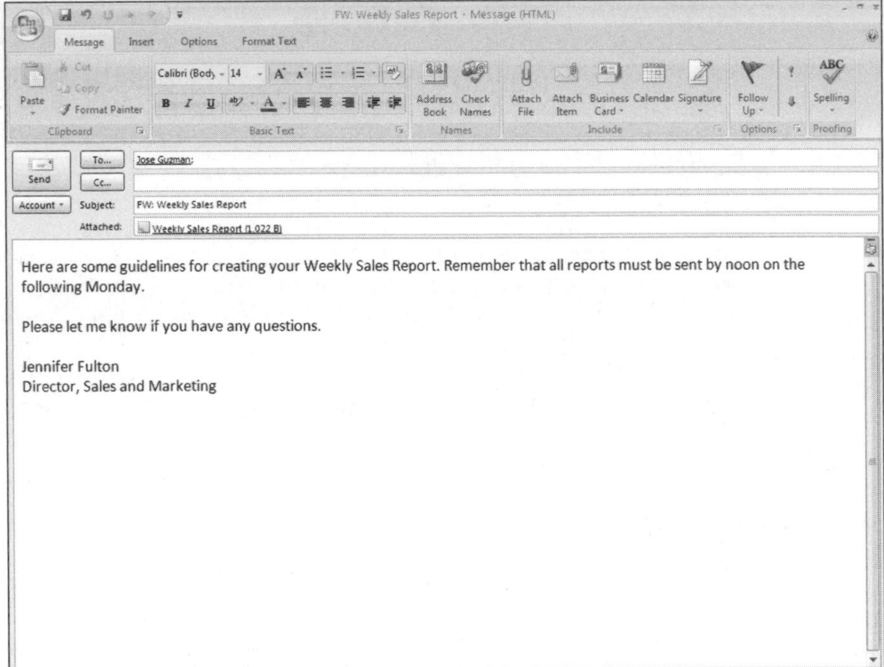

Figure 4-4: Hold the salt, pass the note.

Chapter 5: Taking Notes in Overdrive: OneNote

In This Chapter

- Discovering a whole new way to organize your notes
- Adding notebooks, new pages, and sections
- Creating typed or handwritten notes
- Taking screen shots
- Recording audio or video
- Inserting documents and other files
- Creating links to everything

The idea behind OneNote isn't new — it's as old as writing itself. From the dawn of time, whenever man had something important to remember, he wrote it down — that is, after he invented paper, a writing system, ink, and an eraser. Using OneNote, you, too, can cover your cave with important bits of information — for example, a meeting agenda, a map to the meeting site, flight info, things to do for the meeting, sales charts, images taken at a meeting or class lecture, and meeting/lecture/conference notes. OneNote can gather all sorts of typed or handwritten notes, graphics, audio and video files, Outlook items, and other stuff all in one spot where you can find it. And rather than letting you dump all this glorious information in one big heap, OneNote directs you in various ways in which you can *organize it.*

OneNote is not one of the core Office programs, although if Microsoft asked me for an opinion, it would get my vote. Thus, sadly, OneNote is not included with every version of Office, but it is included in the Home & Student, Ultimate, and Enterprise editions of Office. OneNote is also available separately.

If you have a smartphone or a PDA that's Windows Mobile–enabled, you can connect it directly to OneNote and import data. If your cell phone or your PDA doesn't happen to use Windows Mobile, you can still copy data, such as images you took during a meeting, to the hard drive and then import them into OneNote.

Organizing in OneNote

OneNote is like a bunch of electronic notebooks. You can organize each notebook into sections using tabs, as you might insert tabs into a school binder full of notebook paper. You can add as many note pages in each section of a notebook as you need. Each page in a notebook is just like a piece of paper; you can click anywhere you want and type text or insert a graphic, audio file, Outlook item, or bits of wisdom from the Web (see Figure 5-1). If you have a pen tablet, you can write or draw on it to add information to a page. Stuff you add to a page, such as a typed note, gets placed in a box called a *container.* You use these containers to move stuff around on a page.

Even after you put something on a page, you can still reorganize it however you want, dragging and dropping directions next to a map, or moving a picture of a digital camera next to a bulleted list you're compiling of Web sites that offer the camera and various accessories for sale. To move a note or other object, click the top border of its container, which selects the object. To move the note or object, drag it around on the page.

If you just have to write something down right now, and you don't want to think about which notebook or section it should go into, you can place it in the Unfiled Notes section until you can find or create a place where it should go.

To make it easier to add or move objects around on a page, you might want to temporarily hide all the tabs and the Navigation Bar by clicking the Full Page View button to the right of the menus. To return to regular view, click the Full Page View button again, which you'll find at the front of the Standard toolbar. You can also adjust the view using the Zoom button on the Standard toolbar. For example, you can select 75% to see more of a page or 200% to see something up closer.

One thing you don't see on your tour of OneNote is a Save button. That's because you don't need to save anything you do; OneNote takes care of saving automatically as you work.

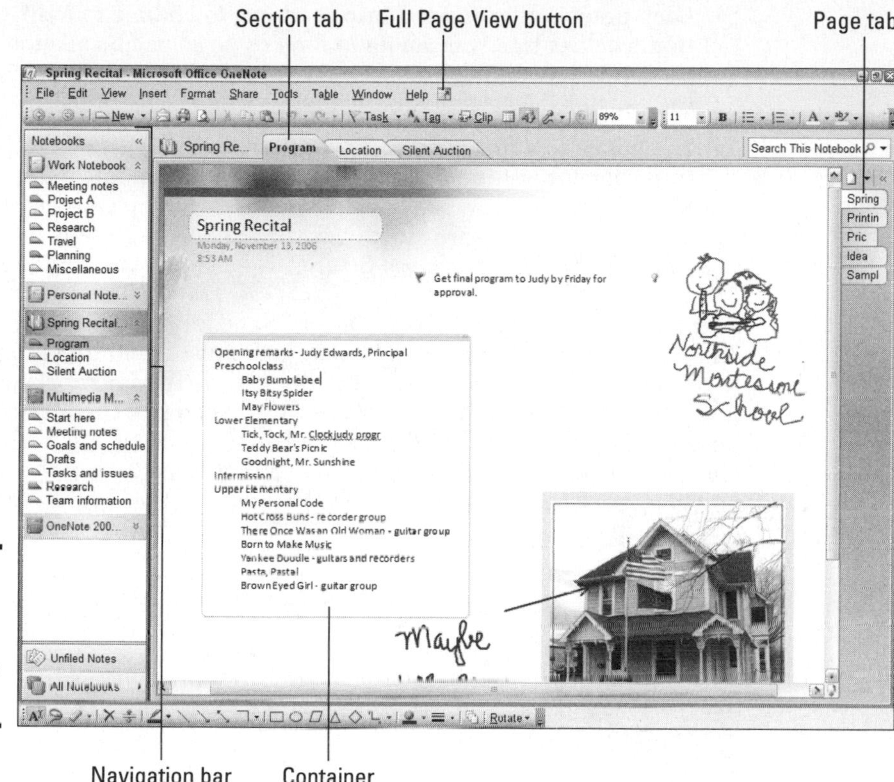

Figure 5-1: OneNote helps you get a handle on your life.

Navigating in OneNote

OneNote has a simple structure. Each notebook is divided into tabbed sections, which are further divided into separate pages. Here's how to get around OneNote:

- **To change notebooks,** click the notebook's button on the Navigation Bar.

- **You can minimize the Navigation Bar and expand it when needed.** An expanded bar lists all your notebooks (see Figure 5-1). When a notebook is expanded, each page in that notebook is listed. You can collapse a notebook's list by clicking its Collapse button or expand it again so that it shows all the notebook's pages by clicking the Expand button. To minimize the Navigation Bar, click the Collapse Navigation Bar button. On a minimized Navigation Bar, each notebook appears as a simple icon; section pages don't appear. To expand the Navigation Bar again, click the Expand Navigation Bar button.

- **Each notebook is divided into sections; to change to a different section,** click its tab. You can jump directly to a specific section in a notebook (even in a different notebook) by clicking that section's name in the expanded Navigation Bar listing.
- **To change to a different page within a section,** click its tab. Each section contains at least one page, but it can contain lots more. The page tab area, by the way, can be expanded so that you can read long page tab names more clearly. Just click the Expand Page Tabs button (it looks like a double left arrow <<). Go ahead — I know you want to.

Another way to navigate around OneNote and all its notebooks, sections, and pages is to use the All Notebooks List. I must admit that I forget about this handy button all the time, but really, it's worth remembering, especially if you have the Navigation Bar collapsed. You can find the All Notebooks List button at the bottom of the Navigation Bar, as shown in Figure 5-2. Once you click it, a menu listing all the notebooks and the sections in them flies out of nowhere; click a section in the listing to jump right on over to that notebook/section.

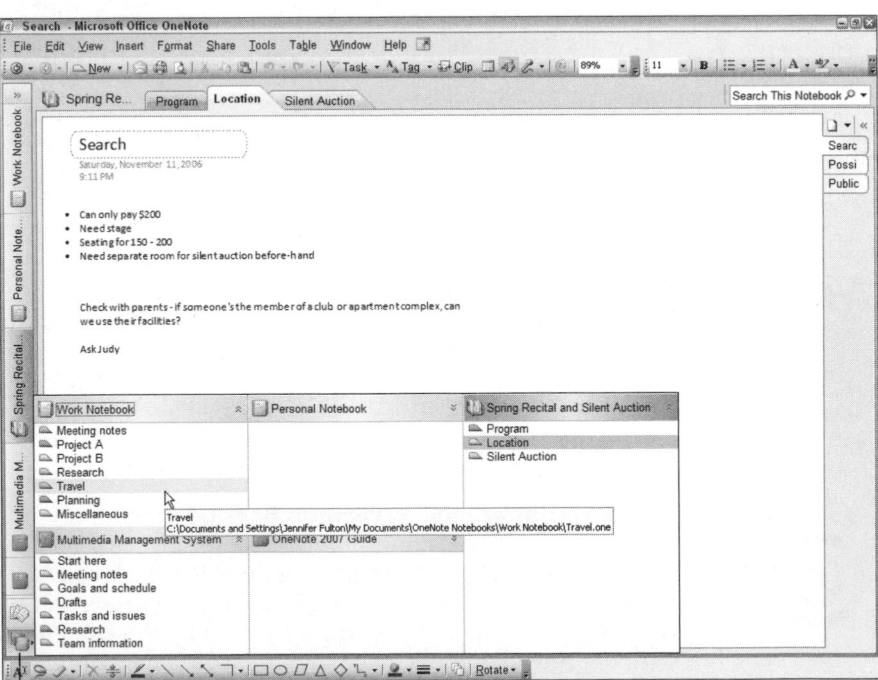

Figure 5-2: List all those notebooks.

After compiling a page in OneNote, you can send it to Word if you want to take advantage of its superior word-processing capabilities: choose File⇨Send To⇨Microsoft Office Word.

Creating a Notebook

OneNote starts you out with two notebooks, one for each part of your life: Work and Personal. You don't have to use these notebooks, but it makes sense to use them, at least at first. To change to a particular notebook, click its icon on the Navigation Bar. Both the Work and Personal notebooks are already divided into sections, with little tabs marking each section. You can rename the tabs or remove them and add your own sections. You can also create your own notebooks, whether or not you keep the Work and Personal notebooks.

To create a new notebook, follow these steps:

1. **Choose File⇨New⇨Notebook.**

   You can also click the arrow on the New button on the Standard toolbar and choose Notebook from the menu. The New Notebook Wizard, shown in Figure 5-3, appears.

New Notebook Wizard
Specify the notebook properties
Name: Multimedia Management Package Search
Color:
From Template:
Personal Notebook
Professional Services Notebook
Research Notebook
Shared Notebook - Group Project
Shared Notebook - Reference Materials
Student Semester Notebook
Work Notebook
Notebook templates on Microsoft Office Online
Next > Cancel

Figure 5-3: Create a new notebook.

2. **Type a name and choose a color.**

   The color appears on the Navigation Bar and may help you quickly identify the notebook.

3. **Choose a template and click Next.**

   Typically, you'll just start with a blank slate by choosing Blank from the From Template list. But if you want another work-like notebook with all the same sections as the original Work notebook, you can choose Work Notebook. Likewise, you can choose Personal Notebook.

   The other templates create a notebook geared for a specific purpose; if you're creating a notebook like one of the ones listed, go ahead and use the template — for example, the Research Notebook template. You can always remove sections and customize it whenever you want.

   You may be able to find a template on Microsoft's Web site that suits your needs; click the Notebook Templates on Microsoft Office Online link to search for one.

   You can share notebooks if you're at work and you want your colleagues to add to it. The Shared templates create shared notebooks, although you don't have to use one to share a new notebook.

4. **Choose whether to share or not and then click Next.**

   You have several choices:

   - **To use the notebook on this computer only,** choose I Will Use It on This Computer.
   - **To use this notebook on several different computers** (such as your work computer and your laptop) but not at the same time, choose I Will Use It on Multiple Computers.

     If you choose this option, then you don't have to manually copy the OneNote data file from one computer to another (for example, from your work computer to your laptop), provided both computers have access to the folder in which the notebook is stored.
   - **To share the notebook** through your company network or an Internet group site such as a SharePoint server, choose Multiple People Will Share the Notebook. For more information on sharing notebooks, see Book VI, Chapter 6.

5. **Choose a folder and click Create.**

   The default folder appears in the Path box (see Figure 5-4); click Browse and choose a different folder if you want. If you're sharing this notebook, and if the folder you choose isn't already shared, the folder's Properties dialog box appears later so that you can share it. For sharing, you can choose any appropriate folder, including a network folder, a SharePoint library, or a high-storage, USB flash drive.

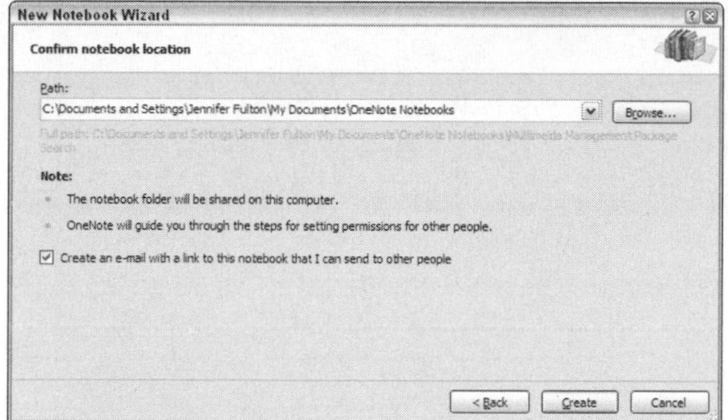

Figure 5-4: Save the new notebook.

At the bottom of the dialog box, you see an option to Create an E-Mail with a Link to This Notebook That I Can Send to Other People. Be sure to select it because it helps you share this notebook. (Even if you don't currently plan on sharing the notebook, you way want to later on, so you may as well ask for the link to be sent to you.) Click Create.

6. **Address the message and click Send and/or complete the Properties dialog box.**

   If you asked for the link to be sent to you, a Message form appears in Outlook. Address the message and click Send to send it. If you opted to share the notebook, the Properties dialog box for that folder appears so that you can set up sharing.

   The new notebook pops open in OneNote.

A button for the new notebook appears on the Navigation Bar, below all the other notebooks. You can move the notebook button up in the navigation list if you like, by simply dragging and dropping it.

If you used a template to create the notebook, you see some sections already set up for you to use; you can rename these sections, rearrange them, or just get rid of them as you see fit. You can also add new sections as needed. Figure 5-5 displays a new, blank notebook so that you can see what one looks like. The current notebook is represented by an open icon on the Navigation pane; when the notebook is closed, it appears as a closed icon in the color you chose when you created the notebook. Notice that the shared notebook (Multimedia Management Research) I created is shown with a special shared icon.

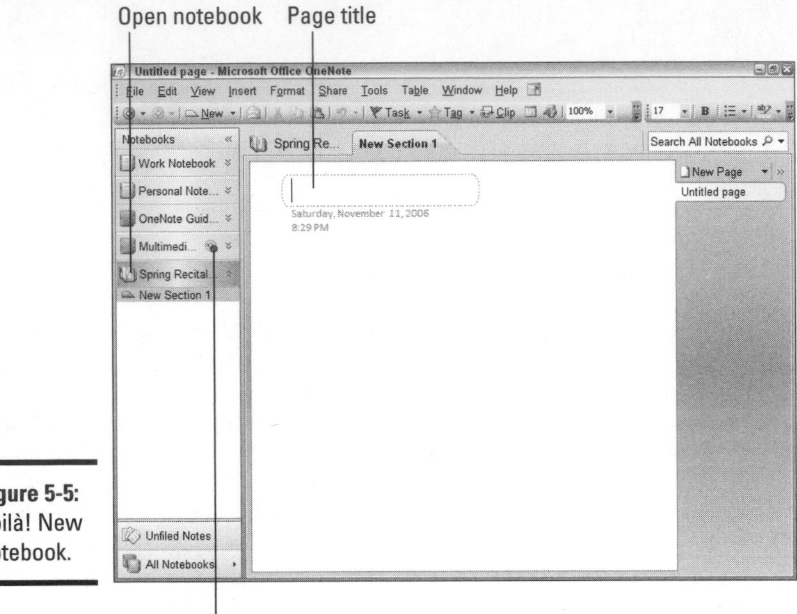

Figure 5-5: Voilà! New notebook.

When you create a new blank notebook, it has one section, and that section has one notebook page. Give the page a title by typing something in that little circle you see at the top of the page. The page title then appears on the right, on the page's tab. If you don't type any title, OneNote just uses the first sentence you type as the page title, at least as far as the page tab is concerned. After you add more pages to this section, you can use this tab to jump right back to this page at any time. You're probably itching to get something down on that nice, empty page. Go ahead; all you have to do is click anywhere you want and start typing.

Each item on a page is saved within its own container. So if you start typing, you see a box forming around what you type. Text automatically wraps within the box, and the box expands to fit the width of the page and the depth of your text, so you have no sizing problems there. The containers surround every object, not just text but graphic images, Outlook items, drawings, and so on. You use these containers to move things around; click the top of a container to select everything in it and then drag the container to move it.

Adding a New Page

Each section starts off with one page. It doesn't take long to fill it, but even before you do, you may want to create a new page instead of dumping everything on the same page. No problem; adding a new page to a section is easy:

- **Click the New Page button** on the right (just above the page tabs) to add a new, blank page.
- **Choose File⇨New⇨Page** to add a new, blank page.

After the page is added, click in the bubble at the top of the page and type a page title. The title appears on the page's tab on the right. You can change this title as often as you feel like it, until you finally get a title that makes sense to you and describes the contents of the page. If you don't type a title, the text from the first note appears on the page tab.

Your next step is to add content to the page. That content can be in the form of text, audio, video, graphic images, charts, tables, bulleted or numbered lists, and just about anything else you can think of. This chapter shows you how to add stuff to a page, but to add a quick note, see the upcoming section "Taking a Note."

To remove a page (or subpage) and its contents, right-click it and choose Delete. To rearrange the order of the pages in a section, click a page's tab, drag it up or down the page tabs, and drop it where you want it. To move a page to a different section, drag the page tab onto a section button on the Navigation Bar and drop it.

Saving yourself from boredom with templates

Instead of adding a boring white page, you can jazz it up by adding a new page with a fancy background or some sample structure. All you need to do is to apply a template when you create the page. Some templates include text sections to get you started on that page. For example, a Project Overview page has a place for the project name and description and a bulleted list for the project goals. To add a new page using a template:

1. **Choose a previously used template or display the task pane.**

   You can choose a template in one of two ways:

   - **Click the arrow on the New Page button** and select a template from the list of ones you've selected before. The template is applied to a new page, and that page is added to the notebook. If you like what you see, you can skip the rest of these steps because you're done.

- **If you don't see something you like, then choose More Template Choices and Options,** and the Templates task pane makes a guest appearance on the right (see Figure 5-6). You can also choose File➪New➪Page from Template to display the Templates task pane.

2. **Choose a template from the task pane.**

   Click the plus sign in front of a category to display its templates to see all the templates. For example, click the plus sign in front of the Business category.

   If you don't like what you see, you can click a different template — nothing's permanent yet. To view even more templates, click the Templates on Office Online link to visit Microsoft's Web site and download a template.

3. **Close the Templates task pane by clicking its Close button (X).**

You can't apply a template to an existing page, but you can create a new page using a template and then copy the stuff from the other page onto it. To copy everything on the page, click outside the borders of the object containers so that you don't select just one, and then press Ctrl+A. Next, choose Edit➪Copy to copy everything, change to the new templated page, and choose Edit➪Paste to paste it all.

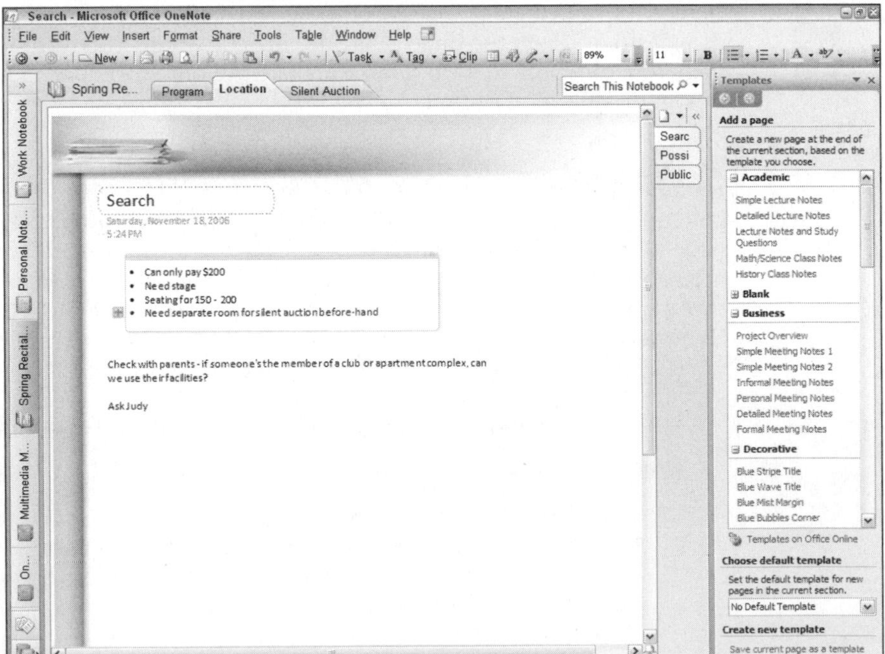

Figure 5-6: No reason why a new page has to be boring.

Hey, gotta template you like a lot? You can make it the default so that you can create new pages using that template easily. This trick is restricted to the current section, however, so change to that section first. Choose File⇨New⇨Page from Template. In the Templates task pane that jumps out, choose the template you want to use in this section most of time, from the Choose Default Template list.

Discovering the subtle truth about subpages

If all you want to do is to continue what's on a page, you can stretch out the current page or add a *subpage.* A subpage has its own title and appears as a small page tab on the right, under the main page's full tab. You can move, copy, delete, and e-mail a page and its subpages as if they were one unit.

To create a subpage, try one of these methods:

- **Click the Page button** on the right and choose New Subpage.
- **Click the New button** on the Standard toolbar and choosing Subpage from the list.
- **Choose File⇨New⇨Subpage.**

A new page is created, and its tab appears under the main page's tab in the page list, as shown in Figure 5-7. Otherwise, a subpage is just like any other page — you can put whatever you want on it. To select a subpage group, double-click the main page's tab. You can then move the group, copy, delete, or e-mail all the pages in the group.

Subpage

Figure 5-7: A subpage appears below the main page.

To make an existing page into a subpage, first drag it up or down the page tab list so that it's under the page you want to act as the main page. Then select both page tabs by pressing Ctrl and clicking them. Right-click and choose Group Pages. The lower page in the selection is changed to a subpage, and its tab is shortened. You can ungroup the pages at a later time and return each one to a main page status. Simply select the group, right-click it, and choose Ungroup Pages.

Adding a Section

Each notebook in OneNote can be divided into little sections. Each section gets its own tab, which runs along the top of the window. (See Figure 5-8.) Each section (and its associated tab) gets its own color, which helps you identify sections with a particular purpose. For example, you might create a new section for each class you're taking, for each major client you handle, or for each person on your team.

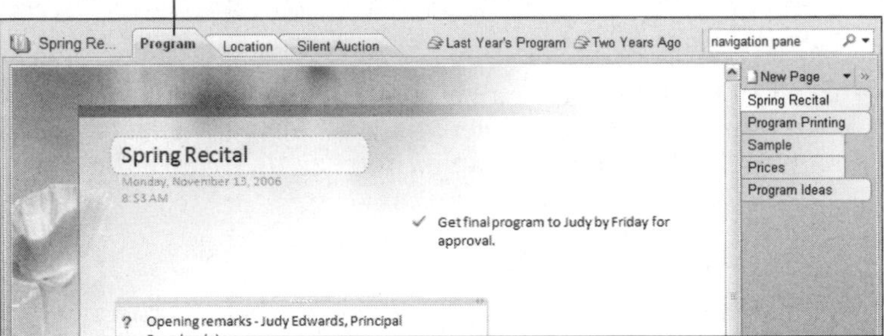

Figure 5-8: Divide your notebook into sections.

You can change the color of a section's tab by choosing Format⇨Section Color and then choosing a color from the list. You don't have to make each tab a different color; use the colors to visually group similar sections.

Each section and its contents are stored as a separate file in whatever folder you choose to create the notebook.

To create a new section in the current notebook, follow these steps:

1. **Choose File⇨New⇨Section.**

   A new section is added to the notebook, and its tab appears at the top of the window, at the end of the list of tabs. You can also click the arrow on the New button on the Standard toolbar and choose Section from the list to create a new section.

The new section tab is highlighted; OneNote is waiting for you to name your new baby.

2. **Type a name for the section and press Enter.**

To move from section to section, click a section's tab. The first page in that section appears. To move to a different page, click the page tab you want to view from those tabs listed on the right.

New sections are added to the end of the tab list, on the right. You can reorder the sections by dragging a section's tab along the line of tabs. A black downward triangle marks the spot; when the triangle is located where you want the section tab to be, release the mouse button to drop it. To move a section to another notebook, expand the Navigation Bar and then drop the tab within the notebook list.

Adding a Section Group

You can create a section group and fill it with as many sections as you like. A section group is still part of a notebook, but it appears to the right of the section tabs as a button. When you click the button, it's as if you're opening a new notebook. You can put one section here, or several. It's just a way of putting a few pages together in an easy-to-get-to place that's away from the main section.

To create a section group, follow these steps:

1. **Choose File⇨New⇨Section Group.**

   You can also click the arrow on the New button and choose Section Group. A new group is created and added to the right of the tabs. The new section group button is highlighted; it's waiting for a name.

2. **Type a name for the new group and press Enter.**
3. **Click the section group button (see Figure 5-9).**

   You're shown a gray page that tells you that no sections are in this group yet.

4. **Click the page to create a section.**

   A section tab is added; type a name for the section and press Enter. The section contains one page. Add whatever you want to this new page. Add pages and sections to this new section group as you like.

5. **Click the Return button (see Figure 5-10) to return to the main sections.**

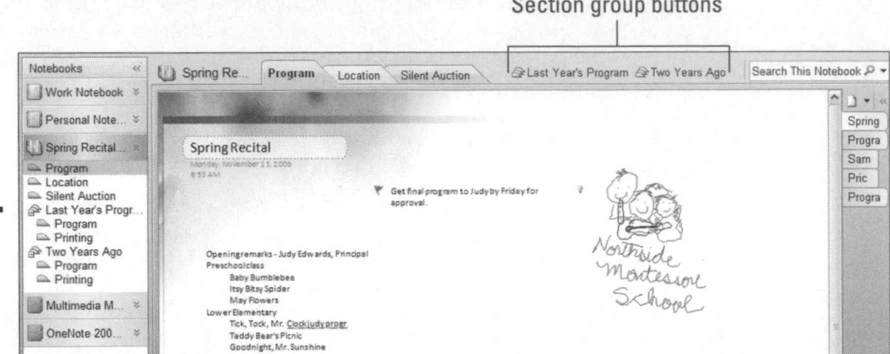

Figure 5-9: A section group is added.

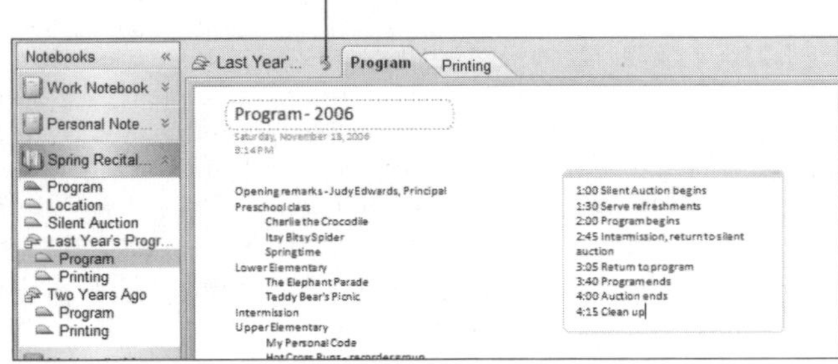

Figure 5-10: Return ticket.

Taking a Note

To add text to a page, just click and type. (Okay, you might take one second to change to the notebook and page you want to store the note on.) Text is stored instantly in a little container with cute borders that cause the text to wrap within it. The container automatically widens to the width of the page and keeps expanding height-wise as you add more text.

If you're not sure where you want to file your new note, you can change to the Unfiled Notes notebook by clicking its icon on the Navigation Bar and then create the note.

You can also resize or move the container:

- **You can resize the container to keep the text in a specific area.** Move the mouse pointer over the right side of a container and drag.

✦ **You can move the container around on the page.** First click the top of the container to select it. Then drag the container wherever you want on the page. To move the container to a different page, section, or notebook, you need to cut and paste it.

Formatting text

I get bored pretty easily, so I format my text to jazz it up, using the buttons conveniently placed on the Formatting toolbar. Of course, you can just type a note and leave it at that. But if you have time, adding formatting may make it easier to find certain information on a page.

I won't bore you with too many details — if you've used any other Office program, you already know how to format: just drag over existing text and click a button on the Formatting toolbar, such as Bold or Italics. To format all the text in a container, click the container's upper border to select everything inside and then apply your formatting. You can also click buttons on the Formatting toolbar to select formats, and then type. Notice that the Bullets and the Numbering buttons are also on the Formatting toolbar so that you can conveniently create bulleted or numbered lists should that strike your fancy (see Figure 5-11).

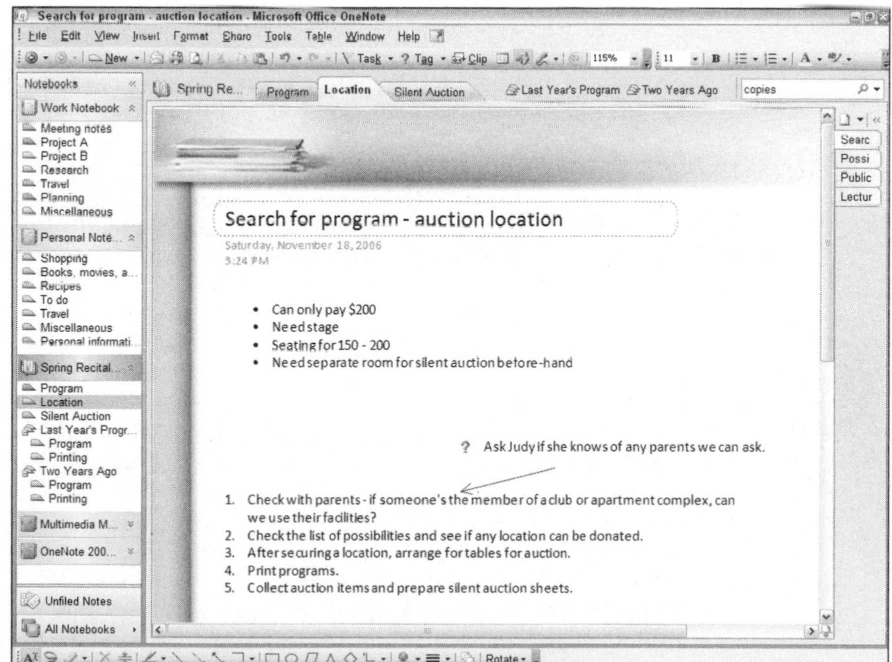

Figure 5-11: Make that text pretty.

A lot of my note-taking involves making lists, so if you're like me, you'll be making lists like crazy. Here's how:

- **Create a bulleted list** by clicking where you want to start the list, clicking the arrow on the Bullets button, and then selecting a bullet style. Type each item on its own line and press Enter to create the next item.
- **Create a numbered list** in about the same way that you create a bulleted list: Click where you want the list to appear, click the arrow on the Numbering button and select a number style, and then type each item pressing enter to add the next item.

Creating a table

I seem to create a lot of tables, which to me, are like long lists that just happen to like standing in neat columns. If you're not sure what a table is, take a look at Figure 5-12. To create a table, follow these steps:

1. **Create column headings.**

   Type the first column heading for your table, press Tab to move to the next column, and type that next heading. Keep pressing Tab to create more columns until you're done.

2. **Add first item.**

   After typing the last column heading, press Enter to add the first row (first item) in the tabled list. Type something in each column; press Tab to move from one column to another.

3. **Add other items.**

   To add another row so that you can create a second item, press Enter. Type something in each column and press Enter to create the next item. Repeat this process to add each item in the table.

You can copy a table directly from an Excel worksheet in order to collect its data together with other notes and material on the same client, project, or job. Just drag over the cells in the worksheet to select them, and then choose Home⇨Clipboard⇨Copy. Switch over to OneNote, click in the page where you want the Excel data to appear, and choose Edit⇨Paste. The Excel data appears in a table, and a link to the Excel workbook appears just underneath the data on the page.

After creating a table, you can make changes to it as you like:

- **To insert a column,** click inside the table and then choose either Table⇨Insert Columns to the Left or Insert Columns to the Right.

- **Add a new row at the end of the table,** simply click in the last column of the last row and then press Enter.
- **To add a new row somewhere in the middle of a table,** click in any row and choose either Table➪Insert Rows Above or Insert Rows Below.
- **To delete a column or row** (and everything in it), click in the column/row and choose either Table➪Delete Columns or Delete Rows.

Borders appear around each cell in the table, but you don't have to stare at them. To turn borders off, choose Table➪Show Borders.

Other stuff you can do with a new page

After typing a bunch of notes or adding graphics, audio files, and such, you may want to add extra space to the bottom of a page. You can do so easily by clicking the Scroll Down by Half Page button at the bottom of the vertical scroll bar. To add space between notes or any object, click the Insert or Remove Extra Writing Space button on the Writing Tools toolbar. Then click and drag to expand the space between objects, as shown in Figure 5-13.

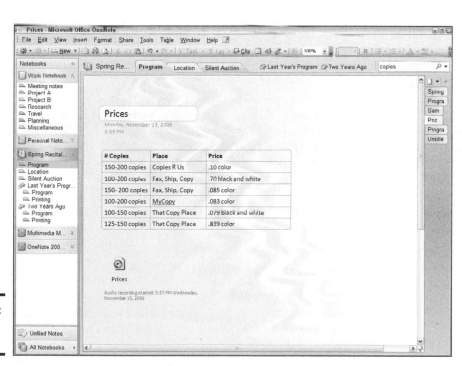

Figure 5-12: Table that idea.

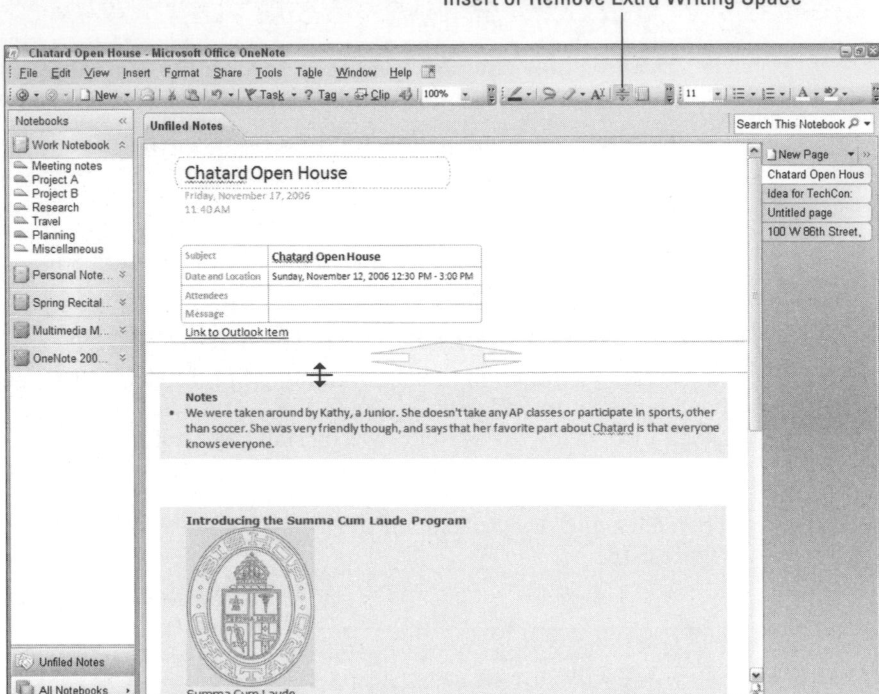

Figure 5-13: Wide open spaces.

Each new page automatically includes a title that you type into a bubble (or skip if you don't want to use a title). Underneath this title are a date and time. This date and time are set when the page is created, and it doesn't change, even if you update the page with new information. To change the date or time that appears at the top of a page:

1. **Click the date or the time you want to change.**

   A calendar or clock icon appears just to the right of the date or time you clicked.

2. **Click the icon that appears on the right (the calendar or the clock).**

   A dialog box appears.

3. **Change the date or time.**

   From the dialog box that appears when you click the icon, change the date and then click outside the calendar, or change the time for the page and click OK.

If you want, you can insert a date and time elsewhere on the page. Choose Insert➪Date and Time or press Alt+Shift+F to insert the current date and time. To insert just the date, press Alt+Shift+D; to insert the time only, press Alt+Shift+T instead.

Creating a Quick Side Note From Any Program

A *side note* is like an adhesive note; you can use it to jot down a quick thought about a telephone conversation, e-mail message, something you saw on the Web, or whatever. The beauty here is that you create side notes when you're not in OneNote, but off working in some other program. Side notes are placed in the Unfiled Notes notebook in OneNote where you can view them later on and then move them into a more appropriate place. Use side notes to gather your thoughts while you work; use OneNote to organize them.

Side notes aren't just for text; oh no. You can drag and drop anything you like into them, including images. You can also select something, copy it to the Clipboard, and paste it into a side note. In fact, you can do anything with a side note you might do with a regular note, including recording audio or video, tagging, creating a task, capturing a screen shot, or drawing with a pen tablet. (See later sections in this chapter for help inserting items into note or side note.)

To create a side note, follow these steps:

1. **From anywhere, click the OneNote button on the Windows taskbar.**

   A side note window appears, as shown in Figure 5-14. You can also press the Windows Logo key on your keyboard, plus the letter N, to create a side note.

2. **Type your note.**

   Again, you can type or write (with a pen tablet), drag and drop, copy and paste, or otherwise use your clever imagination (and the help in this chapter) to put data in the side note.

3. **When you're done, click the window's Close button.**

   A new page is added to the Unfiled Notes notebook, where you can view or relocate it later.

Idea for TechCon: - Microsoft Office OneNote

Idea for TechCon:

- Jermaine's should blog his trip to TechCon
- In the blog, he could share his early impressions of the new products
- He could also share interviews with company reps
- Maybe include videos?
- Would there be a copyright issue with videos?
- He could upload pictures of new products to the ftp site, and we could put them in an image gallery linked to the blog.

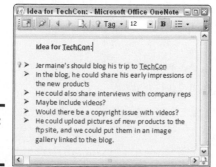

Figure 5-14: Jot down a quick note.

Writing and Drawing Notes by Hand

If you have a pen tablet attached to your computer, you don't have to be confined by a keyboard when collecting your thoughts in OneNote. You can write your notes freehand and draw, doodle, circle something, or highlight an important idea with a star or arrow. Here's what to do:

1. **Activate the pen.**

   To activate the pen so that OneNote doesn't treat it as just another mouse, click the Pen button on the Writing Tools toolbar, as shown in Figure 5-15. There's an arrow on the Pen button so that you can choose a different color, or you can just go with the color shown on the button by clicking the button instead. If you click the arrow to display the pen list, you find a variety of thick and thin pens there, along with some wide highlighters that obviously use semitransparent "ink".

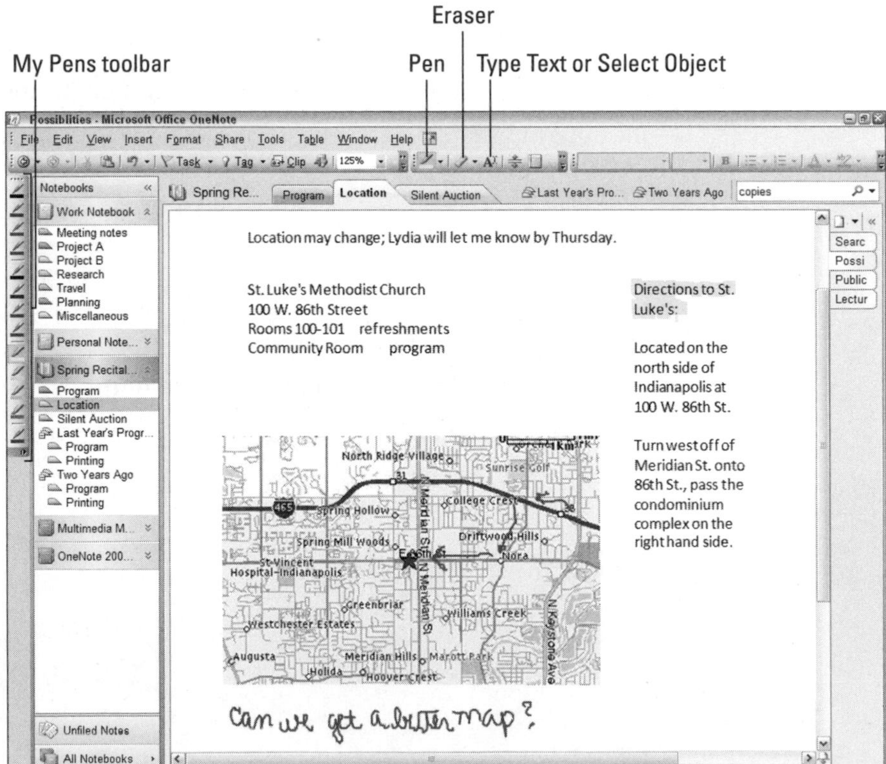

Figure 5-15: Choose a pen.

2. **Use the pen.**

   After choosing a pen, just draw on the tablet surface to create text or a doodle.

3. **Go back to a regular mouse.**

   To return to a regular mouse, click the Type Text or Select Objects button on the Writing Tools toolbar.

If you don't have a pen tablet, you can draw with just a regular old mouse by clicking one of the Pen buttons to activate the drawing feature. However, drawing with a mouse instead of a pen tablet is pretty difficult because a mouse isn't really designed for drawing. OneNote also doesn't recognize that any words you write with a mouse are text; everything is treated as a drawing.

To switch from one pen style to another quickly, display the My Pens toolbar by choosing View⇨My Pens Toolbar. This convenient toolbar hides itself on the side of the window so that it doesn't take up too much room.

If you make a mistake while drawing or writing with the pen, you can use an Eraser, located on the Writing Tools toolbar, to get rid of any stray marks. Use the arrow on the Eraser button to choose what size you want. The Stroke eraser can remove an entire pen stroke with one click, so it's handy but dangerous if that's not what you wanted to do.

You can set options to help you use the pen more intuitively if you want. Choose Tools⇨Options⇨Pen and set these options:

✦ Turn off the Disable the Scratch-Out Gesture While Inking to allow you to erase pen strokes by scratching back and forth over them three times.

✦ Turn on the Use Pen Pressure Sensitivity option to allow you to make the line fatter by simply pressing harder with your pen. This option does tend to make the notebook file larger though, so keep that in mind.

✦ Turn on the Automatically Switch Between Pen and Selection Tool option to allow OneNote to change the pen tool to a pointer when you start doing something that seems more mouse-like, such as clicking on a container.

If you want to select anything you've handwritten, click the Type Text or Select Object button on the Writing Tools toolbar and then drag over any text you want to select. You can also draw around the text with the Lasso Select tool on the Writing Tools toolbar to select all the text. To select a single word, double-click it just as you do in Word.

Adding rules to a page

When I try to write notes, frankly they come out a little awkward, even with a pen tablet. Having ruled paper seems to help though. Trouble is, you can't display the rules on the part of a page that's decorated with a background graphic. So if you created the page using a decorative template, you aren't able to show the rules. But you can extend the page and display the rules there if you want. To display rules on a page, follow these steps:

1. **Click the Show/Hide Rule Lines button on the Writing Tools toolbar.**
2. **Extend the page, if needed.**

   On a page that's not designed for rules (because it uses a background graphic), you need to extend the page to see the rules by clicking the Scroll Down by Half Page button at the bottom of the vertical scroll bar.
3. **Change the rules.**

   Change the type of rules shown using Page Setup: Choose File⇨Page Setup. On the Page Setup task pane that jumps up, choose a Line Style and Line Color from the Rule Lines section.

Converting handwriting to editable text

Here's something that's pretty neat — a way to turn your handwritten scribbles into neat, editable text that looks like you typed it. Another advantage in having editable text (besides the fact that no one will know what sloppy handwriting you have) is that you can format it as well.

You can only convert handwritten text that OneNote recognizes as such. To create convertible handwritten text, you need a Tablet PC — basically a laptop with a swivel monitor that allows you to write on it with a stylus, or some kind of similar handheld device that also runs the Tablet PC operating system. As you write text on such a device, a blue box appears behind it to indicate to you that OneNote recognizes that you're creating text.

To convert text, follow these steps:

1. **Select the text to convert:**
   - **On the entire page,** click the page's tab.
   - **In a note container,** click the top border of the note's container.
   - **Within a note container,** click the Type Text or Select Objects button on the Writing Tools toolbar and then drag over just the text you want to convert or double-click a single word to select just that word.
2. **Choose Tools⇨Convert Handwriting to Text.**

   The selected handwritten text is converted to editable text.

3. Make corrections.

If OneNote converts a handwritten word to something other than what you want, then click the Alternate List symbol or right-click the wrong word and select a different word from the list that appears. If the right word isn't on the list, simply retype it yourself.

Drawing by hand

You can also draw with your pen. To draw straight lines though, you may want to use the buttons on the Drawing Tools toolbar, shown in Figure 5-16. To display the toolbar, choose View⇨Drawing Toolbar. You can use these tools with a regular mouse as well, so don't feel left out if you don't have a pen tablet.

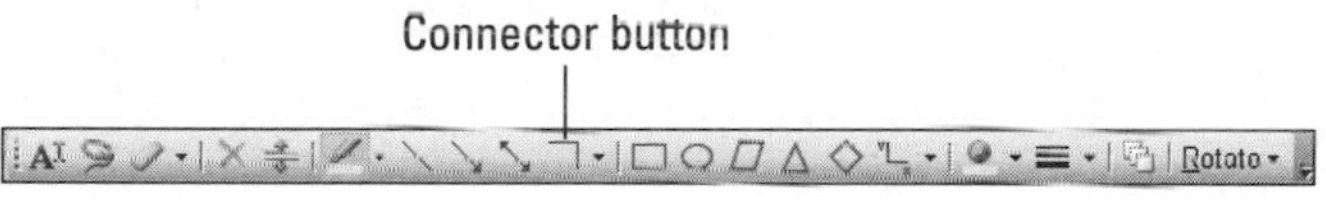

Figure 5-16: Draw lines, arrows, and such.

Here are the drawing tools and how to use them:

- ✦ **To create a line, arrow, or double-headed arrow,** click the Line, Arrow, or Double Arrow button on the Drawing toolbar. Then click on the page and drag to create the line or arrow. The arrow points in the direction you drag, except the line that doesn't have an arrow (duh) and the double arrow (which can't make up its mind, and points both ways).
- ✦ **To create a connector,** click the arrow on the Connector button and select the one you want. You can create connectors that go in two or three directions, and some with arrows on the end. To use the connector shown on the button, just click the button itself. After you select a connector, click near one object you want to connect, and then drag towards the other object. A connector line is created that visually connects the two objects, but not in actuality (in other words, the objects are still free to move about the cabin on their own). If you chose a three-line connector, when you click or drag, a star with six points is created. You can resize or move the star to move it near the objects you want to connect visually.
- ✦ **To create an object such as a rectangle, oval, parallelogram, triangle or diamond,** click the appropriate button. Then click on the page to establish the upper-left corner of the object and drag downward and to the right to create the object.
- ✦ **To change an object's line color or width,** you can make selections from the Line Color and Line Thickness buttons before you draw the line or object, or after you draw it and select it again (by clicking the edge of its container).

- **To create more than one of a certain kind of object,** click the Duplicate Shapes button. This feature allows you to use the line or shape button you select over and over again without having to click it repeatedly. When you're through creating that type of object, click the Duplicate Shapes button again to turn it off.
- **To rotate an object or line,** select it first by clicking it. The handles (small green squares) appear around the object. Next, click the Rotate button on the Drawing toolbar and choose a rotation on the menu that appears. For example, select Rotate Left 45°. You can also flip an object over its vertical or horizontal axis by choosing Flip Vertical or Flip Horizontal.
- **To get rid of an object,** click it to select it and then click the Delete button on the Drawing toolbar or just press Delete.

To select multiple objects, just lasso them. Click the Lasso Select button on the Drawing toolbar and drag to draw a circle around the objects you want to select. This tool is especially helpful in selecting a single object as well, in cases where you drew several objects at the same time, which were then stored in the same container. After selecting some objects, you can then resize the objects by dragging a handle outward or inward; drag a corner handle to resize an object proportionately. You can also change the selected object's line color and width using the Line Color and Line Thickness buttons.

Inserting Images

Notes in OneNote aren't just text — they can contain lots of stuff, including tables, audio and video files, and well, at least according to the heading here, images as well.

Why would you add an image to a note? Well, one reason is to dress it up, with the image acting as a background or just a piece of art on the page. Another reason to add photos is to help you identify things, such as a new client, your kids, or a digital camera you're looking to buy.

Not every image has to be a photo; nope, you can include a piece of clip art or maybe an Internet map showing the fastest route from your hotel to the convention center. You can insert images directly from your computer, digital camera, or scanner. You can also grab them right off a Web page or steal them from your computer screen — see the next section, "Inserting a Screen Shot," for help.

There's something you can do in OneNote with an image (whether it's a screen shot or an inserted image file) that's pretty interesting, and that's search its text. Yep, OneNote does a pretty good job of reading the text in an image, and helping you locate that image again, based on your search text. See Book VI, Chapter 6.

To insert an image file, follow these steps:

1. **Choose Insert⇨Pictures.**

   A menu appears.

2. **Choose either From Files or From Camera or Scanner.**

   Use the From Files option to get an image from your computer or a network folder to which you have access. If you choose this option, the Insert Pictures dialog box appears; browse to the image file, select it, and click Insert.

   Use the From Camera or Scanner option to grab a photo directly from your digital camera (I'm assuming here that you've connected it to your computer) or from your scanner. If you choose this option, the Insert Picture from Camera or Scanner dialog box appears, and you just select your scanner or camera from the Device list, adjust the resolution if desired, and click Insert.

Now, after the image is added to a page as shown in Figure 5-17, you can do what you'd normally do in any other program with an inserted image:

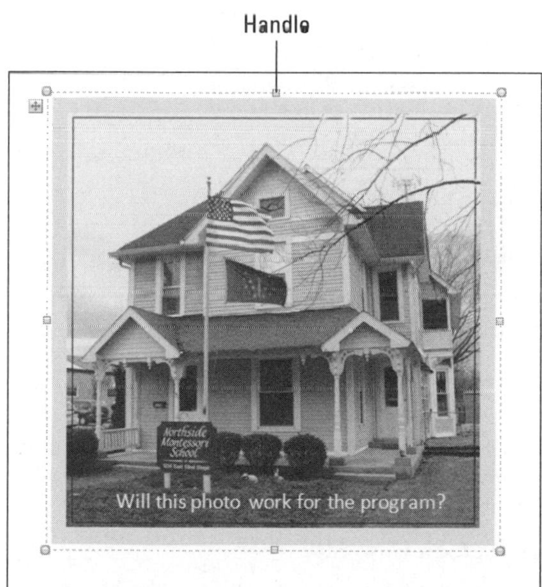
Handle
Will this photo work for the program?

Figure 5-17: Add images to a note.

- **To resize the image,** click its border to display the *handles* (those small squares that surround the image). Drag a handle inward to make the image smaller or outward to make it larger. I recommend using a corner handle to keep the image from getting thrown out of proportion.

- **To move an image on the page,** click its border to select the image and then move the mouse pointer over the image. Drag and drop the image where you want it to live.
- **Add text over top of the image** (as a kind of image caption) by clicking within the image and then just typing. You can format the text as you might format any other text. The text appears over top of the image, in its own container that you can move as needed. (Click the container's border and drag.) You can add as many text captions as you like, by just clicking the image and typing.

If you want to turn your newly inserted image into the page background, right-click the image and choose Set Picture as Background.

Inserting a Screen Shot

Another way in which you can add an image to a page is to simply grab it. The way you normally grab an image is with a screen capture program, or a graphics editor with screen capturing capability. That's what I used to get the images for this book. You're not going to need either one though, because OneNote has screen-capturing capability built right in.

For you Windows Vista users out there, you'll find that OneNote's screen clipper works similarly to Vista's Snipping Tool, except in this case, the screen shots are save automatically in OneNote (instead of within the Snipping Tool window).

To grab a picture of something you see on your screen, follow these steps:

1. **Display the window to capture.**

   If you want to grab something from a Web page, start your browser and display the Web page. If you want to take a picture of a new program or some error message, then display that.

2. **Change back to OneNote.**

   After you have the thing you want to grab a picture of showing on-screen, change back over to OneNote. Click on the page where you want the image to appear once it's captured.

3. **Choose Insert⇨Screen Clipping.**

   OneNote minimizes itself, and the window you had on top comes into view, although it's dimmed. You can also click the Clip button on the Standard toolbar to capture a screen.

4. **Define the area to capture.**

   Click in the upper-left corner of the area you want to capture and then drag downwards and to the right, creating a rectangle. As you drag, the area you select changes to full color while the unselected area remains dim. The area inside the selection rectangle is the area OneNote captures.

   After you release the mouse button, OneNote comes back to the forefront and shows you the image you captured on the page where you clicked, as shown in Figure 5-18. At the bottom of the image, OneNote automatically places a note to remind you that you captured this image yourself, and when. This note helps you easily distinguish captured images from images you've saved on the computer and inserted manually, or images brought in from your camera or scanner (see the section, "Inserting Images".) If you captured a portion of a Web page, a link to that Web page appears as well. This enables you to revisit the page later on if needed.

If you didn't capture the right area, just delete the image (by clicking the container's top border and pressing Delete) and redo these steps again.

The image you just captured, by the way, is placed on the Clipboard so that you can paste it into another program. You can, for example, paste the image into a graphics editor so that you can save the image permanently in a file that you can edit.

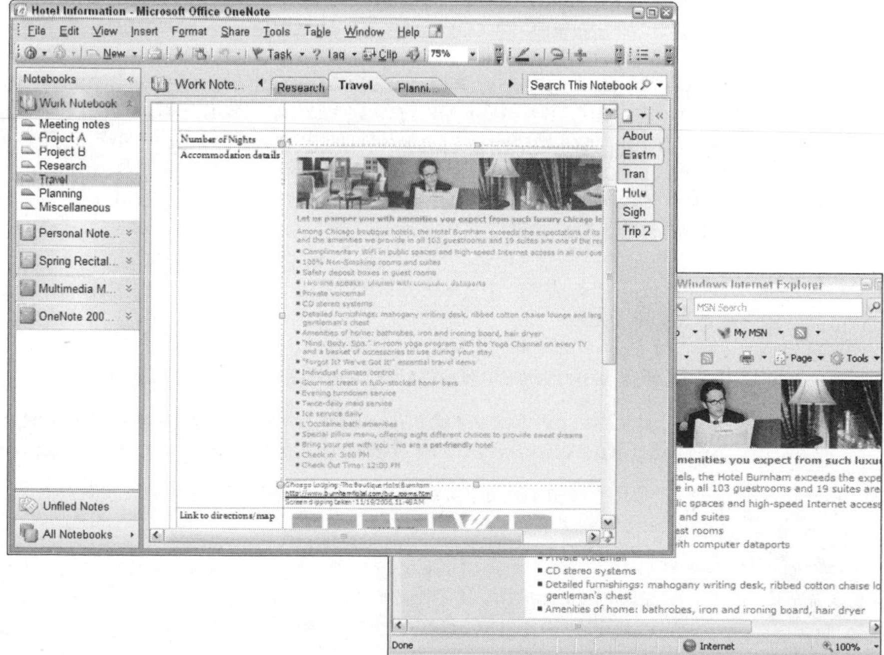

Figure 5-18: Capture an on-screen image.

You can grab a quick image from anywhere by just pressing the Windows Logo button on your keyboard, and pressing S. Drag to define the area to capture, and the image is automatically filed for you on a new page in the Unfiled Notes notebook. You can then move it into whatever notebook you want by using the Cut and Paste commands. You can also drag the entire page onto a notebook on the Navigation Bar to move that page.

When you use this method (Windows Logo key+S) to capture a screen, OneNote places the captured image in the Unfiled Notes notebook. You can change this behavior by right-clicking the OneNote icon on the Windows taskbar and choosing Options⇨Screen Clipping Defaults. For example, maybe you prefer to have OneNote place the capture on the current screen or simply copy it to the Clipboard without inserting it on any page.

Adding Audio or Video

Sometimes, the written word just doesn't tell the whole story; in such cases, you may want to record your thoughts about a note, image, drawing, or other bit of information and store it on a page. Or perhaps typing along while someone's talking may be inconvenient, especially if you're trying to listen and think of questions and comments at the same time. In other cases, trying to create a typed note while someone's talking may be considered rude. But if you consider the possibility of recording someone else, then you don't need to worry that you'll miss the important parts of a lecture or meeting — you can just record it instead.

OneNote provides the recording capabilities; all you have to do is look pretty (or talk pretty, if you're recording audio). Well, okay, you do need to supply a few things for OneNote to perform its magic. To record audio, your computer is gonna need a microphone. (Laptops typically have one built-in, so if your computer is a laptop, you may have just lucked out.) To record video, you need a webcam.

After you install all the necessary equipment, follow these steps to record audio or video:

1. **Click where you want the recording to appear.**
2. **Click the arrow on the Record button, located on the Standard toolbar, and choose either Record Audio Only or Record Video.**

   The current time appears on the page, and the Audio and Video Recording toolbar appears.

   If OneNote is not currently running, you can start an audio recording by right-clicking the OneNote icon at the right end of the Windows taskbar and choosing Start Recording Audio.

3. **Record the audio or video you want.**

   If you want to mark a particular place in the recording or make a comment about it, simply type a note. In Figure 5-19, I typed my notes just under the recording, but you can actually type them anywhere — they'll still be linked. Notes created during a recording are linked to that spot in the recording.

4. **When you're through, click the Stop button on the Audio and Video Recording toolbar.**

   OneNote creates either an audio (`.wma`) or video file (`.wmv`), and adds an icon on the page to represent it.

5. **To play the recording, double-click its icon.**

   If you want to jump directly to a spot at which you made a note, hover the mouse pointer over the note, and you see a Play button just to the left of the text, as shown in Figure 5-19. Click this button to start the recording.

   If you select the See Playback button on the Audio and Video recording toolbar, then as the recording plays, notes you may have typed during that recording are highlighted at the same point in the recording at which you made them originally. In Figure 5-19, for example, the note, "Sign to route," is highlighted as the description of the sign, and how it directs you is being played in the audio file. If you're playing the recording from the beginning, you can still jump to a specific point in the recording that matches a note by clicking the left or right arrow buttons that appear on either side of the time code area on the toolbar.

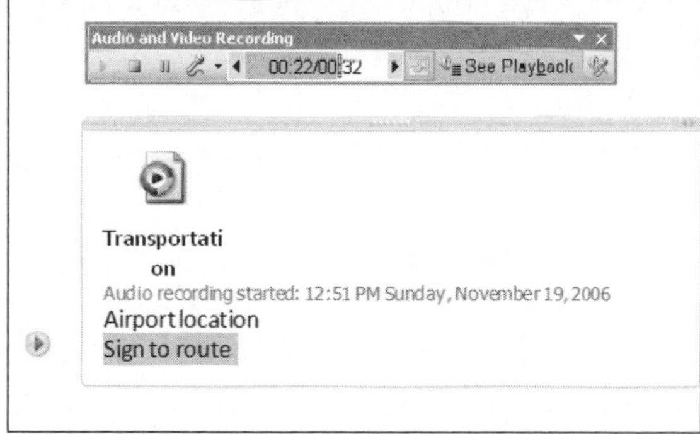

Figure 5-19: Play back your recording.

The recording stops automatically, although you can stop it early by clicking the Stop button. Click Pause to pause the playback temporarily; click the Pause button again to resume.

You can search these notes you make and use them to find a particular recording later on. If you don't make any notes while recording, don't worry. OneNote can also search the text spoken in the audio or video files themselves, although that's not always a guarantee that it'll find what you're looking for because OneNote may not understand each word you say (and thus, may not be able to find that word when searching). See Book VI, Chapter 6 for help in searching.

Inserting a Document or File

It may seem kind of silly to attach a document or a file to a note, because it's often readily available to you, and a link to a document is so much simpler and takes up less room inside the note. (To find out how to link to a document or file, see the upcoming section "Adding Links to Other Pages, Files, or the Internet.")

However, what do you do if you're away on a trip or working at home, and a critical piece of information you need is on the office network? A link to a document on a network you may not be able to connect to doesn't do you much good. If you want to make sure that you always have access to a particular file or files, you can attach them to a page:

1. **Choose Insert⇨Files.**

   The Choose a File or a Set of Files to Insert dialog box appears.

2. **Select the file(s) to insert.**

   Change to the folder that contains the file(s) you want to attach. Press Ctrl and click each file you want to attach.

3. **Click Insert.**

   The file(s) are attached to the current note page. An icon representing each file appears on the page. See Figure 5-20.

If you double-click one of these icons, the associated file opens. You may see a warning telling you not to open the file if you don't trust its source. Good advice under any circumstances. Anyway, click Yes to continue and open the file.

A copy of the file(s) you selected is attached to the page. If someone comes along later and updates the file(s), you'll be looking at an old copy if you open the file(s) through OneNote. A link, on the other hand, always points to the actual, updated file, but it does require that you have access to the folder in which the linked file is located. See "Adding Links to Other Pages, Files, or the Internet" for help.

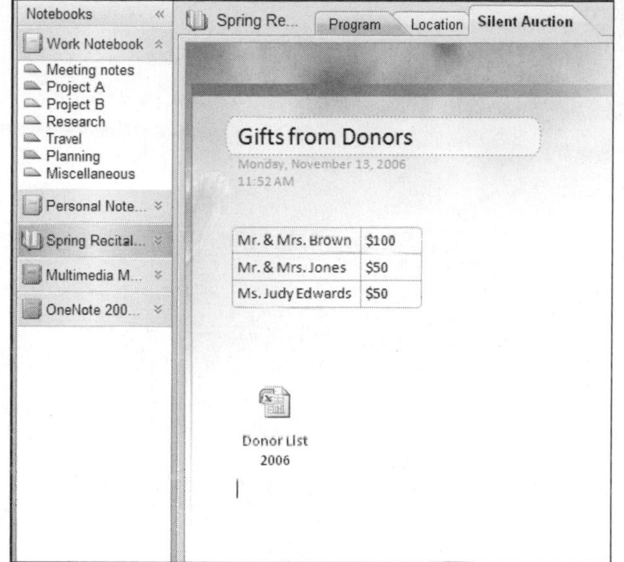

Figure 5-20: Insert files you may need to reference on the road.

Inserting a Picture of a Document

Besides linking and attaching files, you have one other option, and it involves inserting a picture of the document's contents. Instead of calling the result a picture, however, OneNote calls it a *printout,* but you get the idea. You can type text over the top of a picture-page or add notes next to a picture-page, which makes this option good for inserting handouts from a lecture or meeting so that you can annotate them. For example, if you've been given a presentation in PowerPoint format, you can insert it as a printout in OneNote and add your own thoughts as you review the slides. You can also use the drawing tools to circle important information or highlight it. See the section, "Drawing by hand," earlier in this chapter, for info.

To insert a picture of a document's contents, follow these steps:

1. **Choose Insert⇨Files as Printouts.**

   The Choose Document to Insert dialog box appears.

2. **Select the file(s) to attach as a printout.**

   Change to the folder that contains the file(s) you want to attach. Press Ctrl and click each file you want to attach.

3. **Click Insert.**

   The application associated with the file(s) you selected starts, and OneNote loads each file and then "prints" it to the page in the form of a picture (see Figure 5-21).

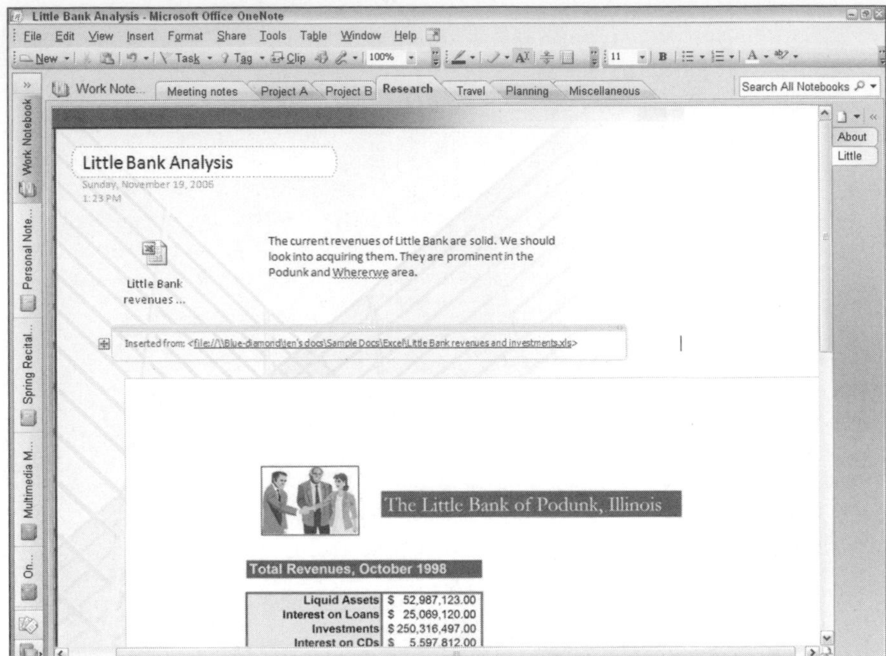

Figure 5-21: Insert a photo of a document.

If you're in a program (such as PowerPoint or Excel, although it can be any program, even non-Office ones) and you want to send the document to OneNote so that you can annotate it, choose File➪Print and then choose Send to OneNote 2007 from the Name list. The result is the same as what's shown here.

An icon representing the file appears; use it to open the actual file if needed (assuming that you have access). Below the icon is a notation reminding you that you inserted this data as a printout from a file, with a clickable link to the file. (I guess OneNote wants to make real sure that you can call up the file if you want to.) Anyway, after the icon and the link, you finally see a picture of each page of the document's contents. Yes, if the document has more than one page, you see more than one picture. And yes, they're pictures, which means that you can drag them around and resize them just like you would any other picture on a notebook page. (See the section "Inserting Images," earlier in this chapter, if you need help with that process.)

OneNote can search the text of a picture-page and help you find something in it if you need to. This feature is real handy when you insert as a printout some lecture handouts or some kind of technical document you need to reference. See Book VI, Chapter 6 for help.

Now, if someone sends you a copy of a note page, and you see one of these funky picture-pages on it, you can double-click the icon or click the link to open the document for printing or editing. If you don't have access to the file's location, however, there's no need to despair. You can still copy the contents of the picture-page and paste it into a document to create a file of your own that you can edit, print, or do anything else with. Just right-click the picture-page and choose Copy Text from This Page of the Printout. If the document is a series of picture-pages in the notebook instead of just one, then choose Copy Text from All the Pages of the Printout instead.

Adding Links to Other Pages, Files, or the Internet

Hyperlinks, or just links as they're called by their closest friends, allow you to jump to some other bit of information with a single click. In OneNote, a link may take you to a different section, a different paragraph on the same page, or to another page altogether. Hyperlinks can also link you to documents and other files, whether they're located on your computer or the network. You can also link to a page out on the Internet.

Linking to other notebook pages

You can create any number of pages in a notebook, in the same section or a different section. You can jump from page to page obviously, by just clicking the section tab and then clicking the page tab. That seems like the long way round to me, though, so I started looking for a shortcut. Turns out you can insert a hyperlink on a page that, when clicked, jumps you right to some other page. Actually, what you create is a link to a specific paragraph on a page, which can be the first paragraph at the top of the page, or somewhere else if that suits you better. If you don't want to link to a particular page but to a whole section, you can do that, too.

You can use page hyperlinks to create a table of contents for a notebook that's going to be used by lots of people (or hey, maybe just for yourself). You can also use page links to point to pages on any kind of list, such as a list of favorites, key concepts, or special terms.

To create a page or section link, follow these steps:

1. **Copy the hyperlink:**

   - **To link to a specific paragraph,** move the mouse pointer in front of that paragraph and right-click. Choose Copy Hyperlink to This Paragraph.

   - **To link to a specific page,** right-click the tab of the page you want to link to, and from the menu that appears, choose Copy Hyperlink to This Page.

- **To link to a particular section,** right-click the section tab and choose Copy Hyperlink to This Section.

 A link to the paragraph, page, or section is created and placed on the Clipboard.

2. **Change to the page on which you want to add the link.**
3. **Choose Edit⇨Paste.**

 The hyperlink appears on the page; if you click the link, the paragraph, page, or section you originally selected appears.

To create a new page instantly and add a link on the current page that points to the new page, type a phrase to use as the link. Then right-click the phrase and choose Create Linked Page.

Linking to files, documents, or Web pages

To create a link to a page on the Internet, you can just type it anywhere on a note page. OneNote recognizes the format of a link and turns your text into a clickable link. You can also copy the link from your browser and paste it onto the page. When linking to a file or other document, you can simply drag and drop the file from Windows Explorer onto a page and create an instant link.

Another way to create a link is a bit slower, but it allows you to insert some text on the page that points to a Web page or document without showing the actual Web address or file path on the page.

To insert a link to a Web page or file on your computer or network, follow these steps:

1. **Choose Insert⇨Hyperlink.**

 The Insert Hyperlink dialog box jumps up.

2. **Type the address you want to link to into the Address box.**

 To link to a file on your computer or network, click the Browse for File button, select the file, and click OK.

3. **Type the text you want to appear on the page in the Text to Display box. Click OK to insert the hyperlink.**

 A link appears in blue text on the page, and when the mouse moves over it, the pointer changes to a hand.

You can change the hyperlink later on (either its address or the link text itself) by right-clicking the link and choosing Edit Hyperlink.

Chapter 6: Maximizing the Power of OneNote

In This Chapter

- Creating Outlook items from within OneNote
- Getting the details of a meeting into a note
- Sharing notes in all sorts of ways
- Protecting your notes from prying eyes
- Reorganizing your note pages
- Tagging important items
- Finding something you've lost

OneNote is a fairly simple application on the surface; click a page and type to create a note. Organize notes on different pages, sections, and notebooks. But it turns out, under this unassuming package lies a pretty powerful assistant. While creating notes and collecting images, charts, and documents, you can create a quick reminder in OneNote to do something. You can also add a quick contact, appointment, or meeting in Outlook, all without leaving the comfort of your little note-taker. If you've already set up a meeting or appointment, you can insert the details on a note page so that you have everything in one place: OneNote.

After you gather lots of stuff in OneNote, you don't need to keep it all to yourself. OneNote lets you easily share your thoughts, whether you choose to e-mail them, blog them, or simply share a file. You can even share pages in a live session where everyone contributes at the same time. On the other hand, if sharing isn't your thing, you can keep your notes safe and secure with a super-secret password and a decoder ring.

Whether you choose to share your notes or keep them all to yourself, you can tag important information to make it easier to find them again. And OneNote certainly gives you lots of ways to search for data, including searching not only text notes but the text in audio and video files and photos, too.

Although you're probably a OneNote expert by now, it bears repeating that stuff you add to a OneNote page is saved automatically for you. So don't go wasting your time looking for a Save button; it's not needed.

Inserting Details of an Appointment or Meeting into a Note

OneNote and Outlook are good buds, working very closely with each other. When needed, you can insert the details of an Outlook appointment or meeting into a note, where you can refer to it as you gather the materials for that appointment or meeting. Okay, it's not a glamorous feature, but hey, it beats typing the details manually or worse yet, forgetting the appointment or meeting altogether.

To insert the details of a meeting into a page, follow these steps:

1. **Choose Insert⇨Outlook Meeting Details.**

   The Insert Outlook Meeting Details dialog box appears, as shown in Figure 6-1. The appointments and meetings for today appear in a list.

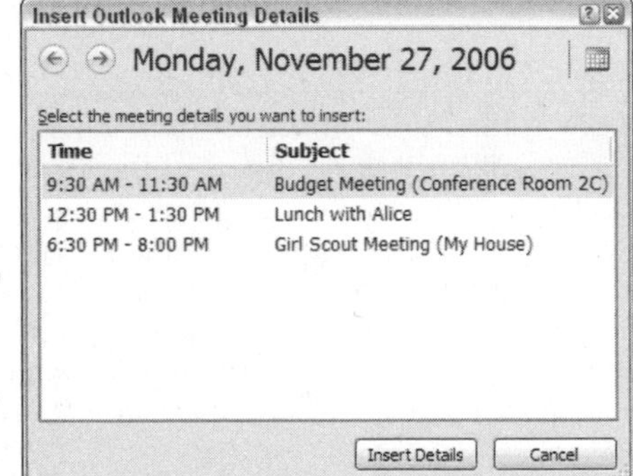

Figure 6-1: Here's your schedule for today.

2. **Change to the date of the appointment or meeting by clicking the Previous Day or Next Day buttons, or clicking the calendar button in the upper-right corner and choosing a date.**
3. **Select an appointment or meeting.**
4. **Click Insert Details.**

   The details of the appointment or meeting, its time, date, location, agenda items, and a list of the attendees are inserted onto the page in a text container. This data isn't connected to Outlook, so if you change something, don't expect Outlook to notice.

Creating an Outlook Task on a Page

Now, here's something cool that Outlook may also be interested in. You can create a task on a page, and it's added to the Outlook Tasks list. If you check off the task, it's checked off on the Tasks list, too. If you spend a lot of time in OneNote, you don't need to switch back and forth just to check on a task.

If you don't want to involve Outlook in tracking tasks you create in OneNote, you can tag an item with a To-Do tag, which creates a check box you can use to track things to do. See the upcoming section "Tagging Important Information."

To add a task on a OneNote page that's also added to Outlook's Task list, follow these steps:

1. **Type the task on a page.**

   For example, click on a page and type **Update slide #4 in Sales presentation** or **Send meeting notes to Alice**. You don't have to select the text, but just keep the cursor in the note container.

2. **Choose Insert⇨Outlook Task. From the sub-menu that appears, choose a due date, such as Today or Next Week.**

   A task flag appears next to the description you typed in Step 1. You can view the task details by hovering the mouse over the description (see Figure 6-2).

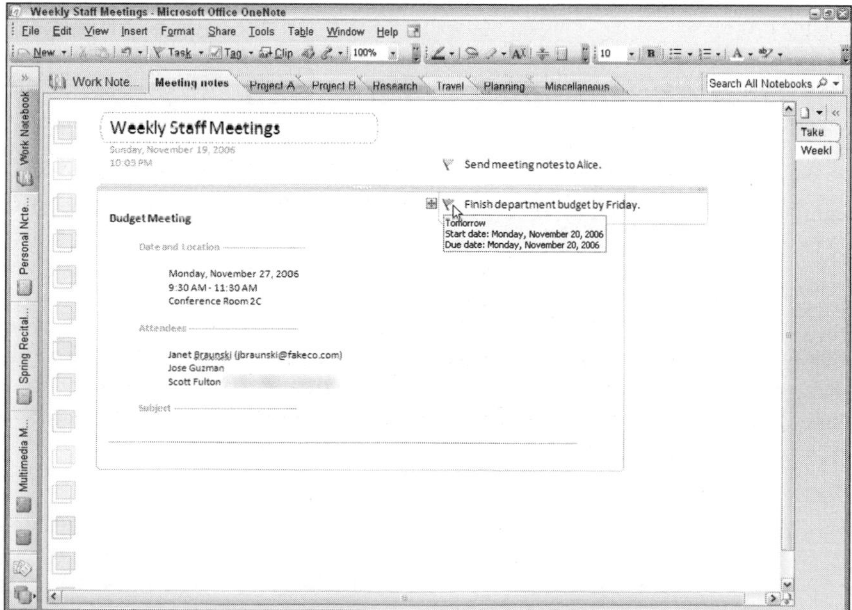

Figure 6-2: Jot down those things to do.

You can also click the Task button on the Standard toolbar to insert a task on a page. The task's due date is set by the type of flag currently showing on the button; to insert a task using a different due date, click the arrow on the Task button and choose a date such as Next Week. After inserting the task flag, type a description, and the task is added to Outlook.

Assume that at some point, you'll get this task done. If you're in Outlook, no problem; just mark that task off in the usual manner. If you're in OneNote, you don't have to switch programs just to check something off your Great Big Jobs list:

- **To check off a task on a page,** click the flag, and it changes to a check mark. You can also click the task description and choose Insert⇨Outlook Task⇨Mark Complete.
- **To change the due date,** click the description, choose Insert⇨Outlook Task, and then choose a different date from the menu.
- **To remove the task from the note page and Outlook,** click the description and choose Insert⇨Outlook Task⇨Delete Outlook Task. The task icon is removed, but the text you typed remains on the page. Select it and press Delete.

  Do not select the task text and press Delete without first removing the task from Outlook, because if you do that, the task is only removed from OneNote and not Outlook.
- **To open the task in Outlook** so that you can add more details or reassign it to someone, click the description and choose Insert⇨Outlook Task⇨Open Task in Outlook.

Creating an Outlook Contact from OneNote

OneNote and Outlook are no strangers to each other; let's face it, they're practically family! And so it shouldn't surprise you that you can use OneNote to send new stuff to Outlook for you. For example, you may be in a meeting, taking notes in OneNote, recording audio or video, or doodling ideas, and bam! Someone breaks your chain of thought and introduces you to some bigwig person you better remember longer than five minutes. To make sure that you do, you instantly decide to add a new name to your Contacts list. But gee whiz, do you have to drop everything and jump over to Outlook just to do that? Nope. OneNote can help you.

To create an Outlook contact from within OneNote, follow these steps:

1. **Choose what to include.**

   Before you create the contact, you need to decide what to send along with it:

   - **To copy the notes on the current page** into the notes section of the new Contact form, click anywhere on the page.
   - **To copy only certain text from the page** into the new contact, select the text by dragging over it. To include all the text in a container, click anywhere within the container.

2. **Choose Tools➪Create Outlook Item➪Create Outlook Contact.**

   An Outlook Contact form appears.

3. **Enter the contact's information.**
4. **When you're done completing the form, choose Contact➪ions➪Save & Close.**

Creating an Appointment or Meeting from OneNote

It may suddenly occur to you, while listening to a lecture or attending a conference, that you need to meet with someone to go over what you've heard or to share your insights. Or maybe, while listening to the Sales Manager drone on and on about this quarter's revenues, you may remember that you forgot to make a note about that dog-grooming appointment you set up for Fido. In any case, you don't need to stop your doodling; you can simply add the appointment or meeting to your Outlook Calendar, without skipping out of OneNote.

To create a meeting or appointment from OneNote, follow these steps:

1. **Choose what to include.**

   First, decide if you want to include any of the notes you've been writing, with the appointment or meeting you want to create:

   - **To copy the notes on the current page** into the notes section of the new appointment or meeting form, click anywhere on the page.
   - **To copy only certain text from the page** into the new appointment or meeting, select the text by dragging over it. To include all the text in a container, click anywhere within the container.

2. **Choose Tools⇨Create Outlook Item⇨Create Outlook Appointment.**

   An Appointment form appears.

3. **Complete the Appointment form.**

   Enter a description in the Subject box. Select the date and time you want the appointment/meeting. (It's automatically set to the current time when I'm going to assume you're already busy.) Type a Location.

4. **Choose Appointment⇨Actions⇨Save & Close.**

   For a meeting, choose Appointment⇨Actions⇨Invite Attendees and select the people you want to attend. Fill in any other information you want and then choose Appointment⇨Actions⇨Save & Close.

Creating Notes about Outlook E-Mail, Contact, Appointment, or Meeting

Because Outlook and OneNote are such buddies, it won't surprise you that you can call up OneNote from Outlook and make it take notes about an important message, contact, or meeting. I mean, what are friends for, right? Basically, all you do is send a selected e-mail, contact, or whatever from Outlook over to OneNote, and it creates a nice little page for it where you can take notes. A link is created in OneNote so that you can flip back to Outlook anytime you're reviewing your notes and take a look at the original item.

To create notes about an Outlook item, follow these steps:

1. **Select the item you want to take notes on.**

   In Outlook, select the e-mail message, contact, appointment, or meeting you want to take some notes on in OneNote. You don't have to open the item, although if it's already open, don't worry about it.

2. **Click the Send to OneNote button.**

   If the item isn't open, you see the Send to OneNote button on the Standard toolbar. If the item is open, you find it on the Ribbon (see Figure 6-3).

3. **Take your notes.**

   The contents of the item you selected are copied into a new note page in the Unfiled Notes notebook in OneNote, as shown in Figure 6-3. Add whatever notes you want to the page; move the page into a real notebook by dragging the tab onto an expanded Navigation Bar, and drop it on a section name.

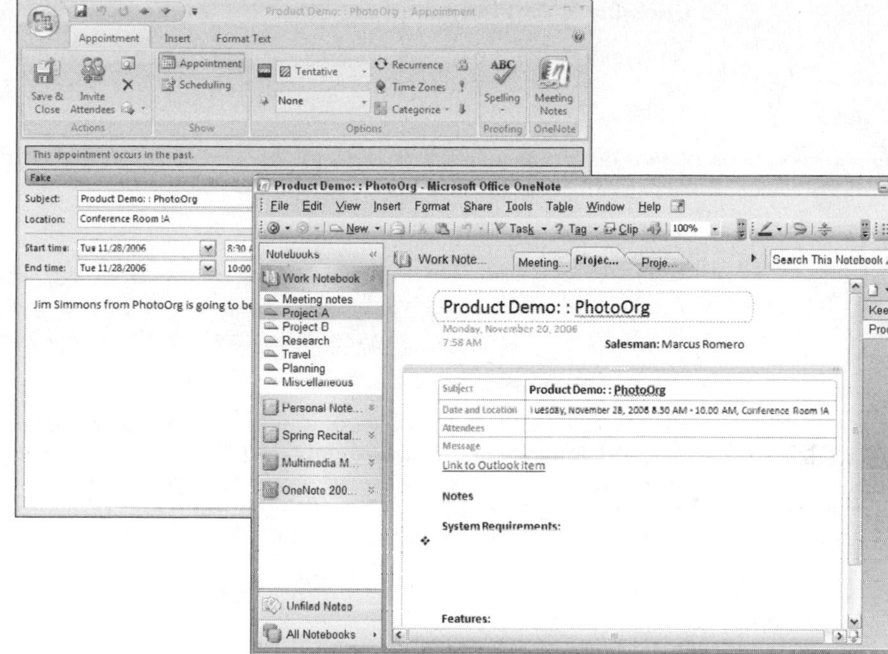

Figure 6-3: Send OneNote a nice little package.

Sending a Page to Someone

One of the reasons why it's so great to gather lots of information in OneNote is that you can share it. And the simplest way to share your notes is to send them in an e-mail message. Best of all, the recipient doesn't need to have OneNote installed to be able to view what you're sending.

To send notebook page(s) in an e-mail message, follow these steps:

1. **Select page(s) to send:**
   - **To select a page,** click its page tab.
   - **To select a page and all its subpages,** double-click the main page's tab.
   - **To select more than one page,** press Ctrl and click each tab.

Notice that you can't send less than one page. If you select a note container, you'll end up sending the entire page. If you want to send only a single note, copy that to a new page and send it that way.

2. **Click the E-Mail button on the Standard toolbar.**

   An e-mail envelope jumps up, as shown in Figure 6-4. You may see lots of page tabs, but only the ones you originally choose to send are selectable.

   If you didn't choose the correct pages, click the E-Mail button again to restore the regular OneNote controls.

3. **Address the e-mail.**

   Address the e-mail. The Subject is based on the first page you choose, but you can change it if you want. Type a message in the Introduction box. The text of the page(s) you selected appears below this introduction.

4. **Click Send a Copy.**

   The e-mail is sent in HTML format, with the text of the pages you selected appearing in the body of the message. A OneNote file is attached for those recipients who may also be using OneNote. All the recipient needs to do is to copy the section file(s) into any OneNote folder to open the page(s) they contain.

E-mail button

Figure 6-4: Send it along.

When you send a note in an e-mail, everything's sent except for any audio or video recordings you may have created. You can tell OneNote that you want recordings included in e-mails by choosing Tools⇨Options⇨E-Mail, and selecting the Attach a Copy of Linked Audio and Video Files option.

You can save your note pages in PDF or XPX format and share them that way. Just select the pages you want or an entire section and then choose File⇨Publish as PDF or XPS (an XML format). You do need to install the PDF/XPS converter for Office, if you haven't already. You can download it from Microsoft's Download Center, located at `www.microsoft.com/downloads`.

Sharing Notes

OneNote loves to share. In fact, it provides many ways in which you can share your OneNote information. For example, you can zip off a quick e-mail message and send along a few note pages if you want; see the previous section, "Sending a Page to Someone." You can also publish your notes in a shared folder and make them available to your colleagues, whether or not they also use OneNote. If you're a blogger, you can add your notes directly to your blog. You can also share a whole notebook and let everyone contribute their ideas.

Sharing a few pages

Rather than sending note pages in an e-mail, if you want to share them with colleagues on your network, why not publish them to a shared folder? Here's how:

1. **Select the page(s) you want to share.**
   - **To select a page,** click its page tab.
   - **To select a page and all its subpages,** double-click the main page tab.
   - **To select more than one page,** press Ctrl and click each tab.
2. **Choose File⇨Save As.**

   The Save As dialog box appears, as shown in Figure 6-5.
3. **Type a name for this collection of pages in the File Name box and change to shared folder.**

   Select the shared folder from the Save In list, or click My Network Places and then navigate to the share folder in which you want to save your OneNote pages.

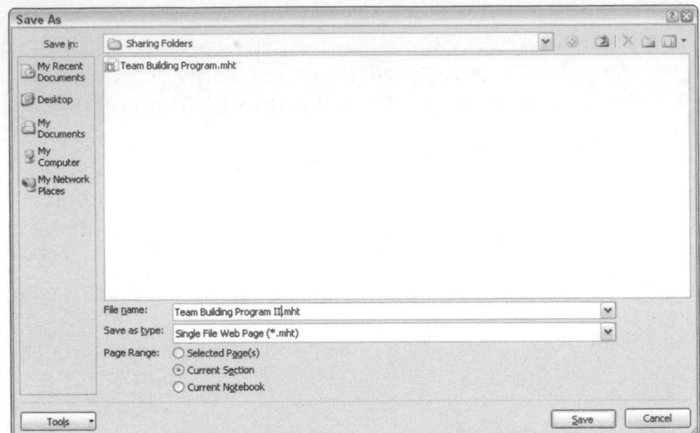

Figure 6-5: Save your notes to share them.

4. **Open the Save As Type list and choose how you want to share your note pages:**

   - **To make the pages readable in a Web browser,** choose Single File Web Page.
   - **To make the pages readable by OneNote users only,** choose OneNote Sections or OneNote Single File Sections.

     Saving your page(s) as a OneNote Single File Section compresses the resulting file, making it much smaller than it might normally be. To use the file, however, your colleagues need to double-click it to expand the file, and then they can open it in OneNote.
   - **To make the pages readable in Word,** choose Microsoft Word Document or Microsoft Word XML Document.

5. **Click Save.**

   The file is saved in the folder you selected, in the format you chose.

Blogging your notes

If you have your own blog, you can publish your notes directly to them instead of retyping all that stuff.

This task assumes that you also have Word 2007 installed, which I bet you do.

Here's what to do:

1. **Select the page(s) you want to blog:**

   - **To select only part of a page,** drag over the text and images you want, or press Ctrl and click the top border of various note containers.

- **To select a page,** click its page tab.
- **To select a page and all its subpages,** double-click the main page tab.
- **To select more than one page,** press Ctrl and click each tab.

2. **Choose File⇨Send To⇨Blog.**
3. **Register your blog.**

   If you've already entered your blog information somewhere in Office, you can skip this step. Otherwise, you see the Register a Blog Account dialog box. Click Register Now and then follow the wizard to enter the information Office needs to post to your blog.

   You can, if hard-pressed for time, skip the process of registering your blog and just create the blog page now by clicking Register Later.

4. **Click Publish.**

   A Word document, such as the one in Figure 6-6, is created, using the page(s) you selected. All pages that you selected in OneNote appear in a single page in Word. You can edit the Word document as you like and then click Publish to post it to your blog.

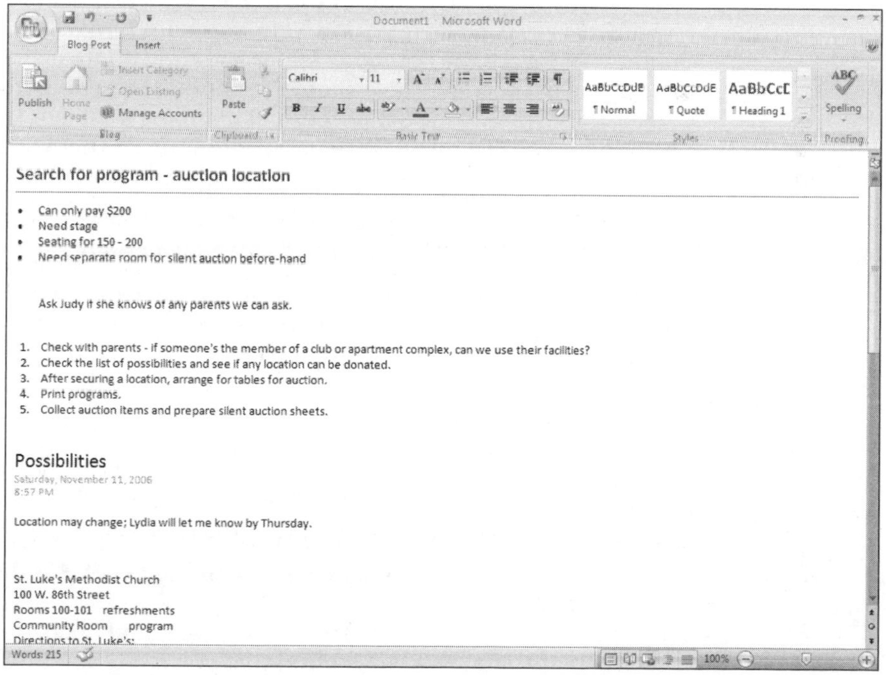

Figure 6-6: Blog it, baby.

Sharing notebooks

Another way you can share OneNote information is to share a notebook. Typically, you designate a notebook to be shared when you create it. (See Book VI, Chapter 5.) You can, however, suddenly share an already existing notebook, should the Ghost of Notebooks Past pay you a visit and unlock your miserly heart. For example, you can share a notebook you've been using for a new project you're involved in and use the newly shared notebook to gather everybody's ideas, notes, suggestions, and (when there's time) actual work on the project.

1. **Close the notebook you want to share.**

   Right-click the notebook's icon on the Navigation Bar and choose Close This Notebook.

2. **Choose File⇨Exit.**

   OneNote closes.

3. **Move the notebook folder.**

   Using My Documents or Computer, move the folder for the notebook you want to share to a shared folder on the network. (See, it's easy to share.) The notebook folder, by the way is in the \My Documents\OneNote Notebooks or \Documents\One Note Notebooks folder on your computer. Just locate the notebook folder and drag it into a shared folder and dump away. It may be a shared folder on your computer that you've created and shared for the purpose of dumping stuff in it that you want people to see, or it could be a shared folder on the network created by your boss for the same reason — to make it convenient for you and your coworkers to share stuff.

4. **Restart OneNote and choose File⇨Open⇨Notebook.**

   The Open dialog box jumps up. Change to the folder to which you just moved the notebook you want to share and then select the notebook file and click Open. The notebook reopens in OneNote so that you can use it again.

5. **Send an e-mail invitation.**

   To let everyone know where your shared notebook is located so that they can open it in their copy of OneNote, choose Share⇨Send Shared Notebook Link to Others. A Message form appears.

6. **Type a Subject and a message, address it, and click Send.**

To stop sharing a notebook, display any page in it and choose Share⇨Stop Sharing Notebook. You need to confirm that you really want to stop sharing; click Yes.

If you get an e-mail notifying you of a shared notebook, just click the link in the message to open that notebook in OneNote. Now, when more than one person has access to a shared network, OneNote has quite a job keeping up with all the simultaneous changes. What it does to resolve this sticky situation is to periodically synchronize the changes being made by a particular user with the data stored in the file. Even so, conflicts may arise, but at least OneNote gives you a way to resolve them.

If you want to see who made changes to a note and when, right-click the note and look at the bottom of the shortcut menu.

First, to see whether a shared notebook contains all the latest and greatest, check out its icon on the Navigation Bar, shown in Figure 6-7. If the synchronization can't be completed, it's probably because you're not connected to the shared folder where the notebook is kept. That doesn't mean you can't keep working, though; your changes are updated the next time you connect. If you're connected but the notebook is just not synchronized yet, you can force OneNote to synchronize it now: Choose File⇨Sync⇨Sync Current Notebook.

If you suspect there's another reason that the notebook couldn't be updated, you can hover the mouse pointer over the notebook's icon on the Navigation Bar, and a ScreenTip tells you what's up.

Synchronization is in progress; hold your horses cowboy.
Everything's in synch.
You're not connected to the shared folder, so OneNote can't synchronize your copy of the notebook.

Figure 6-7: Synchronize your watches and your notebooks.

Sometimes, when you happen to be working on the same note that somebody else is working on in a shared notebook, an error message appears in the yellow information bar at the top of the window. To see how your changes are in conflict with someone else's, click the information bar, and a new page is created. The new page lists the conflicting changes in red. Change back to the real page, make the changes manually if you want, and then delete the Conflicts page.

From time to time, OneNote may run across a section it needs to update, but the section has been moved or deleted by another user. Oops! In such cases, OneNote lists the little lost section in the Misplaced Sections list, along with odd socks and pens without caps. OneNote keeps the data in the lost section in the notebook until it finds where it should go. A button for the Misplaced Sections list appears on the Navigation Bar, just above the All Notebooks button. Click the button to see the list; select a section and click the Delete button on the Standard toolbar to remove it permanently. You can also move the section to a permanent location.

Hosting a Live Sharing Session

There's really no better way to generate new ideas than in a brainstorming session. OneNote makes it easy to share your ideas (even the silly ones) in one or more selected sections of a notebook, shared over the Internet or through your company network. This sharing, by the way, happens in real-time, so you can read each other's work and instantly comment on it. And everyone leaves the session with the same copy of the notes you all created — so no one can claim that she's missing some important bit of information.

Got a pen tablet? You can use it as a pointing device instead of a pen during the sharing session if you want. Choose Tools⇨Pen Mode⇨Use Pen as a Pointer.

Creating a live session

When you create a live sharing session, you designate who to invite and also whether a password is needed to join the session. Passwords can help keep the information you share during the session secure. To start a live sharing session, follow these steps:

1. **Select the section(s) you want to share.**

   To select a single section, click the section's tab. To select more than one section, press Ctrl and click each tab.

2. **Choose Share⇨Live Sharing Session⇨Start Sharing Current Section.**

   The Start Live Session task pane appears, as shown in Figure 6-8.

3. **Enter a password if you want.**

   You can secure the session by requiring a password for each participant to join. To assign a password, type it in the Session Password box on the task pane.

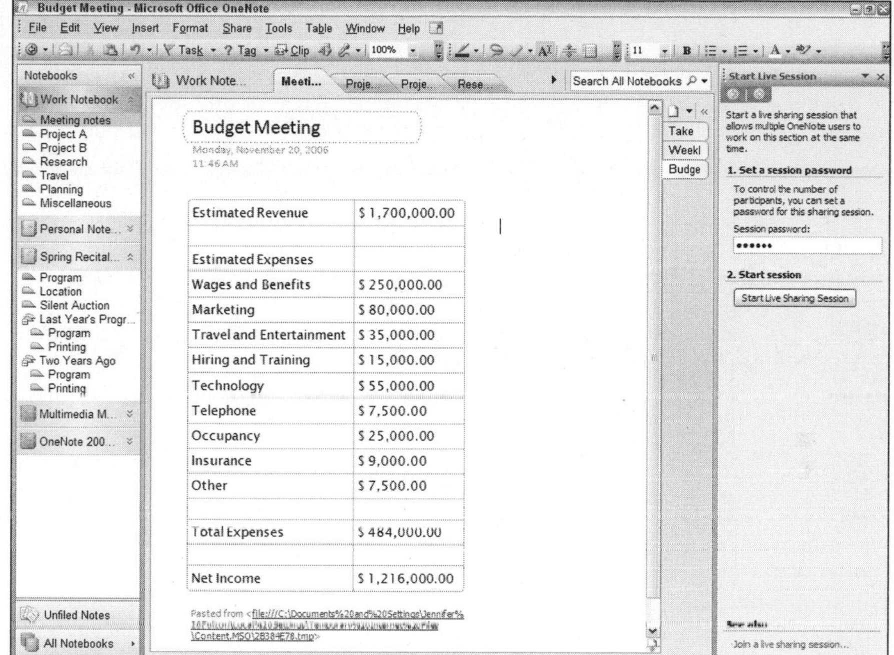

Figure 6-8: Your mind to my mind.

4. **Click Start Live Sharing Session.**

   You may see a warning if you're sharing the entire section instead of just a page. Click OK to continue.

5. **Set limits.**

   OneNote prepares the section(s) for sharing and puts a special icon at the top of each shared section tab. First, select the options that control what participants can do:

   - **To let participants create notes and add other items** to existing pages, on the Current Live Session task pane, choose the Allow Participants to Edit option (see Figure 6-9).
   - **To let participants view pages only,** make sure the Allow Participants to Edit option is turned off.

6. **Click Invite Participants and address the e-mail message that appears.**
7. **Click Send.**

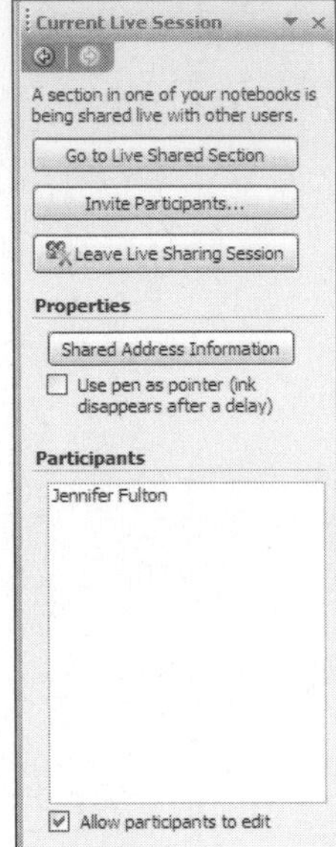

Figure 6-9: Set your own limits.

Joining a live session

If you receive an e-mail message inviting you to a live sharing session, it's easy to join the fun:

1. **Choose Share⇨Live Sharing Session⇨Join Existing Session.**

   The Join Live Session task pane jumps up.

2. **In the Live Sharing Session Address box on the task pane, type the IP address you were sent in the e-mail message you received.**

   You can also simply open the attachment to the e-mail message you were sent to join a session.

3. **If you need to enter a password to join the session, type it in the Session Password box.**

4. **Click Join Session.**

   If you've been given permission to edit, you can add your own notes, images, drawings, and so on to the existing pages (see Figure 6-10).

5. **When you want to leave the session, click Leave Live Sharing Session and then close the task pane.**

   If you're the one hosting the session, you can close it down by clicking Leave Shared Session and then closing the task pane. This step kicks everyone out of the session, so you may want to give everyone a chance to leave gracefully before you pull the rug out.

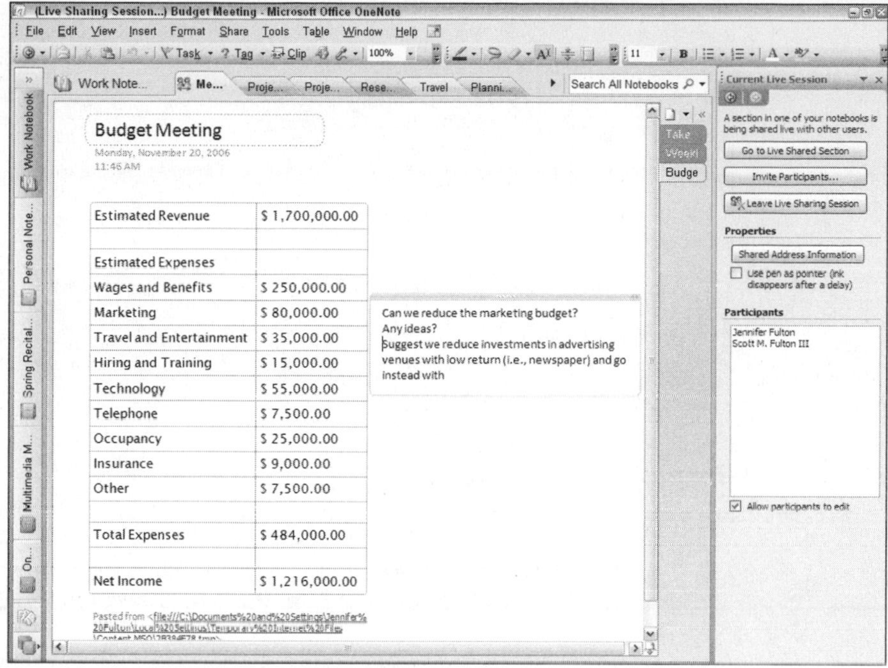

Figure 6-10: Share ideas in a live session.

Just closing the task pane itself doesn't end the session.

Securing Your Notes

You can keep all kinds of notes in OneNote: lecture notes, conference notes, or the daily bits of everyday life. Most of it would probably never cause a fuss, even if it got posted to the Internet. But some of it may be company information that's proprietary, credit information that should be kept private, or simply personal bits of trivia you don't want just any old nosy body to know.

Audio or video recordings aren't protected when you protect a section because they're stored in separate files and aren't part of the notes file.

To password protect a section of a notebook, follow these steps:

1. **Change to the section you want to protect.**
2. **Choose File⇨Password Protect This Section.**

   The Password Protection task pane appears, as shown in Figure 6-11.

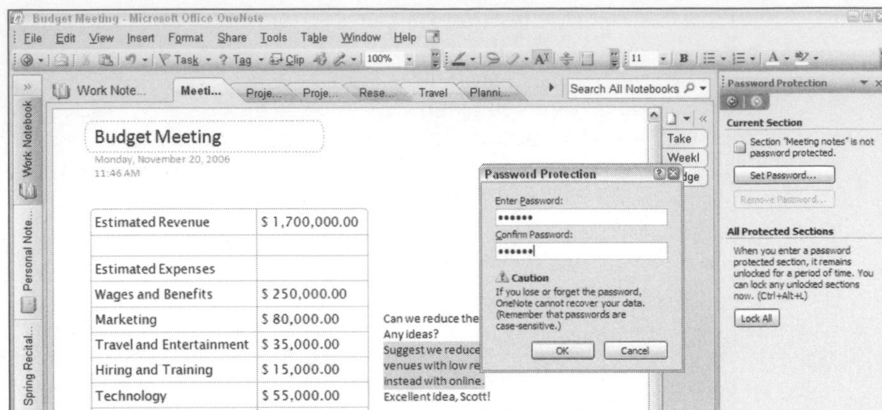

Figure 6-11: Protect your notes from prying eyes.

3. **Click the Set Password button.**

   The Password Protection dialog box appears.

4. **Type the password you want to use in the Enter Password box. Type the same password in the Confirm Password box and click OK.**

You may be asked about backup copies. If this section has existed for awhile, chances are OneNote has backed up the section and if so, that backup file is unprotected. You can click Delete Existing Backup Files to remove these unprotected copies, or you can click Keep Existing Backup Files to keep them until you can move the files to a protected folder.

If you're going to use a password to protect something, you may as well use one that's difficult to guess. Be sure to mix upper- and lowercase letters as well as a few numbers into your passwords to make them more secure.

The section you just password-protected is actually not protected right now. It remains open for you to use for awhile. If you want to lock the section immediately, click the Lock All button on the Password Protection task pane.

You need to remember the password you use, or you won't be able to view the contents of this section again.

To unlock a password-protected section, follow these steps:

1. **Click the section's tab.**

   When a section is password-protected and you click its tab, you're not shown the contents of that section but instead see a sad, gray page.

2. **Click the locked page.**

   The Protected Section dialog box appears.

3. **Type your password in the Enter Password box and press Enter.**

Once unlocked, a section should stay unlocked, right? Well, depending on your options, a section may only stay unlocked while you work on it, and then, after a certain amount of time or right after you switch to another section, it may lock itself again. To view the stuff in that section, you need to reenter your password. Believe it or not, this seemingly crazy behavior actually protects you, should you walk away from your computer and forget to secure it. Now, how to set those options:

1. **Choose Tools⇨Options⇨Passwords.**

   The Options dialog box appears, as seen in Figure 6-12.

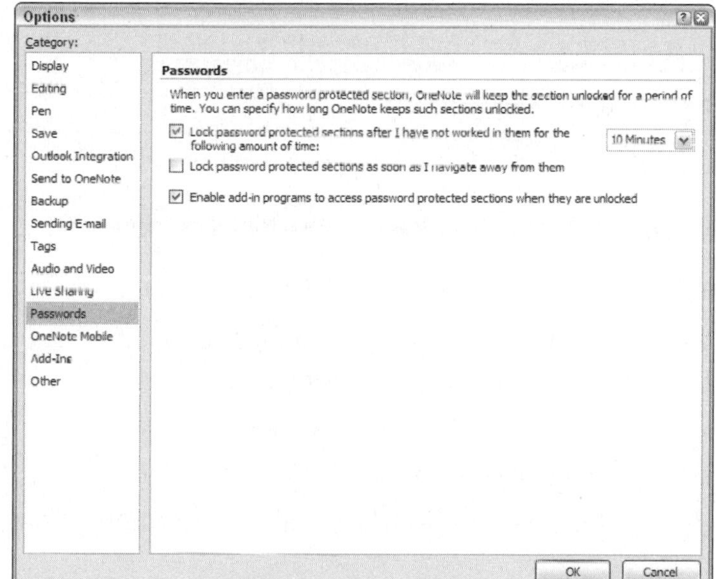

Figure 6-12: Set your password options.

2. **Choose the security options you want and click OK.**

   You have a few options from which you can choose:

   - **To lock a section again after so much time passes,** choose Lock Password-Protected Sections After I Have Not Worked in Them for the Following Amount of Time and then set the amount of time you want.
   - **To lock a section immediately after you change to a different section,** choose Lock Password-Protected Sections as Soon as I Navigate Away From Them.
   - **To allow other applications to access data in unlocked sections,** choose Enable Add-On Applications to Access Password-Protected Sections When They Are Unlocked.

If you have to leave your computer for a moment and you want to lock all your password-protected sections so that no one can access them, choose File⇨Password Protect This Section. In the Password Protection task pane, click Lock All.

You can remove a password from a section, should it become too much of a bother. You can also change a password, something you may want to do if you suspect that you password is no longer that secure.

To remove a password, follow these steps:

1. **Change to the section whose password you want to remove.**
2. **Choose File⇨Password Protect This Section.**

   The Password Protection task pane appears.
3. **Click Remove Password.**

   The Remove Password dialog box appears. To remove the password, you have to prove you know it.
4. **Type the password in the box provided and click OK.**

To change a password, follow these steps:

1. **Change to the section whose password you want to change.**
2. **Choose File⇨Password Protect This Section.**

   The Password Protection task pane appears.
3. **Click Change Password.**

   The Change Password dialog box appears, as shown in Figure 6-13.

Figure 6-13: Change a password if needed.

4. **In the Old Password box, type the current password for this section. Then, in the Enter New Password box, type the new password you want to use.**
5. **Type the new password again in the Confirm Password box and click OK.**

Reorganizing Your Notes

The whole point behind OneNote is organization. Face it, OneNote's the one stop informationarama. So there's probably nothing more frustrating to you than discovering, after working hard to gather lots of data together, that your notes are less than organized.

Selecting pages

The first step in cleaning house is to select what it is you want to move. Here's how:

- **Select a page** by clicking its tab to jump to it and then clicking it again to select the page.
- **Select a main page and all its subpages** by changing to the main page in the group and then double-clicking its tab.
- **Select several unrelated pages** by pressing Ctrl and clicking each page tab.
- **Select consecutive page tabs** by clicking the first page's tab, pressing Shift, and clicking the last tab in the group.

The tabs of selected pages are grayed so that you can tell they're selected.

Moving pages and notes

Pages don't have to stay in the order they were born. Nope, if a page turns out to be more important than you originally thought it might be, once you get some content on it, you can move the page up in the page tab listing. Likewise, you can move less important pages down in the listing. You can also move a page into a different section altogether.

To move a page up or down the page listing, while keeping it in the same section, follow these steps:

1. **Select the page(s) to move.**

   You can move more than one page at a time if you want. See the previous section, "Selecting pages," for help.

2. **Drag the selected page(s) up or down the page tab list.**

   A small black triangle appears to the right of the tabs as you drag.

3. **When that little guy is where you want the pages to be, release the mouse button to drop them.**

You can also move page(s) to a completely different section when that suits you:

1. **Select the page(s) to move.**

   For help, see the previous section, “Selecting pages.”

2. **Drag the selected page(s) over to the section tab you want them located in and drop them.**

To move the page(s) to a section in a different notebook, expand the Navigation pane so that you can see the notebook listing. Drag the selected page(s) over to the Navigation pane on the right, as shown in Figure 6-14. If the sections for that notebook are listed, then simply drop the page(s) on the proper section. If the sections aren’t shown, don’t panic; just hover the mouse over the notebook in which you want to place the page(s). After a moment, the notebook opens, showing you its various sections; drop the page on the section in which you want it to appear. You can then click the tab to display that section, and drag the page up or down the page tab listing on the right to put it where you want it in that section.

You can put notes on a page anywhere you want, but they don’t have to stay there. Every object on the page has its own container. Each text note, for example, is surrounded by a little box.

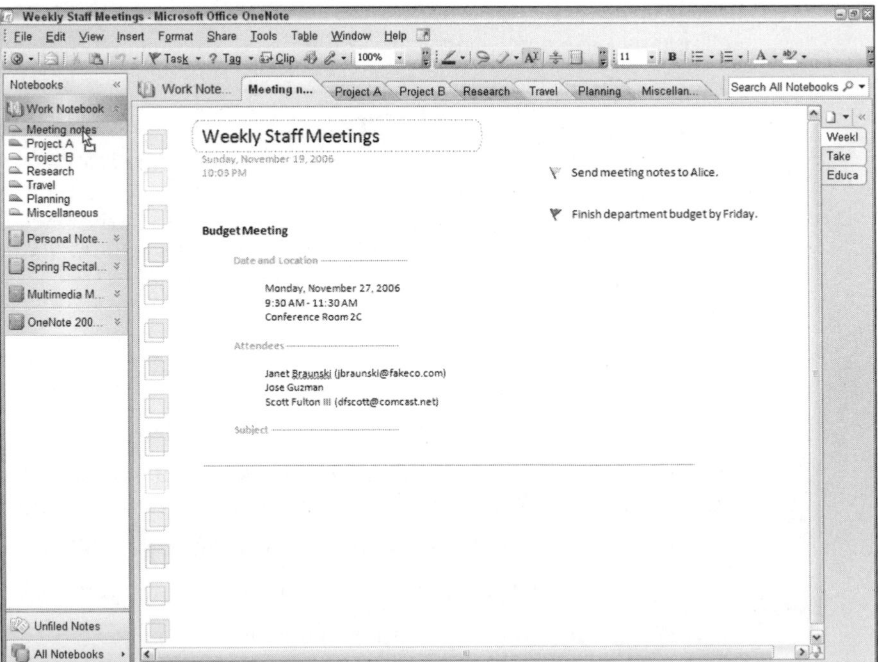

Figure 6-14: Move pages around.

Here are a few tricks of the trade:

- **To move a note somewhere else on the page,** just click the edge of this box (the mouse changes to a four-headed arrow) and drag.
- **To move a paragraph within a note,** move the mouse pointer to the right of the paragraph until it changes to that four-headed hydra-pointer thingie and drag.
- **To merge two note containers** so that only one box surrounds them both, drag one note container over the other while holding down Shift and rubbing your tummy.

You may notice while you're dragging and dropping notes that they seem to snap into place, almost as if invisible lines are on the page, magically causing stuff to line up against them. Well, aliens haven't just landed, but still you're right — there are magic invisible lines on the page that force stuff to line up. If you want something to stay right there and not move you can override the magic lines by pressing Alt as you drag and drop.

Moving sections

There's no reason why pages and notes should have all the fun. If you're rearranging the furniture, why not rearrange sections in a notebook to better suit the way in which you use them?

- **To move a section within the same notebook,** drag its tab along the tab listing and then drop it. As you drag, you notice a little, black down arrow; when the arrow is located where you want the section tab to appear, release the mouse button to drop it.
- **To move the section to a different notebook,** drag its tab over to the expanded Navigation pane and hover it over to the notebook in which you want the section to appear. If the notebook's sections aren't currently displayed, then after a bit, the notebook wakes up enough to show you its list of sections. Drag the mouse down the list until you reach the place where you want the section to appear and then release the mouse button to drop it.

You can also drag sections up or down within the listing on the Navigation pane — within the same notebook, or into a different notebook.

Tagging Important Information

The whole idea behind OneNote is that it's a great place to keep track of a lot of related stuff — notes, images, tables, charts, audio, and video data. But what good is it to collect your things in one place if you can never find them again? In the upcoming section "Searching for Data," I show you how to search for a specific bit of information based on the text it contains. Here, I show you another way in which you can make important information stand out: tags.

OneNote comes with a bunch of tags you can use to highlight whatever you want. There's an Important tag (a star), a Question tag (a question mark), an Idea tag (a light bulb), and many more. When you tag an item, the icon associated with that tag appears to the left of the object's container. The To Do tag is kind of unique, because it puts a check box icon in front of the item that you can actually check off when you get that item done.

What's the difference between adding an Outlook task to a page (as explained in the section, "Creating an Outlook Task on a Page," earlier in this chapter) and simply tagging something with the To Do tag? Well, first of all, the To Do tag item doesn't appear in Outlook, like an actual task does. Also, you can apply a To Do tag to any container, not just text, which makes it different from an Outlook task. Both, however, present you with a way in which you can check off the item after you get it done.

To apply a tag, follow these steps:

1. **Select an object you want to tag.**

   It can be a note, a picture, a drawing, anything. To select it, click the top border of the object's container.

2. **Click the arrow on the Tags button on the Standard toolbar and select a tag.**

   The most frequently used tags are listed first; click More at the bottom of the list to display the rest of the tags. The icon for that tag instantly appears to the left of the selected object, as shown in Figure 6-15.

Create your own tags

Why go with only the tags OneNote suggests? Create your own tags to attach to your notes by clicking the arrow on the Tag button on the Standard toolbar and choosing Customize My Tags. The Customize My Tags task pane appears. Click Add and, in the Modify Tag dialog box shown in the figure, type a name for the tag. Select a Symbol to represent that tag, a Font Color, and a Highlight Color (if desired). The font color and highlight color you select are applied to any note text that uses this tag. Click OK.

You can modify an existing tag you don't plan on using; just display the Customize My Tags task pane, select a tag, and click Modify. Then make any changes you want (for example, change the tag's name) and click OK.

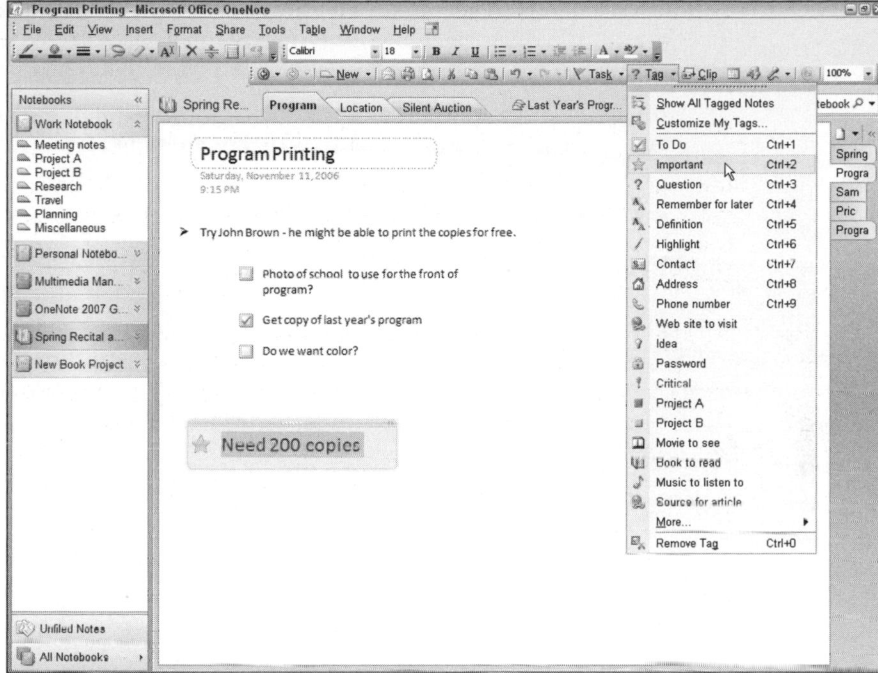

Figure 6-15: Tag, you're it.

Searching for Data

One of the advantages of using OneNote over, say, tons of tiny bits of paper scattered across your desk, snuggled in your pockets, and tucked into the corners of every room in your home is that you can, well, *find your notes when you need them*. And finding them has never been easier, given that you actually let OneNote do the finding for you. Yep, just type some words, and OneNote goes searching through your haystack of notes and finds that missing needle.

The searching goes a lot easier, and you're even able to search within audio and video files if you install Windows Desktop Search. You probably have already installed WDS to make searching in Outlook faster, not to mention the rest of Office and uh, all the files on your computer. But in case you haven't, install it! Choose Tools➪Options➪Other➪Install Instant Search.

If some of the pages you want to search are password-protected, you need to unlock them by entering your password before they can be searched.

Follow these steps to search for OneNote text:

1. **Type some search text in the Search All Notebooks box.**

   You find the box at the top of the OneNote window, to the right of the section tabs, as shown in Figure 6-16. For example, type **sales** or **economics** in the Search All Notebooks box. Here are some search tips:

   - **Use quotes to find some exact phrase,** such as "metal stress."
   - **Upper and lower, it's all the same to OneNote.** So don't worry about typing **John Doe**. If you type **john doe** instead, it still finds a match.
   - **Use OR when you have several search criteria.** For example, if you type **metal OR stress**, you find notes that contain either word, or both. If you type **metal stress**, you find items with both words, although not necessarily together or in that order.
   - **Use NEAR to look for two words within a few words of each other** in the text. For example, type **Joe NEAR cell** to search for Joe's cell phone number.

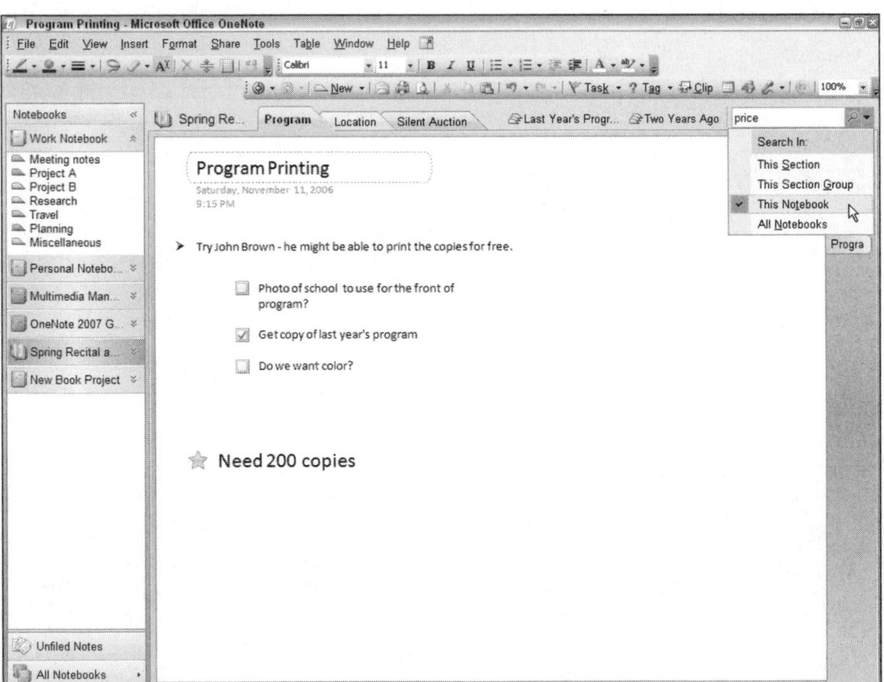

Figure 6-16: Let's search for "price".

- **To find an audio recording, you can try typing just audio or video,** but that may pick up notes, too. If you type audio recording started or video recording started, you get only audio or video files because OneNote marks them with a note that contains the date on which you made the recording, something like Audio recording started 3:59 PM Wednesday, January 15th, 2007. You can also type **audio Wednesday** to find a recording you made Wednesday, although you may find a note that contains a reference to that recording.

2. **Click the arrow on the Search All Notebooks box and select where you want to search: This Section, This Section Group (current section and all open sections), This Notebook, or All Notebooks. Press Enter.**

   REMEMBER

   OneNote remembers the scope of the last search you did, so if you want to search that same area (such as This Section), you don't need to select the search area in Step 2.

3. **Scroll to find the item you were looking for.**

   OneNote searches for items that match your text. The Search All Notebooks box goes away and is replaced by a bright, yellow, search results thingie, shown in Figure 6-17. The first item that matches your search text appears, highlighted on the page in screaming yellow. Actually, all matches are highlighted in screaming yellow, so get used to it.

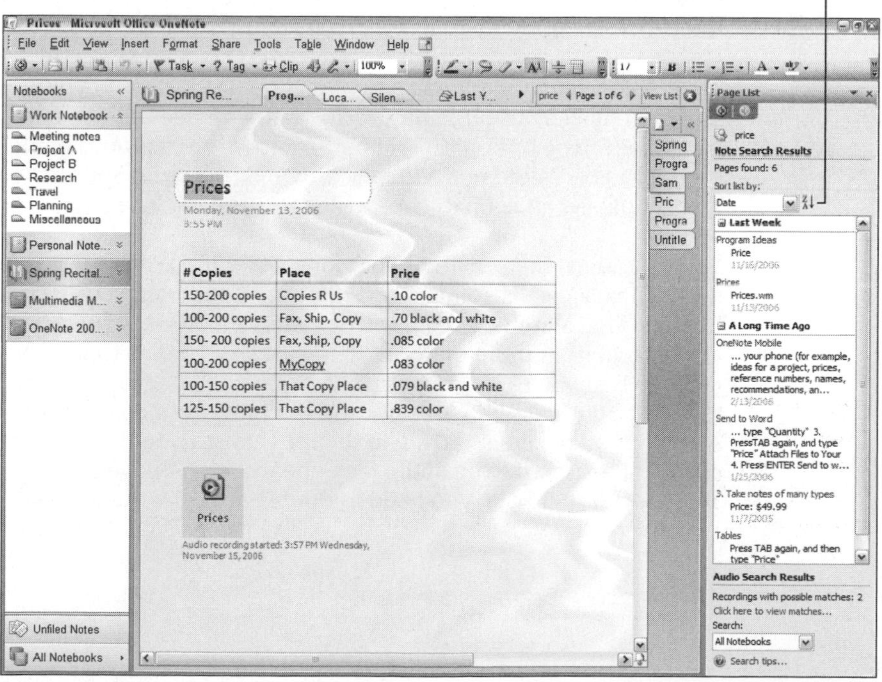

Figure 6-17: The results are in.

Do one of these things to find the item you really want, if the first item isn't it:

- **Click the old search text,** shown on the far left in the search results area, and then type different search criteria.
- **Click the right arrow** on the search results thingie to scroll to the next matching item.
- **Click the left arrow** to return to a previous matching item.
- **Click View List** to display the Search Results task pane, shown in Figure 6-17. You can then scan the list to quickly find the item you want.

The results list in the Search Results task pane is arranged by date (the date associated with the page the note is on). You can sort the results by section or title by choosing that option from the Sort List By list. Display whatever sort you use in reverse alphabetical order by clicking the Sort Descending button.

4. **Once you find some item you think may be the one you're looking for, just click its link in the View List (assuming you displayed it) to view that item.**

At the bottom of the Search Results task pane, you see the results of the audio search. Assuming that you installed Windows Desktop Search, there's a chance it found some text in an audio file that matched your search. To view those matches or to adjust the sensitivity of the search, click the Click Here to View More Matches link (see Figure 6-18).

To enable audio and video searching, you need to have Windows Desktop Search installed, as explained earlier and you need to turn the audio and video searching option on. Choose Tools➪Options➪Audio and Video. Turn on the Enable Audio and Video Searching for Words option. Read the Did You Know box and click Enable Audio Search and click OK.

You can adjust the sensitivity or closeness with which WDS searches through audio files and calls something a match, by choosing a value from the Show Results That Match with Confidence Above list box. A lower value here (such as .10) results in more matches, but with less chance that they really do contain the text you're looking for. A higher value (such as .80) restricts the list to only audio files WDS is really, really almost sure contain the search text. Again, if you see an audio file in the list that may be the one you want, just click it. The icon for the audio file appears on the page where it was inserted. To play the audio file, you need to double-click the audio icon.

Exit Search and
Clear Match Highlighting

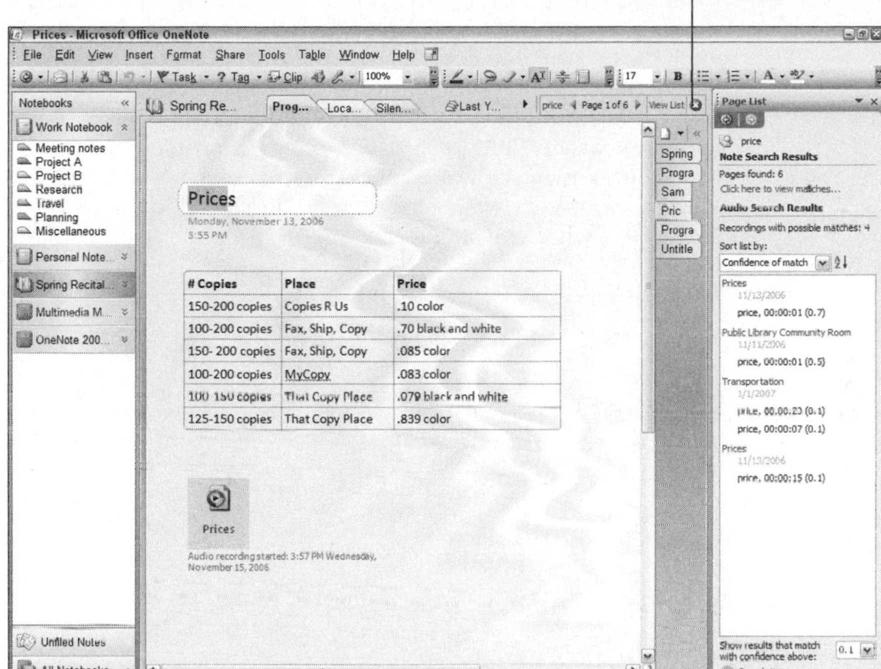

Figure 6-18: Search audio files, too.

Now, even with Windows Desktop Search, an audio file that matches your search text may still be skipped, simply because Windows hasn't had time to index it. (WDS "listens" to the audio file and creates a list of the words in it.) Basically, all that's needed is time, because Windows Desktop Search works in the background. If the audio file is a long one, it may take a while to index it, but in any case, if a file is skipped because it's not indexed, you see a message telling you so on the Audio Search Results task pane. In such a case, you can always try the search again or simply listen to the audio files that were skipped and see for yourself whether one of them is the one you wanted.

After you're through reviewing the search results, click the Exit Search and Clear Match Highlighting button (the red X), located on the screaming yellow search results thingie to the right of the section tabs. The search results thingie goes away, along with all those yellow highlights. Click the Close button on the Search Results task pane (if the task pane is open) to make it go away as well.

Finding notes you wrote recently

If you need to find something you jotted down recently, you don't need to remember exactly what it was. I mean, if you could remember what it was you jotted down, you could just search for its text as explained in the previous section. But pretend you suffer from a rare condition known as "I'm too busy to remember everything I do or say," or ITBREIDOS, as it's known in the trade. And as an ITBREIDOS sufferer, you can remember writing something down, but not what it was about. You do, however, remember that your job, your life, your very well being depend on your finding that little note right now. Here's what you should do:

1. **Choose View⇨Pages Sorted by Date.**

   The Page List task pane pops up on the right (see Figure 6-19).

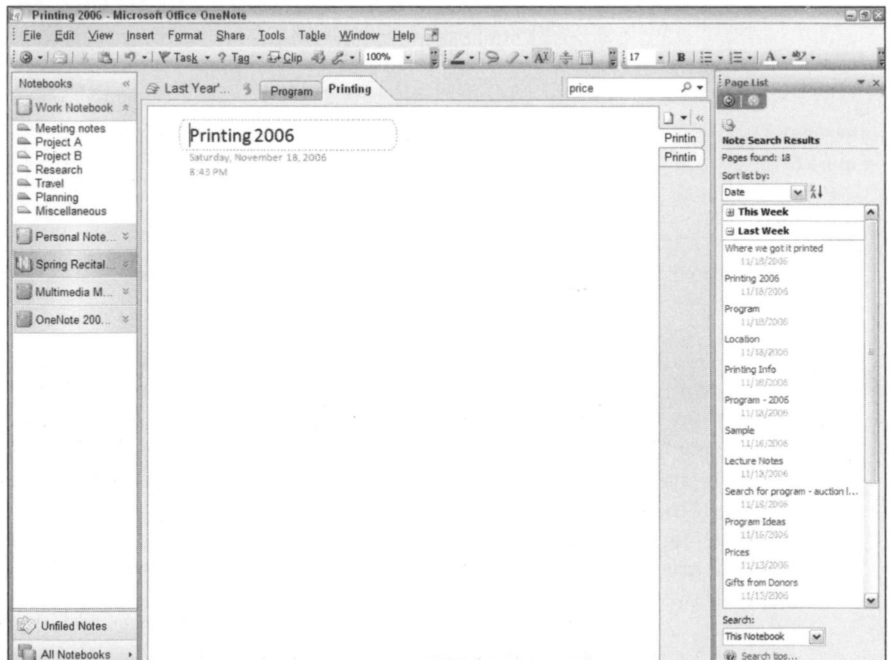

Figure 6-19: ITBREIDOS sufferers unite.

2. **Choose where to search from the Search list.**

   At the bottom of the task pane, choose All Notebooks from the Search list if you can't remember where this mystery note might be. If you think it's located in the current notebook or section, you can narrow the list by choosing a different search area from the Search list.

3. **Review the list and click a note you want to review.**

   You can reverse the sort order so that the oldest notes are listed first by clicking the Sort Descending button to the right of the Sort List By list box. Shorten a long list by collapsing a group — just click the minus sign in front of that group. To expand a group, click its plus sign. To view a particular note, click it in the list.

Other view options can help you find a long lost note. For example, to quickly review all the notes you've either created or changed recently, choose View⇨Pages Changed Recently and then choose a date from the list, such as Since Yesterday or Last Seven Days. To review notes you haven't read (helpful if you were sent a notebook by someone and now you'd like to review the parts you haven't gotten to yet), choose View⇨Pages I Haven't Read.

Finding tagged items

OneNote provides you with a set of tags (icons) you can use to mark items that are important to you in some way. There's a To Do tag, a Critical tag, and a Remember for Later tag. (See the section "Tagging Important Information," earlier in this chapter.) After tagging various items, you can use those tags to locate the items again.

To search for tagged items, follow these steps:

1. **Click the arrow on the Tags button on the Standard toolbar and choose Show All Tagged Notes.**

   The Note Tags Summary task pane appears, listing all the tagged items, grouped by tag, as shown in Figure 6-20. To change how items are grouped, select an option from the Group Tags By list. For example, instead of Tag Name, you can choose Date or Title (page title).

2. **Open the Search list at the bottom of the pane and choose the area you want to search.**

   For example, choose This Section or This Week's Notes and then click Refresh Results as needed. To display only To Do tag items that haven't been completed (checked), choose the Show Only Unchecked Items.

3. **Select an item to view.**

   Click an item in the list to display it on its page.

If you click the Create Summary Page button at the bottom of the task page, a new page is added to the back of the current section. The page that's created simply contains a copy of the items in the task pane, in their current order.

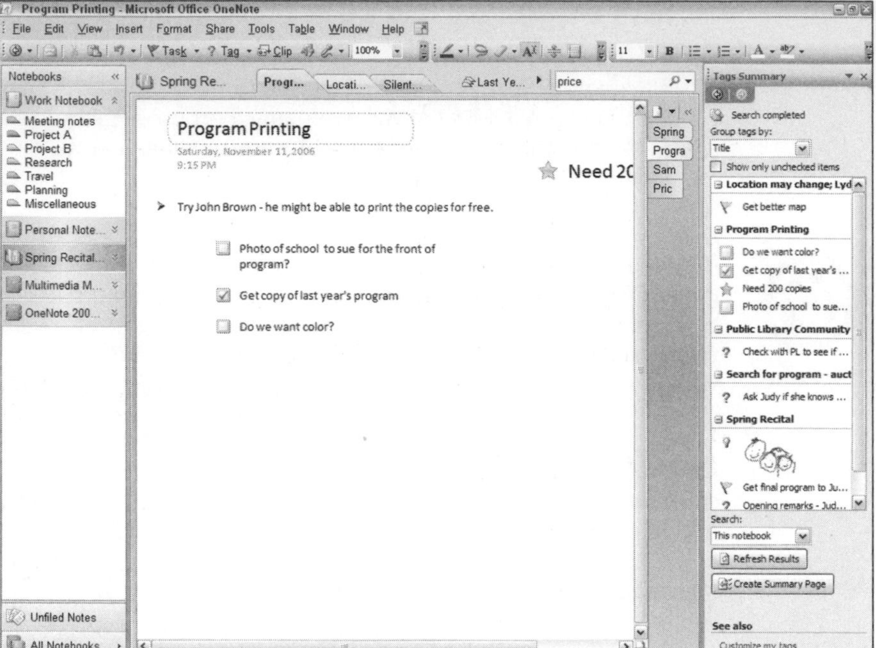

Figure 6-20: Find tagged items.

Chapter 7: Making History in the Journal

In This Chapter

- Getting the Journal to track what you do
- Adding items the Journal doesn't track automatically
- Keeping track of your phone conversations
- Tracking how much time you spend with those pesky clients
- Getting rid of Journal items you no longer want
- Changing the view

Outlook comes with a lot of big guns — Mail, Calendar, Contacts, and Tasks. With these fantastic four, you can keep track of a whole lot of those often-missing parts of your busy, busy life. Notes is a little guy that's typically forgotten, but useful nonetheless. But poor old Journal doesn't even rate a button on the Navigation pane (well, unless you add it). Now, don't let the Journal's lowly status fool you; he really can be a pretty useful guy to have around the computer. With Journal, you can track activities related to particular contacts you select. By activities, I mean things like sending and receiving e-mails from a contact, creating tasks related to a contact, or setting up appointments or meetings with a contact. In addition, the Journal tracks your work on any Office document, so if you know you worked on something in Word yesterday but you can't remember what, Journal can help you. Journal also helps you locate your missing keys (provided you left them in an Office document).

Tracking Activities in Your Journal

You can use the Journal to track the amount of time you spend with a particular contact, or all the things you do every day for your boss that he or she simply doesn't remember (the ingrate). You pick the contacts, and the Journal does the spying — I mean *tracking*.

Best of all, the Journal is painless: You simply turn it on, tell it which contacts to track, and the rest is done for you. Once activities are gathered in the Journal, you can rearrange them in many ways so that you can get a good overview of your activities or quickly locate a specific item. If you find an item you're interested in, by the way, you can open it lickity-split, right from the Journal.

Automatically tracking activities

The Journal is pretty easygoing, watching over everything you do and keeping special track of the things you do. The only thing the Journal asks, basically, is that you turn it on and tell it exactly what to track. From there out, everything's, well, automatic.

To track activities in the Journal, follow these steps:

1. **Choose Tools➪Options➪Journal Options.**

   The Journal Options dialog box rears its head, as shown in Figure 7-1.

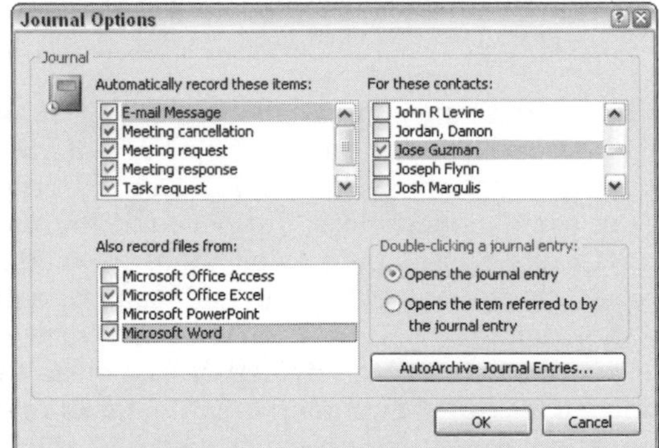

Figure 7-1: Tell Journal what to do.

2. **Select the Outlook items to record.**

   In the Automatically Record These Items list, choose the type of items you want Journal to keep track of. The Journal can track e-mail messages; meeting requests, responses, and cancellations; and task requests and responses.

   You may want to track quite a few things you do every day, such as phone calls, conversations in the hallway, or a teleconferencing or remote work session. You may also like to track faxes and letters related to a particular contact. Well, the good news is you can. The bad news is that you have to add these entries manually. But the process is pretty painless, I assure you. See the upcoming sections "Tracking Journal entries manually," and "Logging phone conversations."

3. **Select the document types you want tracked.**

   Journal can track activities related to your Office documents. For example, it can track when you work on Word documents and where those Word documents are stored. From the Also Record Files From list, select the type of Office documents you want to track. You can choose from the Office programs you have installed, such as Word, Excel, PowerPoint, and Access.

   You don't have to select every program in order to track it; if you work mostly in Word and Excel, then select just them. If you happen to begin work on a PowerPoint presentation that's important and you want to track it, you can add that one file to the Journal. See the upcoming section "Adding previous activities to the Journal."

4. **Select contracts to track.**

   From the For These Contacts list, select the contacts whose Outlook items you want to track. If you choose John Smith from this list and E-Mail Message from the Automatically Record These Items list, then the Journal tracks all e-mails sent to or from John Smith, and you can view them altogether in a list.

   If you forget to track activities related to some contact, you can always add a specific activity to the Journal manually, even if that contact isn't on the preferred list. See the upcoming section, "Adding previous activities to the Journal."

5. **Choose what you want the Journal to do when you double-click and click OK.**

   You can have the Journal open the Journal entry itself, which may contain extra notes related to the item, or just open the item tracked by the entry.

6. **After you make your big decision, click OK to close the dialog box.**

   Well, unlike what you may expect, nothing spectacular happens. No, the Journal doesn't go out and collect a whole bunch of items related to the contacts you choose. Nope, it just sits there, waiting and watching for any new activity related to those contacts. So it's up to you to go make some activities.

You can get old activities into the Journal — but it's going to take a little work on your part. See the section "Adding previous activities to the Journal" for help.

Entries related to the contacts and Office documents you selected are tracked from now on in the Journal. You can stop this tracking whenever you want; see the upcoming section "Turning Off Journal Tracking" for help.

An alternate method of "tracking"

You can view activities related to a specific contact, without doing anything in the Journal. You simply use the Activities tab as described in Book V, Chapter 2. The only problem with relying on the Activities tab is that you can do very little to arrange the items in some kind of order, other than the order in which the activities occurred. To utilize the flexibility of the Journal to review activities related to a specific contact, you must add that contact to the Journal tracking list.

Adding previous activities to the Journal

There's a bunch of reasons why you may want to add activities that have already happened to the Journal. For example, if you forgot to track the activity related to a specific contact until just now, you can catch up by adding those missing entries manually. Or you may have been tracking specific activities for a contact, but not all of them. Again, you can add those missing activities as needed.

To add a previous activity to the Journal, follow these steps:

1. **Select the item you want to add to the Journal.**

   For example, select an e-mail message or an appointment.

2. **Copy the item into the Journal.**

   There are several ways in which you might go about this. The simplest way is to drag the item onto the Journal button on the Navigation pane and drop it. This method assumes, however, that you have a Journal button on the Navigation pane.

   To add the Journal button to the Navigation pane, click the Configure Buttons button at the bottom of pane and choose Add or Remove Buttons➪Journal.

   The second method involves copying and pasting. Choose Edit➪Copy to copy the selected item, and then change to the Journal by choosing Go➪Journal, and choose Edit➪Paste to paste the copy in the Journal.

   With either method, a Journal Entry is created, and the Journal Entry form appears, as shown in Figure 7-2. A shortcut to the item you selected appears in the Notes area; you can use this shortcut later to open the item from the Journal.

3. **Add any details you want, such as the Company name.**
4. **Choose Journal Entry➪Save & Close to save the entry in the Journal.**

For more information on the fields in the Journal Entry form, see the next section, "Tracking Journal entries manually."

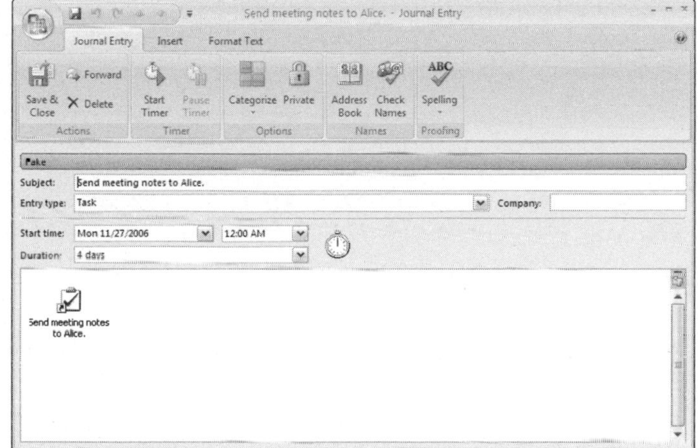

Figure 7-2: Adding an existing task to the Journal.

Tracking Journal entries manually

You can create some Journal entries only by hand. These entries include the types of activities that happen outside of Outlook, such as receiving a fax or making a phone call. Phone calls are a bit special because you can actually track how long you're on the phone, so I cover them in the next section, "Logging phone conversations." Here, I show you how to add a variety of manual entries, including logging a fax, letter, conversation, online collaborative session, or work on a non-Office document.

You can create a manual entry that points to a contact by selecting the contact (not opening it) and choosing Actions➪Create➪New Journal Entry for Contact. You can do so, by the way, for any contact — even contacts whose activities you're not automatically tracking.

To create a manual Journal entry, follow these steps:

1. **Choose File➪New➪Journal Entry.**

   A new Journal Entry form appears, as shown in Figure 7-3.

2. **Type a description.**

   In the Subject box, type a description for the journal entry.

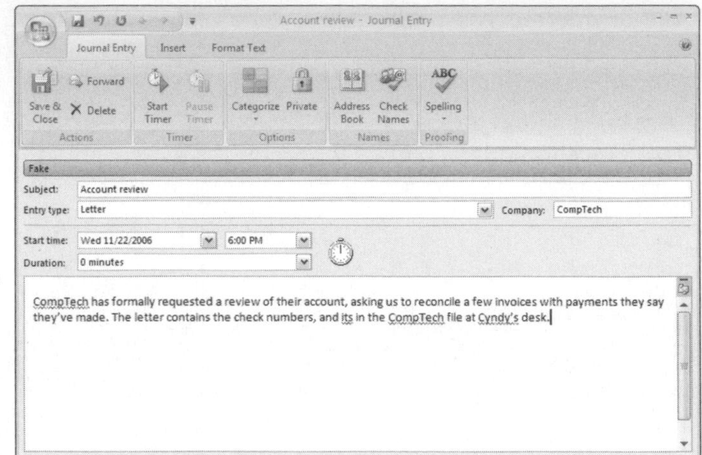

Figure 7-3: Record all sorts of activity in the Journal.

3. **Select an entry type.**

   From the Entry Type list, choose the kind of journal entry you're trying to add, such as a conversation or remote session.

4. **Complete the journal entry.**

   If this item is related to a particular company, type the Company name. If you want to track the amount of time spent on the task related to this entry (maybe for billing purposes), set the start date and Start time. Choose a Duration as well. Set other options as you like, such as adding a category or marking the entry private.

5. **Save the entry and add it to the Journal by choosing Journal Entry⇨Save & Close.**

For timed activities such as a phone call or conversation, you can actually have Outlook time you and figure the duration automatically. See the next section, "Logging phone conversations," for help.

A simple way to add a non-Office document to the Journal is to simply drag and drop it there. Open Explorer, locate the file, and then drag it into the Journal.

Logging phone conversations

If you make a lot of phone calls like me, chances are that unless you write something down about each one, by the end of the day, you've forgotten who you talked to and what you promised them. Luckily, you have Journal by your side to reintroduce you.

To log a conversation with someone, whether or not he's in your Contacts list, follow these steps:

1. **Choose File⇨New⇨Journal Entry.**

   A new Journal Entry form appears, as shown in Figure 7-4.

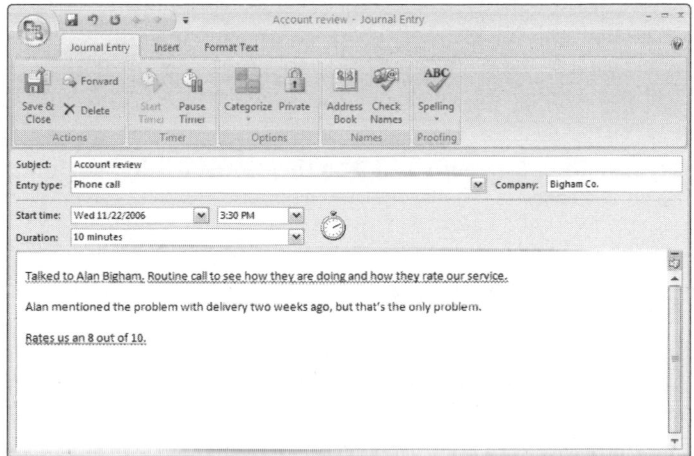

Figure 7-4: Mr. Jones on line 4.

2. **Type a description.**

   In the Subject box, type a description for the phone call.

3. **Select an entry type.**

   From the Entry Type list, choose Phone Call.

   Because you're probably about to be actively engaged in conversation, you can easily leave the rest of the Journal entry details until after the call is completed.

4. **Start the timer by choosing Journal Entry⇨Timer⇨Start Timer.**

   The small clock icon starts spinning, and Outlook tracks the length of the call.

5. **Take notes.**

   Go ahead; if the person you're talking to says something you need to remember, well, there's a big notes area right there. Just click in the large white box and type.

6. **When the call is over, stop the timer by choosing Journal Entry➪Timer➪Pause Timer.**

   The clock stops, and a Duration is calculated.

   You can restart the timer if needed by choosing Journal Entry➪Timer➪Start Timer again.

7. **Complete the journal entry.**

   Now that you have time, complete the Journal entry. If this phone call was related to a particular company, type the Company name. Set other options as desired, such as adding a category or marking the entry private.

8. **To save the entry and add it to the Journal, choose Journal Entry➪Save & Close.**

Changing the Journal View

Obviously, there's no point in tracking all this activity if you can't find a particular entry when you want. That's where the multitude of views the Journal offers come into play. At first, entries appear in a timeline, grouped by entry type, as shown in Figure 7-5.

To change to a different view, click that view in the Current View list, which pokes out at you from the Navigation pane. You see a nice mix of timeline views similar to the By Type view (the default) and list views such as the Last Seven Days view. In a timeline view like the one shown in Figure 7-5 (which is the By Type view), the dates are shown in a ribbon along the top of the window. Other list views include By Contact and By Category. Here are some tips to remember when dealing with a timeline view:

- ✦ Use the vertical scroll bar on the bottom to move from day to day.
- ✦ Click the month name at the top of the window to display a calendar that you can use to quickly jump to a different day or month.

In a timeline view, items are grouped in some kind of group; the one shown here grouped its items by type. Here are some tips for handling groups:

- ✦ To collapse a group, click the minus sign on the gray bar that heads up the group.
- ✦ To expand a group, click the plus sign on its gray bar.

Click month name to display calendar

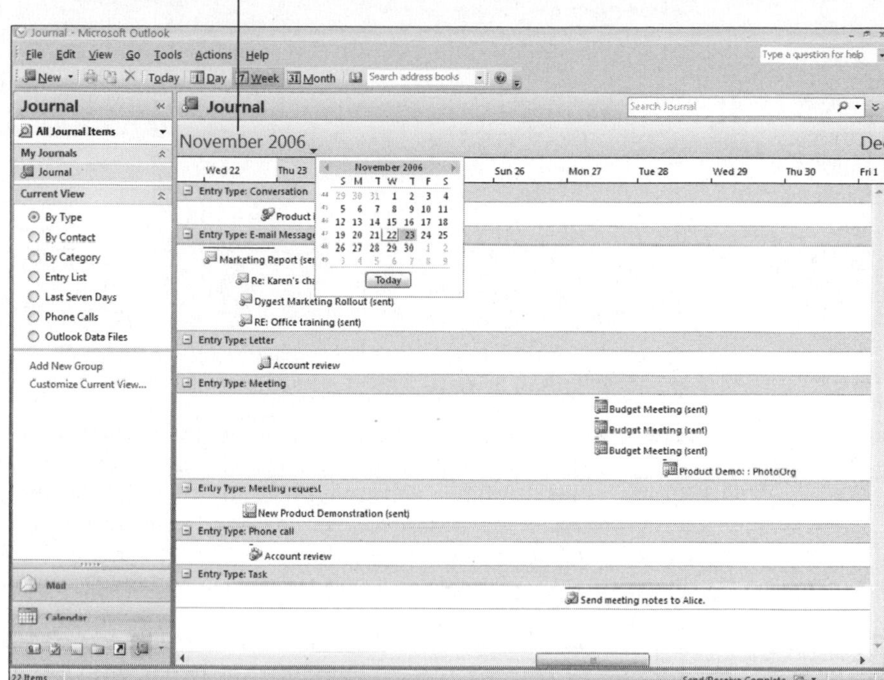

Figure 7-5: The Journal timeline.

Customizing the timeline

Items appear in the timeline with a bar just above them to indicate the duration of that activity — its start and its end. Items aren't shown when they're simply modified unless you customize the timeline.

To customize the timeline to show when items are modified, make sure that you change to a timeline view first and then follow these steps:

1. **Choose View⇨Current View⇨Customize Current View.**

   The Customize View dialog box pops up.

2. **Click Fields.**

   The Date/Time Fields dialog box appears, as shown in Figure 7-6.

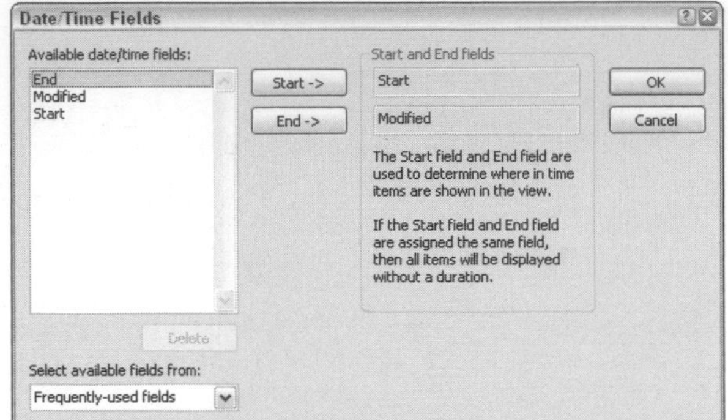

Figure 7-6: Gentlemen, start or modify your engines.

3. **Choose the Start field.**

   The bar that appears above each item begins at the item's start date (creation). If you want the bar to show the range of time from when an item was last modified to when it was completed, then set this first field to Modified. Select Modified from the Available Date/Time Fields list and then click Start.

4. **Choose the End field.**

   To continue the example, if you want the bar to show the range of time from when an item was last modified to when it was completed, then set the second field to End. Select End from the Available Date/Time Fields list and then click End. (If End has already been selected as the second field, you can skip this step.)

5. **Click OK twice.**

   The bars appearing above items change to fit these new parameters. In the example shown in Figure 7-6, I wanted my bar to show when an item was created and when it was last modified.

Using a list view

Another way in which Journal entries can be displayed is in a list view, such as the one shown in Figure 7-7, which is the Last Seven Days view. Other list views include Entry List, Phone Calls, and Outlook Data Files.

In a list view, items are displayed, well, in a list. Each row in the list represents a different entry. The entries are sorted by the column that contains an up or down arrow on its header. The list shown in Figure 7-7 is sorted by the Start column — typically, the item's creation date.

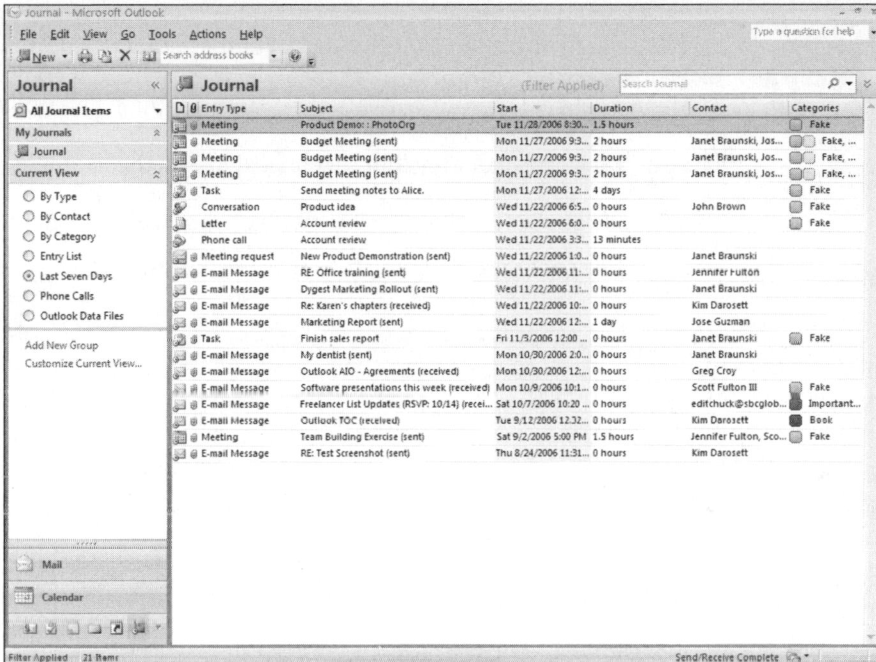

Figure 7-7: A Journal list view.

Here are a few pointers to keep in mind when using list view:

- ✦ To sort a list by a different column, click that column's header.
- ✦ To sort a column in reverse order, click the sort column's header. In the sample shown in Figure 7-7, I could click the Start column header to reverse the sort and arrange items so that the oldest ones appear at the top.

Turning Off Journal Tracking

You can stop the automatic tracking of items into the Journal whenever you like. For example, if you're tracking all items related to a client of yours, but that client has been turned over to a different team or has stopped service or is no longer a problem, you can stop tracking activities for that client. Doing so, however, doesn't remove the related entries from the Journal so you don't have to worry about that. You can, of course, remove any entries you no longer want — see the upcoming section "Removing Journal Entries."

Although you can't share your Journal folder, you can forward Journal entries related to a client or other important contact to another member of your team, if your colleague is taking over. The "means of transportation" from your Journal to your colleague's is simple e-mail. See Book II, Chapter 2.

To stop tracking particular Journal entries, follow these steps:

1. **Choose Tools⇨Options⇨Preferences⇨Journal Options.**

   The Journal Options dialog box appears, as shown in Figure 7-8.

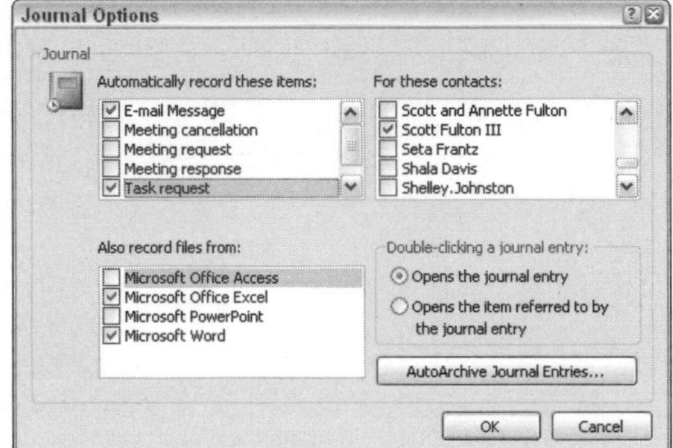

Figure 7-8: Stop Journal in its tracks.

2. **Turn off options.**

   If you no longer want to track items related to a specific contact, then locate that contact in the For These Contacts list and remove its check mark.

   If you want to keep tracking items for the contacts you've selected, but maybe not every specific item you choose earlier, then locate the items you no longer want to track (such as meeting responses) in the Automatically Record These Items list and remove their check marks.

   If you no longer want to track certain Office documents, remove the check marks in front of those document types in the Also Record Files From list.

3. **Click OK.**

   The options you selected are no longer tracked, but the data you've already collected in the Journal isn't removed.

Removing Journal Entries

Even after you stop tracking items in the Journal, those items aren't removed. For example, you may have started out all enthusiastic, tracking everything related to a particular contact: e-mails, meeting requests, meeting responses, task requests and responses, and so on. But now, after turkey, mashed potatoes, green bean casserole, cranberry sauce, and three pieces of pumpkin pie, your Journal is looking overstuffed.

The problem is easily remedied: When needed, you can manually remove any entries you no longer want.

Actually, entries are removed from the Journal all the time, automatically. I'm talking about old entries of course, and the AutoArchive system that copies old entries to an archive file automatically at periodic intervals. The purpose of AutoArchive is, of course, to keep your Outlook data file manageable by reducing its size. See Book IX, Chapter 1 for more information about archiving.

To remove entries from your Journal, follow these steps:

1. **Change views.**

   Change to a Journal view that helps you locate the item(s) you want to remove. Typically, a list view is best because you can sort it easily. List views include Entry List, Last Seven Days, Phone Calls, and Outlook Data Files.

   To change to a different Journal view, select it from those listed on the Navigation pane.

   You can search for Journal items you want to remove. See IX, Chapter 4 for the lowdown on searching.

2. **Select items to remove:**

   - **To select a single item,** simply click it.
   - **To select several consecutive items,** click the first item in the group, press and hold Shift, and then click the last item in the group.
   - **To select nonconsecutive items,** click the first item, press and hold Ctrl, and click each additional item, as shown in Figure 7-9.

3. **Remove the selected items.**

   Press Delete to remove the selected items or click the Delete button on the Standard toolbar.

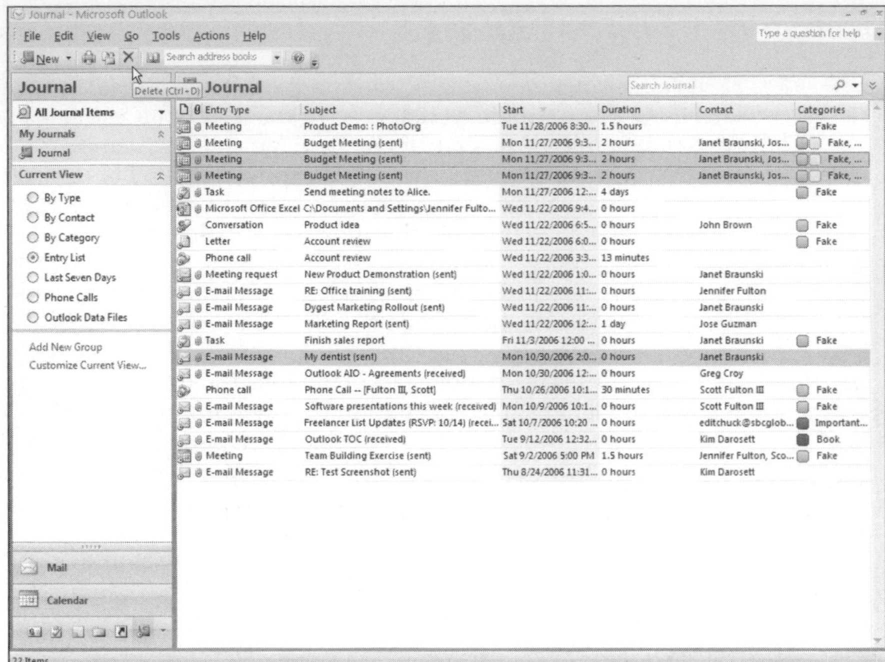

Figure 7-9: When you gotta go, you gotta go.

The items you selected are removed from the Journal, but you can still retrieve them if needed; just drag them from the Deleted Items folder back into the Journal.

Book VII

Working with Business Contact Manager

The 5th Wave
By Rich Tennant
©RICHTENNANT
SPAM KING
MASS E-MAIL MARKETING
A Limited Canker on the Butt
of Society Partnership

Contents at a Glance

Chapter 1: Minding Your Business Contact Manager 537

Chapter 2: Introducing the Basic Business Contact Manager Elements 551

Chapter 3: Working with Opportunities..567

Chapter 4: Reports and Dashboards 577

Chapter 1: Minding Your Business Contact Manager

In This Chapter

- Introducing Business Contact Manager
- Creating a database
- Copying Outlook Contacts into BCM
- Importing other software into BCM

As Microsoft was creating the world of personal computing, it realized the use of cool software could prevent disorganization, and so the company created Outlook. Computer users everywhere rejoiced because Outlook helped them organize their contacts and calendars.

But hark! Microsoft soon heard rumblings about a new type of software — Customer Relationship Management, or CRM. The newly organized wanted to become even more organized. Business people wanted to manage their relationships with their customers (or prospects or leads or vendors), so that all their employees could see who's done what to whom, what's been promised and delivered, what money is owed, and what receivables are coming in. Even nonprofit organizations and soccer moms felt a need to share contact and calendar information with other people.

Enter Business Contact Manager (Business Contact Manager). BCM is the entry-level CRM program that Microsoft has integrated into Outlook. BCM is built right into Outlook as another Address Book.

Comparing BCM and Outlook?

You're probably wondering what the difference is between Outlook and Business Contact Manager. We like to think of BCM as "Outlook on steroids." Here's a list of the main power features in BCM:

- In addition to Contact Records, you can create *Account Records* in BCM. Think of an Account Record as a master record that contains information about a company rather than an individual.
- You can easily link BCM Contact Records to BCM Account Records to help keep track of all the individuals who work at the same company.

- BCM allows more flexibility if you need to add fields to help keep track of your business.
- You can use BCM to set up marketing campaigns and track their effectiveness.
- You can set up Opportunities in BCM to help you track your company's sales process.
- BCM can help you keep track of your client-based projects. It even integrates with Microsoft Small Business Accounting so that you can bill the time from a project without having to re-enter any data.
- BCM integrates with Microsoft Small Business Accounting (SBA). The customers in SBA are the same contacts as in BCM, which means that you don't have to resort to the double entry of your contacts. You can turn Sales Opportunities you start in BCM into Invoices or Sales Orders in Accounting with just a few clicks and no re-entry of data.
- You can share BCM across a network so that everyone in the office sees the same data. You can even let co-workers take a subset of your BCM database with them when they leave the office and synchronize their changes back to yours when they return.
- BCM comes equipped with lots of reports and dashboards to help you keep better tabs on your business.
- Because it's written in SQL Express, BCM is able to hold more contacts than can Outlook.

Knowing Who Should Use BCM

Although anyone can use Business Contact Manager, certain kinds of organizations and individuals are better suited to BCM.

So just who should be using BCM? We think that everyone should be using BCM! Here are a few examples:

- A CEO who needs to know what his salespeople are doing and how his customers are being treated.
- An administrative assistant who wants to automate routine tasks and keep a schedule of various tasks and activities.
- A salesperson who wants to make sure that she's following up on all her prospects.
- A disorganized person who wants to become more organized.
- A smart person who realizes that she'll have more time to play by working more efficiently.

- Anyone who wants to separate his personal contacts from business contacts or keep track of multiple sets of contacts.
- Anyone who needs to track money through a process — whether it's a pledge or donation to a charity.
- A lazy person who knows it's more fun to play than to work.

So what kinds of businesses are ideal BCM candidates? All kinds:

- Large businesses that want to improve communication among employees.
- Small businesses that have to rely on a small staff to complete a multitude of tasks.
- Businesses of all sizes looking for software that can automate their businesses and make them more productive in less time.
- Businesses looking to grow by marketing to their prospects.
- Businesses looking to retain their current customers by providing an excellent level of customer service and developing lasting relationships.

Getting Started in BCM

BCM comes as a free add-on to Outlook 2007 when you purchase Outlook as part of Microsoft Office Small Business 2007, Microsoft Office Professional 2007, or Microsoft Office Ultimate 2007.

You can access the various BCM components in one of three ways:

- Clicking Business Contact Manager on the main Outlook menu bar.
- Clicking the Business Contact Manager Home button on the BCM toolbar.
- Expanding the Business Contact Manager folder toward the bottom of the Folder List.

If you don't see the BCM folders, menu, or toolbar when Outlook opens, you need to tweak your Outlook settings:

1. **From Outlook, choose File⇨Data File Management.**

   The Account Settings dialog box opens in all its glory. You should already be viewing the Data Files tab, as shown in Figure 1-1. If not, go ahead and click that tab. If Outlook isn't properly configured you see only the name of your Outlook account.

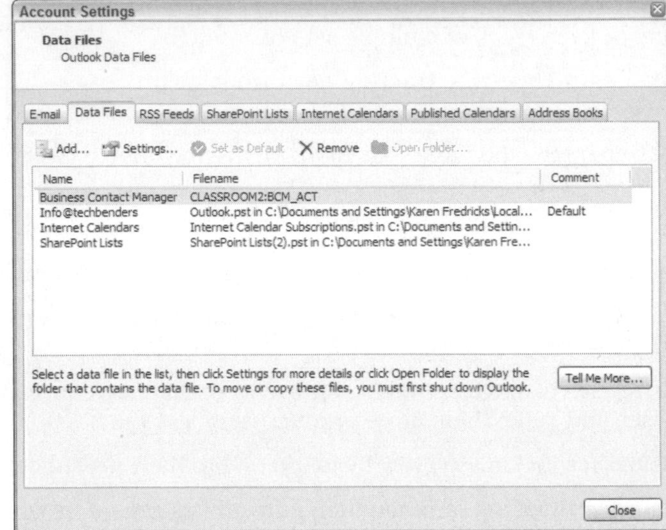

Figure 1-1: The Account Settings dialog box.

2. **Click the Add button.**

   The New Outlook Data File dialog box opens; you can look at Figure 1-2 to get an idea of what it looks like.

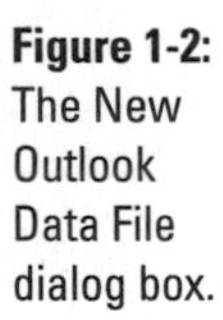

Figure 1-2: The New Outlook Data File dialog box.

3. **Choose Business Contact Manager Database and click OK.**

   Like magic, you're the proud owner of all the BCM tools that you need to get started.

Creating a database

When you first install BCM, you see the cheerful Startup and Welcome to BCM Wizard, which allows you to create your BCM database. Although the Welcome Wizard doesn't hand out coupons like the Welcome Wagon does, it helps you create your all-important database. However, if you missed this wizard or want to create another database, here's what you need to do:

1. **From Outlook, choose Business Contact Manager➪Database Tools➪ Create or Select a Database.**

   The new database dialog box appears, as shown in Figure 1-3.

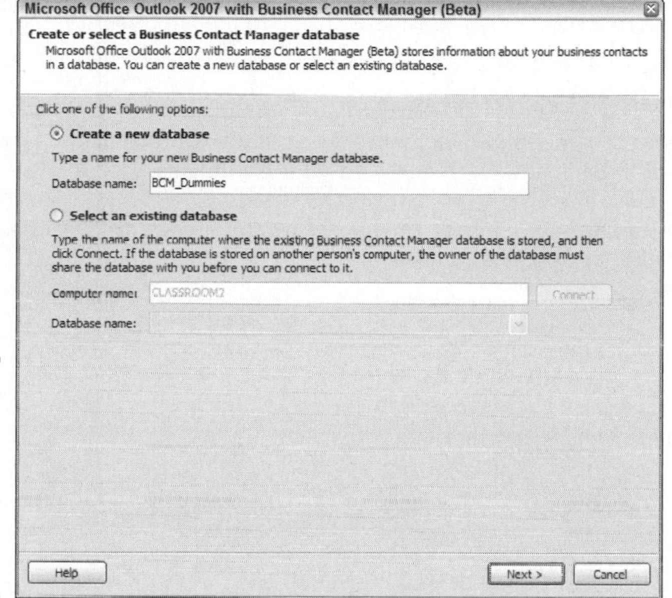
Microsoft Office Outlook 2007 with Business Contact Manager (Beta)
Create or select a Business Contact Manager database
Microsoft Office Outlook 2007 with Business Contact Manager (Beta) stores information about your business contacts in a database. You can create a new database or select an existing database.
Click one of the following options:
Create a new database
Type a name for your new Business Contact Manager database.
Database name:
BCM_Dummies
Select an existing database
Type the name of the computer where the existing Business Contact Manager database is stored, and then click Connect. If the database is stored on another person's computer, the owner of the database must share the database with you before you can connect to it.
Computer name:
CLASSROOM2
Connect
Database name:
Help
Next >
Cancel

Figure 1-3: Creating a new Business Contact Manager database.

2. **Click the Create a New Database option.**
3. **Enter the name of the new database and then click Next.**

   You may want to name your database something that you're able to pick out of a crowd, such as CoolBeans or LetsMakeMoney. You also should avoid spaces in the name, as well as characters such as @#$%^& and *, especially if you don't want your computer to think you're swearing at it. If you don't suggest a name, Business Contact Manager suggests one for you: MSSmallBusiness.

   As quick as a bunny, your database is created.

WARNING!

When you create a database, it opens automatically. Don't sweat when your old one disappears. You can find out how to switch between databases in the next section, "Opening a database."

BCM uses SQL as its database engine. When you create a new database, two data files are actually created: one with an `.mdf` extension and the other with an `.ldf` extension. You can find those files somewhat buried alive deep in the bowels of your computer — or in the Documents and Settings\User Name\Local Settings\Application Data\Microsoft\Business Contact Manager. If you'd like to rename those files, you can stop the SQL service, navigate to that folder, and rename the two files in question.

Opening a database

After you create a database, you may actually want to use it. Here's how you can switch back and forth between your databases.

1. **From Outlook, choose Business Contact Manager⇨Database Tools⇨Create or Select a Database.**

   You can check your progress by looking at Figure 1-4.

Click one of the following options:

Create a new database

Type a name for your new Business Contact Manager database.

Database name: BCM_Dummies2

Select an existing database

Type the name of the computer where the existing Business Contact Manager database is stored, and then click Connect. If the database is stored on another person's computer, the owner of the database must share the database with you before you can connect to it.

Computer name: CLASSROOM2 Connect

Database name: BCM_Dummies

BCM_ACT
BCM_Dummies
MSSmallBusiness3

Figure 1-4: Selecting a previously created database.

2. **Click the Select an Existing Database option.**
3. **Select the name of your database from the Database name drop-down box and click Connect.**

   BCM is a SQL database. That simply means that it must be *connected* to SQL in order to work. (Make sure that you throw in the comment that you "had to connect your database to SQL" the next time you go to a cocktail party.)
4. **Click Next to continue.**

   If you'd like, you can tap your fingers on the desk for a minute while your computer makes a bit of noise and ultimately opens your database.

Finding your current database

Nothing is worse than getting lost in an endless maze of databases. Okay, worse things happen, but not knowing which database you're using can be extremely frustrating — especially if you've spent the day entering tons of contact information only to discover that you entered it into the *wrong* database.

Here's a simple way to get the M.O. on a database that may be MIA:

1. **From Outlook, choose Business Contact Manager⇨Database Tools⇨Manage Database.**

   Ta-dum, the Manage Database dialog box appears.

2. **Click the Backup/Restore tab if it isn't selected.**

   You see a screen that coincidentally matches the one in Figure 1-5. In addition to seeing the name of your current database, you also see the name of your computer, the date and time in which it was created, the owner of the database, and the size of the database.

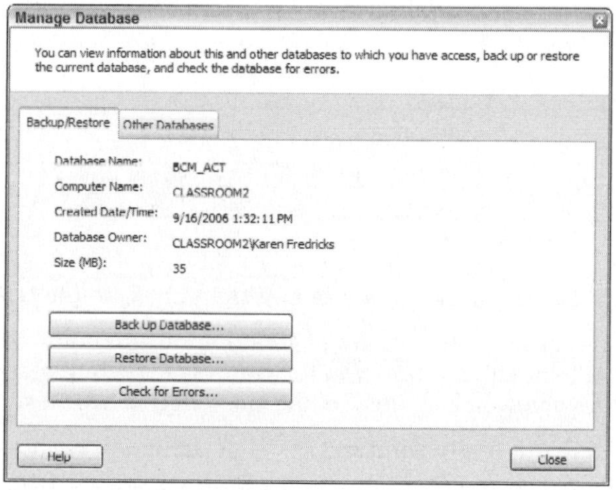

Figure 1-5: The Backup/Restore tab of the Manage Database dialog box.

Deleting a database

Life changes, things happen, and your cheese gets moved. Maybe you created a database for the leads that you purchased, and you now find that you no longer need them. Or maybe you created a database in error and want to get rid of the evidence before the boss sees it. Whatever the reason, it's just as easy to delete a database as it was to create it in the first place. Here's all you've got to do:

1. **From Outlook, choose Business Contact Manager⇨Database Tools⇨Manage Database.**

   The Manage Database dialog box opens.

2. **Click the Other Databases tab.**

   You see a list of most of your database on the Other Databases tab, shown in Figure 1-6. We mention that you see most of your databases because one important one is missing from the list: the database that you're currently in. As a safety precaution, this database is excluded from the list so that you delete only nonactive BCM databases.

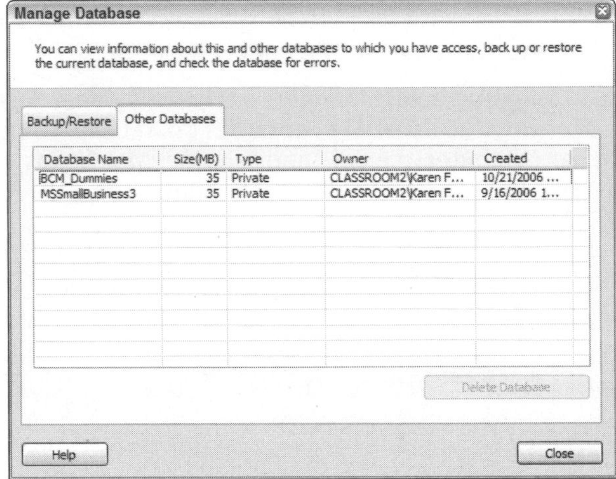

Figure 1-6: The Other Databases tab.

3. **Highlight the database to delete and then click Delete Database.**

   A warning asks whether you're of sound mind and body. Okay, the warning doesn't actually prompt you for your current state of mental health, but it does give you a chance to halt the deletion process.

4. **Click Yes if you really want to get rid of the database in question.**

   Unfortunately, BCM doesn't believe in long, lengthy goodbyes. Wham, your database is gone, permanently (as in forever) so think carefully before clicking that Yes button.

Importing Contacts into BCM

The only thing worse than doing a bunch of work is redoing it all over again. With that thought in mind, BCM has thoughtfully included an Import wizard that can magically transform your old database information into a shiny, new BCM database. If you're using a program like ACT! or Access and decide to switch to BCM, you can do so without losing — or retyping — your data. If you're currently using QuickBooks, you can import your various lists of customers and vendors into BCM. Many of you may even be using an Excel spreadsheet to keep track of your contacts; not to worry — BCM helps you move those contacts easily and painlessly into BCM.

If you have multiple users — salespeople for example — that have each been keeping their own lists of contact data, you can import them into one new BCM Master Database for your company. You can even import a BCM database into BCM database if that's what floats your boat.

Determining your data type

So what specific data types can be brought into BCM? A look at Figure 1-7 shows you the main ones. Four of these options carry the `.bcm` handle because they all involve bringing existing BCM data into your database:

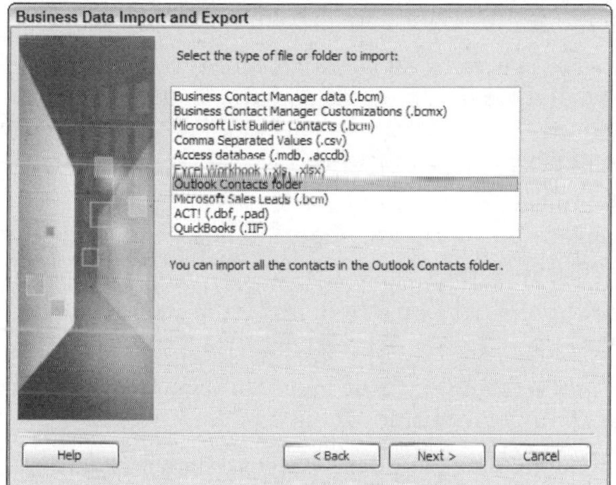

Figure 1-7: The Business Data Import and Export Wizard.

- **Business Contact Manager data (`.bcm`):** Imports all the good stuff, including business contacts, accounts, opportunities, and communication history. Use this option if you accidentally created two separate databases and want to merge them together, or if someone else in your organization is already using an existing BCM database. This option is also a good way to collect data from remote guys; you can import their data into the company database at regular intervals.
- **Business Contact Manager Customizations (`.bcmx`):** Allows you to import your business contacts and any user-defined fields that you may have created for your database.
- **Microsoft List Builder Contacts (`.bcm`):** Use this option to bring in a list of List Builder contact information into BCM.
- **Microsoft Sales Leads (`.bcm`):** Lets you bring in your Business Contact Manager information from any older version.

The rest of the import choices actually involve a two-pronged attack: Your data is converted to a BCM database, and then you need to import that BCM database into your existing database. After you've imported in the information, BCM automatically prompts you to import it into your existing database.

Here are your other import choices:

- **Comma Separated Values (`.csv`):** The one-size-fits-all option for importing data. Basically, if you can get your information *out* of a program, you can get it *into* BCM. CSV is also the format of choice for organizations that run trade shows or that sell prospect lists. All you have to do is ask someone "Can you send me those names in a CSV format?" and you're good to go. BCM's Import function allows you to "map" incoming fields from the CSV file into the fields that BCM stores in its database, which allows you to get the right data in to the right place.

  Most software programs allow for an export to a text file. Even if you're using a (gasp!) DOS-based program, you can probably find a Print to File option that creates an ASCII or "text" file. You can then open that text file in Excel and save it as a `.csv` file.

- **Access database (`.mdb` or `.accdb`):** Depending on the tables you were using, use this option to import in business contact or account information.
- **Excel Workbook (`.xls` or `slsx`):** Import in your business contacts or accounts.
- **Outlook Contacts folder:** Bring in any of your Outlook contacts and plunk them into your business contacts.

  If you plan on building your database with information that another user is keeping in Outlook, you need to wrestle a copy of his `.pst` file from him and open it on your machine. Only then can you import all his contacts.

- **ACT!:** This is actually one of the coolest of the import options. BCM will be able to capture your existing contacts, companies, groups, opportunities, notes, and histories.
- **QuickBooks:** Helpful if you're using QuickBooks. Figure 1-8 shows you the portions of the program that you can export from QuickBooks.

Figure 1-8: Lists that you can export from QuickBooks.

When exporting from QuickBooks, you may find that your import into BCM works better — albeit much slower — if you export your files from QuickBooks one at a time.

Importing data

To import data, you have to follow quite a few steps along the way, but the effort is worth it when you think of all the time saved! BCM comes equipped with an Import wizard that guides you through the process and guarantees that you don't get lost along the way.

1. **From Outlook, choose Business Contact Manager⇨Database Tools⇨ Import and Export.**

   If you're so inclined, you can also choose File⇨Import and Export⇨Business Contact Manager for Outlook. In any event, the Business Data Import and Export dialog window appears.

2. **Select Import and click Next.**

3. **Select the type of data file you're going to import and click Next.**

   For the purpose of this exercise, we're going to pick a `.csv` file. The Business Data Import and Export dialog box appears, as shown in Figure 1-9.

   Not sure which type of data to import? The data choices are explained in full detail in the preceding section.

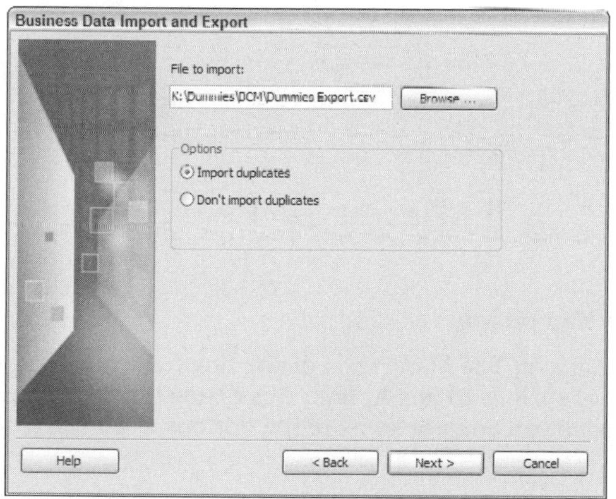

Figure 1-9: The Business Data Import and Export dialog box.

4. **Select the location of your import file and indicate your duplicate option.**

   Here's where you can decide whether you want to import duplicates into your database. For example, you might be importing contacts from various sources that have overlapping contacts. In some cases you might want to include the duplicates to make sure that you won't lose any notes or other pertinent information that might be associated with the contact.

5. **Click Next to continue.**

   In this window, indicate

   - The file you want to import — which seems kind of silly because you just chose it in the previous step.
   - Whether you want to import your data into your Business Contacts or Accounts.

   You can see all your choices in Figure 1-10.

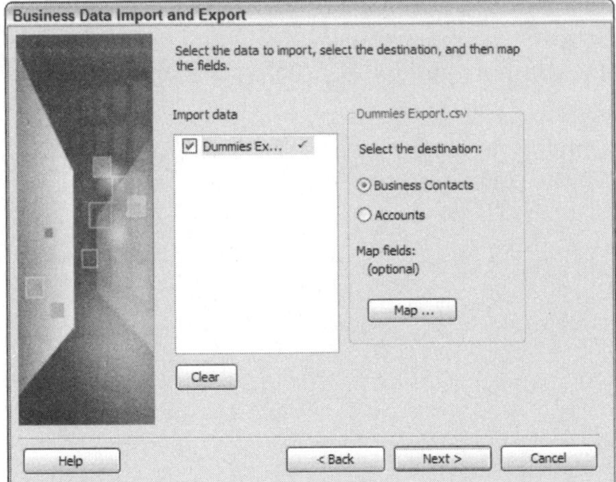

Figure 1-10: Stepping through the Import wizard.

6. **Click the Map button.**

   Holy Guacamole! The Map Fields dialog box (which you can see in Figure 1-11) springs to life. At first, this dialog box seems way too confusing, but once you analyze some of the options, it all starts to make more sense:

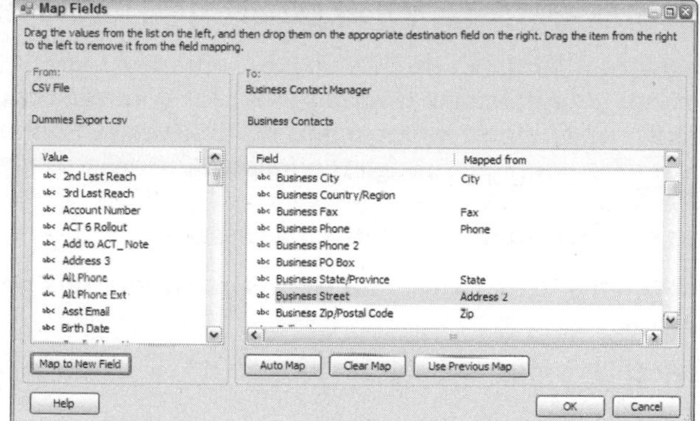

Figure 1-11: Mapping the import file fields to the BCM contact fields.

- Start by clicking the Auto Map button. Any fields from your import file that are an identical match to a BCM field appear in the Mapped from column. (The import fields are on the left, and the BCM fields are on the right.)
- Manually map an import field to a BCM field by dragging it from the From column to the To column. If you look at Figure 1-11, you see several examples of manually mapped fields. Notice that we mapped Business Phone to Phone.
- (Optional) Click an import field and then click the Map to New Field button if you want to import information into your database and BCM doesn't have a field for that information. Fill in the necessary field information in the Add a Field dialog box that opens and click OK.

7. **Click OK to continue and then Next to continue to the end of the Import Wizard.**

   At this point, you see a rather reassuring message that tells you that your information is going to be imported.

8. **Click Next to continue.**

   This part is pretty easy — you get to sit back and watch a moving graphic that illustrates how your data information is flying from your import file into the arms, er, fields of BCM. When your data is finished flying through cyberspace, you're treated to a congratulatory message. Too bad it doesn't include champagne and bon bons!

9. **Click the Close button to close out of the wizard.**

   Give yourself a really big pat on the back — you deserve it!

Moving contacts from Outlook

Entering in new contact data into BCM can be a drag — but not if you're able to *drag* them into your database from Outlook. For your next trick, you can magically transform Outlook contacts into BCM Business Contacts or Accounts. Just drag yourself through the following steps:

1. **Click the Contacts folder on Outlook's folder list.**
2. **Select the contacts that you want to transform into Business Contacts or Accounts.**
   - To select all contacts, hold down the Ctrl key and tap the letter A on your keyboard
   - To select contacts at random, hold down the Ctrl key and click the contacts you want
3. **Right-drag the selected contacts to either the BCM Accounts or Business Contacts folder.**
4. **Select Move if you want to move the contact(s) or Copy if you'd like the contact(s) to appear in both BCM and Outlook.**

   Next time you look, the contact(s) will now be residing happily among the rest of your BCM Business Contacts or Accounts.

Chapter 2: Introducing the Basic Business Contact Manager Elements

In This Chapter

- **Contacting Business Contacts**
- **Accounting for accounts**
- **Linking Outlook to BCM**
- **Working with business projects**

You've got Outlook BCM up and running, and you're anxious to dive right in to it. Well, you've headed to the right chapter! In this chapter, you find out how to create Business Contacts — those people with whom you do business. You'll add in a few Accounts or "super contacts" that represent the main company that those Business Contacts associate with. If you already have contacts in Outlook, this chapter shows you how to move, copy, and link those contacts to Business Contact Manager. Finally, if you're interested in project management, this chapter covers that as well.

Working with Business Contacts

No tour of BCM can be complete without locating your Business Contacts; after all, BCM does stand for Business Contact Manager. As the name Business Contact Manager implies, contacts are the heart and soul of the program. A contact is one person, and BCM comes with many fields of information that can store information about that person. You can have all types of contacts — prospects, customers, friends, enemies, vendors — and each contact has information that is specific to it.

You can find your BCM Contacts in a number of places:

- Click the plus sign to the left of Business Contact Manager on the Navigation pane and then choose Business Contacts.
- Click the Display icon on the Business Contact Manager toolbar and then choose Business Contacts from the menu.
- Choose Business Contact Manager⇨Business Contacts from the main Outlook menu bar.

Adding a new Business Contact

BCM comes configured "out of the box" with more than 50 fields of data that you can store about each contact. You can add more fields if you want to customize BCM to fit the needs of your business.

Here's how you add a new Business Contact:

1. **Click the Business Contacts folder in the folder list.**
2. **From Outlook, choose File⇨New⇨Business Contact.**

   You see the window in Figure 2-1. This area is where you enter all the pertinent info for your new contact.
3. **Start filling in your tidbits of information.**

   The only field you must enter is the Full Name field. However, this field is just the proverbial tip of the BCM contact iceberg. A few things aren't apparent to the naked eye, so we'd like to point them out:

   - Clicking the *Full Name* button brings up a dialog box to enter in a contact's title (Mr., Mrs.), first, middle, and last name, and suffix. You can see what we mean by giving Figure 2-2 a gander.
   - The *File As* field is important because that's how the name is sorted in list views of contact names.

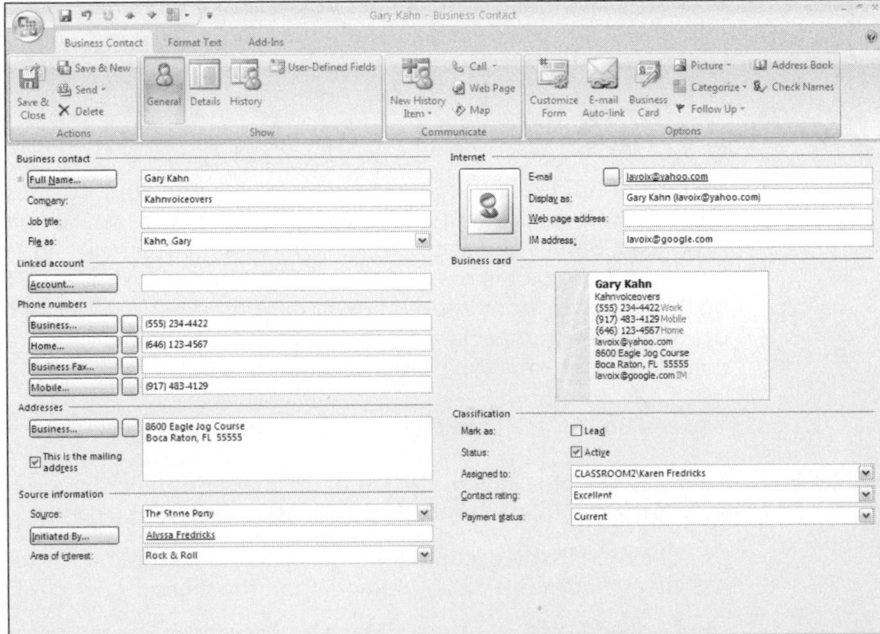

Figure 2-1: Business Contact window.

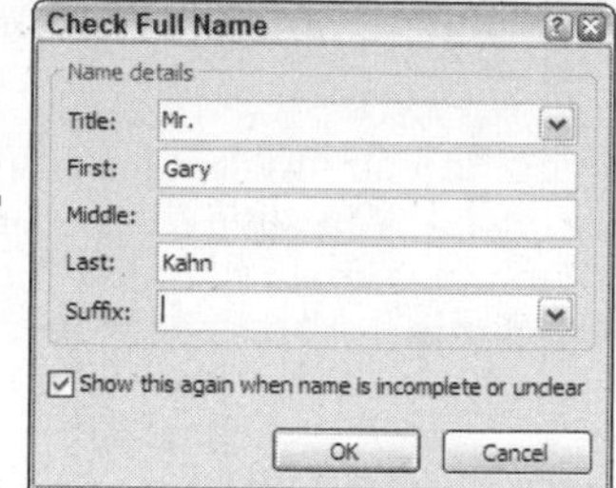

Figure 2-2: The Check Full Name dialog box.

- The *Account* button opens all the Account records if you need to link the Business Contact record to an Account record.
- BCM comes with more *Phone Numbers* than you can shake a stick at. And, if you need more, you can add them. If you click the down arrow after one of the phone fields, you can choose which one you want to use. Although you can store 19 phone fields, you can only display four numbers at a time. Clicking the phone buttons themselves allows you to change the country code for that number.

Don't worry about messing with dashes and parenthesis when entering a phone number — BCM thoughtfully adds them when you leave a phone field.

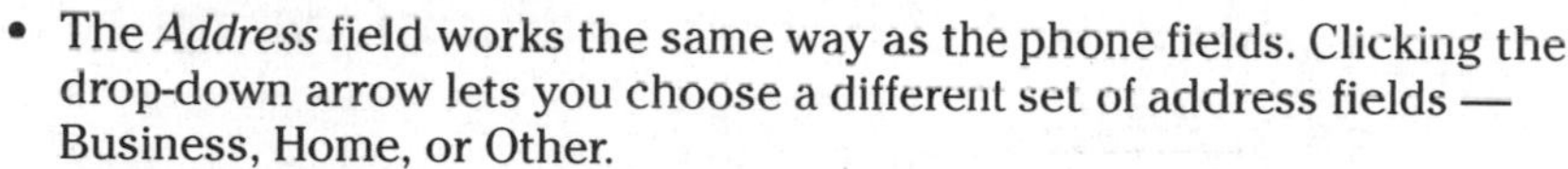

- The *Address* field works the same way as the phone fields. Clicking the drop-down arrow lets you choose a different set of address fields — Business, Home, or Other.
- Several of the other fields include drop-down arrows so that you can select a value from the drop-down list, thus ensuring that your information is entered consistently. If you're familiar with the drop-down list, you can simply type the first letter or so of your intended info, and poof! BCM fills in the rest of the information automatically.
- Clicking on the *Initiated By* button allows you to link this contact to another contact, marketing campaign, opportunity, or business project. This button is a great way of keeping track how this contact came into your world.
- BCM stores three *e-mail addresses;* just click the drop-down arrow to switch between them.
- The Web Page and IM address fields are hyperlinks; give them a click to launch your browser or IM window.
- Click on the *picture* to include a photo (or icon or logo) of that person. This picture is also sent to a Pocket PC or Smartphone when you synch.

4. **Click the Save and Close icon when you've finished entering your contact information.**

   Or click the Save & New button if you had so much fun adding one contact that you just can't wait to do it again. You save the record you were entering and have a new, blank Business Contact screen open so that you can start working on your next victim.

Making changes to a Business Contact

You've worked really hard at adding all sorts of new contacts to your database. Life is good. The birds are singing. Time to go try out that new putter. However, even the best-laid plans of mice, men, and golf carts can get messed up. Perhaps one of your clients has the audacity to change his e-mail address, and another one changes his phone number. You may even have a lowdown, nasty former client decide to take his business elsewhere — and you can't wait to remove all remnants of him from your database.

Fear not — stuff happens, and BCM makes it really easy to deal with change. Simply double-click on the name of the Business Contact that you want to change, make your changes, and click the Save & Close button on the Ribbon to save them.

Adding a Business Contact from an Account record

You may want to picture a BCM Accounts as a super-sized Business Contact. Here's where you can enter information about an organization or large company. In general, you create a Business Contact for a single individual and an Account for a bunch of individuals.

In many cases, if you're dealing with an Account, you're probably dealing with a group of individuals who share several things in common: the same address, main phone number, and signature on the bottom of their paychecks. If you'd like, you can enter all those Business Contacts individually, get a migraine, and storm into your boss's office complaining that you're overworked or underpaid. Or, you can use the following method to enter a bunch of Business Contacts, sneak out to the driving range for an hour, and then storm into your boss's office complaining that you're overworked or underpaid:

1. **Click the Accounts folder on the folder list.**
2. **Find the Account to which you want to add a Business Contact.**
3. **Double-click the Account to open it.**

   The Account record should swing open at this point.

4. **In the Business Contacts section, click on the Add button.**

   The Business contacts section is way on the bottom of the Account screen. When you click it, you're treated to a list of all your existing Business Contacts.

5. **Click the New button.**

   A new Business Contact record opens, just like magic. And, just like magic, the address and phone information are already filled in. The Account name appears in the Account field, and the Web site address is in the Web page field. Talk about automation!

   TIP: You right-clickers in the crowd may prefer to right-click on an Account record and choose Create⇨New Business Contact for Account.

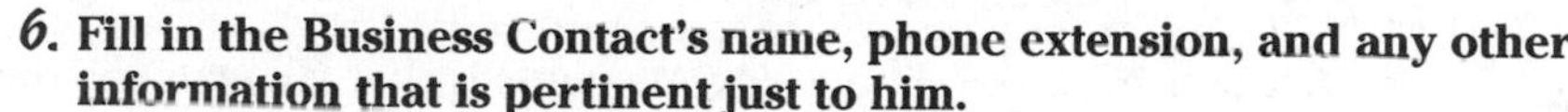

6. **Fill in the Business Contact's name, phone extension, and any other information that is pertinent just to him.**

   BCM is pretty good, but it's not psychic. You have to add these tidbits of information on your own.

7. **Click on Save & Close to save your entries.**

Getting the 411 on Accounts

Accounts are the way to organize several contacts into their company affiliations. You have another entire record of data that you can customize separately from a contact. It can contain fields that are specific to the company instead of the people working at the company. An Account is quite handy if your style of business is to work with multiple people at the same company — the purchasing manager, the production manager, the accounting department. Each contact at that company has his own Business Contact record where you can enter notes about conversations and appointments with that person. All that data rolls up into an Account view so that you or anyone else in your organization can see what's going on with that Account at a higher level.

You may find yourself relying on Accounts even if you're not using BCM to manage a business. You can use Accounts to group all sorts of people together. Perhaps you want to keep track of a soccer team or a PTA or your kid's homeroom class. These groups may translate into your business Accounts.

Face it: Bureaucracy is alive and well and living in most civilized countries. Actually, it probably lives in *un*civilized ones as well. Your database may contain the names of the head guy (also know as The Decision Maker), your main point of contact, the guy who signs the checks, and the person who actually does all the work (the Administrative Assistant). Seems easy at first until the head guy gets fired, the check signer takes off for Brazil — and new people replace both of them.

If you deal with really large companies (generally those that have their own cafeteria and a lot of cubicles), you're probably dealing with numerous Business Contacts as well. The question then becomes "Which do you create first: the Business Contact or the Account?"

In Business Contact Manager, you can

✦ Create an Account and add new Business Contacts to it at the same time.

✦ Create a new Business Contact and add a new Account to it at the same time.

✦ Link a new or existing Account to existing Business Contact records.

✦ Link a new or existing Business Contact to an existing Account Record.

Another huge benefit of using Accounts is that you can link them to Microsoft's Office Accounting software.

It may be tempting for you to create either a Business Contact or Account for every new person you meet. If you've decided to use Accounts, you're much better off entering both the Account and first Business Contact record at the same time. Creating them "on the fly" is much easier than hunting them down and linking them later.

You may have a slight feeling of déjà vu as you read through this section. No, you're not having a flashback to the '60s — you probably just read a section that focuses on adding a Business Contact record. Working with Business Contacts and working with Accounts is a pretty similar process.

Entering Accounts

You can get the Account creation process going in a variety of ways:

✦ Choose File⇨New⇨Account from Outlook's menu bar.

✦ Choose Business Contact Manager⇨Accounts⇨New from Outlook's menu bar.

✦ Click the Accounts folder in the folder list and then click the New button on the toolbar.

✦ Right-click an open area in the Accounts display and select New Account.

Any of these methods lead to Rome and the window you see in Figure 2-3, where you enter each field of information.

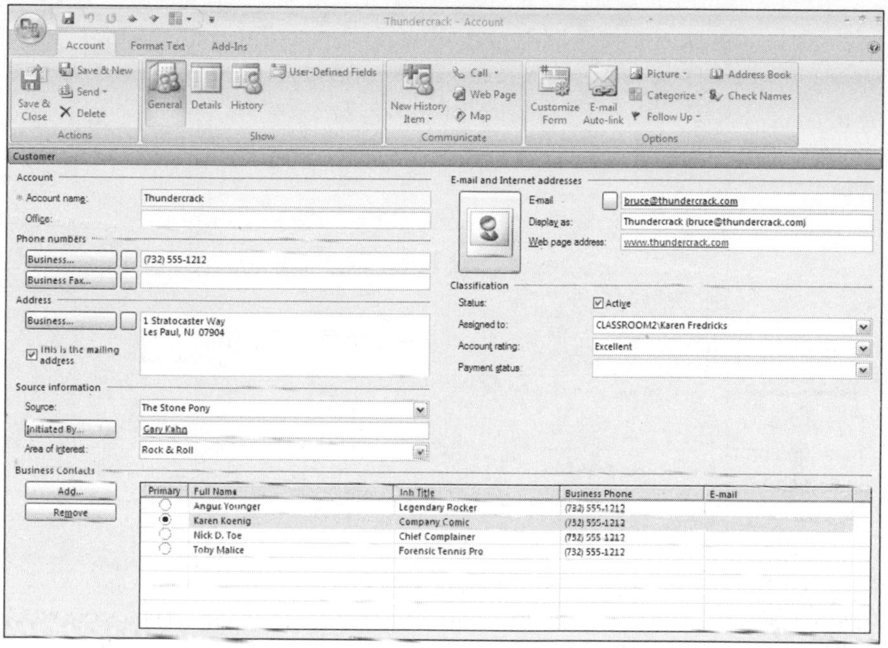

Figure 2-3: The Account record window.

The only field you must enter into BCM is the Account name field. However, you may want to take an extra gander at a few other areas:

✦ **Office:** Use this field to designate different locations or divisions within the company.

✦ **Phone numbers, address, and e-mail fields:** Notice the drop-down arrows to the right of some of the field labels. These arrows are indicators that more fields are lurking behind those innocent-looking arrows. For example, click the E-Mail arrow, and you notice that you can add a second or third e-mail address; unfortunately you're able to see only one of them at a time.

✦ **Initiated By:** Click on this button, and you get a list of all your Business Contacts, Marketing Campaigns, Opportunities, and Business Projects. Select an item from the list so that you can track where all your business comes in from. You can see how this works in Figure 2-4.

✦ **Business Contacts:** Link to a new or existing Business Contact. Simply click the Add button and select the name of the Business Contact that you want to associate with this Account from the Select the Business Contacts to link to the Account dialog box. If you hold down the Ctrl key while selecting those critters, you can associate multiple Business Contacts to the Account at the same time.

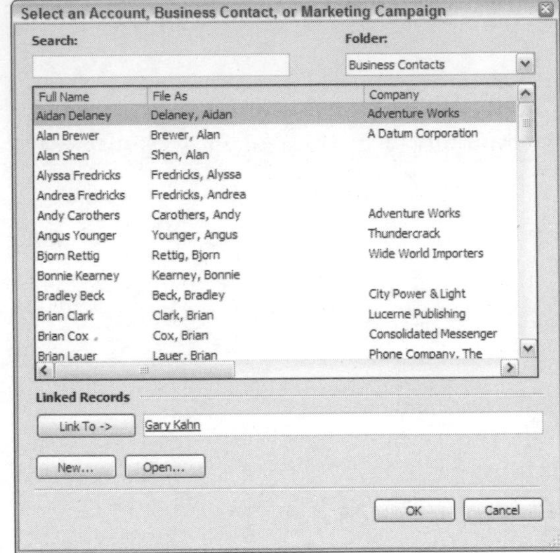

Figure 2-4: Selecting an Initiated By source.

Can't find the Business Contact that you're trying to associate with the Account? Click the New button on the Select the Business Contacts to link to the Account dialog box. BCM snaps to attention and presents you with a brand-new Business Contact window and the keys to the city.

- **Categories:** If you associate a category with an Account (see Book VIII, Chapter 1), the category(ies) appear at the top of the Account screen.

Several fields have a drop-down arrow at the end of them; using these drop-down lists helps ensure the consistency of the database. If you type the first letter of so of a drop-down item, BCM completes the rest of the word for you. If you add in a value that isn't included in the drop-down list, BCM asks whether you'd like to add that item to the drop-down list; if you decline the invitation, BCM prevents you from adding it into the field.

Creating an Account from an existing Business Contact

For generations, we have pondered that age-old question: Which came first, the Account or the Business Contact. Okay, maybe that's not the age-old question, but it's one that we can attempt to answer. In the preceding section, the Account was created first. In this section, you create the Business Contact first and use that Contact to create a new Account.

To create a new Account from an existing Business Contact, follow these steps:

1. **Open a Business Contact record.**
2. **Click on the Account button in the Linked Account area.**

   A list of all your existing Accounts appears.
3. **Click the New button.**

   The Account window shown in Figure 2-3 appears. Notice that the form is already partially filled out with information from the Business Contact screen.
4. **Continue filling in additional Account information.**
5. **Click Save & Close when you're finished.**

Editing an existing Account

After you have a few Accounts under your BCM belt, you need to know a little about their care and feeding — or at least about their editing and deleting. These tasks may seem painfully easy, but we want to make sure that you know what to do if a company moves to Podunk Junction or decides to permanently shutter its doors. You may even be staying up late worrying that you might have entered an Account twice into your database by accident. Go back to sleep — BCM has your back covered!

Changing data in an account record is simple:

1. **Choose Accounts from the folder list.**
2. **Double-click on the Account Record that you want to change.**

   You can delete information by using your delete and Backspace keys or fill in new information for fields that you had originally left empty.
3. **Click Save & Close to save your changes.**

   If you decide you don't want to save the changes, either press the Esc key or click the X in the upper-right corner; when asked if you want to save changes, click No.

Linking Outlook to BCM Records

There is a lot of good — and great — software on the market. Unfortunately, if you purchased several pieces, you may have encountered that word that strikes terror in the heart of computer users everywhere: incompatibility. You know the drill — you install one piece of software only to find that another stops working. And, a call to tech support generally ends with you feeling like a human ping pong ball. The great thing about Outlook and BCM is that they're two very powerful programs combined into one piece of software. No problems with compatibility here because the programs are designed to work together seamlessly.

Linking existing Outlook items to a BCM record

If you have existing Outlook items, you can link them to a BCM record by following these steps:

1. **From Outlook, choose Go⇨Calendar.**
2. **Double-click the appointment that you want to link to a record.**

   Outlook's appointment dialog box opens. It's quite a bit simpler than the one you use to schedule appointments in BCM. However, in Figure 2-5, that special BCM area appears on the Ribbon.

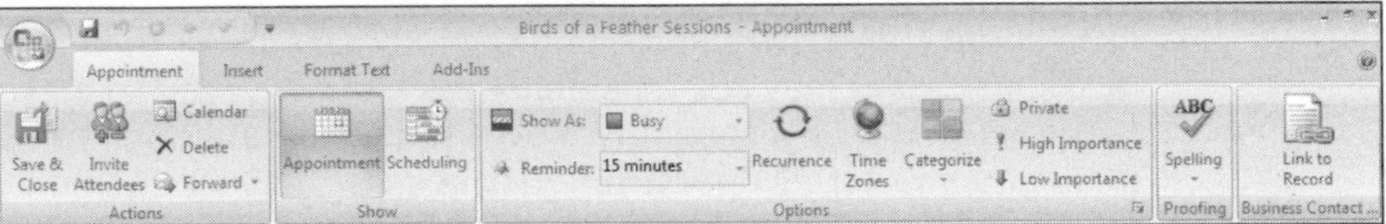

Figure 2-5: Linking an Outlook appointment.

3. **Click Link to Record on the Business Contact Manager area of the Ribbon.**

   The Link to Business Contact Manager Record dialog box opens as shown in Figure 2-6.

4. **Select Account, Business Contact, Opportunity, or Business Project from the Folder drop-down list.**
5. **Type the name of the record you're looking for in the Search box or select the name from the record list.**
6. **Click link to add the Account, Business Contact, Opportunity, or Business Project record to the Linked Records box.**
7. **Click OK to close the Link to BCM record dialog box and then click Save & Close to save the appointment.**

You can link multiple records to an appointment.

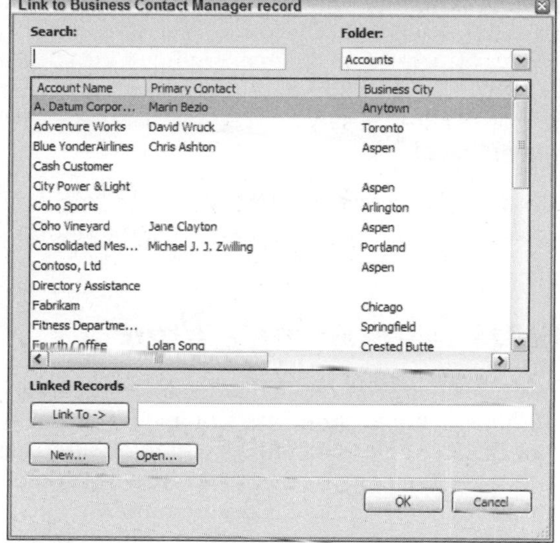

Figure 2-6: Linking an Outlook appointment to a BCM record.

Linking a BCM Record to a new Outlook item

Just as you can link an existing Outlook item to BCM, you can also create a new Outlook appointment, e-mail message, or task that is automatically linked to the open BCM record. The process is a simple one when you follow these steps:

1. **Create or open an Account, Business Contact, Opportunity, or Business Project record.**

2. **Click the New History Item icon in the Communicate section of the Ribbon.**

   To create or open a Business Contact Manager for an Outlook record, on the Business Contact Manager menu, click Accounts, Business Contacts, Opportunities, or Business Projects. To create a new record, on the Standard toolbar, click New, or select and double-click an existing record to open it.

   You can see a sneak preview of the BCM Ribbon in Figure 2-7.

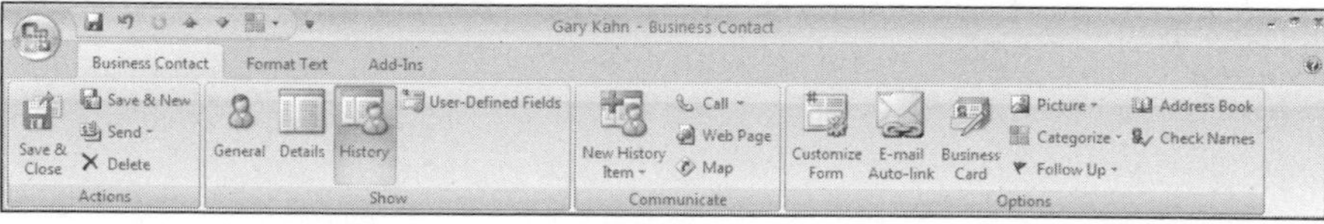

Figure 2-7: The BCM Ribbon.

3. **Select the Outlook item that you'd like to create from the drop-down list.**

   If you choose Task, Mail Message, or Appointment, you're plunked into familiar, Outlook territory.

4. **Fill in the form as usual.**

   There's only one crucial difference than when you're creating those items in Outlook: The new items now link back to a BCM record.

Turning Your Business into a Major Project

As you delve into the various features of Business Contact Manager, you may start thinking of BCM as a "super-sized" version of Outlook. A great example is found in Business Projects. Outlook allows you to create tasks and appointments. BCM takes the concept one — or three — steps further by allowing you to group together all the tasks and appointments that relate to a single project. Even better, you can assign the various project tasks to an authorized user of your Business Contact Manager database.

Projecting your Business Projects

The first step in working on a project is to create it. Okay, that step seems a bit logical, but using BCM can help you take a huge undertaking and break it down into smaller, bite-sized pieces. In BCM, a Business Project, such as a trade show or conference, can include several project tasks that need to be delegated and completed by the various people in your organization. As you think of complete tasks — or think of new ones — you can enter them in BCM where you can track their progress. Alternatively, you can put all your tasks on sticky notes, but then you're going to have to spend a lot of your time praying that no one turns on the paddle fan!

To create a Business Project in BCM, follow these steps:

1. **Click on Business Projects in the BCM area of the Outlook folder list.**

   If you have a lot of projects going on, you can create a subfolder for each project by choosing File➪New➪Folder from the Outlook menu bar.

2. **Choose File➪New➪Business Project.**

   Not surprisingly, the Business Project form appears, and it looks exactly like the one in Figure 2-8.

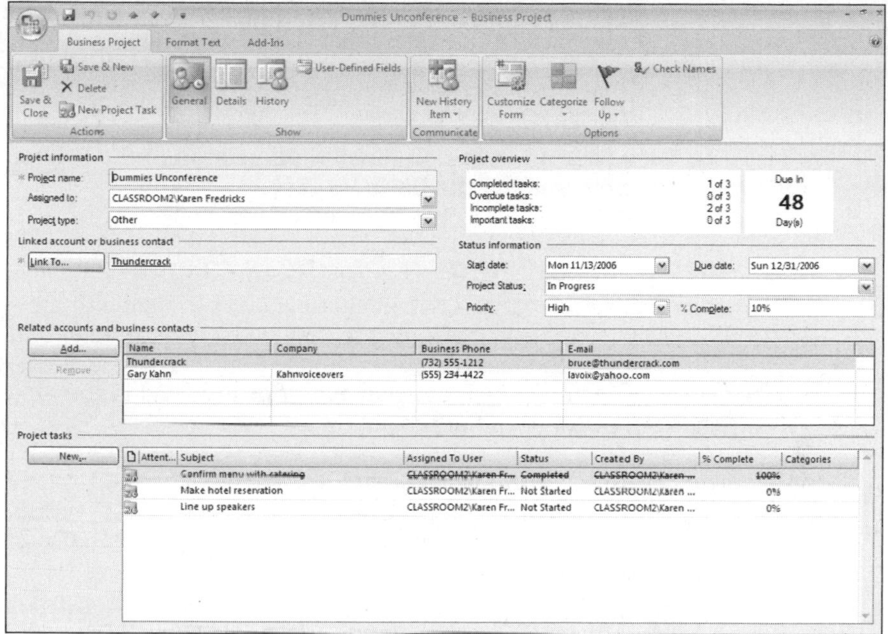

Figure 2-8: Creating a Business Project.

3. **Fill in the pertinent details of the Project.**

   You can start by adding as much — or as little — information as you'd like. Here's a few of your options:

   - *Project Name:* You can't tell a book by its cover, and you can't keep track of your projects without a good title.
   - *Assigned To:* Here's where you can pass the buck — or at least the task — on to someone else in the crowd.
   - *Project Type:* If you have a whole lot of projects going on, you can group them together according to type.
   - *Link To:* If your project revolves around one of your big Business Contacts or Accounts, you can link to it so that you can cross-reference your projects by Account or Business Contact.
   - *Status Information:* Fill in a couple of the important details here, including the start and due dates, the status, and the priority of the project.

   - *Related Accounts and Business Contacts:* Here's where you can add the entire cast of characters that will be working on your project with you.
   - *Project Tasks:* Add as many new tasks to the project as you'd like — and assign them to whomever you'd like!

4. **Click Save and Close in the Actions section of the Ribbon when you're finished creating the Business Project.**

Chipping away at a Business Project

A Business Project can contain multiple tasks assigned to multiple victims. When a project task is assigned to you, you'll want to rise to the occasion and complete the task. As you complete your tasks, you can record that information into Outlook so that everyone involved in the project is able to track the progress of the project.

You can access your project-related tasks in two ways:

- Double-click the task from the BCM portion of the To-Do bar. You can see what this looks like in Figure 2-9.
- Open the Business Project and double-click the Task in the Project Tasks area.

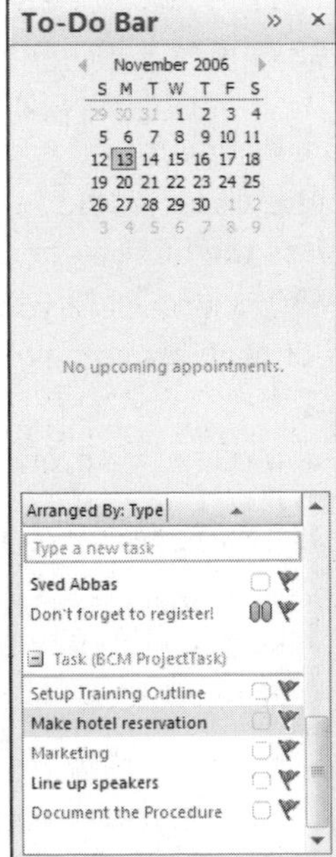

Figure 2-9: Accessing BCM tasks from the To-Do bar.

After you complete and save the task, the latest information from the task appears in the linked Business Project form. If you complete the task, you're able to recognize that important milestone because the task is now crossed off of your project, like the one you see in Figure 2-8.

Tracking your project progress

As the owner of a business, you'll probably sleep better at night knowing that your project is progressing its way on to completion. Or, if your business consists of one overworked and underpaid employee (YOU!), you may sleep better at night knowing that your various Business Projects are extremely well organized. In either case, we assume that you're the Project Manager for this project and that you need to make sure that the project is on track.

As you see that various tasks within a Business Project are completed, you'll want to update the overall progress of the Business Project itself. Here's how you can do just that.

1. **Open the Business Project you want to edit.**

   You can find all your Business Projects neatly arranged in the BCM section of Outlook's folder list. When you double-click one of them, the Business Project form springs to life.

2. **Change the completion status and % complete in the Status information section of the Business Project record.**

   If you refer to Figure 2-8, you see the Project Status field, which is a great place to track the status of the project.

3. **View the important information about the status in the Project overview section.**

   BCM keeps a running tally of where you stand in each of your projects by letting you know how many tasks you've completed, how many are overdo, and how many you still have left to complete. You'll even have a large countdown number reminding you of how many days are left until the "big" day.

4. **Click Save & Close when you're finished editing the project.**

Bidding your project adieu

If you feel that old news is, well, old news, you may want to remove your Business Projects from BCM as they're completed.

When you delete a Business Project, you also lose all the content of that project. You may want to keep completed projects "on file" so that you can refer back to them if you find yourself dealing with a similar project again in the future.

You can archive your older information rather than deleting it.

To delete a Business Project:

✦ Open the Business Project and click Delete from the Actions section of the Ribbon.

✦ Right-click the Business Project on the Folder List and click Delete from the shortcut menu.

In either case, Outlook asks whether you're really, really sure that you want to delete the Business Project. If you are, click OK.

Just in case you accidentally deleted the *wrong* Business Project — or if you just plain changed your mind — you can easily recover the deleted Business Project by dragging it out of the BCM Deleted Items folder. Whew!

Chapter 3: Working with Opportunities

In This Chapter

- **Creating an opportunity**
- **Tweaking existing opportunities**
- **Working with products and services**

In this chapter, you discover how you can use BCM to work with your sales process. You find out how to create an initial opportunity and update the sale as it makes its way through the sales funnel. For good measure, I even show you how to link your BCM opportunities with your SBA opportunities so that you don't have to duplicate your efforts.

Creating a New Opportunity

In BCM, an *opportunity* is a potential sale to a Business Contact or Account, and each opportunity must be associated with either a Business Contact or Account. When you create an opportunity, you're actually creating a new item in much the same way that you create a new Business Contact or Account (you can flip back to Book VII, Chapter 2 for more details). When you create an opportunity, you can include the names of your products or services, specify a sales stage and forecasted close date, and even add your own user-defined fields. If you prefer, you can create a new opportunity directly from a Business Contact or Account record.

After creating an opportunity, you can go to the Opportunity folder, where your opportunities are listed together, or view the Business Contact's or Account's Communication History tab. As if that isn't enough, you can choose from a slew of Opportunities reports or access one of the neat Opportunities dashboards that, like your car's dashboard, shows you graphical representations about what's going on in your business.

You can make your first million — and track it in BCM — in a number of ways:

- ✦ From either the Business Contacts or Accounts folder, right-click the Business Contact or Account and choose Create➪New Opportunity for Business Contact (or Account).
- ✦ While adding or editing a Business Contact or Account record, choose New Communication History Item➪Opportunity.
- ✦ While editing a Business Contact or Account record, choose File➪(the Office logo) New Business Item➪New Opportunity.

Whatever your method, you're immediately transported to the Opportunity's General tab, shown in Figure 3-1.

If you didn't know better, you'd think that you're looking at a Business Contact or Account record, and some of the information you'll be entering is very similar. Here's a rundown of the information to add. These fields hang out together in organized bundles:

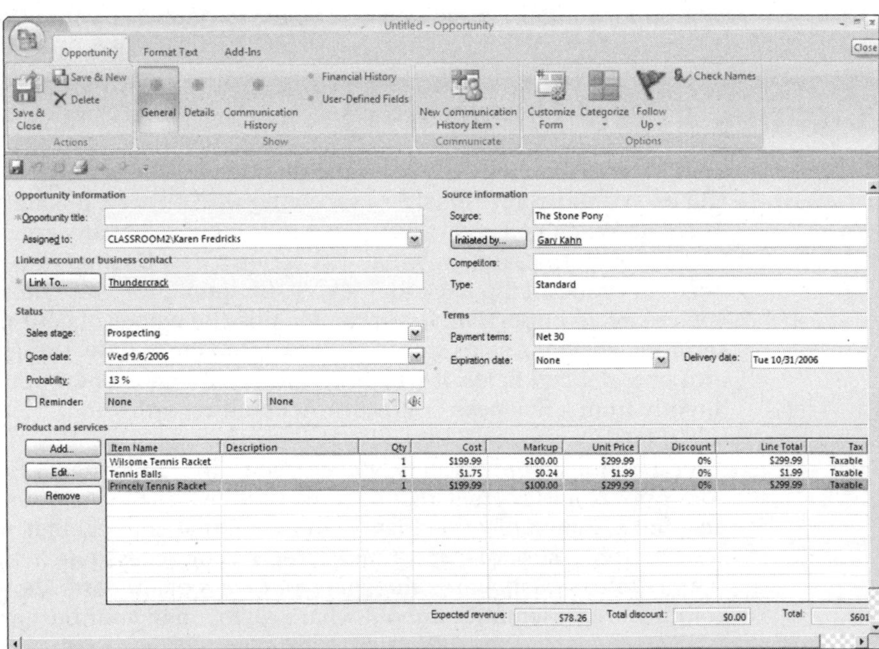

Figure 3-1: Entering a new Opportunity record.

✦ The **Opportunity Information** contains pretty much the "must-have" fields that you need to fill in with opportunity information:

- *Opportunity Title:* This field is mandatory, I guess, so that you can keep your opportunities apart. Feel free to name the opportunity with an important tidbit of information like "This one will finance my kids' education."
- *Assigned To:* This field is where you can add a list of the salespeople in your company and tie them to the opportunity.
- *Link To:* This field is required — it links the opportunity to a Business Contact or Account. Click the button, and a window appears. From here, you can select an account, click the Link To button, and then click OK to attach the Account to the opportunity. If you prefer, change the Folder drop-down list to Business Contacts and link one of your Business Contacts to the new opportunity.

✦ The **Status section** is where you track a deal as it moves through the sales process. It consists of four fields:

- *Sales stage:* You can select a sales stage from the drop-down list. As you select a sales stage, Business Contact Manager adds a percentage to the Probability field.
- *Close date:* You can indicate the date that you think your red-hot opportunity will convert into cold hard cash.
- *Probability:* Although this field changes automatically based on the contents of the sales stage, you can edit the probability manually, if you'd like.
- *Reminder:* You may want to set a reminder to follow up with the people who are trying to give you some of their hard-earned money. The reminder field consists of a date, time, and alarm field. Click the alarm, and you can choose the alarm sound of your choice — a loud "ka-ching" is certainly appropriate.

✦ **Source Information** is where you can record where this opportunity came from — and what little devil may be lurking in the background just waiting to snatch it away from you.

- *Source:* This field contains the main marketing source that helped you reel in the big kahuna. If you're spending money on any type of marketing effort — Web site optimization, direct mail campaign — fill in this field so that you know whether you're getting any bang from your marketing buck.
- *Initiated By:* Just like the Link To field discussed earlier in this list, this field lets you indicate the Business Contact or Account who handed you this deal on a silver platter. This information may prove useful at holiday time when you're trying to decide who gets the great gift basket and who's going to have to contend with the lousy fruit cake.

   - *Competitors:* Win or lose, you may want to know who your competition is.
   - *Type:* You may think of this spot as a do-it-yourself field because the choices you create in this field can help you analyze your business a wee bit better. Maybe you differentiate between commercial and residential sales, or wholesale and retail products. This field is where you can track that important information.

- The **Terms section** lets you indicate the payment terms you're going to extend; the Expiration date lets you know at a glance how long that special pricing is good for. The Delivery date helps you remember when your client should be receiving your product.

Click Save & Close when you're all finished entering the basic Opportunity information. Or, if your business is really on a roll, click Save & New and forge on to your next opportunity.

Finding More Opportunity in Your Opportunities

At times, your head may be swimming with all the Outlook information that you're attempting to cram into it. Don't get discouraged if you don't feel like you're mastering all the bells and whistles at once. One of the fun parts of Outlook is delving deeper and deeper into its features.

The preceding section walks you through the creation of a basic opportunity. This section shows you how you can take the opportunity and run with it. Who knows, you may even score a touchdown — or at least a really large sale!

Wrapping a ribbon around an opportunity

Just as in other records in BCM, the Ribbon at the top of the window gives you a few more places to store your data, as well as a few more functions to help keep track of your opportunities. A few of the areas are specific to opportunities, including

- **Details tab:** You can locate the Details tab by clicking on Details in the Show area of the Ribbon. I'm not quite sure why this tab is called Details when the only thing it contains is a huge area in which you can add time-stamped comments.
- **User-Defined Fields tab:** Found by clicking User-Defined Fields in the Show area of the Ribbon, this tab is where you can add the fields that are specific to the way you and your company do business.
- **Categorize:** The Categorize button (found in the Options section of the Ribbon) isn't specific to Opportunities; you see its identical twins throughout Outlook. However, the concept of using categories is so important that it deserves an extra mention.

Editing an opportunity

You may want to edit an opportunity for two main reasons:

- ✦ You forgot to add some information the first time, or some of your original information requires a bit of tweaking. (That's an official computer term.)
- ✦ You want to track the progress of the opportunity as it makes its way from freezing cold to super hot.

Here's all you have to do to make a change to an existing opportunity:

1. **Click Opportunities from the Business Contact Manager area on the Folder List.**

   The Opportunities list opens (see Figure 3-2).

2. **Double-click the opportunity that you want to edit.**

   Not sure how to find the opportunity you're looking for? You can type your search criterion into the Search box at the top of the Opportunities list.

   The opportunity record appears.

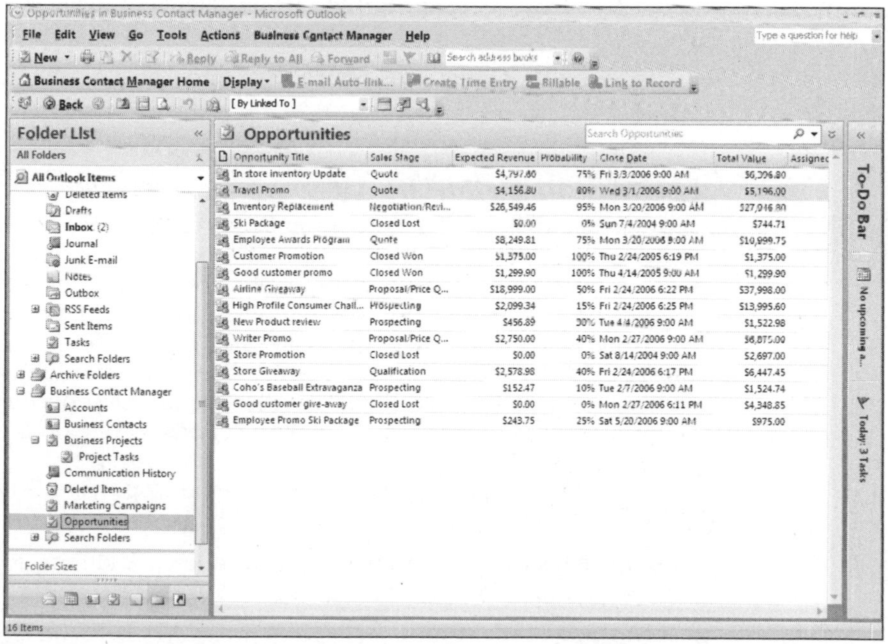

Figure 3-2: BCM's Opportunities list.

3. **Update information as necessary.**

   In addition to adding information that you omitted the first time, you want to make sure that you change the information in the Sales stage field. This update helps keep you on top of the opportunity as it follows along the path of your sales pipeline. Also notice that as you work your way through the stages, the probability of closing becomes higher and higher.

4. **Click Save & Close when you're finished making all your changes.**

Closing the deal

And now the moment you've waited for — drum rolls, please — it's time to close the deal. All those hours of sweat chasing that prospect are going to (hopefully) pay off in spades.

You close a deal in the exact same way that you edit one by opening an existing opportunity. At that point, you select either Closed Won (yippee) or Closed Lost (gasp!) from the Sales stage drop-down list. As you make this change, notice the following:

- All existing fields have gone gray, which means you can no longer enter any additional information into them.
- The probability changes to 100% if you selected Closed Won and 0% if you selected Closed Lost.
- The boss either greets you with a cigar and a slap on the back or a pink slip.

Deleting an opportunity

In general, you're better off marking an Opportunity as Closed Lost rather than just deleting it. You can often gain valuable insight from a Lost Opportunity: Maybe one of your competitors is offering a new product, or someone else is selling a comparable product for half the price. Other times, you may just want to get rid of the evidence: Perhaps the company you were selling to closed its doors for good, or maybe you inadvertently entered in the same opportunity twice. Whatever the reason, the procedure for removing unwanted opportunities is as simple as choosing one of these methods:

- Right-click the Opportunity record from the Opportunities folder list and choose Delete.
- Double-click the Opportunity record to open it and then press the Delete button on the Ribbon.
- Highlight an opportunity record and press Ctrl+D.

As soon as you perform one of the preceding operations, your opportunity disappears. Quickly. Without further warning.

Make a mistake? Fortunately, when you delete an opportunity, it's gone, but certainly not forgotten. It's sitting in the Business Contact Manager's Deleted Items folder just waiting to be rescued. To do so, just drag it to the Opportunities folder. To delete it permanently, give it a right-click in the Deleted Items folder and choose Delete.

Adding Products and Services to an Opportunity

After you create an opportunity, you can add specific products and services to it. If you're like most people, this part is fun because those products and services come with a price tag — which hopefully translates into money in your pocket.

If you open an existing Opportunity record, you see the Product and Services tab that runs along the bottom of the General tab. Here's where you get to count the cash, bill for the beans, dream of the dollars. . . . In any event, the Products and Services portion of the General tab is where you get to add all the line items for your opportunity and sit back while BCM crunches the numbers for you.

Here's how you start counting those beans:

1. **Click the Add button.**

   The Add Product or Service dialog box, shown in Figure 3-3, appears.

Add Product or Service

To add a product or service to the opportunity, enter the relevant information and then click OK.

Item name:	Tennis Balls
Description:	Round yellow objects that bounce
Quantity:	1
Unit cost:	1.75
Markup:	$0.24
Unit Price:	1.99
Line Total (Before Discount):	$1.99
Discount: (%)	0
Line Total:	$1.99
Tax:	☑ Taxable

Help | Add Next | OK | Cancel

Figure 3-3: The Add Product or Service dialog box.

2. **Click the Item Name drop-down arrow and select the name of the product.**

   You can simply type the first several letters of a product name if you're already familiar with the items in your product list.

3. **(Optional) Scroll to the bottom of the list and select Edit This List if you don't see the product you need; if you don't need to add a product, skip to Step 7.**

   The Products and Services dialog box appears. Amazingly, it looks just like Figure 3-4.

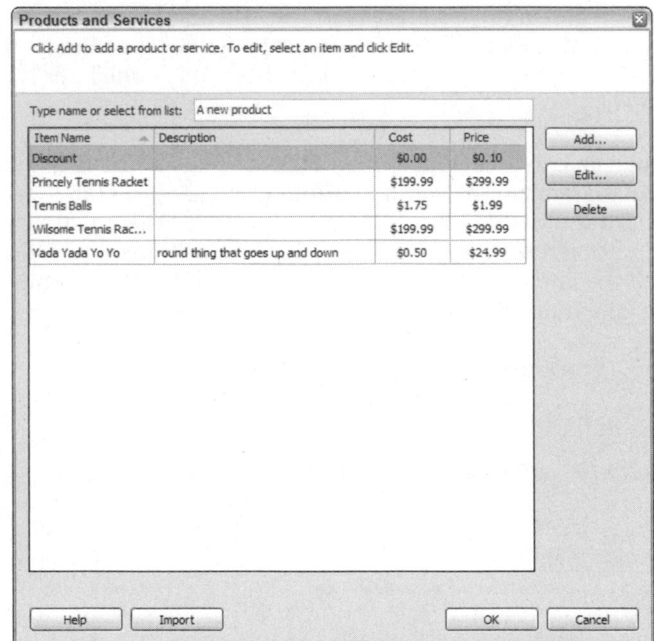

Figure 3-4: The Products and Services dialog box.

All the products and services that you've created in both BCM and SBA are proudly displayed in the Products and Services window.

4. **Click the Add button, and the Add Product or Service dialog box appears.**

   It looks very much like the Add Product or Service dialog box shown in Figure 3-3 except that this one has a Taxable check box and no place to add a discount.

5. **Fill in the juicy details and then click Save to save them.**

   You have to add a unit price, but don't worry — you can over-ride the amount every time you create a new opportunity if you need to.

6. **Click OK to close the Add Product or Service dialog box.**
7. **Enter the quantity that you're going to sell of the item.**

   When you set up your product list, you can set up a default quantity. Feel free to change it each time you create a new opportunity. As you change the quantity, notice that the Line Total (Before Discount) changes as well. You doubting Thomases in the crowd may want to grab a calculator and check the math — don't worry, it's correct!
8. **(Optional) Change the Unit cost and the Unit price.**

   Notice that you can't enter anything into the Markup field because BCM is doing the math for you.
9. **(Optional) Type a Discount percentage.**

   Ooh and aah as the Line Total totals up for you. Okay, you don't have to ooh and aah — or if you do, do it quietly so that the rest of the office doesn't think you have a stomach ache.
10. **Click OK if this product is the only one you're entering or click Add Next if you want to add another product and repeat these steps.**

After you've added Products to an Opportunity, you can:

- ✦ Highlight a line item and click the Edit button if you need to modify one of the products.
- ✦ Highlight a line item and click the Remove button if you want to remove an item from the Opportunity. You're asked whether you're sure you want to remove the item — the answer is Yes.

Also notice that the Total discount and the Total of the Opportunity totals at the bottom of the Product and services table. In addition, the Expected revenue field is calculated based on the probability percentage and the total of all your line items.

Editing or Deleting a Product or Service

You can edit or delete a product or service in the Product and Services dialog box. By now, you probably don't need a road map because you found your way there when you added new products. However, just in case you spilled coffee on your map, here are the necessary directions.

1. **Click Opportunities from the Business Contact Manager folder list.**
2. **Open an existing opportunity by double-clicking it.**
3. **Click Add from the Product and Services area.**

   The Add Product or Service dialog box opens.

4. **Click the Item name drop-down list, scroll to the bottom of the list, and select Edit This List.**

   The Products and Services dialog box springs to life.

5. **Click on a product or service to select it.**
6. **Click Edit to change the item name, description, default quantity, unit cost, or unit price of a product of service or click Delete to remove a product or service.**
7. **Click OK to close the Products and Services dialog box, and then OK again to close the Add Product or Service box.**

You can't edit an item that was synchronized to BCM from Office Accounting — you'll have to do your editing in Office Accounting.

When you delete a product, it doesn't end up in the Deleted Items folder. When you see the rather ominous warning, take heed — the product disappears permanently from the product list.

Chapter 4: Reports and Dashboards

In This Chapter

- Meeting the BCM reports
- Running a report
- Modifying a report
- Drilling through a report
- Working with dashboards

After you build your database, the fun part is sitting back and using it. In this chapter, you find out about the various BCM reports and dashboards. I also include basic information on editing report templates.

Knowing the Basic BCM Reports

BCM comes with a menu of 50 basic reports right out of the box. Chances are good that at least one of the basic BCM reports will give you exactly the information that you're looking for without even having to customize it.

The BCM report menu is divided into seven sections; you'll probably find it to be no small coincidence that these sections reflect seven of the most valuable areas of BCM.

- **Accounts:** Your BCM accounts drive your business, so it's only fitting that BCM comes equipped with 12 Account reports. The title of several of these reports reflects how the accounts are grouped together in the body of the report. Figure 4-1 shows you a sample of the Accounts by Rating report.
- **Activity:** If you're the boss, you may be wondering exactly what your employees are doing all day. If you're the employee, you may want to prove to your boss that you are indeed up to good things during the day. Either way, the Activity reports give proof to the pudding.
- **Business Contacts:** Most of these reports are clones of the Account reports except they're Contact centric rather than Account centric. You can find cool birthday and anniversary reports, such as the one you see in Figure 4-2 should you want to send cards on those red letter days.

Report: Accounts by Rating

File Edit View Action Help

Save Report | Modify Report | Filter Report

Report: Accounts by Rating
Filter Applied: No
Wednesday, September 06, 2006

Account Name	Primary Cont...	Business Pho...	Active	Payment Stat...	Business Fax	Email	Web Page
Rating: Unspecified							
Cash Customer			✔				
Coho Sports		(847) 555-0114	✔		(847) 555-0115		
Directory Assistance			✔				
Fabrikam		(773) 555-0111	✔				
Fitness Department Stores		(217) 555-0115	✔				
Global Sporting Goods		(313) 555-0116	✔				
Hobby Store		(616) 555-0117	✔				
Metro Bike Mart		(613) 555-0118	✔				
Motorless Cycles		(613) 555-0119	✔				
Nearby Sporting Goods		(517) 555-0120	✔				
Pro Sporting Goods		(773) 555-0121	✔				
Recreation Supplies		(630) 555-0122	✔				
Sea View Bike Center		(416) 555-0123	✔				
Sprint Customer Service			✔				
Variety Cycling		(313) 555-0124	✔				
Rating: Excellent							
Adventure Works	David Wruck	(800) 555-1212	✔	Current	(900) 555-1212	info@adventure-...	http://www.adv...
Blue YonderAirlines	Chris Ashton	(800) 555-1212	✔	Current	(900) 555-1212	contact@blueyo...	http://www.blue...
Coho Vineyard	Jane Clayton	(800) 555-1212	✔	Overdue	(900) 555-1212	cineyard@ohovi...	http://www.coh...
Consolidated Messenger	Michael J. J. Zwil...	(800) 555-1212	✔	Overdue	(900) 555-1212		http://www.cons...
Fourth Coffee	Lolan Song	(800) 555-1212	✔	Current	(900) 555-1212		http://www.four...
Lucerne Publishing	Brian Clark	(800) 555-1212	✔	Current	(900) 555-1212		http://www.luce...
Margie's Travel	Olinda Turner	(800) 555-1212	✔	Overdue	(900) 555-1212		http://www.mar...
Tech Benders			✔				
Thundercrack	Karen Koenig	(732) 555-1212	✔			bruce@thunderc...	www.thundercra...
Wide World Importers	Kok-Ho Loh	(800) 555-1212	✔	Overdue	(900) 555-1212		http://www.wid...
WoodgroveBank	Nicole Caron	(800) 555-1212		Overdue	(900) 555-1212		http://www.woo...
Rating: Good							

Figure 4-1: The Accounts by Rating report.

Report: Business Contacts by Birthday

File Edit View Action Help

Save Report | Modify Report | Filter Report

Report: Business Contacts by Birthday
Filter Applied: No
Wednesday, September 06, 2006

Business Contact Name	Account	Business Phone	Mobile Phone	Address -...	Address - City	Address - State
Nicole Caron	WoodgroveBank	(800) 555-1212	(425) 555-1212	216 S. Monar...	Woody Creek	CO
Nicole Holliday		(800) 555-1212	(425) 555-1212			
Nigel Westbury	Adventure Works	(800) 555-1212	(425) 555-1212	1512 3rd Street	Crested Butte	CO
Olinda Turner	Margie's Travel	(800) 555-1212	(425) 555-1212	7031 S Lawre...	Roaring Fork Val...	CO
Ovidiu Burlacu	Adventure Works	(800) 555-1212	(425) 555-1212	789 3rd Street	Toronto	ON
Patrick M. M. Cook	Litware	(800) 555-1212	(425) 555-1212	818 Market St...	San Francisco	CA
Paula Barreto Barreto de Mattos	Contoso, Ltd	(800) 555-1212	(425) 555-1212	121 South Ga...	Aspen	
Rob Young	Variety Cycling					
Ryan Calafato	Adventure Works	(800) 555-1212	(425) 555-1212	789 3rd Street	Toronto	ON
Sam Abolrous	Contoso, Ltd	(954) 234-5678	(425) 555-1212			
Scott Cooper		(800) 555-1212	(425) 555-1212	340 Carriage...	Aspen	CO
Sean P. Alexander	Adventure Works	(800) 555-1212	(425) 555-1212	789 3rd Street	Toronto	ON
Sunil Koduri	Margie's Travel	(800) 555-1212	(425) 555-1212	7031 S Lawre...	Roaring Fork Val...	CO
Susan W. W. Eaton		(800) 555-1212	(425) 555-1212			
Tete Mensa-Annan		(800) 555-1212	(425) 555-1212	338 5th St.	Detroit	MI
Tim O'Brien	Nearby Sporting Goods					
Toby Malice	Thundercrack	(732) 555-1212		1 Stratocaster...	Les Paul	NJ
Toby Nixon	Trey Research	(800) 555-1212	(425) 555-1212	45 Village Sq...	Woody Creek	CO
Tommy TestPerson		(214) 555-6677	(972) 334-5532	123 Main Stre...	Dallas	TX
Birthdays in January						
AlyssaFredricks					Tallahassee	FL
Birthdays in June						
Gary Kahn					Boca Raton	FL
Birthdays in July						
Andrea Fredricks					Gainesville	FL

Figure 4-2: The Business Contact by Birthday report.

- **Leads:** These reports give you different ways to view the new leads that are coming into your database. If you aren't tracking leads, these reports won't mean much to you. However, if you're paying a lot of money to get new leads for your database, these reports are invaluable.
- **Opportunities:** BCM provides you with a variety of Opportunity reports. The Opportunity reports use information that you entered into an Opportunity record. If you aren't using the Opportunities feature, you won't use these reports. An opportunity funnel or pipeline is an important part of the sales process; you can see BCM's version in Figure 4-3.
- **Business Projects:** One of the strengths of Outlook has always been the ability to schedule and follow up on tasks. BCM runs with that concept and takes it to a whole new level. You can think of a project as a supersized task. Whereas a task involves one chore that needs to be done by one individual, a project involves a multitude of tasks that need to be done over a period of time, generally by several individuals. BCM offers a wide range of reports to help you keep track of your projects. Figure 4-4 shows you an example of the Business Projects by Status report.
- **Marketing Campaigns:** It's probably fairly safe to make one major assumption about your marketing campaigns: If they don't result in new business, they are not worth the time and money you spend on them. The BCM marketing reports will give you a handle on your Marketing Campaigns.

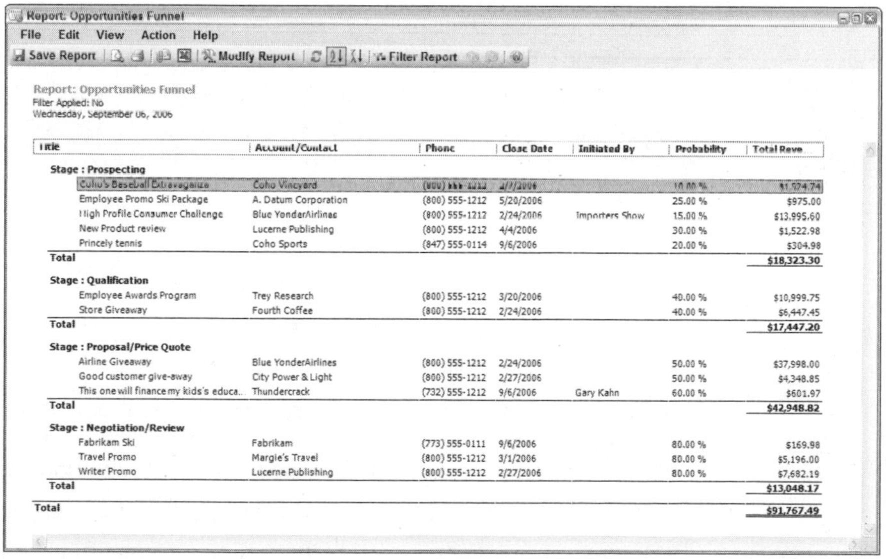

Report: Opportunities Funnel

File Edit View Action Help

Save Report | Modify Report | Filter Report

Report: Opportunities Funnel
Filter Applied: No
Wednesday, September 06, 2006

Title	Account/Contact	Phone	Close Date	Initiated By	Probability	Total Reve
Stage : Prospecting						
Coho's Baseball Extravaganza	Coho Vineyard	[illegible]	[illegible]		10.00 %	[illegible]
Employee Promo Ski Package	A. Datum Corporation	(800) 555-1212	5/20/2006		25.00 %	$975.00
High Profile Consumer Challenge	Blue YonderAirlines	(800) 555-1212	2/24/2006	Importers Show	15.00 %	$13,995.60
New Product review	Lucerne Publishing	(800) 555-1212	4/4/2006		30.00 %	$1,522.98
Princely tennis	Coho Sports	(847) 555-0114	9/6/2006		20.00 %	$304.98
Total						**$18,323.30**
Stage : Qualification						
Employee Awards Program	Trey Research	(800) 555-1212	3/20/2006		40.00 %	$10,999.75
Store Giveaway	Fourth Coffee	(800) 555-1212	2/24/2006		40.00 %	$6,447.45
Total						**$17,447.20**
Stage : Proposal/Price Quote						
Airline Giveaway	Blue YonderAirlines	(800) 555-1212	2/24/2006		50.00 %	$37,998.00
Good customer give-away	City Power & Light	(800) 555-1212	2/27/2006		50.00 %	$4,348.85
This one will finance my kids's educa...	Thundercrack	(732) 555-1212	9/6/2006	Gary Kahn	60.00 %	$601.97
Total						**$42,948.82**
Stage : Negotiation/Review						
Fabrikam Ski	Fabrikam	(773) 555-0111	9/6/2006		80.00 %	$169.98
Travel Promo	Margie's Travel	(800) 555-1212	3/1/2006		80.00 %	$5,196.00
Writer Promo	Lucerne Publishing	(800) 555-1212	2/27/2006		80.00 %	$7,682.19
Total						**$13,048.17**
Total						**$91,767.49**

Figure 4-3: The Opportunity Funnel.

Report: Business Projects by Status

File Edit View Action Help

Save Report | Modify Report | Filter Report

Report: Business Projects by Status
Filter Applied: No
Thursday, September 07, 2006

Title	Account/Contact	Due Date	Percent Complete	Priority
Status : Not Started				
Online Promotional Training	Litware	7/20/2006	95.00 %	Normal
Status : In Progress				
Corporate Seminar on New Products	Lucerne Publishing	5/11/2006	25.00 %	Normal
Telephone System Upgrade	City Power & Light	7/14/2006	72.00 %	High
Status : Completed				
Wimbledon Fund Raiser	Tech Benders		100.00 %	High

Figure 4-4: The Business Projects by Status report.

Running a BCM Report

Creating a BCM report is ridiculously easy — you choose a report by clicking it. Here's the drill for running any one of the out-of-the-box BCM reports:

1. **From Outlook, choose Business Contact Manager⇨Reports.**
2. **Select the category of the report that you want to run.**

   Here's the fun part — you get to pick which type of report. For the purpose of the rest of this chapter, we use an Account report. You can see the BCM Reports menu in Figure 4-5.

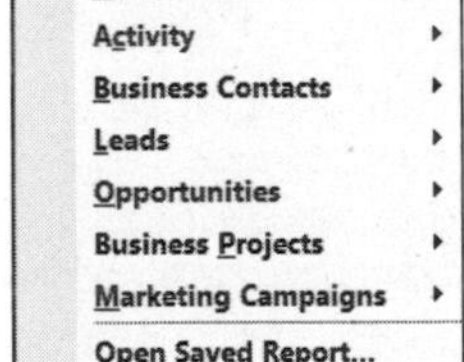

Figure 4-5: Choosing a BCM report.

3. **Select the specific report.**

   In a flash, your report springs to life.
4. **Click a column heading to re-sort your report.**

   By default, most of the BCM reports appear in alphabetical order. If you are left-handed — or just enjoy seeing your reports sorted in *Z to A* order — you can do so with a single click of any column heading.
5. **Change the order of the columns by dragging them to a new location.**

   If you're not thrilled with the order in which the columns appear in the report — or if you just like to exercise a bit of control — drag a column to a new location by holding down your left button on a column head and moving to the left or right.

6. **Print, e-mail, or export your report.**

   Choose from one of the following options:

   - Choose File⇨Print to print the report.
   - Choose File⇨Send E-Mail with Excel Attachment. This one has to be one of the neatest of the report features; BCM thinks about it momentarily and then opens a new e-mail message with your report already attached as an Excel attachment.
   - Choose File⇨Export to Excel to save your report in Excel format.

7. **Choose File⇨Close when you're finished working with the report.**

Giving Your Reports a Facelift

Chances are that you began with a basic report and decided to modify it somewhat — or even give it a complete makeover. Start by tweaking some of the fields already on your report template. You can remove one or two of the existing columns and replace them with columns that are more to your liking. You may want to make the font a wee bit larger to accommodate your 40-something eyes. The more ornery members of the crowd may not be happy with the order in which the fields appear in one of the opportunity reports. Like anything else, it's simple if you know the trick.

Modifying an existing report

Probably the first thing you want to do is decide which fields will — or won't — appear in your report. Being familiar with the structure of your existing database can prove helpful during this process. Thus, you need to know the field names that you're working with. For example, if you want to include the name of a company, you must know that the field is called Account.

Once you make the momentous decision of which fields should appear in your report, follow these steps to get the job done.

1. **Open the report that is closest to what you're looking for.**

   With more than 50 reports to choose from, why choose a report that's not even close to what you're looking for when another report can do the trick quite nicely? For this example, we use the Quick Account List report.

   TIP

   The report window often opens in Normal window size — that is, it's not maximized to its fullest size. You may want to maximize the report window before you start to customize a report.

2. Click Modify Report in the Report toolbar.

At this juncture, the Modify Report dialog box, shown in Figure 4-6, snaps to attention on the right side of your report. The Modify Report dialog box allows you to make changes to the report's fonts, headers and footers, and columns.

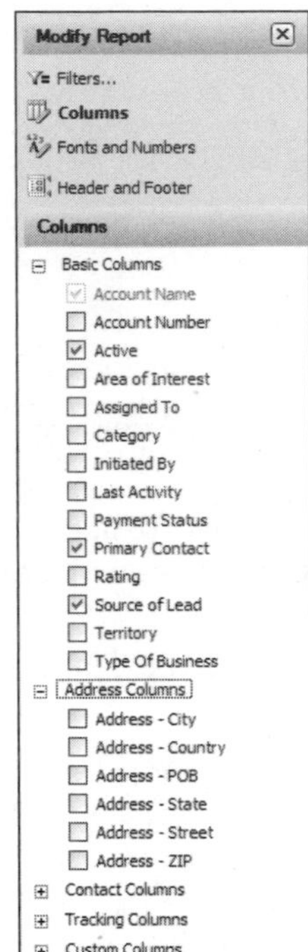

Figure 4-6: The Modify Report dialog box.

3. Click on the plus sign next to one of the column types to display more field choices.

Probably the first way you'll want to modify your report is by adding or removing the columns that you see in the existing database. Each column of a BCM report is based on a field in an Account, Business Contact, Opportunity, and Business Project record.

Depending on the report you selected, you have different columns types available to you:

- *Basic:* Contains the fields for first and last name, title, and Account, as well as other basic fields, including birthday and anniversary.
- *Address:* Provide you with postal address fields, including city, state, and zip code.

- *Contact:* Help you contact an Account or Business Contact, including fax, phone, page, and e-mail address.
- *Mail:* Show the recipient, sender, and date of an e-mail message.
- *Tracking:* Show the date that an Account or Business Contact was created or edited, as well as the person who did the creating or editing.
- *Other:* Includes duration of a phone log and the filename and location of an attached file.
- *Custom:* Contains the fields added to your Account, Business Contact, Opportunity, or Business Project record.

4. **Place a check mark next to any of the fields you'd like to add to your report by clicking them.**

   You can check as many fields as you'd like; the fields you check are added as new columns at the end of the report.

5. **Remove any columns that you don't want to appear in your report by removing the check mark next to those fields.**

   Sorry to be the bearer of bad news, but most paper holds only a finite number of columns. If you add a bunch of columns, you'll probably want to remove a few as well.

6. **Rearrange the columns on your report by dragging them to the left or right.**

   You'll be amazed at how easily you can drag a column — and all the information that it contains — to a new spot on your report.

7. **(Optional) Save the report.**

   You've got two options here:

   - Choose File⇨Save Report if you want to permanently change the existing report.
   - Choose File⇨Save Report As if you'd like to save your modification as a whole new report.

   Either way, BCM cheerfully saves your report for future use using the `.bcr` extension. Could it be that the `r` stands for report? You be the judge!

8. **Click File⇨Close to close the report.**

Filtering out the bad stuff

Another way in which you can modify your BCM reports is by changing the content of the report. You can create filters to determine what data should appear in your report. Although you can create complex queries, the process that you follow is quite simple.

1. **Open the report that is closest to what you're looking for.**
2. **Click Filter Report in the Report toolbar.**

   Alternatively, if you just modified a report, you can click Filters at the top of the Modify Report dialog box. In either case, the Filter Accounts dialog box, shown in Figure 4-7, appears.

   For this example, we use the Quick Account List report. The options you see in Figure 4-7 may be slightly different than the ones you see if you filter a different report. No problem — the concepts work exactly the same.

Figure 4-7: Filtering a BCM report.

3. **Check the options for the data that you want to appear in your report.**

   If you're one of those people who have trouble in deciding what flavor you want at the local ice cream shop, then you may have problems here because you have a lot of choices. However, if you believe the more the merrier, then you should have a field day here.

   Each option represents one of the fields in the Account, Business Contact, Opportunity, or Business Project that you're reporting on. The choices within the option are the values of the drop-down list for that field. In our example of the Quick Account List report, we see the option of Account Status, which represents one of the Account record fields, and the choices of Active or Inactive, which are the two options for that field.

You really have a lot of information to choose from when filtering a report — and not all of it is visible to the naked eye. You notice see scroll bar indicators after many of the fields, which mean that you have more field choices to choose from. If you're interested in seeing — or not seeing — information from a given field, give those scroll bars a scroll.

4. **(Optional) Click Save Filter.**

   The only thing worse than doing work is having to do the same work over again. After you slave over the various filter options, you may want to save your work so that you don't have to save it again later. BCM assigns your saved query the `.bcmq` extension.

   If you already saved a query, you can click Open Filter to open an existing filter.

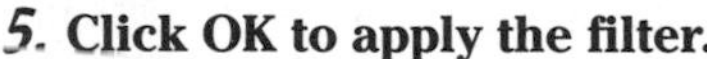

5. **Click OK to apply the filter.**

   At this point, you can print the report, save it, or just close it.

Drilling for Dollars in Your Reports

The entire purpose of a BCM report is to provide you with accurate, up-to-the-minute information. And, before, you hit that Print button, it's always a good idea to review your to make sure that all the report information is correct. For example, one of your best clients may be missing a phone number or may be listed as inactive.

BCM's ability to edit information "on the fly" from within a report is a great way to both modify incorrect and add missing information.

Giving your reports a helping hand

You may consider editing information from within a report a rather handy feature — especially considering that a "hand" is your tool of choice for correcting information. Here's the drill:

1. **Move your mouse over the area of your report where you see inaccurate or missing information.**

   Your mouse cursor turns into a hand.

2. **Double-click on that report item.**

   Zoom! You're transported to the BCM record that stores the information. For example, if you're looking at a Business Contact report and notice that a phone number is missing, give that contact a double-click. The corresponding Business Contact record appears.

3. **Make your changes.**

   In this case, more is more. In addition to missing a phone number, the city and state fields are also blank. You may as well make as many corrections as you'd like.

4. **Save and close the record.**

   Double zoom! You land with a thump back in your report.

Having a refreshing look at your report

Once you've changed the information that appears in your report, you'll probably rush right over to gaze fondly at the new data. But wait. What happened? The new information didn't magically appear! Typically, you first blame yourself and redo the steps you followed to correct information. And, it still doesn't work! At this point in time, you're probably composing a nasty letter to Microsoft in your head complaining about the BCM reports.

Creating an Excel-ent report

As hard as it may be to believe, not everyone you deal with is using BCM, and you have to get the report to them in a manner that they can use. As usual, BCM provides you with two solutions for transporting your report from Point A to Point B, both of which you can access from the BCM reports menu:

- Choose File⇨Export to Excel to create a spreadsheet version of the current report.
- Choose File⇨Send E-Mail with Excel Attachment to create an e-mail message with your report already included as an attached Excel spreadsheet. You can see an example in the figure.

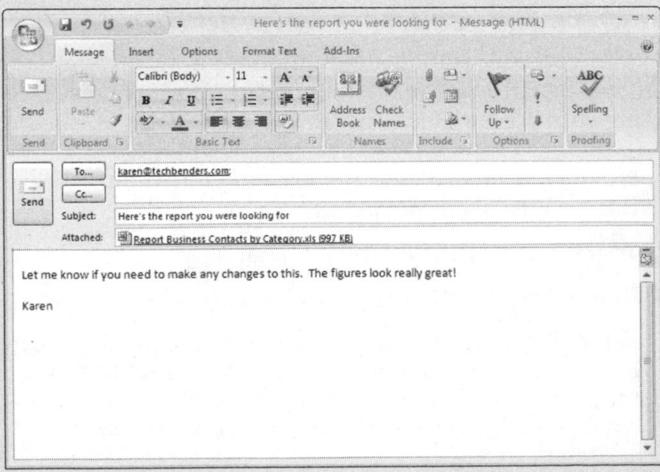

In order to speed up the works, BCM doesn't *refresh* the report information until you tell it to do so. This delay is meant to allow you to correct many items in your report without having to wait for the report to reappear on your screen.

You have your choice of three methods to get that information to appear:

- ✦ Tap the F5 key on your keyboard.
- ✦ Choose View⇨Refresh Report in the Reports menu bar.
- ✦ Click the Refresh Report icon (it looks like two arrows on top of one another) on the toolbar.

Whew! Problem solved.

Working with Dashboards

By definition, a *dashboard* is a panel under the windshield of a vehicle, containing dials, compartments, and instrument controls. In case you're wondering why a book on Outlook is talking about car parts it's because dashboards in computer software are very cool areas that contain several snapshots of your information.

If you look at Figure 4-8, you see a sample of two of the Opportunity dashboards that are found in BCM.

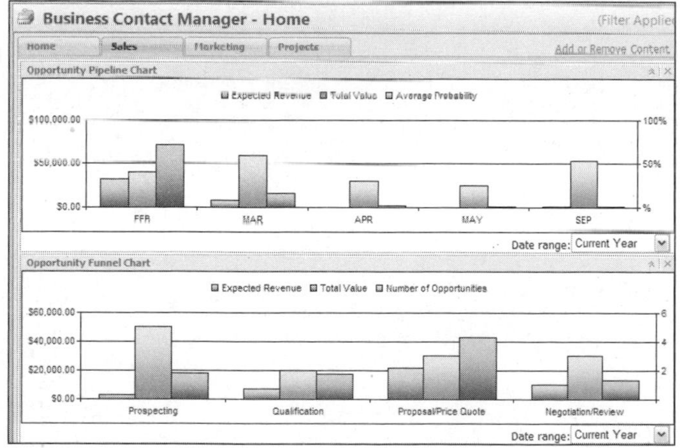

Figure 4-8: A sample of the Opportunity dashboards.

The Opportunity Pipeline Chart shows you the expected revenue, total value, and average probability grouped by month. The Opportunity Funnel Chart shows you the expected revenue, total value, and number of Opportunities grouped by sales stage.

Now comes the best part — you can use several dashboards to help you analyze your Opportunity data. They're simple to find if you follow these steps:

1. **Choose Business Contact Manager⇨Business Contact Manager Home on the main Outlook menu bar.**

   The Business Contact Manager – Home page appears in the main Outlook pane.

2. **Choose Add or Remove Content.**

   If you're not sure where the Add or Remove button is, you'll find it on the top of the Home page. The Add or Remove Content dialog box springs to life.

3. **Select the dashboards that you want to test drive and click OK.**

   You can see the dashboard choices in Figure 4-9.

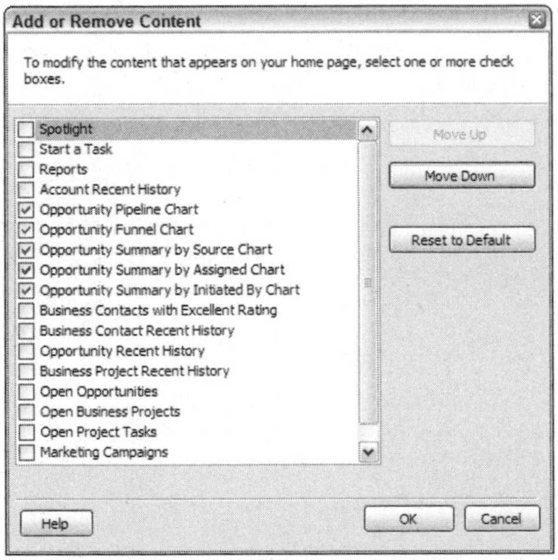

Figure 4-9: The Add or Remove Content dialog box.

Book VIII

Customizing Outlook

"He saw your laptop and wants to know if he can check his Hotmail."

Contents at a Glance

Chapter 1: Organizing Items with Categories 591
Chapter 2: Changing Your View on Outlook 603
Chapter 3: Customizing Outlook Forms 621

Chapter 1: Organizing Items with Categories

In This Chapter

- Grouping similar items together by category
- Adding and removing categories from an item
- Renaming, creating, and deleting categories
- Assigning shortcuts to categories so they're easier to use

It's easy to get overwhelmed with the amount of data Outlook contains. Let's face it: A normal person probably receives hundreds of e-mails a day, maintains hundreds of contacts, and tracks thousands of appointments per year. And some of that stuff should be grouped together somehow because it deals with the same project, company, or special segment of your life — such as your children. But with everything in Outlook organized by type (appointments in the Calendar and people in the Contacts list), how can you show that two dissimilar items belong together? The answer is *categories.*

After assigning a category to a group of items, you can search for them easily. See Book IX, Chapter 1 for help in searching.

Adding a Category to an Open Outlook Item

Outlook comes with seven color categories, all with clever names such as Red Category, Green Category, and so on. The first time you choose a color category to assign to an item, you are prompted to rename it to something meaningful like the Salmon-Colored Category. No, actually you can choose a real name like Dardon Company, Marketing, Department Stuff, Personal, or Kids. If you've got more than one brat (uh, kid), you can create a separate category for each one, making it easier to see what Sadie, Anya, and Joey have scheduled for after school.

First you name your categories and assign them to various Outlook items. Then if you happen to find yourself looking in a mail folder or viewing your Calendar, you can use the colors to quickly identify what category a particular item belongs to. So if a marketing meeting conflicts with an appointment with an important client, you know which one you need to attend (the one with the better food, of course). You can even arrange items in a folder by category so you can quickly group all e-mails related to the Dardon account, for example. And if you run out of color categories, you can create more.

But first, you need to start assigning categories to items so you can group similar things together visually. If you've opened an item such as an e-mail message or an appointment, the Ribbon at the top of the form provides you with a quick way to assign a category:

1. **In the open item, click the Categorize button on the Ribbon.**

   A menu listing all your current categories appears, like the one shown in Figure 1-1. Here, I've already renamed a few categories, but some unnamed ones remain, as you can see.

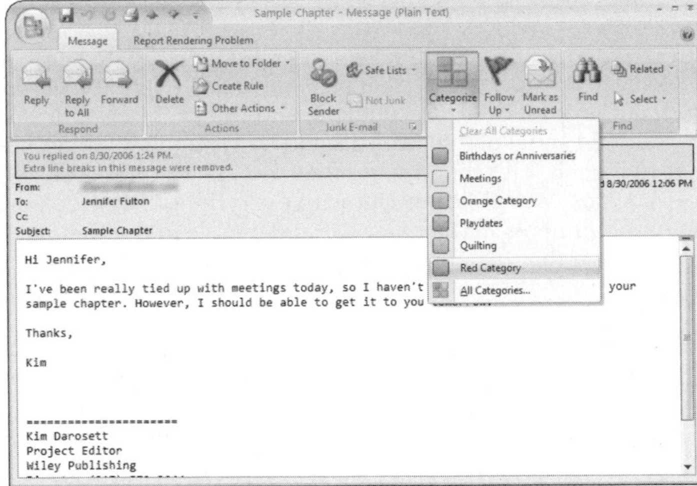

Figure 1-1: You can assign categories when reviewing an item.

2. **Choose a category.**

   If you have more than 15 categories and the one you want to use isn't listed, choose All Categories from the list. The Color Categories dialog box appears. Choose the category you want to assign and click OK. The listing that appears when you click the Categories button on the Ribbon contains the 15 most recently used categories, by the way; so if you start using a certain category often, it shows up on the list.

3. **Rename the category.**

   If this is your first time assigning this category, you are prompted to rename it. Type a Name for the category and click OK. The color you've chosen appears in a band at the top of the form.

When using a category for the first time, you can change the Color assigned to the category and assign a shortcut. See the section, "Managing Your Categories" later in this chapter for help.

You can assign multiple categories to an item by simply repeating the preceding steps. For example, you might assign both the Key Client and Dardon Company categories to the same appointment.

When you close the item, the color appears in the Categories column in most list views, such as the Messages view in Mail. In the Calendar, meetings, appointments, and events appear as little colored rectangles. In some views, the colors don't appear at all, although you can modify a view so that it displays categories. See Book VIII, Chapter 2 to find out how to customize a view.

Adding a Category to an Item without Opening It

There's no reason why you have to bother opening an item to assign a category to it. Sure, it's convenient when opening a series of e-mails or creating a new appointment to take the time to categorize each one using the Categorize button on the Ribbon. But when you assign categories after the fact, it's much easier just to grab a bunch of messages and, boom, assign a category to them.

Here's what you do:

1. **Select the item(s) to categorize.**

   To grab a bunch of items, press and hold Ctrl as you click each one. If the items are grouped together, press Shift and click the first one in the group; then while still holding Shift, click the last item in the group.

   You can sort items to make it easier to select a bunch of them. See Chapter 2 in this minibook.

2. **Click the Categorize button on the Standard toolbar.**
3. **Choose a category.**

   If the category you want isn't on the list, choose All Categories, select the category from the longer list that appears, and click OK.

   If this is your first time assigning this category, you are asked if you want to rename it. So unless you think Red Category fits the category's purpose, type a better name in the Name box. Change the Color for the category, if you like, and assign a shortcut (see the section, "Managing Your Categories" later in this chapter for more info). Click OK.

The color you've chosen appears in the Categories column next to the chosen items, assuming that the Categories column is included in the current view. In the Calendar, items are colored by category, as shown in Figure 1-2.

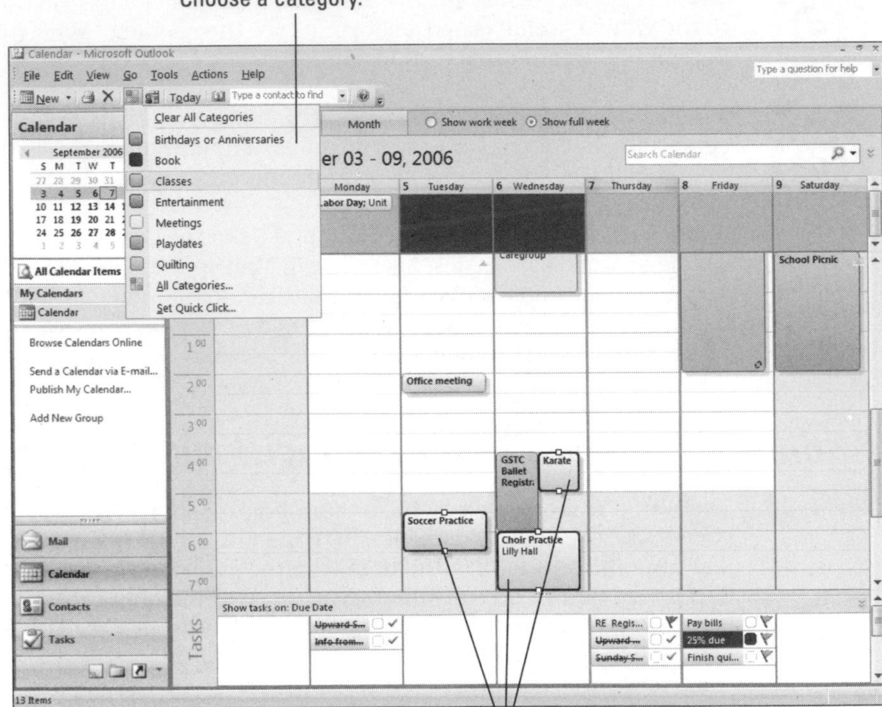

Figure 1-2: You don't have to open items to categorize them.

Assigning a Quick Click Category to an Item

Part of Microsoft's pledge for the Office 2007 redesign was to make all the Office programs easier to use. They certainly made it easy for you to assign a frequently used category to any item you want, assuming the Categories column is displayed in the view you're using. First, you have to set the Quick Click category; then you use it (with a quick click of the mouse) to assign that category to an item.

Here's how to set the Quick Click category:

1. **Choose Categorize⇨Set Quick Click.**

   Click the Categorize button on the Standard toolbar and then choose Set Quick Click from the menu that appears. The Set Quick Click dialog box, shown in Figure 1-3, appears.

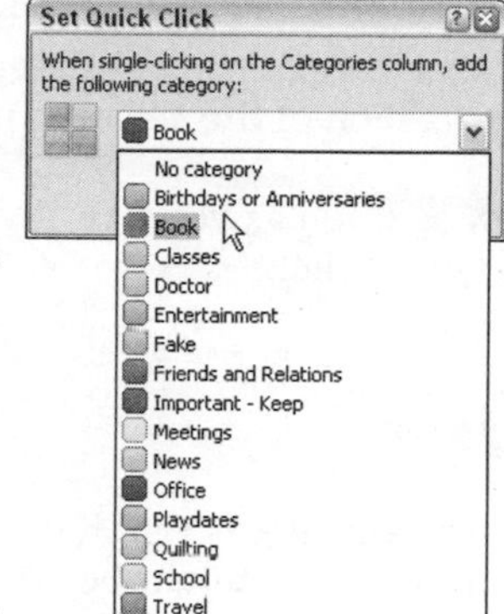

Figure 1-3: Choose which category you use the most.

2. **Select your favorite category.**

   Choose the category you want to be able to assign with a single click and then click OK.

To assign the Quick Click category to an item, the Categories column must be displayed in the current view. It so happens that the Categories column appears in Messages view, the most common view in Mail. If you're there, you're OK. It also appears on the To-Do bar, which you can make appear in any module you like by choosing View➪To-Do Bar. It also appears in most list (column type) views in Calendar and Contacts. Anyway, once the guy shows his head, you just click in the Categories column to assign the Quick Click category to that item, as shown in Figure 1-4.

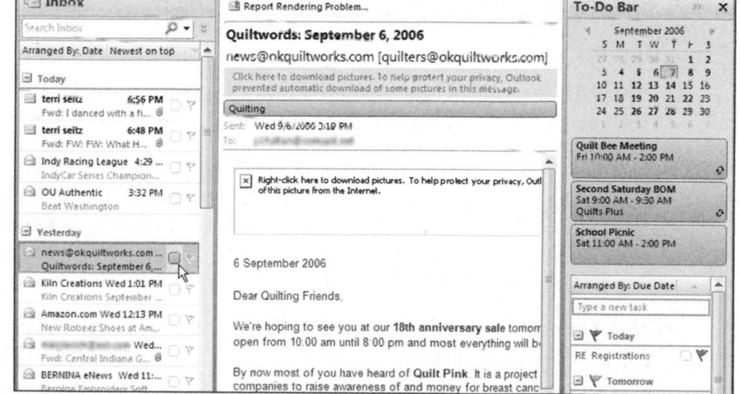

Figure 1-4: Your favorite category is a click away.

One at a time not your thing? No problem, just select multiple items (by pressing Ctrl and clicking each one). Then click once in the Categories column to assign your favorite category to each of the selected items.

You can change the Quick Click category as often as you like; it won't affect items you've already categorized using Quick Click.

Removing a Category from an Item

It's so easy to assign categories to your Outlook items that it can sometimes get out of control. Kind of like a small tattoo — one might be OK, even tasteful. But 20 are just downright hard to look at. Here's how to remove a category from an item:

1. **Select the item or items you want to change.**

   To remove a category from one item, select that item. If you want to remove the same category from several items, select all the items at once. Press and hold Ctrl as you click each item to select it; or click the first item, press and hold Shift, and click the last item in that group. Got 'em selected? Good.

2. **Select the category to remove.**

   Yep, you remove categories from an item one at a time. You can do any of the following:

   - *Click the Categorize button on the Standard toolbar and choose the category you want to remove to deselect it.* See Figure 1-5.

     Categories assigned to an item are highlighted in the Categories list (they appear with an orange border around the color block on the menu).

     You can remove a category from an item that's open; just use the Categorize button on the Ribbon and select the category to remove.

   - *Click the Categories column to remove the Quick Click category* if the Categories column happens to be showing; change to a list view if needed to display it. In Mail and on the To-Do bar however, you can remove any category (and not just the Quick Click category) by clicking in the Categories column. See Figure 1-5.

   - *Right-click to remove a category.* To remove a single category from an item without making a trip to the Standard toolbar or Ribbon, right-click the item and choose Categorize⇨Category to Remove.

   - *To remove all the categories from an item,* choose Categorize⇨Clear All Categories.

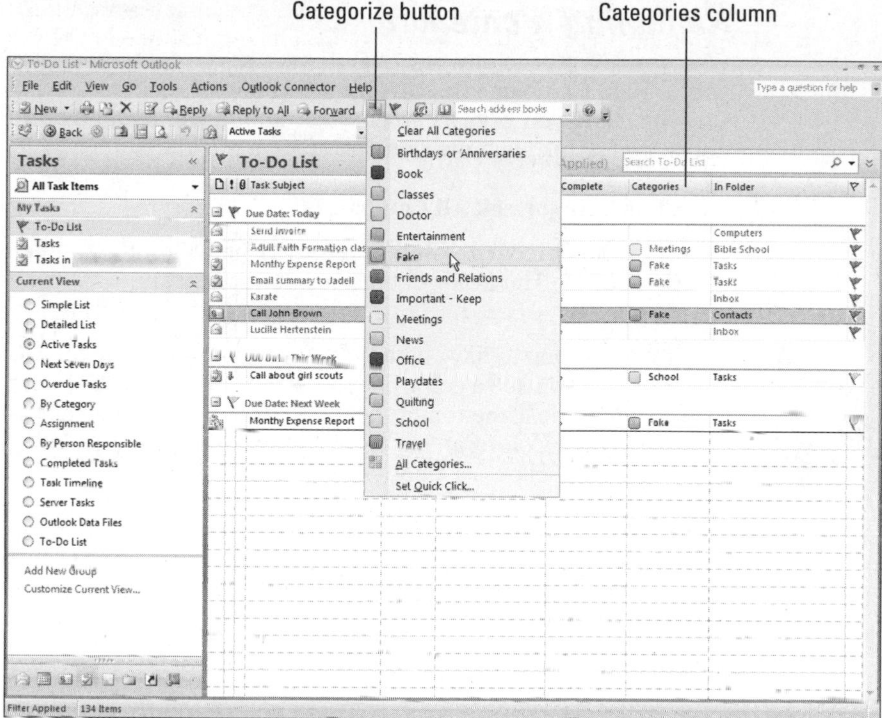

Figure 1-5: Remove unwanted categories from an item one at a time.

Managing Your Categories

Outlook starts you off with seven categories, but as I mentioned earlier, you can easily add more. You can also remove categories that you don't need any more and revisit existing categories at any time to rename them or assign a shortcut key.

A shortcut key is typically two keys, such as Shift+B or Ctrl+V, which are used to activate a command without making a side trip to a menu or toolbar. To use a shortcut key combination, you press both keys at the same time. To prevent you from creating a key combination for a color category that's already used by Outlook to activate some other command, you have a short list of key combos you can choose from. So assign a shortcut key only to the categories you use frequently. Keep in mind that you won't typically need one for the Quick Click category because it's so easy to apply.

Renaming a category

When you first used any one of Outlook's seven categories, you were asked if you wanted to rename the category. If you were sick that day or if you feel that the name you gave a category (even one you created yourself) simply doesn't work for you now, you can change it.

1. **Click Categorize⇨All Categories.**

   Click the Categorize button on the Standard toolbar and choose All Categories. The Color Categories dialog box appears, as shown in Figure 1-6.

   If you happen to have an item open and it has a category assigned to it, then you will see a color bar (or bars, if more than one category has been assigned) near the top of the form window. Double-click this color bar to display the Color Categories dialog box. For example, in Figure 1-3, you can double-click the Quilting color bar.

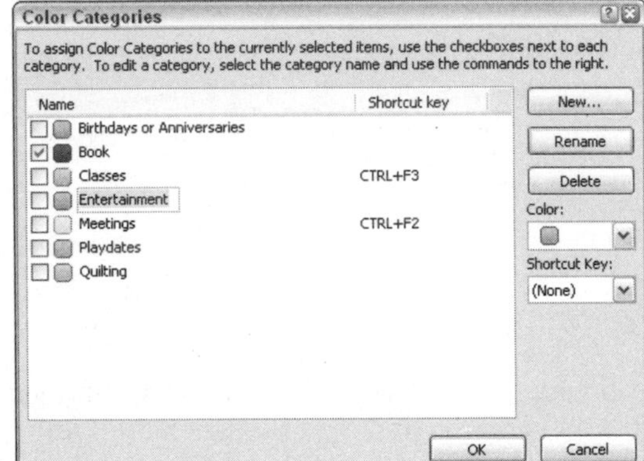

Figure 1-6: Refine your categories with this dialog box.

2. **Select the category to change and click Rename.**
3. **Type a new name and press Enter.**

   If you want to assign the category you're renaming to the currently selected item(s), click the check box in front of the category. Otherwise, just click OK. When you view any item that has this category assigned to it, you see the new category name, even if the category was assigned before you changed the name.

Assigning shortcut keys to categories

When you used any one of the original categories for the first time, you were given a chance to assign a shortcut key to the category. You probably didn't do that unless you had an inkling at the time that this category was going to be an often-used one. In any case, after you discover which categories you use most often, you assign shortcut keys to them so they are easier to reach.

1. **Click Categorize⇨All Categories.**

   The Color Categories dialog box rears its head (refer to Figure 1-7).
2. **Select the category to which you want to assign a shortcut key.**
3. **Select a shortcut key and click OK.**

   To change the shortcut key assigned to a category, open the Shortcut Key list and choose a key combination, as shown in Figure 1-7. If you accidentally choose a combo that's being used by another category, you see a warning. Just answer No and make a different choice.

   The combination you choose appears in the Shortcut key column. You can keep the dialog box open and make all your shortcut assignments by repeating these steps. When you're through, click OK.

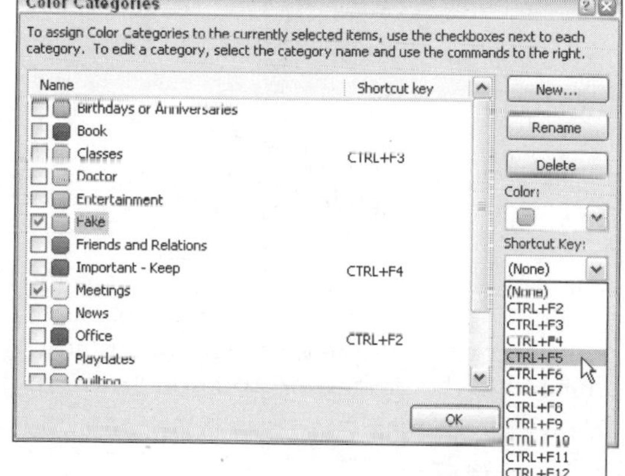

Figure 1-7: Make it easier to assign a favorite category.

To assign a color category to an item using a shortcut key, select the item first. You can select more than one item if you want: Press and hold Ctrl as you click each item; or press and hold Shift, click the first item in a group, and then click the last item. After you've selected the items you want to categorize, press both keys in the shortcut combination to assign the category.

Assigning new colors to categories

When you were creating your initial categories, you probably didn't give much thought to the color used by a category — until you discovered the color was too similar to some other one you use often. No problem; you can just substitute a more suitable color. To change the color assigned to a particular category:

1. **Choose Categorize⇨All Categories.**

   The Color Categories dialog box appears; refer to Figure 1-8.

2. **Select the category to which you want to assign a new color.**

3. **Select a new color and click OK.**

   To change the color assigned to a category, open the Color list as shown in Figure 1-8 and select the color you want the category to use. The color you choose appears next to the category in the list. You can keep the dialog box open and change the colors assigned to other categories. When you're done, click OK.

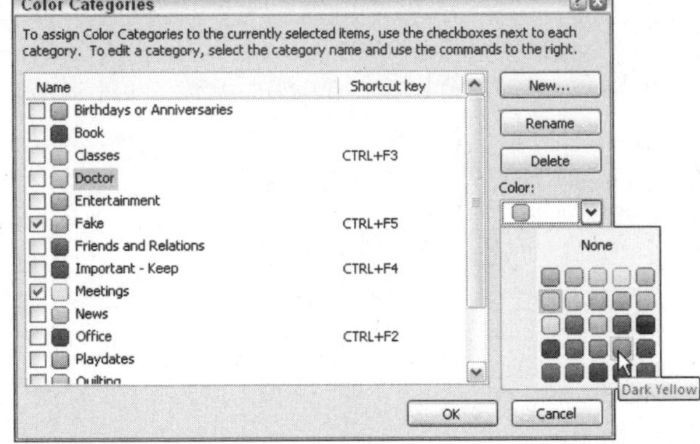

Figure 1-8: Change the color assigned to a category.

After you assign a new color to a category, items that already use that category are instantly changed to the new color. You don't have to do a thing.

Creating new categories

It won't take too long before the seven measly categories Outlook provides start to feel a little too confining. Not to worry; you can add new categories anytime you need to. For example, you might add a Business and a Personal category to help you quickly identify items belonging to each segment of your life. Remember that items can have multiple categories assigned to them, so even though you identify something as Business, you can also further identify it as belonging to Key Clients or My Department.

1. **Choose Categorize⇨All Categories.**

   The Color Categories dialog box pops up (refer to Figure 1-8).

2. **Click the New button.**

   The Add New Category dialog box appears, as shown in Figure 1-9.

Figure 1-9: Add your own categories.

3. **Type a name for the new category.**
4. **Choose a color and assign a shortcut key if you want.**

   Outlook suggests the next color in its list as the color you should use for this new category. If you don't happen to like that color, you can open the Color list and choose a different color for the category. You can also select a shortcut key if you wish. Click OK.

   If you accidentally choose a combo that's being used by another category, you see a warning. See Figure 1-10. Just answer No and make a different choice.

Figure 1-10: Outlook won't let you make a wrong choice.

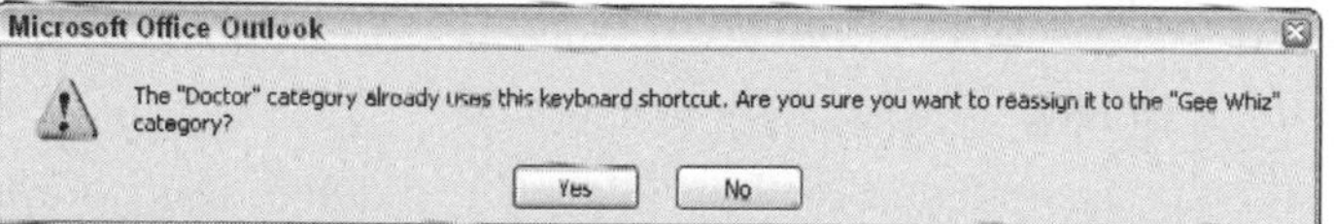

The category you've just created appears in the category list of the Color Categories dialog box. You can make adjustments to the new category (such as selecting a different color) if it turns out that your original choice is too similar to another category you use a lot. You can also create another category by clicking New and repeating these steps. When you've exhausted yourself, click OK to close the dialog box.

Before you close the Color Categories dialog box, be sure to look at what's checked. Any categories with a check mark are applied to the currently selected item(s), whether or not that's what you intend.

Removing a category

Occasionally, clothes go out of style. Take bell bottoms, peasant blouses, and tie-dyed T-shirts for example. No wait — those things are back in again. Well anyway, occasionally categories go out of style, and you find that they just aren't useful anymore. You can keep an unused category in your Outlook closet (for sentimental reasons or in case your children can find some use for it 20 years from now), or you can remove the category.

1. **Click Categorize➪All Categories.**

   The Color Categories dialog box appears (see Figure 1-11).

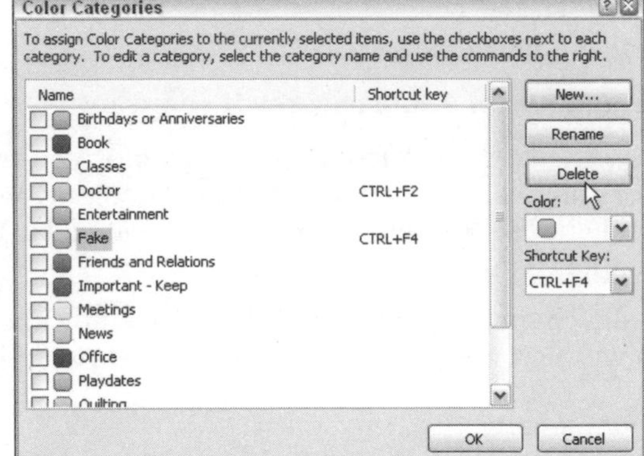

Figure 1-11: Remove categories that are out of style.

2. **Select the category you want to get rid of.**
3. **Click Delete.**

   You are asked if you really, really want to delete this poor little category that's never done anything to you. Click Yes. The category is removed from the list shown in the Color Categories dialog box. Click OK to close the box.

The category you've just deleted obviously can't be used anymore, but some items may still have the category assigned to them. If you want, you can manually remove the deleted category from any items you want. See the section, "Removing a Category from an Item," earlier in this chapter for help.

Chapter 2: Changing Your View on Outlook

In This Chapter

- ✓ **Working with Outlook Today**
- ✓ **Using the Reading pane**
- ✓ **Grouping your items**
- ✓ **Working with views**
- ✓ **Seeing your information in a table**
- ✓ **Looking for unread mail**

A common ailment among computer users is "screen envy." Generally, this disease strikes you when you observe someone else's computer screen and notice that things look a bit different than what you're used to seeing. Unfortunately, some people assume that *different* means *better* and start to worry that the other computer is somehow better than their own.

There are two known cures for screen envy:

- ✦ Realizing that different isn't necessarily better.
- ✦ Mastering the art of customizing your computer screens.

This chapter is devoted to changing the basic Outlook look and feel. You explore the ways in which you can view the various Outlook items, and even how you can change those views should the notion strike you. The chapter even shows you a few tricks to get the most out of your existing views and even how to group your Outlook items together.

Changing Your Outlook Today

The Outlook Today page provides you with a snapshot of your day ahead by giving you a list of the day's appointments and tasks, and gives you a count of the unread e-mail messages in your various mailboxes.

Turning on Outlook Today is a snap — or at least a click. You can access Outlook Today from the Navigation pane by clicking the Outlook Today icon that appears next to name of your data file. Figure 2-1 shows the name of the data file as Tech Benders; the Outlook Today icon appears directly to the left of it.

You can "drill down" into any of the items listed in Outlook Today by clicking them. If you want more details about one of your appointments, for example, just give it a click and you are instantly transported to the original calendar entry.

To exit Outlook Today, all you need to do is click on any of the folders in the Folder List. To return to Outlook Today, click the Outlook Today icon once again.

As with just about every other feature in Outlook, you can customize Outlook Today. If you click the Customize Outlook Today button (shown in Figure 2-1), the Customize Outlook Today dialog box opens, as shown in Figure 2-2.

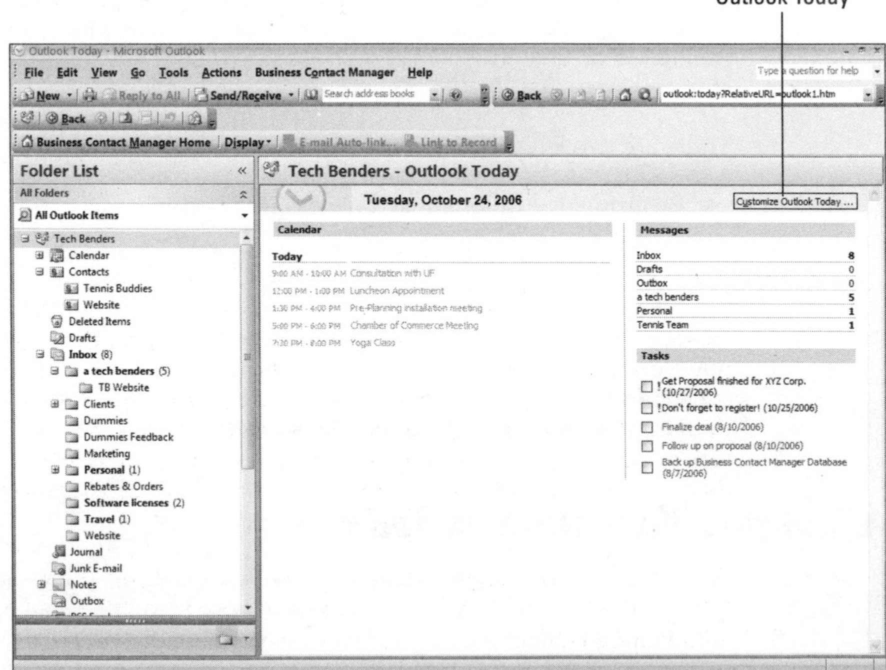

Figure 2-1: Checking out Outlook Today.

Figure 2-2: Customizing Outlook Today.

The Outlook Today customization options are fairly straightforward:

- **Startup:** Click this check box if you'd like to have Outlook Today open when Outlook opens.
- **Messages:** Select the Inboxes that you'd like to include.
- **Calendar:** Show the number of days (1–7) that you'd like to include in your calendar recap.
- **Tasks:** Decide the date range of the tasks as well as how you'd like to see them sorted.
- **Styles:** Choose the color scheme for Outlook Today, as well as the number of columns to show.

Reading Can Be a Pane

The Reading pane allows you to preview various Outlook items without having to actually open them. Although you may associate the Reading pane with viewing the e-mail in your Inbox, you can also use the Reading pane to preview items in the Drafts, Calendar, Contacts, Tasks, Notes, and Journal views. The Reading pane also allows you to open attachments, follow hyperlinks, use voting buttons, and respond to meeting requests. Figure 2-3 shows the Reading pane for a selected e-mail item.

Security is not an issue when it comes to using the Reading pane. You can safely preview your e-mail in the Reading pane without fear of encountering a virus. Previewing an e-mail message doesn't run any potentially dangerous scripts that may be contained in the e-mail.

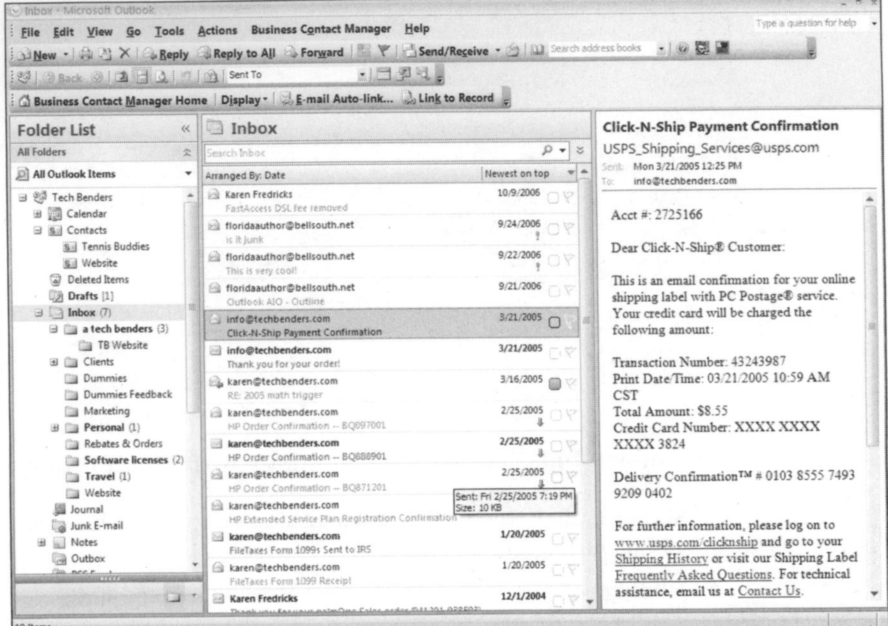

Figure 2-3: The Reading pane.

You may want to experiment with the Reading pane to see whether or not the feature is for you. Here's a few of the ways you may want to customize the Reading pane:

- Depending on your preference, the Reading pane can appear to either the right or bottom of the item that is currently selected. Choose View⇨Reading Pane in the main menu bar, and then choose Right or Bottom.
- If the Reading pane runs along the right side of Outlook, you can change its size by hovering the mouse pointer on the left border of the Reading pane, and when the pointer becomes a double-headed arrow, dragging the border to the left or right.
- If the Reading pane runs along the bottom side of Outlook, you can change its size by hovering the mouse pointer over the top of the Reading pane, and when the pointer becomes a double-headed arrow, dragging the border higher or lower.
- If you feel that the Reading pane is a pain, you can turn it off completely by choosing View⇨Reading Pane in the main menu bar and then choosing Off.

Joining the Group

You can group similar e-mail, contact, task, and project items together to make them easier to view. For example, Outlook automatically groups items by date. The default Inbox groups are Today, Yesterday, Last Week, Last Month, and Older. If you often find yourself buried under a mountain of e-mail, you'll probably like this feature because the newest mail automatically appears in the top of your e-mail heap while the older mail sinks to the bottom. Figure 2-4 shows this feature in action.

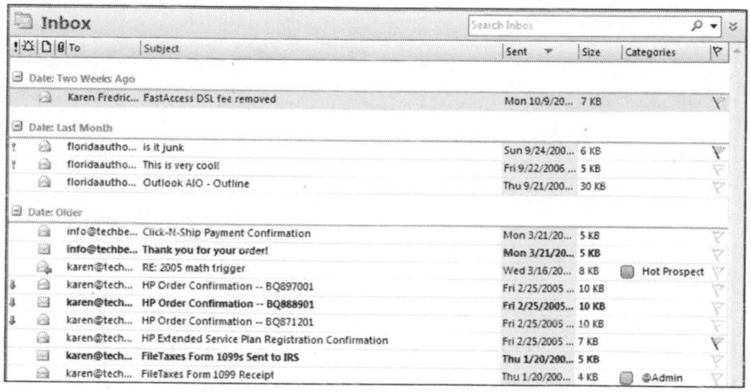

Figure 2-4: An Inbox grouped by date.

To group or not to group

If you'd rather not have your e-mail grouped together by date, choose View⇨Arrange By and then remove the check mark next to Show in Groups. Need to regroup? Put the check mark back.

You can group items together in ways other than by date. You can also group your Outlook items using several pre-defined grouping scenarios. If you choose View⇨Arrange By, you can select one of the pre-defined groupings from the menu that appears.

Getting in with the In Group

For most of you, grouping your e-mail by date or using one of the pre-defined group schemes is more than sufficient to keep you happy, healthy, and well organized. But there's always someone in the crowd who just has to do things a bit differently. For example, you may want to see all your contacts grouped by categories, or your tasks grouped by priority.

Here's how you can group your items together by virtually any field in your database:

1. **Choose View➪Arrange By➪Custom in the main menu bar.**

   The Customize View dialog box opens (see Figure 2-5).

Figure 2-5: Customizing your view.

Can't find the Arrange By option on the View menu? This option only works with e-mail, contacts, tasks, and projects.

2. **Click Group By.**

   The Group By dialog box appears, looking very much like the one shown in Figure 2-6.

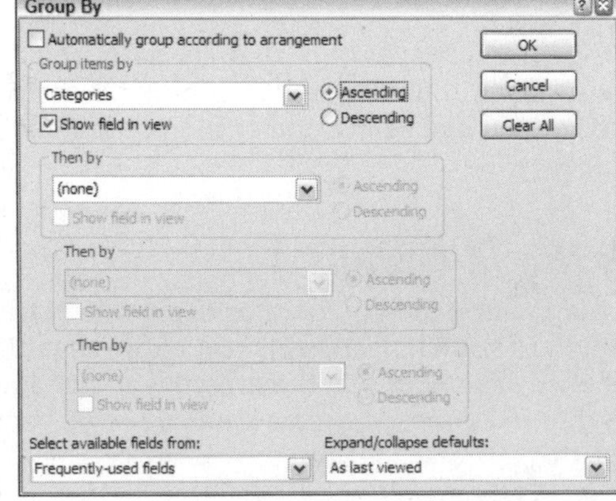

Figure 2-6: Creating custom groups for your Outlook items.

3. **Uncheck the Automatically Group According to Arrangement check box.**

   This sheds some light on the situation because the various Group By options now come to life — or at least, not grayed out like they were before.

4. **Click a field to group by in the Group items by drop-down box.**

   Outlook responds with a list of the most frequently used fields for that item type. If you are grouping contacts, for example, you see choices such as Company, Categories, and State. If you are grouping e-mail, you see choices such as Importance, Subject, and Received Date.

5. **(Optional) Select a different field set from the Select Available Fields From drop-down box if you don't see the field you're looking for.**

   Perhaps you added a new field to track product preference for all of your contacts. If you select User-Defined Fields in Folder from the Select Available Fields From drop-down box, you can group items by product preference.

6. **Choose Ascending or Descending for the sort order of the group headings.**

7. **(Optional) Select the Show Field in View check box if you'd like to display the field that you are grouping items by.**

8. **(Optional) Select a field in the Then By drop-down box to divide each group into subgroups.**

   For example, you may want to group your contacts by category, and subdivide each category into states.

9. **Select the way you'd like to view your groups in the Expand/Collapse Defaults drop-down box.**

   By default you can select All Expanded to show all items; All Collapsed to just show the group headings; or As Last Viewed to keep your groups exactly the way they were the last time you looked at them.

   After you close the dialog boxes you can expand groups by clicking the plus sign that appears in front of the group name, and collapse a group by clicking the minus sign that appears in front of the group name.

10. **Click OK to close the Group By dialog box, and then click OK again to close the Customize View dialog box.**

Viewing Outlook in a Whole New Light

Every Outlook folder displays the items it contains in a layout, or *view*. Views give you different ways to look at the same information in a folder by putting it in different arrangements and formats. There are several standard views available for a folder that you can choose from or you can create custom views. You can switch between views or stick to your tried-and-true favorite view.

You can access the current folder view by the Current View pane at the bottom of the Folder List, or by choosing View➪Current View in the main menu bar.

It doesn't matter how you get there; both methods result in the same five views:

✦ **Table:** Probably the most common view, a table displays your information as rows with columns representing the various fields of information for each record.

✦ **Timeline:** If the Table is the most common view, then the Timeline is the one you'll most rarely, if ever, use. Available only with the Inbox and Tasks folders, each of your items is placed along the appropriate date on the timeline. Think back to elementary school and you'll know exactly what an Outlook timeline looks like; if you can't remember back that far, see Figure 2-7.

Figure 2-7: The Timeline view.

✦ **Day/week/month:** Available with the calendar folder, this view allows you to flip back and forth between a daily, weekly, and monthly view of your calendar.

✦ **Card:** Most commonly used with the Contacts folder, a card view allows you to look at your information in the form of a business card. This view is most often used by Outlook users who are mourning the passage of the rolodex.

✦ **Icon:** Generally used with Notes, Icon view displays your information as a series of sticky notes.

Not all view types are available with all item types. For example, you can't view your contacts in the icon view, or see your Inbox in the Day/Week/Month view.

Tabling the Table View

The table view is one of the most popular views. Its popularity is based in part on the fact that the table view is highly customizable. There are several neat table tricks that you can master so that you, too, can be popular. Okay, these tricks may not make you the life of the party, but they do make you popular around the water cooler if you pass them on to your co-workers.

Adding a column to a table

One of the most common things you'll want to do is to add another column to the current list view. You can accomplish that feat by following these instructions:

1. **Open any folder in list view.**
2. **Right-click a column heading and choose Field Chooser from the shortcut menu.**

   The Field Chooser dialog box opens, as shown in Figure 2-8.

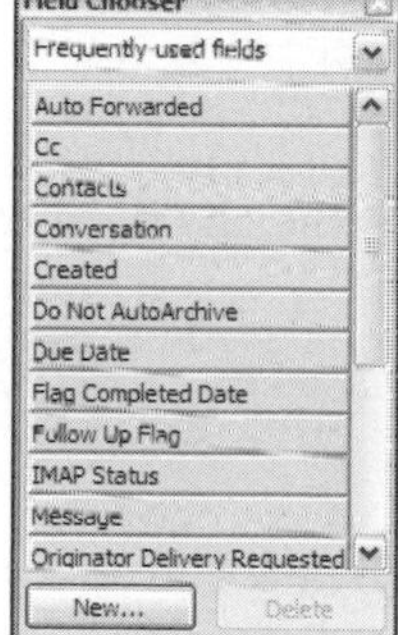

Figure 2-8: Adding new columns to a list view.

You may be wondering why the dialog box is called *Field* Chooser when you're actually trying to add *columns* to the current view. In Outlook the terms *field* and *column* are pretty much synonymous. A field is one of the pieces of information that you enter into a record item; each of the columns in the list view represents one of those fields.

3. **Select the field you'd like to add and drag it to the appropriate spot on the list view.**
4. **(Optional) Click the Frequently-Used Fields drop-down box and select a different set of fields if you don't see the field you're looking for.**
5. **Click the X when you're finished adding new fields to close the Field Chooser dialog box.**

Removing columns

You might decide that one or more of the columns in the list view contain information you don't need. You can remove those columns in two easy steps:

1. **Right-click the column heading that you want to remove.**
2. **Choose Remove This Column from the shortcut menu.**

Worried that you won't be able to get your column back again? Don't be — just read the preceding section about adding columns.

Moving a column

You may think it's a drag if your columns are not in the order that you'd like them to be. A drag is a *good* thing when it comes to column arranging because that's just how you're going to do it, however. Hover the mouse pointer over the column heading you'd like to move, and then click and drag it to your preferred destination. Outlook helps you by flashing two red arrows at you indicating the spot where your new column will end up.

Resizing a column

If you feel like you're seeing spots before your eyes when you gaze at a list of Outlook items, you need to either see your doctor immediately or widen your columns a smidge. When a column is not wide enough to contain all the data, Outlook *truncates* it by placing three little dots at the end of the column.

If you've worked with Excel spreadsheets in the past you're probably already an old pro at this, but just in case you haven't, here's the drill:

1. **Move the mouse pointer to the right edge of the column you want to widen until the cursor morphs into a two-headed arrow.**
2. **Drag the edge of the column until the column is the desired width.**

If you are a real column perfectionist and, like Goldilocks, like to have your columns sized *just right,* you can double-click the right edge of the column header when you see the double-headed arrow. Outlook automatically sizes your column to fit the largest entry in that column.

Sort of sorting your column

You may cringe when a salesperson tells you that something can be done with the click of a button, but when it comes to sorting an Outlook column, he's right. Click the column heading of the column that you want to sort by, and Outlook responds by sorting your table based on that column. Want your contacts in zip code order? Click the Postal Code field. Change your mind and want your contacts listed alphabetically by company? Click the Company field.

If you want to reverse the order of the sort, click the column a second time. After you sort your data, you can tell which field your data is sorted by. If you look carefully at the column headings, one of them has a tiny up-pointing arrow indicating that the data in that column is sorted in ascending order. If the arrow points downward, your data is in descending order.

Sorting Your Data

Any time you look at your Outlook data it is in some kind of order. Unfortunately, that order may not be exactly what you had in mind. In the preceding section, you find out how to quickly sort a table view by clicking on one of the column headers. However, you may want to sort your information by more than one criterion; for example, you might want a list of your contacts sorted alphabetically by state and then alphabetically by the cities within each state. Or you may be viewing your contacts in one of the card views and wondering how in the world you can sort those cards when there are no column headings to click on.

To take your sorting skills up to the next level, follow these steps:

1. **Choose View➪Current View➪Customize Current View from the main menu bar.**

   The Customize View dialog box opens (refer to Figure 2-5).

2. **Click the Sort button.**

   The Sort dialog box opens, as shown in Figure 2-9.

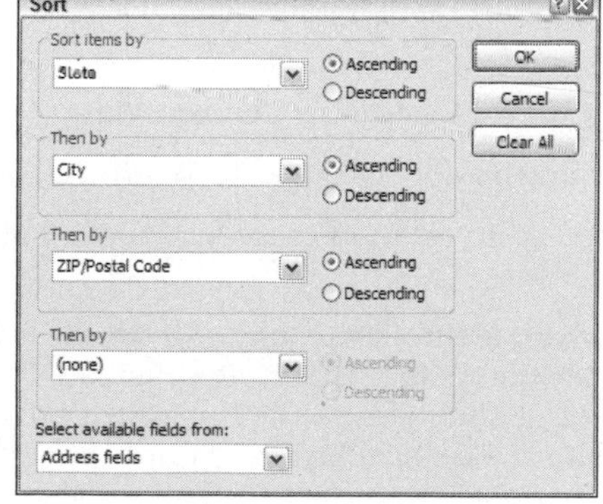

Figure 2-9: Creating a custom sort.

3. **Choose the first field that you want to sort by from the Sort Items by drop-down box.**

4. **(Optional) If you don't see the field you're looking for, select another set of fields from the Select Available Fields From drop-down box.**

5. **Choose Ascending of Descending depending on whether you want your fields sorted from A-Z or from Z-A order.**
6. **Repeat Steps 3 through 5 if you want to create secondary sorts within the main sort.**
7. **Click OK to close the Sort dialog window.**

   Outlook, always eager to please, warns you if one of the fields you chose is not shown in the current view. If you'd like to see the field, answer Yes.
8. **Click OK to close the Customize View dialog box.**

The View from the Top

By now you've probably realized that there are countless ways in which you can customize the various Outlook views. But wait! With the purchase of the knife set you can get even more customizations. And, if you order now, we'll even let you keep those customizations at no extra charge!

Okay, this isn't an infomercial, but the thought of taking a piece of software and totally reformatting it is a powerful thought.

Tweaking an existing view

The preceding sections show you how to group, work with table views, and sort your information. But Outlook still has a few more tricks up its sleeve. Here are a few more ways in which you can customize Outlook even further.

1. **Switch to the view that's closest to what you'd like.**

   Although you can start from scratch if you prefer, it's generally easier to tweak an existing view.
2. **Choose View⇨Current View⇨Customize Current View.**

   The Customize View dialog box opens (refer to Figure 2-5).
3. **For each type of change that you want to make, click a button, and select the options you want.**

   Options that are grayed out are not available with the view you are currently using. Consider switching to another view instead. For example, you may find that you can't add fields to the Business Cards view but that you can add fields to the Detailed Address Cards view.

   The first three options are somewhat of a rerun because we discussed them earlier in conjunction with the table view. If you want to modify other views such as a card view, however, here's your chance to do so:

   - *Fields:* Here's where you can add more fields to any layout.
   - *Group By:* Group all like items together.

- *Sort:* Sort the current layout in the manner of your choosing.

You also have a few new options to play with:

- *Filter:* You can create a filter to include only those items that match a certain criteria. Perhaps you want to quickly access only your Hot Prospects in California, or your e-mail that came in from six key contacts. Figure 2-10 shows you an example of a filter.

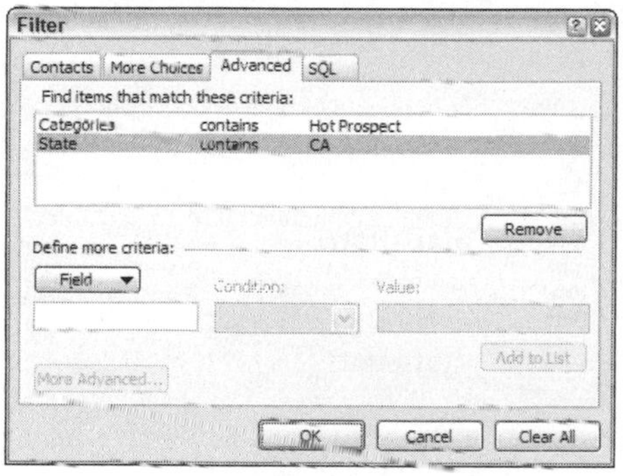

Figure 2-10: Creating a custom filter.

- *Other Settings:* Here's where you can pick the font that you want to use and other settings pertinent to the current view. Figure 2-11 shows you the options that can be changed for the Detailed Address Cards view.

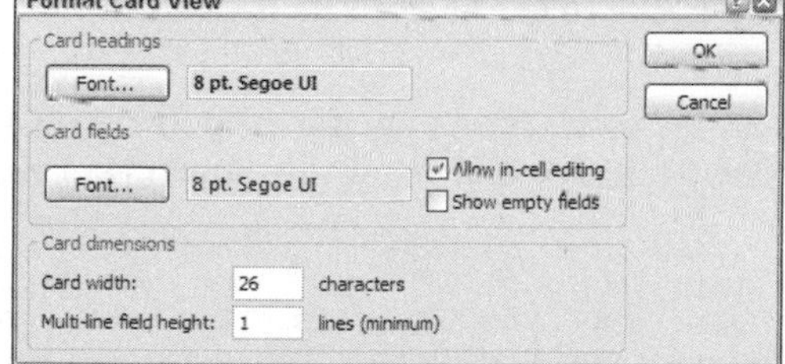

Figure 2-11: Other view settings that you can tweak.

- *Automatic formatting:* This is where you can select a font for specific items. For example, you can have all your unread e-mail show up in magenta or the contracts in your distribution list in green.
- *Format Columns:* If you're working in a table view you can have each of your columns formatted in a different way. You can even rename the column headings if you so desire.

4. **Click OK to close the current dialog box and then OK again to close the Customize View dialog box.**

Resetting a standard view

After you customize the current view, you can sit back and admire your handiwork. If you less than totally thrilled with your masterpiece, however, you can easily reset the view back to its original, pristine form. Here's how:

1. **Choose View⇨Current View⇨Define Views.**

   The Custom View Organizer opens (see Figure 2-12).

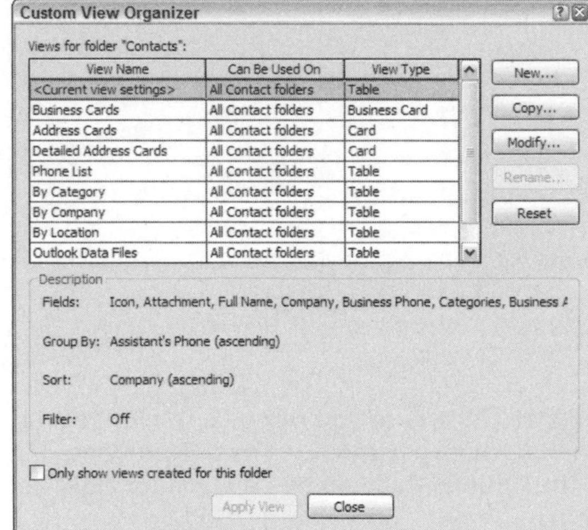

Figure 2-12: Setting your customized view back to the default setting.

2. **Select the view you'd like to set back to its default in the View Name column.**

   As you click the various views, you may notice that sometimes the Reset button is grayed out. That's your tip that the view has never been tinkered with.

3. **Click the Reset button.**

   Outlook prompts you for verification that your passport is up-to-date and that you really want to reset the view back to its original state.

4. **Click OK to the warning and then Close to close the Custom View Organizer.**

Changing the name of a custom view

Ironically, although you can customize a view in more ways than you ever dreamed possible, one thing you cannot do is to rename a predefined view. Try as you might, you can't change Detailed Address Cards to Really Important Address Cards. You can, however, copy a predefined view, give it a name, and then customize it. Follow these steps to do just that:

1. **Choose View⇨Current View⇨Define Views.**

   The Custom View Organizer opens (refer to Figure 2-12).

2. **Select the view that you want to rename in the View Name list and click Copy.**

   The Copy View dialog box opens.

3. **Enter the name of the new view into the Name of New View text box and click OK.**

4. **Click OK to close the Copy View dialog box, and then a final OK to close the Custom View Organizer.**

Creating a view from scratch

Considering that Outlook comes equipped with myriad views, and that all those views can be customized from here to Podunk Junction and back, you may wonder why you would want to create a view from scratch. As the saying goes, different strokes for different folks. And, if you happen to be one of those people who is stroking along differently from the rest of the world — or maybe if you have an adventurous side — here's your opportunity to explore uncharted waters.

1. **Choose View⇨Current View⇨Define Views.**

   The Custom View Organizer opens (refer to Figure 2-12).

2. **Click New.**

   The Create a New View dialog box opens, as shown in Figure 2-13.

3. **Enter a name into the Name of New View box.**

4. **In the Type of View box, select a view type.**

   You have the option of creating a new Table, Timeline, Card, Business Card, Day/Week/Month, or Icon view.

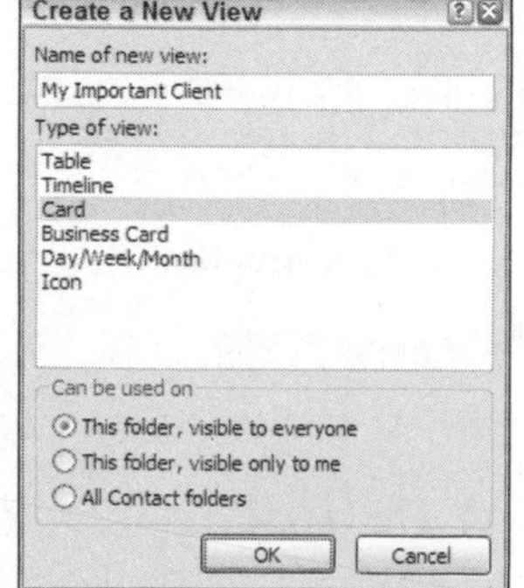

Figure 2-13: Creating a new view.

5. **Select an option in the Can Be Used On area.**

   Your options are to share the view with anyone that you share your Outlook with, horde the view for only your own usage, or apply the view to all folders that can be used with that view type.

6. **Click OK.**

   The Customize View dialog box opens. Try to contain your excitement at finding yourself at old, familiar territory.

7. **Select the options that you want to use.**

   You'll see different options depending on the type of view you are creating. By now, these options — Fields, Group By, Sort, Filter — should seem like old hat to you.

8. **Click OK when you finish selecting options.**

   You land smack dab where you started — in the Custom View Organizer.

9. **Click the Apply View button if you want to use your new view immediately, if not sooner.**

10. **Click Close to close the Custom View Organizer dialog box.**

11. **Choose View⇨Current View from the main menu bar.**

    Wonder of wonders! Your new view now sits proudly on top of all the items in the Current view submenu!

Deleting a custom view

Now that you've had a chance to fool around creating new views, you may realize that the out-of-the-box views are really just what the doctor ordered, and you'd like to simplify your life — and Outlook — by getting rid of your custom views. Not a problem, as long as you follow these simple steps:

1. **Choose View⇨Current View⇨Define Views.**

   The Custom View Organizer opens (refer to Figure 2-12).

2. **Select the view you want to delete in the View Name column.**

   You'll notice that no Delete button appears when you select a predefined view, although you see the Reset button. When you click a view you created, the Delete button appears.

3. **Click the Delete button and click OK when prompted.**

4. **Click Close to close the Custom View Organizer.**

Displaying All the Messages in a Folder

To make it easy to find your unread messages, Outlook displays them in bold text in your Inbox. An unopened envelope appears next to the message in the Table View. In addition, the number of unread messages can be seen next to the name of each of your Inbox folders.

Another easy way to find all of your unread mail is to look at the Unread Mail folder found in the Search Folders area of the Folder List. The Unread Mail folder displays the e-mail messages you haven't read, no matter where they are located.

If you prefer, you can display the total messages in the folder rather than just the unread ones:

1. **Right-click the folder and choose Properties.**

   The Properties dialog box appears before your eyes, just like the one in Figure 2-14.

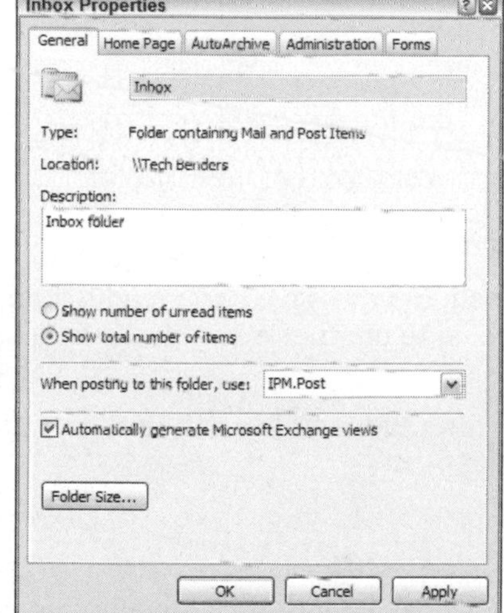

Figure 2-14: The Properties dialog box for Outlook's Inbox.

2. **Select the Show total number of items option.**
3. **Click OK to close the Properties dialog box.**

Reading in the Reading pane

Outlook lets you keep track of your unread messages by both bolding unread messages and keeping a count of them by default for each of your Inboxes. In turn, you need to send a signal to Outlook that you have read a message. You can do this in a number of ways. The most obvious way is by opening a message; Outlook takes the cue and automatically marks the message as read.

If you are using the Reading pane, you can change the default way in which Outlook determines whether a message has been read:

1. **Choose Tools⇨Options, and then click the Other tab.**

   You can see the Other tab of the Options dialog box appears.

2. **Click Reading Pane.**

   Alternatively, if you use the Reading pane, you can right-click the border of the Reading pane and choose Reading Pane Options from the shortcut menu.

   The Reading Pane dialog box opens, as shown in Figure 2-15.

Figure 2-15: The Reading Pane dialog box.

3. **Select the options you want.**

   You can have Outlook consider a message to be read if it appears in the Reading pane, if you move on to another message, or if you hit the spacebar.

4. **Click OK to close the Reading Pane dialog window, and then OK again to close the Options dialog box.**

Manually marking messages

If you prefer, you can send the signal to Outlook manually that you've finished reading a message:

1. **Select the messages you want to change in one of your Inbox folders.**
   - *To select adjacent items, click the first item,* shift-click the last item.
   - *To select nonadjacent items,* click the first item, and then Ctrl-click additional items.
   - *To select all items,* click one item, press and hold the Ctrl key, and then press the A key.
2. **Right-click the selected message(s) and select Mark as Read or Mark as Unread from the shortcut menu.**

Chapter 3: Customizing Outlook Forms

In This Chapter

- Customizing the Quick Access toolbar
- Customizing an Outlook form
- Creating custom fields
- Defaulting a form

If variety is the spice of life, this chapter is certainly one of the spicier ones because it's all about customizing Outlook. You start by learning about the Quick Access toolbar and move on to creating custom forms. You find out how to add a custom field or two and learn a few tips on how to make your form have a bit of extra pizzazz. Finally, you learn how to make your new form the default one that is used each time you create a new Outlook item.

Making Quick Changes to the Quick Access Toolbar

The Quick Access toolbar is a customizable toolbar that appears next to the Ribbon for most Outlook items. Although the Ribbon lists all the functions that are currently available, the Quick Access toolbar contains only those commands that you are most likely to use. For example, if you categorize all your contacts, you can add the Categorize icon to the contact Quick Access toolbar. Or, if you routinely schedule follow-ups directly from incoming e-mail messages, you may want to add the Follow-Up icon to the Quick Access toolbar.

Each of the various Outlook items has its own unique Quick Access toolbar so that you use one Quick Access toolbar when you add or edit a contact record and another Quick Access toolbar when you send or receive e-mail.

In addition to adding buttons to the Quick Access toolbar, you can also move it. You can see the Quick Access toolbar in Figure 3-1.

The Quick Access toolbar can be found hanging out in one of two places:

- ✦ The upper-left corner of an opened item next to the Microsoft Office Button.
- ✦ Directly below the Ribbon.

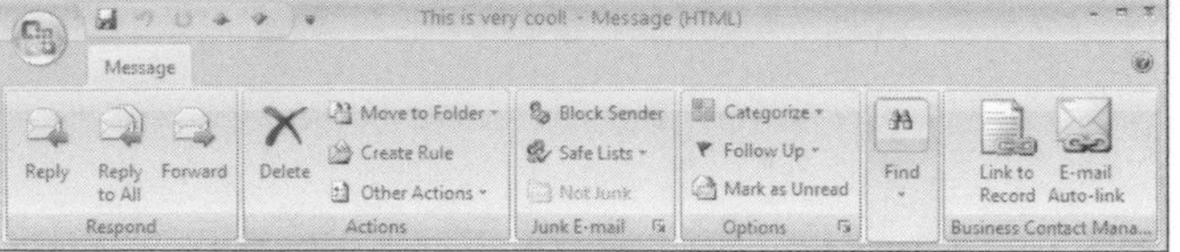

Figure 3-1: Outlook's Quick Access toolbar.

If you don't want the Quick Access Toolbar to be displayed in one of these locations, you can move it to the other fairly easily:

1. **Click the Customize Quick Access Toolbar icon.**

   The last icon on the Quick Access toolbar looks like a down-pointing arrow. If you hover your mouse over it for a moment, a ScreenTip displays, helping to point you in the right direction.

2. **Choose Show below the Ribbon in the Customize Quick Access Toolbar menu.**

   By default, the Quick Access toolbar, shown in Figure 3-1, is located above the Ribbon. If you've already moved it, you pick the Show above the Ribbon option.

You can also right-click the Ribbon and select Show Quick Access Toolbar below the Ribbon as an alternative way to move the Quick Access toolbar.

You may find that the Ribbon takes up a bit too much real estate on the various Outlook forms. If this is the case, consider adding the key features that you use to the Quick Access toolbar and hiding the Ribbon by giving it a right-click and choosing Minimize the Ribbon.

Adding a Quick Access toolbar command from the Ribbon

You can add any one of the commands displayed on the Ribbon to your Quick Access toolbar with the click of a button. This is particularly helpful if you want to hide the Ribbon, but still want to be able to access various Ribbon commands.

1. **Right-click the command that you want to add to the Quick Access toolbar.**

   A shortcut menu springs to life like the one you see in Figure 3-2.

2. **Click Add to Quick Access Toolbar on the shortcut menu.**

   Miraculously, the new command will take a place of honor at the end of Quick Access toolbar.

Add to Quick Access Toolbar
Customize Quick Access Toolbar...
Show Quick Access Toolbar Below the Ribbon
Minimize the Ribbon

Figure 3-2: Adding a command to the Quick Access toolbar.

Quickly adding Quick Access toolbar commands

You find as many commands available to add to the Quick Access toolbar as there are flavors at your local ice cream parlor. Here's how you find them:

1. **Open the Quick Access Toolbar Editor by using one of the following methods:**

   - Right-click the Ribbon and choose Customize Quick Access Toolbar.
   - Click the Customize Quick Access Toolbar icon at the end of the Quick Access toolbar and choose More Commands.

   Both methods lead you to the Customize tab of the Editor Options dialog box. If you want to see it for yourself, take a look at Figure 3-3.

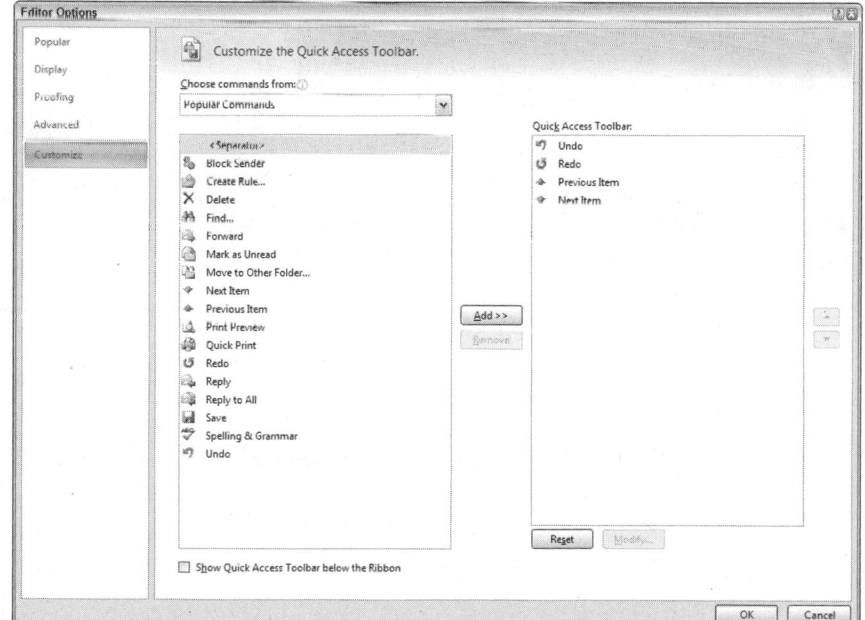

Figure 3-3: The Editor Options dialog box.

The commands that appear on the left side of the screen (in the Choose Commands From area) represent all the commands that you have to choose from. The commands on the right in the Quick Access toolbar area are all the commands that are currently found on the Quick Access toolbar.

2. **Select a command from the left side of the screen and click the Add button to move it to the Quick Access toolbar commands on the right side of the screen.**

   For example, you may want to add the Quick Print button if you routinely print some of your e-mail messages.

3. **Select another list of commands by clicking the drop-down arrow to the right of Popular Commands.**

   Baby, you ain't seen nothing yet! As its name implies, the commands listed under Popular Commands are the most popular commands that you may want to add to the Quick Access toolbar. However, they represent only the tip of the iceberg. You can choose Commands Not in the Ribbon or All Commands to see lots more choices.

   The <Separator> command may leave you wondering. A separator is a vertical line that appears between the various commands on your Quick Access toolbar. You can use a separator to help you organize the various commands into groups. Feel free to add as many separators as you need.

4. **(Optional) Select a command in the Quick Access toolbar section and then click the up or down arrow to change the order of your commands.**

5. **(Optional) Select a command in the Quick Access toolbar section and then click the Remove button to remove a command from the Quick Access toolbar.**

   You may find that you're not sure how a command will work. If you're not sure, go ahead and add the command to the Quick Access toolbar — you can always remove it later.

6. **(Optional) Click the Reset button to reset the Quick Access toolbar to the way it was originally.**

7. **Click OK after you finish adding all the commands that you want to the Quick Access toolbar.**

   Figure 3-4 shows you a sample of a new and improved Quick Access toolbar.

Figure 3-4: A customized Quick Access toolbar.

Playing with Forms

Every time you choose File➪New in Outlook, a form opens that is ready and willing to hold your new information. Although most of you are more than happy to use just the existing forms that come with Outlook, there's always someone in the crowd who just has to have it "his way."

Creating a new form using existing fields

You may have noticed that most things in life can be done in one of two ways: the hard way and the easy way. Frankly, if I am given the option, I generally vote to try the easy route first. That rule applies to Outlook as well — you can design a form from scratch or you can modify an existing form.

Outlook comes equipped with hundreds of standard fields that are ready and waiting to hold your information. You can choose to add any of them to an existing form by following these steps:

1. **From the main Outlook menu bar click Tools➪Forms➪Design a Form.**

   The forms of the Standard Forms Library appear in the Design Form dialog box. These are the forms that appear when you create a new item such as a new contact, message, or appointment. You can see the window in Figure 3-5.

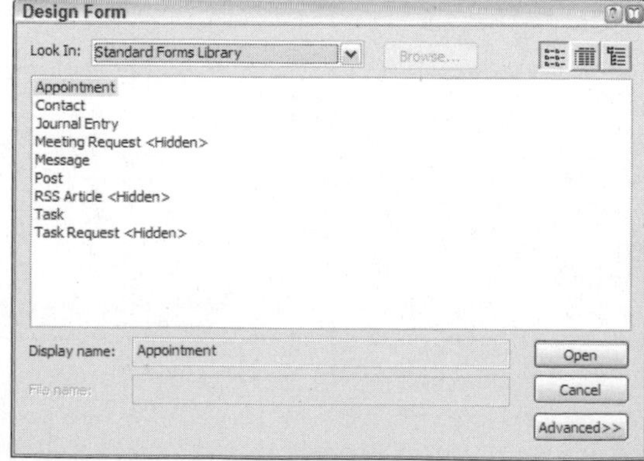

Figure 3-5: The Design Form dialog box.

Unfortunately you can't edit all the Outlook forms. You may notice that a few of the forms include `<Hidden>` after their names; this means that these are specially protected forms that you can't edit.

2. **(Optional) Choose another folder from the Look In drop-down window.**

   For example, if you have already created some custom forms, you find them hanging out in the Personal Forms Library.

3. **Select Contact and then click Open.**

   Although you can customize any of the Outlook forms, you probably want to start with the Contact form because this is the form that holds all the key contact information.

   The Contact Design window opens. You can see what it looks like in Figure 3-6.

   At first glance it looks almost identical to the window that you see when you create a new contact. It has, however, a couple of notable differences:

   - The title bar includes the term *(Design)*.
   - The pretty blue background is replaced by a series of boring gray dots.
   - The Field Chooser tools appear on top of the form.

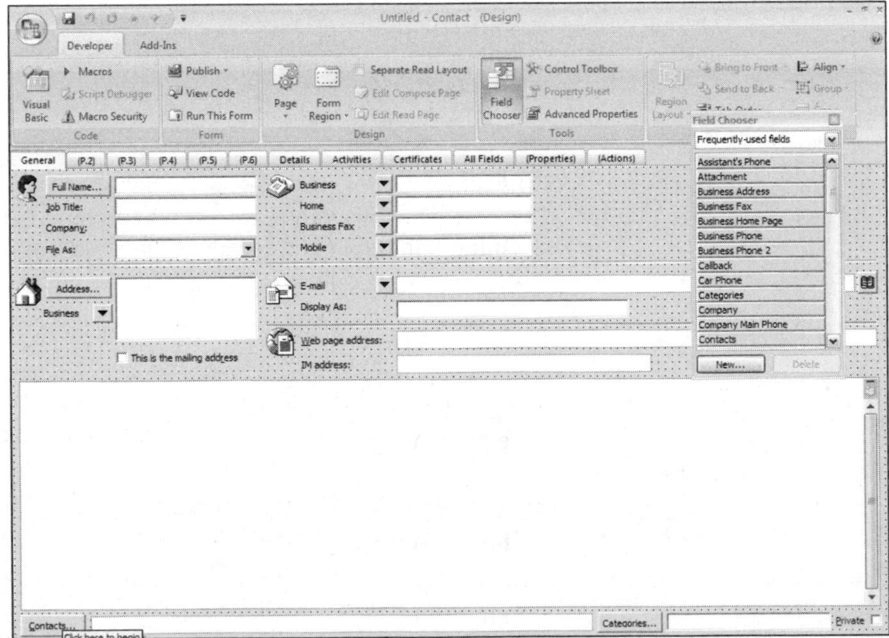

Figure 3-6: The Contact Design window.

You may notice in Figure 3-5 that a lot of the area of the form is taken up by a large white box. This is the area where you generally type notes. You may consider making this box slightly smaller by clicking the box one time so that little "grab" handles appear around the box. You can then place your mouse on one of those grab handles and drag the box borders so that the notes box takes up less space on your form.

4. **Save the form by clicking the Office Button and choosing Save As.**

   You'll have a few things to do here:

   - *Navigate to the folder where you'd like to save the form.* By default, Outlook buries it in a Templates folder, which is as good a place as any to save your template.
   - *Give the form a brand-new name.* Call me silly, but here's the deal: If you save the form using a completely new name, you can go back to the original form just in case something goes wrong. Saving the form using a new name is my vote.
   - *Change the extension type to `.oft`.* You have a few other file extension choices, but using the `.oft` extension ensures you that you'll be able to use the template in Outlook.

5. **(Optional) Add a new page to the form.**

   Notice in Figure 3-6 that the form comes with five additional tabs or pages labeled P.2–P.6. Also notice that the page numbers are surrounded by parenthesis, indicating that these pages are not currently in use. The object of the game is to add these pages to your form (if you need them).

   - Click a tab.
   - Click the Page icon in the Design section of the Form Designer's Ribbon.
   - Click the Display This Page option to display the page.

     A page is automatically displayed if you drag a field onto it.

   - Click Rename This Page and supply a new name for the page.

     Not all things are created equal, and this is certainly the case with Outlook's pages. Don't be upset if you click a page and find that you can't rename it. Some of the pages are system pages and can't be renamed.

6. **Select the field you want to add to the form from the Field Chooser and drag it to the appropriate spot on the form.**

   As you drag the field, notice that both the field and the corresponding label move together to the new location on your form. Unlike some graphic programs, Outlook tries to line up the fields perfectly for you.

The same field can appear multiple times on a form. However, all the fields contain the same piece of information. For example, you may add the phone number on several pages of your form. This enables you to view the same phone number from various areas of your form.

Can't find the Field Chooser? Many users accidentally close it when it is in their way. To bring it back, simply click the Field Chooser icon on the Tools section of the Ribbon.

7. **(Optional) Click a field and press Delete to remove a field from the form.**
8. **Click the Save icon to save your form.**
9. **Click the Publish icon on the Form section of the Ribbon and select Publish Form As.**

   When you *save* a form, you are saving it to your hard drive or network. When you *publish* a form, you are saving it to one of your Outlook folders so that you can use it when creating a new item.

10. **Select the Outlook folder from the Look In drop-down box, give the form a name, and click Publish.**

    You probably want to use the same name that you used when you saved the form in Step 9. You can see what it looks like in Figure 3-7.

11. **Click the Office Button and click Close to close the form.**

Figure 3-7: Publishing a new Outlook form.

Form Beautification 101

If you followed the preceding steps, you are now the proud owner of a new, customized form. You can master a few cool party tricks, however, to provide your form with a little more polish. Although they are not mandatory, they lead to a more professional-looking form — and help you find an avenue for the artistic side of your personality.

1. **Choose Tools⇨Forms⇨Design a Form.**

   The Design Form dialog box opens.

2. **Click the Look In drop-down box and select User Templates in File System.**

   If you were creative in choosing the file location when creating the form, you have to click the Browse button, navigate to the location of your saved form, and click Open.

   From this point forward, all the steps are optional, albeit fun.

3. **Select the form you'd like to tweak and then click Open.**

   True to its word, Outlook opens your form.

4. **Add a colorful background to your form.**

   Although you may be delighted with the silvery blue background of the basic Outlook form, you may want to coordinate your form with the office décor.

   - Right-click the form background and choose Advanced Properties. Alternatively, you can click Advanced Properties on the Tools portion of the Ribbon.
   - Click BackColor on the Properties dialog box.
   - Click the ellipsis button (the three little dots) at the top of the properties window.
   - Select a color and click OK.

5. **Add a colorful background to a specific field.**

   For example, you may want emphasize a field by coloring it yellow.

   - Right-click a field and choose Advanced Properties.
   - Click BackColor on the Properties dialog box.
   - Click the ellipsis button (the three little dots) at the top of the properties window.
   - Select a color and click OK.

6. **Make two or more fields the same size.**

   As you move fields onto your form, you may find that the fields are not all exactly the same size. Although this does not affect your data input, it is annoying — and something you can easily correct:

   - Select the field that is the correct size; this becomes the anchor field and now has white selection boxes.
   - While holding down your Shift key, click any other fields that you want to make the same size as your anchor field.
   - Right-click any of the selected fields and choose Make Same Size⇨Both.

7. **Align two or more fields.**

   When you customize a form, you may notice a series of dots on the form designer. These dots represent the *snap-to grid;* ideally, any new field you place on a form snaps to these dots so that your new fields line up with each other. If for some reason the fields seem slightly out of whack, you can line them up manually as well:

   - Select the field that is in the correct location; this becomes the anchor field and now has white selection boxes.
   - While holding down your Shift key, click any other fields that you want to line up with your anchor field.
   - Right-click any of the selected fields and choose Align.

   You can get an idea of what it's like to align fields in Figure 3-8.

8. **Group several fields together.**

   Although it's easy to drag a field to a new spot on the form, the process becomes tougher if you have to drag a whole bunch of fields at the same time because you have to select them all first. To solve this problem — or at least to make life a wee bit easier — you can group several fields together and then move them around your form en masse. For example, you may have added fields for the names and birthdates of your contact's kids; grouping them enables you to move those multiple fields around in single click.

   - While holding down the Ctrl key, click all the fields you want to group together. Alternatively, you can hold down your left mouse button and lasso all the fields by drawing a box around them.
   - Right-click any of the selected fields and choose Group.

9. **Close and save the form when your beautification project is complete.**

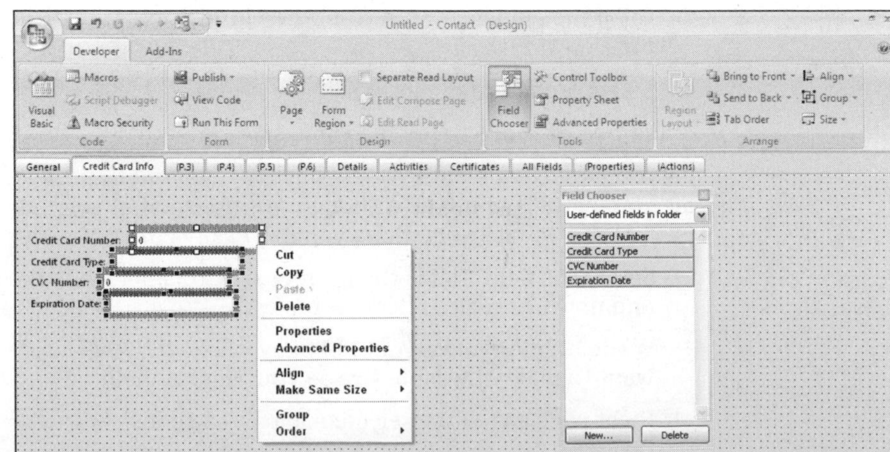

Figure 3-8: Aligning fields on a custom form.

Adding custom-defined fields

I am a firm believer that a little knowledge is a dangerous thing. Although adding a field to Outlook is not a hard thing to do, it is something that should be well thought out and planned in advance. Planning prevents you from adding thousands of contacts to your database, only to find you have to modify each record to include information that was omitted the first time around.

You add new fields by returning to the scene of the crime — or, at least, the place where you created your custom form:

1. **From the main Outlook menu bar, choose Tools⇨Forms⇨Design a Form.**

   The Design Form dialog box opens showing a list of the basic Outlook forms.

2. **Select the name of the form you wish to edit and click Open.**

   Theoretically, it doesn't matter which form you choose because your mission here is to add new fields to the database. In any event, the Form Designer opens with the Field Chooser dialog box prominently displayed.

3. **Click New on the Field Choose dialog box.**

   The New Field dialog box opens as seen on stage, screen, and in Figure 3-9.

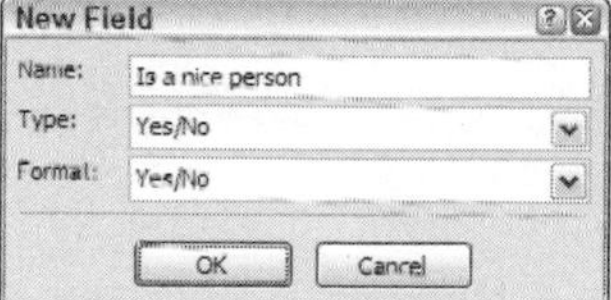

Figure 3-9: Adding a new field to Outlook.

4. **Type the name of the new field in the Name box.**

   If you happen to give the field a name that is already in use, Outlook gently reminds you that the field name is already being used and that you need to come up with a better one.

5. **Select the type of field that you want to add from the Type drop-down list, shown in Figure 3-10.**

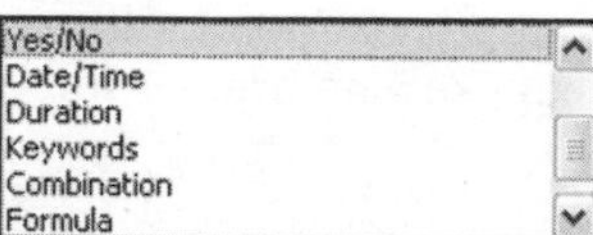

Figure 3-10: The Type drop-down list.

Let the games begin! This is where the real fun starts. You've got a number of choices here. If your field is going to contain a numeric value you can designate the field as a Number, Percent, Currency, or Integer field. If you're tracking time, you can use a Date/Time or Duration field.

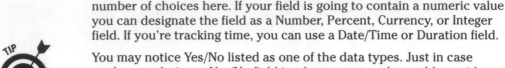

You may notice Yes/No listed as one of the data types. Just in case you're wondering, a Yes/No field is what most people would consider a check box field.

6. **Select a format from the Format drop-down list (see Figure 3-11).**

   You have a variety of options here that depend on the data type you selected. If you chose Date/Time, you can now select the data format that you'd like to use, as shown in Figure 3-11. If you chose Number, you can decide how you want to deal with everything from commas and decimal points to negative numbers.

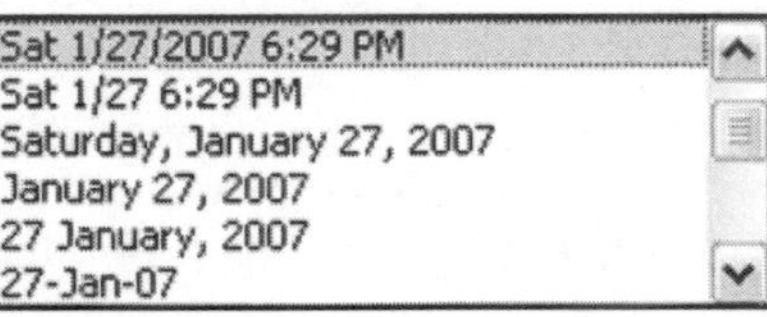

Figure 3-11: The Format drop-down list.

7. **Click OK to add your new field to Outlook.**
8. **Select the User-Defined Fields in Folder option in the Field Chooser dialog box to add your newly created field to your form.**

Using Custom Forms

After you've created your custom forms, the hard part is over. Now you get to pretty much rest on your laurels. However, before you head to the pool with drink in hand, you may want to give a bit of thought as to what you're going to do with the forms now that you've created them.

Making your form the default

After you've created a custom form, you want to associate it with a specific Outlook folder. Associating a specific form to a specific folder can unleash an entirely new aspect of Outlook. Let's say, for example, that you have divided your contacts folder into three subfolders: one for friends, one for customers, and one for vendors. The information that you enter for a customer may be quite different from what you enter for a friend. Although keeping credit card information on file may seem like a no-brainer for your customer contacts, your friends may not be as willing to give you that important tidbit of information. Conversely, you may want to keep the names of your friends' children in Outlook, but you may not need this information for your customers and vendors.

Associating a form with a folder is a two-step process: First, you make the form available in the folder, and then you'll make it the default form that is used any time new items are added to that folder.

1. **From Outlook's Folder list, right-click the folder that contains the customized form and choose Properties.**

   The Properties dialog box opens.

2. **Click the Forms tab and then click the Manage button.**

   The Forms Manager dialog box springs to life, just like the one you see in Figure 3-12.

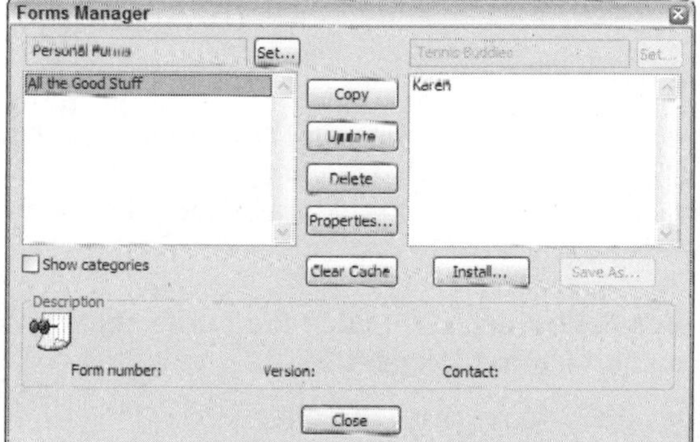

Figure 3-12: The Forms Manager.

3. **Click the Set button, select the location of your form, and click OK.**

   The form now appears in the left side of the Forms Manager.

4. **Select the form you want and then click the Copy button.**

   The form magically appears on the right side of the Forms Manager, which is exactly where you want it to appear.

5. **Click Close to return to the Properties dialog box and select the General tab.**

6. **Select the form in the When Posting to This Folder, Use drop-down box.**

   If you'd like to see this in person, look at Figure 3-13.

7. **Click OK to save your changes.**

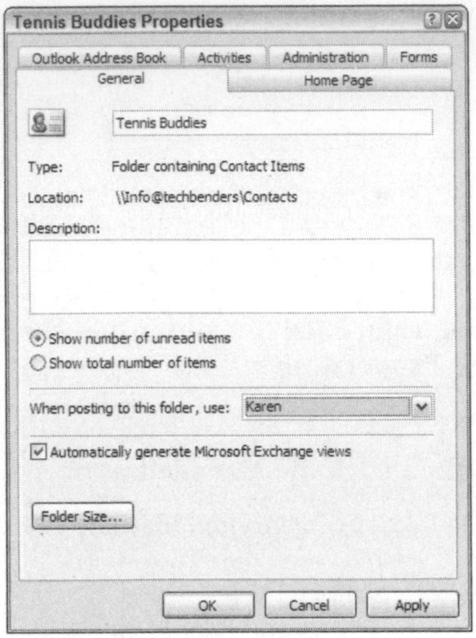

Figure 3-13: The General tab of the Properties dialog box.

Deleting a form

Let's face it — we all like to experiment, and sometimes our experiments aren't successful. This is particularly true in the computer world. If you design a form that isn't exactly what you had in mind, it's very easy to hide the evidence. Here's all you have to do:

1. **From Outlook's Folder list, right-click the folder that contains the customized form, and choose Properties.**

   The Properties dialog box springs to life.

2. **Select the Forms tab and click the Manage button.**

   The Forms Manager appears (refer to Figure 3-12).

3. **Select the form that you wish to delete and click Delete.**
4. **Click Close to close the Forms Manager and then OK to close the Properties dialog box.**

Book IX

Managing Your Outlook Stuff

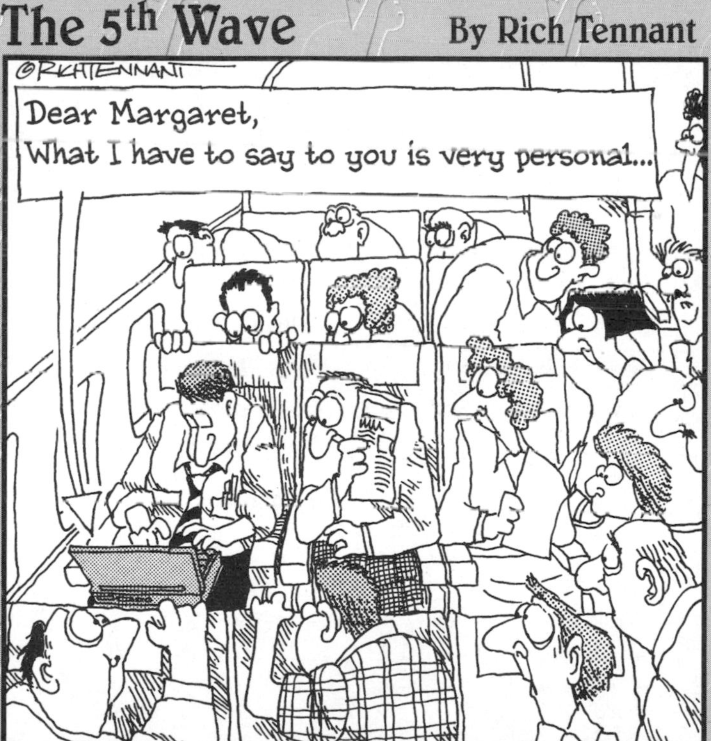

The 5th Wave
By Rich Tennant
©RICHTENNANT
Dear Margaret,
What I have to say to you is very personal...

Contents at a Glance

Chapter 1: Finding a Place for Your Stuff 637
Chapter 2: Playing by the Rules 661
Chapter 3: Making Mincemeat Out of Spam 677
Chapter 4: Seek and Ye Shall Find 689
Chapter 5: Securing Outlook E-Mail 707

Chapter 1: Finding a Place for Your Stuff

In This Chapter

- **Performing common tasks**
- **Using Organize to get organized**
- **Adding new file folders**
- **Reducing the Size of your Outlook data file**
- **Archiving old data**

As George Carlin says, "All you need in life is a little place for your stuff." If this is your first foray into Outlook, you're probably wondering how it could ever get messy and disorganized. As you come to rely on Outlook for each and every aspect of your busy life, however, you accumulate more and more "stuff." This chapter shows how to create folders to hold your stuff. You see how to use the Organize feature and reduce the size of your stuff. You even find out how to put stuff into storage — or in this case, archival folders.

Developing an Outlook Filing System

Out of the box, Outlook comes with a variety of folders aimed at storing your stuff:

- Calendar
- Contacts
- Deleted Items
- Drafts
- Inbox
- Journal
- Notes
- Outbox
- Sent Items
- Tasks

When you first use Outlook, these folders are sufficient for storing your various Outlook items. As your life becomes more complicated, however, so does Outlook. If you want to save some of your thousands of incoming messages, for example, subdividing your Inbox folders for each of your clients is helpful. Keeping your personal contacts in separate from your business contacts is also helpful, so you may want to subdivide your contacts, as well.

So how many folders can you create? The sky is the limit. You really can't outgrow Outlook. You can add new folders as the need arises without worrying that you're going to run out of room in your filing cabinet.

If data management isn't your forte, stop worrying. If you swing open any of the file drawers in your desk, chances are good that you've put your insurance information into a folder marked insurance, and your tax information into a folder marked taxes. That same sense of order applies to Outlook — except you won't have to invest in a bunch of folders and worry about creating neat little labels!

Creating a new folder

The hardest part about creating a new folder is deciding what to name it. The easy part is creating the folder. Here's all you need to do to get started:

1. **Right-click any of the existing Outlook folders, and choose New Folder from the menu that appears.**

   The Create New Folder dialog box opens, as shown in Figure 1-1.

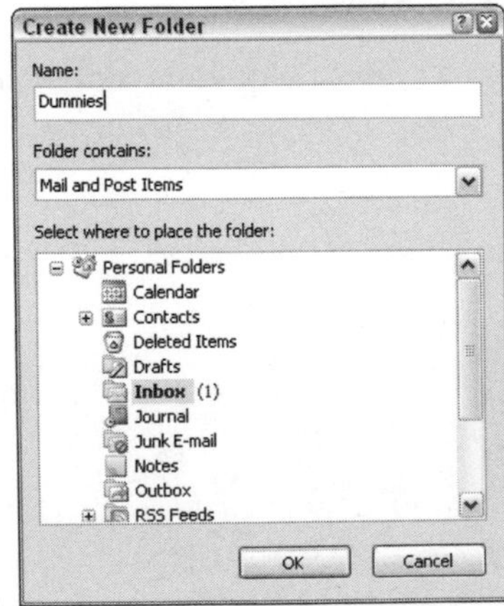

Figure 1-1: Creating a new Inbox folder.

2. **Enter a name for the new folder in the Name text box.**
3. **Select the folder location from the Select Where to Place the Folder list box.**

   If a subfolder or two exists within a folder, a plus sign appears in front of the main folder. Click it, and the subfolders appear.

   TIP

   You might be wondering what to select from the Folder Contains drop-down list. Actually, you don't have to concern yourself with that drop-down list because it defaults to the folder type that you selected in Step 1.
4. **Click OK to close the Create New Folder dialog box.**

   Sigh happily, knowing that you are well on the way to organizational bliss. Figure 1-2 shows a Folder List that has been customized to include new folders.

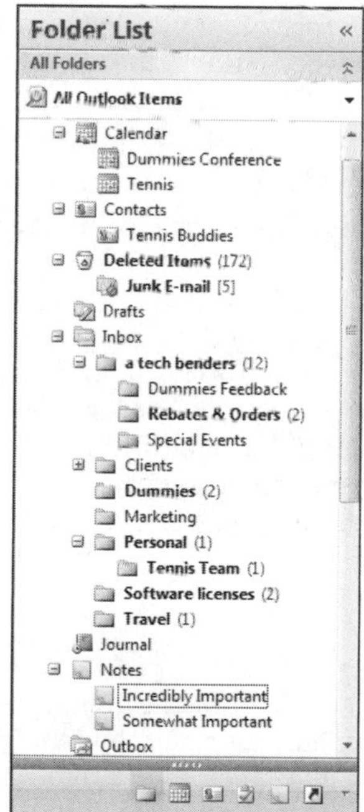

Figure 1-2: An Outlook Folder List that contains new folders.

Moving an item to another folder

The easiest way to move an item to another folder is by dragging it from one folder to the next. Here's how:

1. **Select the item(s) you want to move.**

   Although you can move your items one by one, dragging a bunch of items at the same time is much easier. You can select multiple items in several ways:

   - **To select adjacent items,** click the first item, hold down the Shift key, and then click the last item.
   - **To select nonadjacent items,** click the first item, hold down the Ctrl key, and then click each additional item.
   - **To select all items,** click the first item, and press Ctrl+A.

2. **Drag the selected item(s) to the destination folder.**

   When you drag the items, they disappear from the first folder and find a permanent home in the new folder — unless you move the items again.

   Sometimes, you may want an item to appear in both the original and the new folder. For example, you might store all of your contacts in the Contacts folder but want to copy select contacts into a new folder to make them easier to access. Select the item(s) as outlined in the preceding steps, drag them with the right-mouse button to the new folder, and then choose Copy from the shortcut menu.

3. **Ponder how you can go about organizing your closets that easily.**

Rearranging your folders

When you create new folders in Outlook, they appear alphabetically in the Folder List. Drag as you might, you can't change the order. However, you can drag your folder in order to make it a subfolder of another folder. And if a folder is a subfolder of another folder, you can drag it up to the top of the Folder List to promote it to being a full-fledged folder of its own.

Giving folders the heave-ho

If you've ever attempted to redo an office file system, you know that it can be a lesson in futility; some drawers are filled to overflowing, and others sit empty. Fortunately, Outlook makes manipulating files easy. If you identify a folder you no longer need, deleting it is simple. Just give the folder a right-click and choose Delete from the shortcut menu. Outlook prompts you to click Yes if you really want the folder (and all its contents) to go bye-bye. See Figure 1-3.

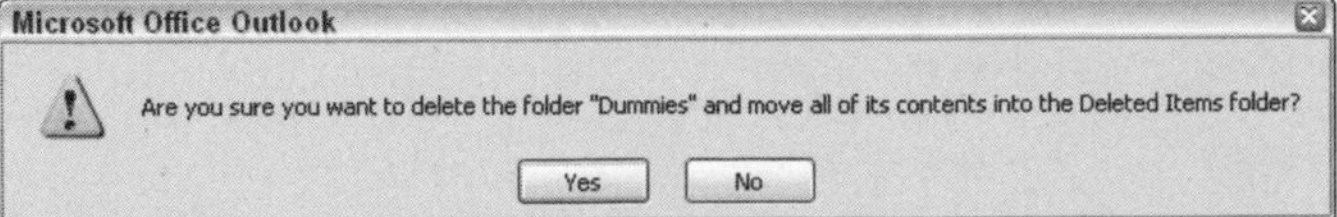

Figure 1-3: Bidding *adieu* to a folder.

Just like you wouldn't walk the tightrope without a net, Outlook comes equipped with a safety net of its own. Don't panic if you accidentally delete a folder. Run, don't walk, to your Deleted Folders; your deleted folder sits there patiently until you clean out the Deleted Items folder. If you want to salvage your folder, simply drag it back to where it belongs.

Moving an item to a different type of folder

Outlook has all kinds of neat party tricks up its sleeve. If you move an item to a different type of folder, for example, all kinds of cool things happen. For example:

- ✦ If you drag an e-mail item to the Contacts folder, Outlook attempts to create a new Contact Record from the e-mail message. It fills in the name and e-mail, and the body of the message appears as a note on the Contact Record.
- ✦ If you drag an e-mail item to the Calendar, Outlook creates an appointment. Change the date and time, if necessary, and you're ready to go.
- ✦ Drag an e-mail item to the Tasks folder, and you are ready to follow-up on an e-mail. Outlook creates a new task — the details of the e-mail become the details of the task (see Figure 1-4).

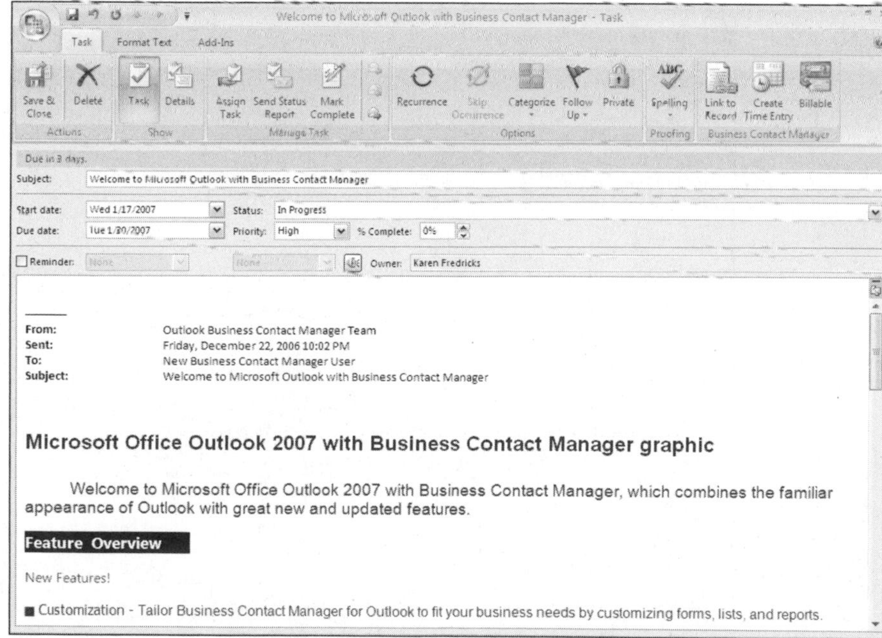

Figure 1-4: Creating a Task from an incoming e-mail message.

- ✦ If you love sticky notes, drag an e-mail message to the notes folder, and Outlook creates one for you instantly.
- ✦ Drag a Calendar activity to the Inbox to remind someone about an appointment. Fill in the contact's e-mail address, and you're ready to go.
- ✦ Drag a contact to the Inbox, and Outlook creates a new e-mail message addressed to the contact.

Getting Organized with the Organize Feature

For many people, the best part of watching *The Jetsons* cartoon was watching the various robots whisking around taking care of their human counterparts. Outlook's Organize feature is kind of like one of those robots.

Follow these steps, and Outlook gets you organized in a jiffy:

1. **Select the Outlook folder that needs organizational TLC.**
2. **Choose Tools⇨Organize from the main menu bar.**

   The Organize window appears at the top of the items in the currently selected folder (see Figure 1-5).

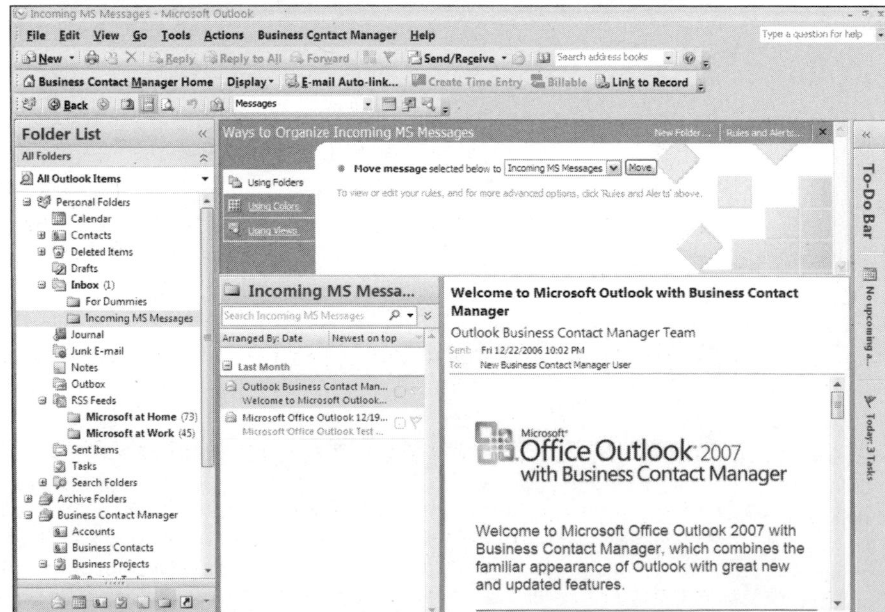

Figure 1-5: The Organize window.

3. Choose an organizational option from the left side of the Organize window.

You have three ways in which you can organize your folder.

- **Using Folders:** Select the items you want and move them to the folder you select in the Move Message Selected Below To list box, shown in Figure 1-5.
- **Using Colors:** This option appears if you select an e-mail folder in Step 1. If you live for color-coordinated highlighters, sticky notes, and folder labels, you'll think you've died and gone to Organizer Heaven. You can select an item in your current folder and assign it a color. Colorizing can be slow-going because you can colorize only one item at a time. Figure 1-6 shows how you can attach a color to an e-mail message.

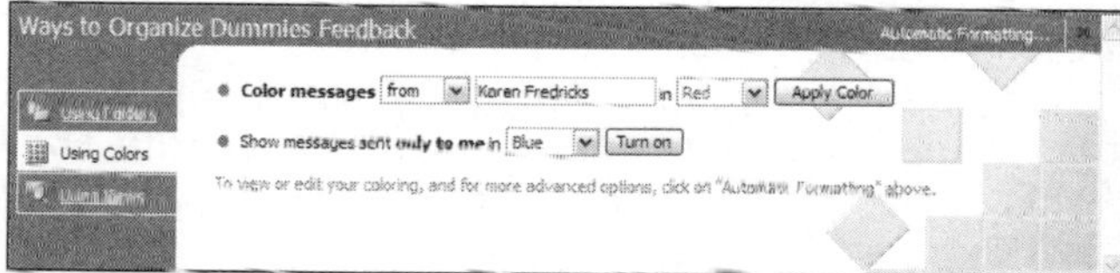

Figure 1-6: Assigning a color to an e-mail message.

You may want to avoid selecting white as your color because it's pretty much impossible to read white wording on a white background.

If you are organizing Contact records, or Calendar, Journal, or Task items, you are given the option to categorize them rather than color coding them.

- **Using Views:** You can change the view for the currently selected folder to make selecting records even easier. For example, using the Sent To view makes it easy to follow-up on tasks for e-mail that was sent to a specific address.

4. Click another folder in the Folder List to close the Organize window.

Playing Favorites with Your Favorite Folders

Most people have favorite things — an old pair of jeans, their blankie — that they'd like to keep nearby at all times. The more you use Outlook, the more folders you create. The more folders you create, the harder navigating through the Folder List becomes. No worries. With Outlook, you can designate *Favorite Folders.*

Favorite Folders are a great way for you to organize your e-mail so that you can find your most important e-mails easily. However, the Favorite Folders do have a few minor limitations:

- ✦ You can add only e-mail folders to Favorite Folders.
- ✦ You can create Favorite Folders from subfolders but not from the main Inbox.

Because Search Folders are based on e-mail, you can create Favorite Folders from them. Then you can customize the folder list to provide quick access to the types of messages you need the most. For example, you can create a Search Folder for all messages that need follow-up, and name it *Needs Follow-up.*

Adding folders to your Favorite Folders

You can literally add a folder to your favorites in the blink of an eye by using one of the following methods:

- ✦ Right-click the folder you want to designate a favorite, and then choose Add to Favorite Folders from the shortcut menu.
- ✦ Drag a folder from the Folder List to the Favorite Folders pane.

Finding your favorites

Creating Favorite Folders is the easy part. Finding them again can be perplexing. When you create a Favorite Folder, you access the folder from either the Folder List or from the Favorite Folders.

Because you can only create Favorite Folders for your e-mail subfolder, you can access them only when you are in the Mail view. Here's what you need to do:

1. **Click the Mail icon at the bottom of the Navigation pane.**

   Figure 1-7 shows you the Navigation pane in Mail view.

2. **Expand the Favorites Folders by clicking the two down arrows.**
3. **Select your Favorite Folder by clicking it.**

Changing the order of your Favorite Folders

After you create a Favorite Folder or two — and find them on the Navigation pane — you can switch their order. You can arrange your favorites in the order that makes the most sense to you; unlike regular folders in the Folder List, your Favorite Folders don't have to be in alphabetical order.

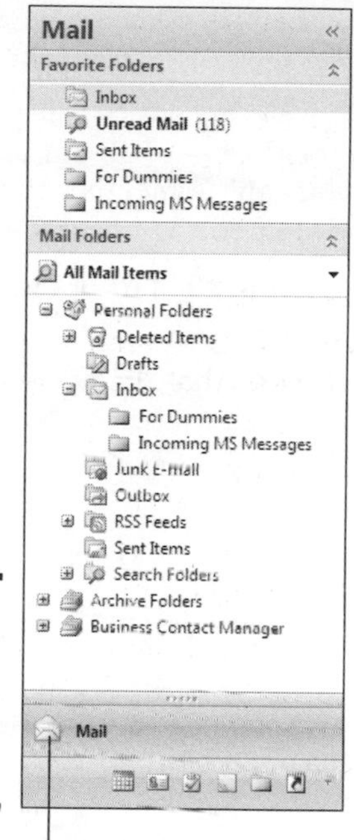

Figure 1-7: The Navigation pane in Mail view.

You can change the order of your Favorite Folders in two ways:

- ✦ Click a folder in the Favorite Folders list and drag it to a new location in the Favorite Folders list.
- ✦ Right-click a folder in the Favorite Folders list and then click Move Up in List or Move Down in List on the shortcut menu.

Linking a Web page to a Favorite Folder

After you use Outlook a while, you may find yourself addicted. You open Outlook first thing in the morning, every morning. You feel pangs of separation anxiety when you close it. Outlook feels so familiar and comfortable, that you are hesitant to wander into other programs on your computer. Don't worry; it's normal to feel this way. When you get to this point (and you will), you may want to add a Web site or two to Outlook so that you don't have to wander away from Outlook into the cruel, hard world of your oh-so-deficient Web browser any more often than necessary.

Even if you're not an Outlook junkie, adding a frequently accessed site or two is another cool way to organize your life. For example, you may have an Inbox subfolder for one of your top clients and include another subfolder to access their Web site directly from Outlook.

Here's how:

1. **Create a new folder in the Navigation pane.**

   You can create any kind of new folder you like — Mail, Contact, or whatever makes the most sense to you. If you can't remember the exact steps flip back to the section, "Creating a new folder."

2. **Right-click the new folder and choose Properties from the shortcut menu.**

   The folder Properties dialog box opens. Note that the dialog box is named after the folder you right-clicked.

3. **Click the Home Page tab (shown in Figure 1-8).**

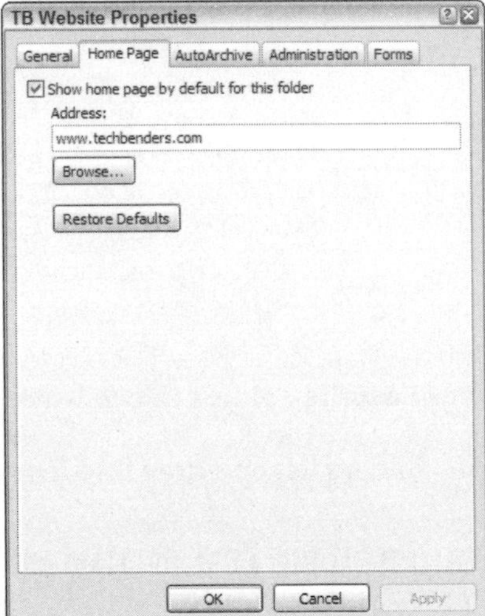

Figure 1-8: Linking a Web site to a new folder.

4. **Enter the address of the Web page you want to use as the folder's home page in the Address text box.**

   Type the Web page address exactly as you would in Internet Explorer. Be sure to include the `http://` and/or the `www.`, if necessary.

5. **Select the Show Home Page By Default for This Folder check box, and then click OK.**

   When you click the folder, the Web page appears in Outlook. As you can see in Figure 1-9, Outlook even opens a Web toolbar.

If you create the Web folder as an Inbox subfolder, you can add it to your Favorite Folders. Simply right-click the folder and choose Add to Favorite Folders from the shortcut menu.

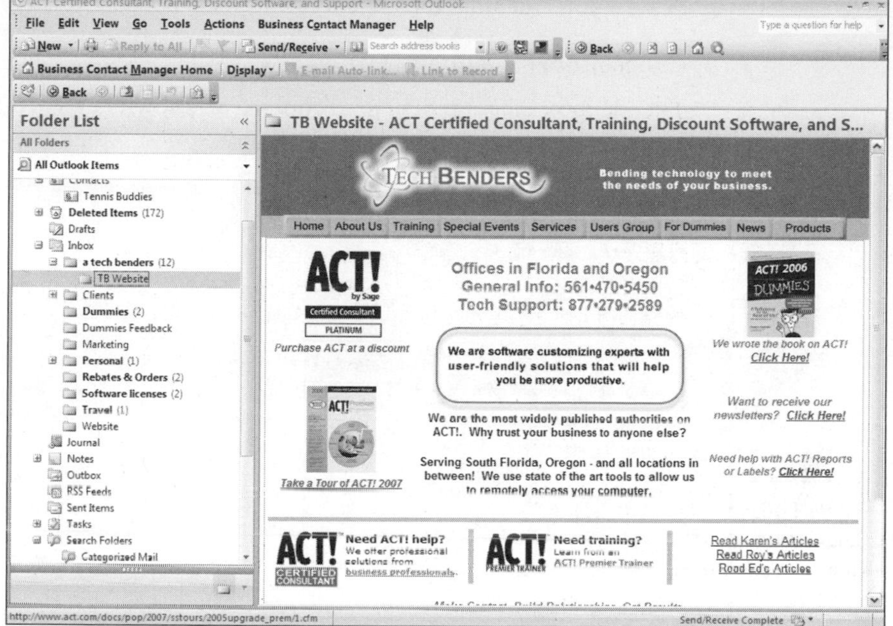

Figure 1-9: An Outlook folder that contains a Web site.

Cleaning Up Your Mess

Needless to say, as you create and receive more and more Outlook items, your Outlook file is going to get bigger and bigger. Having a bloated data file slows down your search when you try to find an item or, even worse, makes Outlook slow to open. You may also find that creating a backup of a large data file takes a lo-o-o-ng time.

Most people have at least a few tools to help keep up with housekeeping at their homes. Similarly, Outlook has several cleanup tools up its sleeve.

Giving your folders a bit of spring cleaning

Having an excessive amount of e-mail is probably the biggest culprit of Outlook data bloat. Theoretically, you could skim through every one of your Outlook folders and start cleaning them. However, Outlook's Mailbox Cleanup tool gives you a bit more direction if you follow a two-step process:

- ✦ Evaluate the size of each of your Outlook folders so that you know which ones are the ones that you'll want to start pruning.
- ✦ Search for items that match specific criteria so that you can apply some logic to exactly which items you get rid of.

Here's how you can start the cleanup process:

1. Choose Tools➪Mailbox Cleanup.

The Mailbox Cleanup dialog box opens, as shown in Figure 1-10.

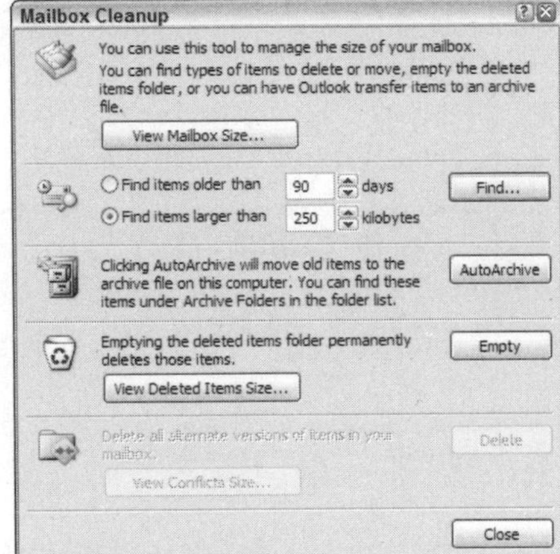

Figure 1-10: Cleaning up your mailbox.

2. Click the View Mailbox Size button and do a bit of sleuthing.

The Folder Size dialog box opens (see Figure 1-11). This dialog box allows you to get a handle on which of your folders are manageable and which ones need to be put on a diet. Oddly enough, even though you clicked the View Mailbox Size button to arrive here, you can view the size of *all* your folders.

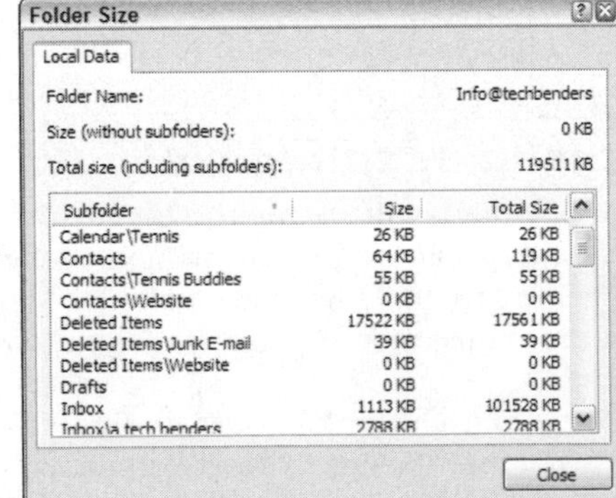

Figure 1-11: Viewing the size of your Outlook folders.

3. **Make note of any of the folders that need to go on a quick weight-loss plan, and then click the Close button.**

   Although the Folder Size dialog box doesn't let you reduce the size of your folders immediately, it allows you to decide which of your folders should be pruned, archived, or deleted entirely.

4. **Select and indicate one of the Find options, and click the Find button.**

   - **Find items older than *x* days:** Enter a number between 1 and 999.
   - **Find items larger than *x* kilobytes:** Enter a number between 1 and 9,999.

   The Advanced Find dialog box opens (see Figure 1-12). By default, you see all the e-mail that matches the criteria you entered.

5. **Click the Browse button to browse to a different Outlook folder.**

   This is where the detective work that you did in Step 3 comes into play. You'll probably want to browse to the folders that you feel are in the most need of cleaning.

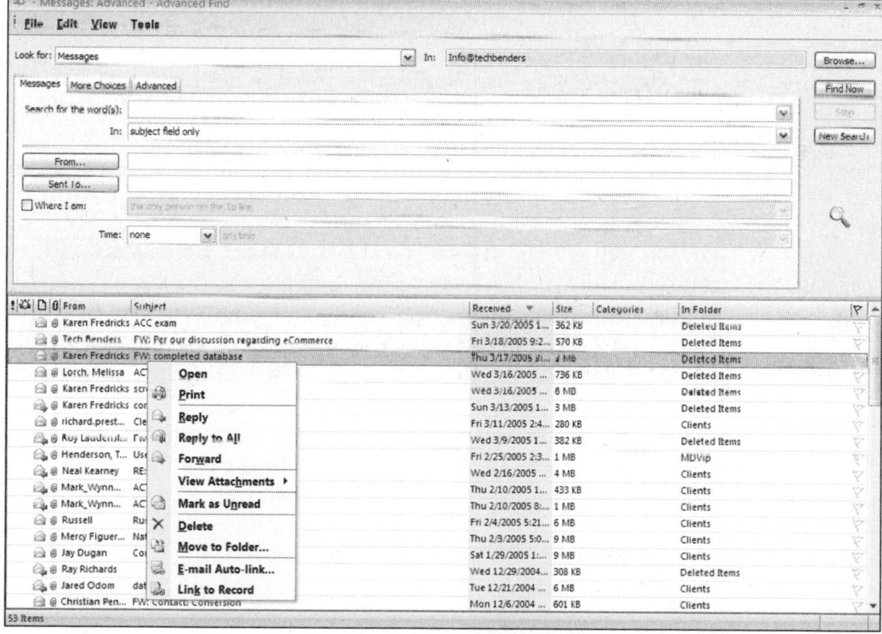

Figure 1-12: Being specific about the Outlook items you want to clean up.

6. **(Optional) Refine your search by filling in additional information in the various search fields of the Advanced Find dialog box.**

   You can create a very targeted search by looking for specific keywords and indicating where to look for them. For example, you might look for the word "contract" in the subject line of e-mail messages. You can even search for messages that were sent from or to a specific individual.

7. **Select items from the Advanced Find pane and give them a right-click. Choose which cleanup option you want:**

   - **Delete** to get rid of the selected items permanently.
   - **Move to Folder** to relocate the selected items to another Outlook folder.

8. **Click the X in the upper-right corner to close the Advanced Find dialog box or click New Search to hunt down more items to clean up.**

   No one said that cleaning up your data would be an immediate process. You may need to hunt through a whole lot of folders, cleaning as you go. By doing a bit of advanced scouting, however, you'll have a good idea of where to start.

   - To view the size of your Deleted Items folder, click View Deleted Items Size.
   - To empty your Deleted Items folder, click Empty.
   - To view the size of your Conflicts folder, click View Conflicts Size.
   - To delete the contents of your Conflicts folder, click Delete.

Sending your data to the trash compactor

When you add new items to your data file, Outlook puts them on the top of the file. When you delete an item, a gap forms in the middle of the data file. Then, when you add new items, some of the information may be in the middle of your data file while the rest of it appears at the top of your data file.

You can reduce the size of your data file by compacting it. Compacting your data file squeezes out all of the air bubbles out of it. Although the procedure takes several minutes, the steps to get there take only a minute:

1. **Choose File⇨Data File Management.**

   The Account Settings dialog box opens (see Figure 1-13).

2. **Select the data file that you want to compact and then click Settings.**

   The Personal Folders dialog box springs to attention, as shown in Figure 1-14.

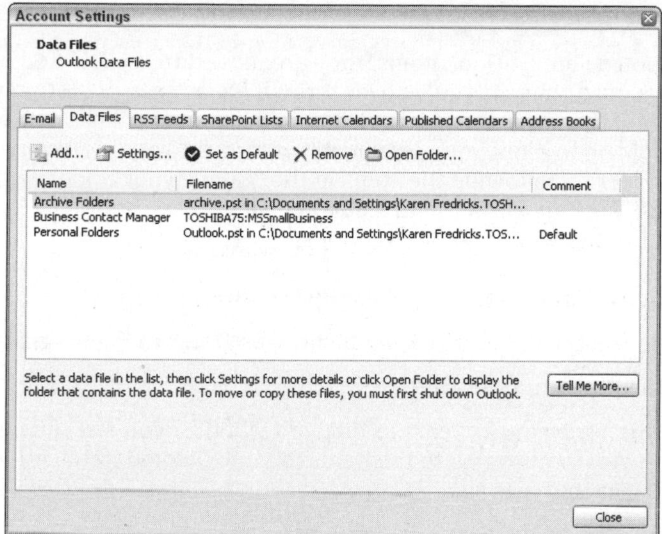

Figure 1-13: Outlook's Account Settings dialog box.

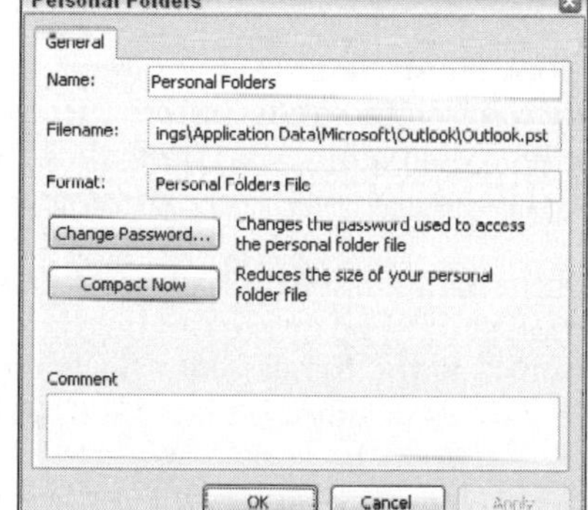

Figure 1-14: The Personal Folders dialog box.

3. **Click the Compact Now button.**

   Wait patiently for Outlook to compact your data file. You may want to wave a dust mop around and explain to the rest of the office that you are cleaning your data file.

4. **Click OK to close the Personal Folders dialog box, and then click Close to close the Account Settings dialog box.**

Emptying the trash

When you delete Outlook items, they are moved to the Deleted Items folder. This is a good thing; if you've ever thrown out a piece of clothing only to find a day later that you really wanted it, you'll know what I mean. However, you can't hold on to all of your deleted items forever. You can empty your Deleted Items folder by following the steps in the "Giving your folders a bit of spring cleaning" section, earlier in this chapter. Or you can get rid of them in one fell swoop by following these instructions:

1. **Choose Tools➪Mailbox Cleanup.**

   The Mailbox Cleanup dialog box opens (refer to Figure 1-10).

2. **Click the Empty button.**

   A stern warning appears asking you whether you are 100 percent positive you want to delete the items in your Deleted Items folder on a permanent basis.

3. **Click Yes to the scary warning message.**

   Say *sayonara* to the contents of your Deleted Items folder, because they are now gone — permanently.

If you prefer, you can have Outlook empty your Deleted Items folder each time you exit Outlook. To empty the Deleted Items automatically, choose Tools➪Options to open the Options dialog box, and then click the Other tab and select the Empty the Deleted Items Folder Upon Exiting check box.

If you set the option to allow Outlook to empty the Deleted Items folder every time you close Outlook, you should be aware of one thing: Outlook deletes the entire contents of your Deleted Items folder permanently without stopping to take prisoners. This process cannot be reversed, so choose this option carefully!

This is one for the archives

Outlook's Personal Folder file (`outlook.pst`) contains all your current data. However, Outlook also allows you to create another file (`archive.pst`) that is used to hold all your items that you no longer use but still want to keep close at hand. Best of all, you can put the archive file in "set it and forget it" mode, which means that Outlook periodically move items from your current Outlook file to your archive file. Talk about speed cleaning!

When you archive a folder, all the items in that folder that match your criteria are moved into an archival folder. Generally, you move old items, making it easier to work with the latest and greatest information. Should you happen to need to look at some of your older items, you can easily access them by looking at the archival folders.

Turning AutoArchive on autopilot

The first thing you'll need to know is how to check to see if AutoArchive is working and, if so, how you can shut it off if necessary. Once you turn on AutoArchive, you can specify which folders you'd like to have Outlook archive for you.

1. **Choose Tools⇨Options.**

   The Options dialog box opens.

2. **Select the Other tab and then click the AutoArchive button.**

   The AutoArchive dialog box opens (see Figure 1-15).

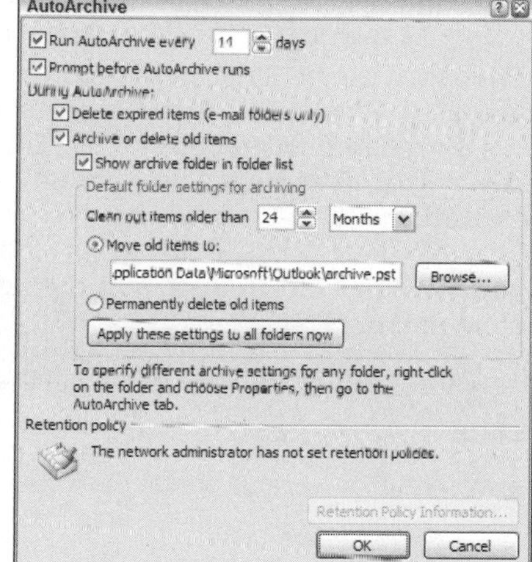

Figure 1-15: Setting up AutoArchive to archive old information automatically.

3. **Choose the AutoArchive options.**

   As you can see from Figure 1-15, Outlook can archive your data in a variety of ways. You can have Outlook:

   - Run AutoArchive every *x* days.
   - Prompt before AutoArchive runs.
   - Delete expired items.

- Show the Archive Folders in the folder list.
- Indicate the time frame used to identify "old" items.
- Indicate whether you want to move items to the archive folders or delete them permanently.

4. **Click OK to close the AutoArchive dialog box, and then click OK again to close the Options dialog box.**

Remove the check mark in the Run AutoArchive every *x* days option if you do not want Outlook to automatically archive your data.

By default, Outlook AutoArchives all your data folders.

Removing AutoArchive from individual folders

By default, the AutoArchive feature archives all your data folders. In general, the whole idea behind archiving is to keep the really important stuff around for posterity. When Outlook archives your data, it moves it into separate archive folders and creates an entirely new `.pst` file.

You may not consider archiving the Deleted Items folder to be necessary. On the other hand, you may have a few folders that are so important, you don't want any of the items in them moved into an archival folder. Therefore, Outlook provides you with a way to turn archiving on — or off — on a folder-by-folder basis. Here's how it works:

1. **Right-click the folder you want to AutoArchive, and then choose Properties on the shortcut menu.**

   Unfortunately, you have to do this on a folder-by-folder basis.

2. **Click the AutoArchive tab.**

   As shown in Figure 1-16, you have several archival options you can choose:

   - Do not archive items in this folder
   - Archive items using the default settings
   - Archive folder using custom settings including moving the archived items to a new folder or deleting them completely

3. **Click OK to close the folder Properties dialog box.**

   From this point forward the folder is governed by the rules you just set each time Outlook runs AutoArchive.

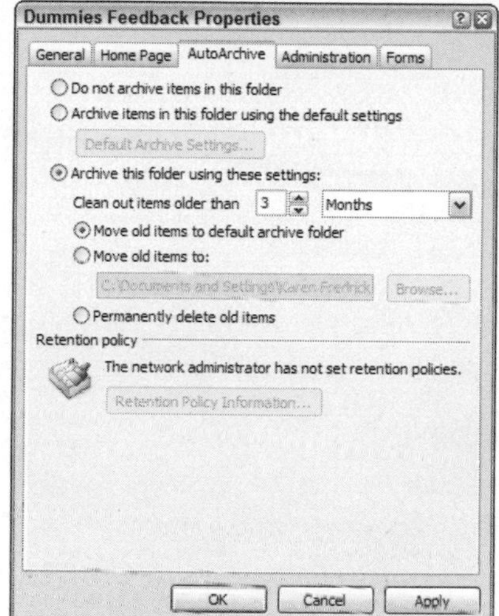

Figure 1-16: Changing the Archive options for an individual folder.

Archiving items manually

As nice as the thought is of archiving your information automatically, you might feel more comfortable doing it on your own time schedule rather than on an automated one. Outlook is cool with that. Here's how you do it:

1. **Choose File⇨Archive.**

   The Archive dialog box opens, as shown in Figure 1-17.

2. **Choose the Folders you want to archive:**

   - **Archive All Folders Using Their AutoArchive Settings:** This option archives all the folders for which you had set archiving options.
   - **Archive This Folder and All Subfolders:** This option archives only the folder you select.

3. **(Optional) Select a date to determine which items you consider "old" enough to archive.**

4. **(Optional) Specify a different filename in the Archive file box if you want to archive your items to a file other than the default archive file.**

5. **Click OK to archive your data or Cancel to exit without archiving.**

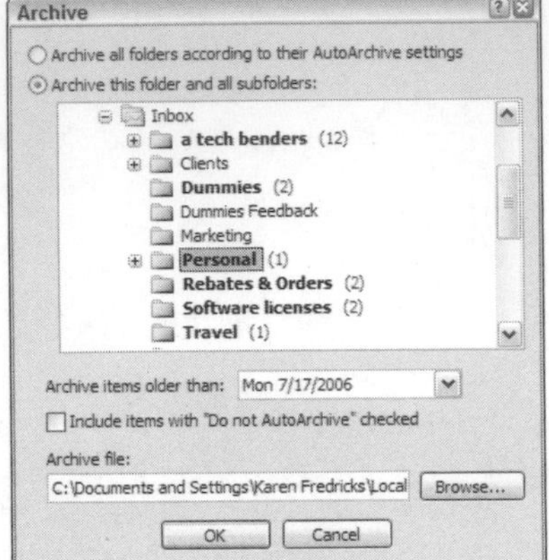

Figure 1-17: Choosing the archive options manually.

Looking into the archives

The cool thing about archiving your Outlook data is that the information you archived is still right at your fingertips — you don't have to go through a lengthy "restore" to get to it.

To get a peek at your archived data, follow these steps:

1. **Choose File⇨Open⇨Outlook Data File.**

   The Open Outlook Data File dialog box appears.

2. **Choose `archive.pst` (or whatever you named your archive file) from the Open Outlook Data File dialog box, and click OK.**

3. **Click the plus sign next to *Archive Folders* at the bottom of the Folder List.**

   The folders you've archived are listed there as shown in Figure 1-18. Click any of the Archive Folders, and the contents appear in the main Outlook pane. You'll notice that the contents of the Archive Folders are somewhat dated because, after all, they contain only those items you deemed old enough to archive.

Restoring from an archive

Don't panic if you accidentally archive too much data and find that you are missing critical information from your regular Outlook folders. You can drag items from an Archive folder back to a regular folder manually, or you can copy the contents of all your Archive Folders back to their original state by importing the `archive.pst` file back into your main `outlook.pst` file.

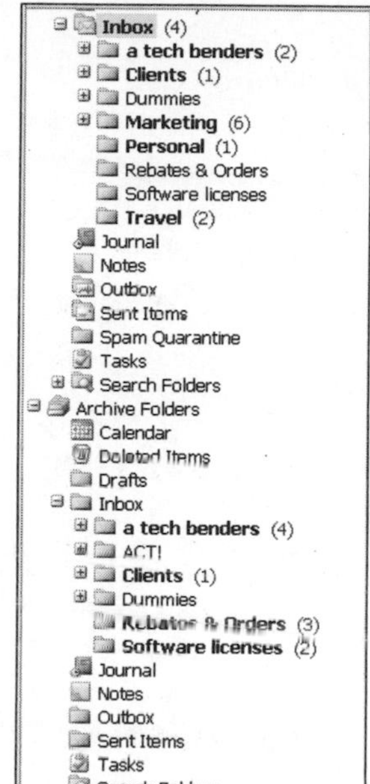

Figure 1-18: Looking at your Archive Folders.

In order to import the `archive.pst` file into the `outlook.pst` file, you need to close the archive file by right-clicking it and choosing Close "Archive Folders" from the shortcut menu.

Follow these steps to restore a file from the archive:

1. **Choose File⇨Import and Export⇨Outlook.**

   Outlook's Import and Export Wizard opens. The Import from Another Program or File option should already be highlighted as shown in Figure 1-19.

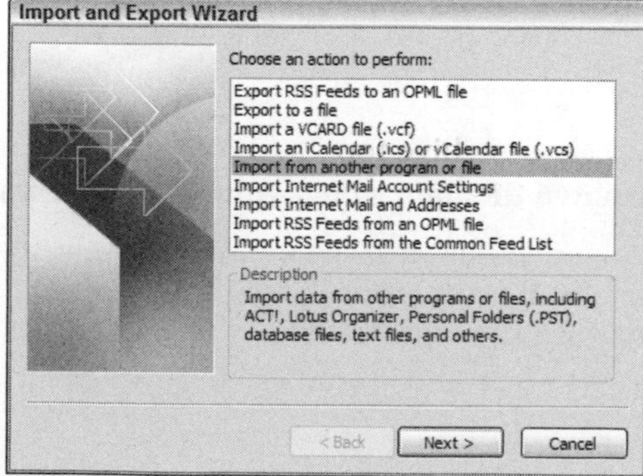

Figure 1-19: Importing your archived information back into Outlook.

2. Click Next to continue.

The Import a File dialog box opens; see Figure 1-20.

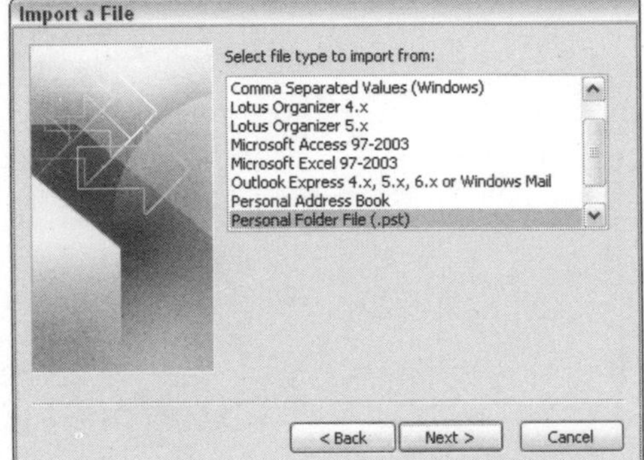

Figure 1-20: Selecting the file type to import into Outlook.

3. Select Personal Folder File (`.pst`) and then click Next.

You'd think that because your selected Outlook in the first step you wouldn't have to indicate in this step as well. So much for logical assumptions! In any event, the next screen of the wizard appears; see Figure 1-21.

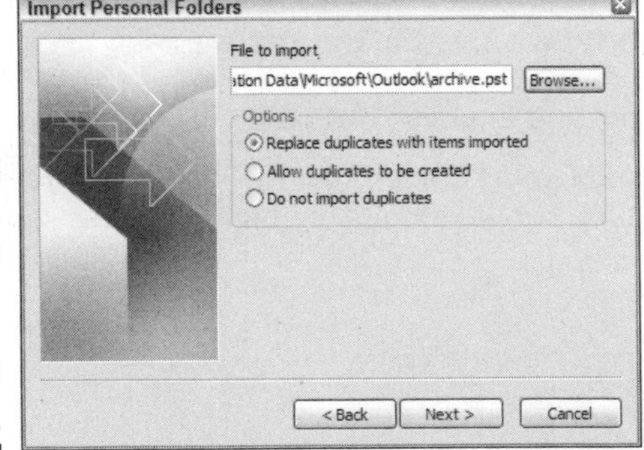

Figure 1-21: Dealing with duplicates when importing an archive file.

4. Browse for your archive file, and select your duplicate import options.

You can replace any duplicates with the imported items, allow duplicates to be created, or not import duplicates. You'll probably find that replacing duplicates with the imported items is your safest bet.

5. Click Next to continue.

The next screen of the wizard appears (see Figure 1-22).

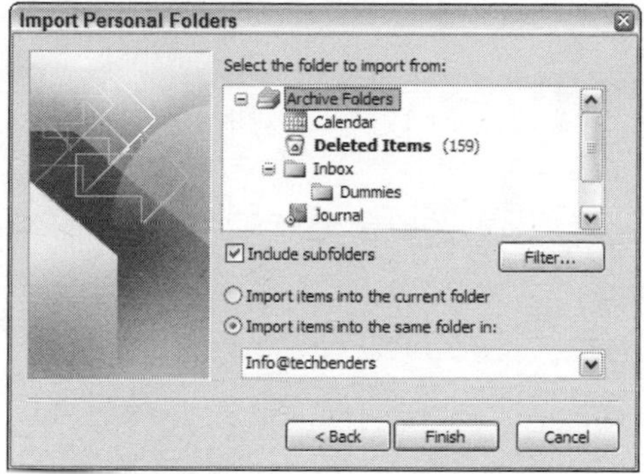

Figure 1-22: Select a folder.

6. Select your import options.

You have a few choices here, as shown in Figure 1-22.

- Select the archive folder you want to import.
- (Optional) Select the Include Subfolders check box if you'd like to include all the subfolders, as well.
- Select the Import Items Into The Current Folder option if you want to restore your archive to one folder or the Import Items Into The Same Folder option if you want the archival items to return to their original location.

7. Click Finish to close the Import Wizard and place all the archived items back to their original homes.

Chapter 2: Playing by the Rules

In This Chapter

- Creating basic e-mail rules
- Creating advanced rules
- Managing the rules

It's always nice to play by the rules — at least, that's probably what your Mother told you when you were little. As an adult, it's even more fun to play by the rules when you get to create them yourself. This chapter shows you how to transform Outlook into a smart mail clerk that grabs all your incoming e-mails and sorts them automatically for you. Best of all, should your life change, you can easily change the rules to better suit your new status without the risk of having several game pieces thrown back into your face.

Making Up the Rules as You Go

You can probably visualize a typical mailroom in your mind: Someone with a huge basket of new mail diligently sorts through the pile and places each piece of mail into the appropriate mailbox. That is the very same concept used by Outlook. As your incoming e-mail pours in, Outlook can sort that mail and place it into the appropriate folder.

Creating the basic game plan

The main purpose of an Outlook rule is to make sure that nothing gets lost in the shuffle. Many situations can arise where a rule can make your life — or at least your e-mail — much more manageable:

- ✦ You have a very important client, and you want to make sure that all his e-mail gets sent to a specific folder and/or flagged for follow-up.
- ✦ You'd like to move any e-mail that you receive from a specific group of contacts to a specific folder.
- ✦ You'd like to move mail that you've sent to various people to specific folders.
- ✦ You'd like all incoming e-mail that contains specific words in the subject line to end up in a specified folder.

- You'd like to have Outlook sound an alarm anytime a message arrives from your boss, spouse, or someone else with high placement on the food chain.

In case you're wondering whether these rules apply to moving junk mail — yes, they do. If you take a peek at the next chapter, you can find out how Outlook makes mincemeat out of spam.

After you decide on your course of action, it's fairly easy to put your plan into play by following these steps.

1. **Click on the Inbox from Outlook's folder list.**

   The rules you are creating work with your e-mail, so it's only fitting that your Inbox becomes your starting line.

   Rules are associated with a specific Inbox. If you have subdivided your Inbox into subfolders, you can create a rule for anyone of those subfolders.

2. **Choose Tools⇨Rules and Alerts.**

   The Rules and Alerts dialog box appears as shown in Figure 2-1.

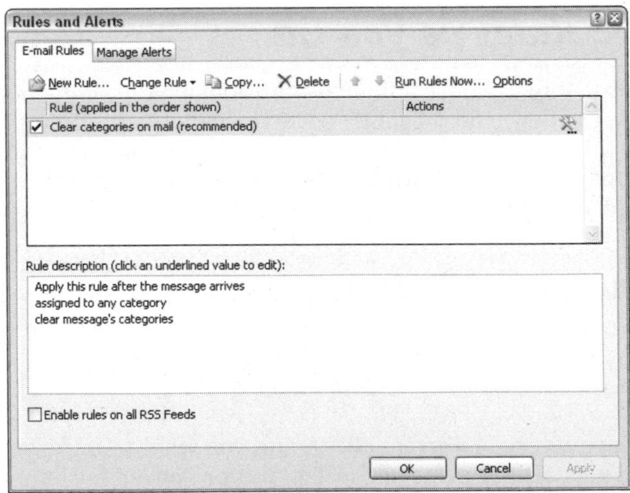

Figure 2-1: The Rules and Alerts dialog box.

3. **Click the New Rule button.**

   If all systems are go, you see the Rules Wizard as shown in Figure 2-2.

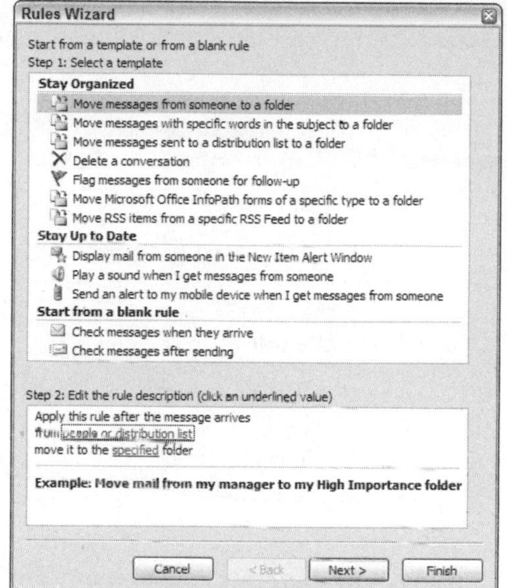

Figure 2-2: The Rules Wizard dialog box.

Notice that the top portion of the window includes three subsections:

- **Stay Organized:** These are rule templates designed to move your data to a new location.
- **Stay Up to Date:** These rule templates determine how you want to be informed when a new message arrives.
- **Start from a Blank Rule:** These are do-it-yourself, non-templated rules that you can use when none of the one-size-fits-all rules seem to fit.

If you scroll down the list of rule options, you notice two things:

- The values that you need to enter in the bottom of the dialog box change.
- Outlook gives you an example of how the rule works.

This is a great way to get a better understanding of how each of the rule templates work.

The Move Messages from Someone to a Folder option is highlighted; that's probably the most common type of rule you'll create.

4. **Click the People or Distribution List link in the Step 2 area of the Rules Wizard dialog box.**

   Outlook bends over backwards to try to make this process as easy as possible for you. Think of this as one-stop clicking because you don't even have to click the Next button to create a basic rule.

   The Rule Address dialog box opens, as shown in Figure 2-3.

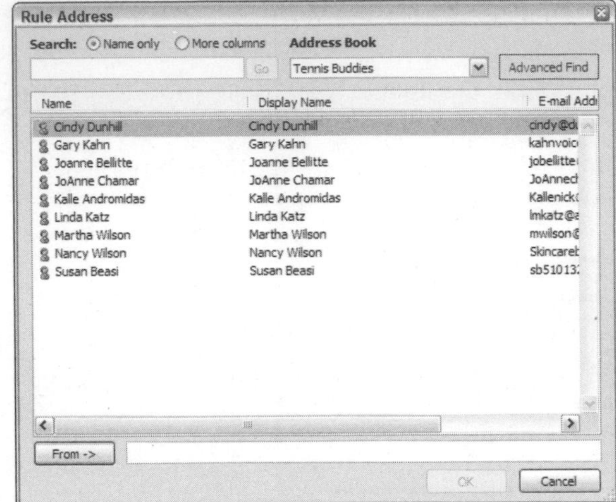

Figure 2-3: The Rule Address dialog box.

5. **Select the names to whom you want this rule to apply and click the From button.**

   If you've created individual contact folders, you can choose one of them from the Address Book drop-down list. You have several ways to select the names:

   - **To select a single name:** Click it.
   - **To select multiple names:** Hold down the Ctrl key and click the desired names.
   - **To search for a contact by first name:** Type the first few letters of the person's first name and then double-click the name when Outlook highlights it.

6. **(Optional) Click the More columns radio button if you can't find a contact.**

   This method is a bit trickier but nothing a beginner can't handle:

   - Type your search criteria (for example, a contact's last name or company) in the Search box and then click the Go button.
   - Double-click the name when it appears.
   - Repeat the process if you'd like to add a few more names, and then click OK when you're finished to return to the Rules Wizard dialog box.

7. **Click the specified folder option on the Rules Wizard dialog box.**

   The Rules and Alerts dialog box, which is slightly different from the Rules and Alerts dialog box that you saw in Figure 2-2, opens. Go figure!

8. **Select the folder to which you want to move the e-mail messages and click OK.**

   You are returned to the Rules Wizard dialog box. The bottom of the window looks something like Figure 2-4.

9. **Click Finish to, well, finish and then OK to close the Rules and Alerts dialog box.**

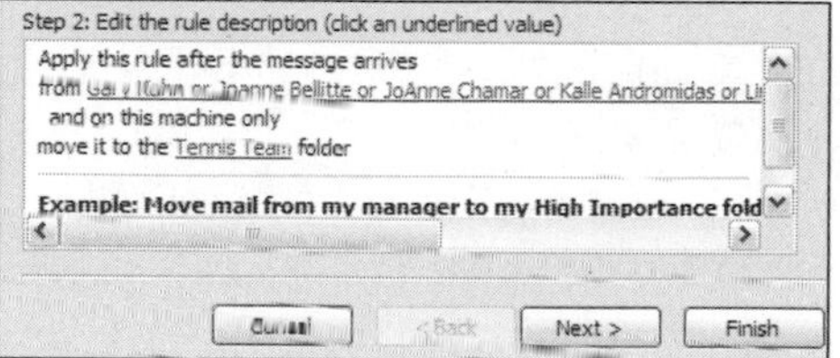

Figure 2-4: A rule moving e-mail from specific contacts to a specified folder.

Adding bells and whistles to your rules

When you were little, you probably made up games with your friends. After a while, you might have decided to tweak the rules of the game a bit — so that they were more in your favor. The previous section shows you how to create a basic rule. In this section, you see how to bend those rules so that they keep you even more organized.

Return to the scene of the crime — or at least of your original rule — to tweak an existing rule. Here's what you need to do:

1. **Click the Inbox from Outlook's folder list.**
2. **Choose Tools⇨Rules and Alerts.**

   The Rules and Alerts dialog box appears.

3. **Select an existing rule and then click the Change Rule button.**

   You can see a sample of the Change Rule menu in Figure 2-5.

4. **Click a rule option, fill in the required information, and click OK.**

   The Rules Wizard dialog box opens as shown in Figure 2-6. Several cool options are available to you here at no additional cost. Best of all, they are easy to implement because each one requires you to select an option or fill in your wording.

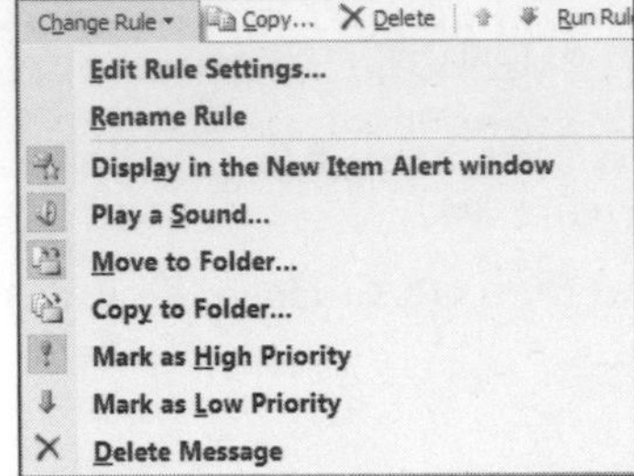

Figure 2-5: Various options for editing an existing rule.

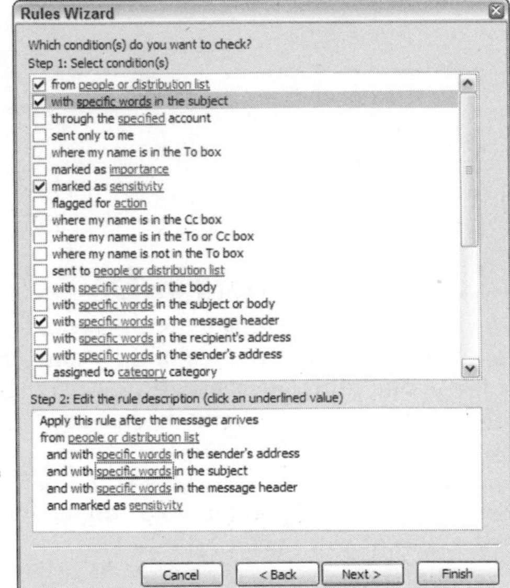

Figure 2-6: The Rules Wizard.

The options work on a toggle basis; the first time you click an option, you're prompted to fill in the required information. The next time you click that option, your preference setting is removed.

- **Rename Rule:** When you originally create a rule using a template, Outlook names the rule for you automatically with a catchy title. For example, if you created a rule to move all the mail from Joe Blow to the Real Important Stuff folder, Outlook would name your rule "Joe Blow." You might want to give your rule a snappy moniker such as "Stuff from the Boss Man."

- **Display in the New Item Alert Window:** Use this option if you are just dying to know when you receive an e-mail from someone. You receive a special Alert just like the one you see in Figure 2-7; this is particularly effective because you can assign a name to the alert, such as Holy Guacamole.

Figure 2-7: A special alert.

- **Play a Sound:** You can assign a sound to play when the special e-mail arrives, such as Beethoven's Fifth or an eloquent Ta-Da.
- **Move to Folder:** Here's your chance to change the folder your e-mail moves to if you're not happy with the location you originally selected for storage.
- **Copy to Folder:** If you want to be doubly sure that your e-mail won't get lost in the crowd, you might consider copying it to a new folder and leaving it in your Inbox until you have followed up on it.
- **Mark as High Priority:** Here's how you can automatically flag an important incoming e-mail as a high priority.
- **Mark as Low Priority:** Tired of your nagging mother or a high-maintenance client? You can have Outlook mark their messages as low priority items.
- **Delete Message:** Use this option to automatically delete an e-mail that arrives from a specific person; this works especially well when dealing with ex-spouses.

When you're finished tweaking your rule, it may look something like the rule you see in Figure 2-8.

5. **Click OK to save your rule.**

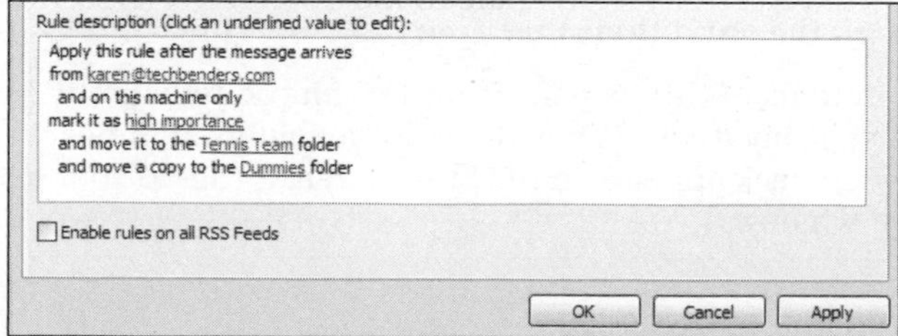

Figure 2-8: A sample of a customized rule.

Taking Rules the Whole Nine Yards

By now you're probably thinking that you have customized your rule in every way possible. But wait. In several situations, you may need an even more sophisticated rule:

- ✦ You want only the e-mails that come in from Mr. Big to be transferred to another folder if they are set at a certain priority level.
- ✦ You are tracking multiple e-mail addresses, and you want the mail clerk (or in this case Outlook) to sort your messages into corresponding folders.
- ✦ You want to move all the bounced e-mail that is returned to you into another folder so that you can take further action later.
- ✦ You want to be on the lookout for e-mail that contains specific words or phrases.

All these situations can be handled through the use of Outlook rules. And, even though you might need a very complex and complicated rule, Outlook comes equipped with a handy dandy wizard to guide you through the process.

1. **Click on the Inbox from Outlook's folder list.**
2. **Choose Tools⇨Rules and Alerts.**

   The Rules and Alerts dialog box appears (refer to Figure 2-1).
3. **Select an existing rule from the Rules and Alerts dialog box, click the Change Rule button and choose Edit Rule Settings.**

   Alternatively, if you are brave and want to develop the rule from scratch, click the New Rule button, select Check Messages When They Arrive from the Rules Wizard dialog box, and then click Next.

   One advantage of choosing the New Rule button is that you can select the Check Messages After Sending option to create a rule that is applied *after* you send a message.

   Both options take you to the Rules Wizard (refer to Figure 2-6).

   Although the Rules Wizard looks a bit daunting at first, it's relatively easy to master.
4. **Select all the conditions that apply to your rule.**

   You can think of this as your favorite Chinese restaurant — feel free to select as many items as you'd like from column A. A description of each item you check appears in the Step 2 area at the bottom of the Rules Wizard window.

5. **Fill in the details for each condition that you selected by clicking the underlined words in the Rules description area, filling in the appropriate details, and clicking OK.**

   Figure 2-9 shows an example of the dialog box that opens when you click the specific words option.

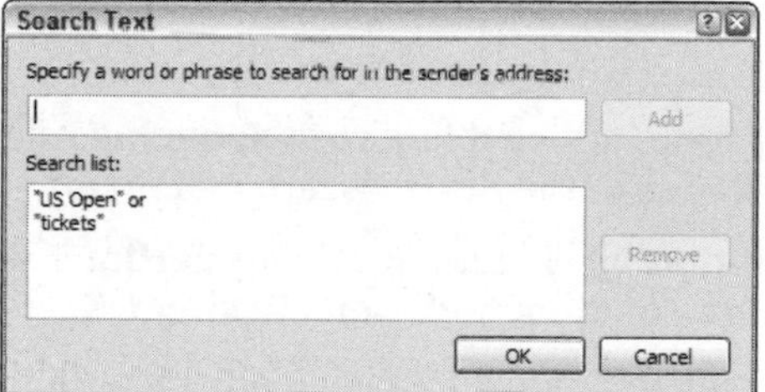

Figure 2-9: Adding specific words to the rule's searching criteria.

6. **Click Next in the Rules Wizard to continue.**

   The second screen of the Rules Wizard is shown in Figure 2-10.

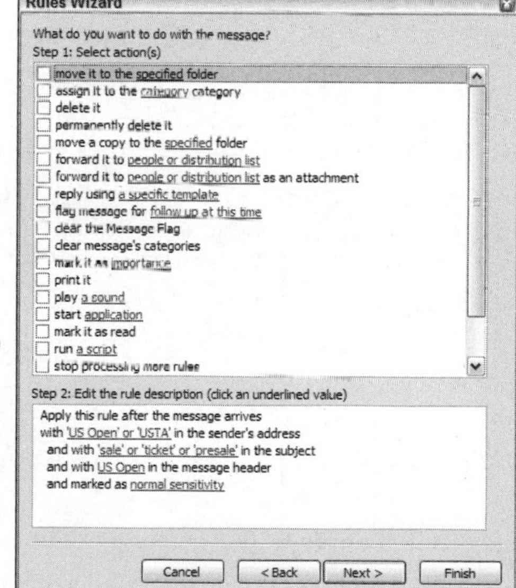

Figure 2-10: Determining the course of action your rule is going to take.

7. **Select the actions that you want Outlook to take.**

   Several courses of action are available to you. Here are a few that you might find particularly useful:

   - Assign the e-mail to a category.
   - Forward the e-mail to someone else.
   - Flag the message or mark it as important.
   - Print the message.

   As you select each action, notice that a corresponding rule description appears in the Step 2 area of the Rules Wizard dialog box.

8. **Edit the rule description by clicking on the underlined values, filling in the appropriate information, and then clicking OK.**

   For example, if you selected Category as one of your actions, you click on category in the rule description area and select one of your categories.

9. **Click Next to continue.**

   The third screen of the Rules Wizard opens as shown in Figure 2-11.

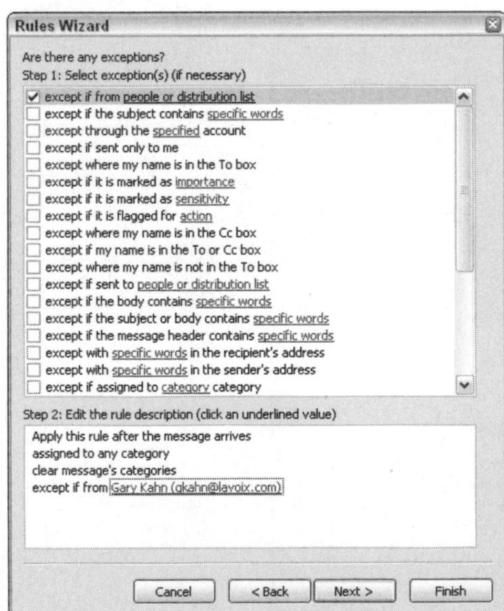

Figure 2-11: Creating exceptions to the rule.

10. **(Optional) Select any exceptions to the rule. Then edit the rule description by clicking the underlined value, filling in the appropriate information, and then clicking OK.**

    If you believe that there is an exception to every rule, here's your chance to prove your point. For example, you might want to run a rule except when the message comes from a specific person or already has been assigned a category.

11. **Click Next to continue.**

    Finally! You've arrived at the last step of the wizard; see Figure 2-12.

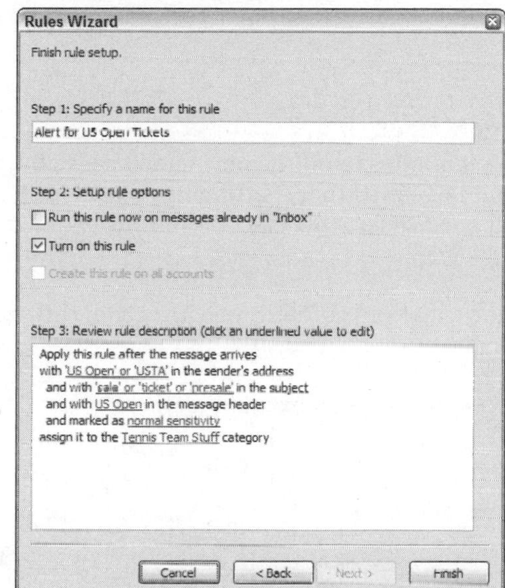

Figure 2-12: The last step of the Rules Wizard.

12. **You have a few more simple choices to make.**

    - Specify a name for the rule.
    - Indicate whether you want to run the rule on existing messages in your Inbox.
    - Indicate whether you want to turn on the rule.

    You might also give your rule the once over for accuracy.

13. **Click Finish to close the Rules Wizard and then OK to close the Rules and Alerts dialog box.**

14. **(Optional) Give yourself a high five as you think about how organized you've become!**

Bending the Rules

Although you may not agree that rules are meant to be broken, you might want to bend them a bit. You might want to temporarily turn off a rule or use one of your rules for the basis of another rule.

Running with the rules

After you create your rule, you may find that it's not working. You may go back and double-check the rule for accuracy, following the preceding steps to no avail. In life, the best solution is often the simplest solution. This idea is particularly true in the computer world. Your rule might not be working because you've never run it on your existing e-mail — or maybe the rule is just not turned on.

Teaching old e-mail new rules

When you create a rule, it applies to all the new e-mail that pours into your Inbox. But how about all the e-mail that's sitting in your Inbox waiting for you to take action? You need to run the rule on your Inbox one time to take care of all your existing e-mail.

If you create a new blank rule from scratch, you are given the option to run the rule on existing e-mail.

Follow these steps to run your rule on existing mail:

1. **Click the Inbox from Outlook's folder list.**
2. **Choose Tools⇨Rules and Alerts.**

   The Rules and Alerts dialog box appears (refer to Figure 2-1).
3. **Click the Run Rules Now button.**

   The Run Rules Now dialog box, shown in Figure 2-13, appears before your eyes.
4. **Select the rules that you want to run.**
5. **(Optional) Select a different Inbox folder by clicking the Browse button and selecting a different folder.**
6. **Click the Apply Rules To drop-down arrow to select the type of messages on which you want to run the rule.**

   You can run the rule on all messages, unread messages, or read messages.
7. **Click Close to close the Run Rules Now dialog box and then OK to close the Rules and Alerts dialog box.**

Figure 2-13: Applying a new rule to existing e-mail.

Making sure the rule is turned on

Conversely, your rule might be working too well, and you want to turn it off for a while so that you can think about what you want that rule to accomplish.

Here's what you do to turn a rule off — and back on again:

1. **Click the Inbox from Outlook's folder list.**
2. **Choose Tools➪Rules and Alerts.**

   The Rules and Alerts dialog box appears (refer to Figure 2-1). A slight feeling of déjà vu may be coming over you because you've definitely been here before!
3. **Clear the check box in front of the rule you want to turn off.**

   When you want to turn the rule back on again, make sure that you place a check mark in front of the rule once again.
4. **Click OK to finish.**

Cheating with the rules

Over the years, you've probably discovered a whole bunch of computer shortcuts. Most of us love shortcuts because they help us to get more things accomplished in less time. The same theory holds true with rules. After you spend hours slaving over a rule (or at least tell your boss that you've spent hours), you might want to clone your rule. Maybe you set up a cool rule to move all the e-mails from Mr. Big to the Mr. Big folder, mark them as important, and categorize them as green for money. Now you want to do the same thing for Mr. Grande. Or maybe one of your co-workers is so impressed by your Inbox organizational skills that she is willing to trade you a large plate of chocolate chip cookies for your list of rules.

Copying a rule

In general, it's easier to tweak an existing rule rather than to start over again from scratch. Copying a rule enables you to take an existing rule, clone it, and then make minor modifications to it. Here's all you need to do:

1. **Click on the Inbox from Outlook's folder list.**
2. **Choose Tools⇨Rules and Alerts.**

   The Rules and Alerts dialog box appears.
3. **Select the rule that you want to clone.**
4. **Click the Copy button.**

   The Copy Rule To dialog box opens (see Figure 2-14). By default, the new rule applies to your Inbox.

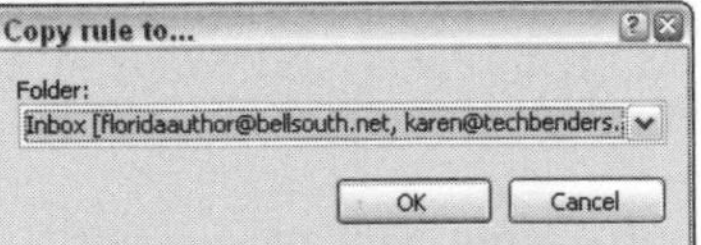

Figure 2-14: The Copy Rule To dialog box.

5. **Click OK to close the Copy Rule To dialog box.**
6. **Click OK to finish.**

   Your cloned rule now appears in your list of rules with a snappy name like "Copy of Mr. Big Rule." At this point you can modify the rule following the steps in the earlier section, "Creating the basic game plan."

Importing and exporting a list of rules

Every office generally has two types of computer users: those who can figure out most things and those who ask for help from the ones who can figure out most things. Because you've been reading this book, you are probably in that first group of computer users. Being in the know has a decided advantage: You can use your power to extract payment from the other, less-computer-literate members of the crowd.

Should one of the computer-challenged members of your office compliment you on your rules, you can export your list of rules and then import them into his copy of Outlook. Not only does this save a great deal of time, but you also look like a hero.

Exporting a list of rules

Exporting a list of rules is easy, if you follow these steps:

1. **Click on the Inbox from Outlook's folder list.**
2. **Choose Tools⇨Rules and Alerts.**
3. **Click the Options button.**

   The Options dialog box, just like the one shown in Figure 2-15, opens.

Figure 2-15: Exporting a list of rules.

4. **Click the Export Rules button.**
5. **Give the Export file a name, save it to the location of your choice, and click the Save button.**

   Outlook automatically assigns the `.rwz` extension to the file.

6. **Click OK to close the Options dialog box and then OK again to close the Rules and Alerts dialog box.**

It never hurts to have a backup. If you save the export file to an external source, you have a backup of your Outlook rules just in case something wacky should happen in the future.

Importing a list of rules

After you've successfully created an export file, you can import your rules to another computer. The rules in the import file are added to existing Outlook rules.

The going rate for a good list of Outlook rules is one large plate of cookies!

Import your rules with these steps:

1. **Click the Inbox from Outlook's folder list.**
2. **Choose Tools⇨Rules and Alerts.**
3. **Click the Options button on the Rules and Alerts dialog box and then click the Import Rules button in the Options dialog box.**
4. **Navigate to the location of the rules' export file, select the file, and then click Open.**
5. **Click OK to close the Options dialog box and then OK to close the Rules and Alerts dialog box.**

Although importing doesn't remove or override any of your previously created Outlook rules, importing adds duplicate rules of the same name. For example if you have a Mr. Big rule, and you import another Mr. Big rule you are left with two Mr. Big rules. Although the math is simple, you have to decide which rule you want to keep and which one you want to delete.

Throwing your rules out the window

Easy come, easy go. Over a period of time, a rule may no longer be necessary; maybe you are no longer working with that big client.

Follow these steps to delete a rule:

1. **Click the Inbox from Outlook's folder list.**
2. **Choose Tools⇨Rules and Alerts.**

   The Rules and Alerts dialog box appears.
3. **Clear the check box in front of the rule you want to turn off.**

   When you want to turn the rule back on again, make sure that you place a check mark in front of the rule once again.
4. **Click OK to finish.**

Chapter 3: Making Mincemeat Out of Spam

In This Chapter

- **Moving junk mail out of your life**
- **Dealing with the junk**
- **Dealing with phishing**
- **Using the Outlook postmark**

Like it or not, spam has become a way of life for anyone using e-mail. Outlook tries its very best to help you manage the seemingly endless piles of junk mail that are delivered right to your door — or in this case, your Inbox. This chapter shows you how Outlook sorts through your incoming e-mail and moves any suspicious messages to the Junk E-Mail folder. You'll also learn how to protect yourself from any phishing scams designed to bilk you out of your hard-earned money. Finally, you learn about the Outlook Postmark that offers you another level of e-mail protection.

Maintaining Your Junk

If the problem weren't so serious, the thought of maintaining your junk mail would almost sound humorous. However, there are a few things that you should do to ensure that Outlook's e-mail filter gives you the level of protection that you need.

Changing the level of protection in the junk e-mail filter

By default, the junk e-mail filter in Microsoft Office Outlook 2007 is turned on, and the protection level is set to Low, which is the setting that is designed to catch the most obvious spam. You can make the filter more aggressive by changing the level of protection.

1. **Choose Actions⇨Junk E-Mail⇨Junk E-Mail Options.**

   Alternatively, you can right-click any of the e-mail messages in your Inbox and choose Junk E-Mail⇨Junk E-Mail Options.

   In either case, the Junk E-Mail Options dialog box opens, as shown in Figure 3-1.

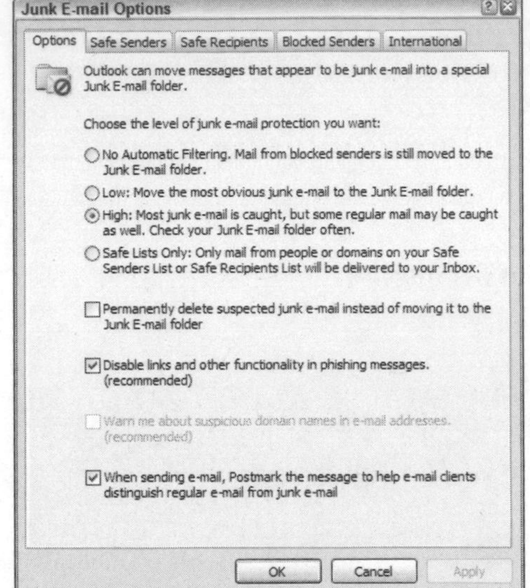

Figure 3-1: The Junk E-Mail Options dialog box.

2. **Select the level of protection that you want on the Options tab.**

   - **No Automatic Filtering:** This level turns off the automatic junk e-mail filter. However, Outlook continues to move message from people on your Blocked Senders List to the Junk E-Mail Folder.
   - **Low:** This option filters out only the most obvious junk e-mail messages.
   - **High:** Use this option if a lot of spam is still appearing in your Inbox. Just make sure that you check your Junk E-Mail Folder very carefully because chances are pretty good that some legitimate e-mail is going to be sent there.
   - **Safe Lists Only:** Choose this option if you only receive e-mail from a limited number of people and your Inbox is flooded with spam. Outlook will only deliver messages from your Safe Senders List to your Inbox; the rest is neatly deposited in your Junk E-Mail Folder.

3. **(Optional) Select the option to permanently delete suspected junk e-mail instead of moving it to the Junk E-Mail folder.**

   Unless you only receive e-mail from a very limited number of people, this option is probably not one that you want to use. Outlook automatically — and permanently — deletes any messages that it perceives to be spam.

4. **Select the option to disable links in phishing messages.**

   Graphics can give an ordinary e-mail message a bit of extra pizzazz. Legitimate e-mailers often link to graphics on their Web sites to avoid embedding a large graphic in the body of an incoming e-mail.

Unfortunately, spammers often embed links in graphics that send a signal to the spammer when you open a graphic, making you a prime candidate for more spam. Selecting this option makes you a less likely target for spam.

5. **Select the option to Postmark your messages.**

   You can learn more about this feature in the section, "Giving Your Mail a Postmark."

6. **Click OK to save your changes and close the Junk E-Mail Options dialog box.**

Giving senders your seal of approval

Although you might often think that a lot of garbage is landing in your Inbox from your boss or one of your co-workers, you'd probably prefer to take a look at it before Outlook banishes it to the Junk E-Mail folder. Outlook's junk e-mail filter is fairly accurate; there is always the possibility, however, that e-mail from one of your VIPs is mistakenly marked as junk. To be on the safe side, you can add names to the Safe Senders List. E-Mail addresses that appear in the Safe Senders List are never treated as junk:

1. **Choose Actions⇨Junk E-Mail⇨Junk E-Mail Options.**

   The Junk E-Mail Options dialog box springs to attention.

2. **Click the Safe Senders tab.**

   You can see what it looks like in Figure 3-2.

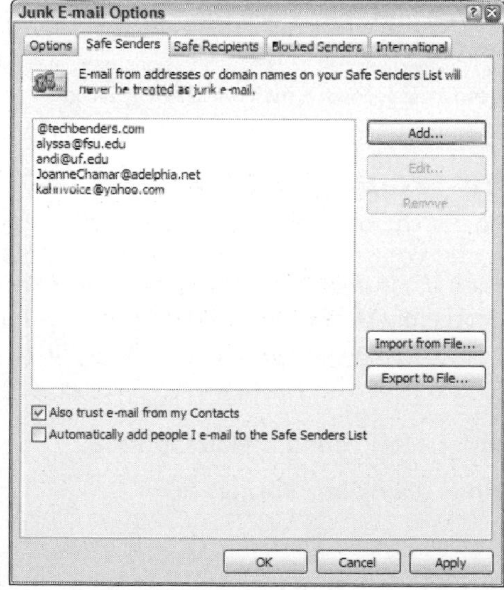

Figure 3-2: Adding Safe Senders to the junk e-mail filter.

3. **Click the Add button.**

   The Add Address or Domain dialog box appears (see Figure 3-3).

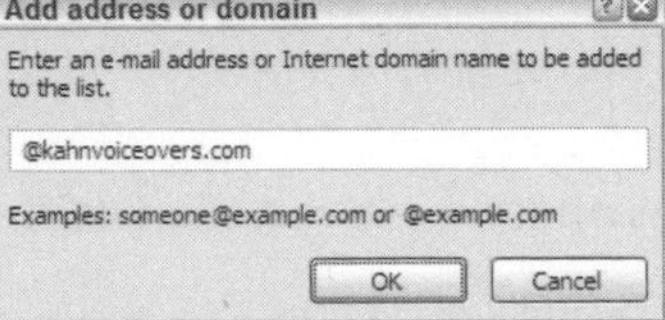

Figure 3-3: The Add Address or Domain dialog box.

   In the Enter an E-Mail Address or Internet Domain Name to Be Added to the List box, enter the e-mail address or domain name that you want to accept e-mail from. You can type *@domain.com* or simply *domain.com* to include all the e-mail addresses from a company.

4. **Click OK to close the Add Address or Domain dialog window.**

   Outlook returns you to the Junk E-Mail Options dialog box.

5. **(Optional) Select the Also Trust E-Mail from my Contacts check box if you want all your Contacts to be considered safe senders.**
6. **(Optional) Select the Automatically Add People I E-Mail to the Safe Senders List check box if you want to add people that you e-mail who might not be included among your contacts.**
7. **(Optional) Select a name and then click the Remove button to remove a name from the Safe Senders List.**
8. **(Optional) Select a name and then click the Edit button to change a name on the Safe Senders List.**
9. **Click OK to close the Junk E-Mail Options dialog box.**

Ensuring that your recipients make the list

Rest assured that you are not the only one out there battling e-mail demons. Your friends, colleagues, and your enemies are all dealing with spam. Short of reviewing this book, they must decide for themselves the best way to resolve their junk mail problems. However, by adding their e-mail addresses to Outlook's Safe Recipients list, you can ensure that your mail, at least, reaches them unscathed.

1. **Choose Actions⇨Junk E-Mail⇨Junk E-Mail Options.**

   The Junk E-Mail Options dialog box springs open.

2. **Click the Safe Recipients tab.**

   You might be yawning about now because the routine for adding a Safe Recipient is pretty similar to that of adding a Safe Sender. For added excitement, take a peek at the Safe Recipients tab shown in Figure 3-4.

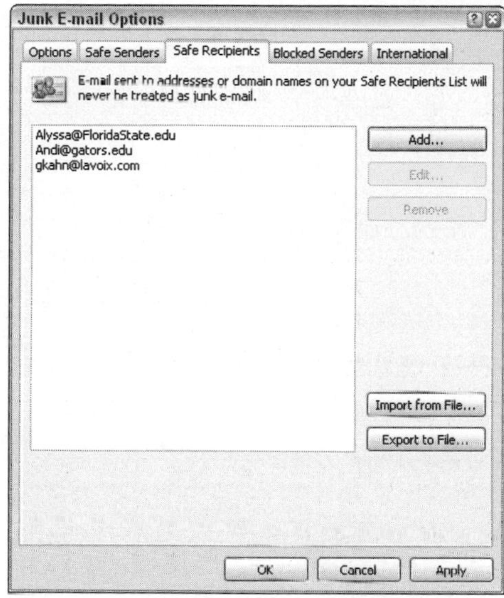

Figure 3-4: Adding safe recipients to the Junk E-Mail options.

3. **Click the Add button.**
4. **Enter the name or address that you want to add to the Enter the E-Mail Address or Internet Domain Name to Be Added to the List box.**
5. **Click OK to close the Add Address or Domain dialog box and OK again to close the Junk E-Mail Options dialog window.**

Blocking a name from your Inbox

You can easily block messages from a specific sender by adding the sender's e-mail address or domain name to the Blocked Senders List. Messages from addresses or domain names in this list are always treated as junk. When you add a sender to the Blocked Senders List, Outlook moves any incoming message from that sender to the Junk E-Mail Folder, regardless of the content of the message.

1. **Choose Actions⇨Junk E-Mail⇨Junk E-Mail Options.**

   The Junk E-Mail Options dialog box opens.

2. **Click the Blocked Senders tab.**

   Just in case you're wondering, you can see the Blocked Senders tab in Figure 3-5.

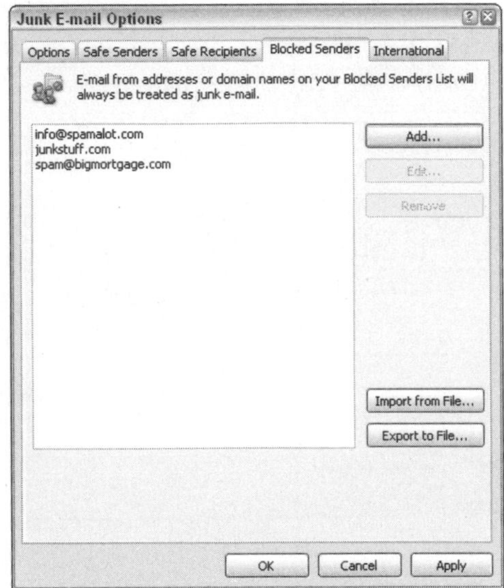

Figure 3-5: The Blocked Senders tab.

3. **Click the Add button.**
4. **Enter the name or address that you want to add in the Add address or Internet domain list box.**

   You can add specific e-mail addresses such as `spammer@junk.com` or an entire Domain Name such as `junk.com`.
5. **Click OK to close the Add Address or Domain dialog box and OK again to close the Junk E-Mail Options dialog window.**
6. **Smile devilishly to yourself as you think of all those nasty spammers who you have permanently denied entrance to your Inbox.**

Putting Junk in Its Place

Outlook comes equipped with a junk e-mail filter that evaluates incoming messages and moves anything that it thinks might be spam to a special Junk E-Mail folder. By default, Outlook's e-mail filter is set to Low, which means that it finds only the most obvious junk e-mail. Once the junk is captured, you can read all these suspicious messages at a later time. If you prefer, you can manually relegate a message to the Junk E-Mail folder.

Delegating a message to the junk pile

No spam filter system is perfect, and Outlook is no exception. While Outlook will find the most blatant spam, you'll still find a wayward message in your Inbox wanting to help you decrease your mortgage and increase your — well, you can fill in the blank on that one!

Should you spot a piece of spam lurking in your Inbox, here's how to get rid of it:

1. **Right-click the suspicious message in the Inbox folder and choose the Junk E-Mail option.**

   Figure 3-6 shows the context menu.

Add Sender to Blocked Senders List
Add Sender to Safe Senders List
Add Sender's Domain (@example.com) to Safe Senders List
Add Recipient to Safe Recipients List
Mark as Not Junk...
Junk E-mail Options...

Figure 3-6: The results of right-clicking an item in the Junk E-Mail folder.

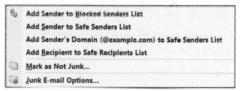

2. **Select an option.**

   The options are pretty self-explanatory:

   - Add Sender to Blocked Senders List
   - Add Sender to Safe Senders List
   - Add Sender's domain to Safe Senders List
   - Add Recipient to Safe Recipients List
   - Mark as Not Junk

   If you choose the first option, you'll be treated to the message you see in Figure 3-7. Like the message says, your e-mail will be zapped to the Junk E-Mail folder. In addition, any new messages that you receive from the same sender will move immediately to the Junk E-Mail folder, leaving you with at least one less piece of spam to deal with!

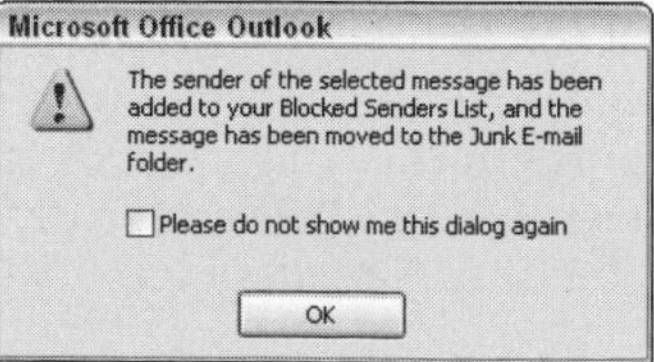

Figure 3-7: Dealing with spam that lands in your Inbox.

Sorting through your junk mail

Any message that is caught by the junk e-mail filter is moved to the special Junk E-Mail folder. You find the Junk E-Mail folder in the Deleted Items folder on Outlook's folder list. You can recognize it by the red mark, indicating that you can't delete the folder.

Because no spam filter is foolproof, you might want to skim through the messages in your Junk E-Mail folder from time to time to make sure that Outlook didn't mistake something really important for a piece of junk mail. If a message is legitimate, you can move it back to the Inbox or any other folder and mark it as not junk.

It's pretty easy to sort through your messages and take the appropriate action:

1. **Right-click a message in the Junk E-Mail folder and choose the Junk E-Mail option.**

   The context menu is exactly what you see in Figure 3-6 in the preceding section.

2. **Select an option.**

   The options are pretty self-explanatory:

   - Add Sender to Blocked Senders List
   - Add Sender to Safe Senders List
   - Add Sender's domain to Safe Senders List
   - Add Recipient to Safe Recipients List
   - Mark as Not Junk

The Mark as Not Junk option provides you with two features for the price of one. It moves the e-mail back to your Inbox, and it adds the sender to the Safe Senders List. You can also click the Not Junk icon on Outlook's toolbar to achieve the same goal.

Taking out the trash — permanently

When you delete a message, Outlook automatically moves it to the Deleted Items folder. At that point, you have to delete the message from the Deleted Items folder if you want to permanently remove it. The same process holds true for the Junk E-Mail folder; when you delete one of the messages, it is moved to the Deleted Items folder where you have to deal with it once again.

After you have skimmed through your Junk E-Mail folder and picked out anything salvageable, you might want to get rid of the true junk once and for all. Here's how you can do just that:

1. **Right-click the Junk E-Mail folder in the folder list.**

   The context menu opens like the one you see in Figure 3-8.

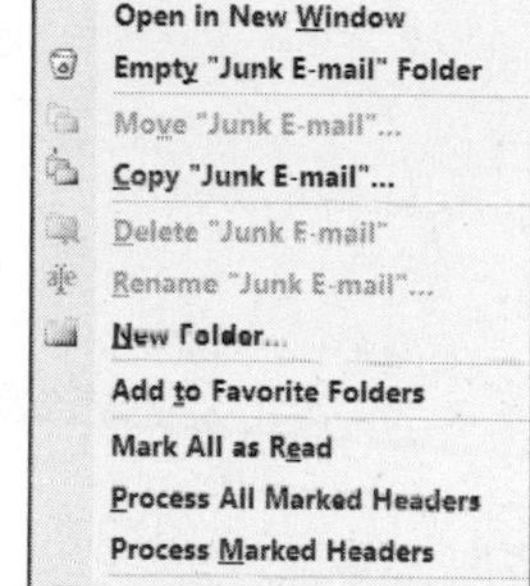

Figure 3-8: The Spam folder's context menu.

2. **Click Empty "Junk E-Mail" Folder on the context menu.**

   You receive a warning asking you if you are sure that you want to permanently delete all the items in the Junk E-Mail folder.

3. **Click Yes to remove those annoying junk messages from your life permanently.**

Protecting Yourself from Phishing Attacks

Phishing is a particularly dangerous type of spam. A phishing message tries to get personal information such as your bank account number and password. Phishing messages sometimes include links to fake Web sites that urge you to enter and submit your personal information; these Web sites may look exactly like the real McCoy.

Because you might have trouble distinguishing a phishing e-mail message from a legitimate one, the junk e-mail filter evaluates each incoming message to see if it contains suspicious links or was sent by a spoofed e-mail address. Like a protective mother, Outlook tries its best to keep you safe from danger if it suspects phishing by:

- ✦ Sending the message to the Junk E-Mail folder and converting it to plain text.
- ✦ Disabling the links in the message.

- Preventing you from replying to the message.
- Blocking any attachments in the suspicious message.
- Showing you the scary warning seen in Figure 3-9 if you try to open a link inside the e-mail message.

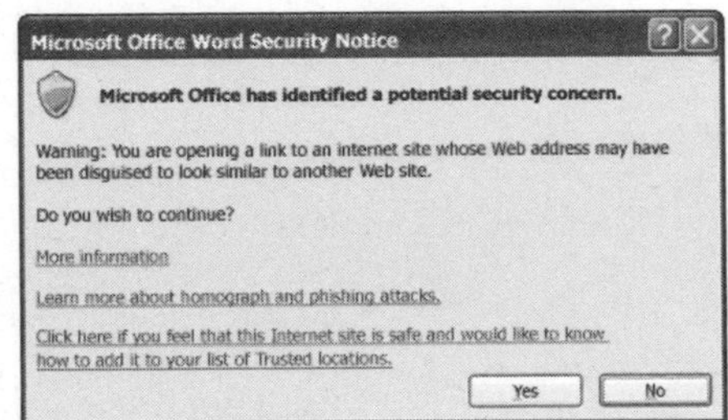

Figure 3-9: Outlook's scary message when you try to open a suspicious link.

Changing the phishing options

To adjust Outlook's phishing options, follow these steps:

1. **Choose Actions⇨Junk E-Mail⇨Junk E-Mail Options.**

   You end up on the Options tab of the Junk E-Mail Options dialog box. If you're dying to know what it looks like, take a peek back at Figure 3-1.
2. **Check Disable Links and Other Functionality in Phishing Messages (Recommended) check box.**

   By default, this option is checked, but it never hurts to double-check.
3. **Check the Warn Me about Suspicious Domain Names in E-Mail Addresses (Recommended) check box.**

   This enables Outlook to continue to warn you if it detects a fake domain.

Enable or disable links in phishing e-mail messages

The annoying thing about spam is that it's just so hard to detect. If you set the filter too low, your spam might start to outnumber the good stuff. If you set your filter too high, chances are good that some legitimate mail will be sent off to the Junk E-Mail folder. If that happens, you need a way to salvage the e-mail so that you can once again access the links that appear in the messages.

If you want to resurrect an e-mail that has been falsely identified as being part of a phishing operation, here's what you do:

1. **Move the message back to your Inbox.**

Ten tips on how to help reduce spam

This chapter talks about using Outlook's spam filter tools. However, you can do a few other things to reduce your risk of spam.

- **Block pictures in HTML messages:** By default, Outlook blocks automatic picture downloads if the content is linked to a server. If you open a message that has graphic linking back to a server when this feature is turned off, the server is notified that you are downloading a graphic — and that your e-mail address is a valid one.
- **Turn off read and delivery receipts and automatic processing of meeting requests:** Spammers sometimes resort to sending meeting requests and messages that include requests for read and delivery receipts. Responding to meeting requests and read receipts helps spammers to verify your e-mail address.
- **Limit the places where you post your e-mail address:** Be cautious about posting your e-mail address on public Web sites, such as newsgroups, chat rooms, bulletin boards, and so forth. When visiting public sites, you might want to use an e-mail address that is different from your main e-mail address. Remove your e-mail address from your personal Web site.
- **Review the privacy policies of Web sites:** When you sign up for any online service or newsletters, review the privacy policy of the site carefully before you reveal your e-mail address or other personal information. If the Web site does not explain how your personal information will be used, consider not using the services at that site.
- **Watch out for check boxes that are already selected:** When you shop online, companies sometimes add a check box that is already selected, which indicates that it is fine with you if the company sells or gives your e-mail address to other businesses. Clear that check box!
- **Don't reply to spam:** Never reply to an e-mail message — not even to unsubscribe from a mailing list — unless you know and trust the sender, such as when the e-mail message comes from a service, an online store, or newsletter that you have signed up with.
- **If a company uses e-mail messages to ask for personal information, don't respond by sending a message:** Most legitimate companies don't ask for personal information to be sent in e-mail. Be suspicious if they do.
- **Don't contribute to a charity in response to a request sent in e-mail:** Unfortunately, some spammers prey on your goodwill. If you receive an e-mail appeal from a charity, treat it as spam.
- **Don't forward chain e-mail messages:** Besides increasing overall e-mail volume, you lose control over who sees your e-mail address.
- **Create a secondary e-mail address that you use when filling out Web forms and making purchases:** Hotmail, Google, and Yahoo! all provide e-mail addresses free of charge. Use these when making an online purchase or accessing a Web site that requires an e-mail address.

You can do this by simply dragging the message from the Junk E-Mail Folder to the Inbox or by clicking the Not Junk icon on Outlook's toolbar.

2. **Open the message and click the InfoBar at the top of the message on the text that says Click on the InfoBar to Enable Functionality (Not Recommended).**

   You can now use any of the links in the e-mail.

Giving Your Mail a Postmark

The Outlook E-Mail Postmark is a new technology from Microsoft designed to help stop junk e-mail. Outlook assigns a Postmark to any e-mail that you send that might be considered junk mail by another computer. Most users won't notice the time it takes to create a single Postmark. However, because spammers generally send thousands of e-mail at a time, the process slows down spammers quite a bit. When your message is received by another user of Outlook 2007, her version of Outlook recognizes the postmark and makes sure that your message is delivered.

Before sending a message, the junk e-mail filter in Outlook evaluates whether the message has spam characteristics that make it likely to be categorized as spam by the recipient's spam filter. If the message does not have spam characteristics, Outlook does not postmark the message.

Outlook E-Mail Postmarking is turned on by default. If you decide that you don't want the feature turned on, you can turn it off by following these steps:

1. **Choose Actions⇨Junk E-Mail⇨Junk E-Mail Options.**

   The Junk E-Mail Options dialog box opens.

2. **Click the Options tab.**
3. **Uncheck the When Sending E-Mail, Postmark the Message to Help Recipient E-Mail Programs Distinguish Regular E-Mail from Junk E-Mail check box.**
4. **Click OK to close the Add Address or Domain dialog window and click OK again to close the Junk E-Mail Options dialog window.**

Chapter 4: Seek and Ye Shall Find

In This Chapter

- **Using an Instant Search**
- **Searching with a Search Folder**
- **Finding someone quickly in the Address Book**
- **Finding your way around the Navigation pane**
- **Playing with Shortcuts**

Creating information is only half the fun; after it is created, you want to be able to find it again. Learning Outlook is like driving a new car — it takes you a while to figure out where all the button are, but once you do, using them becomes second nature. This chapter shows you how to find anything instantly using the Instant Search pane. You can create Search Folders if you're constantly hunting down the same items over and over again. The Address Book enables you to find that one special contact in a heartbeat. You can master the Navigation pane so that everything you need is right there at your fingertips, and you can even start to use Shortcuts as a super-fast way to arrive at your intended destination.

Getting Instant Gratification with Instant Searching

As its name implies, Instant Search is a new Office 2007 feature that helps you find items instantly. When you first ran Outlook, you might have noticed a prompt asking you if you'd like to *index* Outlook; presumably you clicked Yes — even if you weren't quite sure what that meant. Creating an index of your Outlook content means that ultimately you'll be able to find things a bit faster. Instant Search in Outlook works by accessing indexed content. Outlook indexes all of your items — even the attachments. Once the initial indexing takes place, Outlook continues to index your new content in the background.

The Instant Search pane is available in Outlook's Mail, Calendar, Contacts, Tasks, Notes, Folder List, and Journal views. When you click any of these folders, you see the Instant Search bar displayed prominently at the top of your list of items. You see a sample of the Contacts Instant Search pane in Figure 4-1.

Figure 4-1: Instant Search pane.

Enabling Instant Search

Instant Search requires certain Microsoft Windows search components in order to function. If you're using Microsoft Windows Vista, you're in luck: Vista already comes equipped with Windows Desktop Search, so Instant Search is enabled automatically.

If you're not running Vista and you don't already have the Windows Desktop Search component installed, the first time you run Outlook a dialog box prompts you to download the software. Go ahead and do so. The screen prompts walk you through saving and installing the Search component. After you download the software, you must restart Outlook in order for Instant Search to function. If you don't enable Instant Search, you can still search — but not as quickly as if you had enabled Instant Searching.

Fiddling with the Instant Search options

To change the Instant Search options, choose Tools⇨Instant Search⇨Search Options from the main menu bar. Or you can click the arrow in the Instant Search pane and then click Search Options. After you choose the command, the Search Options dialog box opens, as shown in Figure 4-2.

The Search Options dialog window is divided into several sections:

✦ **Indexing:** The main reason that Instant Search works so quickly is that Outlook indexes all of your Outlook data when you originally install Instant Search and then retains information about the contents of the various items. When you perform an Instant Search, Outlook uses this information to speed up the searching process.

  You can choose the accounts you want Outlook to *index,* or store in its memory. In case you jump the gun by trying to perform an Instant Search before Outlook has had a chance to index your information, you can ask Outlook to prompt you by selecting the Prompt Me When Search Results May Be Incomplete Because Messages Are Still Being Indexed check box, located at the bottom of the Indexing section of the Search Options dialog box.

  If you choose not to index any of your Outlook accounts, you are, in essence, disabling Instant Search. Although the Instant Search pane still appears, Instant Search is no longer functional.

- **Search:** By the default, the search results appear in the Instant Search pane as you type; the more you type, the shorter the list of results becomes. If you prefer not to see search results until you press Enter or click the Search button, you can deselect this option. You can also speed up your searches by limiting the number of results shown in the Instant Search pane. When your search returns an extremely large number of results, Outlook limits the number that is shown by displaying only the most recent items. Finally, if color isn't your thing or yellow isn't your color, you can change the highlighting preference that Instant Search uses when returning your results.
- **Deleted Items:** You can have Outlook look through your Deleted Items folder when you perform an Instant Search by selecting the check box in the Deleted Items section of the Search Options dialog box. This option is not selected by default. By default, Outlook assumes that you don't want to search through your deleted items; however, if you frequently delete various items without also deleting them from the Deleted Items folder, you might want to place a check mark next to this item.
- **Instant Search pane:** By default, an Instant Search searches through only your currently selected folder; after you see the results, you can choose to search your other folders by clicking the Try Searching Again in All Mail Items option, as described in the next section. If you select the All Folders option, Instant Search looks through all your Outlook folders without prompting you. Typically, if you have a rough idea of where an item might be lurking, the default setting of Only the Currently Selected Folder is fine.

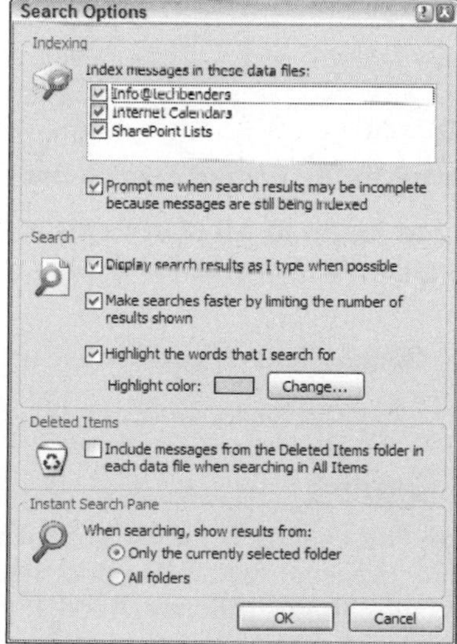

Figure 4-2: The Search Options dialog box.

Searching instantly

Although you can search through any Outlook folders, probably one of the best uses of Instant Search is for searching in your e-mail. To find a certain message, do the following:

1. **Select the Inbox folder you want to search.**
2. **Type your search text in the Instant Search box.**

   Let your imagination run wild! You can search for a specific sender, a phrase in the subject line, or a word in the body of an e-mail. You soon see why this is called the Instant Search because the results of your search appear instantaneously as soon as you type the first couple of letters of your search string.

   Your results appear in the Instant Search Results pane with the search text highlighted. It is not necessary to click the Search button to start the search. As you type more characters, your results narrow to reflect your search criterion. You can see the results of an Instant Search in Figure 4-3.

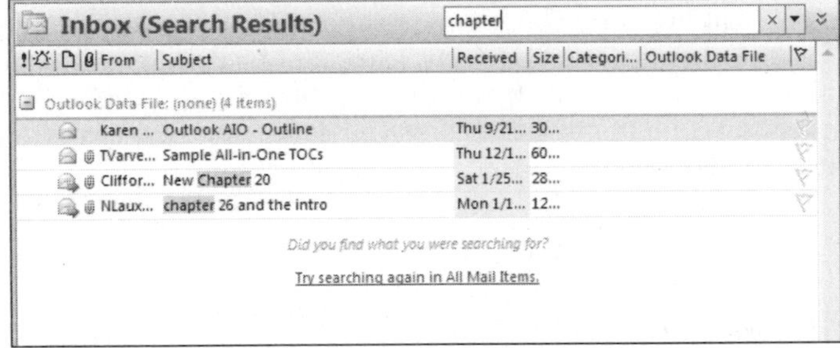

Figure 4-3: The results of an Instant Search.

3. **Double-click the item you want in the Instant Search pane results.**
4. **(Optional) Click Try Searching Again in All Mail Items at the bottom of the Search Results pane if you'd like to include all your mail folders in the search.**
5. **(Optional) Click the X in the Instant Search pane to clear the search and start a new one.**

Refining your Instant Search

Chances are excellent that you can find exactly what you're looking for the first time you use an Instant Search. However, you might find that the Instant Search works too well and returns more items than you need. If you find that you have to filter through a long list of items, you want to add a few more criteria to your search so that the Instant Search provides you with a "short list."

Although the word *query* sounds much more technical — and scary — than *search,* it's a very easy process:

1. **Click the Expand the Query Builder arrow in the Instant Search pane (see Figure 4-4).**

Figure 4-4: Query Builder arrow.

The Instant Search pane magically expands to include a Query Builder. The Query Builder offers you more search criteria choices, like the ones you see in Figure 4-5.

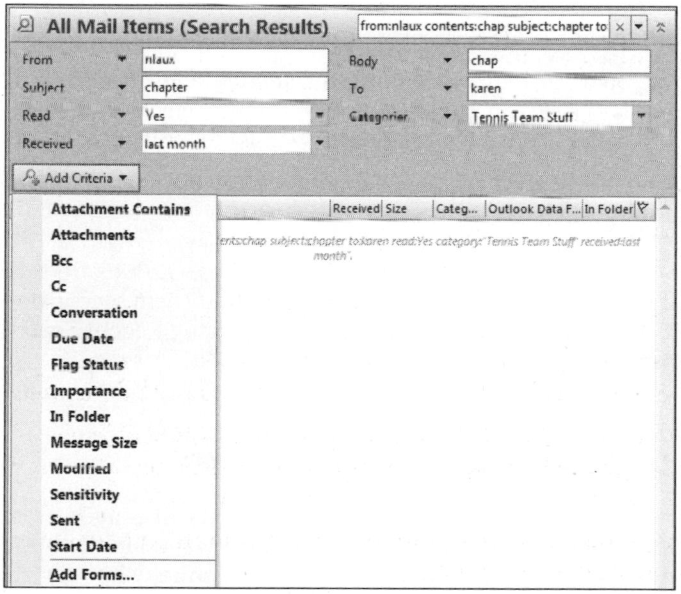

Figure 4-5: Building an advanced Instant Search.

2. **Type your search text in the From, Body, Subject, or To lines of the Query Builder.**

   If you are looking for an e-mail from a specific person, for example, enter a message with a specific subject, or one that contains a certain phrase in the body of the e-mail.

3. **(Optional) Click the Add Criteria button to display more search fields in the Query Builder.**

   The Query Builder expands once again to include even more fields to have Outlook search through. Talk about having it *your* way! You can search for just about anything your little heart desires from attachments and categories to sent dates.

4. **Click the fields that you want to appear in the Query Builder.**

   As you select the search fields you want from the list, they are added to the Query Builder. You can even select the Add Forms option to navigate to any forms in which you have created customized fields. The search fields that you add are specific to where you are within Outlook, such as Mail, Calendar, Contacts, Tasks, Notes, Folder List, or Journal.

5. **(Optional) Click a search field label and select Remove from the drop-down list to remove a search field.**

   Although you don't have to use them, the search fields that you add become permanent fixtures in the Instant Search pane unless you remove them.

6. **Enter your search criteria in the new search fields.**

   As you enter information into the search fields, the Instant Search box displays it. If you are familiar with the search query syntax, you can type your query in the Instant Search box instead of using the search fields.

7. **View the search results in the list below the Instant Search pane and double-click the item you want.**

Although you can't save your Instant Searches, Outlook does display up to ten of your most recent searches. You can find them by clicking the drop-down arrow in the Instant Search pane, choosing Recent Searches, and then selecting the search that you want from the list.

Searching through the Search Folders

A Search Folder is a virtual folder that contains all e-mail items that match specific search criteria. The information in a virtual folder appears there automatically; you can't move information manually into a virtual folder. For example, the Unread Mail Search Folder allows you to view all unread messages from one neat and tidy location — the Unread Mail Search Folder — even though the messages may be physically located in different Mail folders. The Unread Mail Search Folder is updated automatically; the next time you access it, any messages that you've read no longer appear there. You'll find these virtual Search Folders at the bottom of the Outlook Folder list.

Using Instant Search is the quickest way to find *any* Outlook item.

As you see in Figure 4-6, you find the Search Folders toward the bottom of Outlook's Folder list.

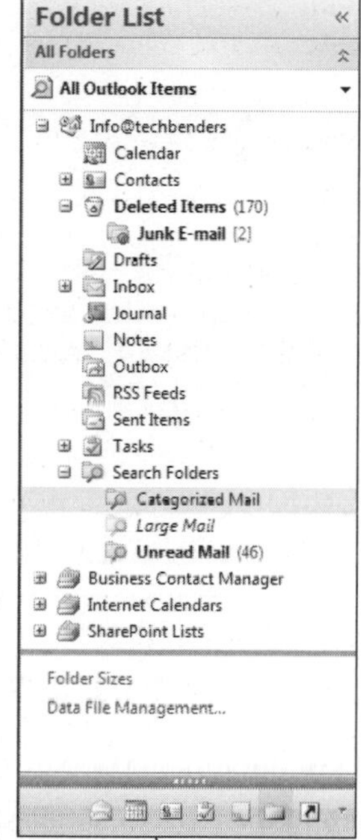

Figure 4-6: Viewing Outlook's Search Folders.

By default, three Search Folders exist:

- **Categorized Mail:** Includes any e-mail to which you have assigned a color category.
- **Large Mail:** Includes e-mail that is larger than 100K.
- **Unread Mail:** Includes e-mail you've never read.

In addition to the three default Search Folders, Outlook includes several other predefined Search Folders. You can customize a predefined Search Folder with your own search criteria, or you can create your own custom Search Folder by defining specific search criteria. See the following sections to find out how to do all these nifty (and useful) things.

Adding a predefined Search Folder

You can add a ton — or at least over a dozen — predefined Search Folders to your Folder List at the drop of a hat.

1. **Right-click Search Folder in the Folder List and choose New Search Folder.**

   The New Search Folder dialog box opens, as shown in Figure 4-7.

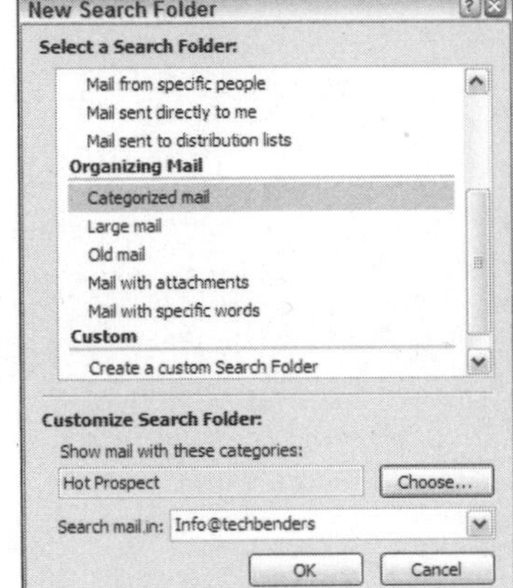

Figure 4-7: Creating a predefined Search Folder.

2. **Select a Search Folder option.**

   You've got a bunch to choose from including:

   - **Reading Mail:** Creates Search Folders for unread, flagged for follow-up, or important e-mail.
   - **Mail from People and Lists:** Creates Search Folders for e-mail sent to or from specific people or distribution lists.
   - **Organizing Mail:** Creates Search Folders for categorized, large, or old e-mail or for e-mail that contains attachments or specific words.

3. **(Optional) In the Customize Search Folder section of the New Search Folder dialog box, specify the search criteria to use if prompted.**

   Figure 4-7 shows an example of a Search Folder that includes all the e-mail that has been categorized as a Hot Prospect.

4. **(Optional) Select a different mailbox in the Customize Search Folder area.**

5. **Click OK to close the New Search Folder dialog box.**

   The new Search Folder now appears in all its glory with the rest of your Search Folders. Its name reflects the criterion that Outlook uses to move e-mail into it.

6. **(Optional) Right-click the folder and choose Customize this Search Folder to rename the search folder or select different search criteria.**

   The Customize *Folder Name* dialog box opens. As shown in Figure 4-8, you can give your Search Folder a new name, change the criteria, or associate the Search Folder with a different mailbox.

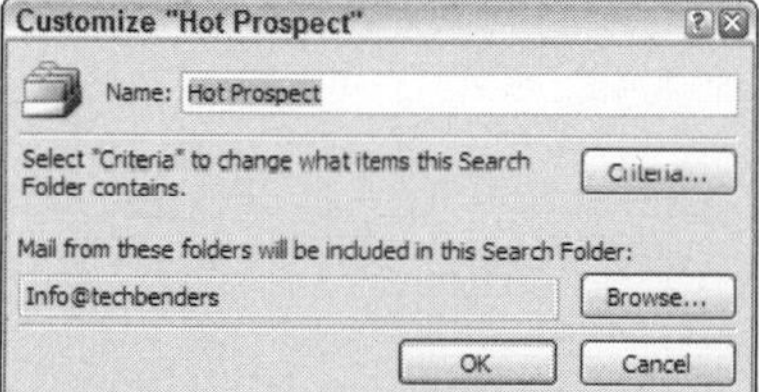

Figure 4-8: Renaming a Search Folder.

Creating a customized Search Folder

One of the things you may find most endearing about Outlook is its capability to perform tasks in multiple ways. This chapter is a great example of Outlook's flexibility. Keep in mind, however, that you don't have to use all of Outlook's search features; you can find the one that makes the most sense for your needs and stick with it.

As an alternative to performing an Instant Search (see "Getting Instant Gratification with Instant Searching," earlier in this chapter), you may want to create your very own personalized Search Folder. Here's how you can do just that:

1. **Right-click the Search Folders and choose New Search Folder from Outlook's Folder List.**

   The New Search Folder dialog box opens (refer to Figure 4-7).

2. **Click Create a Custom Search Folder and then click the Choose button.**

   If you can't find that option, it's because it's hiding all the way down at the bottom of the Search Folder options. If you find it, the Custom Search Folder dialog window opens up; it's exactly like the one in Figure 4-7.

3. **Type a name for your custom Search Folder.**

4. **Click Criteria to select the criteria for the Search Folder.**

   The Search Folder Criteria dialog window appears. By default, the Messages tab is displayed.

5. **Select the options for the type of search you want the Search Folder to perform.**

   As shown in Figure 4-9, you can search by word, by the location within the e-mail, or even by the sender or recipient.

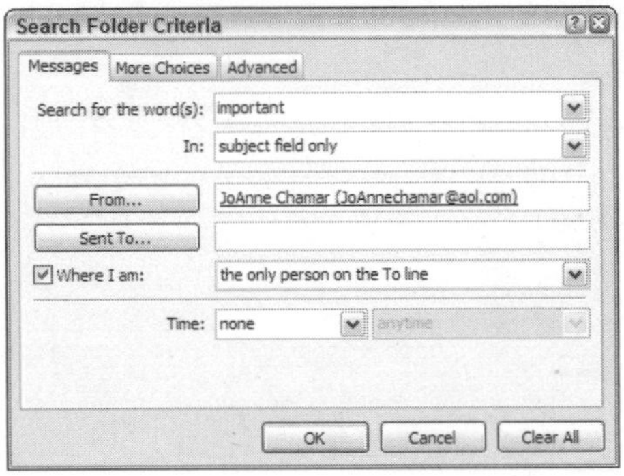

Figure 4-9: Creating a custom Search Folder.

6. **(Optional) Click the More Choices tab.**

   The More Choices tab appears, as shown in Figure 4-10. As its name suggests, the More Choices tab gives you a few more choices of search criteria including e-mail category, read status, importance, and flagging status. You can also search for e-mails that have attachments or that are of a certain size.

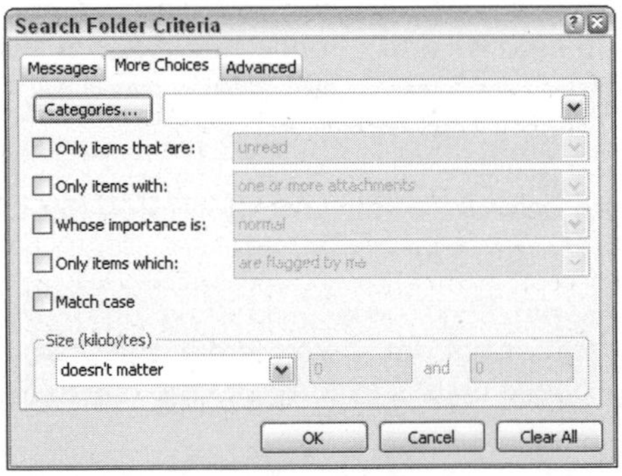

Figure 4-10: Further refining your search.

7. **(Optional) Click the Advanced tab to include customized fields as part of your search criteria.**

   The Advanced tab appears, as shown in Figure 4-11. Not surprisingly, you can get really advanced here. For example, you might be looking for everyone who has a fax number but not an e-mail address so that you can create a list of everyone who needs to receive your monthly newsletter by fax.

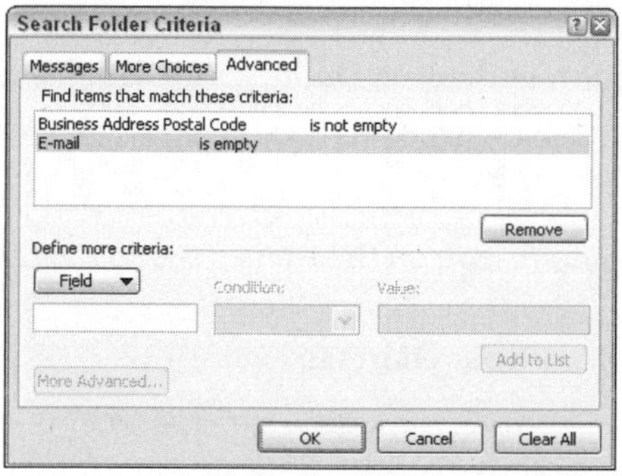

Figure 4-11: Adding customized fields to your search criteria.

8. **Click OK to close the Search Folder Criteria dialog box and then click OK again to close the Custom Search dialog box.**
9. **Just for good measure, click OK one last time to close the New Search Folder dialog box.**

Deleting a Search Folder

Because the Search Folders are virtual folders, deleting a Search Folder does not delete the e-mail messages shown in the Search Folder from their original locations. However — and this is a *big* however — although the Search Folders are virtual ones, the e-mail they contain are real, live e-mail messages. If you delete a *message* from one of the Search Folders, the message is also deleted from the Outlook folders where it is stored.

The easiest way to delete a Search Folder is to give it a right-click and choose Delete *[Search Folder Name]* from the context menu. You are prompted one last time to verify whether this is really your intention; click yes to the warning, and the folder is out of your life. If you change your mind and decide you really do want to use that Search Folder, feel free to create it again. You may, however, receive some annoyed looks from your computer.

Searching 101 — Finding Names in the Address Book

The first sections of this chapter focus primarily on searching through your e-mail. You can also use the Address Book to look up names when you address messages.

A contact must have either an e-mail address or a fax number in order for his name to appear in an Address Book search.

1. **Open the Address Book.**

   You can accomplish this feat in a number of ways:

   - Choose Tools⇨Address Book on Outlook's main menu bar.
   - Click the Address Book button on the Standard toolbar.
   - Click the To, Cc, or Bcc buttons on a new e-mail message.
   - Click the Address Book icon on the Names section of the new message Ribbon.

   You can see the results of your efforts in Figure 4-12.

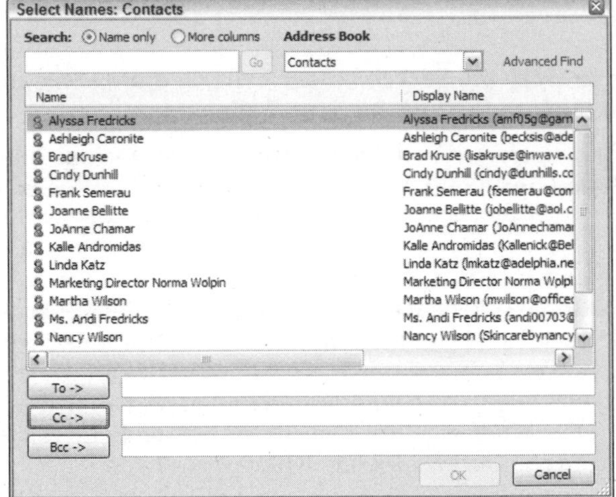

Figure 4-12: Outlook's Address Book.

2. **Select the address book that you want to search in the Address Book drop-down list.**

   Typically, if you're using Business Contact Manager, you'll have address books for your Accounts and Business Contacts in addition to your Outlook Contacts. (See Book II, Chapter 1 for more on address books.)

3. **Type the name you are searching for in the Search box.**

   By default, Outlook looks for contacts on a first-name basis. If you have several Susans in your address book, you can continue typing a few of the first letters in the last name.

4. **(Optional) Click More Columns, type your search criteria, and click Go if you can't find the person you're looking for.**

   You can search for a person by just about any tidbit of information: last name, title, city. You can search by more than one criteria if you include a comma after each criterion.

5. **Right-click the name and select Properties to view the contact record of the person you found.**

   You can now edit the contact information as you see fit.

Taking the Pain out of the Navigation Pane

The Navigation pane runs down the left side of the Outlook window (refer to Figure 4-6). The Navigation pane is totally customizable; you can add items, resize, minimize, or get rid of it completely if you so desire.

Getting turned on by the Navigation pane

You might want to play around with the various Outlook views until you find the one that you are the most comfortable with. If you feel that the Navigation pane is taking up a bit too much of your Outlook real estate, you can easily turn it off by choosing View⇨Navigation Pane⇨Off from Outlook's main menu bar.

If you closed the Navigation pane and are frantically trying to get it back, choose View⇨Navigation Pane⇨Normal. The Navigation pane reappears.

Playing hide and seek with the Navigation pane

You can save space in Outlook by minimizing the Navigation pane. If you do this, you have the best of both worlds: Most of the time the Navigation pane is fairly unobtrusive, but you can maximize it again with the click of a button.

You have several ways to hide or show the minimized Navigation pane:

- ✦ Click the double arrows at the top of the Navigation pane.
- ✦ Choose View⇨Navigation Pane⇨Minimized from the Outlook menu bar.
- ✦ Hover your mouse over the right edge of the Navigation pane; when your cursor transforms into double arrow, drag the border all the way to the left.

You can restore the Navigation pane to its original state in as many ways as you can minimize it:

- ✦ Click the double arrows at the top of the Navigation pane.
- ✦ Choose View⇨Navigation Pane⇨Normal from the Outlook menu bar.
- ✦ Hover your mouse over the right edge of the Navigation pane; when your cursor transforms into double arrow, drag the border all the way to the right.

Finding your way around the Navigation pane buttons

The buttons at the bottom of the Navigation pane enable you to zoom in on one specific part of Outlook. For example, you may be working with your contacts and want a quick way to access your various contact lists and to view those lists in a variety of ways.

You can view the Navigation Pane button as either large buttons that run vertically or as small buttons that run horizontally across the bottom of the Navigation pane. Figure 4-13 shows the buttons in their miniaturized state.

Figure 4-13: Economy size.

You notice the horizontal splitter at the top of the buttons. If you hover your cursor over it, and when the pointer turns into a double-headed arrow, drag the splitter bar up as far as it will go, the buttons expand, as shown in Figure 4-14.

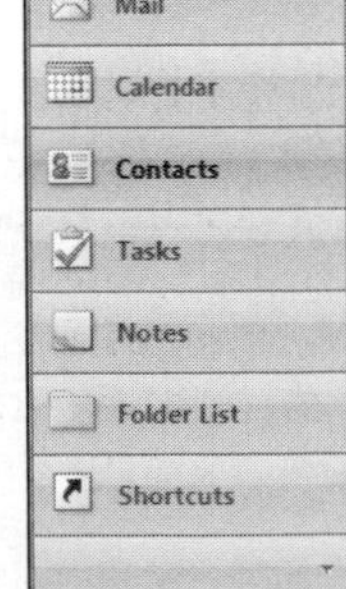

Figure 4-14: Viewing the Navigation pane buttons.

Building better buttons in the Navigation pane

You can add buttons to or subtract buttons from the Navigation pane. No matter how you view the Navigation pane, notice the Configure buttons icon (cleverly disguised as a tiny arrow) at the bottom of the Navigation pane. If you click it, you have several options from which to choose:

- **Show More Buttons:** Displays all the Navigation pane buttons.
- **Show Fewer Buttons:** Displays the most commonly used Navigation pane buttons.
- **Navigation Pane Options:** Opens the Navigation Pane Options dialog box, which enables you to select the buttons you want, as well as to place them in the order you want. You can even click the Reset button to set the buttons to their original states. Figure 4-15 shows the Navigation Pane Options dialog box.

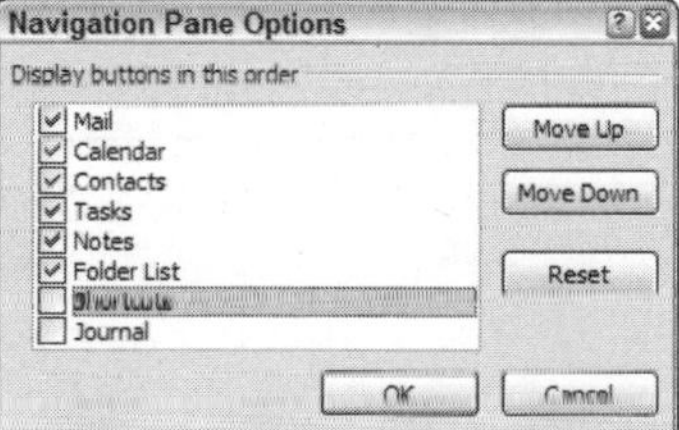

Figure 4-15: The Navigation Pane Options dialog box.

- **Add or Remove Buttons:** Allows you to select the buttons that you want to appear on the Navigation pane by clicking them.

You can remove all the buttons from the Navigation pane, and you can maximize the folder pane space by dragging the horizontal splitter bar to the bottom of the Navigation pane. You can even turn off the Navigation pane. However, you can't remove the row of small buttons at the bottom of the Navigation pane if the Navigation pane is visible.

Pushing the right button

After you're comfortable with the location of the Navigation pane buttons, you may want to take them out for a test drive. The best way to familiarize yourself with them is by giving each of the buttons a click. Figure 4-16 shows you the results of clicking the Contacts icon. You can see that you have ready access to your various contact lists. You can indicate whether you want to view your contacts in a variety of card formats or in category or zip code order. Many other options are available, of course. See Book V, Chapter 1 for the full scoop on the Contacts view.

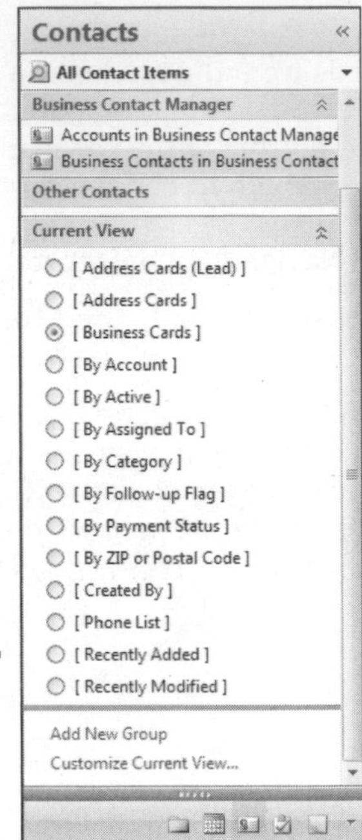

Figure 4-16: The Contacts view.

Fiddling with the Folder List

The Folder List enables you to view all your folders including your Inbox and any subfolders you create. The Folder List displays all Outlook items, including the Calendar, Contacts, Notes, and Tasks. This view might become one of your favorites because it is extremely easy to navigate.

You can access the Folder List by clicking the Folder List button at the bottom of the Navigation pane. If you want to keep the Folder List as your main view in the Navigation pane while you are working, do not click the other buttons at the bottom of the Navigation pane. If you want to move around in your various Outlook items, click the appropriate folder, icon, or name in the Folder List itself. To view subfolders, click the plus sign next to the folder.

Working with Shortcuts and Shortcut Groups

Everyone loves a shortcut, and Outlook is no exception. If you'd like to be able to access parts of Outlook at the click of a button — and the Navigation pane buttons just don't do the trick — then you can create a shortcut to any of your Outlook folders.

You can organize Shortcuts into groups and arrange the Shortcut groups on the Navigation pane so that they are easy to find, even if you switch the view other than the Folder List.

Creating a Shortcut

Because a Shortcut is designed to save you time, it only stands to reason that you can create one in a short amount of time. Here's how you can quickly add a Shortcut to the Navigation pane:

1. **Choose Go⇨Shortcuts from the main Outlook menu.**

   The Shortcuts pane opens.

2. **Click Add New Shortcut in the Shortcuts pane.**

   The Add to Navigation Pane dialog box opens, as shown in Figure 4-17.

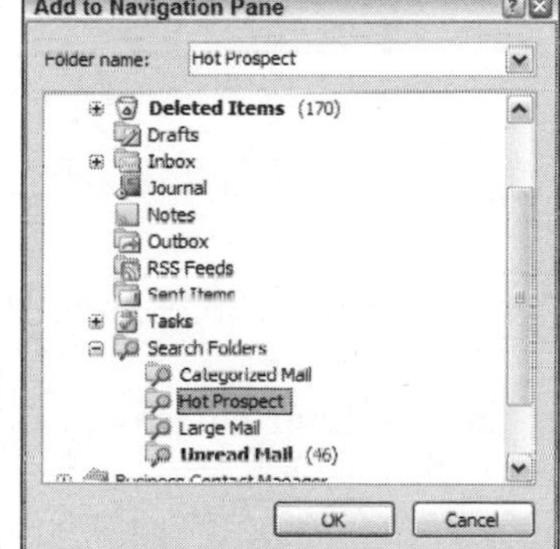

Figure 4-17: Adding new Shortcuts.

3. **Select the folder for which you'd like to create a Shortcut and click OK.**

   Your new Shortcut now appears in the Shortcut pane. You can access that folder with a single click of the Shortcut.

If you find yourself having trouble navigating back to the Shortcut pane, you can get there with the click of a button — or at least the click of a Navigation Pane button. By default, a Shortcut button automatically appears at the bottom of the Navigation pane.

Tweaking a Shortcut

After you create a Shortcut, you can change it again in a jiffy. Simply right-click a Shortcut, and you'll be able to delete the Shortcut, rename the Shortcut, or move the Shortcut up or down in the Shortcut pane.

Creating a group of Shortcuts

If you're a real Shortcut junkie and create lots of Shortcuts, you may want to create groups within the Shortcut pane to help organize them all. Here are the short steps needed to create a Shortcut group:

1. **Choose Go⇨Shortcuts from Outlook's main menu.**

   The Shortcuts pane opens.

2. **Click Add new Group and then type a name for the group in the box that appears.**

   You can see what this looks like in Figure 4-18.

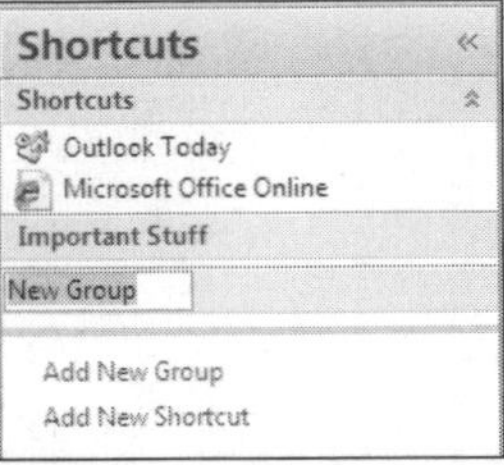

Figure 4-18: Adding a new Shortcut group name.

   You are now the proud possessor of a new Shortcut group in the Shortcut pane.

3. **Drag any existing Shortcuts to the new Shortcut group.**

Tweaking a Shortcut group

Because Shortcuts — and the groups that contain them — are so easy to create, you may find yourself taking advantage of them more and more often. For example, you might create a VIP group of Shortcuts that allow you to flip to the Inboxes of your key clients. Just as your life can change at the drop of a hat, you may need to change the Shortcut groups equally quickly.

By right-clicking a Shortcut group, you can

✦ Add a new Shortcut to the group.

✦ Rename the Group.

✦ Remove the Shortcut group.

✦ Move the group up or down the Shortcut pane.

It's nice to know that Outlook is so thoughtful that it even provides you with shortcuts for dealing with your shortcuts!

Chapter 5: Securing Outlook E-Mail

In This Chapter

- Giving Outlook a password
- Working with the Microsoft Outlook Trust Center
- Addressing security issues
- Using digitally signed e-mail
- Using the Information Rights Manager

You may want to put on a dark trench coat and don a pair of sunglasses while reading this chapter because it deals with ways you can protect yourself from e-mail spies. Adding a password is a simple way to ensure that others aren't accessing your e-mail. You also need to know about security alerts and what to do if you receive one. Your espionage toolkit won't be complete without information on digitally signed and encrypted e-mail and the Information Rights Manager. And, of course, remember that your martinis should be shaken not stirred.

Working with Passwords

Probably the simplest way to protect your Outlook information is by giving it a password. A password prevents intruders from opening your Outlook and sneaking a peek at your entire life including all your contacts, appointments, and e-mail. However, it won't prevent someone from grabbing your password if you write it down on a sticky note and stick it on your monitor.

To add a password to your Outlook file, follow these steps:

1. **Choose File⇨Data File Management from Outlook's main menu bar.**

   The Account Settings dialog box opens like the one you see in Figure 5-1.

2. **On the Data Files tab, select the Personal Folders file (`.pst`) for which you want to create a password and then click Settings.**

   The Personal Folders dialog box opens.

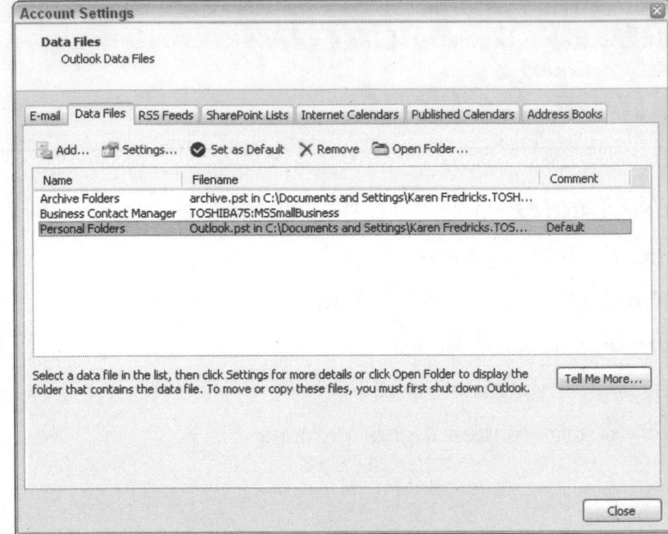

Figure 5-1: The Account Settings dialog box.

3. **Click the Change Password button.**

   The Change Password dialog box opens, as shown in Figure 5-2.

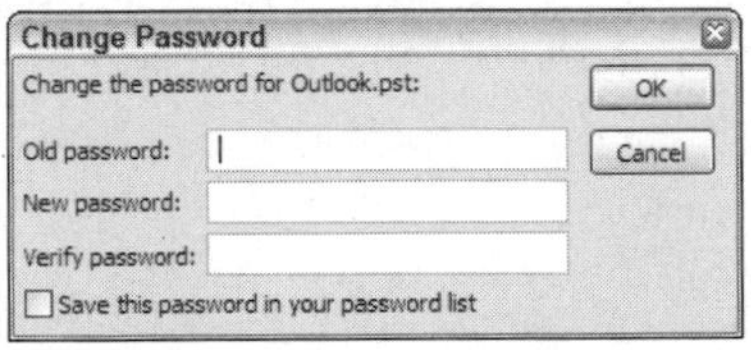

Figure 5-2: Changing an Outlook password.

4. **Type your new password in the New Password text box.**
5. **Type your new password in the Verify Password text box just to be sure you have spelled the new password correctly.**
6. **Don't select the Save This Password in Your Password List check box.**

   Guess it kind of seems funny to give a "non" instruction, but this one is worth mentioning. If you check this box, you won't have to fill in your password when you open Outlook because Outlook will remember it for you. And, if you don't have to enter a password, what's the point of having one in the first place? By checking this box, any spy or questionable person will be able to access your Outlook file without having to supply a password because you have already supplied if for them!

7. **Click OK twice to close the Change Password and the Personal Folders dialog boxes, and then click Close to close the Account Settings dialog box.**

   The next time you open Outlook, you are greeted with the cheerful message you see in Figure 5-3. Okay, maybe it's not such a cheerful window; but if you type your password and click OK, you gain admission into the exciting world of Outlook.

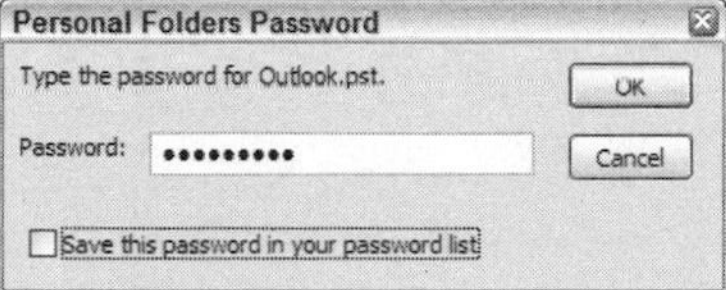

Figure 5-3: Entering your password.

Remember your password! If you forget your password, you're pretty much up the proverbial creek. If you have a lot of passwords to remember, you might consider purchasing password wallet software that will help you to organize your passwords. Or, at the very least, jot that password down in a *very* safe place!

You might rest easier at night knowing that your Outlook is password protected. No one can open your Outlook if he doesn't have the password. However, nothing prevents an intruder from walking off with all your data if you don't close Outlook when you aren't using it.

Guarding Your Privacy

You might snicker at the thought of wearing a trench coat and sunglasses when you use your computer, but allowing a stranger access to your computer is no laughing matter. You should be aware of the information Outlook is sending to the outside world. These options can be found in Outlook's Trust Center.

Microsoft developed the Trust Center to handle security and privacy settings for all the 2007 Microsoft Office programs. The idea was to replace the various security settings used in earlier versions of Office with a more streamlined security system. Microsoft designed the Trust Center to work in the background. In previous versions of Office, warning signs asking you to take some form of action frequently popped up while you were working. Unfortunately, you might not have understood the question — much less the answer. Hopefully, the Trust Center will automatically provide you with the best level of protection without having to nag you to change various settings.

Although you can access the Trust Center from any of the Office products, here's how you can get to it from Outlook:

1. **From Outlook's main menu bar, choose Help➪Privacy Options.**

   The Outlook Trust Center opens (see Figure 5-4).

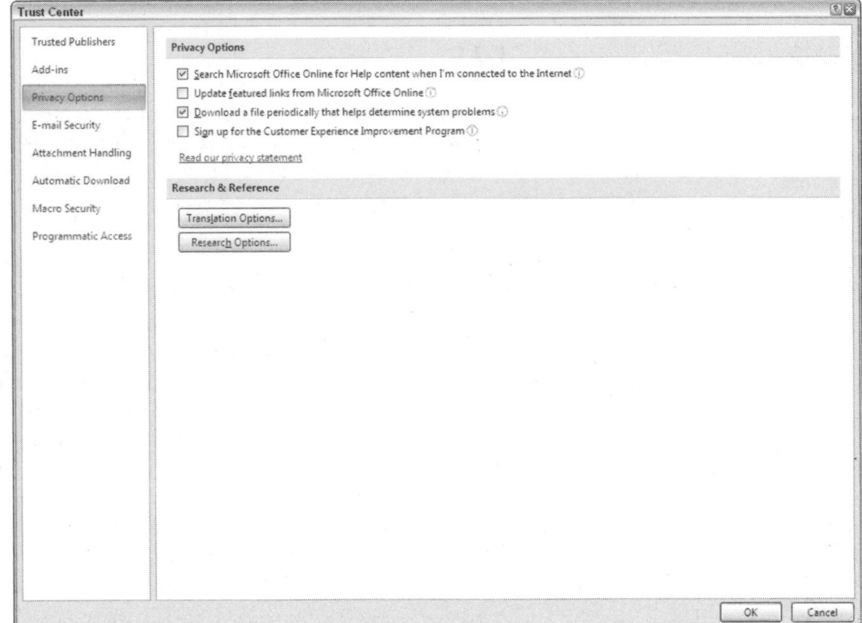

Figure 5-4: The Privacy Options of the Outlook Trust Center.

2. **Check the privacy options you want:**

   - **Search Microsoft Office Online for Help Content When I'm Connected to the Internet:** This option allows you to get the latest and greatest Help articles hot off the presses — or in this case, the Web site.
   - **Update Featured Links for Microsoft Office Online:** This option enables you to download cool templates to use in your mail merges from the Microsoft Office Online Web site. You also have links to various helpful sites in the Business Contact Manager dashboards.
   - **Download a File Periodically That Helps Determine System Problems:** You've probably seen the message that pops up periodically telling you that your computer has just thrown a hissy fit and asking you if you'd like to be a tattletale and tell Big Brother Microsoft all about it. Checking this option sends that information automatically.

- **Sign Up for the Customer Experience Improvement Program:** The jury is still out on this option. Basically, you are allowing Microsoft to monitor your computer to make sure you're happy. You might wonder what your computer is gossiping to Microsoft about — I know I sure am!

3. **Click OK to close the Trust Center.**

Grappling with Macros

A macro is a tiny program that automates a series of tasks. Typically, programmers write macros to run various commands on your computer. Unfortunately, some macros can put you and your computer at serious risk. For example, a hacker could write a macro to run a virus on your computer

Handling a macro security warning

If the Trust Center detects a macro in one of your documents, it calls the FBI and runs a background check. Okay, the Trust Center doesn't really call the FBI, but it does check out the macro pretty thoroughly to ensure that it was created by a *trusted publisher.* If the Trust Center detects a problem, the macro is disabled by default, and a dialog box appears to notify you of a potentially unsafe macro.

You might be wondering how Microsoft determines whether or not a macro is from a Trusted Publisher. Most software vendors that have worked directly with Microsoft are Trusted Publishers. However, there are thousands of less-known software programs that are quite trustworthy — even though they weren't created by a trusted publisher. The bottom line is that if you receive a security warning, make sure that you can verify the publisher.

When a security dialog box appears, you have the option to enable the macro or leave it disabled. You should enable the macro only if you are sure it is from a trustworthy source. You can click Trust All Documents from This Publisher in the security dialog box if you are sure the macro is from a trustworthy source. This adds the publisher to your Trusted Publishers list in the Trust Center.

Depending on the situation, the security dialog box describes the specific problem. The following table lists the possible problems and offers advice on what you should or should not do in each case.

Changing the macro settings in the Trust Center

You might want to change the macro settings in the Trust Center to set the level of protection that you are the most comfortable with. You can open the Trust Center and fiddle with the macro settings by following these steps:

1. **Choose Tools⇨Trust Center.**

   The Trust Center opens front and center (refer to Figure 5-4).

2. **Click the Macro Security tab, as shown in Figure 5-5.**

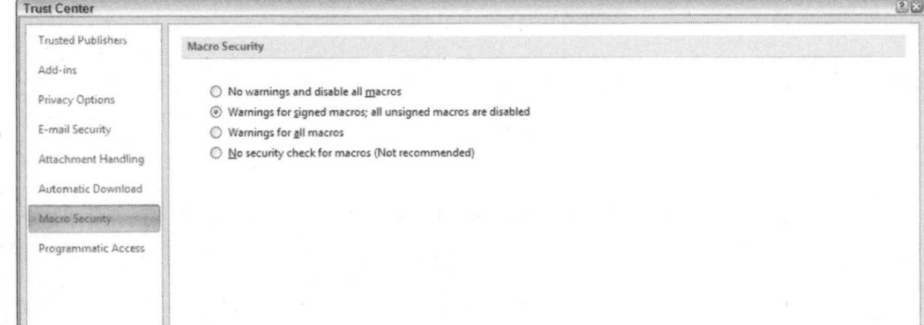

Figure 5-5: The Macro Security tab of the Trust Center.

3. **Select the macro security option that you want:**

   - **No Warnings and Disable All Macros:** Outlook disables all macros and does not issue macro warnings.
   - **Warnings for Signed Macros; All Unsigned Macros Are Disabled:** Outlook allows a macro to run if it is digitally signed by a trusted publisher. If the publisher is not on the Trusted Publisher list, you are notified, and Outlook disables the macro.

     Not sure what a digitally signed macro entails? You find out more about this added level of security in the section "Sending via Certified E-Mail," later in this chapter.
   - **Warnings for All Macros:** Outlook disables all macros, but sends you an alert if it finds one.
   - **No Security Check for Macros (Not Recommended):** This option allows all macros to run. This is not a good choice because it leaves you susceptible to viruses.

Help! Someone's Sending E-Mail on My Behalf

You might be happily working away one day when, out of the blue, one of the following security warnings appears:

- A program is trying to access e-mail address information stored in Outlook. If this is unexpected, click Deny and verify that your antivirus software is up-to-date.

- A program is trying to send an e-mail message on your behalf. If this is unexpected, click Deny and verify that your antivirus software is up-to-date.
- A program is trying to perform an action that may result in an e-mail message being sent on your behalf. If this is unexpected, click Deny and verify that your antivirus software is up-to-date.

Needless to say, these warnings can be quite traumatic. Many of the recent viruses attacked Outlook, took over the Address Book, and started sending e-mail to all contacts. Small wonder that Outlook feels compelled to issue a warning!

One of two harmless situations can occur that will prompt these warnings:

- A program started automatically that uses Outlook to send e-mail messages. For example, your accounting software might interface with Outlook.
- You started a program that is designed to send automatic e-mail. For example, you might be using a program to send e-mail newsletters to your entire client base.

Answering the security warning

When you receive one of these security warnings, you have two possible options:

Deny: Choose this option if you did not expect a program to access Outlook, or if you are at all unsure as to what program is attempting to access Outlook. The chances are pretty good that a virus is knocking on your door — or at least trying to gain entry to Outlook.

Allow: Choose this option if you clicked a command or started a program that you know is supposed to access Outlook data or send e-mail messages using Outlook. For example, you might be using a marketing product that automatically sends out e-mail at pre-assigned time intervals.

Preventing future security warnings

Installing an antivirus program and keeping it up-to-date may prevent this security warning from appearing again. However, be sure of a few things:

- Your antivirus software must be updated regularly. Most antivirus programs enable you to get automatic updates when you are online. Unfortunately, some computer users never bother to update their virus protection.

✦ Many new computers come bundled with antivirus software. Unfortunately, this software usually requires a yearly renewal; typically, if you don't pay for the renewal you are not protected from the latest and greatest — or nastiest and most lethal — of viruses. If your antivirus software subscription expires or has been inactive, you may get the security warning again when a program attempts to access Outlook. Guess you might consider this a case of pay now or pay later!

✦ Your antivirus software works with Outlook so that all incoming e-mail is automatically scanned for viruses.

Outlook's Trust Center actually checks for the presence of antivirus software and determines when a warning should be issued. To view these settings:

1. **Choose Tools⇨Trust Center from the main menu bar.**

   Outlook's Trust Center plays Open Sesame. To see it live, refer to Figure 5-4.

2. **Click the Programmatic Access tab.**

   The nice part here is that you only have to click the tab rather than trying to pronounce the darn things. If you look at the bottom of the tab, you see the status of your antivirus software just as it appears in Figure 5-6.

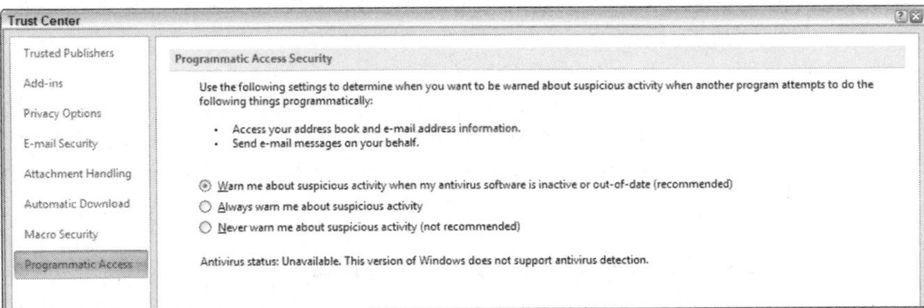

Figure 5-6: The Trust Center's Programmatic Access tab.

3. **Select one of the Programmatic Access security settings.**

   • *Warn Me About Suspicious Activity When My Antivirus Software Is Inactive or Out-of-Date (Recommended):* This is the default setting in Outlook; if your antivirus software is not working, you'll be warned if something tries to tinker with your e-mail or Address Book.

   • *Always Warn Me about Suspicious Activity:* This is the most secure setting; you are always prompted when a program tries to access Outlook.

- *Never Warn Me about Suspicious Activity (Not Recommended):* This option is for those of you who love jumping out of airplanes without first checking to see that your parachute is operational. That's probably why it's not a recommended setting.

4. **Click OK to close the Trust Center and breathe a big sigh of relief.**

Kicking the HTML out of Your E-Mail

In the Middle Ages, e-mail was limited to plain old black and white. With the dawning of the age of enlightenment — or at least HTML — e-mail took on all the colors of the rainbow. We all tried to outdo one another by including lots of gorgeous graphics in our electronic missives. Unfortunately, hackers also saw the advantages of HTML and started embedding links to evil Web sites from seemingly innocent graphics. And yes, your computer could be infected just by opening or previewing an e-mail.

Unfortunately, viruses are part of a vicious circle that is, well, very vicious. As soon as a new virus arrives on the scene, programmers scramble to plug up the hole that let the virus in. In the meantime, the unscrupulous virus creator finds *another* security breach and creates *another* virus. And so it goes.

If you are concerned that reading HTML-formatted messages will put you at greater risk for contracting a virus, you can have Outlook automatically display the messages that you open in plain text. Although it's not a guarantee, you are at somewhat less of a risk.

1. **Choose Tools⇨Trust Center from the main Outlook menu bar.**

   Not surprisingly, the Trust Center opens.

2. **Click the E-Mail Security tab.**

   You can check it out for yourself in Figure 5-7.

3. **Select the Read All Standard Mail in Plain Text check box in the Read as Plain Text area.**

   Optionally, you can include messages signed with a digital signature by selecting the Read All Digitally Signed Mail in Plain Text check box.

4. **Click OK to close the Trust Center.**

Bored with dull text e-mail? If you want to view a plain-text message in its full glory, click the InfoBar and choose either the Display as HTML or Display as Rich Text option.

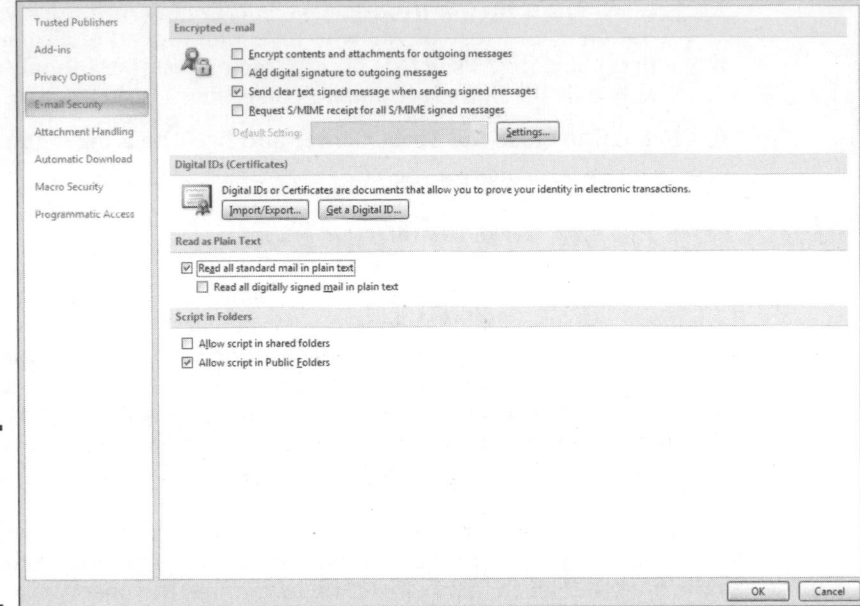

Figure 5-7: The E-Mail Security tab of the Trust Center.

Sending via Certified E-Mail

Outlook uses e-mail certificates to make the transmission of e-mail a more secure process. In order to do this, you obtain a digital ID from a certificate authority. After your message is certified, your certificate is sent along with it to prove to your recipient that you are exactly who you say you are. A digital ID also verifies your identity should you be asked to "sign" a document electronically.

Getting a digital ID from a certifying authority

Although the thought of obtaining a digital ID may strike you as being more high-tech than you bargained for, it's actually a pretty easy process if you follow these steps.

1. **Choose Tools⇨Trust Center from the main menu bar.**

   Once again, you find yourself smack in the middle of the Trust Center.

2. **Click the E-Mail Security tab.**

   You probably hate reruns as much as I do, but if you look at Figure 5-6, you can follow along here quite nicely.

3. **Click the Get a Digital ID button in the Digital IDs (Certificates) area.**

   At this point, you take a trip out to the Internet. You can select from a number of providers. After you've signed up for the service, you receive your digital ID and instructions via e-mail.

Although there is usually a slight fee for this service, the price is certainly worth it. You can't overstate the gratification of a good night's sleep knowing that you have good security on your system.

Putting your digital ID to work

After you obtain a digital ID, you want to start using it for all your outgoing e-mail. Here's how you do it:

1. **Choose Tools⇨Trust Center from the main menu bar.**

   The Trust Center opens (refer to Figure 5-5).

2. **Click the E-Mail Security tab.**
3. **Click the Settings button in the Encrypted e-mail section.**

   The E-Mail Security dialog box opens. At this point, you have one of two options:

   - If you have a digital ID, the settings to use the digital ID are automatically configured for you. Click OK to close the E-Mail Security dialog box.
   - If you don't have a digital ID, click the Get Digital ID button. You then hurtle through the Internet and land in a Microsoft Web site that will explain how to get a digital ID. Don't forget to click OK when you return from your cyber-travels to close the E-Mail Security dialog box.

4. **(Optional) Select the Encrypt contents and attachments for outgoing messages in the Encrypted E-Mail tab.**

   Choosing this option encrypts all your outgoing messages to any of your contacts who also have a digital ID.

   Although choosing this option ensures that every future message you send is encrypted, you need to know a few more things about e-mail encryption. Read the section, "Sending Encrypted or Digitally Signed E-Mail," later in this chapter, for further details.

5. **(Optional) Select the Add Digital Signature to Outgoing Messages check box.**

   This adds your digital ID to all your outgoing messages.

6. **(Optional) Select the Request S/MIME Receipt for All S/MIME Signed Messages.**

   S/MIME offers you another layer of protection. You can learn a bit more about it in the section "Sending a message with an S/MIME receipt request," later in this chapter.

7. **Click OK to close the Trust Center.**

Exchanging e-mail certificates

You must exchange certificates in order to send encrypted messages to someone. The preceding section explains that these certificates are issued by a certification authority. Like a driver's license, they can expire or be revoked. Fortunately, these certificates are not influenced by your driving habits.

You can exchange certificates in a number of ways:

- Send a digitally signed message. When the recipient adds your e-mail name to his contacts, your certificate is added as well.
- Certificates are actually special files with the `.cer` extension. You can send an e-mail message with your `.cer` file attached. The recipient can then import the certificate into your contact record.
- You can burn the `.cer` to a CD and deliver it to your intended recipient. You might want to meet in a dark corner of a neighborhood bar as you exchange `.cer` files.
- If you work on the same network, you can post the certificate somewhere where your recipient can access it.
- Create a contact card that includes your `.cer` file and send the recipient your card.

Arranging for the clandestine exchange of certificates is the hard part. After you receive a certificate into your nervous, sweaty hands, you add it to the recipient's contact record. You can accomplish this secret exchange of information in one of two ways, as described in the following sections.

Adding a certificate from a digitally signed e-mail

If someone sends you an e-mail with a digital signature, it's a snap to add the sender's certificate to his contact record:

1. **Open a message that has been digitally signed.**
2. **Right-click the name in the From box, and then click Add to Outlook Contacts on the shortcut menu.**
3. **(Optional) Select Update information of selected Contact if the Duplicate Contact Detected dialog box appears.**

The certificate is now stored in the contact's record. You can now send encrypted e-mail messages to this person.

Adding a certificate from a .cer file

If you receive a certificate on a CD or another format — and have sworn on a stack of Outlook bibles that you won't share the confidential information with anyone else under penalty of death — you can easily add the certificate to an existing contact record. Here's what you do:

1. **Click the Contacts folder on the folder list.**
2. **Open the contact record to which you want to add the certificate.**

   With any luck, the contact record should spring open. If you need help opening the contact record, see Book IV, Chapter 2.
3. **Click the Certificates icon on the Show section of the Ribbon.**

   If you already have a certificate for the contact, you see it listed here. If not, continue to the next step.
4. **Click the Import button.**
5. **Navigate to the secret location of the certificate; select it and click Open.**

   The certificate is now attached to the contact record.

Sending Encrypted or Digitally Signed E-Mail

When you were little, you might have sent secret messages by writing on a piece of paper with lemon juice and then holding it up to the sun. Unfortunately, lemon juice and keyboards don't mix so you need to find another method for sending secret messages.

When you encrypt an e-mail message, Outlook converts the message from readable text into scrambled text. The recipient needs a private key provided by the sender in order to be able to decipher the message. The plot thickens because the recipient must receive this key from the sender of the e-mail.

This is a separate process from digitally signing a message. A digital signature verifies that you are who you say you are. Encrypting a message renders the message unreadable except by recipients who hold the special key. The wearing of black trench coats and dark glasses is optional.

Encrypting or using a digital signature

In the preceding section, you see how you can automatically send encrypted messages or use digital signatures every time you send a message to someone who also has a digital ID. However, you might prefer to encrypt your outgoing messages only on an *as-needed* basis. Here's how you can do that:

1. **Compose a new e-mail message.**
2. **Click the Message Options button in the Options group section of the Ribbon.**

   The Message Options dialog box opens.
3. **Click the Security Settings button, located at the top of the Message Options dialog box.**

   The Security Properties dialog box opens (see Figure 5-8).

Figure 5-8: Encrypting or adding a digital signature to a message.

4. **(Optional) Select the Encrypt Message Content and Attachments check box if you want to encrypt this message.**
5. **(Optional) Select the Add Digital Signature to This Message check box if you want to add a digital signature to this message.**
6. **Click OK to close the Security Properties dialog box and then click OK again to close the Message Options dialog box.**
7. **Click the Send button to send your encrypted e-mail message on its way through cyberspace.**

Now might be a good time to take off that trench coat and, for heaven's sake, get rid of those dark glasses before you ruin your eyes!

Sending a message with an S/MIME receipt request

An S/MIME (Secure Multipurpose Internet Mail Extension) is an e-mail security feature used to request confirmation that a message was received unaltered. It results in a message attesting to the fact that your message arrived unscathed to its intended destination. The verification even includes information about who opened the message and when it was opened.

In the previous section, "Putting your digital ID to work," you see how to request a receipt for all encrypted messages that you send. Here's how you can request a receipt for a single message.

1. **Compose a new e-mail message.**
2. **Click the Message Options icon in the Options area of the Ribbon.**

   The Message Options dialog box opens.
3. **Click the Security Settings button.**

   The Security Properties dialog box opens (refer to Figure 5-8).
4. **Select the Add digital signature to this message check box.**
5. **Select the Request S/MIME receipt for this message check box.**
6. **Click OK two times to close the dialog boxes.**
7. **Click the Send icon to send your message.**

Setting a message expiration date

Just as an expiration date can prevent you from eating something that is no longer fit for consumption, adding an expiration date to a message can prevent your messages from circulating when they are no longer timely. When you set an expiration date for a new message, you are ensuring that the message can no longer be viewed after a specified period of time.

To set an expiration date, follow the following steps:

1. **Create a new message.**
2. **Click the Options icon in the Options section of the Ribbon.**

   The Message Options dialog box appears.
3. **Select the Expires After check box, and then select a date and time in the Delivery Options section of the Message Options dialog box.**
4. **Click Close to close the Message Options dialog box and then Send to send your e-mail hurtling on its way to your recipient.**

Understanding the Information Rights Management Program

The Information Rights Management (IRM) is a free Outlook add-on that allows you to specify what can and can't be done with the e-mail that you send. For example, you can keep your e-mail from being printed, forwarded, or copied. After you determine the ground rules for a message using IRM, your recipient can't amend the rules because they are stored in the message file itself.

How IRM watches your back

IRM provides you with a whole other layer of protection by controlling what happens after your e-mail leaves your Outbox, careens its way through cyberspace, and lands in your recipient's Inbox.

Here's a list of some things that IRM can do:

- ✦ Prevent the recipient from forwarding, copying, modifying, printing, faxing, or cutting and pasting the e-mail content.
- ✦ Prevent the e-mail from being copied by using Window's Print Screen feature.
- ✦ Restrict the content for all recipients of the e-mail.
- ✦ Provide the same level of protection for attachments, as long as the attachments are files created by using other Microsoft Office programs.
- ✦ Support file expiration so that content can no longer be viewed after a specified period of time.
- ✦ Allow you to sleep better at night because you don't have to worry that your confidential e-mail is being passed around the office.

When you need to watch your own back

It seems that there will always be a vicious circle between the good guys and the bad guys. As soon as antivirus software finds a cure for one virus, a new virus appears on the horizon. As cool as IRM sounds, it doesn't keep you totally protected. As the saying goes, where there's a will, there's a way.

Here's a list of some of the things that IRM *can't* do:

- ✦ Prevent your message from being erased, stolen, tortured, or transmitted by malicious programs such as Trojan horses, keystroke loggers, and spyware.
- ✦ Keep your message from being lost, mangled, or mutilated as the result of a computer virus.
- ✦ Prevent someone from retyping your message.
- ✦ Stop your recipient from taking a digital photograph of your message, although, I hope, the flash will invoke temporary blindness.
- ✦ Prevent your message from being copied by third-party screen-capture programs.
- ✦ Help you overcome OCD and other paranoid manifestations.

Configuring your computer for IRM

IRM does not appear magically when you install Outlook — if you want to use it, you have to do a bit of detective work to find and install it. Fortunately, this section provides you with a treasure map — and you won't even have to fight off pirates to use it.

1. **Choose Start⇨Control Panel.**
2. **Depending on your operating system, do one of the following:**
   - **Microsoft Windows Vista:** Choose Programs⇨Installed Programs⇨Install a program from the network. In the list of programs, choose Windows Rights Management Services Client and then click Add.
   - **Microsoft Windows XP:** Choose Start⇨Control Panel⇨Add or Remove Programs. In the left pane, click Add New Programs. From the list of programs, click Windows Rights Management Services Client and then click Add.

Alternatively, Outlook prompts you to download the Windows Rights Management Services Client the first time you try to open an e-mail in which the sender used IRM rules.

Sending a message with restricted permissions

By now you're probably feeling like James Bond. You've laid the groundwork by tweaking all the security settings to your liking. All systems are go to send an e-mail using restricted permissions. The hard work is over, and now you're off to win the spying game!

To send a message with restricted permissions, follow these steps:

1. **Create a new Outlook e-mail message.**
2. **Click the Microsoft Office Button and then click Permission.**

   You notice a rather ominous-looking message in the InfoBar at the top of the message that is intended to send chills down your spine. If you want to be scared, sneak a peek at Figure 5-9.
3. **Address and send the message.**

If you attach a document that was created in any of the Microsoft Office 2007 products to a message with restricted permission, Outlook automatically applies the same restricted permissions to the attachment. If the attached document has already been rights-managed in its originating program, those permissions remain in effect.

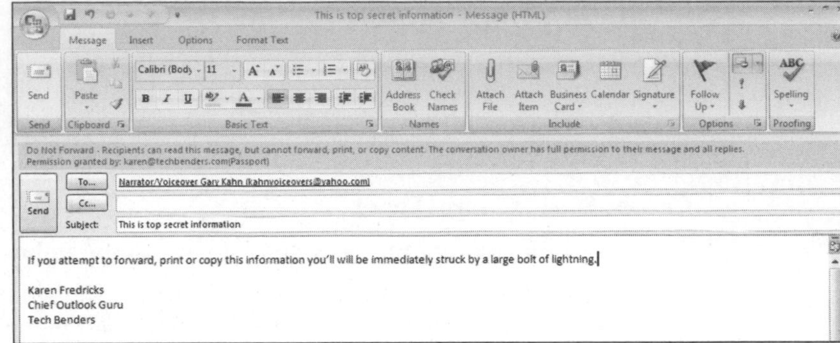

Figure 5-9: A scary e-mail heading when you use IRM.

Using a different account for IRM e-mail

Just like spies become masters of disguise, you might want to associate a different alias with your IRM-restricted messages. After you've set up your e-mail accounts, it's easy to associate one of them with an outgoing message.

1. **Create a new e-mail message.**
2. **Click the Microsoft Office Button, and then choose Permission⇨Manage Credentials.**

   The Select User dialog box opens.
3. **In the Select User dialog box, do one of the following:**
   - Select the e-mail address for the account you want to use.
   - Click Add, type your credentials for the new account, and then click OK.
4. **(Optional) Select the Always Use This Account check box if you always want to use the selected account to send IRM messages.**
5. **Click OK to close the Select User dialog box.**
6. **Click Send to send your IRM message.**

Viewing messages with restricted permissions

When you receive a message with restricted permission, you can identify it by the special icon that appears next to the message in the message list of your Inbox.

If you attempt to open and view a message with restricted permission without first obtaining a certificate, Outlook gives you the option to obtain one. You can open the message after you have installed a certificate.

If you reply to the message, your reply carries the same restrictions as the original e-mail.

Book X

Out and About: Taking Outlook on the Road

"My spam filter checks the recipient address, http links, and any writing that panders to postmodern English romanticism with conceits to 20th century graphic narrative."

Contents at a Glance

Chapter 1: Staying in Touch No Matter Where You Are 727

Chapter 2: Turning Your E-Mail Accounts into Roadies 751

Chapter 3: Printing Your Stuff and Taking It with You 767

Chapter 1: Staying in Touch No Matter Where You Are

In This Chapter

- **Letting Outlook handle e-mail while you're out of the office**
- **Getting someone else to handle your e-mail and appointments**
- **Managing Mail and Calendar for someone else**

Outlook makes handling life's little nuisances pretty easy. For example, Outlook can automatically organize and categorize incoming mail, remind you to leave early for a dentist's appointment, and even nag you to pick up your laundry. But what about vacations or business trips where you're out of the office for several days in a row? Do you just let e-mail flood the Inbox, or can Outlook help you there as well, and notify people that you're out of town so they won't expect an immediate response?

Perhaps you're a busy professional, with a nice assistant who not only keeps track of where you need to be *right now,* but even stops drop-in clients at the door so you can get there on time. As nice as that may sound, the system tends to break down every now and then, especially when you make an appointment and forget to tell your assistant, or vice-versa. Is there any way for Outlook to help you keep your appointments in one place that both of you can access and make changes to? The answer to all of these questions is a resounding, "Yes!" as you see in this chapter.

Letting the Out of Office Assistant Handle Mail While You're Gone

Every time I leave the office for even just the afternoon, I return to find my Inbox full of messages. Some are junk, and some are important. But I don't know which until I take the time to go through them all. Wouldn't it be nice to have someone sitting in for you while you're out, deleting the junk, forwarding the stuff that's important to a colleague so it gets acted on in a timely manner, and letting everyone else know that you're not ignoring them, you're just out of the office until tomorrow? Well, actually, you do have someone who can sit in at a moment's notice, and he's called the Out of Office Assistant.

The Out of Office Assistant is available to help you only if you work on an Exchange network. If you don't, you're not totally out of luck. You can still do some things to get Outlook to help you with e-mail management. See "What to Do if You Have a POP3 or IMAP E-Mail Account," later in this chapter.

You can use the Out of Office Assistant to send an instant reply to anyone who e-mails you while you're away. What the reply says is up to you: "I'm out of the office; see Bill if you need immediate assistance" or "Leave me alone. I'm on vacation, you bug!"

You can set up rules to process your e-mail automatically, too. For example, you may want e-mails from particular people passed on to someone in your company, and you may want junk newsletters and such automatically deleted.

Turning the Assistant on or off

To turn the Out of Assistant on, follow these steps:

1. **Choose Tools⇨Out of Office Assistant.**

   The Out of Office Assistant dialog box jumps up to help, as shown in Figure 1-1.

   If you use Outlook on an older Exchange network (and not Exchange 2007), your dialog box has fewer options. For example, you can create only one outgoing message that then goes to both people in your organization and out. Also, you can't format the message, or set the Office Assistant to turn on at a later time.

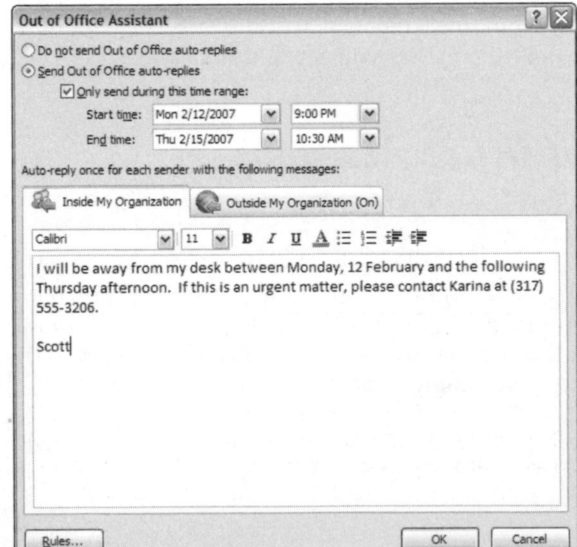

Figure 1-1: One assistant you don't have to hire.

2. Choose Send Out of Office Auto-Replies.

3. Set limits, if desired.

If you want to limit the time when the Assistant is active (for example, you want to set it up to work while you're on vacation next week, but not actually turn it on right now), then set a Start date and time, and an End date and time.

4. To create a message for e-mail received from people you work with, click the Inside My Organization tab located in the middle of the Out of Office Assistant dialog box, and then click inside the text box and type a message.

5. To create a message for e-mails received from people you don't work with, click the Outside My Organization tab as shown in Figure 1-2 and then click inside the box and type your message. Make sure that the Auto-Reply to People Outside My Organization option is turned on.

You can format the text for your outgoing message(s) however you like by using the buttons just above the text boxes on each tab.

Out of Office Assistant
Do not send Out of Office auto-replies
Send Out of Office auto-replies
Only send during this time range:
Start time: Mon 2/12/2007 9:00 PM
End time: Thu 2/15/2007 10:30 AM
Auto-reply once for each sender with the following messages:
Inside My Organization | Outside My Organization (On)
Auto reply to people outside my organization
My Contacts only | Anyone outside my organization
Calibri 11 B I U
Thank you for contacting my office. I will be away from my desk from Monday, 12 February, until the following Thursday afternoon. However, I will be checking e-mail periodically, so please let me know how I can return your inquiry.

Yours,

Scott Fulton
Rules... OK Cancel

Figure 1-2: Create a message for people outside your company.

6. Decide which "non-colleagues" you mean:

- **To use this auto reply only with people outside your company who are listed in your Contacts,** choose the My Contacts Only option, located just above the formatting buttons.

- **To use this auto reply with anyone who sends you an e-mail who is not in your company** even if he isn't in your Contacts list and chances are you don't know him, choose the Anyone Outside My Organization option.

If you choose the My Contacts Only option, the contact who e-mails you must be listed in your Exchange Contacts list — this can be the main list, or one you create — it just can't be a contacts list in an offline folder, or a personal folder you're using with a POP3, IMAP, or HTTP account.

Letting rules control the Assistant

With the Rules Wizard, you can create a set of rules to handle your e-mail while you're out — for example, you can move it from one folder to another, forward it to a colleague, or delete it. These rules are different from the ones I discuss in Book IX, Chapter 2, in that they only come into effect when you turn on the Out of Office Assistant.

To create a rule that limits what the Out of Office Assistant does with certain e-mails when you're at the spa (or wherever), follow these steps:

1. **Choose Tools⇨Out of Office Assistant⇨Add Rule.**

   The Edit Rule dialog box pops out, as shown in Figure 1-3.

Figure 1-3: You make the rules.

2. **Tell Outlook when to apply this rule.**

   In the When a Message Arrives That Meets the Following Conditions section, select the conditions that define the kinda e-mail you want to do something special with. For example, maybe you want to do something special when an e-mail arrives from your boss, or with a Subject line that includes "Blackford account" or just "Blackford."

   For the lowdown on how to select conditions that define the e-mail you want to affect and to set Advanced rules options, see Book IX, Chapter 2.

3. **If necessary, you can get nitpicky on which e-mails you want to affect by clicking Advanced and specifying additional conditions. After you're done, click OK.**

   In the Advanced dialog box (see Figure 1-4), you can further define the e-mails you want this rule to apply to. For example, you might want to do something special with large e-mails, e-mails received on a particular day or days, e-mails with attachments, and so on. After making selections, click OK and you return to the Edit Rule dialog box (refer to Figure 1-3).

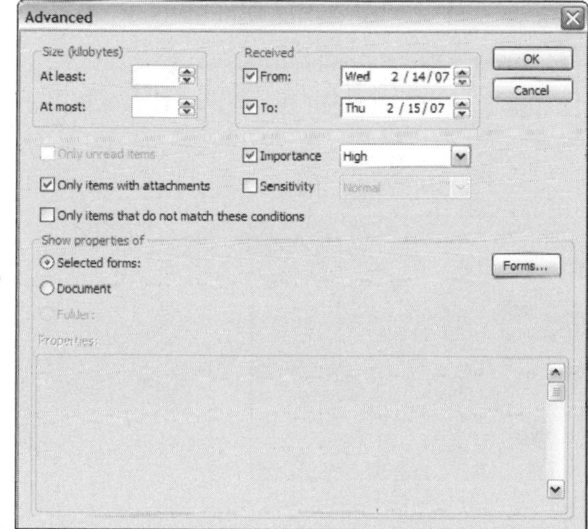

Figure 1-4: Set more options to define which e-mails you want to rule.

4. **If you want this particular rule to be applied last, after all other rules, then select the Do Not Process Subsequent Rules options.**

   Normally, rules are applied in the order in which they are listed, until every rule has been applied, but turning on this option changes that.

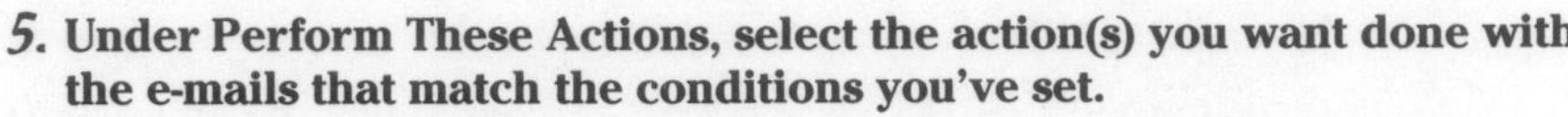

5. Under Perform These Actions, select the action(s) you want done with the e-mails that match the conditions you've set.

If you're creating a rule that deletes specific e-mail, then for obvious reasons, after that rule is applied, Outlook won't go looking at the rest of the rules to see if any more might apply to the e-mail. You can change the order of rules to have Outlook do something to the e-mail before its deleted, if you want. See the upcoming section, "Changing the rules," for help.

6. Click OK.

The rule is added to your other Out of Office rules. To create more rules, just click Add Rule and then rinse and repeat Steps 2 to 6.

Changing the rules

Just because you created some rules doesn't mean you're stuck with them. You can modify rules to make them work the way you want them to work. You can also delete rules you don't need.

To modify an existing rule, follow these steps:

1. Choose Tools⇨Out of Office Assistant.

Your rules are displayed in a list, in the Out of Office Rules dialog box, as shown in Figure 1-5.

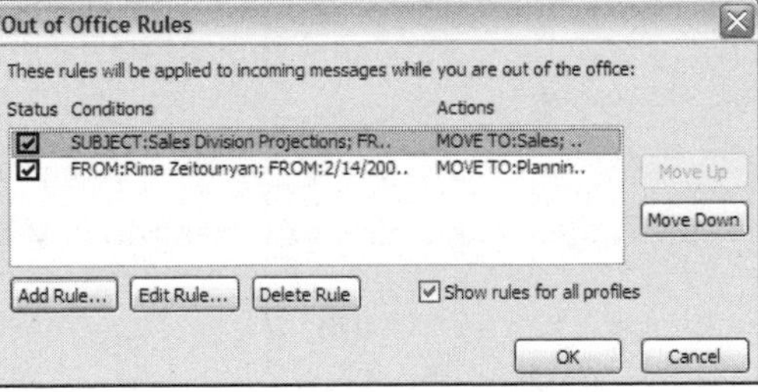

Figure 1-5: Select the rule you want to change.

2. Select a rule and click Edit Rule.

The Edit Rule dialog box appears (see Figure 1-6).

3. Make changes and click OK twice.

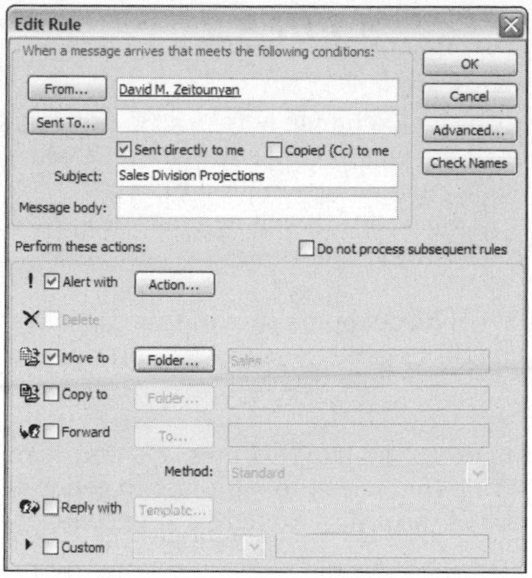

Figure 1-6: Rules aren't set in stone.

To change the order in which rules are applied, follow these steps:

1. **Choose Tools⇨Out of Office Assistant.**

   The Out of Office Rules dialog box appears. Refer to Figure 1-5.

2. **Select a rule to move up or down in the list.**

   Rules are applied in the order in which they appear in the list, so moving a rule up means that it will be applied before some other rule. Moving a rule down means that it will be applied after other rules have been applied to an e-mail message.

3. **Click Move Up or Move Down.**
4. **Repeat these steps to adjust the order of other rules. When you're done, click OK.**

To remove a rule completely, follow these steps:

1. **Choose Tools⇨Out of Office Assistant.**

   The Out of Office Rules dialog box appears. Refer to Figure 1-5.

2. **Select a rule to delete.**
3. **Click Delete Rule.**

   This is so much fun, why not remove other bothersome rules, like that red stoplight thing? I mean, why do I have to let others go first just because they have a green light? I like red.

4. **Then click OK when you're done.**

What to do if you have a POP3 or IMAP e-mail account

Well, okay, not everyone has an Exchange network. So not everyone can just wiggle their fingers and call the Out of Office Assistant to take over when they're away from their desk. Assuming you don't have an HTML account, and that you at least use POP3 or IMAP, well, you can at least do something to handle e-mail when you're away.

Some HTML (Web-based) e-mail accounts provide simple ways to handle incoming e-mail, so you might be able to use a Web interface to set up a system.

Here's the basic plan: You create a plain text message and save it as a template. Then you create a rule that uses the template to generate outgoing messages while you're out of the office. So here's stage one, creating the template:

1. **Choose File⇨New⇨Mail Message.**

   A new mail message for pops up.

2. **Choose Options⇨Format⇨Plain Text.**

   The message is changed to plain text rather that HTML format. Plain text means you're not going to be able to apply any formatting, but you can at least get your message out, as you can see in Figure 1-7.

3. **Type the message you want people to get while you're gone.**

   Outlook, being a bit of a control freak, keeps track of each and every e-mail you receive while you're gone, and sends the reply only once to each one, even if somebody sends you a bunch of e-mail. So keep that in mind when you design your message.

4. **To save the message as a template, click the Microsoft Office Button and choose Save As⇨Save As.**

   The Save As dialog box pops up.

5. **In the Save As Type drop-down list, select Outlook Template.**

6. **Type a filename for your template, like** Out of Office, **and click Save.**

7. **Close the message.**

   Because you saved your message as a template, and you don't want to send it to anyone just now, close the e-mail message and do not save any changes.

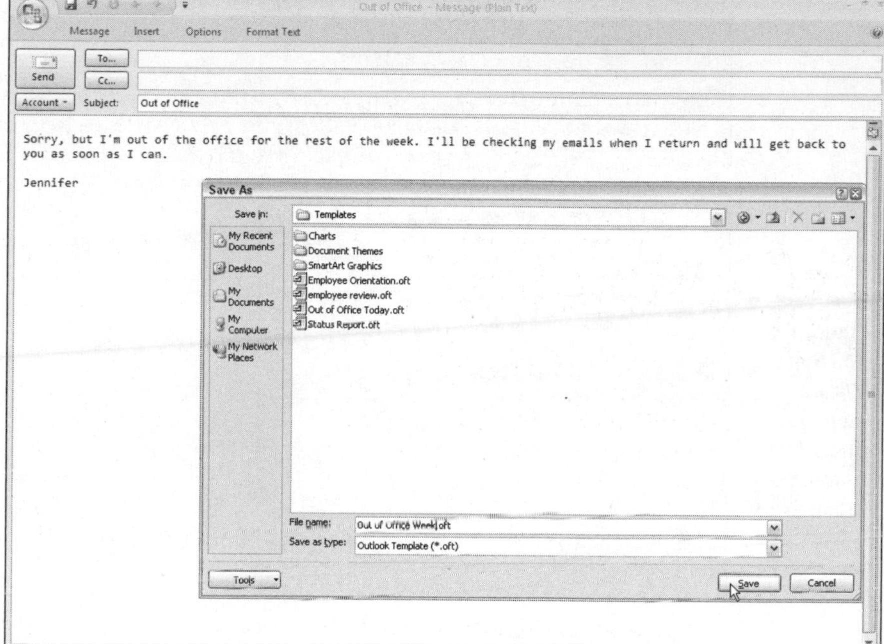

Figure 1-7: Create the message you want to send when you're out of the office.

You created a template for your out-of-office replies. Now, onto stage 2, creating a rule to use it:

1. **Choose Tools⇨Rules and Alerts⇨New Rule.**

   The Rules Wizard dialog box appears. See Figure 1-8.

2. **In the Start From a Blank Rule section, Select Check Messages When They Arrive and click Next.**

3. **Set conditions to define which messages get replies.**

   For example, you can send replies only to messages sent directly to you and no one else by choosing Sent Only to Me.

   You can set more limiting conditions if you want, or select none at all if you want this to apply to all incoming e-mail. Click Next. If you set up a rule that applies to every message you get, click Yes.

4. **In the What Do You Want to Do With the Message? list, choose Reply Using a Specific Template, as shown in Figure 1-9.**

5. **Click the A Specific Template link shown in the bottom of the dialog box.**

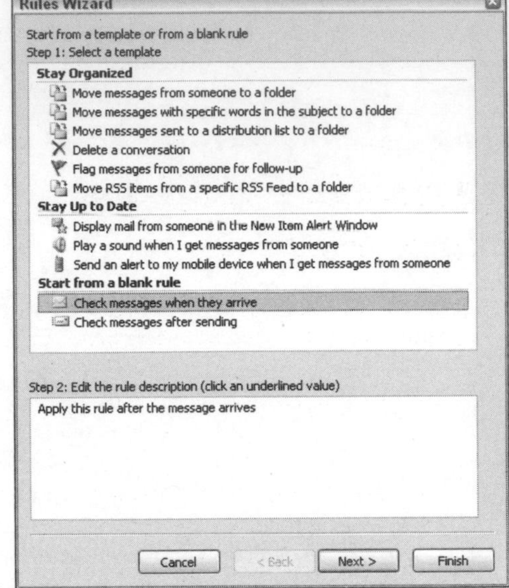

Figure 1-8: The Rules Wizard steps you through the process of creating an e-mail rule.

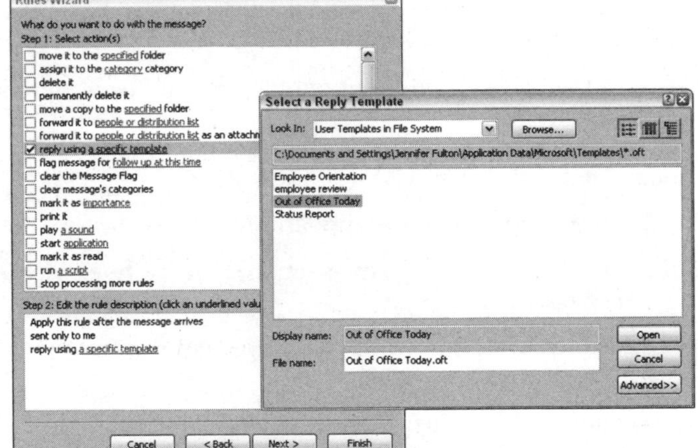

Figure 1-9: Send out auto-replies using a template.

6. **Choose User Templates in File System from the Look In list.**
7. **Select the template you just created, and click Open. Then click Next.**
8. **Select any exceptions and click Next.**
9. **Type a name for the rule in the Step 1: Specify a Name for This Rule box, select the Turn On This Rule option, and click Finish.**
10. **Click OK.**

Now, assuming that you leave Outlook (and your computer) on, and that you have Outlook set up so that it automatically checks for e-mail every once in a while, then when you get an e-mail, a reply is automatically created using your template.

Assigning a Delegate to Handle E-Mail and Appointments While You're Gone

If you work on an Exchange network, you can designate someone to act as your delegate, meaning that she can take over your day-to-day Outlook operations, including sending e-mails, accepting meeting requests, canceling appointments, and so on. Whether you can get her to do your laundry and walk the dog is another story.

Now, there is a different kind of sharing, which is typically more equal, and that involves simply sharing folders. For example, you can share your Calendar with someone, and he can share his with you. This sharing might involve only being able to view items in the folder, or it can involve various permission levels all the way up to being allowed to not only view, but create, change, and delete items in the folder. See Book IV, Chapter 3 for Calendar; Book V, Chapter 4 for Contacts; and Chapter VI, Chapter 3 for Tasks. Although you can use these same techniques to share an e-mail folder, typically you use delegate access to allow them to perform certain tasks *acting as you,* as described in this section.

For delegate access to work, both you and your personal workhorse must not only be on the same Exchange network, but also using the same version of Outlook. Typically, the network administrator makes sure that everyone has the same software so this shouldn't be a problem. In addition, for someone to have access to the e-mails you want her to answer, those e-mails must arrive in your regular Exchange mailbox — either the Inbox or some custom folder, and not into a Personal Folder you've created (a completely different data file, with a `.pst` extension).

Assigning a delegate

When you assign a delegate to take over some of your Outlook calendar duties, he can not only respond to meeting and task requests (by accepting, declining, or tentatively accepting them) but also receive meeting and task responses (responses to meeting or task requests you've sent). When people get these meeting/task replies, however, the From field reads something like *Delegate Name* on behalf of *Manager Name.* That way, people know it's not actually you responding, but someone acting on your behalf. For very special delegates, you can adjust the permissions to allow them to do even more, basically acting as your replacement. Don't worry; no matter how many tasks you allow him to perform for you, your delegate can't take over your corner office.

To assign a delegate, follow these steps:

1. **Choose Tools➪Options.**

   The Options dialog box appears.

2. **Click the Delegates tab and then click the Add button.**

   The Add Users dialog box jumps up, as shown in Figure 1-10.

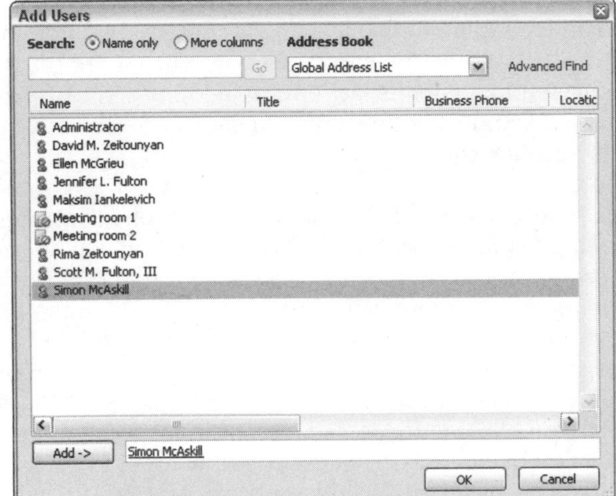

Figure 1-10: Add a delegate.

Now, if that ol' Add button isn't active, you may not be connected to the Exchange network. Check the status bar to make sure that you're connected properly and that the network is not down for some reason. If you're connected, then the problem is that you're trying to create delegate access to a Personal Folder (`.pst` file). Sorry, can't do that. Try again with your regular Exchange Inbox.

3. **From the people listed, select a workhorse (uh, delegate) to take over your job while you're gone. Then click Add and OK.**

4. **Set what you want them to do.**

   By default, a delegate can reply to meeting requests, and process meeting replies you receive. They can also respond to task requests and task replies. You can allow a delegate to do more if you want by changing settings in the Delegate Permissions dialog box, shown in Figure 1-11.

Even though the Inbox permission level is set to None, with the Delegate Receives Copies of Meeting-Related Messages Sent to Me option turned on, your delegate automatically receives your meeting requests and replies in her Inbox. She doesn't need a higher level of permission for your Inbox unless you want her to read, send, or delete e-mails on your behalf. The Calendar and Tasks permission level is set to Editor to allow the delegate to read and respond to task/meeting requests and task/meeting replies and do other stuff, as explained here.

Delegate Permissions: Simon McAskill
This delegate has the following permissions
Calendar: Editor (can read, create, and modify items)
☑ Delegate receives copies of meeting-related messages sent to me
Tasks: Editor (can read, create, and modify items)
Inbox: None
Contacts: None
Notes: None
Journal: None
☑ Automatically send a message to delegate summarizing these permissions
☐ Delegate can see my private items
OK | Cancel

Figure 1-11: You can allow your delegate to do more for you.

For any Outlook module, such as Inbox or Contacts, choose a permission level from the appropriate list box:

- *Reviewer:* Delegate can read items only.
- *Author:* Delegate can read any item, create new items, and change or delete the items he creates only.
- *Editor:* Delegate can read any item, create new items, and change or delete any item, even if the delegate did not create the item.

5. **To allow your delegate to see items you've marked as private, select the Delegate Can See My Private Items option.**

   This option allows a delegate to see all private items in your Exchange data file, regardless of the folder they are in.

6. **To create a message to your delegate that summarizes the permissions you've just set, choose the Automatically Send a Message to Delegate Summarizing These Permissions option.**
7. **When you're through setting options and having fun, click OK.**

   You return to the Options dialog box. See Figure 1-12.

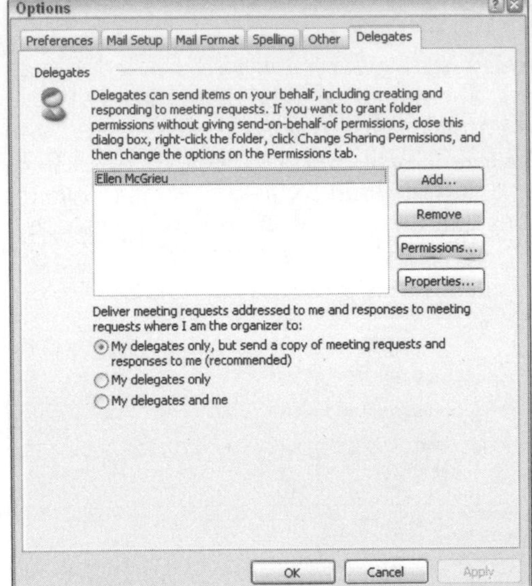

Figure 1-12: Set additional options for your delegate.

8. **Set whether you want copies and then click OK.**

   With the Delegate Receives Copies of Meeting-Related Messages Sent to Me, your delegate gets your meeting requests and replies. You can ask to get copies of these items placed in your Inbox, or bypass that altogether. You might want the copies, for example, so you can review what went on while you were gone. Select the option you want:

   - **To get copies of the meeting requests and replies that come in while you're gone,** choose the My Delegates Only, But Send a Copy of Meeting Requests and Responses to Me option.
   - **To allow meeting requests and replies to go to your delegate's Inbox only,** choose the My Delegates Only option.
   - **To place the original meeting requests and replies in both your delegate's Inbox and yours so you can also reply to them,** choose My Delegates and Me.

   The problem with this last option is that you might both reply differently, and who knows what Outlook would do with that.

If you choose the Automatically Send a Message to Delegate Summarizing These Permissions option in Step 6, your delegate gets an e-mail letting him know his duties and the permission levels you set. Your delegate can now take over the tasks (replying to meeting requests, for example) that you have assigned them. See "Managing Someone Else's E-Mail and Calendar," later in this chapter, for more help.

Changing a delegate's permission levels

To change what a delegate can do for you, follow these steps:

1. **Choose Tools⇨Options. Click the Delegate tab.**

   The Options dialog box jumps up, with the Delegates tab showing. See Figure 1-13.

2. **Select the delegate you want to change, and click Permissions.**

   The Delegate Permissions dialog box peeks out (see Figure 1-13).

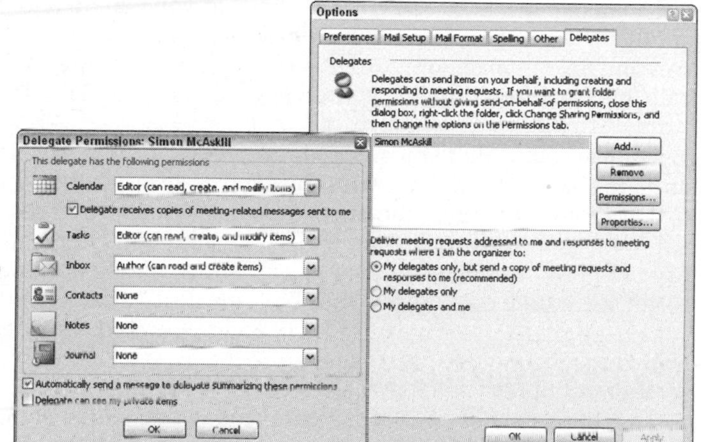

Figure 1-13: Changing the permissions you gave.

3. **Make changes to the various permissions levels.**

   To change the access level for one of your Outlook modules, such as Contacts or the Calendar, open the permission list and make a selection: Editor, Author, Reviewer, or None.

4. **Set other options as desired, and then click OK twice.**

You can also remove a delegate altogether, which you may want to do once you get back to work:

1. **Choose Tools⇨Options⇨Delegates.**

   The Options dialog box appears, with the Delegates tab open. Refer to Figure 1-12.

2. **Select the delegate you want to remove.**

   From the list of delegates, click a name to select it.

3. **Click Remove.**

   The delegate is removed from your Permissions lists and no longer is able to access your various Outlook folders. Your delegate doesn't get any e-mail letting him know that he's now "off the hook," so you might want to drop an e-mail yourself to thank him for his hard work and to tell him to stop reading your mail.

Managing Someone Else's E-Mail and Calendar

You might be given access to somebody else's Outlook folders in several ways. If someone wants to control exactly what you can do and doesn't want you acting on her behalf, you were probably given access to a shared folder. You can find help managing these folders in Book IV, Chapter 3 for Calendar; Book V, Chapter 4 for Contacts; and Chapter VI, Chapter 3 for Tasks.

This section assumes that you are given a different kind of access — delegate access — to someone's folders. With this kind of access, when you create items, you do it by acting on the other person's behalf. If you send a task request, for example, everyone knows that it came from you, but on behalf of someone else. So, no, you can't plan an eight-hour "doing nothing" meeting just to get some time off, without your boss eventually catching on.

Displaying somebody else's folders

When someone sets you up as a delegate, you get an e-mail detailing exactly which folders you have access to and what you can do there. The first thing you'll probably want to do is to display that person's folders in your Outlook, so you can keep an eye on them.

Although delegate access is great, unless the person also makes his mailbox visible, you can't access it through the Navigation pane. To make a mailbox visible on the Exchange network, you need to change to Mail and right-click the Mailbox - *your name* folder in the Navigation pane and choose Change Sharing Permissions. Select the Folder Visible option and click OK. Then tell your delegate that everything's set.

To add somebody's folders to Outlook so you can see them each time you start the program, follow these steps:

1. **Choose Tools⇨Account Settings.**

   The Account Settings dialog box appears (see Figure 1-14).

2. **Select your Exchange account and click Change.**

   The Change E-Mail Account dialog box appears. See Figure 1-15.

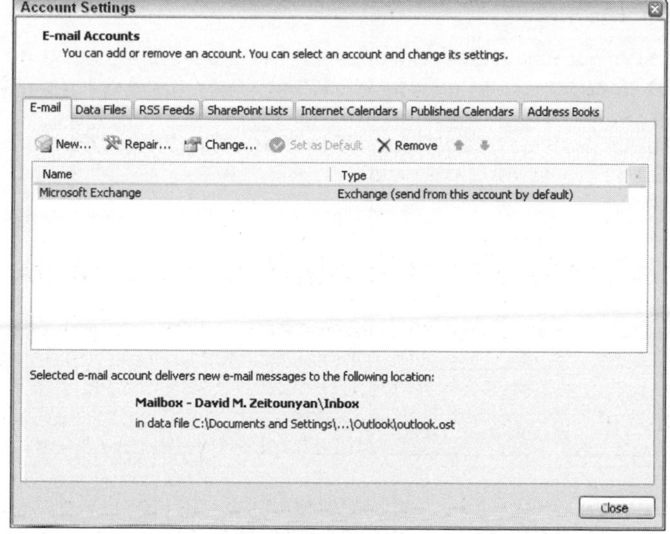

Figure 1-14: Getting a peek at somebody's Outlook folders.

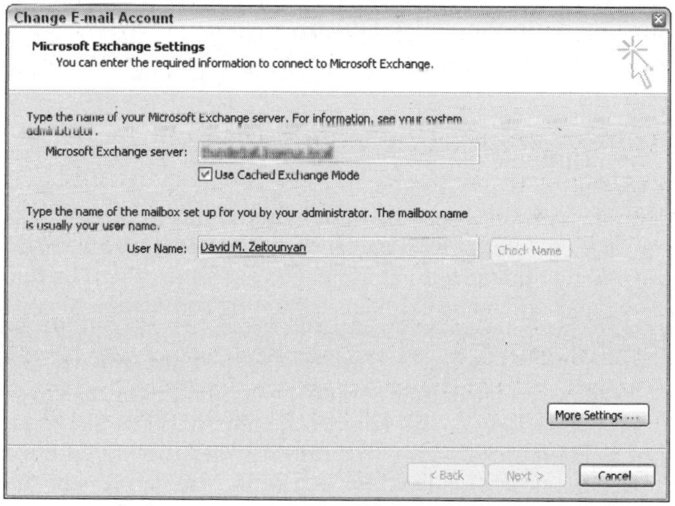

Figure 1-15: The Change E-Mail Account dialog box.

3. **Click the More Settings button. Click the Advanced tab in the More Settings dialog box. Then click the Add button.**

   The Add Mailbox dialog box opens, as shown in Figure 1-16.

4. **Enter the name of the person whose folders you want displayed in your Outlook, and click OK.**

   The person's name appears in the list at the top of the Advanced tab in the Microsoft Exchange dialog box.

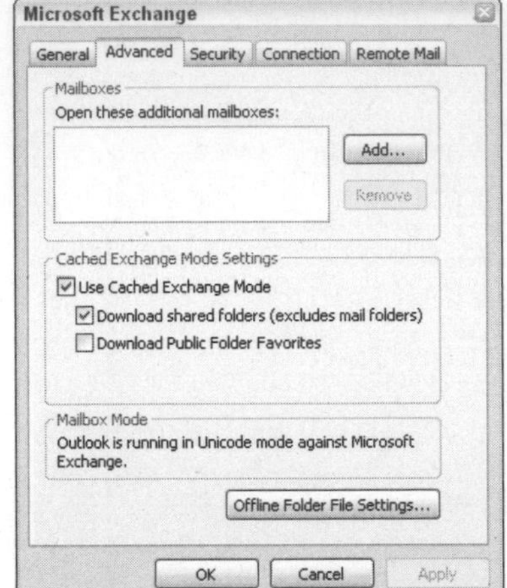

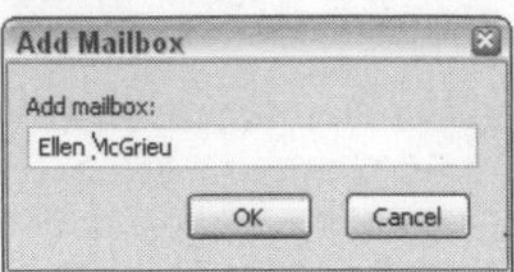

Figure 1-16: Add somebody's mailbox to yours.

5. **Click OK in the More Settings dialog box.**

   You return to the Change E-Mail Account dialog box.

6. **Click Next and then click Finish.**

   The Account Settings dialog box peeks back out.

7. **Click Close.**

8. **Restart Outlook.**

Assuming the person whose name you typed has granted you access to some or all their folders, you can access her folders from the Navigation pane within the appropriate module. For example, if you have Editor access to the Calendar so you could handle meeting requests and replies, you also have permission to view that person's calendar and to make appointments and events. After following the previous steps conveniently provided here by *moi,* you can now access that person's calendar easily, as shown in Figure 1-17. Here, I've switched over to my Calendar, and I've clicked the Calendar in Mailbox - Ellen McGrieu link (I found it under the My Calendars category) to view her calendar side-by-side with mine. You can repeat this process in any other module you've been given access to, such as Tasks, to view its items and perform your duly designated duties as delegate.

When you gain access to someone's Contacts folder, you need to click only that folder in the Navigation pane at any time to display its contacts.

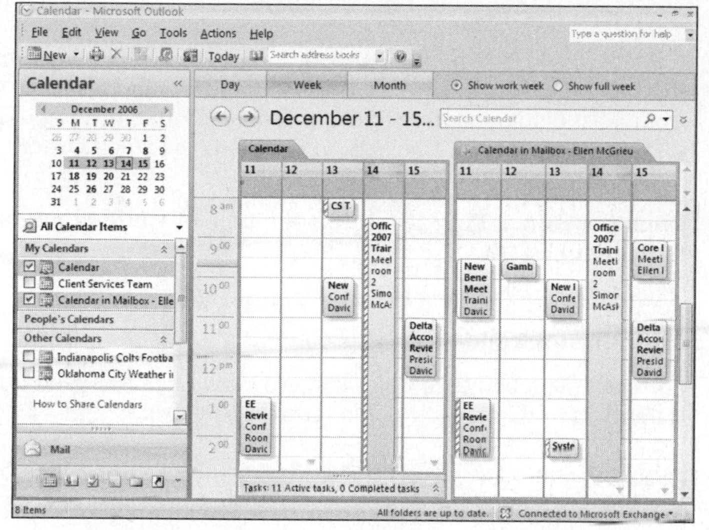

Figure 1-17: Now you can access the folders.

If you don't want to see somebody's folders hanging out with yours, causing you to accidentally add your appointments to their Calendar or vice versa, you can display their folder just when you need it. As you change to a different module, or exit Outlook, that folder is removed from view and you'll need to repeat these steps to see it again. To temporarily display someone's folder in your Outlook (assuming you have permission), follow these steps:

1. **Choose File⇨Open⇨Other User's Folder.**

   The Open Other User's Folder dialog box appears, as shown in Figure 1-18.

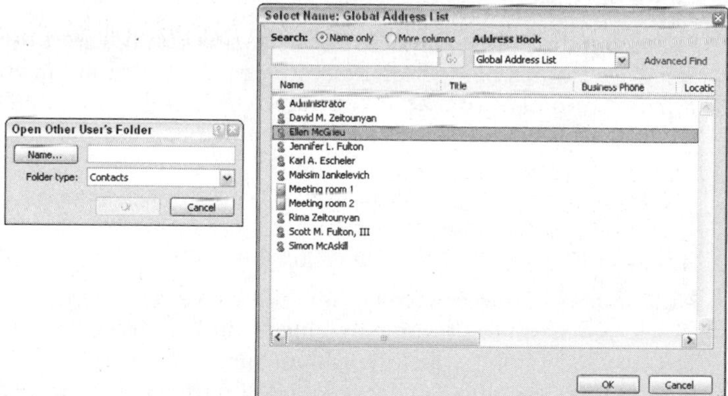

Figure 1-18: Spying on another user, kinda.

2. **Designate a mailbox to open.**

   In the Name box, type the name of the person whose mailbox you want to open temporarily, or click the Name button and select that person from a list displayed in the Select Names: Global Address List dialog box (refer to Figure 1-18). Click OK to return to the Open Other User's Folder dialog box.

3. **From the Folder Type list, select the type of Outlook module you want to open. Click OK.**

   The folder you chose is added to the Navigation pane.

4. **Click that folder to display its contents.**

   For example, change to Calendar and click Ellen McGrieu under My Calendars to display her calendar next to yours.

If for some reason you haven't been given access to the folder you wanted to open, you'll see a message asking if you'd like to request access. Click Yes.

Dealing with meetings and tasks as a delegate

Well now, you're pretty well set. You have the folders for that special someone who's stuff you promised to take care of, appearing right there in your Outlook, all nice and ready to go. All you need to do now is sit back and wait for a meeting or task request or reply to come in, assuming that's what you're taking care of. If you're in charge of other things as well, such as adding or canceling appointments, well, just go ahead and take care of that too.

Here's how to deal with meeting or task requests that come in for the person you're covering for, follow these steps:

1. **Open the task or meeting request you want to reply to.**

   Assuming the colleague whose stuff you're handling left the Delegate Receives Copies of Meeting-Related Messages option on, any incoming meeting requests appear in your Inbox, where you can easily deal with them. If your colleague didn't choose this option when she set you up as a delegate, then you need to actually check that person's mailbox for the requests (assuming you have at least Reviewer access for that). Once found, double-click the request to open it, as shown in Figure 1-19. The InfoBar reminds you that this request is actually for someone else.

   Now, unless you were given at least Reviewer access to your colleague's Inbox, you need to do some digging to find and reply to task requests because they don't appear automatically in your Inbox. With Editor access to Tasks, you can use the steps in the preceding section to display your colleague's Tasks folder, and then when task requests come in, they appear in the listing in bold (until you open them, that is).

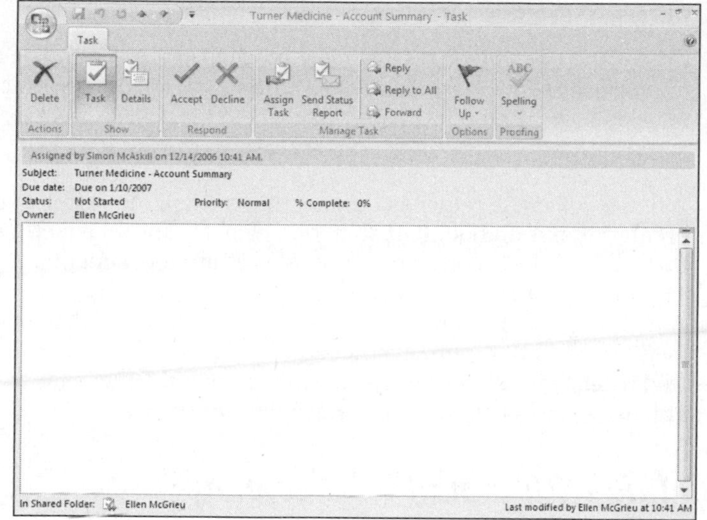

Figure 1-19: As delegate, you can open up somebody else's requests.

To help you quickly identify task requests, sort your colleague's Tasks list by person responsible. Choose View➪Current View➪Person Responsible.

2. **Decide what to do.**

   As the delegate, hopefully you've been given some guidelines on how to determine whether or not to accept a meeting or task request. If not, there's always the Magic 8 Ball. Click Accept, Decline, or Tentative. If appropriate, you can (for a meeting request, that is), propose a different time by clicking Propose New Time.

3. **Choose whether or not to comment.**

   In the dialog box that appears, choose Edit the Response Before Sending to type a comment in your reply before sending it; choose Send the Response Now to just send the reply; or choose Don't Send a Response to cancel your reply. Click OK.

The sender of the meeting or task request gets your reply, clearly marked with your name, and the name of your colleague. This helps everyone know that you're acting as someone's delegate.

To create a meeting request or task request on behalf of someone else, follow these steps:

1. **Open the other person's Calendar or Tasks folder.**

   See the preceding section, "Displaying somebody else's folders," for help accessing someone's folders.

2. **Choose File⇨New⇨Meeting or Task.**

   Create the meeting or task request in the usual manner. For help in creating meeting requests, see Book IV, Chapter 4. For help with task requests, see Book VI, Chapter 3.

3. **Click Send.**

   When a colleague receives the meeting or task request, he sees that you created it, but on behalf of someone else. He knows exactly who's asking the favor, and who owes him one if he ultimately accepts.

When meeting replies come in, you simply need to open the messages to have Outlook add that person's Accept, Decline, or Tentative added to the meeting total. For task replies, you need to open the message as well, so you can at least see whether or not she accepted the task.

Dealing with e-mail as a delegate

Managing a few meeting replies or task requests that come in while someone's on vacation should probably amount to very little work on your part. Of course, if it's your full-time job to manage someone's schedule, that's another matter altogether. Still, dealing with appointments, meetings, and a few stray task requests is nothing compared to dealing with a steady stream of incoming e-mail. I mean, I know how much e-mail I get on any given day, and if I had to double that by taking on someone else's e-mail, I'd probably never be able to leave the office.

To send out a new e-mail on someone's behalf, follow these steps:

1. **Choose File⇨New⇨Mail Message.**

   A message form jumps up.

2. **Add your colleague's name to the From box.**

   Now, normally, the From box doesn't show up in the message form. To make it show, choose Options⇨Fields⇨Show From. Then either type the name of the person you're creating the e-mail for in the From box, or click the From button and select the name. See Figure 1-20.

3. **Complete the e-mail.**

   The rest is familiar: address the e-mail, type a Subject, and enter your message, or rather, your colleague's message, in that big white box at the bottom of the form. If you need help creating the e-mail, see Book II, Chapter 1.

4. **When you're finished, click Send.**

   The recipient knows that you sent the e-mail, but he also knows that the message was ultimately from someone else.

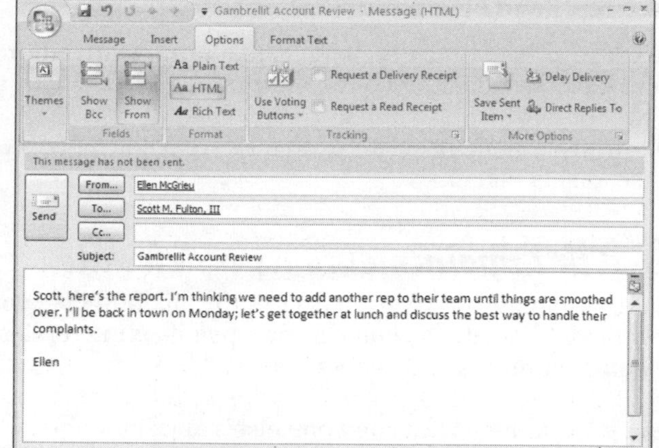

Figure 1-20: Sending an e-mail that's not from you.

To reply to somebody else's e-mail, you need to be able to view the contents of her Inbox first. See the section, "Displaying somebody else's folders" for help. After you display her Inbox, here's how to do the rest:

1. **Select the message you want to reply to.**

   It's hiding in your colleague's Inbox.

2. **Click Reply.**

   A message form appears, as shown in Figure 1-21. If you have the From box displayed, you'll notice that your colleague's name automatically appears there.

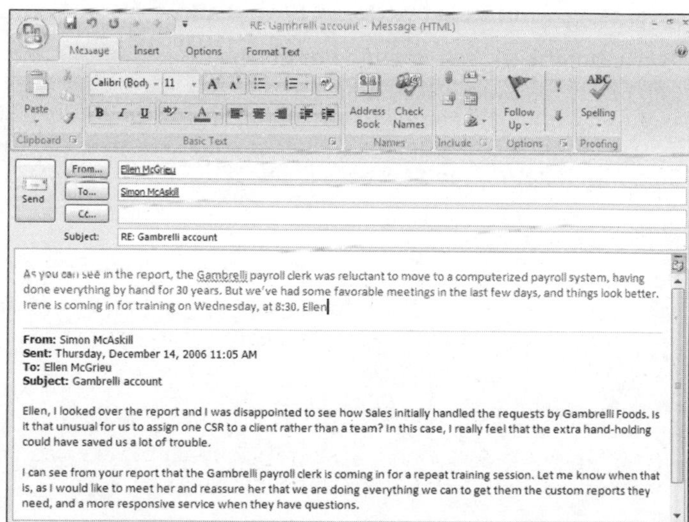

Figure 1-21: Ghost writer.

3. **Type the reply and click Send.**

   The message arrives in the recipient's mailbox, clearly addressed from you, acting on the behalf of your colleague.

You can follow these same basic steps to forward a colleague's e-mail to someone else, on his behalf.

Dealing with appointments as a delegate

As a delegate, assuming you're given access to somebody's Calendar, you can not only reply to meeting requests and open meeting replies, but you can add appointments and events.

Follow these steps to deal with someone else's appointments:

1. **Change to your colleague's Calendar.**

   The calendar should be listed on the Navigation pane; if not, see the previous section "Displaying somebody else's folders" for more info. If the calendar is listed, select it to make that calendar active.

2. **Choose File⇨New⇨Appointment.**

   An appointment form appears.

3. **Complete the appointment.**

   Complete the appointment as normal: Add a Subject, Location, Start Time and Date, End Time and Date, and so on. If you need help in creating an appointment, see Book IV, Chapter 1.

4. **Choose Save & Close to save the appointment.**

5. **Choose Appointment⇨Actions⇨Save & Close.**

   The appointment appears in your colleague's Calendar and not yours.

Follow these same basic steps to add an event to somebody else's Calendar. For help in creating a meeting on behalf of someone else, see the section, "Dealing with meetings and tasks as a delegate."

Chapter 2: Turning Your E-Mail Accounts into Roadies

In This Chapter

- Keeping in touch even when you're out of the office
- Making your company's Exchange e-mail vacation friendly
- Utilizing Web mail as an out-of-office solution
- Going live with Windows Live Mail

E-mail, once it's set up and working properly, is pretty much a "forget about it" kind of thing. You drive to work, get a cup of coffee, sit down at your desk, and start slogging through all the messages. At the end of the day, you go home, get another cup of coffee, sit down at your desk, and start slogging through your personal messages. It's when you break the routine that trouble starts. You go on vacation, but you'd like to check to see if your boss has responded to your request for more personnel. Or you go on a business trip and need to check e-mail every day. It's not like you can drag your desktop computer with you on that trip, even if you wanted to. And taking your laptop along doesn't take your e-mail too, or at least, your e-mail connection.

So what's a person to do? I have to assume everybody has this problem because in recent months, solutions abound everywhere you look: With a smart phone, you can dial and get your e-mail from any location. With a PC Card, it's easy to connect your laptop to the Internet and get e-mail. These two solutions, however, assume that you have a cooperative e-mail account, such as Web mail, that allows you to connect through the Internet and grab your messages. Problem is, most corporate accounts aren't Web-mail–based, so it's tough to take them along with you on a trip. And personal e-mail isn't always much better, depending on the kind of account you have. In this chapter, I discuss various options and what you can do to get your e-mail from the road.

Taking E-Mail on the Road

Okay, I've outlined the basic problem, which is "Doctor Jennifer, I get my e-mail on my home computer and now I'm going on vacation and I want to be able to use my laptop to check e-mail while I'm gone but I really like the idea of keeping all my e-mail in one place. What do I do?"

The lowdown on e-mail accounts

Many e-mails accounts wear more than one hat, meaning that you can connect to them using a variety of protocols. Most personal accounts, for example, use either POP3 or HTTP protocols to retrieve and post e-mail. When you use POP3, it gets the mail from the server and then deletes it. HTTP is a whole different animal. With HTTP, you bypass Outlook and use your Web browser to manage e-mail. The Web interface allows you to look at e-mail and delete it from the server when you want; otherwise, it's kept on the server. So if you mostly use POP3 to dump your e-mail into Outlook, you can go on vacation and use the hotel's computer and its Internet connection to check e-mail using HTTP. As long as you don't delete messages, you can get them again using Outlook when you get home.

Some personal accounts use IMAP to retrieve and post e-mail messages. With IMAP servers, the e-mail is left on the server and copied to Outlook. When you delete a message in your Inbox, it's marked for deletion from the IMAP server, and the next time you connect, that message is deleted permanently.

You can change these behaviors and get Outlook to leave the messages on the server when desired, so you can download them into a more permanent location (such as your home computer) when you're ready.

Yes, Virginia, there is a Santa Claus, and it's Outlook and its ability to beat your e-mail server into submission. You see, in most cases, when you get your e-mail using Outlook on your home computer, that's it — the e-mail is deleted from the server, and it ain't comin' back, baby. So how do you tell the server, "Look, I wanna get these e-mails, but I wanna save 'em too." Luckily, that's pretty easy. You just need to tell Outlook what you want, and it tells the e-mail server to leave your messages alone.

Getting e-mail messages on a second computer without deleting them

Here's how you can tell Outlook to retrieve e-mail off a POP3 server without deleting them:

1. **Choose Tools⇨Account Settings⇨E-Mail.**

   The Account Settings dialog box jumps up, with the E-Mail tab displayed. See Figure 2-1.

2. **Select the account to change.**

   From the list that appears on the E-Mail tab, select the account you want to change. (Refer to Figure 2-1.)

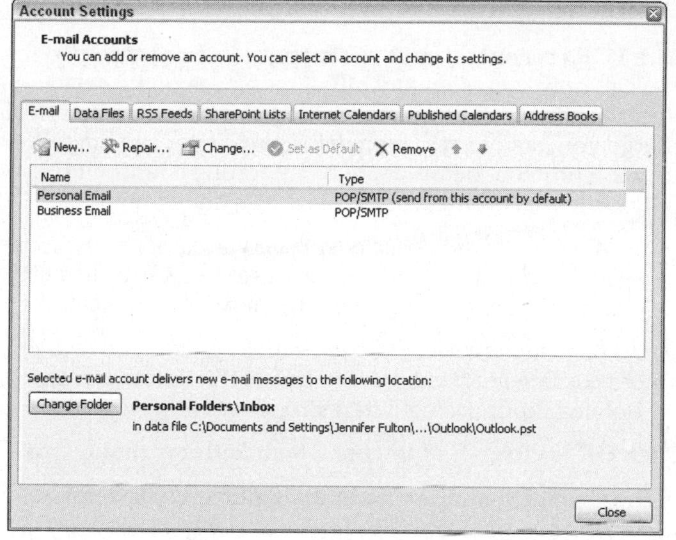

Figure 2-1: The Account Settings dialog box.

3. **Click the Change button, and the Change E-Mail Account dialog box appears. Click the More Settings button.**

   The Internet E-Mail Settings dialog box pops out. (Refer to Figure 2-1.)

4. **Click the Advanced tab and turn on the Leave a Copy of Messages on the Server option, as shown in Figure 2-2.**

   This feature tells Outlook to leave your messages alone.

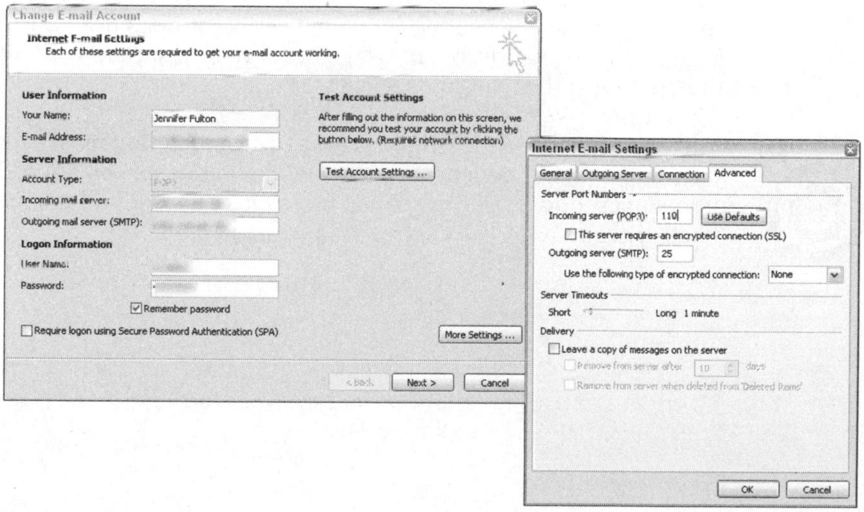

Figure 2-2: Keep a copy for yourself.

5. **Set deletion options.**

   With POP3 accounts, your ISP is only going to be so patient; typically you can only keep so many MB of messages on its server and then it'll either send you an evil e-mail telling you to fix it, cancel your account, or charge you lots of extra money for going over the limit. Well, you can stop the problem before it starts by setting a limit on the messages Outlook leaves on the server. Here are your options:

   - *To remove the messages after a set period of time,* choose Remove From Server After *XX* Days. Then set the *XX* to the actual number of days you want messages left up there on the e-mail server.
   - *To remove messages from the e-mail server when you empty them out of your Deleted Items folder,* choose the Remove From Server When Deleted From "Deleted Items" option.

6. **Click OK to close the Internet E-Mail Settings dialog box.**
7. **In the Change E-Mail Account dialog box, click Next.**
8. **Click Finish.**

Downloading message headers only

Another way in which you can deal with the problem of checking e-mail while you're away from your main computer is to just check message headers. The message header, or Subject, should tell you whether an e-mail is important enough to bother downloading. After downloading a message, you can tell Outlook to remove it from the server, or keep it there, depending on your needs.

Message headers appear in the Inbox looking just like normal e-mail. When you click a message header, though, its content does not appear in the Reading pane. In addition, message headers are marked with a special icon, a telephone and envelope (see Figure 2-3).

You can, when needed, tell the server to stop deleting messages you download, and to keep them around for a while on the server. For help, see the preceding section, "Getting e-mail messages on a second computer without deleting them."

Message Header icon

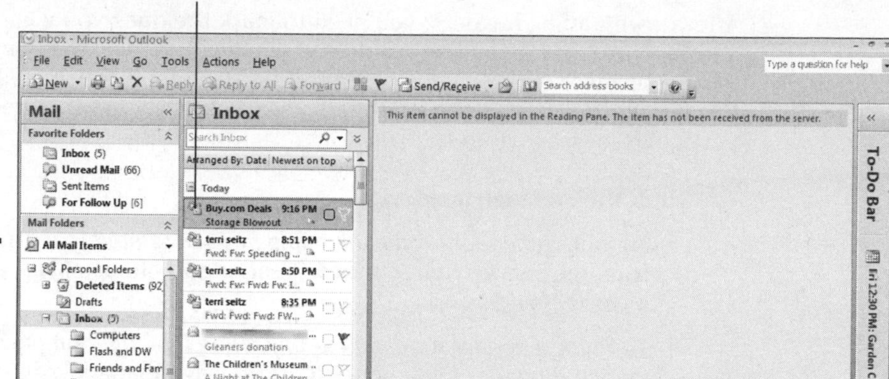

Figure 2-3: Message headers and their icons.

Viewing headers has some advantages. You can delete junk mail and spam without downloading those messages to your system and possibly infecting it. You can keep most e-mail on the server for later downloading (possibly at your main computer) and get only the messages you need now. Also, by scanning headers, you can process e-mail more quickly and get back to that well-deserved vacation.

To download message headers, leaving the actual messages on the server, follow these steps:

1. **Choose Tools⇨Send/Receive.**

   The Send/Receive submenu appears.

2. **From the submenu that appears, choose the e-mail account whose message headers you want to get.**

   Another submenu appears, listing commands that are valid with that e-mail account.

3. **Choose Download Inbox Headers.**

   Outlook checks the e-mail server for that account and downloads just the message headers.

You can set up a Send/Receive Group to download message headers only all the time for a particular e-mail account, To find out how to do it, see Book III, Chapter 5.

Acting on message headers

After downloading headers, you need to mark the ones you want to act on and then process them. For example, if you want to view the contents of a particular message, you need to mark it for download. You can also mark headers for deletion, if you've already decided that you won't need to read a particular message. Here's how:

1. **Mark the message headers:**

   - *To mark a header for downloading to your computer,* with removal from the server, right-click the header and choose Mark to Download Message(s).
   - *To mark a header for downloading while leaving it on the server,* right-click the header and choose Mark to Download Message Copy.
   - *To mark a header for deletion,* right-click it and choose Delete. You can also select a header and press Delete. The header is marked with strikethrough, to indicate that it's set for deletion.

   Messages marked for deletion are not removed from an IMAP server until you say "Boo!" Well, actually, the items are deleted only when you physically yank them from the server's greedy hands by issuing a purge command. Select the e-mail folder containing the items you want to delete from the server, and then choose Edit⇨Purge⇨Purge Marked Items in *foldername.*

   You can process several message headers at one time; just press Ctrl and click each header you want to select, or press Shift, click the first header in a group, then select the last one in the group while still pressing Shift. After you select the headers to process, right-click the group and choose the appropriate command from the shortcut menu that appears.

2. **To process the marked headers, choose Tools⇨Send/Receive⇨ *accountname*⇨Process Marked Headers.**

   You can also click the Send/Receive button on the Standard toolbar and choose *accountname*⇨Process Marked Headers. See Figure 2-4.

   You can't process message headers if they've been moved from the Inbox to another e-mail folder.

After you process them, message headers marked for downloading are placed in your Inbox. Message headers you marked for deletion are removed from the server.

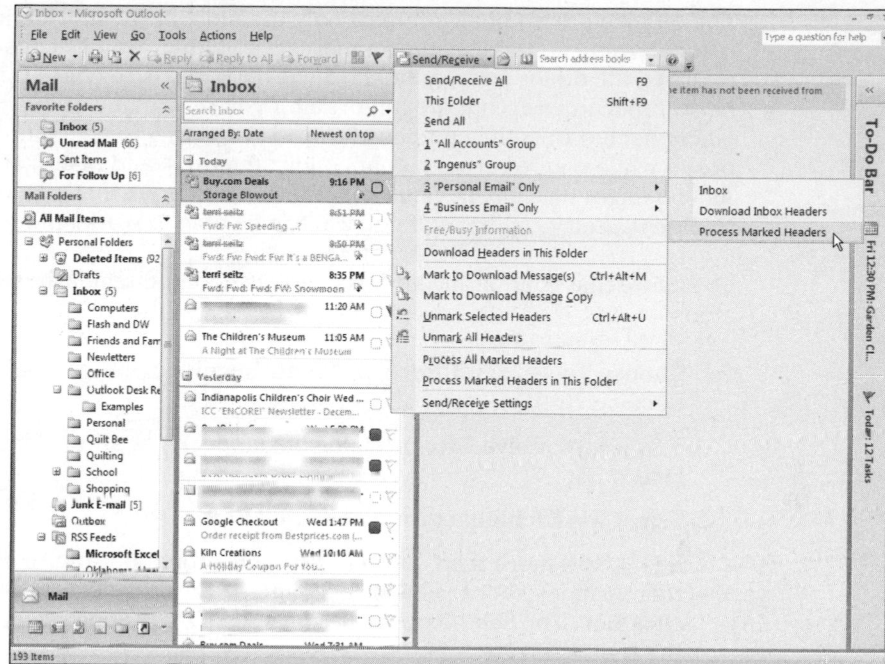

Figure 2-4: Ready, set, mark your header!

Taking Microsoft Exchange on the Road

It seems a little funny to be talking about taking Exchange on the road, seeing as though it's designed to be used on a company network. But the reality is, even though you may have a desk downtown, chances are you spend very little time at it. Or, even if you do keep your desk chair warm from 8:00 to 5:00, your work probably doesn't stop just because you're sitting in your living room. So what should you know about taking Outlook out on the road? This section helps you fill in the blanks.

Downloading the Offline Address Book

For Exchange users, the Global Address List is king. It contains a list of everybody in the corporation, their e-mail addresses, and other information such as employee ID, department name, and phone number or extension. While you're connected to Exchange, Outlook resolves e-mail addresses by looking them up in the Global Address List. If you use Exchange in Cached Exchange Mode, Outlook looks up addresses in the offline address book, in order to reduce network traffic and the number of times it has to run back to the server to check stuff.

The offline address book contains only the most basic information needed to resolve e-mail addresses and get messages on their way. Because Outlook refers to the offline address book whenever it needs to check up on somebody, it becomes even more important if you're working offline (temporarily disconnected from the company network) or trying to get some e-mail composed while you're between connections (Outlook and plane) at the airport. As you might imagine, having an offline address book that's at least kinda up-to-date is pretty important if you want to be able to work offline.

To ensure that your offline address book is updated regularly, follow these steps:

1. **Choose Tools⇨Send/Receive⇨Send/Receive Settings⇨Define Send/Receive Groups.**

   The Send/Receive Groups dialog box appears, as shown on the left in Figure 2-5.

2. **Select the Exchange group and click Edit.**

   If you have more than one Send/Receive group, be sure to select the one that includes your Exchange account. After you select the right account, click Edit. The Send/Receive Settings dialog box appears, as shown on the right in Figure 2-5.

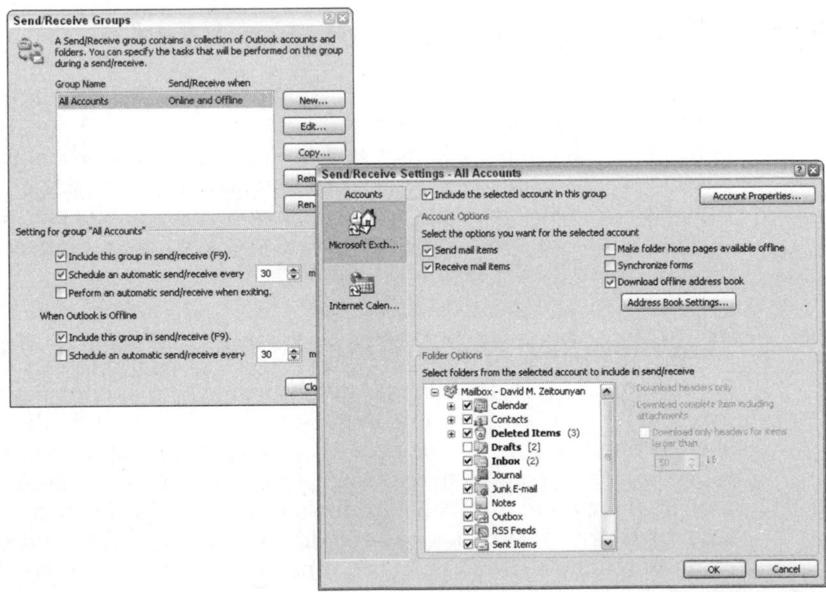

Figure 2-5: Keep that offline address book up-to-date.

3. **Choose Download Offline Address Book.**

   In the Account Options section, choose the Download Offline Address Book option.

4. **Click Address Book Settings.**

   The Offline Address Books dialog box appears, as shown in Figure 2-6. Select how much detail you want to store in the offline address book: Full Details or No Details. Typically, it's best to go with Full Details.

   If you're part of a really, really, super big organization, there may be more than one address book, so be sure to select the one you want from the Choose Address Book list. Click OK about a billion times.

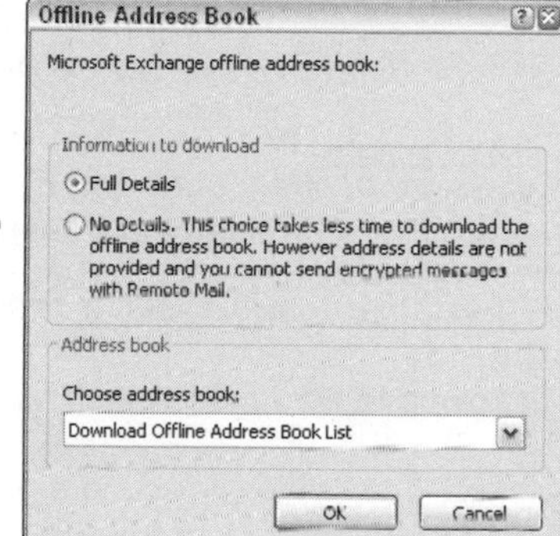

Figure 2-6: Set your offline address book options.

With the preceding option turned on, Outlook automatically updates the offline address book about once a day or so. You can get Outlook to update the offline address book immediately by following these steps:

1. **Choose Tools⇨Send/Receive⇨Download Address Book.**

   The Offline Address Book dialog box appears (refer to Figure 2-6).

2. **In the Information to Download section, click either Full Details or No Details, depending on how much data you want to download right now, and how long you want to wait for it.**

3. **Click OK.**

   The offline address book is downloaded.

Changing the Cached Exchange Mode settings to download headers only

Normally, when you use Outlook on an Exchange network, it works just like any other e-mail account. At regular intervals, the server is checked for new mail, and when it's found, that new mail is placed in your Inbox. If you have a slow network connection, you may want to tell Outlook to download only message headers to your computer. Here's how:

1. **Choose File⇨Cached Exchange Mode.**

   A submenu pops up. See Figure 2-7.

2. **Choose a download option.**

   Choose an option from the submenu that appears:

   - *To have Outlook download complete messages,* choose Download Full Items.
   - *To have Outlook download message headers only,* and then download the message content when you click on a header, choose Download Headers and Then Full Items.

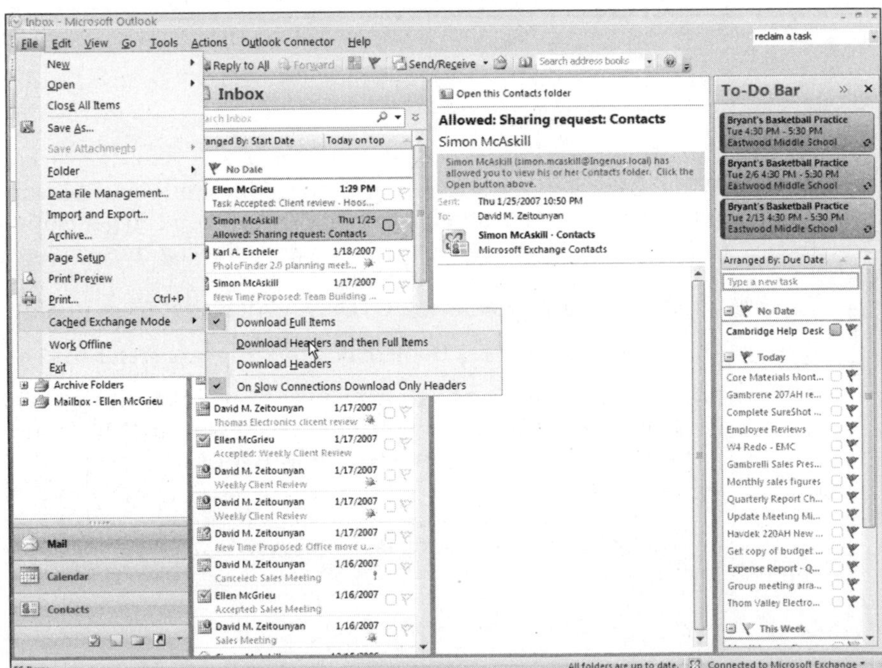

Figure 2-7: Download headers only if you want.

- *To have Outlook download message headers only,* choose Download Headers. When you click on just a header, you see a short preview of the message in the Reading pane, as shown in Figure 2-8. Click the Download the Rest of This Message Now button to download the actual message.
- *To have Outlook download headers only when the network connection is slow,* then choose either the Download Full Items or the Download Headers and Then Full Items option first, and then choose On Slow Connections Only Download Headers.

You can also click the Connected to Microsoft Exchange button on the status bar to display a menu from which you can select these same settings, and also take yourself offline, where you don't receive any messages or even check for them. Working offline allows you to speed up your computer to do other work, rather than letting it constantly check for e-mail over a slow network. It also prevents any messages you're creating from going out, until you are completely sure you want the world to see them.

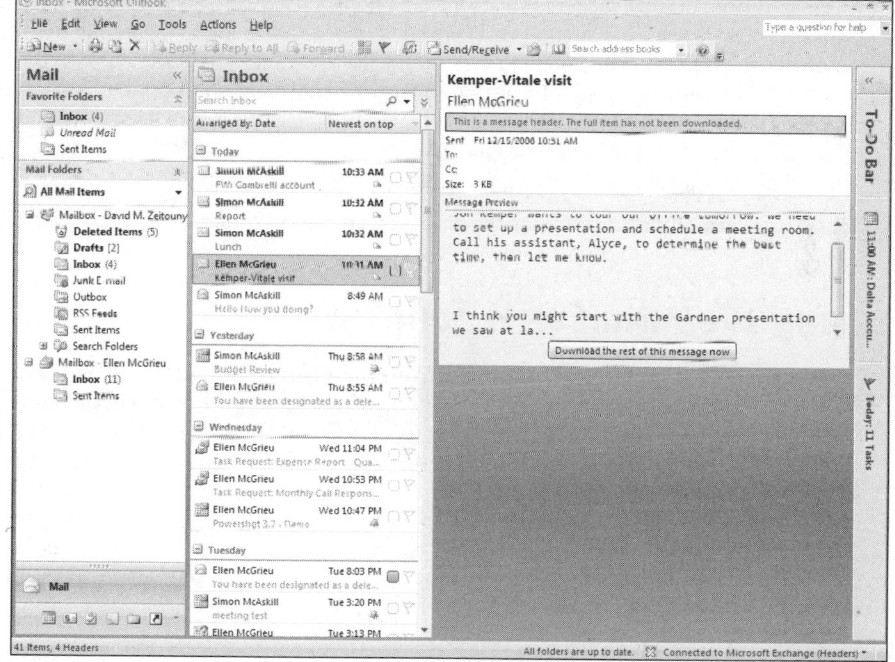

Figure 2-8: Click a header to see a preview of your e-mail.

What to do when you're out of the office

Normally, you connect to Exchange over your company's network. If you need to connect to Exchange when you're out of the office, your system administrator has several options. In a lot of cases, she'll set up a VPN, or *virtual private network,* that you can use to connect via the Internet. Connecting through a VPN is great because you typically have access to the complete network, so it's really just like being in the office. The downside is that the connection process, in order to maintain high security, is often complicated and time-consuming.

Another alternative that your system administrator may use is Outlook Anywhere (assuming your company network uses Exchange Server 2007). This option also connects you to the company's network using the Internet, but it provides access only to e-mail and nothing else on the network. Connecting through Outlook Anywhere is fairly painless and fast, so if you and your colleagues only need e-mail access when you're out of the office, it's a good way to go. Typically, if your network system administrator decides to go the Outlook Anywhere route, she'll also do the setup on your computer. But if you're using your personal laptop or home computer to connect, don't expect her to pay you a house call.

To turn on the Outlook Anywhere option for your home computer, choose Tools➪Account Settings, select your Exchange account, and choose Change➪More Settings➪Connection. Still with me? Good. In the Outlook Anywhere section, turn on the Connect to Microsoft Exchange Using HTTP option. Click Exchange Proxy Settings, and then type the Internet address your system administrator told you to use, in the Use this URL to Connect to My Proxy Server for Exchange box. If the administrator babbled something about a secure sockets layer, turn on the Connect Using SSL Only option. Set other options as instructed by the administrator, and be sure to make a selection from the Proxy Authentification Settings drop-down list. Click OK.

Using Web Mail as a Solution

For a gal or guy on the go, Web mail (an HTTP account) is the way to go in style. Web mail is HTTP based, which means that it's accessible from anywhere you can find an Internet connection. Sounds like heaven, right? Well, it's not bad, but it's not Outlook. With Web mail, you often have clumsy interfaces that make it difficult to scan through your messages quickly, and to get rid of the ones you no longer want. And they typically don't interface with Outlook, so if you're using Web mail while on a trip, you have to enter e-mail addresses manually to send any messages (that's assuming you know the addresses to use).

Don't get me wrong — my home account comes with an HTTP interface, and I don't care how clumsy the thing is, it's really convenient because I can use it basically anywhere. I just wish it had all my e-mail addresses so I didn't have to remember them when I go on a trip. Of course, once I enter e-mail addresses manually into the Web interface of my home e-mail account, they stay there, but I'm just not into manual stuff anymore.

So what's a gal to do? Go hunting for a Web account that does interface with Outlook, and wouldn't you know I found one? It's called Windows Live Mail.

Creating a Web-Outlook connection

Here's the lowdown, in manager-speak: You're going to leverage the power of your existing Web-based e-mail (specifically, Office Live Mail, Windows Live Mail, Hotmail, or MSN e-mail), along with the Microsoft Office Outlook Connector add-in to create a richly featured Web mail-Outlook experience. In other words, with the help of a magic gizmo called Microsoft Office Outlook Connector, you're gonna download your Web-based e-mail into Outlook. You also can send e-mail through the Web account, using the Outlook interface and its valuable list of contacts.

So the first thing to do is to install the Connector and configure it to work with your Web-based e-mail account. Here's how:

1. **Install Microsoft Office Outlook Connector.**

   Get yourself a copy of Microsoft Office Outlook Connector and install it. I found my copy at `www.microsoft.com/downloads`. Close Outlook and install the Connector program.

2. **Restart Outlook.**

   The Microsoft Office Outlook Connector dialog box pops up, as shown in Figure 2-9. If not, choose Tools⇨Account Settings⇨E-Mail⇨New⇨Other⇨Microsoft Office Outlook Connector to start it.

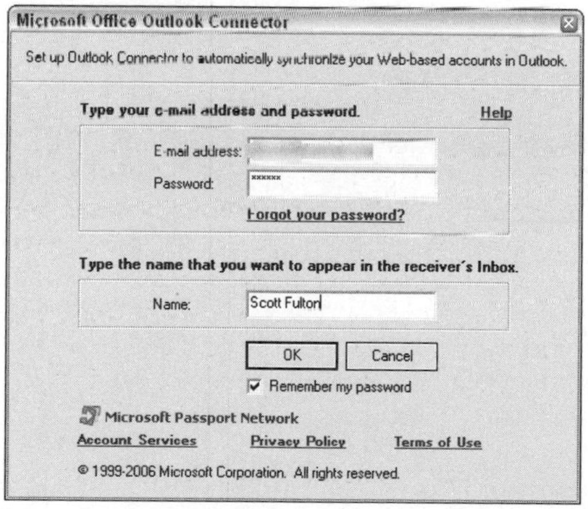

Figure 2-9: Setting up the Outlook Connector.

3. **Enter your E-Mail Address and Password from one of the Connector-compatible accounts, such as a Windows Live or Hotmail account. Select the Remember My Password option if you like. Type your Name as you want it to appear in e-mail messages and click OK.**

   A message appears telling you that a new e-mail account has been added to Outlook.

4. **Click Yes to close down Outlook and restart it.**

   Your compatible account (the Windows Live Mail, Hotmail, or MSN account) appears in the Navigation pane, in Outlook.

You can now create e-mail messages using Outlook, and send them through your Web account. You can also download Web mail into Outlook. To change to your Web account, just select it from the Navigation pane in Outlook.

If you have more than one e-mail account set up in Outlook, normally, everything is sent using the main account. So if someone gets an e-mail from you and clicks Reply, he sends his reply to your main e-mail address. If you're using Outlook to help you send and receive e-mail for a Web-based account, you might want replies to any messages you send to go back to that e-mail address. To send an e-mail from Outlook using your Web account, you need to select that account from the Account list in the Message form, as shown in Figure 2-10. (See Book III, Chapter 5 for more information on using multiple accounts in Outlook.)

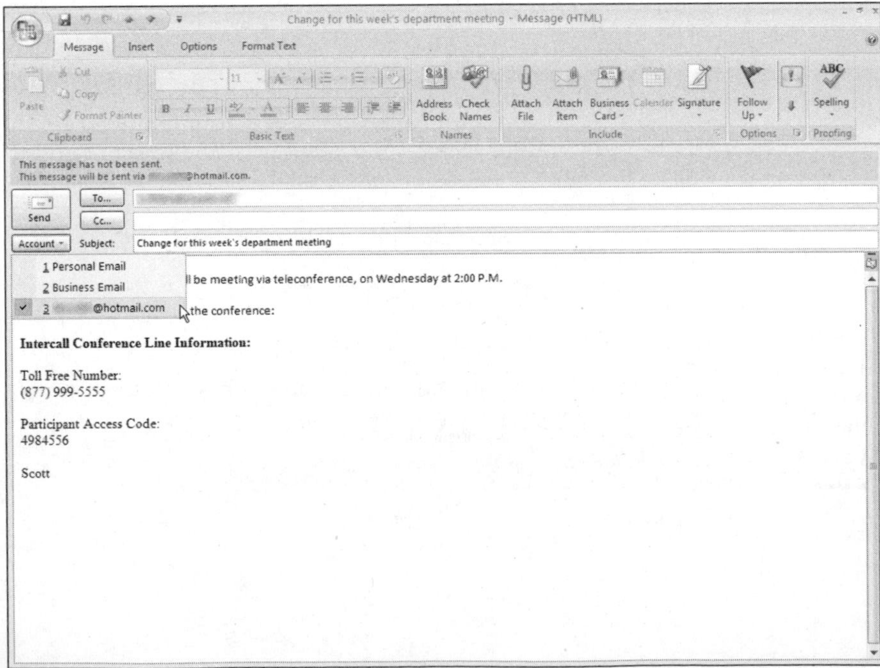

Figure 2-10: Sending an e-mail from your Web account.

Checking on your Web connection

Now that you have Microsoft Office Outlook Connector installed, let's review: Somebody e-mails your Web account, and that mail gets bounced down to Outlook. Occasionally, all this redirection gets you dizzy, and you may not remember whether you're connected to your Web account. If your Web account happens to be Windows Live Mail, well lucky you, because you can easily check its status from within Outlook.

1. **Select any folder in your Web account.**

   On the Navigation pane, click any folder in your Web account, such as the Inbox.

2. **Click the Server Status button.**

   The Server Status button is located at the right end of the status bar. After you click it, a menu appears.

3. **Read the menu.**

   - *To check whether you're connected,* just look next to Mail, Calendar, or Contact. If it says Connected, you're all set.
   - *To see how much online storage you still have left on your account,* look at the top of the menu, after the word *Storage.*
   - *To view a report that summarizes your account,* choose Detailed Report.

Importing Outlook contacts to Windows Live Mail

If you have a Windows Live Mail account, you can import the e-mail addresses in your Contacts list so that you don't need to retype them in Windows Live Mail. Need to go on a trip? No problem — if your contacts are up on Windows Live Mail, you can log in from anywhere with an Internet connection and be assured that you'll be able to send e-mail to anyone you need.

To import Outlook contacts, follow these steps:

1. **Log on to Windows Live Mail.**
2. **Choose Contacts⇨Import Outlook Contacts.**
3. **On the left side, in the Navigation pane, click Contacts.**
4. **Click Import Outlook or Outlook Express Contacts.**

   The Windows Live Contact Import Wizard appears.

5. **Click Next.**

6. **Type your Windows Live ID and password and click Next again.**

   The Select Contacts dialog box opens.

7. **Select the contacts you want to import and click Next.**

   By default, Windows Live Mail wants to grab all the Outlook contacts it can. You don't have to let it, though. Just uncheck any contacts you don't want up on the Web. If it's quicker, you can click Uncheck All and then check the contacts you want to import.

   You see a message telling you just how many contacts you selected for import.

   You can only import 1,000 contacts into Windows Live Mail.

8. **Click Next and then click Close.**

   The contacts are imported into Windows Live Mail.

Chapter 3: Printing Your Stuff and Taking It with You

In This Chapter

- Printing messages so that you can refer to them
- Printing the documents attached to a message
- Printing an entire list of items
- Printing a name and address list for contacts
- Printing a distribution list of contacts
- Printing a blank calendar so that you can mark it up

In today's electronic age, where everyone has more electronic gizmos hanging off their body than a space-age robot, it seems almost quaint to think of printing something on paper. "Look Jimmy, in that museum case over there. That's a paper calendar. Grandpa used to carry one just like that, to and from school, through the snow, in bare feet, just so he could keep track of his homework assignments."

But let's face it. As much as we'd like to pretend we live in the 21st century (oh, that's right, we do), there are times when paper is a happy sight. For example, when you suddenly discover that a new client's office isn't where you thought it was, you're real glad to see that little piece of paper sitting there on the passenger seat — the printout containing the directions to the client's office that they sent to you anyway, even though you reassured them a thousand times that you knew exactly where they were located. Yep, it was a lucky thing your assistant printed that message for you because she knows you couldn't find a tree in a forest. Or the printer connected to your computer.

There are other things you might want to print out from Outlook, for times when your PDA, cell phone, and laptop are unavailable. If you're heading into a meeting of company bigwigs, for example, it would be nice to know that everybody's name is right there in your pocket, in case you suddenly can't recall who the VP of Marketing is this week, and there he is, heading right across the room at you. When traveling, it might be nice to just whip out that paper containing your schedule, rather than squeeze out of your seat, retrieve the laptop from the overhead, and wait five minutes for it to start up. This chapter shows you practical and creative ways that you can have fun with paper.

The tasks in this chapter assume that your computer is attached to a printer, either directly or through a network, and that the printer has paper, ink, and a valid driver's license.

Printing a Message and Any Attached Documents

If you receive a message that contains important information you need to carry with you when you're not at your computer, you can just print it out. For example, the message may contain directions to the off-site meeting, your itinerary for a business trip, your flight number and confirmation information, and other important data.

In addition, sometimes a message comes to you, dragging some of its buddies (attachments). When you want, and without much fanfare, Outlook can print out the message's attachments, too. It's important to note here that you don't have to print the attachments just because they are there, though.

Although Outlook tries hard to print a message's attachments, there are limits. If the attachment is zipped, for example, it won't print. Also, you must have a program compatible with the attachment installed on your computer, in order for Outlook to print it. In addition, if the file is a non-Office file, even if you have a compatible program installed, the attachment may only open in that program and not automatically print.

If you just want to print a message and any attachments and you're not in a mood for messing with options, you can select the message and then click the Print button located on the Standard toolbar.

To print a message and its attachments, follow these steps:

1. **Select the message to print.**

   Change over to Mail, and in the message list, click the message you want to print. Do not open the mail message — at least, not if you want to be able to print attachments.

2. **Choose File⇨Print.**

   The Print dialog box, shown in Figure 3-1, appears.

3. **From the Name list, select the printer to use. If you want to print attachments, select the Print Attached Files option.**

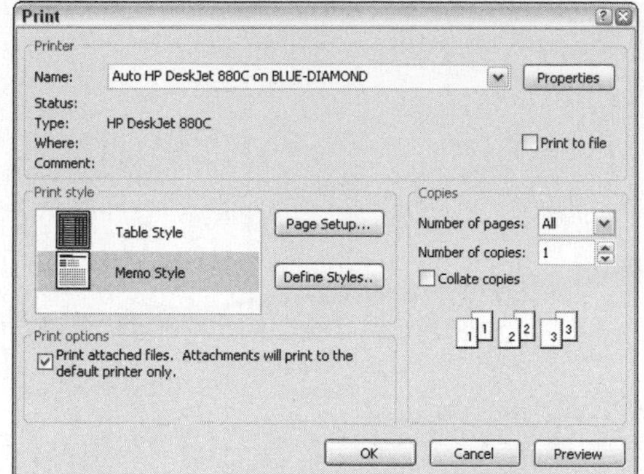

Figure 3-1: The Print dialog box.

4. **To produce multiple copies of your printout, enter the number of copies you want in the Number of Copies box.**

   If you print more than one copy, you might want to give that Collate option a click and save yourself the trouble of putting the pages in order after they are printed. If you don't select the Collate option, then Outlook prints multiple copies of page one and then the copies of page two, and so on. With the Collate option, it prints one set: page one, two, etc. and then it prints the next set.

   WARNING!

   Outlook prints the message using the printer you choose, but the attachments (if you decide to print them) are printed on your computer's default printer, regardless of which printer you choose from the Name list. So if you're printing attachments, be sure that the default printer is the one you want to use to print them.

5. **To change the page setup, click Page Setup, make the changes you want in the dialog box that appears, and click OK to close the dialog box.**

   - *To change the font of either the report title or its data,* on the Format tab as shown in Figure 3-2, click either Font button, choose a font, size, and font attributes such as bold, and then click OK.
   - *To remove the gray shaded areas of the printout,* turn off the Print Using Gray Shading option on the Format tab.
   - *To change the paper type or orientation,* click the Paper tab, as shown in Figure 3-3. Select a paper size from the Type list. For example, for 8.5 x 11 paper, choose Letter. From the Size list, choose how you want that paper size utilized. For example, you might choose 1/2 Sheet Booklet or Franklin Day Planner Classic. To change the page orientation, choose either Portrait or Landscape. The sample changes to show what your choice means.

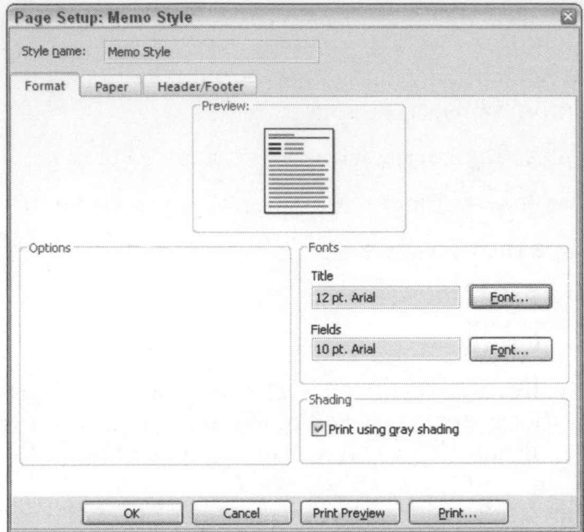

Figure 3-2: The Format tab.

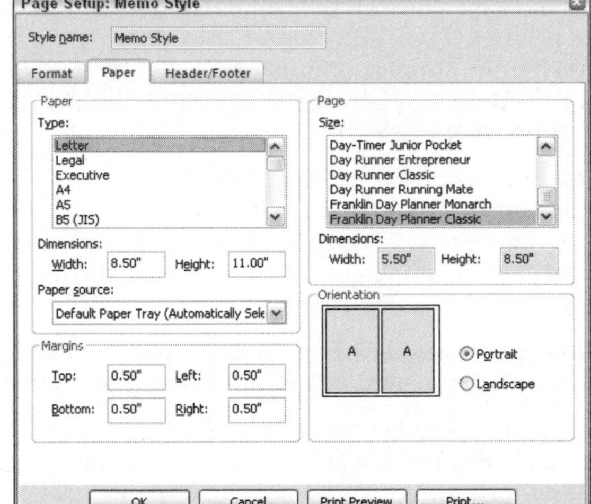

Figure 3-3: With page setup, you can change the format of the printout.

You can change other things on the Paper tab although that's kinda rare. You can enter custom dimensions for some paper type you can't find in the Type list, for example. You can also adjust the Margins.

- **To add a header or footer, click the Header/Footer tab, shown in Figure 3-4.**

  A header, by the way, prints at the top of every page in a printout, and a footer prints along the bottom, so this only makes sense if you're printing something that's more than a single page. Anyway, in the Header area, there are three boxes; click in the box where you want something to appear. For example, to have your name appear on the left, click the left box. Then either type what you want, or click a button to insert an option.

Page: Displays the current page number on each page.

Total Pages: Inserts the total number of pages in the printout.

Date: Inserts the current date.

Time: Inserts the current time.

User Name: Inserts your name.

Choose the Reverse on Even Pages option to reverse the order of the header or footer items on even-numbered pages. For example, if you inserted your name on the left, you could print it on the right on page two.

6. **Click OK.**

The message is immediately printed. You might see a message reminding you to open only attachments you know came from a trusted source, and therefore probably do not contain any viruses. (Outlook must "open" the attachments in a compatible program to print them.) If you see such a message, and you're sure the file is safe, click Open to continue.

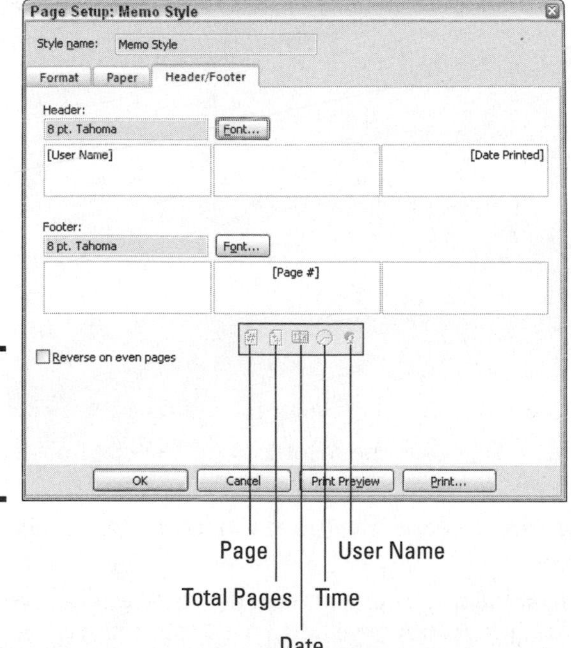

Figure 3-4: Adding a header or footer.

Printing the Contents of Any Other Single Item

You don't have to limit yourself to simply printing messages. Oh no; if you want to print the details of a task or appointment, you certainly can. There's no particular mystery about it either. You basically, almost, follow the same steps as listed in the preceding section, "Printing a Message and Any Attached Documents."

If you just want to print an item and you don't feel like dealing with setting options, you can choose the item and then click the Print button located on the Standard toolbar.

If you want to customize your print options, you need to take a few extra steps to set up printing. Here are the steps.

1. **Open the item to print.**

   Open whatever you want to print — an appointment, meeting, task, contact, or note.

2. **Choose Microsoft Office⇨Print⇨Print.**

   The Print dialog box, similar to the one shown in Figure 3-5, appears.

Figure 3-5: Print whatever you want, such as a contact or a task.

3. **From the Name list, select the printer to use. Then choose any option you want:**

   - *If the item has any attachments and you want to print them,* select the Print Attached Files option.
   - *To print more than one copy,* change the Number of Copies value.
   - *To collate multiple copies,* select the Collate Copies option.

If you choose to print attachments to the item, they print on the default printer, regardless of the printer you choose from the Name list.

4. **To change the page setup, click Page Setup. The Page Setup dialog box appears (refer to Figure 3-3). Make the changes you want, and then click OK to close the dialog box.**

   For help, see the preceding section, "Printing a Message and Any Attached Documents."

5. **Click OK.**

   The item prints.

Printing a List of Items

Sometimes, you don't need the contents of an item printed; you just need a list. You can print your Tasks list, for example, or a list of contacts. The process is fairly simple. First, you select a view that displays the items you want to print, and then you begin the print process. Outlook offers a lot of options along the way, so put your decision cap on.

To print a list of items:

1. **Change to the folder that contains the items you want to print.**

   Want to print tasks? Well then, change over to the Tasks folder.

2. **Rearrange or filter the list.**

   You can rearrange the order of the items before printing; if you're in a list view, you simply click the column button of the column you want to sort by. For example, click the Due Date column to sort a list of tasks by their due date. If you're using a non-list view, you must customize it to sort it. See Book VIII, Chapter 2 for help.

   In addition, you don't have to print all the items in the folder, although Outlook will print everything it sees, unless you make a selection:

   - *To select multiple items,* press Ctrl and click each one.
   - *To select contiguous items,* press Shift, click the first one in the group, then click the last one while still holding down Shift.

   If you're in Calendar and using one of the Day/Week/Month views, it doesn't matter what you select, so you may as well not bother. You limit your selection in a different way, as shown in Step 3.

   Some views automatically hide certain items, so by choosing one of them, you can limit the size of your printout without having to select anything. For example, the Last Seven Days view in Mail displays only the e-mails received in the last week.

Another way to limit the view is to filter it so that it only displays items of a particular type. You filter a list by customizing the view; see Book VIII, Chapter 2, for the lowdown.

If you display a list using some kind of grouping, such as categories, you can collapse the groups you don't want to print so that they are not visible.

3. **Choose File⇨Print.**

   The Print dialog box appears (see Figure 3-6). Choose a printer to use from the Name list.

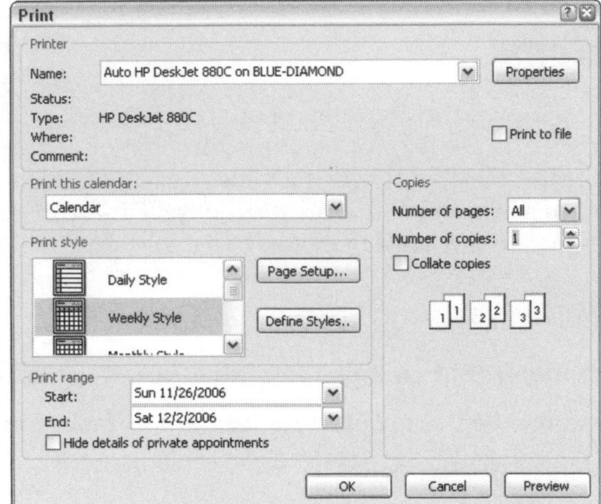

Figure 3-6: Printing a list of items.

4. **Select a print style.**

   You have several options to choose from, depending on the kind of items you're trying to print:

   - *Table Style:* Prints items in a long list. If you choose this option, you can print the entire list (despite what you might have selected) by choosing the All Rows option. To print only your selected items, you must choose the Only Selected Rows option.
   - *Memo Style:* Prints the contents of each item, typically two to a page.

   If you're printing Calendar items, you have a few more styles to choose from. But first, you must select which items to print by setting the Start and End print range.

   You can hide the details of Calendar items marked as private by selecting the Hide Details of Private Appointments option. Now that you've got that settled, select Table, Memo, or one of these Calendar print styles:

- *Daily Style:* Prints Calendar items one day per page (work hours only), with a daily task list.
- *Weekly Style:* Prints Calendar items in a weekly view (work hours only).
- *Monthly Style:* Prints Calendar items in a monthly view.
- *Tri-Fold Style:* Prints Calendar items with each page divided into three sections. The detail for a single day is shown on the left, the daily task list is shown in the middle, and a weekly summary of the week is shown on the right. See Figure 3-7.
- *Calendar Details Style:* Prints Calendar items in a long list, with full details, grouped by day.

You can preview any style before printing by clicking the Print Preview button. Click Print in the preview to return to the Print dialog box.

5. **(Optional) Print multiple copies of your printout by changing the Number of Copies value. Collate those copies by selecting the Collate Copies option.**

To change the paper type, page orientation, or similar options, click Page Setup and follow the instructions in the section, "Printing a Message and Any Attached Documents," for help.

6. **When you're ready, click OK to print your list of items.**

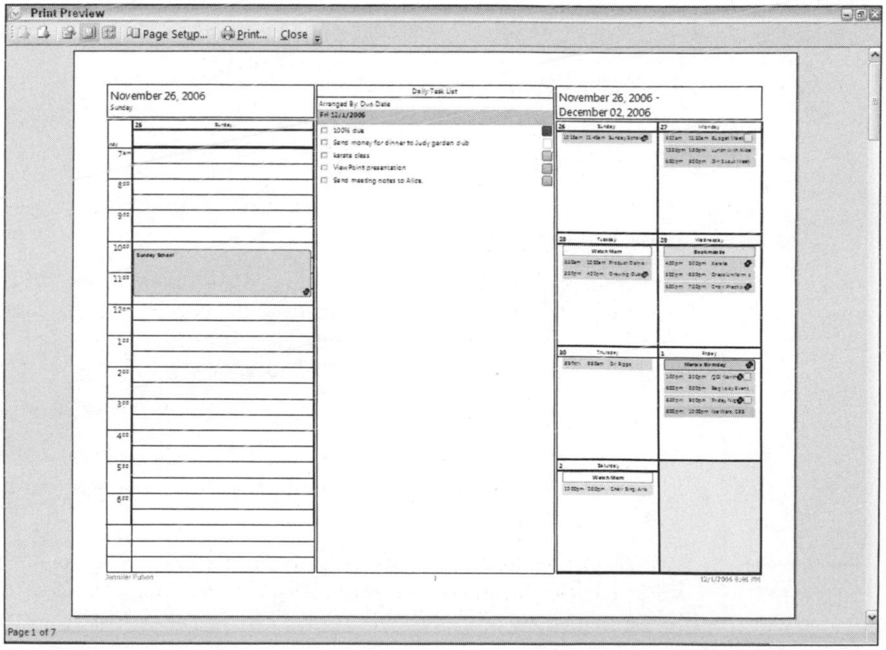

Figure 3-7: A triple threat.

Printing Contact Names and Mailing Addresses

A name and address listing is pretty standard stuff and pretty useful to have around. If you carry a day planner, for example, you can print your contacts and have their data handy wherever you go. Of course, for those of you with laptops, PDAs, and smart phones, the thought of a paper printout may seem laughingly simplistic, and well, you'd be right. Still, when the power runs out on your expensive electronic device and the nearest outlet is a mere two or three hours away, depending on airport security and the length of the taxi line, the thought of a simple paper name and address listing is comforting.

To produce a name and address list, follow these steps:

1. **Click the Contacts button in the Navigation pane.**
2. **Choose View➪Current View➪Address Cards, or click the Address Cards option in the Navigation pane to switch to Address Cards view. See Figure 3-8.**
3. **Choose View➪Current View➪Customize Current View.**

   Without choosing this command, Outlook prints everything in the Contacts list. So if you want to print names, addresses, and phone numbers, you're ready to print without completing this step. If you want to print selected contacts, complete this step, and the Customize View: Address Cards dialog box appears. See Figure 3-9.

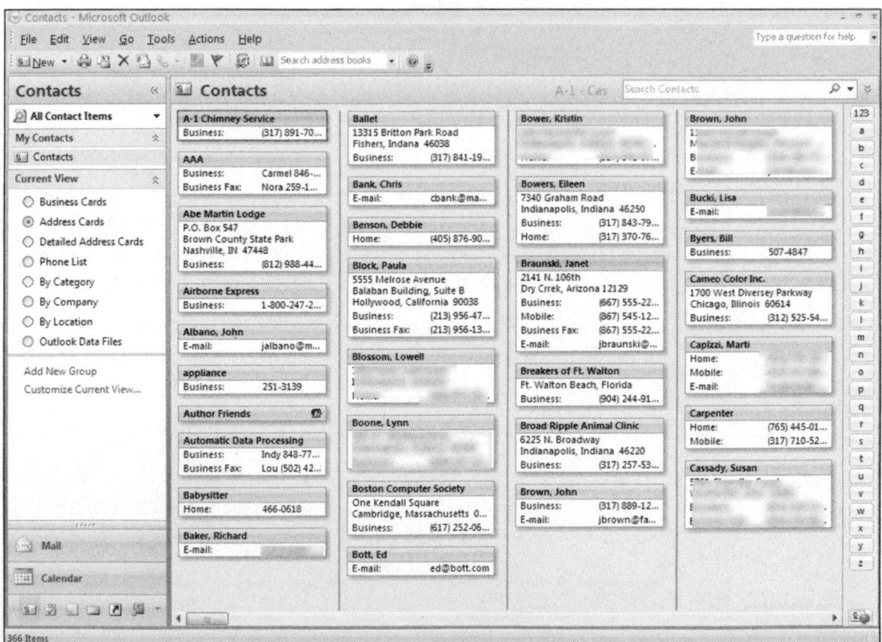

Figure 3-8: Address Cards view.

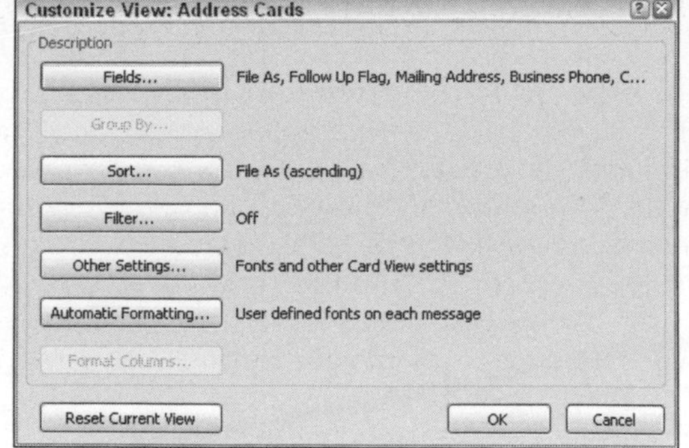

Figure 3-9: Create your own name and address list to print.

4. **Click Fields.**

   The Show Fields dialog box appears, as shown in Figure 3-10.

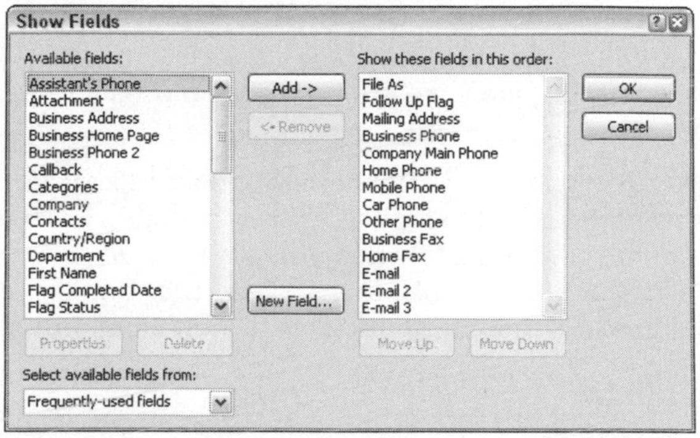

Show Fields

Available fields: Assistant's Phone, Attachment, Business Address, Business Home Page, Business Phone 2, Callback, Categories, Company, Contacts, Country/Region, Department, First Name, Flag Completed Date, Flag Status

Add -> | <- Remove | New Field...

Show these fields in this order: File As, Follow Up Flag, Mailing Address, Business Phone, Company Main Phone, Home Phone, Mobile Phone, Car Phone, Other Phone, Business Fax, Home Fax, E-mail, E-mail 2, E-mail 3

OK | Cancel | Properties | Delete | Move Up | Move Down

Select available fields from: Frequently-used fields

Figure 3-10: Add or remove fields to print.

5. **Select the fields to show by choosing them from the Available Fields on the left and clicking the Add button. To remove a field, select it from the Show These Fields In This Order list on the right, and click the Remove button. When you're done, click OK twice.**

   You're returned to the Outlook window, and your custom view of Contacts is displayed. For more help in customizing a view, see Book VIII, Chapter 2.

6. **Select items to print and choose File⇨Print.**

   You can print only certain names and addresses by selecting those cards first. Press Ctrl and click each one. Then choose File⇨Print. The Print dialog box appears (see Figure 3-11).

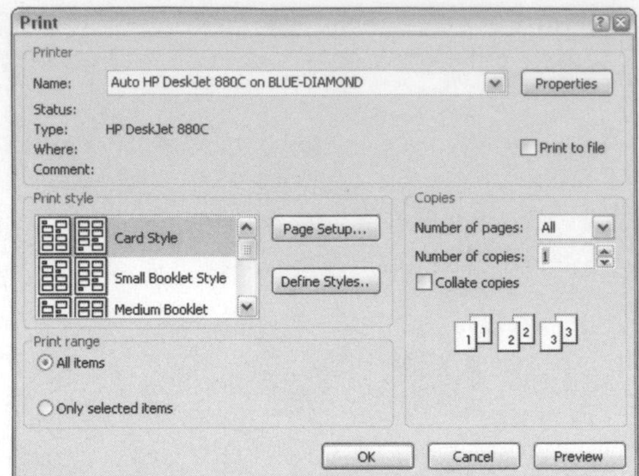

Figure 3-11: The Print dialog box.

7. **Choose a printer from the Name list.**

8. **Select a print style.**

   Select a style from the Print Style list:

   - *Card Style:* Prints the information you see on the address cards, in alphabetical order.
   - *Small Booklet Style:* Prints the names and addresses like a small book, two pages on each side of a piece of paper. Each paper is printed on both sides, and when you put them in order, you can create a little address book. Each page in the "book" is divided into two columns of contacts, so the font is a bit small but still readable.
   - *Medium Booklet Style*: Similar to Small Booklet Style but this style creates a booklet in a larger font. Each page in the resulting "book" contains only one column of contacts. It's a bit more readable although bulkier because it would take more pages to print the same number of contacts than if you'd chosen Small Booklet Style.

     To print using Small Booklet or Medium Booklet Style, your printer must be set up for double-sided printing.

   - *Memo Style:* Prints the contents of each contact, typically two per page. This style prints only the currently selected contacts, so if you want to use this style, you'll need to select the contacts you want to print. Also, with this style, you're also given the option to Print Attached Files.
   - *Phone Directory Style:* Prints only contact names and phone numbers in a long list.

9. **Print multiple copies of your printout by changing the Number of Copies value. Collate those copies by selecting the Collate Copies option.**

To change the paper type, page orientation, or similar options, click Page Setup and follow the instructions in the section, "Printing a Message and Any Attached Documents," for help.

10. **Click OK to print your contacts.**

Printing Contact Names and E-Mail Addresses

If you travel a lot, you may have found that the easiest way to keep in touch with the office and your family is to use e-mail. Sure, a cell phone is instantaneous, but only workable if you call during work hours or before the kids are in bed. If you're at a convention or a conference, your hours are not always your own to spend how you like. You may be scheduled for one talk after another, followed by special networking sessions late at night. By the time you stumble back to your hotel room, it's a bit too late to be making phone calls.

The beauty of e-mail is that you can always send a message off, even in the middle of the night. You're not be disturbing anyone, and you can go to bed knowing that your message will be read the next day, whether you're in that work session or not. The problem with e-mail is that it requires an Internet connection. True, that's not usually a problem, given that most hotels have some kind of Internet connection available. But unless you've carted your laptop with you or your PDA with e-mail addresses, having an Internet connection won't help, even if you can easily borrow one. You can solve that problem by printing the contacts and addresses you use most often and carrying them with you.

To produce a name and address list, follow these steps:

1. **Change to Phone List view by clicking the Contacts button in the Navigation pane, and clicking the Phone List option in the Navigation pane to switch to Phone List view.**

   You also can change to Phone List view by opening the Contacts window and choosing View➪Current View➪Phone List.

   Figure 3-12 shows Phone List view.

2. **Customize the view to show e-mail addresses by choosing View➪Current View➪Customize Current View.**

   The Customize View: Phone List dialog box appears.

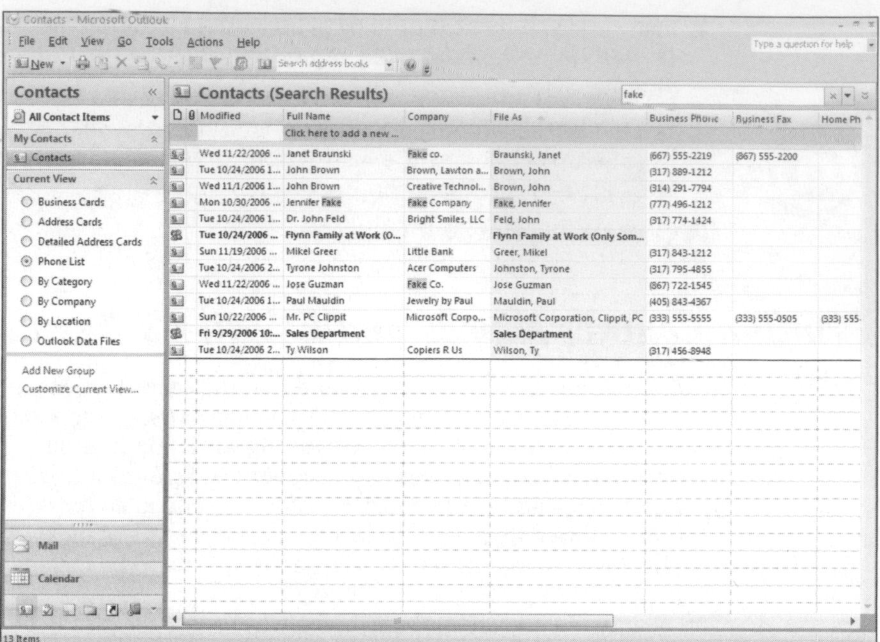

Figure 3-12: Phone List view.

3. **Click the Fields button.**

   The Show Fields dialog box appears, as shown in Figure 3-10.

4. **Choose E-Mail Fields from the Select Available Fields list.**

   The list of Available Fields on the left narrows to those that contain e-mail addresses.

5. **Select one or all of the e-mail fields from the Available Fields on the left side of the dialog box, and click the Add button.**

   You can make other changes to the view as well; see Book VIII, Chapter 2 for help. When you're ready, click OK twice.

6. **Select items to print, and choose File➪Print.**

   You can print only certain contacts by selecting those cards first, before you begin the print process. Press Ctrl and click each contact you want. Then choose File➪Print. The Print dialog box appears (refer to Figure 3-11).

7. **Choose a printer from the Name list. To print only selected contacts, choose the Only Selected Rows option.**
8. **Change to landscape orientation by clicking Page Setup, and in the Page Setup dialog box that appears (shown in Figure 3-13), click the Paper tab and choose the Landscape option. Click OK.**

   Most list views look better if printed in landscape orientation. You can change other page setup options, as well. For more information, see the previous section, "Printing a Message and Any Attached Documents."

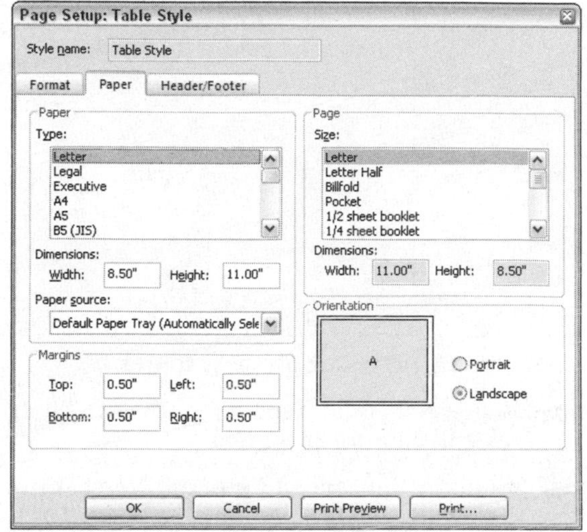

Figure 3-13: Change page setup.

9. **Print multiple copies of your printout by changing the Number of Copies value. Collate those copies by selecting the Collate Copies option.**
10. **When you're ready, click OK to print your contacts.**

Printing a Blank Calendar

Sometimes, having a blank calendar printout is handy, especially if you're out of the office or away from home and you need to jot down an appointment or meeting. To print a blank calendar, however, you need to create one first. Thankfully, that's not difficult.

To print a blank calendar:

1. **Choose File➪New➪Folder.**

   The Create New Folder dialog box appears, as shown in Figure 3-14.

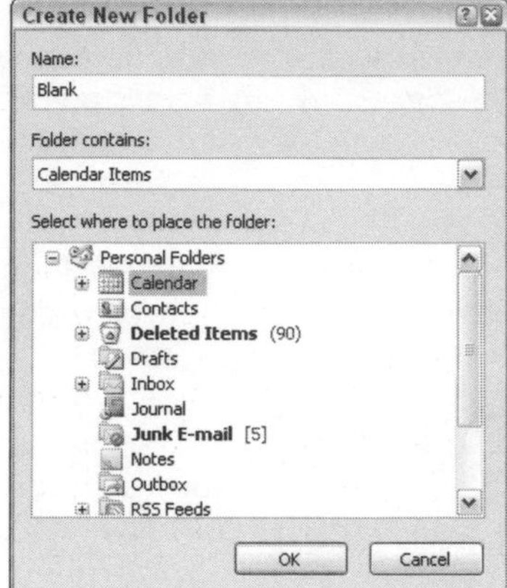

Figure 3-14: Creating a blank calendar.

2. **In the Name box, type a name for the new folder.**

   I used the name, Blank, so I could remember never to fill it. That way, I'll always have a blank calendar for printing.

3. **From the Folder Contains list, select Calendar Items. Choose Calendar from the Select Where to Place the Folder list. Click OK to create the blank calendar.**

   The calendar is added to the My Calendars list on the Navigation pane.

4. **In the Navigation pane in Calendar, under the My Calendars section, click the check box for the new, blank calendar you just created. The blank calendar appears.**

5. **Choose File➪Print.**

   The Print dialog box appears.

6. **Select the calendar to print from the Print This Calendar list. Choose the print style you want, select the print range, set any other options you want, and click OK.**

   See the section, "Printing a List of Items," for help with making selections.

Index

Numerics and Symbols

! (exclamation point) character, 176
; (semicolon) character, 88
3-D effects, 153

A

accdb (Access database) file extension, BCM data type, 546
Accepting Task dialog box, 432–433
Access, data importing, 79–82
Access database (.mdb/.accdb), BCM data type, 546
Account button, Business Contact, 553
Account Records, 537, 554–562
Account Settings dialog box
  account checking order, 221–222
  address book attachment, 95–97
  BCM configuration, 539–540
  compacting data files, 650–651
  connection type, 67
  default account, 220–221
  displaying other user's folders, 742–744
  e-mail account, 57–59
  file password assignment, 707–709
  IMAP sent e-mail folder paths, 227–228
  ISP settings, 66
  naming/renaming e-mail accounts, 64–65
  removing news feeds, 201
  reply address, 64–65
  retrieving e-mail without deleting, 752–754
Accounts by Rating report, BCM, 578
ACT!, 79–82, 546
Active Tasks view, 419–420
Activities tab, 524
Add Address or Domain dialog box, 680
Add Contact Picture button, 354
Add Holidays to Calendar dialog box, 259, 262
Add Mail dialog box, 743–744
Add New Category dialog box, 600–601
Add New E-Mail Account dialog box, 95–97
Add New E-Mail Account Wizard, 57–61
Add New Group link, 30
Add New Member dialog box, 207
Add or Remove Buttons button, 703
Add or Remove Content dialog box, 588
Add Product or Service dialog box, 573–576
Add to Navigation Pane dialog box, 30, 705
Add Users dialog box, 738–739
Address Book dialog box, 98–99
Address Book Import Tool dialog box, 76–77
address books
  access methods, 700
  attaching, 95–97
  e-mail address resolving process, 99–101
  Eudora contact import, 76–77
  Global Address List, 94
  importing, 98
  LDAP (Lightweight Directory Access Protocol), 94
  Outlook Mobile Service, 94
  search order settings, 98–99
  search queries, 699–701
  searches, 101–102
Address box, 354, 356
Address Cards view, 364, 776–779
Address column, 582
Address field, 553, 557
Addressing dialog box, 98–99
adjacent items, 640
Advanced dialog box, 731–732
Advanced E-Mail Options dialog box, 185–186, 227
Advanced Find box, 407–408
Advanced Find dialog box, 649–650
Advanced Options dialog box, 346–348, 452
Advanced toolbar, 337
alerts, 185–187, 667. *See also* notifications
alignments, 153, 630
All Accounts group, 214
All Notebooks List button, OneNote, 458
all-day events, 247–250
annotations, 209
anti-virus software, 713–715
AOL, 54–55
Appointment Recurrence dialog box, 251–253

appointments
Account Record linking, 560–561
archiving, 256
attachments, 246
availability, 274–275
Calendar module display, 234–235
category selections, 246
changing, 254–255
copying/pasting, 258
creating, 43–44, 243–247
date shifting, 257
Day view, 235–237
delegate handling, 750
drag-and-drop, 48–49
event conversion, 255
file attachments, 246
forwarding, 280–281
group schedules, 277–279
hiding/displaying, 408
importance marking, 246
jumping to, 237
locations, 244, 258
meeting conversion, 255
versus meetings/events, 230–231, 301
Month view, 239–241
notes, 246, 447
OneNote, 493–494
overlapping, 245
recurring, 251–254
reminders, 245, 247, 255
removing, 255–256
reorganizing, 51
scroll bars, 236
shorten/lengthen, 258
spell checking, 246
start/end times, 244–245
subject editing, 258
subject entry, 244
task links, 416–417
time management, 274–276
time shifting, 256
To-Do Bar, 25
Week view, 238–239
Archive dialog box, 655–656
Archive Folders, 656–657
archive.pst file, 652, 656–657
archiving, 566, 652–659
Arrange By button, 123–124
arrows, drawing, 477
Assigned To field, 563, 569
Assignment list, 431
Assignment view, 430–431
as-you-type spell checking, 128
Atom, news feeds, 195
Attachment Options pane, 110–111
attachments
BCM reports, 586
blocked file formats, 116–117
business cards, 375, 381–382
compressing, 108
download canceling, 188
files, 108–111
forwarding task, 436–438
item insertions, 156–157
news feeds, 197
notes, 453–454
opening, 116–117
pictures, 114–116
previewing, 20–22
printing, 768–771
restricted permissions message, 723
RTF (Rich Text Format), 21
saving to a file, 117–118
viruses, 18, 108, 118
attendees
canceling meetings, 311–312
e-mailing all, 313–314
meetings, 303–306, 310–311
Audio and Video Recording toolbar, OneNote, 482–484
audio clips, 482–484, 513, 516–517
Author permissions, 266, 387, 440, 739
AutoArchive dialog box, 533, 653–655
AutoComplete, 100–101
AutoCorrect, 128, 130
AutoCorrect in E-Mail dialog box, 130
AutoPreview, 19–20
auto-replies, 729–730
AutoResolve, 99–101

B

Back button, Calendar module, 241–242
background colors, 629
backgrounds, 142–145
Basic column, 582
basic rules, functions, 661–665
BCM (Business Contact Manager)
advantages, 537–538
Account Records, 537, 556–558
Account reports, 577–578
account settings, 539–540
Activity reports, 577
adding a Business Contact to an Account Record, 554–555
.bcm, data type, 545
Business Projects, 562–566, 579–580
client-based project tracking, 538
component access, 539
contact addition, 552–554
Contact Records, 537
dashboards, 538, 587–588
data importing, 547–549
databases, 540–544
editing contact, 554
existing item links, 560–561
exporting reports, 586
importing contacts, 544–550
Invoices or Sales Orders in Accounting, 538

Leads reports, 579
locating/displaying contacts, 551
Marketing Campaign reports, 579
marketing campaign tracking, 538
mass mailings, 205
modifying reports, 581–583
moving contacts, 550
network sharing, 538
opening a database, 542
Opportunities reports, 579
Opportunity creation, 567–570
Opportunity dashboards, 587–588
overview, 2
report editing, 585–587
reports, 538, 577–580
Ribbon display, 561
running reports, 580–581
Sales Opportunities, 538
sales process, 538
SBA (Microsoft Small Business Accounting) integration, 538
SQL Express language, 538
supported data, 545–546
switching between open databases, 542–543
tracking flexibility, 538
who should use, 538–539
BCM Deleted Items folder, 566
bcm file extension, 545
bcmx file extension, 545
blank calendars, 781–782
blind carbon copy (Bcc), 88, 103–104
Blocked Senders List, 683–684
bloggers, 195, 498–499
body text, 88–89
Bold button, 106
brightness/contrast, 145
Browser button, 649
browsers, 199–201, 369–370
bulleted lists, 159, 470
Bullets or Numbering dialog box, 159
business cards, 163–164, 356, 375–384
Business Cards view, 364, 383–384
Business Contact, 552–555, 558–559
Business Contact by Birthday report, 578
Business Contact Manager (BCM)
advantages, 537–538
Account Records, 537, 556–558
Account reports, 577–578
account settings, 539–540
Activity reports, 577
adding a Business Contact to an Account Record, 554–555
.bcm, data type, 545
Business Projects, 562–566, 579–580
client-based project tracking, 538
component access, 539
contact addition, 552–554
Contact Records, 537
dashboards, 538, 587–588
data importing, 547–549
databases, 540–544
editing contact, 554
existing item links, 560–561
exporting reports, 586
importing contacts, 544–550
Invoices or Sales Orders in Accounting, 538
Leads reports, 579
locating/displaying contacts, 551
Marketing Campaign reports, 579
marketing campaign tracking, 538
mass mailings, 205
modifying reports, 581–583
moving contacts, 550
network sharing, 538
opening a database, 542
Opportunities reports, 579
Opportunity creation, 567–570
Opportunity dashboards, 587–588
overview, 2
report editing, 585–587
reports, 538, 577–578
Ribbon display, 561
running reports, 580–581
Sales Opportunities, 538
sales process, 538
SBA (Microsoft Small Business Accounting) integration, 538
SQL Express language, 538
supported data, 545–546
switching between open databases, 542–543
tracking flexibility, 538
who should use, 538–539
Business Contacts link, 557–558
Business Data Import and Export Wizard, 545–549
Business field, 354, 356
Business Projects, 562–566
Business Projects by Status report, 580
businesses, BCM (Business Contact Manager) candidates, 538–539
Busy marker, 275–276
buttons. *See also* commands
Navigation pane, 15–16, 524, 702–703
Ribbon command groupings, 35
ScreenTip help, 14
By Category list view, 364–365

By Category view, 450, 528–529
By Company view, 355
By Contact view, 528–529
By Location view, 352
By Type view, 528–529

C

Cached Exchange Mode, 760–761
Calendar Address dialog box, 298–299
Calendar Details Style, 775
Calendar module
 Advanced toolbar, 337
 all-day events, 247–250
 appointment creation, 43–44, 243–247
 appointment display, 234
 appointment forwarding, 280–281
 appointment location editing, 258
 appointment subject editing, 258
 appointments/events, 254–258
 color editing, 344–345
 Daily Task List, 234–235, 410–412
 Date Navigator, 241–243, 345–348
 date/time display, 236
 Day view, 235–237
 default reminder time setting, 343–344
 Delete button, 255–256
 e-mail information insertion, 283–286
 entire network calendar sharing, 264–266
 events display, 234–235
 Go To Date command, 243
 Google Calendar import, 296–298
 Google Calendar sharing, 292–300
 group schedules, 277–279
 grouping calendars by purpose/type, 334–337
 holidays, 258–262
 iCalendar format, 281–283, 329–331
 jumping to appointments, 237
 meetings display, 234–235
 Microsoft Exchange sharing, 264
 Microsoft Office Online publishing, 286–289
 Month view, 239–241
 multiple calendar creation, 328–329
 multiple calendar display, 332–334
 Navigation pane, 348
 Outlook Today 605
 overview, 2, 12
 personal (unshared) calendar uses, 327
 printing a list, 774–775
 printing blank calendars, 781–782
 quick meeting schedule, 302
 Recurrence button, 251–254
 removing canceled meetings, 311–312
 removing iCalendars, 331
 scroll bars, 236
 share methods, 328
 shared calendar permissions, 269–270
 sharing invitation, 264–265, 273
 Show As list, 274–275
 snapshots, 328
 specific people calendar sharing, 266–269
 switching between views, 235
 time grid editing, 339–343
 time management, 274–276
 view differences, 234–235
 viewing Other People's Calendars, 270–273
 Web server calendar publishing, 290–291
 Week view, 238–239
 work day, 338–339
 work week, 337–339
Calendar Options dialog box, 338–339, 341–342, 345
Calendar Properties dialog box, 265–266
Call Status dialog box, 372
carbon copy (Cc), 88, 103–104
Card Style, 778
Card view, 610
categories, 591–602, 695
Categories column, 558, 593–597
Categorize button, 449, 570, 592–593, 596–597
Categorized Mail Search Folder, 694
Category to Remove command, 596
Cc. *See* carbon copy (Cc)
`cer` file extension, 718–719
certifying authority, 716–719
chain e-mail, 687
Change E-Mail Account dialog box, 742–743
Change E-Mail Account Wizard, 63
Change Password dialog box, 508, 708–709
change picture, 146
character sets, 147
charity contributions, 687
charts, 148–149
check boxes, 687
Check Names dialog box, 100, 130
chicklets, Web page news feeds, 196

Choose a File or a Set of Files to Insert dialog box, OneNote, 484
Choose Document to Insert dialog box, 485
Choose Form dialog box, templates, 170
Clear All Categories command, 596
Clear Formatting button, 107
client-based projects, 538
clip art, 145–147
Clipboard, 257–258, 470
Close button, 36
Close date field, 569
Closed Lost button, 572
Closed Won button, 572
collaboration
  appointments/meetings/events forwarding, 280–281
  calendar information via e-mail, 283–286
  calendar sharing, 264–273
  Google Calendar sharing, 292–300
  group schedules, 277–279
  Microsoft Office Online calendar publishing, 286–289
  time management, 274–276
  Web server calendar publishing, 290–291
Collapse Navigation Bar button, OneNote, 457
colleagues, Out of Office Assistant message replies, 729
Color Categories dialog box, 336, 592–593, 598–602
colors
  background, 142–145
  calendars, 344–345
  category assignments, 593–594, 599–600
  completed tasks, 420
  custom colors, 139–141
  default categories, 591–592
  flagged message header, 175
  folder organization, 643
  form background, 629
  message enhancements, 138–141
  message reply text, 121–122
  Month view display, 240
  notes, 449, 452
  object lines, 477
  overdue items, 410
  overdue tasks, 420–421
  text formatting, 107
  To-Do item flags, 400–401
Colors dialog box, 142–143
columns
  adding/removing, 114
  arrangements, 114
  BCM report modification, 582–583
  moving, 612
  OneNote tables, 470–471
  removing from a table, 612
  reordering BCM reports, 580
  resizing, 114, 612
  sorting, 612–613
  table addition, 611
  table view sorts, 114
COM Add-Ins dialog box, 109
Comma Separated Values (.csv), data type, 546
command buttons, 14
commands, 13, 35, 622–625. *See also* buttons
comments, 122–123, 315
Company box, 352
Competitors field, 570
Complete column, 422
compress pictures, 146
compressing (zipping), 108
conditional rules, 668–671
Configure Buttons button, 16, 524
Conflicts folder, 650
connections, 61–62, 66–68
connectors, drawing, 477
Contact column, 583
Contact Design window, 626–628
contact information, signatures, 161–166
Contact Records, 537
Contacts lists
  activity tracking, 374
  adding distribution list members, 207
  Address Cards view, 364, 776–779
  address maps, 368–369
  automatic Journal tracking, 523
  basic rule selection, 664
  business card appearance editing, 375–378
  business card sharing, 381–382
  business card templates, 378–380
  Business Cards view, 364, 383–384
  By Category list view, 364–365
  certificates, 718–719
  contact addition, 351–355
  contact editing, 355–357
  contact sharing invitations, 388–390
  creating a contact, 357–358, 380–383
  deleting duplicates, 359–362
  Detailed Address Cards view, 364
  Duplicate Detection, 359–360
  e-mail address resolving process, 99–101
  e-mail address selection, 87

Contacts lists *(continued)*
existing contact template application, 380
IM (instant messaging), 190–192
importing into BCM, 544–550
information types, 351, 352–354
information updates, 360
item associations, 374
list views, 352, 364–365
manual Journal tracking, 525–526
marking as private, 385
Microsoft Exchange sharing, 385–392
name checking, 130
printing e-mail addresses, 779–781
printing mailing addresses, 776–779
printing names, 776–779
Quick Contacts, 38–39
reusable business cards, 378–380
same company/multiple employee, 358–359
Search Contacts box, 366–367
search groups, 367–368
search queries, 365–368
Select From list, 356–357
share permissions, 386–387
shared permission editing, 390–392
sharing with everyone on the network, 386–388
sorts, 362
specific people sharing, 388–390
speed dial list, 373–374
switching between views, 363–365
telephone calls, 371–374
To-Do item assignment, 401–402
viewing other shared, 392–394
virus concerns, 351
Web page browsing, 369–370
Windows Live Mail import, 765–766
Contacts module
creating in OneNote, 492–493
drag-and-drop creation, 49–50
Eudora import, 76–77
Outlook Express import, 78–79
overview, 2, 12
views, 114
Contacts Properties dialog box, 386–387, 390–391
containers, 456–457, 468–469
content filters, 583–585
contents, 166–168, 772–773
context menus, 50
contextual errors, 131–132
Contributor
shared calendar permissions, 266
shared contact permissions, 387
shared task permissions, 440
conversation tracking, 123–124, 526–528
Copy Rule To dialog box, 674
Create a New View dialog box, 335–336
Create New Building Block dialog box, 167
Create New Folder dialog box, 328–329, 638–639, 782
Create New Group Schedule dialog box, 277–278
Create New Theme Colors dialog box, 140
Create New Theme Fonts dialog box, 141
crops, object, 154
csv (Comma Separated Values) file extension, 546
Current View list, 528
Current View menu, 235
Custom column, 583
Custom dialog box
Flag for Me, 176–177
Flag for Recipients, 174–176
message flags, 174–177
To-Do item flags, 400
Custom flag, 400
Custom View dialog box, 529–530, 608
Custom View Organizer dialog box, 335–337, 616–618
custom views, 616–618
Customer Experience Improvement Program, 711
Customize dialog box, 697
Customize Outlook Today dialog box, 604–605
Customize View dialog box, 361–362, 613–615
Customize View: Business Cards dialog box, 383
Customize View: Phone List dialog box, 779–781

D

Daily Style, Calendar item printing, 775
Daily Task List
Calendar module display, 234–235
deleting To-Do items, 406
hiding/displaying, 411
item arrangement by start date, 412
marking items as complete, 404–406
minimizing/maximizing, 412

recurring tasks, 418
removing completed tasks, 412
removing flags, 405
task creation, 410–412
dashboards, 538, 587–588
data
Access import, 79–82
Act! import, 79–82
BCM importing, 547–549
compacting files, 650–651
Eudora contact import, 78–79
Eudora Light message import, 75
Eudora Pro message import, 75
Excel import, 79–82
Lotus Organizer import, 79–82
OneNote searches, 513–520
Outlook Express, 70–71, 78–79
Outlook Today sorts, 613–614
viewing archived data, 656
Windows Mail message import, 70–71
data files, database creation, 542
data types, BCM support, 545–546
databases, 540–544
Date Navigator
appointment creation, 43–44
Calendar module, 241–243
customizing, 345–348
font appearance, 346–348
hiding/displaying, 408
month-to-month jumps, 346
multiple month display, 346
To-Do Bar, 24–25, 346
Date/Time Fields dialog box, 529–530
dates
Day view display, 236
flags for yourself, 177
message expiration, 182–183
message flags, 174
Month view, 240–241
note display, 452
OneNote, 472
Week view, 238–239
Day view
all-day events, 248–250
Calendar module, 235–237
calendar time grid, 339–341
Daily Task List, 411–412
Date Navigator, 242
Outlook Today, 610
Delay Delivery button, 182
Delegate Permissions dialog box, 741
delegates
appointments, 750
assigning, 737–740
displaying other user's folders, 742–746
e-mail handling, 748–750
meeting requests, 740, 746–748
permissions, 739–742
private item viewing, 739
removing, 741–742
task requests, 746–748
Delete button, 37, 255–256
Delete key, 37
Deleted Folders, 641
Deleted Items, 691
Deleted Items folder, 37–38, 641, 650, 652, 684–685
delivery receipts, 177–178, 687
Design Form dialog box, 625–626, 629–631
Desktop, notes, 453
Desktop Alert Settings dialog box, 187
Desktop Alerts, 90–91, 186–187
detail fields, 354–355, 356
Detailed Address Cards view, 364
Details tab, 570
Dial button, 371
Dialing Options dialog box, 373–374
Dialog Box Launcher button, 35, 146–147
diamonds, drawing, 477
dictionaries, adding to, 130
digital IDs, 716–719
digital signatures, 718–720
Direct Replies To button, 229
Display As name, 354
distribution lists, 205–209
document pictures, 485–487
documents
automatic Journal tracking, 523
hyperlinks, 155
OneNote insertion, 484–485
OneNote links, 488
printing with message attachments, 768–771
restricted permissions message, 723
domains, 680, 683–684, 686–688
double-headed arrows, 477
down arrow character, 176
down-arrow key, 18
Download Pictures, 115–116
Drafts folder, 27, 36, 90, 111–112
drag and drop, 46–51, 453
drawing, 159–160, 474–478
Drawing toolbar, 477–478
due dates, 413, 327
Duplicate Contact Detected, 360
Duplicate Detection, 359–360

E

Edit Business Card dialog box, 376–378
Edit Rule dialog box, 730–733
Edit Signature dialog box, 164, 166
Editor
  delegate permission, 739
  shared calendar permissions, 265, 267
  shared contact permissions, 387
  shared task permissions, 440, 441
Editor Options dialog box
  context error checking, 131–132
  grammar checking, 134
  Quick Access toolbar commands, 623–625
  spell checking messages, 128
effects, 138–141, 153
e-mail. *See also* messages
  account profiles, 229–230
  adding your name to a reply, 122–123
  address resolving, 87
  all meeting attendees, 313–314
  Bcc (blind carbon copy), 103–104
  BCM report attachments, 586
  BCM reports, 581
  blocking/unblocking file formats, 116–117
  business card sharing, 381–382
  calendar information insertion, 283–286
  Cc (carbon copy), 103–104
  certificate exchanges, 718–719
  certificates, 716–719
  conversation tracking, 123–124
  creating a contact, 357–358
  delegate handling, 748–750
  Desktop Alert, 90–91
  digital signatures, 719–720
  distribution list messages, 208
  download canceling, 188
  draft save times, 112
  encryption, 717, 719–721
  file attachments, 108–111
  flags, 174–177
  forwarding, 125
  HTML format, 104–105, 715–716
  inline comments, 122–123
  linked images, 114–116
  live sharing session invitations, 503
  marking message as unread, 91
  message creation, 85–90
  message expiration date, 721
  message formats, 104–106
  message replies, 118–124
  message reply text colors, 121–122
  message retrieval, 90–93
  note attachments, 453–454
  OneNote pages, 495–497
  opening attachments, 116–117
  Out of Office Assistant rules, 730–733
  Outlook E-Mail Postmark, 688
  Outlook Express message import, 70–71
  plain-text format, 105
  Quick Click Flag, 400, 402–403
  reading messages, 91–93
  received mail folder path selection, 223–226
  Reply button versus Replying to All button, 118–119
  resending messages, 125
  restricted permissions, 723–724
  retrieving without deleting from a POP3 server, 752–754
  RTF (Rich Text Format), 105
  saving as drafts, 111–112
  saving attachments, 117–118
  security warnings, 712–715
  sending to alternate e-mail addresses, 228–229
  sending to multiple recipients, 87–88
  sent mail folder paths, 226–228
  sharing invitation, 264–265, 273
  signature inclusion, 165–166
  subject entry conventions, 88–89
  task assignments, 416
  text formatting, 106–107
  text formatting when copying into a reply, 120–121
  To-Do item assignment, 399–401
  viewing unread only, 92–93
  Voting buttons, 179–181
  Windows Mail message import, 70–71
  workflow process, 53–54, 56

e-mail accounts
All Accounts group, 214
checking order, 221–222
configuration, 56–62
connection testing, 61–62
default settings, 220–221
Eudora, 75–78
HTTP protocol, 752
IMAP (Internet Message Access Protocol), 55, 752
IRM associations, 724
ISP settings, 65–68
naming/renaming, 64–65
Outlook Express, 71–74
password settings, 62–64
POP3 (Post Office Protocol 3), 54–55, 752
profiles, 56–57, 229–230
providers, 54–55
remote computer access, 751–757
reply address settings, 64–65
Send/Receive groups, 214–218
sending messages from alternate accounts, 222–223
signature associations, 164–165
Windows Mail, 71–74
workflow process, 56
E-Mail Address field, 553, 557
e-mail addresses
adding to Safe Senders List, 679–680
contact editing, 356
contact information, 353
distribution list updating, 209
e-mail account setup, 59, 60
hyperlinks, 155
printing, 779–781
resolving, 39–40, 87, 99–102
search queries, 101–102
security warnings, 712–713
sending mail to alternate addresses, 228–229
server conventions, 86–87
spam reduction, 687
verification process, 99–101
E-Mail button, 496
E-Mail Options dialog box, 112, 120–121
E-Mail Security dialog box, digital IDs, 717
e-mail servers, 86–87
emoticons, 194
Empty button, 652
encryption, e-mail, 717, 719–721
End field, 530
end/start dates, 249
end/start times, 244–245
Entry List view, 530, 533–534
Entry Type list, 526, 527
Esc key, 36
Eudora Light, 75–77
Eudora Pro, 75–77
events
adding holidays to a calendar, 258–262
all-day, 247–250
appointment conversion, 255
versus appointments, 230–231
archiving, 256
Calendar module, 234–235
category selections, 249
changing, 254–255
copying/pasting, 258
date shifting, 257
Day view, 235–237
delegate handling, 750
forwarding, 280–281
group schedules, 277–279
importance marking, 249–250
location entry, 248–249
Month view, 239–241
recurring, 251–254
reminders, 249
removing, 255–256
saving, 250
start/end dates, 249
subject editing, 258
subject entry, 248–249
Week view, 238–239
Excel
automatic Journal tracking, 523
copying a table to OneNote, 470
copying/pasting voting responses, 181
data importing, 79–82
exporting BCM reports to, 586
Excel workbook, 546
Exchange network, 26
exclamation point (!) character, 176
Expand button, 16–17
Expand Navigation Bar button, OneNote, 457
expiration date, 182–183, 721

F

Favorite Folders
folder addition, 644
limitations, 644
locating, 644
Navigation pane, 16, 30–31
reordering, 644–645
Search Folder support, 644
Web page links, 645–647
Featured Links, 710
Field Chooser dialog box, 611

Field Chooser tools, 626–628
fields
  business card appearance editing, 376–377
  contact information, 352–354
  custom-defined, 631–632
  form alignments, 630
  form creation, 625–628
  form groupings, 630
  form sizing, 629
File As box, 353
File As field, 552
file formats
  blocking/unblocking, 116–117
  PDF/XPS converter for Office, 497
  switching between, 127
files
  `archive.pst`, 652, 656–657
  archiving, 652–659
  attachment previewing, 20–22
  compacting, 650–651
  compressing (zipping) before attaching, 108
  e-mail attachments, 108–111
  hyperlinks, 155
  OneNote insertion, 484–485
  OneNote links, 488
  `outlook.hoi`, 260–262
  `outlook.pst`, 652, 656–657
  password assignment, 707–709
  restoring archived data, 656–659
  saving e-mail, 117–118
  saving image, 116
  viewing archived data, 656
Fill Effects dialog box, 144
Filter Accounts dialog box, BCM, 584–585
Filter dialog box, 336
filters, 583–585, 682–685
Find Related Messages, 407
Flag column, 422
Flag for Me, 176–177
Flag for Recipients, 174–176
flags
  assignment editing, 403
  colors, 400–401
  contact/To-Do item, 401–402
  e-mail messages, 174–177, 399–401
  Flag for Me, 176–177
  Flag for Recipients, 174–176
  High Importance (!), 176
  low importance (down arrow), 176
  messages for yourself, 176–177
  Quick Click Flag, 400, 402–403
  removing from items, 405
  Tasks list clearing, 419
  To-Do items, 176–177
Folder List
  collapsing/expanding subfolders, 22
  custom Search Folder addition, 697–699
  hiding/displaying, 22–23
  Navigation pane, 15
  navigation techniques, 704
  overview, 16
  predefined Search Folder addition, 695–697
  search folders, 22
  shared folder display nonsupport, 23
  sizing, 23
Folder List button, 15
Folder Size dialog box, 648–649
folders
  archiving, 652–659
  AutoArchive, 653–655
  basic rule creation, 664–665
  color organization, 643
  copying rules between, 674
  creating, 638–639
  deleting, 640–641
  displaying other users, 742–746
  Drafts, 27
  favorite, 16, 30–31
  Favorite Folders, 643–647
  Instant Search process, 692
  manually archiving, 655–656
  moving items between, 639–642
  moving message receipts, 178
  news feed storage, 196
  Organize window, 642–643
  Outlook default, 637–638
  path selections, 639
  received e-mail paths, 223–226
  recovering deleted, 641
  removing AutoArchive, 654–655
  reordering, 640
  restoring archived data, 656–659
  root, 26
  rule settings, 667
  sent e-mail paths, 226–228
  shortcuts, 704–706
  subfolder indicators, 639
  viewing archived data, 656
Font Dialog Box Launcher button, 107
fonts
  custom, 139–141
  Date Navigator, 346–348
  message, 138–141

message formatting, 106–107
note appearance, 452
printing message with attachments, 769
footers, 770–771
For Follow Up folder, 406–407
Format Business Card View dialog box, 383–384
Format Painter button, 107
forms
appearance, 628–630
background colors, 629
closing without saving changes, 36
creating, 625–628
custom, 632–634
custom-defined fields, 631–632
default setting, 632–633
deleting, 634
Distribution List, 206–208
field alignments, 630
field groupings, 630
field sizing, 629
item creation, 34–36
Microsoft Office Button, 34–35
publishing, 628
Quick Access toolbar, 34–35
Ribbon, 35
Save & Close button, 36
Forms Manager dialog box, 633
Forward button, 125, 341, 242
Free marker, 274–276
Free/Busy Time, 266
Free/Busy Time/Subject Location, 266
freehand notes, OneNote, 474–478
frequency, recurring appointments/meeting/events, 252
Full Name box, 352
Full Name button, 552
Full Name field, 552
Full Page View button, OneNote, 456–457

G

gif format, 115
Global Address List, 94
Go menu, 12
Go To Date command, 243
Google, calendar sharing, 292–300
Google Calendar
adding to Calendar module, 329–331
iCalendar export, 292–296
importing, 296–298
subscription process, 298–300
`webcal://` link, 330
Google Gmail, 54–55
Gookin, Dan (*Word 2007 For Dummies*), 106
gradients, backgrounds, 143–145
grammar checking
checking before sending message, 89
enabling/disabling, 133
improper word/phrase identification, 132
Research pane lookups, 133
Grammar dialog box, 133
graphics
phishing message, 678–679
SmartArt, 147, 150–152
gray shading, 769
grids, calendar time editing, 339–343
Group By dialog box, 608–609
group schedules, 277–279
Group Schedules dialog box, 277–279
groups
calendar by purpose/type, 334–337
Contacts list searches, 367–368
detailed task creation, 414
distribution lists, 209
form fields, 630
Journal timeline views, 528–529
objects, 153
Outlook Today, 607–609
Send/Receive, 214–218
shortcut, 704, 706

H

hackers, 190
handwritten notes, 476–477
headers
Cached Exchange Mode, 760–761
downloading to remote computers, 747–757
marking for action, 756
marking for download, 218
printing message with attachments, 770–771
headings, Month view display, 240–241
Help system, 14, 709–711
High Importance
appointment marking, 246
detailed task creation, 414
event marking, 249
message flags, 176
High, junk e-mail protection level, 678
High Priority, 667
holidays, 258–262
Home field, 354, 356
HTML format
e-mail, 104–105
virus concerns, 715–716
HTML messages, 687

HTTP protocol
e-mail accounts, 55, 752
Web mail, 762–766
hyperlinks. *See also* links
message insertion, 154–156
Quick Parts, 166–168
signature inclusion, 164
text formatting, 155

I

iCalendars
adding to Calendar module, 329–331
calendar sharing, 281–283
Google Calendar, 292–298
removing, 331
`webcal://` link, 330
Icon view, Outlook Today, 610
Idea tag, OneNote, 512
IM (instant messaging)
contact addition, 191–192
Contacts list, 190
message reply, 193–194
Microsoft MSN Messenger, 191
Microsoft Office Communicator, 191
Microsoft Windows Messenger, 191
online status display, 191–193
online status editing, 194
security risks, 190, 194
sending messages, 191–194
Windows Live Messenger, 190–194
workflow process, 189–190
IM address field, 553
images. *See also* pictures
backgrounds, 143–145
e-mail attachments, 114–116
message insertion, 145–147
moving, 480
OneNote insertion, 487–480
Quick Parts, 166–168
resizing, 479
saving to a file, 116
text over, 480
trusted sources, 116
IMAP (Internet Message Access Protocol)
e-mail account, 55
out-of-office message replies, 734–737
sent e-mail folder paths, 227–228
IMAP servers, e-mail accounts, 752
Import and Export Wizard
Eudora contact, 78–79
Eudora Light message, 75
Eudora Pro message, 75
Excel data, 80–82
importing address books, 98
importing/exporting news feed lists, 204
Outlook Express contact, 78–79
Outlook Express message, 70–71, 77–78
restoring archived files, 657–659
Windows Mail message, 70–71
important tag, OneNote, 512
Inbox
basic rules, 662–665
Instant Search process, 692
junk mail removal, 683–684
marking messages as read, 620
message blocking, 681–682
Indexing, Instant Search preference settings, 690
InfoBar
blocked file format, 116
contact To-Do item, 401
Display as HTML, 715
Display as Rich Text, 715
Download Pictures, 115–116
Find Related Messages, 407
flagged message, 175
linked image, 115
message information, 18, 20
recurrent item, 253
recurring tasks, 419
trusted image, 116
unsent message, 88, 89
voting options, 180
Information Rights Management (IRM)
configuration, 723
e-mail account, 724
e-mail security, 721
protection layers, 722
restricted permissions message, 723–724
shortcomings, 722
viewing restricted permission messages, 724
Initiated By button, 553, 557
Initiated By field, 569
inline comments, 122–123
Insert Business Card dialog box
business card sharing, 381–382
signature inclusion, 163–164
Insert Chart dialog box, 148–149
Insert File dialog box, 109–110
Insert Hyperlink dialog box
message links, 154–156
OneNote, 488
Insert Item dialog box, 156–157

Insert Outlook Meeting
Details dialog box, 490
instant messaging (IM)
contact addition, 191–192
Contacts list, 190
message reply, 193–194
Microsoft MSN Messenger, 191
Microsoft Office Communicator, 191
Microsoft Windows Messenger, 191
online status display, 191–193
online status editing, 194
security risks, 190, 194
sending messages, 191–194
Windows Live Messenger, 190–194
workflow process, 189–190
Instant Search
accessing, 689–690
preference settings, 690–691
Query Builder, 693–694
results display, 692
search criteria, 692–694
Windows Desktop Search, 690
Instant Search pane, 691
Instant Search Results pane, 692
Internet
live sharing sessions, 502–505
VPN (virtual private network), 762
Internet Connection Wizard, 71–73
Internet E-Mail Settings dialog box
connection type settings, 67–68
IMAP sent e-mail folder paths, 227–228
naming/renaming e-mail accounts, 65
reply address settings, 65
retrieving e-mail w/o deleting, 753
Internet Explorer, 199–201
Internet Free/Busy Address field, 354
Internet Message Access Protocol (IMAP)
e-mail account, 55
out-of-office message replies, 734–737
sent e-mail folder paths, 227–228
Internet Service Provider (ISP)
account information settings, 65–68
e-mail accounts, 54–55
invitations
distribution list messages, 208
live sharing sessions, 503
meeting members, 303–306
meeting updates, 310–311
sharing tasks, 441–442
specific people contact sharing, 388–390
Invoices or Sales Orders in Accounting, 538
IRM (Information Rights Management)
configuration, 723
e-mail account, 724
e-mail security, 721
protection layers, 722
restricted permissions message, 723–724
shortcomings, 722
viewing restricted permission messages, 724
ISP (Internet Service Provider)
account information, 65–68
e-mail accounts, 54–55
items. *See also* To-Do items
Account Record linking, 560–562
adding previous activities, 524–525
appointment organization, 51
automatic Journal tracking, 522–523
category assignments, 591–594
category removal, 596–597
contact associations, 374
creating from forms, 34–36
creating from New button, 33–34
creating notes, 494–495
deleting, 37, 51
disabling Journal tracking, 532
drag-and-drop creation, 47–50
drag-and-drop reorganization, 51
editing techniques, 36
Instant Search process, 692
list printing, 773–775
manual Journal tracking, 525–526
message insertion, 156–157
moving between folders, 639–642
printing single item contents, 772–773
Quick Click Category assignment, 594–596
Quick Parts insertion, 168
recurrent item editing, 253–254
removing from the Journal, 533–534
restoring after deleting, 38
sorting in table view, 114
tasks arrangements, 51

J

Join Live Session task pane, 504–505
Journal button, 524
Journal Entry form, 524–528
Journal module
  versus Activities tab, 524
  activity tracking, 521–528
  AutoArchive system, 533
  By Category view, 528–529
  By Contact view, 528–529
  By Type view, 528–529
  contact activity tracking, 374
  Current View list, 528
  disabling automatic tracking, 531–532
  Entry List view, 530
  forwarding entries, 532
  Last Seven Days view, 528–529, 531
  list views, 530–531
  Outlook Data Files view, 530
  overview, 2, 12
  Phone Calls view, 530
  phone conversation logs, 526–528
  removing entries, 533–534
  switching views, 534
  telephone call entry, 372–373
  timeline views, 528–530
  views, 114, 528–531
Journal Options dialog box, 522–523, 532
jumps
  appointments, 237
  Calendar module navigation, 241
  Date Navigator, 346
  Go To Date, 243
Junk E-Mail folder, 683–685. *See also* spam
Junk E-Mail Options dialog box
  enabling/disabling Postmarks, 688
  Inbox message blocks, 681–682
  phishing attack settings, 686
  protection levels, 677–679
  Safe Senders List, 679–681

L

language, spell checking, 130
Large Mail Search Folder, 694
Last button, 124
Last Seven Days view
  Journal module, 528–529, 531, 533–534
  Notes module, 450
ldf file extension, 542
Lightweight Directory Access Protocol (LDA), 94
limits
  live sharing sessions, 503–504
  Out of Office Assistant, 729
  recurring tasks, 418
lines, 477–478
Link To field
  Business Projects, 563
  Opportunities, 569
Link To pane, hyperlink insertion, 154–155
links. *See also* hyperlinks
  Add New Group, 30
  BCM records to items, 561–562
  image attachment concerns, 115
  items to BCM records, 560–561
  Manage Public Calendar, 330
  meetings/tasks, 416–417
  Navigation pane tasks, 16
  OneNote, 487–488
  People or Distribution List, 663
  phishing messages, 678–679, 686, 688
  Share My Tasks Folder, 441
  tasks/appointments, 416–417
  Web page/Favorite Folders, 645–647
  webcal://, 330
list (table) view
  hiding/displaying items, 113–114
  sorting items, 114
list views
  Contacts list, 364–365
  Journal module, 530–531
  quick contact, 352
  removing Journal items, 533–534
lists
  bulleted, 470
  distribution, 205–209
  holiday, 260–262
  message, 159
  numbered, 470
  printing items, 773–775
  Show As, 274–276
Live Local, contract address maps, 368–369
live sharing sessions, 502–505
locations
  all-day events, 248–249
  appointment entry, 244
  appointment/meeting/event editing, 258
  meeting information, 304, 308
logon information, 61

logs, phone, 526–528
Lotus Organizer, 79–82
Low, junk e-mail protection level, 678
Low Importance
  appointments, 246
  detailed task, 414
  event marking, 250
Low Priority, rule settings, 667
Lowe, Doug (*Word 2007 All-In-One Desk Reference For Dummies*), 209–210

M

macros, security warnings, 711–712
Mail button, 26
Mail column, 583
Mail dialog box, 229–230
mail merge, 209–211
Mail module
  flagged message, 407
  message creation, 85–90
  message reply, 41–42
  Messages view, 14
  Outlook Today, 26
  overview, 1, 11–12
  reading messages, 41–42, 91–93
  Reading pane, 17–22
  retrieving e-mail messages, 90–93
  sending quick messages, 39–40
  shared calendar access, 273
  switching views, 113–114
Mail Setup dialog box, 229
Mailbox Cleanup dialog box
  Deleted Items folder, 652
  folder size, 648–649
  two-step process, 647
mailing addresses, 776–779
Manage Database dialog box, 543–544
Manage Public Calendar link, 330
MAPI (Messaging Application Programming Interface), 55
maps, contact address, 368–369
Mark Complete command, 422
mass mailings
  Business Contact Manager, 205
  distribution lists, 205–209
  Word mail merge, 209–211
Maximize button, 28
`mdb` (Access database) file extension, 546
`mdf` file extension, 542
Medium Booklet Style, 778
Meeting form
  editing existing meetings, 308–311
  meeting time change, 325
  response reply prevention, 324–325
meeting invitations, 208
meeting requests
  accepting, 314–315
  automatic handling, 318–319
  comment additions, 315
  declining, 314–315
  delegate assignments, 740
  delegate handling, 746–748
  meeting members, 304–306
  meeting updates, 310–311
  new time proposals, 316–318
  reply prevention, 323–325
  spam reduction, 687
  tentatively accepting, 314–315
  time change proposal prevention, 325
meeting responses
  accepting/declining time proposals, 320–322
  automatic handling, 322–323
  reply prevention, 323–325
  time change proposal prevention, 325
  tracking, 319–325
meetings
  accepting meeting request, 314–315
  accepting/declining time proposals, 320–322
  alternate time/day, 306, 310
  appointment conversion, 255
  versus appointments, 230–231, 301
  availability adjustments, 274–275
  Calendar module display, 234–235
  canceling, 311–312
  changing to recurring, 309
  contact searches, 307
  creating in OneNote, 493–494
  date/time editing, 310
  Day view, 235–237
  declining meeting, 314–315
  delegate handling, 746–748
  editing existing, 308–311
  e-mailing all attendees, 313–314
  forwarding, 280–281
  group schedules, 277–279, 302
  information display, 302–303

meetings *(continued)*
inviting/uninviting members, 310
location information, 304, 308
marking as private, 309
meeting requests, 304–306, 314–319
member invitations, 303–304
Microsoft Exchange, 302–306
Month view, 239–241
new time proposals, 316–318
recurring, 251–254
reminders, 309
reply prevention, 323–325
response tracking, 319–325
scheduling, 301–308
start/end date/time, 305–306, 308, 310
subject editing, 258
subject entry, 303, 308
task links, 416–417
tentatively accepting a meeting, 314–315
time change proposal prevention, 325
time management, 274–276
Week view, 238–239
members, meeting invitations, 303–306
Memo Style, 774, 778
menu bar, 13–14
Message form
alternate addresses, 228–229
Bcc (blind carbon copy), 88
Cc (carbon copy), 88
e-mail message, 85–90
message body, 88–89
subject entry, 88
message headers
Cached Exchange Mode, 760–761
downloading to remote computers, 754–757
marking for action, 756
marking for download, 218
Message Options dialog box
delivery delay, 182
digital signatures, 720
encryption settings, 720
expiration dates, 183
message expiration date, 721
sending e-mail to alternate addresses, 228–229
S/MIME receipt request, 721
Voting buttons, 179
message replies, 687
Message tab, 107
messages. *See also* e-mail
attachment previewing, 20–22
automatically deleting, 667
AutoPreview, 19–20
bulleted lists, 159
business card sharing, 381–382
changing before sending, 36
chart insertion, 148–149
color enhancements, 138–141
content previewing, 17–20
conversation tracking, 123–124
creating, 85–90
creating a contact from, 357–358
delivery delay, 181–182
Delivery Receipts, 177–178
delivery rules, 181
digital IDs, 716–719
distribution lists, 208
drag-and-drop creation techniques, 47–48
e-mail retrieval, 90–93
expiration date, 182–183, 721
flagged message searches, 406–408
flagging for yourself, 176–177
flags, 174–177
font enhancements, 138–141
forwarding, 125
grammar checking, 132–134
hyperlinks, 154–156
image insertion, 145–147
Inbox blocking, 681–682
InfoBar display, 18, 20
item insertion, 156–157
marking, 620
marking as unread, 91
Message view groupings, 14
moving to Junk E-Mail folder, 683
numbered lists, 159
object manipulation, 152–154
Out of Office Assistant, 729–733
Outlook Today, 605
printing, 768–771
quick message sending, 39–40
QuickStyles, 157–159
Read Receipts, 177–178
reading, 17–22, 41–42, 91–93
recalling, 183–185
replacing recalled, 183–185
replies, 41–42
Reply button versus Reply to All button, 118–119
resending, 125
resolving e-mail addresses, 39–40

saving as drafts, 111–112
security warnings, 712–713
sending to multiple recipients, 87–88
shape drawing, 149–150
signature inclusion, 165–166
SmartArt, 147, 150–152
S/MIME receipt request, 720–721
special effects, 138–141
spell checking, 89, 128–132
stationery enhancements, 134–137
symbol insertion, 147
table insertion, 147–148
templates, 168–170
text boxes, 159–160
themes, 134–137
To-Do item assignment, 399–401
viewing unread only, 92–93
virus risks, 18
Word themes, 137–138

Messages view, 14
Messaging Application Programming Interface (MAPI), 55
microphones, OneNote audio recordings, 482–484
Microsoft Exchange
Cached Exchange Mode, 760–761
calendar sharing, 264
contact sharing, 385–392
Desktop Alerts, 186–187
displaying other users' folders, 742–746
e-mail delegate assignment, 737–742
e-mail replies, 120
Global Address List, 94
meeting scheduling, 302–306
message delivery delay, 181–182
offline address book, 757–759
Out of Office Assistant, 727–733
Outlook Anywhere, 762
recalling/replacing messages, 183–185
sent e-mail folder paths, 226–227
shared contact permission editing, 390–392
sharing contacts with everyone, 386–387
specific people contact sharing, 388–390
viewing other shared contacts, 392–394
Voting buttons 179–181
VPN (virtual private network), 762

Microsoft LDAP Directory dialog box, 96–97
Microsoft List Builder Contacts (`.bcm`), BCM data type, 545
Microsoft Office 2007 All-in-One Desk Reference For Dummies (Peter Weverka), 147
Microsoft Office Button, 34–35
Microsoft Office Communicator, 191
Microsoft Office Online
business card templates, 378–379
notebook templates, 460
publishing a calendar, 286–289
Trust Center component, 710
Word themes, 137

Microsoft Office Outlook Connector, 763–765
Microsoft Office Outlook dialog box
iCalendar addition, 330–331
news feed selections, 198
sharing news feeds, 203–204

Microsoft Sales Leads (`.bcm`), BCM data type, 545
Microsoft Small Business Accounting (SBA), BCM integration, 538
Minimize button
Navigation pane sizing, 15–16
window sizing, 28–29

Miscellaneous Field page, 356–357
modems, telephone call, 371
Modified field, 361–362
Modify Report dialog box, BCM, 582
modules
Calendar, 1, 12
Contacts, 2, 12
customized buttons/commands, 13
Folder List display, 22–23
hiding/displaying To-Do Bar, 24
interface elements, 13–14
Journal, 2, 12
Mail, 1, 11–12
moving between, 12–13, 15
New button item, 33–34
Notes, 2, 12
pane sizing, 27–28
Standard toolbar, 13
switching views, 113–114
Tasks, 2, 12
views, 14, 113–114

Month view
Calendar module, 239–241
Date Navigator, 242–243
Outlook Today, 610

Monthly, recurring tasks, 418
Monthly Style, Calendar item printing, 775
mouse
drag-and-drop, 46–51
OneNote note drawing, 475
right-dragging, 50
Move Message Selected Below To list box, 642–643
MSN Messenger, Outlook compatible IM, 191

N

Name text box, 639
Navigation Bar, 456–457
navigation buttons, 15
Navigation pane
adding/removing buttons, 524, 703
appointment creation, 43–44
Assignment view, 430–431
browsing news feeds, 197–199
business card views, 383–384
button sizing, 702
button techniques, 703–704
Calendar module display, 235
calendar view list, 348
Configure buttons, 15–16
Configure Buttons button, 524
Contacts list views, 363–365
Current View list, 528
Expand button, 16–17
flagged message display, 406–408
Folder List button, 15
Folder List display, 22–23
hiding/displaying, 16, 701
hiding/displaying buttons, 16
interface element, 13–17
Journal button, 524
Minimize button, 15–16
minimizing/maximizing, 701–702
moving between modules, 13, 15
multiple calendar display, 332–334
navigation buttons, 15
note creation, 447
Notes button, 15
Other People's Calendars, 270–273
Outlook Today, 26, 604
removing iCalendars, 331
Share My Tasks Folder link, 441
shared contact folder display, 387
shared task folder, 442
shortcut addition, 705
Shortcuts button, 15–16
sizing, 16–17
splitter bar, 702
task links, 16, 416–417
viewing assigned tasks, 430–431
viewing others' shared tasks, 444–446
views, 114
Navigation Pane Options button, 703
.NET Passport, 191
networks
entire network calendar sharing, 264–266
live sharing sessions, 502–505
notebook share permissions, 460–462
OneNote sharing, 497–502
shared calendar permission editing, 269–270
sharing contacts with everyone, 386–387
sharing tasks, 439–442
specific people calendar sharing, 266–269
specific people contact sharing, 388–390
stopping shared tasks, 443–444
New button
e-mail message creation, 85–86
item creation, 33–34
module specific actions, 14
New Call dialog box, 371–373
New Field dialog box, 631–632
New Internet Calendar Subscription dialog box, 299
New Meeting Request With command, 302
New Notebook Wizard, 459–462
New Outlook Data File dialog box, 540
New Profiles dialog box, 230
New RSS Feed dialog box, 196
New Search Folder dialog box, 696–699
New Signature dialog box, 163
news feeds
attachments, 197
browsing, 197–199
folder paths, 196
importing/exporting lists, 204
Internet Explorer synchronization, 199–201

reading articles, 202
removing, 201
RSS (Really Simple Syndication) setup, 196–200
sharing, 203–204
Next button, 124
Next Seven Days view, 419
Next Week flag, 399
No Automatic Filtering, 678
No Date flag, 399
nonadjacent items, 640
non-colleagues, Out of Office Assistant message replies, 729–730
None
shared calendar permissions, 266
shared contact permissions, 387
shared task permissions, 440
Nonediting Author
shared calendar permissions, 266
shared contact permissions, 387
shared task permissions, 440
note blogging, 498–499
notebooks
creating, 459–462
e-mailing pages, 495–497
moving pages/notes, 509–511
moving sections, 511
naming conventions, 459
network sharing, 500–502
new page addition, 463–466
OneNote navigation, 457–458
Outlook appointment details insertion, 490
Outlook meeting details insertion, 490
Outlook task creation, 491–492
page links, 487–488
page selections, 509
page sharing, 497–498
page templates, 463–465
recent note search, 518–519
section addition, 466–467
section groups, 467–468
section passwords, 505–508
share permissions, 460–462
subpages, 465–466
tagged item search, 519–520
templates, 460
text search, 514–516
Notepad, `outlook.hoi` file editing, 260–262
Notes button, 15
Notes List view, 450
Notes module
accessing, 15
appearance, 451–452
appointments, 246
By Category view, 450
category assignments, 449
colors, 449
date/time display, 452
default color, 452
distribution lists, 209
drag-and-drop creation, 50
Last Seven Days view, 450
note creation, 45–46, 448–449
notes display, 449
Notes List view, 450
Outlook Data Files view, 450
overview, 2, 12
phone logs, 527
sharing notes, 453–454
size settings, 452
sorts, 451
sticking to the Desktop, 453
switching between views, 450–451
views, 114, 450–451
Notes Options dialog box, 451–452
notifications. *See also* alerts
message arrival, 185–187
recalled messages, 184–185
numbered lists, 159, 470

O

objects
alignments, 153
cropping, 154
deleting, 478
drawing, 477
duplicating, 478
effects, 153
formatting, 152
grouping/ungrouping, 153
line widths, 477
manipulation, 152–154
moving, 152
reshaping, 152
resizing, 152, 154
rotating, 152, 154, 478
selections, 152
shadows, 153
text wrapping, 153
3-D effects, 153
Office Communicator, 191
Office field, Account Records, 557
offline address book, 757–759
Offline Address Books dialog box, 759

OneNote
All Notebooks List button, 458
Audio and Video Recording toolbar, 482–484
audio clip insertion, 482–484
audio/video search, 513, 516–517
automatic saves, 456
bulleted lists, 470
containers, 456–457, 468–469
copying a table from Excel, 470
custom tag creation, 512
data searches, 513–520
date/time editing, 472
document insertion, 484–485
document links, 488
document picture insertion, 485–487
Drawing toolbar, 477–478
e-mailing notebook pages, 495–497
exporting to Word, 459
file insertion, 484–485
file links, 488
Full Page View button, 456–457
handwritten note to text conversion, 476–477
hiding/displaying the Navigation Bar, 456–457
Idea tag, 512
image insertion, 478–480
images, 480
important tag, 512
live sharing sessions, 502–505
meeting information gathering, 306, 308
moving pages/notes, 509–511
navigation techniques, 457–459
New Notebook Wizard, 459–462
new page addition, 463–466
note blogging, 498–499
notebook creation, 47, 459–462
notebook navigation, 457–458
notebook page links, 487–488
notebook section passwords, 505–508
notebook sections, 511
notebook share permissions, 460–462
notebook sharing, 500–502
numbered lists, 470
organization tool, 455–457
Outlook, 490–495
overview, 2, 46
page selections, 509
page sharing, 497–498
page templates, 463–465
PDA support, 456
pen tablets, 474–478
Personal Notebook template, 460
Question tag, 512
quick side notes, 473
recent note search, 518–519
recording audio/video clips, 482–484
recording playback, 483
reorganizing notes, 509–511
Research Notebook template, 460
resizing images, 479
ruled pages, 476
screen shots, 480–482
section addition, 466–467
section groups, 467–468
section navigation, 458
shared notes, 497–499
smartphone support, 456
subpages, 465–466
table creation, 470–471
tagged item search, 519–520
tags, 511–513
text formatting, 469–470
text search, 514–516
To-Do tags, 491
Unfiled Notes section, 456–457
video clip insertion, 482–484
Web page links, 488
Work Notebook template, 460
writing space adjustments, 471–472
Zoom button, 456–457
Open a Shared Calendar dialog box, 270–271
Open Other User's Folder dialog box, 745–746
Open Outlook Data File dialog box, 656
Open Recurring Item dialog box, 253–254
Open Shared Contacts dialog box, 392–393
Open Shared Tasks dialog box, 444–445
Opportunities
BCM sales processes, 538
creating, 567–570
dashboards, 587–588
deal closing, 572
deleting opportunities, 572–573
deleting products, 575–576
editing opportunities, 571–572
editing products, 575–576
information fields, 568–570
product/service addition, 573–575
Ribbon elements, 570
searches, 571
Opportunities list, 571–572

Opportunity Funnel Chart, 587–588
Opportunity Funnel report, 578
Opportunity Information fields, 569
Opportunity Pipeline Chart, BCM, 587–588
Opportunity Title field, 569
Options dialog box
  default reminder time setting, 344
  delegate assignment, 738–740
  e-mail message formats, 105–106
  emptying Deleted Items folder, 37
  exporting rules, 675
  notebook section passwords, 507–508
  removing delegates, 741–742
Organize window, 642–643
orientation, 769
Other column, BCM reports, 583
Other People's Calendars, viewing, 270–273
Out of Office Assistant
  auto-replies, 729
  enabling/disabling, 728–730
  limits, 729
  message creation, 729
  removing rules, 733
  rules, 730–733
Out of the Office marker, Show As list, 275–276
Outbox folder
  changing messages before sending, 36
  sent mail processing, 89
Outlook 2007 Calendar Views, 334–337
Outlook Address Book, 94. *See also* address books
Outlook Anywhere, 762
Outlook button, 28–29
Outlook Connector, 763–765
Outlook Contacts folder, 546
Outlook Data Files view
  Journal module, 530
  Notes module, 450
  removing Journal items, 533–534
Outlook E-Mail Postmark, 688
Outlook Express
  contact import, 78–79
  Eudora address book import, 76–77
  importing e-mail account information from Eudora, 76–77
  importing e-mail from, 70–71
Outlook Express Import dialog box, 76
Outlook Import Tool dialog box
  Eudora, 75
  Eudora Light, 75
  Outlook Express, 70–71
  Windows Mail, 70–71
Outlook Mobile Service, 94
Outlook Today
  Card view, 610
  configuration settings, 604–605
  custom view, 617–618
  customizing, 27
  data sorts, 613–614
  Day view, 610
  deleting custom views, 618
  Drafts folder, 27
  exiting, 604
  folder message display, 618–620
  groups, 607–609
  Icon view, 610
  interface elements, 26–27
  marking messages, 620
  Month view, 610
  naming customs views, 616–617
  Navigation pane access, 604
  Reading pane, 605–606, 619–620
  root folder, 26
  standard view resetting, 616
  Table view, 610–613
  Timeline view, 610
  view editing, 614–615
  views, 609–613
  Week view, 610
  weekly activity overview, 27
`outlook.hoi` file, holiday list creation, 260–262
`outlook.pst` file, Personal Folder file, 652, 656–657
ovals, drawing, 477
Overdue Tasks view, 419
Overlay view, 333

P

Page Color menu, 142–143
Page List task pane, 518–519
Page Setup dialog box
  printing contact names/e-mail addresses, 781
  printing message with attachments, 769–771
page sharing, OneNote, 497–498
page templates, 463–465
panes, sizing, 27–29
paper type, 769
parallelograms, 477
Password Protection task pane, 505–506, 508

passwords
  e-mail account settings, 62–64
  e-mail account setup element, 59– 61
  file assignment, 707–709
  live sharing sessions, 502, 504
  notebook sections, 505–508
  strong password conventions, 64
patterns
  backgrounds, 143–145
  recurring appointments, 252–253
PDA (portable digital assistant), OneNote, 456
PDF/XPS converter for Office, 497
pen tablets
  live sharing sessions, 502–505
  OneNote note drawing, 474–478
People or Distribution List link, 663
permissions
  delegates, 739–742
  distribution lists, 209
  entire network calendar sharing, 265–266
  notebook sharing, 460–462
  shared calendar editing, 269–270
  shared contacts, 386–387, 390–392
  task sharing, 439–440, 443–444
Personal Folders dialog box, 650–651, 707–709
Personal Forms Library, creating forms from existing fields, 626
personal information, spam reduction, 687
Personal Notebook template, 460
phishing messages, enabling/disabling links, 678–679, 686, 688
Phone Calls view
  Journal module, 530
  removing Journal items, 533–534
Phone Directory Style, printing contact names/mailing addresses, 778
Phone List view
  contact creation, 352
  contact display, 355
  deleting duplicate contacts, 361
  printing contact names/e-mail addresses, 779–781
Phone Numbers field
  Account Records, 557
  Business Contact, 553
pictures. *See also* images
  adding to Business Contact, 553
  contact information, 354, 356
  e-mail attachments, 114–116
  message insertion, 145–147
  signature inclusion, 164
  spam reduction techniques, 687
plain-text format
  pros/cons, 105
  signature formatting issues, 166
  Trust Center display settings, 715–716
podcasts, RSS (Really Simple Syndication), 195
POP3 (Post Office Protocol 3)
  Desktop Alerts, 186–187
  e-mail accounts, 54–55, 752
  out-of-office message replies, 734–737
POP3 servers, retrieving e-mail without deleting, 752–754
Post Office Protocol 3 (POP3)
  Desktop Alerts, 186–187
  e-mail accounts, 54–55, 752
  out-of-office message replies, 734–737
Postmarks, spam reduction techniques, 688
PowerPoint, automatic Journal tracking, 523
Preview File button, attachment previewing, 20
Print button, message with attachments, 768–771
Print dialog box
  list of items, 774–775
  printing blank calendars, 782
  printing contact names/e-mail addresses, 777–781
  printing message with attachments, 768–771
  printing single item contents, 772–773
printing
  BCM reports, 581
  blank calendars, 781–782
  contact mailing addresses, 776–779
  contact names, 776–779
  e-mail addresses, 779–781
  list of items, 773–775
  messages with attachments, 768–771
  single item contents, 772–773
priorities, rule settings, 667
privacy guarding, Trust Center, 709–711
privacy policies (Web sites), spam reduction, 687
Probability field, Opportunities, 569

products
adding to an opportunity, 573–575
deleting, 575–576
editing, 575–576
Products and Services dialog box, 576
profiles
choosing between multiple, 230
e-mail account configuration, 56–57
e-mail accounts, 229–230
Programmatic Access, Trust Center security settings, 714–715
programs
Programmatic Access security settings, 714–715
security warnings, 712–713
Project Name field, Business Projects, 563
Project Tasks area, accessing Business Project tasks, 564
Project Tasks field, Business Projects, 564
Project Type field, Business Projects, 563
Properties dialog box, message display, 619
Propose New Time button, meeting time proposals, 316
Protected Section dialog box, unlocking password-protected sections, 506
publishing
calendar to a Web server, 290–291
calendar to Microsoft Office Online, 286–289
forms, 628
OneNote note blogging, 498–499
Publishing Author
shared calendar permissions, 266
shared contact permissions, 387
shared task permissions, 440
Publishing Editor
shared calendar permissions, 265
shared contact permissions, 387
shared task permissions, 440

Q

queries
Address Book search, 699–701
Contacts list search, 365–368
e-mail address search, 101–102
Instant Search criteria, 692–694
Query Builder, 693–694
Question tag, OneNote, 512
Quick Access toolbar
accessing, 621
command addition, 623–625
form window element, 34–35
relocating, 621–623
Ribbon command addition, 622–633
saving images to a file, 116
Quick Access Toolbar Editor, command addition, 623–625
Quick Click, start date settings, 45
Quick Click Category, item assignments, 594–596
Quick Click Flag, e-mail messages, 400, 402–403
Quick Contacts, creating, 38–39
quick messages, sending, 39–40
Quick Parts
category assignments, 167
description text, 167
insertion options, 168
item insertion, 168
naming conventions, 167
reusable text/images, 166–168
saving, 167
saving as a template, 167
selection techniques, 166–167
signatures, 162
quick side notes, OneNote, 473
Quick Task, adding to To-Do bar, 44–45
QuickBooks, BCM data type, 546–547
QuickStyles, text enhancements, 157–159

R

RDF, Outlook supported news feeds, 195
Read Receipt, message tracking, 177–178
Reading pane
attachment previews, 20–22
AutoPreview, 19–20
Calendar module display, 235
conversation tracking, 123–124
forwarding messages, 125
hiding/displaying, 18
Info Bar display, 18, 20
interface element, 17–22
message content previews, 17–20
message display, 619–620

Reading pane (continued)
  message replies, 41–42, 118–124
  Outlook Today, 605–606
  positioning, 18
  Propose New Time button, 316
  reading messages, 41–42, 91–93
  reading news panes, 202
  Remove From Calendar button, 311–312
  scroll bars, 17
  shared calendar access, 273
  sharing news feeds, 203
  veining unread messages only, 92–93
Reading pane dialog box, message display options, 620
Really Simple Syndication (RSS)
  browsing recommended news feeds, 197–199
  importing/exporting lists, 204
  Internet Explorer synchronization, 199–201
  news feed setup, 195–200
  Outlook supported types, 195
  podcasts, 195
  reading news feeds, 202
  removing news feeds, 201
  sharing news feeds, 203–204
  workflow process, 195
reassigned tasks, 435–436
Recall This Message dialog box, 184
recipients
  adding to Safe Recipients List, 683–684
  adding to Safe Senders List, 680–681
  certificate exchanges, 718–719
  message flags, 174–176
  recalled message notifications, 184–185
  sharing invitation, 264–265, 273
  voting response, 180–181
recolor, image enhancements, 146
records, detailed task creation, 414–415
rectangles, drawing, 477
Recurrence button, Calendar module, 251–254
Recurrence dialog box, recurring appointments/meeting/events, 251–253
recurrent meetings, editing existing meetings, 309
recurrent tasks
  creating, 417–419
  removing, 419
  Task Request form, 427
Rejecting Task dialog box, task requests, 432–433
Related Accounts and Business Contacts field, Business Projects, 564
Reminder field, Opportunities, 569
reminders
  all-day events, 249
  appointments, 245, 247
  calendar time setting, 343–344
  detailed task creation, 414
  flags for yourself, 177
  meetings, 309
  message flags, 174–175
  recurring appointments/meeting/events, 253
  removing from appointments/events, 255
  To-Do item flags, 399–401
remote computers
  downloading message headers only, 754–757
  e-mail retrieval, 752–754
  marking message headers for action, 756
  Outlook Anywhere, 762
  VPN (virtual private network), 762
Remove From Calendar button, canceled meetings, 311–312
Remove Password dialog box, notebook section passwords, 508
Reply button, versus Replying to All button, 118–119
Reply to All button, cautions/concerns, 42
reports (BCM)
  Accounts, 579
  Accounts by Rating Report, 578
  Activity, 577
  assigned task status, 433–435
  BCM support, 538
  Business Contact by Birthday Report, 578
  Business Projects, 579–580
  Business Projects by Status, 580
  content filtering, 583–585
  e-mail attachments, 586
  e-mailing, 581
  exporting, 581
  exporting to Excel, 586
  information editing, 585–587
  Leads, 579
  Marketing Campaigns, 579
  modifying existing, 581–583
  Opportunities, 579
  Opportunity Funnel, 579
  printing, 581

refreshing, 586–587
reordering columns, 580
running, 580–581
sorts, 580
Research Notebook template, notebook creation, 460
Research pane
grammar lookups, 133
word lookups, 130–131
reset picture, image enhancements, 146
resource providers, meeting invitations, 303–306
Resource Scheduling dialog box, meeting requests, 318–319
Response column, voting messages, 180
reusable text/images
Quick Parts, 166–168
templates, 168–170
Reviewer
delegate permission, 739
shared calendar permissions, 266–267
shared contact permissions, 387
shared task permissions, 440, 441
Ribbon
adding commands to Quick Access toolbar, 622–623
BCM display, 561
Categorize button, 592, 596–597
command groupings, 35
Delay Delivery button, 182
Delete button, 37
Dialog box launcher, 35
Direct Replies To, 229
form window element, 35
hiding/displaying, 622
message flag display, 176
minimizing/maximizing, 35
Opportunities buttons, 570
Recurrence button, 252–254
Save & Close button, 36
Scheduling Assistant button, 302–303
Send to OneNote button, 494–495
tab navigation, 35
themes, 134
Tracking button, 178
Rich Text Format (RTF) files
attachment preview nonsupport, 21
pros/cons, 105
root folder, Outlook Today, 26
rotation, object enhancements, 154
rows, OneNote tables, 471
RSS (Really Simple Syndication)
browsing recommended news feeds, 197–199
importing/exporting lists, 204
Internet Explorer synchronization, 199–201
news feed setup, 196–200
Outlook supported types, 195
podcasts, 195
reading news feeds, 202
removing news feeds, 201
sharing news feeds, 203–204
workflow process, 195
RSS Feed Options dialog box, news feed setup, 196–197
RTF (Rich Text Format) files
attachment preview nonsupport, 21
e-mail messages, 105
Rule Address dialog box, basic rule creation, 663–664
ruled pages, OneNote addition, 476
rules
advanced rules, 665–667
alert settings, 667
automatically deleting messages, 667
basic rules, 661–665
conditional settings, 668–671
copying, 674
creating new, 662–665
deleting, 676
editing existing, 665–666
enabling/disabling, 673
folder settings, 667
importing/exporting, 674–676
message delivery, 181
Out of Office Assistant, 730–733
out-of-office message replies, 735–737
priority settings, 667
reasons for, 661–662
renaming, 666
running on existing e-mail, 672–673
templates, 663
Rules and Alerts dialog box
advanced rules, 665–667
basic rules, 662–665
conditional settings, 668–671
deleting rules, 676
enabling/disabling rules, 673
importing rules, 676
received mail folder paths, 223–226
running on existing e-mail, 672–673

Rules Wizard
basic rule creation, 662–665
conditional rules, 668–671
editing existing rules, 665–667
out-of-office message reply rules, 735–736
received mail folder paths, 223–226
Run Rules dialog box, 672–673

S

Safe Lists Only, junk e-mail protection, 678
Safe Recipients List, 680–681, 683–684
Safe Senders List
adding domain to, 680, 683–684
adding names to, 679–680, 683–684
recipients, 680–681
trusted image sources, 116
Sales Opportunities, BCM Invoices or Sales Orders in Accounting, 538
Sales stage field, Opportunities, 569
Save All Attachments dialog box, 117–118
Save & Close button, 36
Save As dialog box
iCalendar format, 281–283, 292–293
template creation, 170
Save As Web Page dialog box, 290–291
SBA (Microsoft Small Business Accounting), BCM integration, 538
Scheduling Assistant button, 302–303
screen shots, OneNote, 480–482
ScreenTip, command button help, 14
scripts, image attachment concerns, 115
scroll bars
appointment viewing, 236
message navigation, 17
Search, Instant Search preference settings, 691
Search Address Books box, 365–366
Search Contacts box, 366–367
Search Folder Criteria dialog box, 697–699
Search Folders
adding custom to Folder List, 697–699
adding predefined to Folder List, 695–697
categories, 695
deleting, 699
e-mail w/attachments search, 117
Favorite Folder support, 644
Folder List element, 22
virtual folders, 694
Search Options dialog box, 690–691
searches
Address Book, 699–701
Contacts lists, 365–368
distribution list members, 207
e-mail address, 101–102
e-mail w/attachments, 117
flagged messages, 406–408
folder cleanup, 649–650
Instant Search, 689–694
meeting contacts, 307
OneNote data, 513–520
opportunities, 571
Search Folders, 694–699
Unread Mail Search Folder, 694
Windows Desktop Search, 513, 516–517
section groups, OneNote notebooks, 467–468
sections, OneNote notebook addition, 466–467
Secure Multipurpose Internet Mail Extension (S/MIME), 720–721
security
digital signatures, 718–720
encryption, 717, 719–721
file passwords, 707–709
HTML format concerns, 715–716
IM (instant messaging) risks, 190, 194
IRM (Information Rights Management), 721
macros, 711–712
message expiration date, 721
notebook section passwords, 505–508
phishing attacks, 678–679, 685–686, 688
privacy issues, 709–711
S/MIME receipt request, 720–721
spam protection levels, 677–679
strong password conventions, 64
Trust Center, 709–711
security warnings, 712–715
Select Attendees and Resources dialog box
Exchange meetings, 303–304
inviting/uninviting members, 310
meeting invitations, 306–308
Select From list, 356–357
Select Members dialog box, 206–207
Select Names dialog box, address box search, 101–102

Select User dialog box, IRM/e-mail account associations, 724
Select Where to Place the Folder list box, 639
selections
appointment category, 246
distribution list members, 206–207
event category, 249
folder paths, 639
notebook pages, 509
objects, 152
Quick Parts, 166–167
semicolon (;) character, multiple message recipients, 88
Send a Calendar via E-Mail dialog box, 283–285
Send button
resending messages, 125
sending messages, 89–90
Send to OneNote button, Outlook item notes, 494–495
Send Update to Attendees dialog box, 310–311
Send/Receive button
retrieving e-mail messages, 90
sending e-mail messages, 89
Send/Receive groups
adding/removing accounts, 218
content controls, 215, 216
creating, 214–218
enabling/disabling, 219
folder paths, 215, 216
frequency controls, 214, 217
functions, 214–216
limitation controls, 214, 217
marking headers for download, 218
offline support, 215, 216
receive option settings, 218–219
Send/Receive Groups dialog box, 758
Send/Receive Progress dialog box, 188
Send/Receive Settings dialog box, 758–759
Sent folder, 125
Sent Items folder, 407
server information, e-mail account setup, 61
servers, e-mail, 56, 86–87
services
adding to an opportunity, 573–575
deleting, 575–576
editing, 575–576
Set Quick Click dialog box
category item assignments, 594–596
Quick Click Flag, 402–403
shadows, object enhancements, 153
shapes, Quick Parts, 166–168
Shapes tool, 149–150
Share My Tasks Folder link, sharing tasks with specific people, 441
shared folders, Folder List display nonsupport, 23
shared tasks, 443–444
SharePoint, 110–111
sharing
business cards, 375, 381–382
e-mail invitation, 264–265, 273
entire network calendar sharing, 264–266
Google Calendar, 292–300
iCalendar format calendars, 281–283
Microsoft Exchange contacts, 385–392
notes, 453–454
OneNote notes, 497–499
shared calendar permission editing, 269–270
specific people calendar sharing, 266–269
Tasks lists, 438–444
viewing other shared contacts, 392–394
shortcut groups, 704–706
shortcuts
adding to Navigation pane, 30–31
category assignments, 593, 597, 598–599
creating, 705
deleting, 705
grouping, 30–31
moving, 705
renaming, 705
shortcut groups, 704–706
Shortcuts button, favorite folder access, 16, 30–31
Show As list, appointment/meeting availability, 274–276
Show Fewer Buttons command, 703
Show Fields dialog box
printing contact names/mailing addresses, 777
printing names/e-mail addresses, 780
Show More Buttons command, Navigation pane, 703
side notes, OneNote, 473
side-by-side view, multiple calendar display, 332–333
signatures
adding to e-mail messages, 165–166
business card inclusion, 163–164
business cards, 375

signatures *(continued)*
certificates, 718–719
contact information, 161–162
creating, 162–165
e-mail account associations, 164–165
e-mail entry conventions, 89
hyperlink inclusion, 164
picture inclusion, 164
Quick Part, 162, 166–168
removing from a message, 166
sending e-mail, 719–720
text formatting issues, 166
Signatures & Stationery dialog box
default stationery setting, 136
reply text colors, 121–122
signature creation, 162–165
Skip Occurrence command, recurring tasks, 419
slsx (Excel workbook) file extension, BCM data type, 546
Small Booklet Style, printing contact names/mailing addresses, 778
SmartArt, message enhancements, 147, 150–152
smartphones, OneNote support, 456
S/MIME (Secure Multipurpose Internet Mail Extension), 720–721
S/MIME receipt request, e-mail messages, 720–721
snapshots, calendar sharing, 328
Sort dialog box, 613–614
sorts
Assignment list tasks by owner, 431
BCM reports, 580
contact lists, 362
Junk E-Mail folder, 684
notes, 451
Outlook Today data, 613–614
table (list) view, 114
task status, 431
sounds
alerts, 667
Desktop Alerts, 90–91, 186–187
message arrival, 185–187
Source field, 569
Source Information fields, 569–570
spam. *See also* Junk E-Mail folder
contact list concerns, 351
image attachment concerns, 115
junk e-mail filter, 677–679
junk mail designations, 683–684
phishing attacks, 678–679, 685–686, 688
Postmarks, 688
reduction, 687–688
special characters, message insertion, 147
special effects, 138–141
speed dial list, telephone contacts, 373–374
spell checking
adding words to a dictionary, 130
adding words to AutoCorrect, 130
appointments, 246
before sending message, 89
Contact list names, 130
context errors, 131–132
disabling/enabling as-you-type corrections, 128
language selections, 130
misspelled word identification, 129
Research pane lookups, 130–131
selecting from a list of suggestions, 130
Spelling dialog box, 130
SQL Express language, BCM, 538
Standard Forms Library, 625
Standard toolbar
buttons/commands change with modules, 13
Categorize button, 449, 593, 596–597
Delete button, 37
Dial button, 371
E-Mail button, 496
Forward button, 125
Full Page View button, 456–457
interface element, 13–14
New button, 14, 33–34
Print button, 768
Reply button versus Reply to All button, 118–119
Search Address Books box, 365–366
Send to OneNote button, 494–495
Send/Receive button, 89, 90
Tags button, 512
Task button, 492
Today button, 241–242
Zoom button, 456–457
Start field, Journal timelines, 530
Start from a Blank Rule template, 663

Start Live Session task pane, OneNote, 503–504
start/end dates
  all-day events, 249
  meetings, 305–306, 308, 310
start/end time
  appointment entry conventions, 244–245
  meetings, 305–306, 308, 310
Startup and Welcome to BCM Wizard, 540
Startup, Outlook Today configuration setting, 605
stationery
  e-mail message, 134–137
  setting as default, 136–137
status, task sorting, 431
status bar, download progress display, 188
Status Information field, 563
status reports, assigned tasks, 433–435
Status section, 569
status tracking, 414
Stay Organized template, 663
Stay Up to Date template, 663
Store Folder dialog box, 73–74
Store Location dialog box, 73–74
street addresses, contact editing, 356
strikethrough text, expired message display, 182
strong passwords, conventions, 64
styles
  Outlook Today configuration setting, 605
  QuickStyles, 157–159
subfolders
  collapsing/expanding in Folder List, 22
  folder indicators, 639
  manually archiving, 655–656
  reordering folders, 640
Subject box, Journal Entry form, 525–526, 527
subject line, e-mail entry conventions, 88
subjects
  all-day events, 248–249
  appointment entry conventions, 244
  appointment/meeting/event editing, 258
  detailed task creation, 413
  meeting entry, 303, 308
subpages, OneNote notebooks, 465–466
Subscription Options dialog box, 299–300
subscriptions
  Google Calendar, 298–300
  iCalendars, 330–331
symbols, message insertion, 147
system problems, Trust Center, 710
system tray
  e-mail message alert display, 91
  hiding/displaying Outlook icon, 29, 186

T

table (list) view
  hiding/displaying items, 113–114
  sorting items, 114
Table Style, printing a list of items, 774
Table view, Outlook Today, 610–613
tables
  column addition, 611
  column removal, 612
  column sorts, 612–613
  message insertion, 147–148
  moving columns, 612
  OneNote creation, 470–471
  resizing columns, 612
Tablet PC, OneNote handwritten note to text conversion, 476–477
tabs, Ribbon navigation, 35
tags, OneNote, 511–513
Tags button, OneNote tag selections, 512
task assignments
  accepting/declining, 432–433
  forwarding, 436–438
  progress tracking, 429–431
  reassigning reassigned tasks, 435–436
  reclaiming after reassigning, 428–429
  status reports, 433–435
  task request creation, 426–428
  viewing assigned tasks, 430–431
Task button, OneNote, 492
Task for, updating task changes, 421
Task form, 413–415
task links, 16
Task Options dialog box
  assigned task progress tracking, 429–430
  overdue task color, 421
Task Properties dialog box, 439–440

Task Recurrence dialog box, 417–418
Task Request form, 426–428
task requests
  accepting/declining, 432–433
  delegate handling, 746–748
  forwarding, 436–438
  reassigning reassigned tasks, 435–436
  reassigning tasks, 426–428
  reclaiming reassigned tasks, 428–429
taskbar. *See also* Windows taskbar
  message alerts, 185–187
  minimizing/maximizing programs, 28–29
Tasks lists
  Active Tasks view, 419–420
  clearing flags, 419
  completed task colors, 420
  deleting tasks, 419
  deleting To-Do items, 406
  hiding/displaying, 408
  marking items as complete, 404–406, 422
  Next Seven Days view, 419
  overdue task colors, 420–421
  Overdue Tasks view, 419
  printing items, 773–775
  reassigned task viewing, 430–431
  recurring tasks, 419
  removing flags, 405
  To-Do List view, 419, 423
  views, 419
Tasks module
  appointment/meeting links, 416–417
  change updating, 421
  creating in Daily Task List, 410–412
  creating in OneNote, 491–492
  deleting, 419
  detail recording, 414–415
  detailed task creation, 413–417
  drag-and-drop creation techniques, 50
  due dates, 413
  e-mail assignments, 416
  ending sharing, 443–444
  groupings, 414
  marking as complete, 422
  marking as private, 439
  Outlook Today configuration setting, 605
  overview, 2, 12
  permission settings, 439–440, 443–444
  priority settings, 414
  Quick Task, 44–45
  rearranging, 421
  recurring, 417–419
  reminders, 414
  reordering, 51
  sharing with entire network, 439–441
  sharing with specific people, 441–442
  sorting, 421
  start date settings, 45
  subject entry conventions, 413
  To-Do Bar category, 24–25
  versus To-Do items, 397–398
  tracking, 414
  viewing others' shared tasks, 444–446
  views, 114
telephone
  contact calls, 371–374
  conversation logs, 526–528
templates
  business cards, 378–380
  creating, 168–170
  creating a contact from, 380
  existing contact application, 380
  notebook pages, 463–465
  notebooks, 460
  out-of-office message replies, 734
  Quick Parts, 167
  reusable messages, 168–170
  rules, 663
  Word as resource, 169
Tentative marker, Show As list, 274–276
Terms section, Opportunities, 570
text boxes, message enhancements, 159–160
text formatting
  e-mail messages, 106–107
  hyperlinks, 155
  message replies, 120–121
  OneNote, 469–470
  QuickStyles, 157–159
  signature issues, 166
Text Highlight Color button, text formatting, 107
text wrapping, object enhancements, 153
textures, backgrounds, 143–145
Theme or Stationery dialog box
  default stationery/theme setting, 136–137
  message enhancements, 135–136

themes
e-mail message, 134–137
setting as default, 136–137
Word themes, 137–138, 141–142
Themes menu, Word themes, 137–138, 141–142
This Week flag, To-Do items, 399
time grid, calendar editing, 339–343
Time Zone dialog box, calendar time grid editing, 342–343
time zones, message flags, 175
Timeline view
Journal module, 528–530
Outlook Today, 610
timers, phone logs, 527–528
times
appointment entry conventions, 244–245
appointment shifting, 256
appointment/meeting management, 274–276
Day view display, 236
flags for yourself, 177
meeting information, 305–306, 308
meeting time change proposal prevention, 325
meeting time proposals, 316–318, 320–322
message flags, 174–175
note display, 452
OneNote, 472
Week view display, 238
To box, Task Request form, 427
To field, contact information, 354
Today button, Calendar module navigation, 241–242
Today flag, To-Do items, 399
To-Do bar
accessing Business Project tasks, 564
Appointments, 25
Appointments section, 408
Calendar module display, 235
category groups, 24
completed item display, 409
customizing, 25
Date Navigator, 24–25, 346, 408
deleting To-Do items, 406
hiding/displaying, 24, 397
incoming e-mail/item assignment, 399–401
interface elements, 13–14, 24–25
marking items as complete, 404–406
minimizing/maximizing, 24
more appointment and meeting display, 409
more/less task/To-Do item display, 408
multiple month display, 409
overdue item colors, 410
Quick Task addition, 44–45
rearranging tasks/To-Do items, 409–410
removing flags, 405
sorting tasks/To-Do items, 409
task name editing, 404
task tracking, 397–402
Tasks, 24–25
Tasks list, 408
To-Do items, 24–25
width adjustments, 408
To-Do Bar Options dialog box, 409
To-Do items. *See also* items
clearing flags, 419
contact assignment, 401–402
deleting, 406
flag assignment editing, 403
incoming e-mail assignment, 399–401
marking as complete, 404–406
message flags, 176–177
removing flags, 405
task name editing, 404
versus tasks, 397–398
To-Do Bar category, 24–25
To-Do List view, Tasks lists, 419, 423
To-Do tags, OneNote, 491
Tomorrow flag, To-Do items, 399
tracking
assigned tasks, 429–431
automatic Journal, 522–523
Business Projects, 565
contact activity, 374
Delivery Receipts, 177–178
detailed task creation, 414
e-mail conversations, 123–124
Journal module, 521–528
manual Journal, 525–526
meeting request response, 319–325
Read Receipts, 177–178
To-Do bar tasks, 397–402
To-Do tags, 491
voting responses, 180

Tracking button, message tracking, 178
Tracking column, BCM reports, 583
Tracking Options dialog box
  delivery/read receipts, 178
  meeting responses, 322–323
  voting responses, 181
triangles, drawing, 477
Tri-Fold Style, Calendar item printing, 775
Trust Center
  anti-virus software, 713–715
  digital IDs, 716–719
  macro settings, 711–712
  plain-text display settings, 715–716
  privacy guarding, 709–711
  Programmatic Access security settings, 714–715
  trusted images sources, 116
Trusted Publishers, macro issues, 711
Type field, Opportunities, 570

U

Unfiled Notes section, OneNote, 456–457
Unread Mail Search Folder, 694–695
unread messages, viewing only, 92–93
updates
  anti-virus software, 713–714
  contact information, 360
  distribution list e-mail addresses, 209
  Featured Links, 710
  marking task as complete, 422
  meeting requests, 310–311
  news feeds, 197
  offline address book, 758–759
  opportunity information, 572
  task changes, 421
  Task Request form, 427
user information, e-mail account setup, 61
user-defined fields, contact editing, 356–357
User-Defined Fields tab, Opportunity Ribbon, 570
username, e-mail account setup element, 59, 60
users
  BCM (Business Contact Manager) candidates, 538–539
  e-mail certificate exchanges, 718–719

V

video clips
  OneNote insertion, 482–484
  OneNote search, 513, 516–517
View Conflicts Size button, 650
View Deleted Items Size button, 650
View Mailbox Size button, 648
View menu, display selections, 14
viewing area, interface element, 13–14
views
  business cards, 383–384
  Calendar module, 234–241, 348
  Contacts lists, 363–365
  folder organization, 643
  Journal module, 528–531
  multiple calendar display, 332–333
  Notes module, 450–451
  Outlook Today, 609–613
  resetting a standard view, 616
  switching between, 113–114
  Tasks lists, 419
virtual folders, Search Folders, 694–699
virtual private network (VPN), Microsoft Exchange, 762
virus
  attachment risks, 18
  contact list concerns, 351
  file attachment, 108
  HTML-formatted messages, 715–716
  image attachment concerns, 115
  message opening risks, 18
  security warnings, 712–713
Voting buttons, Microsoft Exchange, 179–181
VPN (virtual private network), Microsoft Exchange, 762

W

Web feeds. *See* RSS (Really Simple Syndication)
Web mail
  connection creation, 763–765
  connection testing, 765
  HTTP protocol, 762
  Microsoft Office Outlook Connector, 763–765
  Windows Live Mail import, 765–766
Web Page Address box, contact browsing, 369–370
Web Page address field, Business Contact, 553
Web pages
  chicklets, 196
  contact browsing, 369–370
  Favorite Folders link, 645–647
  hyperlinks, 155
  OneNote links, 488
  testing, 370
Web servers, publishing a calendar, 290–291
Web services, e-mail account provider, 54–55
Web sites
  file compression, 108
  Google Calendar, 298, 329
  Internet Calendar Directory, 330
  Microsoft, 330
  Microsoft Office Outlook Connector, 763
  RSS feeds, 199
  Windows Live Messenger, 191
`webcal://` link, iCalendars, 330
webcams, OneNote video recordings, 482–484
Week view
  all-day events, 248–250
  calendar time grid editing, 339–341
  Daily Task List item creation, 411–412
  Date Navigator techniques, 242–243
  Outlook Today, 610
Weekly field, recurring tasks, 418
Weekly Style, Calendar item printing, 775
Weverka, Peter (*Microsoft Office 2007 All-in-One Desk Reference For Dummies*), 147
windows
  multiple calendar display, 333
  sizing techniques, 27–29
Windows Control Panel, e-mail account profiles, 229–230
Windows Desktop Search, 513, 516–517, 690
Windows Live Contact Import Wizard, 765–766
Windows Live Mail
  contact importing, 765–766
  e-mail account provider, 54–55
Windows Live Messenger
  contact addition, 191–192
  emoticons, 194
  message reply, 193–194
  online status display, 191–193
  online status editing, 194
  Outlook compatible IM, 190–191
  security risks, 190, 194
  sending messages, 191–194
Windows Mail, importing e-mail from, 70–71
Windows Messenger, Outlook compatible IM, 191
Windows System Tray, e-mail message alert display, 91
Windows taskbar, 185–187. *See also* taskbar
Windows Vista
  hiding/displaying Outlook icon, 29
  IRM configuration, 723
  Outlook Express message import, 70–71
Windows XP
  hiding/displaying Outlook icon, 29
  IRM configuration, 723
wizards
  Add New E-Mail Account, 57–61
  Business Data Import and Export, 545–549
  Change E-Mail Account, 63
  Import and Export, 70–82, 98, 204, 657–659
  Internet Connection, 71–73
  New Notebook, 459–462
  Rules, 223–226, 662–671, 735–736
  Startup and Welcome to BCM, 540
  Windows Live Contact Import, 765–766

Word 2007 All-in-One Desk Reference For Dummies (Doug Lowe), 209–210
Word 2007 For Dummies (Dan Gookin), 106
Word
  automatic Journal tracking, 523
  exporting OneNote page to, 459
  mail merges, 209–211
  mass mailings, 209–211
  message themes, 137–138
  OneNote note blogging, 498–499
  template source, 169
  themes, 141–142
words
  adding to a dictionary, 130
  adding to AutoCorrect, 130
  context error checking, 131–132
  grammar checking, 132–134
  Research lookups, 130–131
  spell checking, 128–132
work day, calendar display, 338–339
Work Notebook template, notebook creation, 460
work week, calendar display, 338–339
Work Week view, Calendar module, 237
workspaces, SharePoint file attachments, 111
writing space, OneNote adjustments, 471–472

X

`xls` (Excel workbook) file extension, BCM data type, 546
XML feeds. *See* RSS (Really Simple Syndication)

Y

Yahoo! Mail, e-mail account provider, 54–55
Yearly, recurring tasks, 418

Z

zipping (compressing) files before attaching, 108
Zoom button, OneNote, 456–457